**Don't miss the first two books
in the *Echoes In My Mind* series:**

In **Father Was A Caveman**, the first book in this heart-warming series, you will be transported back to the 1920s through the 1930s with this delightful American family as the father pursues his dream to be a caveman. He thinks of his life as ideal until unknown forces and a bushwhacker's bullet almost destroys life as he knows it. Then an unexpected ally appears and helps him restore order to their lives.

In **We Were Vagabonds**, the second book in the series, the father leaves his caveman job behind to do his part for the war effort. From the nation's capital to the Deep South, the family's thrilling story continues as they take to the road with life on the home-front during World War II. Then putting away their vagabond shoes they plant their roots in a small town where dreams come true.

Along Came A Soldier

June Harman Betts

authorHOUSE®

AuthorHouse™
1663 Liberty Drive
Bloomington, IN 47403
www.authorhouse.com
Phone: 1-800-839-8640

©2010 June Harman Betts. All rights reserved.

No part of this book may be reproduced, stored in a retrieval system, or transmitted by any means without the written permission of the author.

First published by AuthorHouse 6/8/2010

ISBN: 978-1-4490-9306-8 (e)
ISBN: 978-1-4490-9304-4 (sc)
ISBN: 978-1-4490-9305-1 (hc)

Library of Congress Control Number: 2010905467

Printed in the United States of America
Bloomington, Indiana

This book is printed on acid-free paper.

DEDICATION

This book is dedicated to the soldier who made
the journey a pleasure.

ACKNOWLEDGEMENTS

I want to sincerely thank my daughter, Janice Large, for her moral support, for her many suggestions for additional stories, for the many hours she has spent as my editor and advisor. She has truly been my partner in bringing this completed book to you. I also want to thank Mike and Eric Large for the many times they came to my rescue when I ran into 'technical difficulties' with my computer.

The Dash Of Life

Our lives are the dash between two dates
The length and width we can't anticipate
Our lives end with a period or dot.
We impact others, whether we know it or not.

Our dashes and dots form a new creation
Like Morse Code or Binary Code need translation
As authors and artists tell the story
Presenting the characters in all their glory.

Our dashes and dots become a piece of art
Each life offering a special part
Coming together in a beautiful design
Some muted, some colorful, all one of a kind.

To My Mom, June Harman Betts
Thanks for your creations
Janice Jean Large 3/31/2010

PROLOGUE

As the old man sat alone at his table, he thought about a special day he had spent with his two year old grandson, Richard. The young lad was so ornery and happy to play with his grandpa's unlit pipe. He remembered fondly that when he had placed his dress hat on the little boy's head, how it had slipped down over his eyes, bringing uncontrollable giggles from the youngster.

Now that little boy was eighteen years old, across the ocean in Europe serving in the United States Army. Cruel World War II was raging, separating grandsons from grandfathers, separating sons from mothers.

His grandson had a tremendous love for his mother who was devastated by the thought that her oldest son was in harm's way.

He reached up to his wall calendar, flipped the page, and thought, "Goodbye 1943. Hello 1944." Then the old man picked up his pen and began writing a poem honoring his grandson's love for his mother.

On Leaving For War

Tomorrow I must leave you, darling Mother
To this World's War I must go
Do not weep too much for me, dear Mother
I never before knew that I loved you so

You have always been my guarding angel, Mother
From my childhood days to the present day
Always working and doing everything for me, Mother
Whether it be in my work or play

This war has taught me a severe lesson Mother
That you are the dearest sweetheart I've ever had
I never knew how much you meant to me, dear Mother
It's the only thing that makes me feel so sad

When the train leaves the station to carry me to war
Your sweet face will be before me always, dear Mother
A part of myself like the wheels are to a car

All the girls I've had fade from my vision, Mother
None but yours can ever hold their place with me
I hardly know what the war is about, dear Mother
I am so very young and so carefree

My prayers will be at night for you, dear Mother
I will always pray God keeps you happy and well
All the time I'm away from home mother
Hoping I will soon be back with you to dwell

May God keep you always the same darling Mother
And bring this war to a sudden end
Remember I will always think of you, dear Mother
And to my little brother, Gene and Dad, my love I send.

With a sigh, he finalized the poem by penning his signature…

Written by EE McNamee
January 3rd, 1944
On Richard leaving for war

⁓

He put the paper aside on his table and slowly walked into the bedroom where he joined his wife, Lula, who was already snuggled comfortably under the covers. She asked, "What have you been doing? I've been waiting for you to come to bed."

Even in the dim light, she could see the twinkle in his eye, as he replied, "I've been writing a poem for Richard about how much he loves his mother."

Lula smiled sleepily and the last words she said before she fell asleep were, "Our daughter, Rowena is fortunate to have a son who is so dedicated to her."

⁓

Five days later, as the old man sat in his easy chair, Lula came into the room dressed in her bright green coat and hat, and announced to him, "Rowena, Little Kenny and I are going to the store. I'm planning to make chicken and dumplings for you tonight." She lightly kissed his cheek, before heading for the door.

His daughter leaned over dropping a kiss on the top of his head, and said with a smile, "Love you, Papa."

Little Kenny poked his head in the door, calling out, "Happy New Year, Grandpa!" Then the three of them whisked out the door into the sunshine.

As he reread the poem he had written a few days before, a prayer formed in his heart, "Thank you Lord for giving my grandson such a pure, strong love for his mother. Please keep him safe in the battles he faces in this treacherous war. Bring him home to his family, so he can lead a long healthy life serving you, Lord. I pray that he finds a wife to love, to share his life, and I pray that they will make each other happy."

As this prayer was offered up, he experienced a crushing pain in his chest followed by a great feeling of peace as he felt the comforting arms of Jesus as He lifted him and carried him through the open gates of heaven.

After the paper with Richard's poem dropped off his lap and fell to the floor, the room was quiet except for the ticking of the mantle clock until the door burst open and his wife, daughter and little grandson came into the room. "We're home!" Lula called out.

When she saw her husband so still in the chair, she rushed to him, dropped to her knees, put her head on his chest and listened for the sound of his heartbeat. Hearing none, tears spilled down her checks as she raised her head, looked at her daughter and grandson and cried out, "He is gone."

SHOULD I OR SHOULDN'T I?

June noticed the young dark haired soldier as he entered the theater lobby. A petite curvaceous blond clung to one arm while a dignified older brunette woman walked sedately beside them. "Isn't that sweet? He must have just gotten home from the war and is taking his girlfriend and his mother to the movie," June thought. When they stopped at her concession stand, and bought three boxes of popcorn, she found his friendly somewhat flirtatious manner puzzling. "Hmm," she murmured under her breath as she watched the trio disappear from her sight. For a brief moment, she looked into the darkness and wondered about them. Then she busied herself with other customers and didn't give them another thought.

For the last few months June had been working at the Midland Theater in downtown Newark, Ohio. First starting as an usherette at the Midland, then being given the job to work the concession stand at the Midland's sister theater, the Auditorium. While the new job hadn't offered an increase in her thirty-five cents an hour salary, it had included a whopping commission of ten percent. This had amounted to a penny for each box of popcorn she popped, boxed and sold. When cowboy movies starring Roy Rogers and his girlfriend, Dale Evans, were shown, she could actually sell one thousand boxes a night for the grand sum of ten dollars in commission.

The job offered two perks that she considered as valuable as the money she made. She could attend any movie at either theater free of charge. Also her position in the lobby afforded her a front row seat to the comings and goings in her small part of the world.

Four months earlier, Newark had joined the rest of the world in a massive celebration of the end of World War II, the war that had engulfed the major part of the world for a large part of her life. Now the men who had fought so bravely were returning home to get on with their lives. For many of them, it meant getting reacquainted with the women they had left behind.

Always a romantic, June would often stand behind the counter and watch happy, young couples surge through the lobby and imagine romantic scenarios about each one. In her minds eye, every young couple who passed by was part of a bittersweet story of young lovers who had been torn apart by this long agonizing war. As she had done many times, she sighed at the thought of the soldier and his girl finally being reunited.

∼

She was so deep in her daydream that she was startled when she heard a male voice say, "Hi there! How about some more popcorn?"

Turning toward her customer, she was surprised to see the dark-haired soldier. "Back so soon?" She exclaimed. "You certainly haven't eaten three boxes of popcorn already, have you?"

A glint of mischief was in his grin and in his voice when he replied, "You'd better not let your boss hear you say that. He might think you are trying to cut back on sales."

She quickly glanced around to make sure Mr. Tysinger, the theater manager, hadn't heard her comment. Assured he was nowhere in sight, she returned the young man's gaze and in her most dignified manner asked, "How may I help you?"

His grin had widened and there was a sparkle in his brown eyes as he responded, "I'll have three boxes of popcorn and a date with you." Astonished by his last four words, she was momentarily speechless. Only a few minutes ago he had walked in with two girls and now he was asking her for a date!

While he stood waiting for an answer, she boxed the popcorn and handed it to him. "That will be thirty-one cents," she said.

He placed three dimes and a penny in her outstretched hand and said, "I also asked for a date. How about it?"

Her smile matched his as she quipped, "The date? It is December 21, 1945."

"I didn't ask the date, I asked you for a date. You'd say yes if you knew how much trouble I had getting rid of all that popcorn so I'd have an excuse to come out here and talk to you."

She could feel her cheeks turning pink when she looked into his mocking eyes. Straightening her shoulders, and pulling herself to her full height of five foot seven inches, she returned his smile, but her voice sounded haughty to her own ears when she gave him her answer, "I don't go out with people I don't know."

"You mean you would go out with me if we were properly introduced?" he asked.

"I...I" she stammered. Then her voice took on a cutting edge when she asked, "What about your girlfriend?"

"You mean the girls I came in with?" he asked.

"Yes, it seems you have left your girlfriend and mother alone for too long. Don't you think it is time for you to go back to them?"

Her words had a sobering effect on the young soldier. He nodded curtly and muttered, "You may be right." With these words, he spun on his heels and strode away without a backward glance. She was surprised at the sense of disappointment she felt as she let her gaze follow his departing figure. Although she had made an effort to hide her feelings from him, she had enjoyed the give and take of their bantering.

As she filled the orders of the surge of customers who stopped at the concession stand, she wondered if she would ever see him again.

～

She soon found that all thought of the fresh young soldier was wiped from her mind by the steady stream of customers who stopped by her booth. She'd been too busy to give them more than a cursory glance as she went about her usual routine of filling the popper with corn, adding the oil, popping the corn, boxing it, and filling their orders. That was why she hadn't even looked at the next customer before she'd automatically asked, "How many please?"

"No popcorn this time! I don't think I could stuff another bite down my throat or down the girls'," a familiar sounding male voice said. Before she could reply, he added, "And I don't think the janitor will be very happy when he finds most of the first boxes on the floor!" In response to her quizzically raised eyebrow, he said, "The girls wouldn't eat it fast enough to suit me, so I sort of accidentally spilled it."

June tried to give him a cool look, but she couldn't keep the laughter from her eyes at his words. Pictures raced through her mind of the cantankerous old janitor's reaction to the mound of popcorn he was going to have to dispose of tonight. "You'd better not be around when he sees it," she warned him. She hadn't been aware that one of the usherettes was standing beside him until the girl cleared her throat to get their attention.

At the sound, the soldier turned to the chestnut-haired girl and smiled before saying to June, "You said you didn't go out with anyone until you'd been properly introduced. It appears that we have a mutual friend." When he finished speaking, he let his eyes move first to the young girl in the booth then to the usherette who was standing beside him. When June didn't reply, he said, "Phyllis and I went to school together, and she has agreed to introduce us." The usherette was beaming when she made the introductions. The persistent young man's name was Dick, and he'd just returned from two years of military duty in Europe...including being part of Patton's Third Army during the Battle of the Bulge. Turning to Dick, she informed him that the blond girl's name was June and that she was a junior in high school.

Undaunted by hearing that she was still a student, Dick repeated his request for a date by reminding her that she'd told him the only thing standing in the way of her going out with him was the fact that they hadn't been introduced. "You can't use that as an excuse any more," he stated. "We have been properly introduced now, and Phyllis can vouch for my good character," he added as he and the usherette exchanged conspiratorial grins.

"You can't back out now," Phyllis informed her. Then she snapped her fingers as if an idea had just occurred to her. "Why don't you ask him to the staff Christmas party next weekend?"

June flushed and tried to get out of inviting him by saying, "I don't think he would want to..."

Before she could say anymore, he interrupted. "Of course I would! I love parties! Besides, where I've been there hasn't been much of a chance to go to parties." His voice had dropped, and a note of sadness had crept into it as he uttered the last few words.

At first June sympathized with him, but one look at his face and she knew he was teasing her. "He's trying to play on my sympathy," she thought, as she moved her arm back and forth as if she were playing the violin. He laughed at her charade and said, "You won't believe it, but I do play the violin!"

While June was absorbing this bit of information, Phyllis said, "Aren't you going to ask him to the party?"

"Yes, aren't you going to ask me?" he asked.

"What about your girlfriend?" June said. "Hasn't she been waiting for you while you were overseas?"

"You mean Dixie?" he exclaimed. "We're just friends. I bumped into her and her sister on my way to the movie and asked them to come with me. She's not my girlfriend."

She reluctantly let go of the scenario she'd imagined of the young lovers being reunited and the returning soldier taking his girlfriend and his mother to see the movie. June giggled when she remembered thinking about how sweet it all was. This persistent soldier might be a lot of things, she thought, but she didn't think sweet was one of them.

Before the movie ended and the audience started to spill out into the lobby, June finally capitulated and found herself agreeing to let him come to the party with her. "That wasn't too painful, was it?" he teasingly asked. As the two women he'd brought to the movie made their way toward them, June scribbled the time and the date of the party on a scrap of paper and handed it to him. Before slipping it into his shirt pocket, he glanced at it and exclaimed, "Is this a joke? Are you telling me this party doesn't start until eleven p.m.?"

June and Phyllis both laughed at his bemused expression and explained that the party was going to be held on the stage behind the movie screen, and it couldn't start until the film was over. He might have thought this was a ruse on June's part to avoid going out with him, but Phyllis had certainly demonstrated that she was on his side. He was pretty sure he wouldn't have had this invitation without her help. Before he had a chance to say anymore, though, Dixie and her sister had joined him. "Don't tell me you're buying more popcorn!" Dixie exclaimed. "I don't think I'll ever eat another kernel as long as I live!"

Dick chuckled, and arm-in-arm with the two girls, he sauntered away. Before they reached the large double doors, he turned and mouthed the word, "Saturday." Then with a jaunty salute, he disappeared into the swirling snow of the night.

Before she was again deluged with customers, June turned to Phyllis and sarcastically exclaimed; "You were a lot of help!" Her friend grinned wickedly and replied, "Yes, wasn't I? You know, I think that without my help, you'd have let him get away!"

The look June cast her way clearly showed what she thought of her friend's interference. Undaunted, Phyllis said, "You just don't want to admit it, but you really wanted to go out with him...I just sped it up a little." To June's comment that she sure did, the usherette replied, "You'll have fun! He seems like a pretty nice guy!"

Hands on her hips, June faced her friend and repeated, "He seems like a nice guy?" Her blue eyes were flashing fire when she added, "I thought you said you knew him!"

For a split second, Phyllis lowered her eyes and studied the pattern on the floor before she replied, "I meant to say, he is nice. You don't think either one of us would have said we knew each other if we didn't?"

These words caused June to visibly relax. "She's right," she thought. "He will be fun to go out with! After all it's not as if we're getting married or anything! It's just a date!" It wasn't until later when she was ready to fall asleep and she started mulling over the events of the night that the thought crept unbidden into her mind that just possibly Phyllis and Dick hadn't really known each other. "I'm sure getting suspicious," she mused before she dismissed the thought from her mind. It was to be much later before she found out what had happened behind the scenes that night.

Apparently, after she'd first brushed Dick off with her comment that she didn't date strangers, he'd set out to find someone to introduce them. Not having seen anyone he knew, he'd approached the usherette and explained his dilemma. After he'd pulled the poor lonely service man routine, he'd been able to talk her into pretending that they were former classmates. Of course, by the time June discovered this it was too late to turn back.

~

The next morning at breakfast when she mentioned her upcoming date to her stepmother, Polly, her reaction was what June had expected. She wasn't pleased that her daughter was going out with a stranger. It hadn't taken long while her daughter was talking for her to figure out that if he had been overseas for a couple years, he would have to be at least twenty or twenty-one. "You're only fifteen!" she reminded June. "He's too old for you!"

"Mom!" June wailed. "I'll be sixteen next month!"

She looked at her daughter and sighed. She knew the two of them needed to talk more about her upcoming date, but for now she had to turn her attention to her eleven-month-old son, Freddy. He had somehow managed to get his hands on the bowl of cereal that she'd left next to his high chair, and was about ready to dump it on the floor. As she made a mad dash across the room in an effort to protect her just scrubbed linoleum, she felt her unborn child give her a strong kick in the ribs. "Just what I need," she thought. "Another rambunctious one!"

June had seen the near calamity and being closer to the high chair had reached it first and caught the cereal in mid-air. While some of it did splatter on the floor, it only took a few seconds for her to remove all traces of it. One look at her flushed face told June that this was not going to be a good day for her twenty-six year old stepmother. Five months pregnant with this second child, and unable to get any sleep because of the baby's colic, she was totally exhausted. "Sit down!" June good-naturedly commanded. "I'll get you a cup of coffee, and feed the baby."

Polly didn't require any coaxing. She gratefully sank into the chair and accepted the strong, steaming brew. As she watched her daughter spoon the cereal into the baby's mouth, she thought about the changes the last few months had brought. In January of 1945, this little redheaded baby boy had made his entrance into the world, and five months later she'd discovered that she was again pregnant. During the last few months of her first pregnancy, the doctor had told her that she would have to stay in bed if she wanted to carry the baby to full term. Her rather helpless mother had left her home in Mississippi and braved the northern winter to come to Ohio to care for her. "I don't think that she could have managed though if June, Cecil, and Burrel hadn't pitched in to help," Polly thought.

She hadn't told anyone, but since she had been so nervous when she was carrying Freddy, and even worse since his birth, she blamed herself for his colic. Although the doctor had told her there was no medical basis for this supposition, she was convinced that his lack of sleep was making her tense, and this very tenseness was contributing to his belly-aches and sleeplessness. Although the doctor had explained that she would have no problem carrying this second child, she couldn't keep the worry from creeping into her mind. Although she was the step-mother of three (this girl sitting across from her, and her two brothers Cecil and Dickie) and the birth-mother of Freddy, she found herself feeling like a little girl who wanted her mother.

Although she appreciated that the few minutes June had taken to feed the baby and entertain him had given her enough of a respite that she felt more able to face the day, she still wasn't any more happy about her daughter going out with this stranger. Shoving back a lock of red hair that had fallen onto her forehead, she removed the baby from the highchair and balancing him on her hip, turned to June and said, "We'll talk more about this later. Now I have to give Freddy his bath." June hurriedly completed her chores, and as she started out the door she called over her shoulder that she was going across the street to talk to her cousin Rose. Six months her junior, Rose was not only her cousin, but also her best friend. Since Rose was such a levelheaded girl, June had always confided in her and valued her opinion.

Before she was halfway across the street, she could smell the aroma of cinnamon and spices. She didn't need to be told that her Aunt Mabel and her cousins Rose, Inez, and Annamae were baking goodies for the holidays. She opened the door and called out, "That smells wonderful!"

She was answered by a chorus of voices telling her to come on out to the kitchen. Not needing to be coaxed, she ambled into the midst of their cookie baking. By the looks of the platters of goodies covering every available surface, it was obvious they had been at this chore for a long time. "Can't we take a little break now?" Annamae asked. With a smile at her younger daughter, Aunt Mabel agreed, but admonished them not to go far as they still had quite a bit more baking to do.

In response to June's whispered plea to talk to her alone, Rose filled a small plate with cookies, had June pour each of them a cup of coffee, and together they made their way to Rose's room. Sitting on her cousin's bed, she glanced across the street where she could see the angels she had carefully stenciled onto her own bedroom window. Following the direction of her gaze, Rose commented that they looked especially nice when the light was on in June's bedroom. "I've always liked the thought of having a guardian angel," June murmured softly.

Rose smiled at her cousin's flight of fancy before asking, "What's going on? What did you want to talk to me about?"

June swallowed the last bite of her cookie before she told Rose about the soldier she'd met the night before. The brown-eyed girl listened quietly until she finished speaking. Then she said, "I don't see any problem. He sounds alright to me."

"I guess so," June grimaced. "But like Mom said, he is older than I am!" When Rose didn't reply, she lowered her voice slightly when she added, "But if she or Dad say I can't go out with him, that'll be it. I'm not going to argue with them."

"Don't you want to date him?" Rose asked.

"I'm not sure," she replied. "I was kind of forced into asking him to the party. He and Phyllis were pretty insistent!" June tossed her head sending her straight blond hair flying around her shoulders. Then she exclaimed, "Besides that, I'm not sure I want to go out with a guy who brings one girl to the movies, stuffs her full of popcorn, then when she's watching the movie, he asks another girl for a date!" June looked at Rose for her reaction and to her surprise, she saw that she was laughing. "What's so funny?" June demanded.

"He didn't just desert one girl, he deserted two! From what you said, he came in with two girls! And he forced all that popcorn down their throats!" she whooped. "Don't you think that's funny?"

Her cousin's hilarity was contagious, and much to her surprise, June found herself giggling along with her. The noise had attracted Annamae and her older sister, Inez, who popped their heads through the door to find out what was going on. After Rose filled them in, they joined her in encouraging June to go on the date. "Besides," Inez said, "from what you've said, since you arranged to meet him at the party, you don't know how to get in touch with him, so if you did decide to cancel out," she hesitated a second, for effect, before she added, "If you want to avoid him, it looks like you are going to have to stay at home and miss the party." Inez had made a good point, one June hadn't thought of. No way was she going to miss this party. Besides, with all the people who would be there she wouldn't have to be alone with him for a moment. "There is safety in numbers," she mused. Then thinking of a couple of the usherettes who, she was sure, would make a play for him, she giggled as the thought crossed her mind that if he gave her any trouble, she'd turn them loose on him.

That evening, while she and Polly were sitting in the living room with her father, Burrel, watching Freddy using one of the large cushioned maple chairs as a walker, she found herself hesitantly broaching the subject of her upcoming date using Inez's rationale with her father. A quiet man, he sat in silent contemplation for a few seconds while he watched his youngest son maneuver the chair across the wide planks of the bare floor. His glance idly flicked to the oval braided rug that was rolled tightly in a bundle against the wall. Polly had told him that she had done that because it only frustrated the baby when it got in his way. Burrel let his eyes shift from his son to his daughter before settling on his wife's face. Her flashing eyes and tight lips reflected her disapproval at the prospect of their daughter going out with this young soldier. Before saying anything, he turned his attention to the blond girl. She looked anxious, but not particularly rebellious. "Did you tell her she couldn't go?" he asked his wife.

Her head moved from side to side as she responded, "No, not really. I just reminded her that he is too old for her to date."

Burrel downed the last drop of his coffee, and grinned before reminding her that the girl in question was going to be sixteen in a month. "Besides," he said, "I agree with June, there is safety in numbers. She's going to be at a party, and if I know those kids, there will be a lot of them around all the time."

With a flounce of her skirts and a muttered, "Humph," Polly got up and went to baby Freddy's rescue. He had somehow managed to shove the chair up against the wall and unable to move it, he was howling in frustration. Once she'd gotten the baby out of his dilemma, she looked at the Christmas tree in its strange position. Freddy had been so fascinated by it that they had been forced to put the tree inside the playpen and keep Freddy out. Smiling ruefully at the peculiar sight, she returned to her seat and brought the conversation around to the subject of Christmas.

With the exception of Freddy, who was fascinated with the tree and other holiday trappings, they were feeling ambiguous about the upcoming holiday.

They were looking forward to the baby's first Christmas, and a visit between Christmas and New Year from Burrel's thirteen year old son, Dickie, who lived with his mother, Priscilla, fifty miles away in Mansfield. On the other hand, this was going to be the first Christmas Burrel's oldest son, Cecil, had spent away from home. Seventeen years old, he'd joined the navy in August and was now stationed at Camp Perry, Virginia.

Everything appeared so normal in that cozy living room, that December of nineteen hundred forty-five, that no one could have foretold that this would be the last Christmas they would spend together as a family until after this red-headed infant and his unborn sibling were of school-age. But for this night, having settled the question of June's upcoming date, they'd said goodnight and gone to their rooms.

THE FIRST DATE

A few nights later, as June got ready for the party, she found herself smiling at the memory of the baby's reaction to his first Christmas. They'd all been amused to see that he'd been as fascinated by the bright wrapping paper and ribbons as by the contents of his gifts. One of the presents Santa had left for him was a toddler style rocking horse, with a seat flanked on each side by a wooden cutout in the shape of a mild looking steed. As she watched him ride it, her mind flashed back to the carousel that had seemingly sprung up on the grounds outside their house at Seneca Caverns when they'd been young children and their father had been the cavern's first manager. She smiled inwardly at the memory of what had seemed like a magical ride as she and her brother Cecil, had been allowed to choose from all the horses on the Merry-Go-Round. At that time she would never have dreamed of the changes that would take place in their lives, or that their future would include this red-headed woman and the little carrot-topped cowboy.

As she fastened the clasp of the pink gold locket she'd received from her parents for Christmas, she admired the delicate roses carved into its surface. She liked the way it looked against the pink wool of the sweater set she was wearing. Her mother, Priscilla, and stepfather, Bill, had given the sweaters to her for Christmas after she'd dropped some not too subtle hints to her Mom about being the only girl at Newark High School who didn't have one of these twin sets. As she studied herself in the mirror, she liked the way the set looked with her pink, white and blue plaid pleated skirt, white bobby socks, and saddle shoes. She dabbed some Evening In Paris perfume, her gift from her brother Dickie, on her wrists and behind each ear before she tore down the steps to join her friend Evelyn. Since they were neighbors and both girls worked for the Midland and Auditorium theaters, they were going to walk together to the party. A few minutes later, when they stepped through the door into the snow filled night, June was surprised to realize that she missed the teasing she'd always gotten from her older brother, Cecil. She could imagine his comments, if he'd been here now, about her being all gussied up for someone she wasn't even sure she wanted to date.

All of Newark lay blanketed in snow as if God had answered the prayers of the returning veterans for a white Christmas. As the two girls strolled along the almost deserted streets, they could hear the crunch of the snow under their feet and see it clinging to every bare tree branch. Sounds of laughter spilled from many of the houses they passed as people celebrated the first peacetime Christmas in the last four years.

When the two girls neared the Midland Theater, the door to a nineteen thirty-eight Chevrolet opened and the young soldier stepped out. He was smiling when he greeted them. When June introduced them, Evelyn moved to his side as if he were her date rather than June's. Although Dick was friendly when he acknowledged the introduction, his actions made it clear June was the one he wanted to be with. This action was repeated again when he met Mary. Although she tried to move in on him too, he was friendly, but nothing more.

While June and Evelyn had been friends and neighbors since June had moved to Newark almost three years before, she had only met Mary a few months earlier when they had started working together. Raven haired, blue-eyed Evelyn and Mary with her ash blonde hair and blue eyes were both beautiful, and June knew they couldn't resist flirting with every boy they met. Usually this didn't bother her, but tonight she flashed them a look that fairly shouted, "Back off!" Happily for June, Dick didn't respond to their attentions.

When they entered the movie house they found that it had been transformed. The movie screen and backdrops had been raised and the entire stage had been opened for their festivities. A brightly lighted Christmas tree was standing in one corner of the stage, garlands of green and red tinsel had been looped from wall to wall, and long food laden tables helped fill the wide expanse of the bare stage. After enjoying the party on the stage, some of the young staff decided it would be fun to explore the empty theater's dim, cavernous recesses. June and Dick and several of the others made their way to the balcony where they sank into the comfortable seats and watched the tableau unfold on the stage below them. Someone had brought a record player and some records. While the watchers could barely hear the music, they could see the dancers going through the gyrations of the jitterbug.

They also saw one of the ushers plant a kiss on the lips of an unsuspecting usherette and laugh as he pointed to the mistletoe suspended above her head. "Hmmm," Dick murmured, as he looked around for a sign of the mystical green plant. Although he didn't see any, this didn't deter him as June soon discovered when she found herself being soundly kissed. In response to her startled exclamation, he uttered one word, "Mistletoe!" as he gestured into the darkness. She couldn't see any, but then the light wasn't very good. Besides, who was she to argue?

Just in case he saw anymore of the "kissing plant", she decided she'd better lead him back to the stage. "Sorry, I can't offer you any popcorn," she quipped as they filled their plates from the platters heaped high with food. Sitting on the edge of the stage, they balanced their Pepsi and plates on their laps while they ate. They'd barely finished eating when the lights on the stage were dimmed as a signal that the party was over.

"Time to go!" June said as she slipped into her coat, pulled on her mittens and loosely wrapped her pink angora scarf around her head. Calling goodnight to her co-workers, she strolled along beside him until they got to the Chevrolet. "This is my dad's car," Dick said as he opened the door for her. "I have my name on several lists to buy one," he added. "But I'm afraid it's going to be a long wait."

Before he closed the door, Mary and Evelyn rushed from the movie house with requests for a ride home. "Hop in!" he told them as he held the back door open for them. Mary told him where she lived and let him know that since he'd have to pass her house on his way home, he might as well take the other girls home first. He didn't respond other than to ask Evelyn where she lived. Once he'd established this, he drove directly to Mary's house first then dropped Evelyn off at hers. He did this despite the fact that both girls had singly and jointly protested.

Once they had the car to themselves, he expelled his breath in relief and said, "That was a close call! For a moment there, I wasn't sure I was going to escape their clutches."

"You won't have to worry about them once they see that…" June said, before clasping her hand over her mouth. She was mortified to think that she'd almost told him that they'd quit their flirting once they found out she was interested in him. Since he'd figured out what she was about to say, he chuckled softly as he shifted into gear and maneuvered the car around the mound of snow that Evelyn's father had shoveled away from the curb.

When they arrived at June's home on Lawrence Street, she could see the dim light Polly had left burning in the hallway. Since it was after three o'clock in the morning, she hadn't really expected anyone to be waiting up for her. When she turned to see if her cousin Rose's light was on, she almost bumped into the young man who was sitting beside her. He'd slid over close to her and was holding a pale sprig of greenery above her head. "This time," he murmured, "you can't say that you can't see the mistletoe." Moving closer to the door, she laughingly asked, "Where did you get that?"

"From the stage," he said. "The janitor was just going to throw it out, and I figured I had a better use for it!" The teasing tone had crept back into his voice as he added, "You know you can have years of bad luck if you break a tradition." While she sat looking skeptical, he said, "You have heard about kissing under the mistletoe, haven't you?" She nodded, then leaned toward him and gave him a little peck on the lips before opening the car door and stepping into the cold brisk night. Before she'd made it to the first step of the front porch, he was beside her. "I want to see you again tomorrow night," he said. After she told him she would be working until almost ten p.m., he told her that he would be there when she got off. "Before I walk you home, I'd like to take you over to Drummond's for something to eat," he said referring to a sandwich shop down the street from the Auditorium.

When he returned to the car, she opened the door and stepped into the hallway. As she crossed the hallway, she was humming one of the tunes she'd heard earlier at the party. She almost jumped out of her skin when she heard a husky sounding voice from the living room whisper, "Shhh. I just got the baby back to sleep."

In the dim light, she could make out the form of her mother sitting in the rocking chair with the sleeping baby cuddled in her arms. As she had so many times lately, June immediately felt guilty at the thought that her racket could have awakened him, and she found herself stammering an apology. As she observed Polly's slumped shoulders and listened to the tiredness in her voice, she wished there was something she could do to help her. With every inch of her being, she loved and appreciated this redheaded woman who had become her stepmother four years earlier.

As her eyes adjusted to the dim light, she thought she could see a difference in her mother's expression. She didn't recognize it at the time, but what she was looking at was determination. That night while June had been at the party, and the young mother had been holding her baby and trying to sooth his colic pains, she'd come to a decision...one that was going to make a big difference in the lives of everybody in this household.

Unaware of the change that was soon to occur in her life, June quietly tiptoed up the steps to her room, undressed and slipped under the covers. Looking at her watch and realizing that it would only be a few hours before the early morning sun would be streaming through her windowpanes, she found herself thinking about the evening and feeling glad that she hadn't cancelled her date. Her last thought before she fell asleep was of how much fun the young soldier was to be with and how much she was looking forward to their next date.

BROTHERS

The next day she met her thirteen-year old brother, Dickie, at the bus station when he arrived to spend the rest of his Christmas vacation with the family. Since they had been separated for nearly three years when their parents were divorced and had only been reunited a little more than two years, they enjoyed every minute they spent together. Today was no exception. Walking home to the house on Lawrence Street, suitcase in hand, they joked about the time he'd first visited and how he'd managed to talk Polly into buying a huge watermelon...insisting it wasn't too heavy for him to carry the mile and a half home. "I'd never admit it to Polly," he said. "But there were times when I didn't think I was going to make it."

Remembering the nasty looks Polly had received from people along their trek from downtown, June laughed and said, "I thought for sure Mom was going to be tarred and feathered before we made it to our front door." The suitcase proved to be much lighter than the humongous watermelon had been, and neither one of them was tired when they got home. In fact, after Dickie had stowed his gear in Cecil's bedroom and they'd lunched on a bowl of soup and a sandwich, they set off for downtown again, this time for the Auditorium Theater where Dickie went to see the movie while June relieved her friend in the booth. Since June's shift didn't end until after the first evening movie was over, their father, Burrel, stopped for Dickie on his way home from work. As June saw her father's happy smile of greeting as his son scooted in beside him, her friend Mary stopped at her concession stand and said, "How come I didn't know about this younger brother? Where have you been keeping him?"

June grinned before she replied, "He may look older but he is only thirteen so don't get any ideas."

"Don't be silly," Mary replied. "I knew you had an older brother and a baby brother, I just didn't know you had another stashed away somewhere."

"He's not exactly stashed away. He lives in Mansfield with our mother and her second husband. When my Mom and Dad were divorced, Mom took Dickie, while Cecil and I stayed with Dad." June sighed before she went on to say, "Mom and Dad disagreed on custody issues but with a lot of help from my stepmother Polly, we finally got together and now I get to go visit Mom in Mansfield and Dickie spends time with us here."

∼

True to his word, the young soldier was there that night when she got off work. In fact, he'd come early in time to attend the movie with his brother. When June saw the wide glass doors swing open and the two of them saunter into the lobby, alarm bells went off in her head. "Uh oh!" she thought. She knew, Gene, the dark haired teenaged boy who was with him. She realized that Dick must be the brother Gene had told her about. Until this moment she hadn't connected the last name of her new acquaintance with that of her friend. Having done so, she felt decidedly uncomfortable as the memory flashed through her mind of the last time she'd seen Gene. She remembered how furious she'd been when he'd bombarded her with the words, "You're like all the other girls…You're uniform crazy!" His words dripping with sarcasm he'd added, "I have a brother in the army. You'll just love him!"

When they stopped at her booth, she heard Dick say, "I guess you know my brother, Gene." Her mind raced with the thoughts of how she'd asserted months earlier to Gene that she was prepared to hate his brother on sight.

"So much for that prediction," she mused as her lips twisted into a rueful smile.

Later that night, in Drummond's Sandwich shop while they were washing down their thick juicy cheeseburgers with chocolate milkshakes, Dick's eyes sparkled mischievously as he questioned her about having known his brother. "Gene was telling me a little about it, but I'd like to hear the rest of the story," he informed her.

A little embarrassed, she explained that a few months earlier she'd met his brother through a mutual friend and that they'd become friends. An avid moviegoer, Gene had gotten into the habit of hanging around until she got off work, then he'd walk her home. "One night," she said, with a laugh, "we were laughing and talking…really enjoying each other's company so much that after he walked me home, I returned the favor and walked him home."

He frowned when she said this, before saying, "You mean he let you walk all the way home from South Third Street by yourself?"

"Oh, no!" she exclaimed, "He walked me home again." She took a sip of her milkshake before she continued, "There had never been anything romantic between us…not even a kiss," she said. "That's why I was so surprised when he asked me to go steady."

"My brother always had good taste," Dick murmured.

June responded with a slight smile and a toss of her head before she hesitantly said, "I told him that I'd dated a boy named Butch, before he had enlisted in the navy, and that I'd been writing to him all the time he was in the service." Dick's steady gaze was making her feel so uncomfortable that all she wanted to do was get this story over with and change the subject. "When I told him that I was going to see Butch when he came home, Gene got mad and told me that I was uniform crazy like all the other girls, and that I would love his soldier brother." Her face had turned crimson when she told Dick that she'd said to Gene, "I'm prepared to hate your brother on sight."

"And did you?" he teased.

"Did I what?" she stammered.

"Hate me on sight," he said.

Noticing the glint of amusement in his eyes, she kept her voice light when she replied, "Obviously not, or I wouldn't be sitting here with you, would I?"

Almost as an afterthought, as they stepped out into the crisp night air, he casually asked if she were still writing to this sailor. When she informed him that she not only wrote to him but to several of her brother's navy buddies, he chuckled before saying, "Then I guess it wouldn't do me any good to ask you to go steady with me, would it?" Since this was only their second date, she didn't take his comment seriously nor did she dignify it with a response.

She thoroughly enjoyed the rest of her Christmas vacation. The days seemed to fly with her time divided between her brother, Dickie, and her new friend, Dick. Once the holidays were over, Burrel and June reluctantly took Dickie to the bus station and stood waving goodbye until the bus turned onto Mt. Vernon Road and disappeared from their sight. As she slid into the front seat beside her father she murmured, "I always hate to see him leave."

As he looked into her sad eyes, he reminded her of how much better it was now compared to two short years ago when Dickie hadn't been allowed to visit them at all. She knew he was right, and that she shouldn't complain about the brevity of his visits. The fact that Dickie was now allowed to come to Newark, and she could visit her mother and Dickie in Mansfield was doing a great deal to eradicate some of the pain of their three-year separation. When she voiced this opinion to her father, his warm smile and pat on her hand told her as clearly as words that he understood and shared her feelings. With their thoughts on what she'd just said, they rode the rest of the way home in companionable silence.

∼

Shortly before her sixteenth birthday, Dick received his orders to go to Camp Attebury in Indiana to receive his honorable discharge from the army. When he told her he'd be gone for a couple weeks, her mental calculations told her he wouldn't be back in time to help celebrate her birthday. Before he left, he'd let her know when she could expect him to return. That date passed without a word from him, but she managed to console herself with the thought that he must have been delayed. She knew that before he'd left there had been some confusion with his orders. Originally he'd been told to report to Indiantown Gap in Pennsylvania, but just before leaving, he'd received new orders sending him to the camp in Indiana. She rationalized that the reason he hadn't returned was that once he'd gotten there he'd probably been sent elsewhere.

Any thought though that this was some kind of military snafu was wiped from her mind one evening by a few careless words from her cousin Inez's husband, Bob. "When I was downtown today, I saw that soldier that you've been seeing. When did he get back?"

She managed to mutter that she didn't know before she was able to make her escape from her uncle's house to her own home across the street. When she reached the privacy of her room, it came home to her that despite his jesting banter about going steady and teasing about getting married, there had been nothing serious between them. As she sat in front of her vanity mirror and ran the brush through her hair, she smiled ruefully at her reflection and muttered under her breath, "Why should I take anyone seriously who would bring two girls to a movie then ask me for a date?" Brushing more vigorously than usual, she thought, "As Mom says, he's certainly not the only fish in the sea!"

As if to prove this old adage to be true, she went to a basketball game with one of Cecil's friends, a tall lanky sailor named John who was attending college at Denison University in Granville as part of the navy's V12 program. She'd also accepted a date with a co-worker to go to the Chatterbox for a frosted malt after work. While she enjoyed the dates, this didn't keep her from looking up every time she saw a dark-haired soldier approach her concession booth. While several men in uniform passed through the lobby, none of them were the one she was looking for.

After awhile, she had given up expecting to see him again, but one Saturday night she looked up and there he was standing beside her counter. When she'd thought of him, it had always been as a soldier in uniform, but tonight he was wearing civilian clothes. Dressed in a dark green tweed suit, a white shirt, and bright colored tie, he looked decidedly different from the soldier she was used to seeing. This feeling of strangeness, plus her resentment because he hadn't bothered to call since he'd returned, caused her to remain cool and aloof. Without so much as an explanation...let alone an apology...he asked if she'd like to go out to eat after she got off work. In her most haughty voice, she told him she'd already made other plans. Undaunted, he asked about the next night, and the next, until he wore her down, and she finally agreed to go out with him.

Since the next day was her day off, she and Dick decided to go to the Newark High School basketball game. She was glad to escape from the house and the tension that was building up between her parents. Neither one had told her what was going on, but she had been able to piece together enough from words they'd let drop to know that Polly wanted to do something and that June's father was violently opposed to it. Whatever was going on, it was making everyone in the household unhappy. Not for the first time, June wished her brother, Cecil, hadn't joined the navy. She missed having him around and being able to bounce her problems off of him. As she slipped into her coat, hat, and gloves and headed for the front door to greet her date, she wondered what her brother would think of this young man or what he'd make of what was going on between their parents.

Later that night, after they'd yelled themselves hoarse cheering for the home team, and had later soothed their throats with frosted malts at the Chatterbox, June found out why he had waited so long to come see her. She was bemused, amused, and a little angry when on the walk home he blurted out what was on his mind, "I was telling Dad how I've been joking about us getting married, and he said I'd better watch what I say. You might think I'm serious."

His words stopped her in her tracks. "Serious! About g-g-getting married?" she sputtered. Then with her hands on her hips she turned to face him and eyes flashing, she snapped, "You can tell your father that he doesn't have to worry about me. I'm only sixteen years old, and I have no intention of marrying you or anyone else...for a very long time!"

In response to his plea for her not to be mad, she said, "I'm not angry, but I do think your father is a little presumptuous. If he knows you at all, he should know that you joke around about everything. Maybe some other girl might think you were serious, but I sure didn't."

He spent the next few minutes trying to placate her by apologizing and telling her how much he'd missed her. Still smarting a little from what he'd said, she was careful not to let him know that she'd missed him too. "I wouldn't give him the satisfaction," she thought as they neared the house on Lawrence Street. When they got to the porch steps, she quickly told him goodnight and whispered that they had to be quiet or they would wake baby Freddy. Then she tiptoed across the porch, silently opened the door, and slipped through the doorway into the hall, leaving him standing on the porch looking at the closed door.

As she made her way up the stairs, she frowned at the thought of Dick's father's warning. She'd known that when he was talking about getting married, he was just joking. "What else would I think?" she thought as she slipped under the covers, pulled them under her chin, and promptly fell asleep.

As she had expected, he was waiting for her when she got off work the next night. Cheerful, teasing and joking, he acted as if he'd forgotten all about his father's warning...and her reaction. When they were walking home he said, "Some friends of mine are going skating at Ye Olde Mill Skating Rink near Utica on Saturday night and have asked us to go along. Do you want to go?"

"I would love to!" she exclaimed before she added, "I don't have to work this Saturday so it will work out fine for me."

Her excitement took a nosedive, though, when she told her step-mother about their plans. "I've told you before that he is too old for you," Polly exclaimed. "He's an adult and you're still a child."

Offended at being considered a child, June stated, "I'm sixteen. That is hardly a child!"

"He's almost 5 years older than you!" Polly reminded her.

Her step-mother realized that statement had weakened her argument when June came back with, "Isn't Dad sixteen years older than you are?"

"That's not the only reason I don't want you to go," Polly said. "We don't really know him or this other couple you're going with. What do you know about them?"

Intrigued by the bits and pieces of the conversation her father overheard, he ambled into the room and asked, "What's going on here?"

"Dick has asked me to go skating with him and another couple at Ye Olde Mill Rink near Utica. Mom doesn't want me to go," June bemoaned.

June's father turned to his wife and asked, "Why don't you want her to go?"

Polly replied, "He's too old for her and besides they'd be going with a couple she doesn't even know! She's trying to grow up too fast!"

After her father asked a few more questions, he agreed with his daughter and though her mother stomped out of the room in disgust, June was allowed to go. Although her date was familiar with the mill, that snowy night was the first time June had been there.

Bright light was spilling through the upstairs windows when they stopped in the parking lot of a large rustic building. They could hear the snow crunch beneath their feet and the sound of lively music and laughter spill out into the otherwise stillness of the night as the large double doors were thrown open and a large group of young people surged in. They followed them to the large room at the top of the steps. As her eyes adjusted to the brightness, she could see people of all ages twirling around the floor to the popular music. Dick's strong arm held her up as they joined the throng, and her skates seemed to take on a life of their own. Then before the last note was played and their skates removed, June decided that she was going to have to change her mother's mind about this young man.

Though Polly remained cool toward him for a while, his friendliness and strong personality soon won her over and she discovered that they were actually kindred souls.

From then on June and Dick were inseparable, taking in all the movies in town, going to school basketball games, and skating at the rink upstairs over The Olde Mill.

∽

All during the war, automobile factories had made tanks and other military vehicles. No new cars had come off the assembly line since 1942, and millions of servicemen were coming home anxious to buy a new car. Despite Dick having his name on the list at every automobile agency in Newark and surrounding towns, he still hadn't been able to buy a car. Every dealer he'd contacted had only shrugged and told him to be patient, that he wasn't the only returning serviceman. Consequently, except for rare times when he could borrow his father's car, they had to walk or ride the bus everywhere they went.

Tired of waiting, he'd looked into buying a used car, but due to the shortage, people were hanging on to them. In the rare case someone did decide to sell, they could get more for a used one than dealers were able to receive for a new one. "I never dreamed that I wouldn't be able to buy a car when I got home," Dick complained. "I've been saving for one ever since I went into the army. My paycheck was a whole fifty dollars a month, but the army took out ten dollars each month for insurance and another ten for dry cleaning and laundry. That left me with thirty dollars a month. Since I didn't drink or smoke, I was able to save half of what was left of my pay. I sent that home to Mom every month, and she put it in the bank for me." He went on to tell her that once he went overseas, he received a whopping ten dollars a month raise and an additional stripe, making him a Private First Class.

One warm spring evening as June was getting ready to go to work, she was surprised when Dick showed up at her front door. After he greeted her he said, "I've come to take you to work."

Excitedly, she cried, "Did you get a car?"

His eyes sparkled, as he grabbed her by the hand and pulled her to the porch where he exclaimed, "I've got us some transportation. There it is! A bright shiny red one."

Puzzled, she looked around for the car, but the only thing she saw by the curb in front of her house was a red bicycle with bright chrome fenders. The familiar older cars parked along both sides of the street belonged to her neighbors. Puzzled, she asked, "What's the joke?"

"No joke," he replied. "I borrowed my brother Kenny's bike to take you to work."

She refrained from expressing the thought that he must be out of his mind. Instead, she said, "I didn't even know that you had a bike. Did you just get it?"

He reminded her that it was his brother's bike, then he added. "I got it for Kenny when I got home from the army. I was hitchhiking home and my last ride dropped me off downtown in Columbus. I happened to pass a Cussins and Fearns store where they had a display of bicycles in the window. Since Kenny is only eight and seemed disappointed when I didn't bring anything to him when I got home from overseas, I'd been thinking about buying him a bike. On the spur of the moment, I went inside and before I had time to think about it, I plunked down twenty-nine dollars and wheeled it out of the store."

"Twenty-nine dollars?" she parroted. "That's almost a whole month's pay for you!"

He responded that his little brother was worth it. After absorbing this bit of information, she asked, "How in the world did you get it home? Did your dad come over and pick you up?"

He snorted in reply, "My dad? Are you kidding? I rode it home! I was tired of hitchhiking! That's why I bought it in Columbus." She looked at him doubtfully since she knew it was at least thirty-five or forty miles from Columbus to Newark, but after she heard the rest of his story, she believed him.

"I actually enjoyed pedaling through the maze of traffic in Columbus, but after a few miles on the highway, my legs started to get tired. I was a little cold, and I began to feel I had made a big mistake. Then a truck pulled up at a stop sign beside me, and I told the driver my tale of woe and asked if I could hang on to his truck for awhile so I could rest my legs. When he noticed my uniform, he agreed. He seemed to keep his speed down while I held on to the truck and coasted along beside him. We had only gone a few miles before I heard a siren and saw the red flashing lights of a police car coming up behind us. The trucker and I both got a lecture from the state highway patrolman on the danger we had put me in, but neither of us was cited. I think that was because of my uniform too. I was pretty sorry to see that trucker go, and the farther I pedaled the more sorry I became. It took me three and a half hours to get from Columbus to my house, but I finally made it." He smiled proudly when he added that Kenny's excitement when he saw the bike had made it all worthwhile.

When he finished talking, she glanced at her watch and exclaimed that she was afraid she was going to be late for work. "That's why I'm here," he said. Then grinning impishly, he said, "Hop on." At first she demurred, but he talked her into it, and while he pedaled, she rode on the bar between the seat and the handlebars until they got to the movie theater. When a few of her co-workers teased her about her new method of transportation, she lightheartedly said, "It beats being late," but secretly she had enjoyed it. While she'd rather have found a car parked at the curb, this had been an experience to remember, as were all their times together.

∼

While things were going well with her social life, the situation at home continued to deteriorate. Having walked in on an argument between her father and stepmother, she was now aware of the problem. Polly wanted to move to Mississippi so she could be close to her parents when the baby was born and have some help with Freddy and the new baby after it arrived. "We tried that once before," June heard her father say. "And it turned out to be a disaster!" After a slight hesitation, he'd demanded, "Don't you remember? I couldn't begin to get a job. That's why we moved back here in the first place." He'd raked his hand through his thick blond hair and cast a pleading look her way before he'd added, "Besides June will be going into her senior year of school in a few months. I know she wouldn't want to go to another school."

"I know all of that," she'd replied. "But what you don't understand is that if I go to Mississippi, Mama will be there, and there will be household help. Lee took care of me when I was a baby, and she's still working for Mama and Daddy." Sighing deeply, she'd added, "I'll be able to get some sleep...for a change."

"We can't uproot this entire family to move someplace where I know I won't be able to get a job," he announced through tight lips, before adding, "And that's all there are to it!" That expression usually preceded by, "Hursh I-med-i-ate-ly!" always signaled the end to any conversation. Not this time, though, as Polly had made up her mind and no matter what he had to say, she wasn't going to change it.

June waited until after breakfast the next morning before broaching the subject to her stepmother. Then while they sat sipping coffee and watching Freddy try to escape from the confines of his playpen, she said, "I overheard you and Dad talking last night. I just want you to know that I don't want to move back to Mississippi. Dad was right, it would be awful to leave Newark before I graduate. Besides, I have a lot of friends here that I wouldn't want to leave behind."

"Especially that young man you've been seeing!" Polly said. "I want the entire family to go, but if you and your dad want to stay here, that's up to you!" she said. "But Freddy and I are leaving." June couldn't tell whether the unshed tears in Polly's eyes were from frustration or disappointment, but there was no doubt in her mind that her young mother meant what she was saying. When June reiterated that she just couldn't go, in her ears, her voice sounded like the little girl she'd been when this redheaded woman had come into her father's life after her parents' divorce. Although she knew that this woman had given her a home and a mother's love when she'd so desperately needed it, she still couldn't bring herself to say that she would go with her. Instead, her eyes brimming with tears, she pleaded, "Please don't go. We're a family and we need you here. I know that you are tired, but I can help you with Freddy so you can rest."

Polly sighed before she replied, "I know you would try to help but with school and your job, you wouldn't have the time."

"How about your mother? She came the last time. Couldn't she come up this time?"

Polly smiled ruefully before she said, "You know how helpless Mama is! The only reason we got by when I was pregnant for Freddy and had to stay in bed for months was because of all that you, Cecil and your dad did to help."

"Dad and I still would," June replied.

"You're forgetting that we have a colicky baby who won't let me sleep day or night and another will be here in a couple months." She wiped the tears from her eyes before she added, "I am exhausted and just have to have some help! I don't want to leave you and your dad, but I don't see any other answer."

"I remember the last time we were there and Dad had to come back here to get a job. Is the job situation any better now?" June asked.

Polly replied, "There's nothing in that area in his field now, but I'm sure something will come up soon. He can join me when it does. We'd be with Mama and Daddy and you could graduate from the same school that I did. I could put in a good word for you with the teachers since the ones I had are most likely still there."

June couldn't resist teasing Polly when she heard that. "Are you sure they would want me when they find out I'm your daughter?"

For the first time since they'd started talking, Polly laughed before she said, "I guess I shouldn't have told you about some of my high school escapades." Then in a more sober tone she asked if that meant that June had changed her mind and would want to go.

June replied, "I really don't want to go, but I'll face that if Dad gets a job down there. For now, though, I need to be here with him."

Their conversation was interrupted by a frustrated screech from Freddy who had thrown his favorite toy out of the playpen and was reaching frantically for it.

～

Despite all June and Burrel's efforts, Polly who was seven months pregnant took her young son and left her husband and daughter behind and boarded a plane for the flight to Mississippi. The two who had been left behind had a difficult time without her. The house was too empty when they returned in the evenings, and they missed her smiling face and Freddy's chatter.

Since Polly had never wanted anyone in her kitchen, June hadn't learned to cook. Burrel had some cooking experience, and Aunt Mabel was generous enough to invite them to eat with them occasionally. With a few trips to the lunch counter at Woolworth for a cheeseburger, fries, and a milkshake, they did manage to fight off the hunger pangs.

The baby was due in May, and Burrel had promised Polly that he would be there. They had already arranged for June to stay across the street with her cousin Rose while he was gone. Before leaving for Mississippi, though, Burrel made a quick trip to West Virginia to see his father, Ulysses. While he was there the word came that the baby, a beautiful dark-haired boy had been born. Without returning to Newark, he headed for Mississippi. When he arrived, he could tell by looking at his new son that something was wrong. He looked pale and listless. "I think we'd better take him to the doctor and see what's wrong," he told his wife. "He doesn't look as if he's getting enough to eat. Maybe your milk isn't rich enough for him." He was familiar with this condition as his younger sister Nellie had lost five babies before the doctor in West Virginia had discovered the problem.

Barely taking time to greet his mother-in-law or father-in-law, he picked up his newborn son and bundled him in a blanket and with Polly in tow, he drove directly to the doctor's office. The doctor took one look at what had been a healthy, strapping baby only a few days earlier, and told the new mother that she would have to put him on a bottle. She didn't take kindly to the news, as she had been looking forward to breast feeding this infant. Despite her protests, the doctor was adamant when he told her that the baby's life might have been in danger if they had waited much longer. Chagrined, the new mother almost collapsed in her husband's arms as she cried in gratitude that he'd arrived when he did and had recognized the symptoms.

Burrel stayed at the Srite home for a couple weeks with Polly, Freddy, and the new baby who had been named William Cecil...the first name after Polly's father, Will Srite, and the middle name after two important men in Polly's life, her oldest brother and Burrel's oldest son. He was able to stay long enough to see his new son change from the pale wan infant he'd first seen to a rosy cheeked baby. Before leaving, he echoed a comment Polly had already heard several of her friends and family members make, "He is really a beautiful baby."

The new mother smiled and said, "I can't believe that I told the doctor to put him back when he told me that I had another boy! I really had my heart set on a girl this time."

Rubbing her shoulder, she told him that when she'd complained to the big strapping nurse, the woman had slapped her on the shoulder and told her she should be ashamed for even thinking such a thing when she had such a nice baby. The new father chuckled and said, "I know how you felt when you first found out, but I bet you wouldn't exchange him for a girl now, would you?"

She grinned before replying, "I'd like to see someone try to get him away from me!"

They'd been sitting in rocking chairs on the front porch enjoying the soft balmy springtime breeze while they'd been talking. "That's one thing I like about the South," he said. "The weather is so nice. If I could only find a job here, I might be able to work things out so that I could join you."

"Have you even looked?" she asked.

"I've been scouring the want ads, and today I checked at the union hall in Jackson," he replied. In response to the question in her eyes, he explained that there weren't any jobs for electricians anywhere within a hundred-mile radius. She assured him that she'd keep her eyes open. She'd also have her sister, Ruby, and her dad talk to some of their friends to see if they knew about any that might become available. "Don't you want to come back to Newark?" he asked that night after they'd turned in.

"Not now," she replied. "It's so nice to have someone here around the clock who can help me with these babies. They're just too close together for me to handle both of them. Especially if the baby would turn out to be as colicky as Freddy has always been."

"I guess it wasn't such a good idea having them so close together," Burrel muttered.

He could hear the laughter in her voice as she replied, "I seem to remember that they were both little surprises." He let out a whoop that Polly's parents could hear through the thin walls. The sound of merriment made Polly's parents wonder if the little family might get back together.

WHO'S WINNING?

While all these things had been going on in her parents' lives, and June's junior year in high school was winding down, she'd continued to spend a major portion of her free time with Dick. A couple months earlier, while they'd been sitting in her Uncle Mace's living room, Dick had made a surprising announcement that had almost ended their relationship. He told her he'd been dating a girl before he went into the army, and she had written to him while he was overseas. He concluded his confession by saying that before he'd boarded the ship for the states, he had written and told her he'd visit her in Florida when he got home. He looked startled at June's quick response, "You mean you said you would go see her and you didn't?" He had expected her to be angry at the news, but in his wildest dreams, he hadn't expected her to be concerned about his neglect of the other girl. "Did you ask her to wait for you?" June asked accusingly.

"No!" he exclaimed. "We only had a few dates before I went into the army."

"But you said she wrote to you all the time you were in the service. And I suppose that means you wrote to her too?" June said in a questioning voice. When he slowly wagged his head up and down, her expression clearly showed her disappointment in him. He went on to say that he'd clearly intended to take a train to Florida to see the girl, but once he came into the Auditorium that night, and she sold him those first three boxes of popcorn, all thoughts of any other girl had gone out of his mind.

"Why are you telling me about it now? Did you change your mind?" she asked.

He was quick to respond that he hadn't changed his mind, but something had happened that had made him remember his promise. "Her brother came to see me this afternoon. He'd heard that I was home, and he just wanted to let me know that his sister was expecting a visit from me." After a slight hesitation, he stammered, "I-I-I suppose...I really should go see her."

June surprised him by replying, "I certainly would hope so!" Then with a defiant tilt to her chin, she told him that she thought he should have gone when he first got home. This reaction was too much for him. He had fully expected her to say that she didn't want him to go, then he would have given in and told her that if she felt that way about it, he'd just tell the other woman that he wouldn't be seeing her again.

This discussion led to their first quarrel, with June insisting that he go, and Dick that he didn't want to date anyone except her. Before the evening was over, he'd found himself asking her to go steady. After all the words that had passed between them during the last couple hours, June was reluctant to tell him that she couldn't, but she finally did. Displeased with her answer, he demanded to know why she wouldn't go steady with him. "Is there someone else," he asked. He couldn't imagine that her answer would be yes, but it was. "But you haven't dated anyone else for the last couple months," he exclaimed. His eyes took on a suspicious glint when he added, "Or have you?"

Before she had a chance to reply, Rose looked into the room to say hello but when she saw the air was charged with what was going on between them, she hastily made her exit saying, "I think I'll take this magazine to bed with me, and read for awhile." As she placed the newest issue of her father's labor union journal under her arm, the ludicrousness of her choice of reading material seemed to break the ice.

"There's a copy of Modern Screen around here somewhere," June blithely called after her. "It might be lighter reading." Looking for the first time at the magazine she was carrying, Rose's laughter rang out as she headed for the kitchen.

Once she was gone, June returned her attention to the man sitting beside her. "Do you remember when I was telling you about the argument I had with your brother when I told him that I was writing to a sailor?" she asked.

He nodded and said, "But you've never mentioned him since. I just thought he was out of the picture." She explained that he hadn't been discharged yet but when he was, she wanted to be free to see him. June had discovered that Dick had a habit of hiding his true feelings behind jokes and teasing, and this was no exception. No way was he going to let her know if he were upset. In fact, when he left a short time later, Aunt Mabel commented on what a good mood he'd been in. June shook her head in puzzlement as she watched him take two steps at a time on his down the stairs leading to the street. "Strange," she mused. "I thought for a minute he was angry."

∼

A couple weeks later, June received a phone call from the sailor's mother inviting her to attend a Newark High School basketball tournament game in Worthington. The call came as a surprise to her as she had only met the woman once a few months earlier when she had taken a gift to her. At the theater June had been watching a newsreel of the war, and had recognized her sailor friend, Butch, in the film. She had gone to the projectionist and talked him into cutting out a section of the film and giving it to her. Then she had taken the slice of film to Passman's photo lab and Mr. Passman had developed it into a print for her. The sailor's mother had appeared to be pleased by June's action, but had not contacted her until now.

June's first thought was that the sailor must be home, and this was his and his mother's way of surprising her. As it turned out, she was surprised but not in the way she had anticipated. It wasn't Butch in the car who showed up to pick her up, but his older brother. He had just received his discharge from the navy and his mother remembering June's kindness had wanted the two of them to meet. Although June was disappointed that Butch wasn't home, she couldn't graciously find a way to back out, so she smilingly acknowledged the introduction and got into the car with Gene. As she sat beside him, she marveled at the coincidence of both her male friends having brothers with the same first name.

The game turned out to be exciting with Newark ahead by a slight margin. Sitting next to Gene, she had just turned to make a comment about what a good job the Newark team was doing when she became aware someone had sat down next to her. She didn't even glance his way until a male voice said, "Who's winning?"

Without looking toward the sound of the voice she replied. "We are!"

His muttered reply of, "It's always good to know who's winning!" caused her to sharply turn toward him. She was surprised to see that the voice belonged to Dick. Unable to contain her amazement, she exclaimed, "What are you doing here?" He explained that he'd stopped at her uncle's house and that her aunt had told him she'd gone to the game...with some friends. Casting an appraising glance at Gene, he asked, "Is this the sailor?"

Flustered, she replied, "No! I mean yes! That is, he is a sailor, but..." Before she could finish her sentence, he stood up and wove his way through the cheering throng. The whistle had blown, and Newark had just won the game, but June didn't feel very happy about it. In fact, she had a sinking feeling that she had just lost something more important than a ballgame.

She didn't have long to wait to see what Dick's reaction was going to be. The next day she had a letter from him telling her that when he asked who was winning, he wasn't talking about the game. He went on to say that when he'd played violin in the Licking County Symphony Orchestra, he'd never liked playing second fiddle, and he wasn't going to start now. He concluded the letter with the words, "It's been nice knowing you. Maybe we'll see each other around town sometime."

Hoping that time would help him cool down, she fully expected to see him waiting to walk her home after work the next day, but it didn't happen. Nor did it the next or the next. Hurt and disappointed, she decided to concentrate on school and spending time with her friends. One of those friends was Vonnie Garver who was dating Dick's best friend, Dale Bennett. A few months earlier, when Dale returned from his stint in the marines, Dick and June had introduced them. It had been a case of love at first sight, and the two of them were already discussing marriage. Vonnie's prattle about her romance made June happy for her friend, but only added to her own depression about the breakup with Dick.

Later that week when her aunt called her to the phone, June whispered, "Is it Dick?" The older woman shrugged her shoulders when she handed the phone to her and whispered in return that all she knew was that it was a man. June only had to hear the voice say, "Hello," to know that the caller wasn't the young soldier she'd been hoping to hear from. Instead, it was the sailor, Gene, who wanted to know if she'd like to go to a movie on her night off. Her spirits brightened somewhat as she accepted his invitation. She was aware that her feelings were beginning to change. While earlier she had been brooding over Dick's reaction and feeling guilty, now she was becoming irritated. "The least he could have done was listen to me," she thought. Besides, Gene was a really nice man, and she was looking forward to seeing him again.

They went out together a few more times, and became good friends. Her original opinion of him increased every time she saw him. He was truly one of the nicest persons she'd ever met. One night when he came to see her, he told her that he had good news. His brother, Butch, was coming home. "He'll be here next week. You may be interested to know that when I talked to him on the phone, he said one of the first things he was going to do was come to see you when he got back to Newark."

June could feel her face flush in pleasure while she listened to him speak. She'd already told Gene about how she and Butch had been friends before he enlisted, and that she'd been writing to him ever since he'd left Newark for boot camp. She'd explained that all the time when he'd been somewhere in the South Pacific, she'd dutifully sent letters to him in care of the Fleet Post Office in San Francisco. "It was always a challenge trying to read his letters with the way the censors used to chop them up!" she bemoaned. Gene chuckled in response and told her that sometimes servicemen would write something that the censor thought might give away a military secret. "Is that what my brother was trying to do?" he asked.

"I don't know, but it must have been," June said. "The letters I got from him would read something like this," she quipped. "Dear June, Today we," she said, as she made a scissoring motion to indicate that the next few words had been cut out. Then laughingly she went through the rest of the imaginary letter with only an occasional word remaining before she got to the signature which was left intact.

Their conversation for the rest of the evening was about his brother, and how much they were looking forward to seeing him. When she told him goodnight at the end of the evening, they knew this would be their last date. As much as she wanted to see both of them, she realized that according to the unwritten rules of dating, it would never work.

―――

A few days later, she had a wonderful reunion with the returning sailor. They spent hours walking and talking about everything that had happened to each of them since the last time they'd been together. Their steps seemed to automatically take them to a little soda fountain downtown beside the Midland Theater where he'd broken the news to her a couple years earlier that he had enlisted in the navy. As June sat across the table from him, and listened to the words to the song, *It Seems Like Old Times*, she thought that the words were appropriate. It did seem like old times in some ways, but in other ways it didn't. As before, she felt happy being with him, but as she smiled into his gray eyes, she found herself thinking about a pair of mischievous brown ones.

She had always thought of Butch as very handsome with his blond hair and gray eyes, and she was aware that time had made him even more attractive. "What a nice face," she thought, but as much as she liked it, the face of another person kept dancing through her thoughts. As she listened to him talk, gently teasing her about the time she'd sent him fur lined gloves for Christmas when he was on an island with an average temperature of one hundred-fifteen degrees, she couldn't keep the picture of the dark haired soldier out of her mind. The picture remained clear, even as she quipped, "How was I expected to know where you were? The censors had cut so many holes in your v-mail letters that all I could read was my name and your signature. You could have been in the Aleutians for all I knew."

He flashed his white teeth in a grin while he talked about how they weren't even allowed to write about the weather as the military brass thought that might give away some military secrets. While he regaled her with stories about some of the happenings on his ship, she was remembering how much fun it was to be with him. One particularly poignant evening they'd spent together months before she met Dick edged into her mind.

She remembered it as a warm evening late in May of nineteen forty-four. She had been looking forward to seeing a movie that was playing at the Grand Theater in downtown Newark. Since she was unable to convince Rose to go with her, she had decided to go alone. Halfway through the movie she had been so intent on the action taking place on the screen that she had barely noticed when someone slid into the seat next to her. This had changed in an instant, though, when her seatmate whispered her name and she felt a familiar hand on her arm. Several moviegoers had shushed her when she'd cried out, "Butch, it can't be you. I thought you were in the South Pacific!"

Butch had laughed and said, "I'm home now," before he suggested that they leave and go to the ice cream shop by the Midland Theater so they could talk. Once they'd settled into their favorite booth and Butch had ordered banana splits, he'd told her that he had to leave the next morning. He explained that there was scuttlebutt that something big was in the works but they weren't sure what it was. He just knew that the landing ship on which he was stationed was going to be part of it. "I was given this one day to come home and see my family, but I couldn't leave without seeing you."

After they had finished their ice cream, they'd walked the short distance to her home on Lawrence Street. When they had neared the house June had noticed the one light shining through the window and realized that her brother Cecil wasn't home yet. She'd explained this to Butch and added, "Mom is visiting Dad who is working out of town. It's a nice night so we can sit here on the porch and talk." She smiled when she remembered how that simple decision had almost gotten her into trouble with her mother.

Noticing her smile Butch asked, "What are you smiling about?'

June replied, "I was just remembering the night you came home for the overnight leave and we sat on the porch all night and talked. Just as the sun came up and you were kissing me goodbye, a neighbor stepped out on her porch and saw us. She let me know in no uncertain terms that she was going to tell Mom what I had been up to as soon as she got home."

Butch laughed, "I remember that night and how we had so much to talk about that we talked until we were hoarse. I guess with us not knowing what I might be going back to, we just didn't want to say goodnight. As I recall, some talking and some kissing were the extent of what we were up to when we spent that night together on your front steps."

"Cecil could attest to that with the way, since once he got home, he kept popping out to ask when I was coming in," June said. "He told me the next morning that he didn't go to bed all night. After I told Mom about the possibility that you would be going into a big battle, she was very understanding and wasn't mad at all."

Butch said, "I'm sure when you heard about D-Day on June 6th you realized that was the big secret mission."

"I figured it out when I read the headlines about the navy being involved, including LSMs like the one you were on, in landing men on the beach at Normandy. I sat through the newsreel a couple times just to be sure that I heard everything about what they're calling D-Day."

When he replied, June felt that momentarily, although he was sitting across from her, his mind was back in the battle. "Our ship was part of a large fleet that landed troops on the beach at Normandy that day. It is hard to put into words the noise and the chaos as the fighting went on."

Now that the war was over, and he again sat across from her in their favorite restaurant, she reached across the table for his hand before she said, "I'm glad you are safely home."

Happy as she was to be with him, though, she couldn't keep thoughts of Dick from intruding into their pleasant evening together. "I need some time to think," she mused, "without either of them around." She surprised herself almost as much as she did her companion when she blurted out the words, "I'm going to spend a couple weeks in Mansfield with my real mother."

In response to his startled expression, she told him that her father was still in Mississippi with her stepmother, her baby brother, Freddy, and the newborn baby, Billy. "Mom has been wanting me to visit now that school is out. She knows that once Dad gets back, I'll want to stay home and take care of him. While she'd been talking, she'd scribbled her mother's address on a napkin and handed it to him. While he was carefully folding it and putting it in his wallet, she said, "If you want to write, I'd love to get a letter from you that hasn't been chopped up by the censors." He grinned and said that he would write, and maybe come to see her while she was gone. "That is if I can borrow Dad's car," he explained. "I hear it is impossible to buy a car now days."

~

For the next couple weeks, while she was in Mansfield, June tried to get both young men out of her mind as she enjoyed being with her mother and her brother, Dickie. During the day, though, she was alone while her mother and stepfather were working, and Dickie was caddying at the golf course. The first couple days she rattled around the house all day, sometimes reading or listening to the radio. Mrs. Shier, her mother's next door neighbor came to her rescue by introducing her to Audrey, a girl her age who lived down the street. The two girls soon began spending their afternoons at the swimming pool. One such afternoon, June did something she was soon to regret. She and her new friend spent the entire afternoon sitting on the side of the pool, feet dangling into the water while they chatted and flirted with a couple boys Audrey had introduced to her. Audrey with her dark complexion didn't have to worry about burning but with her fair skin, June should have been cautious. Although, during the afternoon, she could feel the effects of the sun, she ignored it. If she felt too hot, she'd jump into the pool and swim around for a few minutes. By the time they started their trek home, she was beginning to feel uncomfortable. Later that night her mother rubbed vinegar over the burned area, but it didn't remove any of the sting. The next morning when she looked in the mirror, she let out a groan that could be heard throughout the house. Her face was so red that she hardly recognized herself. It didn't take long for her to discover that her appearance was the least of her problems. The sunburn was so bad that even the touch of the lightest clothing caused her to cry out in pain. She was so miserable that she didn't need to be told by her mother to stay in the house that day. The pain made her aware that her days of sitting beside the pool were over for the rest of her visit.

She was to discover when she returned home that the burn was more serious than she had realized. Her father, who had come back during her absence, was tempted to tease her about her red face, but when he saw how much pain she was experiencing, he immediately took her to see Doctor Smith. The tongue-lashing he received from this crotchety female doctor took him back eighteen years to the one she'd given him after he'd taken his eight month pregnant first wife, Priscilla, over the rough roads to visit her parents in Rocky Fork. He could remember as vividly as if it had only been yesterday how furious the doctor had been when the trip had brought on Priscilla's labor, causing Cecil to be born a month early.

Now, the doctor was telling him that he should have had more sense than to allow his daughter to fry herself. While the doctor was still muttering something under her breath about what this younger generation was coming to, June sprang to her father's defense taking all the deserved blame herself. She withered under the doctor's frigid stare, though, and listened quietly while she was told how serious the burn on the upper part of her legs was. Doctor Smith gave her a shot of penicillin to eradicate the infection that had already begun and some salve to put on it twice a day, and scolded both of them again before they managed to escape to the safety of Burrel's car.

June wasn't too happy about the doctor's parting remark, though, as she'd told her to stay off her feet for a few days. There was so much going on at the movie house that she really didn't want to miss a minute of it. An air of excitement had been filling the Midland theater because of the upcoming visit of the actor, Anthony Quinn, and his co-stars to promote his new movie, *Back To Bataan*. June and the rest of the staff had been invited to a party backstage so they could meet this crew from Hollywood. June explained all this to her father on the ride home from the doctor's office. Once he'd ascertained that this event was still a few days away, he assured her she wouldn't have to miss it. While she waited for the infection to clear, her feelings were ambiguous. She wanted to go to the party, but she hated the way she looked. The big day finally arrived, and June was hoping a miracle had happened overnight and that her skin would be back to its usual hue, but one look in the mirror told her that she still looked like somebody masquerading as a lobster.

"My one chance to meet a movie star, and I have to look like this," she wailed to Rose. Her cousin told her to quit worrying about it, and then she added that at least June was getting to meet him. Her expressive brown eyes seemed to say that she would be willing to change places with her. Feeling guilty at being so insensitive, June left her cousin for the walk downtown.

This party reminded her of the last one she'd attended on this stage. Only now, the glittering stars weren't on the Christmas tree, but were the human variety from Hollywood. Anthony Quinn was more handsome than he looked on the screen with his broad shoulders, blue black hair, tan skin, and flashing white smile. He was friendly...spending as much time with the members of the staff as he did with the dignitaries who'd also been invited.

When June and an usherette hesitantly approached him, he very graciously complimented each of them on their "pretty blue eyes". While both girls responded with radiant smiles, he lightly teased June about the dangers of too much sun. "A good many young girls find that out when they first come to Hollywood," he added seconds before the mayor and his wife literally drug him away to talk to some of the city officials. As the two girls watched him join the stodgy looking group June turned to her friend and smiled. The evening had turned out much better than she had anticipated. Star-struck like most girls her age, she was delighted, even remotely, to be compared with the girls in Hollywood.

~

A few days later she received a letter postmarked Columbus. According to the return address it was from a Richardo Butterinski. Carrying the letter into the house, she let the name roll around in her mind, "Richardo Butterinski, Richardo Butterinski." She thought she'd seen that handwriting before, but she wasn't sure. She did know, though, that she didn't know anyone by that name. After she slit open the envelope and saw the words scrawled across the pages of white stationary, she exclaimed. "Good heavens! It's from Dick!" Since she was alone, she felt foolish talking to herself. Before she settled down to read the letter, she looked around as if she expected criticism from the furniture or the clock on the wall. As she slowly absorbed his words, she could feel herself relax. He'd started by telling her that while he was taking advantage of the GI bill of rights and going to school, he was staying with his Uncle Alvin, his Aunt Mary, and their five-year-old son, David. He went on to say that he was doing well in school. The letter continued in this vein for several pages before she came to the part that she really wanted to hear...how much he'd missed her. Telling her that his uncle was going to let him borrow the car on Saturday, he concluded by saying he'd like to come to Newark to see her. As a P.S., he told her to drop him a line if this wasn't convenient. Then in his most jaunty manner, he'd said he hoped he didn't hear from her. (Since that would mean she didn't want to see him again.)

She practically flew across the street to share her news with Rose. Waving her letter in the air, she bounded up the stairs to her cousin's room. "Whoa!" Rose exclaimed. "What's going on?" She'd been sitting in front of her vanity table brushing her hair when her cousin had burst into the room. She let her brush drop onto the tabletop as she turned to hear what June had to say. Tossing the letter onto Rose's lap, she said, "Look what I got today!"

Rose picked it up and looked at the return address before she said, "Who in the world is Richardo Butterinski?"

Although she had asked the same question when she first saw the envelope, she was impatient with Rose's question. Grabbing the letter and turning to the last page, she said, "It's from Dick! He's coming over on Saturday!"

Always practical, Rose reminded her that she had to work that night. June groaned before saying, "I'll just have to trade with someone. There's no way I'm going to write and tell him not to come. If I did, he would probably think I didn't want to see him. This is the first I've heard from him since he sent me that letter saying he wasn't going to play second fiddle, and maybe we'd see each other around town. If he wants to make up, I'm not going to discourage him."

Rose agreed with everything she was saying, and encouraged her to get busy if she wanted to talk someone else into working for her.

As it turned out, her good friend, Juney Hickman, volunteered to take the evening shift for her. June had to work during the afternoon, though, causing her to get home only a few minutes before Dick was expected. As she approached Rose's house she saw an unfamiliar car parked a few doors down the street. She'd never seen one quite like it. While most cars of the day were painted one or two colors, this one was three toned. Curious she dashed into the house calling out, "Have you seen that monstrosity parked down the street?" Her question was met with silence, but Rose was making shushing motions and pointing toward the closet. "Uh oh," June thought before she whispered, "Whose is it?"

As if in response, Dick poked his head out of the closet. His eyes were gleaming with amusement when he informed her that the monstrosity in question belonged to his Uncle Alvin. June could feel her face burning, but she felt better when she realized that he thought it was funny. That didn't keep him from teasing her about it, though. "Things must be back to normal," she mused. "If he's kidding around, he must not be angry at me anymore for being out with Gene."

Before the night was over, she found that anger was the furthest thing from his mind. As she soon discovered, he was thinking more in the line of love. Later when they were finally alone, he asked her if she would marry him when she graduated from high school the following year. While she wasn't quite ready to make that much of a commitment, she did agree to go steady. "How about being engaged to be engaged?" he asked. That sounded good to her as she had already decided that he was the man she wanted to marry...when she was old enough to get married.

When she accepted his proposal, he joked about buying some Cracker Jacks so he could get a ring for her. She went along with his bantering by saying that would suit her fine...for now. She told him that she really didn't want a ring until they were ready to become officially engaged. They both agreed that would be sometime during her senior year of school, and that they would be married in June, following her graduation. He told her that by then he would not only be out of school but would have been working in his dad's barber shop for a few months. Neither one would have guessed that July night, but those carefully made plans were doomed to go awry.

Now June had the unpleasant task of telling Butch that she wouldn't be seeing him anymore. Imparting the news wasn't as difficult as she had thought it would be. As it turned out, he wasn't surprised since she had mentioned Dick's name several times in the last few days. Although their parting was amicable, June felt as if she were losing one of her best friends as she watched him walk out of her life. She consoled herself, though, with the thought that now she could relax and enjoy the decision she and Dick had made about their future.

❧

While the two of them were happily planning their future, June was concerned about her father. He seemed to be rattling around the house like a little lost boy trying to be strong and brave. She knew him too well, though, not to realize that he was lonely without his wife and two babies. One evening after they'd gotten home from one of their usual dinners of hamburgers at Woolworth's Five and Ten Cent store lunch counter, June broached the subject. "Dad," she said. "I think you should go back to Mississippi."

"Do you want to go?" he asked. While his spirits had briefly brightened at her words, her reply brought them plummeting.

"No, I can't leave here now," she said. "I'll be a senior this fall, and I want to graduate from Newark High School." She didn't add, but it was foremost in both their minds, that she didn't want to leave Dick.

He informed her that he couldn't leave her here if he went to Mississippi. "But, Dad," she replied. "I'm old enough to take care of myself. In less than a year, I'll be out of school and on my own. I don't feel right being the reason you can't be with Mom and Freddy and Billy."

He reminded her that there weren't many jobs in his field in Mississippi. "At least around Peelihatchie and Brandon," he added. Thinking that she could see a crack in his armor, June spent a long time that night trying to convince him that he wouldn't have to worry about her. She would get along fine. Before they turned in for the night, he had promised to think about it. They both knew, though, that even if she talked him into it, the job situation would be a real obstacle to overcome.

As if fate were intervening, he received a letter from his wife a few days later informing him that her sister Ruby had talked about Burrel to a friend of hers who owned a construction company. He'd told her that he had an opening for an electrician and Burrel could have the job if he wanted it, but he'd need to be on the job in a month.

He carried the letter around a few days before he mentioned it to June. Torn between his responsibilities to his young family in Mississippi and his daughter in Newark, he wasn't sure what to do. After wrestling with the problem, he decided to talk to her mother, Priscilla, in Mansfield. Since she had consciously avoided being anywhere near him since she'd left him five years earlier, he wasn't sure she would see him. Not taking that chance, he decided to make this a surprise visit.

❧

The next day. dressed in his blue suit, starched white shirt, blue striped tie, clean shaven, with every hair in place, he got in his freshly washed car to begin the hour and a half trip to Mansfield. Before he shifted into gear, though, he cast a quick glance across the street at his brother Mace's house. Since he knew what Mace would say if he saw all the pains he had taken with his appearance, he hoped to leave without talking to him. He breathed a sigh of relief as he shifted into gear…his brother was nowhere in sight. His relief didn't last long as he noticed Mace, newspaper in hand, hurrying toward him. Burrel eased over to the curb and Mace slid in beside him and asked, "Where are you going all spruced up like that?"

"I told you about the letter I got from Polly about the job in Mississippi. I would like to go but I don't want to leave June here. I'm going to Mansfield to see if Priscilla will let her stay with her."

"Hmmn, you want to go to Mississippi to be with Polly but you look like you're dressed for a date to go see Priscilla. What's going on?" Mace asked.

Somewhat defensively, Burrel replied, "This is the way I dressed when Priscilla and I were together. Why should I look any different now?"

Mace said, "Just remember. She's the one who left you, so don't start thinking about all the good times. Just remember the rough time you, June and Cecil had after she left."

"For heaven's sake, Mace!" Burrel exclaimed. "I'm not trying to get her back. I am just going to ask her if June can live with her until she is out of school."

Mace grinned at his younger brother's reaction before he said, "I'm going to go in the house, have a cup of coffee and read my newspaper." Before he walked away, though, he added, "Drive carefully and remember you have a wife and two sons waiting for you in Mississippi."

Finally on the road, he thought about what his brother had said. Had he taken extra pains with his appearance because he was finally going to see Priscilla again? He didn't think so, but he wondered if his brother might be right. Since he didn't want these thoughts as company on the trip, he flipped on the radio to a music station. This didn't help though as the car was filled with the sound of Doris Day singing "Sentimental Journey."

He hummed along with the words as he drove by the little country store he had managed for her father in St. Louisville while he, Priscilla, and their baby son, Cecil, lived in the little saltbox style house down the road. The combination of hearing the song and seeing the country store opened a floodgate of memories of Priscilla. The happy times and the bad times were jumbled together in his mind. "No one would believe that I fell in love with her before we even met. When I saw her picture on the mantel it only took one look at the clear blue eyes, the long blonde hair tied back with a blue ribbon, the warm, friendly smile and I knew she was the one for me." He smiled inwardly as he thought of how her sister Della, whom he'd been dating, had unwittingly brought them together and how his brother Mace and sister-in-law Mabel had conspired to keep her mother occupied so he could court Priscilla. He remembered the night he'd slipped the white gold ring, with the tiny diamond, on her finger and they'd vowed that this was going to be forever.

As he remembered their life together, he felt a pang of regret. Life had seemed so good and he had loved her more than life itself. Then it was over and she was gone. He knew that he shared the blame for the marriage's failure but he still didn't know what he had done.

He had thought he would never love again until Polly came into his life. The thought of his young redheaded wife and their two sons waiting for him in Mississippi brought his thoughts back to the present and his reason for being here. As he entered the Mansfield city limits he hoped he hadn't made a mistake not calling Priscilla first to let her know he was coming to talk to her. "Too late now," he mused as he drove down Arlington Avenue and stopped in front of the white house where she and Dickie lived with her second husband, Bill.

A few minutes later a city bus stopped at the corner and Priscilla got out. He watched her as she walked toward the house. His first thought was, "My lovely Priscilla." His second thought was, "Good Lord! Was Mace right?" He wrestled with the idea and reason won. "It's just that nonsense about a sentimental journey and all the memories I rehashed on the way up here." Every inch of his being told him, "That was then and this is now."

As he watched her, he noticed that she appeared only mildly curious about the strange car parked in front of her house. When he stepped out of the car, and she realized it was her former husband, her curiosity turned to alarm. For a moment he thought she was going to turn and walk away from him. Before she could act on her apparent impulse, he called out to her, "Priscilla, I need to talk to you about June."

Alarmed, she said, "About June? Has something happened to June?"

He assured her that nothing had happened to their daughter. "She is fine."

Her welcome was barely lukewarm. She didn't even invite him into the house. Instead they stood on the front steps and talked. Aware that his presence made her uneasy, he immediately got to his reason for being there. "I have a job possibility in Mississippi, but I don't want to leave June in Ohio. I was wondering if she could come live with you until she graduates."

Priscilla was as surprised by his request as she had been by literally finding him on her doorstep. "What does June think of this idea?" she asked.

Burrel shook his head and glumly replied that he hadn't said anything to her about it yet. "I didn't want to mention it until I had your answer."

"Why doesn't she want to go to Mississippi?" Priscilla inquired.

He explained that their daughter said she wanted to stay in Newark to graduate, but he felt the real reason she didn't want to go was because of the young man she'd been seeing. "They're talking about getting married when she graduates."

This news surprised June's mother. She hadn't heard from her daughter for awhile, and now she knew the reason. "I don't understand how it would help having June stay here with me if what she wants is to graduate from Newark High School. Fifty-five miles is a little far to commute!" she exclaimed.

Burrel raked his hand through his dark blond hair as he told her that he was convinced that the main reason she didn't want to leave Newark was because of Dick. "He's going to school in Columbus and only comes to see her on the weekend," he explained. "He could just as easily come to Mansfield as to Newark." While Priscilla still looked skeptical, he added, "Besides, June had a hard time in school when we were in Mississippi before. I'm sure that's also in the back of her mind."

While she mulled over what he'd just said, Burrel stood and restlessly shifted his weight from one foot to the other. He'd been so focused on waiting for her reply that he hadn't been aware of his son, Dickie's, approach until he heard the familiar voice say, "Hi, Dad!" While father and son exchanged broad grins, Dickie marveled at seeing his parents together. This was something he had never expected to see...*and though he didn't know it at the time, it was something he was never to see again.*

After he went into the house, Burrel continued to try to convince his former wife to let their daughter spend the next few months with her. "As much as she's always missed you, I think she would be so happy being here with you and Dickie that she wouldn't mind changing schools again."

Burrel's eyes brightened at her next words, "Of course I would love to have June live with me." The brightness quickly disappeared, though, when she continued, "I would have to talk to Bill about it first, though, and I would need to have you sign over legal custody to me."

While she was speaking, he had been vigorously shaking his head from side to side. The mention of her second husband hadn't made him very happy, but the real pain had come when she'd asked him to sign legal papers. He knew there was no way he could find it in his heart to relinquish custody of his daughter. Sadly, he said goodbye to Priscilla and Dickie and drove back to Newark.

On his return trip to Newark, when he again passed the little store in St. Louisville, he thought about how much simpler life had been then. "That was yesterday," he mused. "What I want to do now is to think about tomorrow."

～

After he returned to Newark, he told June about the letter from his wife, Polly, but not about his visit with her mother. When June heard that the job problem had been solved, she decided to take matters into her own hands. An advertisement she'd seen in the paper for a live-in baby-sitter seemed like an answer to her prayers. According to the ad, the job entailed taking care of one school age child evenings and after school in exchange for room and board and a small salary. By the time she told her father about her idea, she'd already been hired.

Her employer was a pretty blond divorcee named Charlotte Ankrom who needed someone to baby-sit her eight year old son, Jimmy, while she worked. The hours would work out fine for June, as she and Jimmy would get home from school at the same time. When June told her about the prospect of her father going to Mississippi, Charlotte told her that she wanted to talk to him... to reassure him that she would be in good hands. "I want you to think of this as your home," she said. "You'll be like one of the family."

Her new employer explained that with the exception of Jimmy, this would be a household of women. In addition to June and Charlotte, a young former war bride from Australia named Yvonne lived in the household. A few months earlier, she and hundreds of her countrywomen, all married to American soldiers, had boarded a ship for the United States. While the journey may have had a happy ending for the other brides, for Yvonne it was a different matter. When the ship docked, before she even stepped foot on American soil a message was delivered from her husband telling her not to come. He'd changed his mind and no longer wanted to be married to her. Apparently, he'd erroneously expected the cablegram to reach her before she left Australia. When she'd received it, she'd been completely devastated by the message. Since she was a complete stranger in this country, the only thing she knew to do was to follow through with her original plan to travel to Newark. Charlotte went on to say that when Yvonne arrived on her husband's doorstep, she'd hoped that she could change his mind. The young bride was to be disappointed, though, as he continued to be adamant that he wanted the divorce. Shortly afterwards, she'd answered an advertisement Charlotte had placed in the local paper for a boarder. "The two of us hit it off right away, and she is now living in my spare bedroom and working for a local business."

June soon found that it took some tall talking to persuade her father that it would be alright for her to stay in Newark. In fact, he wouldn't give his permission until after he'd met and talked to Charlotte. Although she was young and vivacious, he could tell that she had a level head on her shoulders. Once she had assured him that June would be like one of the family, and that she would have a home with her as long as she needed it, he felt more confident about the situation. He also elicited a promise from her that if they had any problems or she felt June needed him, she would write or call him immediately.

Feeling better about the situation, he finally agreed to let June accept the job and stay in Newark while he left for Mississippi. Just to be on the safe side, though, before he left, he talked to his brother, Mace and his sister-in-law, Mabel, about keeping an eye on her while he was gone.

Both he and his daughter had important matters to take care of before June could start her new job or he could leave to join Polly, Freddy, and Billy in Mississippi. June had to turn in her resignation at the Auditorium and Burrel had to sell the house on Lawrence Street. Both actions made June feel sad, but she felt that in the long run this would be better for everyone.

Saying goodbye to her father and her home was one of the most difficult things she'd ever done. As she watched his heavily laden car turn the corner onto Buena Vista Street on the first mile of his journey to Mississippi, though, she managed to console herself by thinking about what the future had in store for both of them.

LIFE IS FULL OF SURPRISES

She liked her job, the women she was living with, and the little boy she was baby-sitting. Although Jimmy was full of mischief, June could usually handle him. If she couldn't, she could call on Dick who a short time earlier had graduated from school and was now working as an apprentice in his father's shop at 54 South Second Street just off the downtown square in Newark. Except for a short trip he'd taken to Michigan with his brother Gene to try to buy an automobile, he came over to see her almost every evening. He'd written her, "My whole-hearted reason for going 690 miles up into Michigan was to secure an automobile so I could go see a certain gal once in awhile. But it seems my mission was a complete failure because we still haven't got a car." He went on to say that he'd first gone to Toledo, then to Detroit, and Pontiac, but always the answer was the same, "No cars." Some dealers had hinted that if he'd just slip five hundred dollars under the table, they might be able to move his name to the top of the list.

When he got home he told her that he had even started looking for a used car, but much to his surprise, he found that since new cars were so difficult to buy, used cars were scarce and very expensive. His dad had let a returning serviceman talk him into selling his 1938 Chevrolet for a few dollars over what he'd paid for it new, and now his parents were without transportation. "I tried to tell Dad that if he sold it he wouldn't be able to buy a new car, but he didn't believe me," he told June. "He's had his name on the list every since he sold it, but he's not having any better luck than I am."

It was hard for her to believe that fall of 1946 that there were no cars available. She'd lived through the shortages during the war years, but now in peacetime with all the factories going full blast it was impossible for them to keep up with the demand for automobiles. "Just think," he reminded her. "Millions of men have come home from overseas, and I imagine almost every one of them is trying to buy a car. Several men had more points accumulated than I did, so they got to come home sooner. That way they were able to get their names on the list before I did."

"I never did understand that point system," June said. "What's it all about?" she asked. He patiently explained that points were given for number of months in the service with additional points for time served overseas, and even more for each battle a serviceman had been in.

"A lot of men were in from 1941, when the war started until it was over in '45," he explained. "Since I didn't go in until the fall of '43, was overseas eighteen months and served in three battles, several of the older ones were in longer than I was. Consequently, they had earned a lot more points so they got to come home sooner."

She tried to assure him that someday his name would have to come to the top. He flashed his cocky grin and quipped, "Well at least I do have my bicycle. It will still get me over here anytime I want to come, but this winter will be a different matter." He interrupted her reminder that city buses were as close as the nearest street corner by saying, "Of course, we could go ahead and get married, and I wouldn't have to worry about it."

Her eyes were sparkling when she wiggled her third finger left hand in front of his face and replied that they weren't even officially engaged yet. Taking her hand in his, a serious expression crossed his usually cheerful face when he fervently declared, "You're going to marry me someday. Don't even joke about it!" Then while she studied his serious eyes, he hinted that he would have a surprise for her on their next anniversary.

That would make it November 21st, the eleven-month anniversary of the night they'd first met. Although he wouldn't say anymore, she knew he was talking about an engagement ring. It might have been better for both of them, though, if that little conversation had never taken place. As it happened, their different interpretations almost led to disaster. While June was jubilantly telling her friends that they were engaged and that she suspected he was giving her an engagement ring on their next anniversary, Dick was telling a completely different story.

June found this out from the most unlikely source, her old friend, Butch, who had called and asked her for a date. Feeling very prim and proper, she'd informed him that she was engaged to marry Dick. A few nights later, he called back and told her that he'd seen Dick uptown and that when he'd mentioned the engagement, Dick had denied being engaged. Butch had gone on to say that if her "fiancée" didn't consider himself engaged, he didn't know why she should. Hurt, angry, and embarrassed, she replied, "You're right!" Then she went on to tell him that, she'd love to have him come over to the house any night that week but she wouldn't be able to go out with him, though, until on the weekend when her employer would be home.

He promptly took advantage of the invitation and became a frequent visitor. The next time Dick called, she coldly told him that she was busy, but after repeated calls she finally agreed to see him. When he came to the house, she waited until she'd gotten Jimmy to bed before she told him that she was seeing her old friend

Butch again. He was angry, but no more than she was when she repeated what Butch had told her. "I turned down a date with him because I considered myself engaged to you, then you tell him, of all people, that we weren't engaged!"

He tried to explain that when he'd talked to Butch, he'd meant that they weren't officially engaged yet. She stormily replied, "Did you or didn't you tell him that we weren't engaged?"

Taken aback by her anger, he responded, "No...that is... yes, but that isn't what I meant!" He tried to placate her by apologizing and joking about learning to keep his mouth shut in the future. Then he spent the next couple hours doing the absolute opposite by talking and trying to convince her that Butch had misunderstood what he'd said. And that he really wanted to marry her.

After they talked it out and finally made up, June couldn't resist saying, "For someone who vowed to keep his mouth shut, you've done a good job of talking tonight." She grinned when he teasingly reminded her that the best thing about fighting was the fun of making up. "It might be," she replied. "But I don't like to fight." A few minutes later when they kissed goodnight, they promised each other that this was going to be their last battle. As it turned out, that was a promise they weren't going to be able to keep and as they were soon to learn, the next fight was to have a totally unexpected outcome.

～

Completely unaware of what the next few weeks would bring, June vowed to herself that she was only going to see Dick, and nobody else, from now on. While she meant to keep that promise, circumstances in the form of Danny, an old friend of hers and of Butch, intervened. Always a romantic, June couldn't resist Butch's call to help Danny and his girlfriend, Donna, elope. He explained they were deeply in love, that her parents didn't approve of Danny and were trying to keep them apart. "They want to get married," he said. "And if they go to Kentucky they don't have to wait three days. There's no waiting period there at all."

To June this sounded like a modern day version of Romeo and Juliet, and she couldn't resist conspiring with Butch to help the young couple. She agreed to his suggestion that Donna spend that night with her, and then bright and early the next morning, the four of them would go to Kentucky so the young lovers could be married.

She'd always liked Danny and was excited at the prospect of being his bride's maid-of-honor. Although she'd never been part of an elopement, her friend Vonnie had told her about the little place across the Ohio River from Cincinnati where people went to be married. She and Dick's friend, Dale, had been secretly married there in August. Vonnie had told her that all a man and woman had to do was cross the bridge into Kentucky and the "marriage people" would take over.

Although June had been forewarned, she wasn't prepared for the contingent of people who swarmed around the car...waving placards that read "Weddings!"

and asking if they wanted to get married. Almost overwhelmed by the carnival atmosphere, the four inhabitants of the car could only stare wide-eyed at the people around them. Seconds later, when Danny tried to ease through the throng, one man jumped on the car and clung to it as if he were part of the paint job. Before they could react, the words began to spew from his mouth, "Want to get married? Come with me. You don't have to worry about anything. I'll take care of everything."

Not seeing any way to shake him, they let him direct them to a doctor's office where Danny and Donna got their pre-marriage blood tests and to the courthouse for their license. Once this was accomplished, he took them down a cobble stone street to the office of a justice-of-the-peace. When their guide threw open the door to a dim, shabby looking office, they were greeted by a short, pudgy, swarthy skinned man. For some reason she couldn't quite fathom, June took an instant dislike to him. His fawning manner reminded her of a snake-oil salesman or the con men she'd seen in the movies. She managed to put her personal feelings aside, though, as she basked in the happiness that radiated from Danny and Donna as they repeated their wedding vows. It was obvious that they were too blinded by their new status to be aware of the shabbiness of their surroundings or the oiliness of the man who had just pronounced them man and wife. "Oh, well," June mused. "They may not mind, but when I get married, it's not going to be in a place like this." She shuddered at the rest of her thought, "Or by a man like him!" When Butch leaned over and quipped, "Why don't we tie the knot too?" June just smiled but didn't take him seriously.

The little wedding party enjoyed the rest of the day. Following the ceremony, June and Butch took the newly-weds to a little restaurant that they found on a quaint little street in Cincinnati. Since none of them drank alcoholic beverages, they toasted the young couple with glasses of lemonade. As Butch raised his glass he said, "May the two of you be as happy fifty years from today as you are today." Then turning and flashing his winning smile at June, he added, "And may the four of us still be friends." While June joined in the toast, she knew that although this day was one that would forever live in her memory, this would be the last time they would be together like this.

She knew that while Danny and Donna would be starting on their married life together, June would be returning to Dick and Butch to a girl he had been seeing. A dark cloud crossed her mind at the thought of what her soon to be official fiancée would say when he found out about this little adventure of hers. Although she briefly considered not telling him, she quickly discarded that idea. "I don't think that's the way to have a good relationship," she mentally rationalized as she tagged along behind her three friends as they trooped back to the car and the return trip to Newark.

She and Dick managed to weather the storm caused by her trip to Kentucky, and their romance flourished despite the comments made by their friends. Dale informed Dick that he'd better give some serious thought to marrying such a fickle girl. Furthermore, he advised him to wait until he was sure he could trust her. His wife, June's friend, Vonnie, told her, "I've always believed in fate. I think it was my destiny to marry Dale, and that you and Dick met just so you could introduce us."

Even though June didn't agree with her friend's beliefs, she managed to conceal her irritation when she replied, "I guess you're entitled to your opinion, but I can assure you that Dick and I are going to get married...just as soon as school is out." Although she believed every word she'd spoken, she was soon to discover that fate had something else in store for her.

Though June still worked for Charlotte during the week, she'd taken a Saturday job at the Betty Gay Dress Shop downtown on the square, where Vonnie worked. Things were tense for awhile, but their friendship won out and her irritation was forgotten.

∼

For several weeks now, Dick had continued to hint about the surprise he had for her on the twenty-first of November, that special eleven month anniversary of the day they first met. At work and school, June and Vonnie spent every free moment discussing it and counting down the days. Finally the long anticipated night arrived and June found herself spending an unusually long time preparing for this date. After running the brush through her hair for the one hundredth stroke, she slipped into Charlotte's bedroom so she could inspect herself in the full-length mirror. Turning so she could see herself from all angles, she was pleased with the results of her efforts. She could see that the color of the two piece sweater set, with a matching gold pleated skirt complimented the soft blond of her hair. Peering into the mirror, she applied a rose colored lipstick, then dabbed Evening In Paris perfume behind her ears and on her wrists before fastening her gold locket around her neck. Twirling around, sending the pleats swirling around her knees, she thought, "All I need to make this outfit complete is a diamond on the third finger left hand."

She was already wearing one on her right hand. A couple years earlier, her mother, Priscilla, had the diamond that her first husband, June's father, had given her as an engagement ring remounted in a more modern setting. While June thought it was lovely and treasured it, she was looking forward to the one she knew she would be receiving tonight. After a final glance in the mirror, she skipped downstairs and settled herself in a comfortable chair and waited for Dick to arrive. As she could hear the clock in the hallway tick away the seconds, she waited and waited and waited some more. No matter how hard she strained to hear, the familiar sound of his footsteps or his jaunty tapping at the door never came.

She picked up a magazine and idly turned the pages, but as the seconds turned to minutes and the minutes to hours, she wasn't aware of a single word she had read. Her mind was too full of all the horrible things that could have taken place. "Surely," she fretted, "if something had happened to him, somebody would have let me know." As the silence of the house echoed around her, she realized that he wasn't coming. "He promised me a surprise," she fumed, "but never in my wildest dreams would I have thought that the surprise would be that he'd stand me up!" With this thought in mind, she stomped up the stairs and into her room where she threw herself across her bed. Charlotte, Jimmy, and Yvonne had gone out for the evening so she could have the house to herself for this important occasion. June was to hear them return before she was finally able to stop the hurt, angry thoughts from racing through her mind, and give in to the escape of sleep.

⁓

The next night, she and Dick had planned to go with Dale and Vonnie to see the high school's production of *January Thaw*. "I'm not going!" she stormily told Vonnie. Then barely able to hide the pain she was feeling, she asked, "Can you believe he promised to bring me an engagement ring, then he didn't even show up?" Her eyes reflected her hurt and anger, while she continued to insist that she wasn't going.

"You should at least give him a chance to explain. For all you know, he might have a good explanation," Vonnie said. Then she reminded June that he'd overlooked some of her actions. "Such as going to Kentucky with your friends."

June finally gave in and agreed to go on the date, but when Dick showed up at her door with Dale and Vonnie and tried to greet her with a kiss and a comment about how pretty she looked, the cold fury in her eyes stopped him in his tracks. "Whoa," he thought, "I'm going to have some tall talking to do tonight if I'm going to get out of this mess." He mentally reassured himself that being the romantic she was she would forgive him once he told her what he had accomplished the night before.

"Maybe not!" he mused as he glanced at her as she sat stiffly next to him in the darkened auditorium. When she returned his gaze, her usually warm, smiling eyes were filled with a cold fury. While on the stage the actors were playing out the scenes of *The January Thaw* the only time during the entire evening when he noticed a hint of a *June Thaw* was when her friend Evelyn appeared on the stage. There was no sign of any warming toward him during the rest of the play or later when they stopped on Mt. Vernon Road at the 400 SHOPPE for cheeseburgers and milk shakes.

While the two couples sat in a booth facing each other, Dale and Vonnie couldn't hide their discomfort and soon found themselves making rather flimsy excuses to escape. Vonnie yawned and murmured something about having to get up early to go to work the next day. Dale took his cue from that and heartily exclaimed, "I have an early morning tomorrow too. We'll just leave you two here." While he held Vonnie's coat for her, he lamely added, "We'll see you later."

As they hurried toward the door, Vonnie's words made their way through the sound of the jukebox and the chattering voices to the booth where June and Dick were sitting. "There's going to be a big fight tonight," she'd said.

Dick reached for June's hand and tried to hold it in his as he murmured, "I heard that. Let's prove her wrong." Feeling the warmth of his hand holding hers, she wanted to relent, but the hurt and anger were too strong. Instead she wrenched her hand free, jumped out of her seat, grabbed her coat, and rushed out the door. By the time he had paid the bill and gotten outside she was half a block away. "Wait a minute," he shouted.

When he saw that she wasn't going to stop, he sprinted after her. As he began to outdistance her, like a mantra he repeated, "Wait! I can explain. I can explain."

After a few minutes of this maddening race, he was surprised to see her stop and turn to face him. Feet planted apart, hands on her hips; she waited until he was within a few feet of him before she demanded to know why he'd stood her up. Before he could reply, she announced, "I told you before I wouldn't tolerate being stood up. Now, if you have a good explanation, I'm ready to listen."

The scorn in her eyes caused a pang of dread to settle in the pit of his stomach. When the night before, he had so blithely gone off on what he'd considered his good deed, he hadn't given a thought to how it would effect June. Twenty-four hours later the seriousness of his escapade was catching up with him, and he fervently hoped he was going to be able to undo the harm he'd done to this girl he loved.

"First things first," he informed her. "It's too cold to stay out here and talk. Let's go back to your place, and I'll try to explain what happened." She had been too angry to feel the cold that had been seeping through her clothes, but once he mentioned it, she realized she was chilled to the bone. Still keeping her distance, she hurried back to the warm sanctuary of Charlotte's house.

Charlotte greeted them cordially before disappearing into the kitchen murmuring something about fixing some hot chocolate. June grinned, despite her anger, at the thought that her employer hadn't been very subtle about giving them some privacy to work out their problems. Charlotte was to tell June later that if she'd known what was going to happen later that night, she might not have been so quick to leave them alone.

When they were in the living room, Dick sat on the couch and patted the seat next to him as an invitation for June to join him. With as haughty a look as she could muster, she deliberately sat in the chair she'd occupied for so long the night before. It was close enough for her to hear his impassioned plea, but too far for him to touch her.

He tried for his usual lighthearted tone when he started to talk, but the seriousness of her gaze was contagious, and he found himself taking on a somber manner as he began to explain. "First of all, I know I had hinted that I was going to have your ring last night," he began. While her eyes dared him to come up with an explanation she could accept, he continued to say that he had taken his mother with him to help him pick out the ring, but they hadn't been successful in finding one he thought was good enough for her. He lowered his eyes when he added, "I felt bad about showing up empty handed..."

"So rather than come without a ring and explain, you decided it would be better just to stand me up!" June cried.

His dark brow shot up toward his hairline when he almost shouted his response, "No. It wasn't that way at all. I left home to come over here...but I met my two uncles, John and Raymond, downtown. You remember my Uncle John, don't you?" he asked. Surprised at the turn the conversation had taken, June could only nod. "Uncle John has been so lonely since his wife died that when I saw him, all I could think about was trying to do something to help him," he explained.

Totally confused now, June opened her mouth to speak, but she changed her mind. Watching her intently, Dick wasn't sure, but he thought he had observed a chink in her armor at the mention of his Uncle John. He knew that the few times June had met his uncle, she'd felt compassion for him. A few months earlier this young man had lost his wife and their unborn baby. She remembered that she had told him several times how pretty she thought John's six year old daughter, Rosemarie, was and how much she admired the way the two of them were managing to pick up the pieces and go on with their lives.

When June asked what he'd done to help his uncle, Dick knew he was on his way to being home free. "At least she is listening," he reflected before he went on with his story. "Raymond said that they were going to a dance at the Druid's Club. That's when I decided to go along with them. I thought I might be able to introduce John to someone."

"A woman?" June asked.

"Yes," Dick replied. Noticing a dark cloud flicker across June's face, he hurried on with his explanation that he thought John might be shy and need some moral support. The familiar look of mischief was dancing in his eyes when he added, "You know me. I'm never shy. I just figured if he got cold feet, I could egg him on."

Despite herself, June was curious. "Did you? Did he meet someone?"

"As a matter of fact, he met a girl named Jean Nutter. I knew her when she lived next door to Dale Bennett on Eddy Street." Almost as an afterthought, he added, "She works in the office at Woolworth Five and Ten Cent Store." Then looking like the cat that had swallowed the canary, he announced that he had also fixed up his other uncle, Raymond, with one of Jean's co-workers from Woolworth. "Her name is June Snelling," he said. He was watching June's reaction to his account and was sure the thaw he'd been hoping for all evening was beginning to take place. "I stuck around until Uncle John had gotten a date with Jean and Raymond with June." He sounded sincere when he explained, "As I left them and started to your house, I couldn't believe the time on the courthouse clock. It was midnight! I had no idea so much time had passed. I was certain by then that you would be sound asleep." Although she was still unhappy about being stood up, she was intrigued by his story. For the next few minutes she quizzed him about the two couples. He responded by telling her that he wouldn't be surprised if something came of their meeting. *His words proved to be prophetic as before another six months had passed, Raymond and June had tied the knot as had John and Jean.*

Tonight, though, Dick found himself asking June to be understanding and to forgive him. He looked so sincerely repentant that June couldn't remain angry. Once she forgave him, they soon rediscovered the fun of making up. When, a few seconds later, Charlotte walked into the living room with steaming cups of hot chocolate, she was just in time to see Dick draw June into his arms. Without saying a word, she discreetly returned to the kitchen. If she'd stayed a few seconds longer she would have heard Dick say, "Let's get married."

Sitting on the couch next to him, with her head nestled against his shoulder, she replied, "I told you that I would marry you as soon as I graduate. Even after last night, I haven't changed my mind." When he replied that he meant that he wanted to get married that night, June's eyes flew open in surprise. She quickly moved away from him so that she could look into his eyes. As she studied them for a teasing or mocking note, she could find no hint of laughter or mischief in them. The words, "But why? Why tonight?" escaped from her lips as she stared at him in astonishment.

Taking her hand in his, he murmured, "Too many things have happened in the last few months that have almost caused us to break up. I love you, and you're the only girl I've ever wanted to marry. We could do what Dale and Vonnie did…go to Kentucky and get married and if it would make it easier for you at school we could keep it a secret until after you graduate." His voice trailed off as he added, "That is, if you want to."

The idea was beginning to appeal to her. Like Dick, she didn't want anything to happen to keep them from getting married. Since things were working out alright for their friends, Dale and Vonnie, she couldn't see any reason why it wouldn't for them too. She further rationalized that since she had been an emancipated minor for the last few months, answering to no one except herself, the decision would have to be hers…and Dick's. Maybe if she'd had the security of her family still being together in the house on Lawrence Street, or if she had gone to Mississippi with them or to Mansfield to live with her mother, she would have waited until she graduated. Now, though, she was on her own, and since they planned to get married in less than seven months, she could see no reason to wait.

While these thoughts were forming in her mind, a practical thought intruded. "What about a car? How are we going to get to Kentucky?"

His eyes were sparkling when he replied, "That's the best part. My Aunt Thelma and her family are visiting us from Cincinnati. I'll just borrow her car.

I've always been her favorite nephew, and she'll be really happy to be part of all this!"

Looking at her watch and noticing that the hands were past the midnight hour, June asked, "Won't they be asleep?"

Without hesitation, he replied that they would be, but he'd just leave a note telling his aunt that he was borrowing the car. June shook her head in astonishment. She couldn't imagine borrowing any of her relative's cars without talking to them first, but she realized that all families are different.

Before leaving, June informed Charlotte of their plans, and asked for her help in keeping it a secret. Her employer's response startled June. "I can't do that. You're putting me on a spot. I promised your father that I would look after you." Charlotte looked worried as she pleaded with them not to rush into anything. Then seeing that she wasn't going to change their minds, she told June, "If you do this, you will have to write and tell your father." While the young couple mulled over her words, she straightened her shoulders and pulled herself up to her full five feet and announced, "If you don't tell him, I'll have to!"

They talked it out over hot chocolate. Before they left for Dick's home to pick up the car, June had agreed to write to her father. In return, Charlotte told them that when they got back, she, Jimmy, and Yvonne would let them have the house to themselves for their wedding night. This announcement brought big grins to their faces as they said their good-byes and set off on their big adventure.

∽

When they arrived at Dick's parent's darkened house at 171 South Third Street, they quietly let themselves in. The only sound that reached their ears was of their own footsteps as they tiptoed across the bare floor. Once they'd made their way to the kitchen, June looked on while Dick scribbled a note to his aunt. He looked around for the car keys and once he found them on the kitchen table, he slipped them into his pocket and motioned for June to come along with him to the car. Before they left the dimly lighted kitchen, June asked, "Are you sure this is going to be alright with your aunt? I don't want to start off on the wrong foot with your family."

Without hesitation, he replied, "I'm certain. My Aunt Thelma would do anything for me." Neither could have predicted it, but the next time they stepped foot in this kitchen, this confident young man was going to be in for a rude awakening.

They arrived in Cincinnati just as the sun was peeking over the horizon. The trip through Columbus and several small towns along route forty had taken several hours. Since the heater in the car didn't work, there were times during that long ride that they felt they were traveling by dogsled. The cold air oozed in through every crack and crevice in the car's chassis. The temperature outside had dipped into the high twenties, and it hadn't felt much warmer inside. Their spirits remained high, though, as they stayed bundled in their heavy coats, scarves and gloves and snuggled close together.

The lights of the city of Cincinnati had been a welcome sight to the cold travelers. Especially the neon signs spelling out the word **RESTAURANT** or more simply **EATS**. Dick drove by the first few places, but at June's urging he eased into a parking place at the third. The exterior didn't need neon signs to welcome them. There was something about the small shingled structure with the crisp white organdy curtains criss-crossed across the sparkling windowpanes that struck a cord in June. It reminded her of a cozy cottage rather than the chrome and leather diners that were then in vogue. When they entered and she saw its maple tables covered in blue tablecloths, June felt as if she were walking into the home she'd had on Lawrence Street. She pointed that out to Dick, and he readily agreed with her.

Over a breakfast of bacon, eggs, toast, and coffee, they made plans for their day. First they needed to find a jewelry store where they could pick out an engagement ring for June and wedding bands for each of them. Then they would cross the river into Kentucky, where they could be married. "I want to be married by a minister," June said. "When we cross the river, there will be people who work for the justice-of-the-peace trying to get us to come to their boss." There was a note of determination in her voice when she continued, "I wouldn't feel married unless a minister performed the ceremony."

Although he knew it would be easier to turn everything over to the marriage mill people, he agreed with June since it was also important to him to have a religious ceremony. "This is our one and only wedding, so we want to do it right," he murmured.

Before leaving the restaurant, Dick got directions to a nearby jewelry store. When the clerk in the store opened for business, his first customers were Dick and June. While he surmised by their appearance and their manner that they were probably eloping, he didn't think it was his place to discourage them. Once he'd set trays of rings before them, it only took minutes to select June's diamond and a plain gold wedding band for each of them.

Then while June basked in the pleasure of being officially engaged they set off for Covington, Kentucky. She had the feeling of deja vu when they crossed the river. As she and her friends had been greeted, now she and Dick were greeted by a frenzied crew of men who shouted, "Getting married?" Then like a Pied Piper each one yelled, "Follow me!"

"Wow! I'd heard about this, but I didn't think it was going to be this bad," Dick exclaimed as he tried to maneuver his way through the throng. He managed to shake off all except one particularly aggressive man who had jumped onto the running board and wouldn't release his hold on the car door until Dick pulled the car to a stop.

The man's words tumbled over each other as he chanted, "I can take care of everything for you. First you have to go to the lab for a blood test, then to the courthouse for a license before you can get married. Let me take care of all that for you, okay?"

June leaned across Dick to inform the man that they wanted to be married by a minister. "No problem!" he exclaimed. "I'll handle everything for you." With what they thought was an understanding, the young couple agreed to let him take charge. Then for the next couple hours, he stuck to them like paper on the wall. June began to realize this was the man who earlier had taken Danny and Donna to the sleazy justice-of-the-peace.

Feeling uncomfortable with this realization, she whispered this information to her new fiancée, then asked, "How are we going to get rid of him? I can feel my skin crawl at the thought of that greasy little man marrying us."

When Dick saw tears begin to form in her eyes, he slipped his arm around her waist and pulled her close while he assured her that he would take care of everything. Then he firmly added, "We want to be married by a minister, and we will be!"

They had now gotten their blood test and were waiting for the clerk to finish filling out the marriage certificate. When the clerk started to hand it to them, their constant companion reached for it but Dick said, "I'll take that." The dark cloud that flashed across the face of the justice-of-the-peace's man clearly showed his displeasure. His cheerful reply of, "Now all that's left is the ceremony!" sounded false to their ears.

His eyes didn't quite meet theirs as he instructed them to follow him. "Just where are we going?" Dick asked. "And what denomination is this minister you're taking us to see?"

He stammered over his words when he replied that the man wasn't exactly a minister, but that he had a license to perform marriage ceremonies. Every word he spoke made June more certain that he was taking them to the sleazy justice-of-the-peace. Just to be sure, she asked, "Is this place you're taking us on a cobblestone street?"

His eyes widened in surprise at her question, before he reluctantly admitted that it was. The stubborn thrust of June's chin told Dick all he needed to know. His soon to be wife had made up her mind, and he did not intend to try to change it. "We told you at the start that we wanted to be married by a minister," Dick firmly stated before he asked, "Can you take us to one, or not?"

When the man admitted that he couldn't...or wouldn't, Dick took June by the hand and led her to the car. Before he closed the car door, he informed the man that although they appreciated all he had done, they were going through with their original plan and seek out a minister.

While the man stood open mouthed, Dick put the car into gear, and drove away. The young couple grinned at each other and simultaneously declared, "That was a narrow escape!" Then with license in hand, they rode out of the town in search of a preacher. After they left the narrow streets of Covington, they drove into the country. When they entered the tree lined streets in the small town of South Gate, they saw a matronly looking woman with her arms laden with packages plodding along the sidewalk. Dick immediately stopped and explained that they were looking for a minister so they could get married.

Smiling brightly, she came over to the car and started giving them some complicated sounding directions to the nearest parsonage. At the look of confusion on Dick's face, she volunteered to show them. "Great!" Dick exclaimed before instructing her to, "Hop in!"

After the woman was in the car, she apparently got a closer look at June's face. Her pursed lips and stern voice showed her disapproval when unexpectedly she demanded to know June's age. "You look too young to get married!" she exclaimed. "And I don't think I want to be any part of an elopement!" she added.

Dick had started to ease the car away from the curb, but at the sound of her words, he stopped, got out of the car, and opened the door for her. "We wouldn't want you to do anything you didn't want to do!" he announced. The woman had no choice, but to step out of the car, but before he had a chance to close the door behind her, she gave it one more try. "Please, Kids, think this over. Marriage is a serious business, and it takes some real maturity to make it work."

Dick politely thanked her for the advice, but his manner made it clear he wasn't going to listen to any of it. As Dick drove away, June turned to see the woman standing on the sidewalk shaking her head from side-to-side. Then before they turned the corner, June saw her gather her packages closer and resume her journey.

"That was strange!" she muttered. "You'd have thought she was my mother!" Dick squeezed her hand and reassured her that they were doing the right thing. "I wasn't going to let that woman upset you...or plant doubt in your mind," he said.

Her voice was strong and sure when she replied, "I'm more sure of this than anything I've ever done. You didn't have to worry that she could talk me out of it." While they'd been talking they'd topped a hill, and a white clapboard church had come into view. "Look!" she'd exclaimed. "That looks like what we've been looking for."

No one was at the church, but printed on the marquee was the name of the minister and the address of the parsonage. A few minutes later, they found themselves standing at the door of a red brick house. In response to their knock, a pretty young woman opened the door. Following close behind her was a tow-headed boy of about two. Once Dick explained that they wanted to get married, she invited them in. "My husband is painting the bathroom," she said. "I'll tell him that you're here."

Their first glimpse of the Reverend Thomas Harrison was when he stepped into the hall in his paint splattered clothes. June noticed that some of the yellow paint had speckled through his crisp dark hair, giving the appearance that he was a brunette with blond overtones. She managed to contain the giggle that she could feel welling up inside her. Never in her wildest dreams had she expected to be married by a house painter.

After a quick shower and a change of clothes though, he more closely resembled June's idea of how a preacher should look. His wife had removed her apron and along with a neighbor stood up with them as their witness. They'd had a few tense moments when Reverend Harrison had asked June if her parents knew she was getting married. Her answer that she didn't live with her parents seemed to satisfy him.

Then he had asked if they wanted anything special in their ceremony. June promptly responded with the request that the word obey be changed to "cherish." At Dick's raised eyebrow, she whispered, "I've never thought that word obey had a place in a wedding ceremony." Since he knew how fiercely independent his soon to be bride was, he nodded his understanding. If that was what she wanted, that would be fine with him. All that mattered to him, at this moment, was that she would become his wife.

Then in the front parlor of that country parsonage, with the sun filtering through the organdy curtains, the smell of paint mingled with the tantalizing aroma of freshly baked cookies, they looked into each other's eyes, and made their promise to love, honor, and "cherish" each other. Then with their heart's full of love, they sealed their vow with a kiss. Although they didn't know what their future might hold, they looked forward to it with excitement! After they signed the marriage license, the young minister and his wife served lemonade and cookies to the new husband and wife. Although there had been no wedding bouquet for June to toss or shower of rice to walk through, the young couple was ecstatic with their new marital status. With the good wishes of the young preacher and his wife ringing in their ears, they started on the return journey to Newark...and the welcome reception Dick had promised her they would receive from his family. Totally unaware of what was in store for them, they happily anticipated their welcome home.

Despite the beautiful picture that Dick had painted of his family, June had begun to feel apprehensive. When Dick brought the car to a stop in front of the house on Third Street, her stomach felt as if dozens of ballerinas were pirouetting inside it. Noticing her hesitation, her new husband urged her out of the car by saying, "There's no need to be afraid. My family loves me and since I love you, they're going to love you too."

She wasn't sure whether it was his words, the love shining from his eyes, or the warm kiss he gave her, but by the time they stepped out of the car, she was feeling as confident as he sounded. The lights spilling from every window, the warmth emanating from the humongous coal stove that dominated the living room and the music blaring from the record player heightened this feeling when they entered the house on Third Street. Dick had flung the door open and called out, "We're home!"

Then holding June's hand in his and smiling broadly, they'd walked into the midst of the storm. Before either of them could say or do anything more, they were pelted by a chorus of angry words. "Where have you been?" "How dare you steal my car?" "I almost reported my car stolen." "What have you done to my boy?" were just a few of the things that managed to penetrate June's consciousness. She found herself secretly smiling at that statement. Since she wasn't quite seventeen, compared to her husband's twenty-one, it seemed more like the other way around. Interspersed with these questions and statements were some words that shocked June's young ears. All the while, the last record that had been placed on the record player played over and over...and over again. Neither the young bride nor groom would ever hear that song, *The Sheik of Araby*, without remembering this wedding reception. *In fact, fifty years later when they celebrated their golden wedding anniversary, they would joke about playing that record...for old time's sake.*

Maybe that far in the future, they would be able to laugh about it, but that night while they were being wounded by the sling and arrows of Dick's mother and aunt's angry words, they felt more like crying. June was accustomed to seeing Dick's eyes full of warmth and mischief, and it was painful to see the hurt that was welling up in them. When he was finally able to interrupt the tirade, he asked, "Didn't you get my note about borrowing your car, Aunt Thelma?"

Sparks seemed to fly from his aunt's angry brown eyes as she responded, "Sure, but you didn't say anything about getting married!"

Dick valiantly tried to defend his actions by reminding her that he'd said in the note that he and June were going to Kentucky. "What did you think people go to Kentucky for?" he asked.

June felt her entire body flush in anger and embarrassment at her response. "We thought you'd just gone over to Columbus and shacked up!"

She felt like screaming, "Shacked up? Good heavens, we haven't been to bed in two days!" As she stood in the middle of this bright kitchen and looked at the remnants of the party that had apparently been taking place before their arrival, she heard a calm masculine voice from the other room, "Why don't you leave them alone?" Two more male voices added their support to the first one's request. "Yes, leave them alone," came from a handsome dark haired boy. A tall lanky, sandy-haired man had added, "Relax! They haven't done anything wrong."

That was the first June realized there were other people in the house. She recognized the first speaker as Dick's father, Forest, and the little boy as her new brother-in-law, Kenny. The second man and the trio of blond, blue-eyed children who were staring wide-eyed at the tempest whirling around them were strangers to her. She was to find out later that they were Thelma's family, her husband, Scottie, and their children, Ronnie, Jimmy, and Carol.

The women went on with their inquisition as if no one had spoken. While Dick was fending their questions, June slipped out the door into the cold darkness. She felt she needed to breathe some fresh air and be alone to contemplate what she had gotten into. As if she expected her dad to hear her, she looked up at the star studded sky and whispered, "Dad, I wish you were here!" Future generations can be thankful that her father was a thousand miles away, otherwise they might not have come into existence.

Before her thoughts went any further, Dick joined her. His presence served to remind her that she really loved him. As he put his arm around her and pulled her close, she realized that even if her father showed up at this moment, she wouldn't go through with the annulment that a few seconds ago she had seriously contemplated.

Her love and compassion only increased when she saw the raw pain and embarrassment on her young husband's face. He tried to put a light note on the happenings of the last few minutes by saying, "You can't say that I didn't promise you that my family would give you quite a reception. You'll probably never have another like it."

"One is enough for any lifetime," she fervently replied.

She could feel his arm tighten around her waist when he explained that he'd finally gotten through to them that they had actually gotten married. "I also gave my aunt twenty dollars, and I guess, in her mind, that changed it from stealing her car to borrowing it."

That reception they were trying to make light of had a lasting effect on the newlyweds. Dick was embarrassed about being so naive about his aunt's feelings for him and he never again quite let his guard down. June was deeply disturbed that what was to be the most beautiful day in her life had been destroyed by what they were always to refer to as THE RECEPTION.

Standing in the yard of her young husband's family home, she made a vow that night that if they ever had children, she was going to do everything in her power to see that they had beautiful memories of their wedding day. *In years to come, that was a vow she was to keep.*

After the events of the evening, the privacy of Charlotte's house beckoned them to Eddy Street. Having returned Thelma's keys, they had no choice except to walk. Happy to be free of the house on Third Street, it didn't take long to travel the mile and a half to their destination. With the house almost in sight, though, as they were crossing Shields Street, Dick said, "Dale lives less than a block from here. Do you want to stop and give him the news?" June knew that since Dale and Vonnie had become secretly married, they'd spent every weekend night either at her house or his. She was certain then that if Dale were at his house Vonnie would be there too. With this in mind, she readily agreed.

As they walked up the steps onto the porch, they could see that the downstairs was ablaze with light, but when Dick knocked on the door, no one responded. Dick grimaced and said, "There doesn't seem to be anyone at home. I guess we'll have to wait and tell them tomorrow." He soon discovered how mistaken he was when they turned and started to leave. Before they'd made it to the bottom of the steps, the door opened and Dale called out, "Whoa! Don't leave. Von and I want to know where you two have been since last night!"

Clearly surprised by Dale's statement, Dick exclaimed, "Where we've been! How did you even know that we were gone?"

Dale laughingly replied, "I imagine every friend either of you have knows that you were gone all night. Your mother has been all over town trying to find out where you went."

"Oh, no!" June moaned. There went their plan to keep the marriage a secret until after she graduated. Before either she or Dick could respond, they heard footsteps on the stairs, and heard Vonnie call out, "Is that Dick and June?"

"Yes, Honey. Our wandering friends have returned," Dale replied. Vonnie's blue eyes were sparkling and the corners of her lips were turned up in the beginning of a smile as she and her husband exchanged knowing glances.

"You'd better be able to tell us you're married. If not, your reputation is ruined," she said.

June's only response was to hold out her left hand and wiggle it in front of her friend's face. "You did it!" Vonnie exclaimed. "You got married."

"Officially engaged for all of four and a half hours and married for...," June glanced at her watch before she continued, "Eight hours." Then as if what Vonnie had first said had just sunk in, she cried, "What do you mean, my reputation is ruined? Who else knows that we were gone?"

"Dick's mother came to the store this morning and talked to all the clerks. She told every one of us that you and Dick had been gone all night, and she wanted to know if anyone knew where you were," Vonnie explained. "When I heard that Charlotte had called this morning and reported you off work, I just figured you'd had a big fight after we left and didn't feel like coming in, but when Dick's mother showed up I didn't know what to think."

With every word her friend spoke, June could feel her heart sink. This was especially so when Vonnie told her that one of the people June's new mother-in-law had spoken to had been their boss. "Was Betty upset?" June asked. Upon being told that she hadn't been very happy about it, the flustered newlywed muttered, "That's great! First my reputation is shot, now I'll probably lose my job."

There was more to come as June found out when Vonnie continued to relate what had been going on while they had been blithely going about the business of getting married. "When she left the store, she said she was going to Woolworth and talk to Martha," she said, referring to June's friend and schoolmate. "Then she was going to the Midland and Auditorium to check with the people you used to work with."

Things seemed to have gone from bad to worse. Neither she nor her new bridegroom had anticipated any of these complications, and she knew that she was going to have to repair the damage done by her well-meaning mother-in-law as best she could. First they would have to put a stop to the gossip by announcing their marriage. Then she would deal with her supervisor at the dress shop and with whatever flack that would come her way from the school officials.

While the girls had been talking, the men had disappeared into the kitchen. When they reappeared, they were carrying four bottles of Coca-Cola and tall glasses filled with ice. "This calls for a celebration!" Dale called out. "Come on, Von. Let's drink to our friends being as happy in their marriage as we are in ours." After they'd emptied the contents of the bottles into their glasses, the young couples clinked their glasses together and drank a toast.

While they sat and sipped their drinks, Dick and June filled them in on their experiences since they'd parted from them less than twenty-four hours earlier. Having eloped to Kentucky in August, their listeners could readily identify with what they were saying.

Then Dale regaled them with stories of what it was like to be secretly wed. "You're probably going to be better off being open about being married," he said. "We've probably stirred up quite a bit of speculation among our parents' neighbors. Every time I leave Von's house in the morning, one of her neighbors is peeking from behind her curtains. Since she never sees me arrive, our excuse that I just dropped in to see Von before I go to work is wearing pretty thin."

When Von brushed her hand dramatically across her brow and intoned, "I guess, I'm just a fallen woman," they all laughed. Then in a more serious vein Vonnie added, "I'm glad that our families know the truth. They have been very supportive. You know that Mom thinks it's probably going better with me at school since they don't know." When her last remark brought a gasp from June, Vonnie was immediately contrite.

Although, she hastened to assure June that she probably wouldn't have any problems, and June concurred, neither girl believed it. Feeling like Scarlet O'Hara in Gone With he Wind, June flippantly quipped, "I'll worry about that tomorrow."

In response to that remark, Dick sat his glass on the coffee table and said, "Speaking of tomorrow, it's almost here. I think it's time we head for Charlotte's house, don't you?"

With Dale's teasing remark, "We'd throw some rice, but it's already cooked," ringing in their ears, they took their leave of their friends and resumed their trek.

When Dick was sure they were out of earshot, he asked, "Do you think we might have interrupted something?" Remembering the time it had taken Dale to answer the door, and Vonnie's slightly mussed appearance when she appeared on the stairs; she agreed it was quite possible. Then she thought of how difficult it must be to try to steal some time to be alone, and she was glad that her mother-in-law's actions were forcing them to come out in the open. Young as she was, she realized at that moment that no matter what the future might hold for them, it would be better from the beginning to face it together as husband and wife.

THE MARRIAGE BEGINS

It didn't take them long to cover the distance between Dale's home and Charlotte's. As they approached the white frame house, they could tell by the dimly lighted interior that June's employer, true to her word, had made sure the newly-weds would have the house to themselves. As if he couldn't quite believe their good fortune of finally being alone, Dick cautiously opened the door and called out, "Is anyone at home?" When his question was met by no sound other than the ticking of the mantle clock, he turned and grinned at his bride before scooping her into his arms and carrying her across the threshold. Then, he turned and firmly closed the door behind them...effectively closing out the rest of the world.

As they were to discover early the next morning, the effectiveness of that gesture wasn't to be very long lasting. The sun had barely peeked over the horizon when the sound of something striking the windowpanes brought them both awake. "Must be hail," Dick muttered sleepily. Then, half opening one eye and peering through the narrowed slit, he added, "That's strange, I don't see any sign of rain, snow, or hail." The words had barely passed his lips before a barrage of small objects again smacked against the glass. This was followed by a feminine voice calling, "Richard, Richard." A second female voice took up the cry. While June's eyes swiveled from her bridegroom's startled face to the window, she heard a groan escape his lips as he grumbled, "I don't believe it! It's Mom and Aunt Thelma!"

While June was thinking, "Now I know why people don't tell anyone where they're going on their honeymoon!" Dick threw back the covers, jumped out of bed and in a couple strides was standing at the window. His appearance brought a volley of words from the women. June sat up in bed, pulled the covers up, and tucked them under her chin while she strained to hear what they were saying. From the snippets of conversation she could hear, she realized the women were apologizing and inviting them to the house on South Third Street for breakfast.

She mentally groaned but put on a bright face when her husband asked, "What do you want to do?"

Although she was thinking that she'd rather step into a den of lions than to go back into that house, she managed to murmur that whatever he decided would be alright with her. Relieved, he called down to the waiting women and let them know to expect them in about an hour.

This time when the newly-weds entered the house, the reception was a welcome contrast to the one they'd received the night before. No longer shrill and accusing, the voices were now warm, friendly, and teasing. Some of the ribald comments that were made at the breakfast table left the young bride blushing and speechless. This was especially true when they came from Lula, Dick's maternal grandmother. Although June had never known either of her grandmothers, she knew that this raven-haired, brown-eyed woman didn't fit her conception of someone in that lofty position. While her conversation was friendly, to June's ears, it went a step beyond being "just ornery" with her suggestive jokes. Short, plump, and given to wearing bright colors, as were her two daughters, she made June feel both welcomed into the family and uncomfortable at her outspokenness.

While words flowed around her, June surveyed her surroundings. Although she'd been in this room for hours the night before, she'd bordered on a state of shock and hardly noticed anything. Now, though, she became aware that this house managed to touch all her senses. The colors were vibrant with the bright shades the women wore vying with the multicolored flowers on the wallpaper. While the sultry sound of Peggy Lee singing a love song came from the record player, the smell of the bacon frying was permeating the room. All the while she was engulfed in the comforting heat from the coal-burning stove in the middle room.

When June tasted the perfectly cooked eggs and bit into the crusty home-baked cinnamon rolls, she realized that she was going to be no match for her mother-in-law's excellent cooking. As she was uttering words of praise for the cook's culinary skills, the thought flickered across her mind that she'd be a real disappointment to her husband. Having been exposed to this kind of food all his life, what was he going to think of the pitifully few things she knew how to cook? As if reading her mind, he put his warm hand in hers and squeezed it reassuringly. She didn't realize it then, but her minimum variety of menus would match his limited preferences for food.

∽

For minutes, she'd been absorbed in her thoughts and had lost track of the conversation swirling around her until she heard Dick's mother ask where they planned to stay. A look of surprise, almost of shock, crossed his face before Dick blurted out that he'd thought they'd stay here! Without hesitation, his mother responded, "Oh, no! You're not staying here!" While all the people seated around the table stared in amazement, she firmly added, "It would never work out.

No house is big enough for two women!" While the words seemed to sting her husband, June was jubilant. Her heart had sunk at the prospect of living in this house of strangers. It was going to take her some time to get used to people who never had a thought they didn't express. Coming from a more reserved family, as a young bride, *she couldn't imagine that someday she was going to appreciate this blunt woman and love her almost as much as she did her mother, Priscilla, and step-mother, Polly.*

For the moment, though, she had to be concerned about her young husband. Twice in as many days, he'd had his illusions shattered. First, the ones he'd harbored about his aunt, now his own mother, who'd never denied him anything had refused to let him bring his bride to live in his own home. Now it was her turn to give his hand a reassuring squeeze while confidently explaining to the people still seated at the table that her employer had told her that they could stay at her house as long as it took them to find a place of their own. Smiling brightly, she added, "I'm sure we won't have any problem finding one." Catching the eye of Thelma's pre-teen daughter, Carol, June grinned at her while she explained that all they needed was a three-room apartment. It was obvious from the way the girl looked at the newlyweds that she admired her older cousin and had wholeheartedly accepted her new cousin-in-law, as had her handsome older brother, Ronnie, and rambunctious younger brother, Jimmy. From the moment June met them, she liked all three of them and their light-hearted father. This was a feeling that was only to grow stronger as the years went by.

A few minutes later, when June and Dick put their heads together over the classified ads in the local paper, The Advocate, she realized the folly of her confident statements. There was no category for either houses or apartments for rent. On the other hand the listing headed "Wanted to Rent" scanned one entire column and spilled over into the next one. The newlyweds exchanged bemused glances before Dick muttered, "Looks like finding an apartment isn't going to be any easier than trying to buy a car."

No one could tell the depth of the disappointment June felt when she patted his hand and cheerfully reassured him that they would find something. Dick turned a pleading look on his father when he asked, "Dad, how about one of your houses? Are any of them going to be vacant?"

His father glumly wagged his head from side to side before replying that with all the men coming home from overseas, they'd snapped up every vacant property in town. His voice rose as he continued, "If my renters wanted to move, they'd have as hard a time as you are in finding another place." He went on to tell them that with the rent control that had been set up during the war and was still in effect, he wouldn't be allowed to ask anyone to vacate. "You wouldn't believe all the rules the government has. I don't have any control over my properties at all," he grumbled.

After June and Dick said goodbye to his family, they started the long walk to Lawrence Street to break the news of their elopement to Uncle Mace and Aunt Mabel. As they were trudging along, Dick grumbled, "You'd think with the eight or nine houses Dad and Mom have, we'd be able to rent one of them, wouldn't you?"

June laughed and told him that she was sure they'd be comfortable at Charlotte's. "My bed is only a three quarter size one, so we'll be cozy." He grinned and told her he didn't think that would be too much of a problem. For the rest of their trek, they joked about pitching a tent on the courthouse lawn if they couldn't find anything else. Neither anticipated as they ascended the steps to June's uncle's house that the solution to their problem would soon be at hand.

The first person they saw when June opened the front door and they walked into the hallway was her cousin, Rose. "Where have you been?" Rose cried. Her large, expressive brown eyes were filled with concern when she added, "Dick's mom told Vonnie that you took her sister's car and were gone all night. Vonnie called me to ask me if I knew anything about it." Rose's voice had taken on an accusatory tone when she added, "I had to admit that I didn't know where you were."

"No one knew except the two of us," June replied as she nonchalantly trailed her left hand across her face as if brushing an invisible substance from her cheeks. Rose stared at her cousin for a second before she saw the sparkling diamond and narrow gold band June was sporting. "Good heavens!" she exclaimed. "You got married!"

Annamae had wondered into the hall in time to hear her sister's announcement. "Married! That's great!'" she exclaimed as her face lit up with a wide beaming smile.

The sound of her words had made their way into the dining room where the rest of the family was still sitting around the table talking and drinking coffee. Inez called out, "Who got married?"

Excitedly showing the newlyweds into the room, Rose announced, "These two." Then as if that wasn't explanation enough, she added, "June and Dick!"

A jumble of voices followed Rose's announcement. Among the words of surprise and congratulations, June was almost certain she heard at least one, "Oh, no!" Looking from one face to the other, she could see only happiness reflected in all eyes except the troubled blue ones of her Uncle Mace. Never one to keep his concerns to himself, he said, "I wish you had talked to me about this. I promised your dad I would keep an eye on you!" Then running his hands through his dark hair, in a woebegone sounding voice he said, "I don't know what your dad is going to say."

"Hursh," Aunt Mabel instructed. "Burrel will take it alright. They're already married. He might be upset at first, but he'll be okay about it." Uncle Mace grumbled a little more before finally giving them his blessing.

Aunt Mabel asked them to join them for lunch, but having just finished breakfast they refused, but they did pull up a couple of chairs and have some coffee. Sitting around the table, besides June's aunt and uncle and cousins, Rose and Annamae, were Inez, her husband, Bob Cochran, and their baby daughter, Sandy. Aunt Mabel's sister Neva Dunn, her husband, Kenny, and their little daughters, Linda and Mary Lou filled the other chairs.

Amidst all the questions and chatter, the newlyweds heard one question that changed their smiles to looks of gloom. "Where are you going to live?" Neva asked. When June glumly replied that they hadn't been able to find a place...that they'd be staying at Charlotte's until they found something else, Neva replied that she might be able to help them out.

As everyone at the table turned inquiring eyes on this young woman, she went on to tell them that she had an extra bedroom, and that her husband, Kenny, could fix up a kitchen for them in their basement...that is, if they'd be interested. With visions of the long list of "Wanted to Rent" ads swirling through their minds the newlyweds readily accepted her offer. "When can we move in?" Dick inquired. Neva's husband, Kenny, asked that they give him about a week to get things set up in their basement kitchen.

That settled, Aunt Mabel turned to June and asked if she'd told her mother yet. June had to admit that she hadn't. "I thought I would write to her tonight."

While June was speaking, her aunt had been nodding negatively. When the last words were out of June's mouth, Aunt Mabel said, "I think you need to call and tell her. You can call from here if you want to."

Shortly after this statement was made, the people around the table dispersed with the men retiring to the living room and the women clearing off the table and going into the kitchen to take care of cleaning up after their meal. To the background sound of the clatter of the dishes and pots and pans in the kitchen and the news coming from the radio in the living room, June remained in the dining room where she placed her call. With her new husband standing beside her, his hands on her shoulders giving her moral support, she spoke into the mouthpiece. "Mom," she said. "This is June."

"I know," her mother replied. Her voice held a hint of alarm when she asked, "Is everything alright? Nothing's wrong, is there?"

June took a deep breath before she replied, "Everything's fine, Mom. In fact everything is wonderful!"

Since June wasn't in the habit of calling long-distance, Priscilla was puzzled by this apparently casual call. In an effort to glean additional information, she asked if June planned to come to Mansfield soon. In response, June said, "We will be up soon."

"We? Is Rose coming with you?" Priscilla asked.

Although June could feel the furious pounding of her heart and the sweat beading on her forehead, none of this was evident in her casual sounding reply, "I'll be bringing Dick. We got married yesterday."

The sound of her mother's gulp traveled across the lines. It was followed by silence...dead silence. Then, her voice unnaturally bright, she parroted, "You got married yesterday?" June could picture her mother with the receiver clutched in her hand as she tried to assimilate this message. If her mother was disappointed or alarmed by what her daughter had just sprung on her, she managed to muster her resources and hide her feelings behind a facade of congratulations and best wishes. Before ending the conversation, she asked to talk to her new son-in-law. After June nervously handed the phone to Dick, she could tell from his end of the conversation that her mother was graciously welcoming him into the family.

Instead of hanging up the phone when they finished talking, Dick handed the phone back to her, "Your mom wants to talk to you again," he said. June beamed as she listened to her mom tell her that she wanted to have a party for them. "I'll invite all the Mansfield relatives." After June passed this bit of news onto her husband, her mother concluded the conversation by saying that she'd write with the date and time.

"Whew!" June breathed as she hung up. "Now, all I have to do is let Dad know." Although she tried to sound disappointed, her voice didn't quite ring true when she continued, "I guess I won't be able to call Dad since Granddad doesn't have a phone. I'll just have to write to him."

That night, after they returned to Charlotte's house, June sat down and composed the letter. "I bet he'll call when he gets this," June said as she placed the envelope in the mailbox. Although she waited anxiously for a call or, at the least, a letter in return, neither happened. Her father was as silent as if he'd never heard the news.

⁓

Returning to school loomed as a big hurdle in June's mind. Her first Monday, as a bride, she could feel the butterflies battling in her stomach when she walked into her homeroom. By the time she returned from lunch, she was beginning to relax though, thinking that the administration either wasn't aware of her new status or that it was going to be ignored.

Hearing her name booming over the intercom brought her head up from the Spanish assignment she'd been reviewing. Over the sound of the blood pounding in her ears, she heard the school secretary firmly request her immediate presence in the principal's office. On reluctant feet, she made her way down the three flights of stairs and the long hall until she was in the outer office. The secretary looked up, smiled at her, and motioned for her to be seated. "He will be with you in a moment," she said, before returning her attention to the papers on her desk.

June consoled herself with the thought that this wasn't going to be too bad. Within the next hour, though, she was to discover that it was even worse than she could possibly have imagined. The principal acted as if she had committed a crime against the entire school...that the very presence of a married student was going to contaminate the innocent minds of the rest of the students. Her feeble attempt at humor when she said, "They're around their parents who are married, and it doesn't seem to hurt them," only brought another onslaught of angry words and contempt from him.

After what seemed like hours, she began to understand that, though he wasn't specifically saying it, he wanted her to quit school. This realization, at first, stunned her, then she became angry. The white haired man sitting across from her gradually became aware that the frightened girl who'd entered his office was changing. If he'd had any doubt, this was erased from his mind when she raised her downcast eyes and firmly announced, "I'm not quitting school. I plan to graduate with my class in six months. If that isn't satisfactory to you, I'm sure my husband and my father will be glad to come in and talk to you about it."

The principal had been surprised at the change in her demeanor. Her eyes were now flashing, her lips were tightened into a thin line, and her dimpled chin was thrust forward in a challenging position. It was obvious, to him, that if he persisted in his original intent, he would have a fight on his hands. With a barely audible sigh, he reversed his position entirely by saying, "It won't be necessary for either of them to come in. I just want to extend my good wishes."

June smiled in return, but her smile wasn't so much in response to his words as to the thought that had been running through her mind that he'd just saved himself from one of her father's "talking tos." She had no doubt that her father would have rushed to her defense. He had always treasured education, a value instilled in him by his own father who had been a schoolmaster in a one-room schoolhouse. She knew her father would never have allowed anyone to deprive her of her education.

That night when she told Dick about the encounter, he gave her a big hug and told her that he was proud of her. He laughed aloud when she explained to him about one of her father's talking tos. "When we were growing up, Dad didn't spank us, but if we ever did anything that disappointed him, that's what he called the little talks he gave us. By the time he got through telling us how much he'd always expected of us and how disappointed he was that we'd let him down, we would be so ashamed of ourselves for ever putting him through it that we'd promise never to do it again."

"Whew," Dick exclaimed. "I hope your dad doesn't ever have to give me one of those." She could tell by the mischievous glint in his brown eyes that he was teasing her, but pretended to be serious when she replied that he'd better watch his step or she'd sic her dad on him.

Dick's eyes brimmed with laughter when he said, "I think the principal would be surprised to find out that some of his students aren't as innocent as he thinks they are." June was soon to discover, first hand, the truth in her husband's remark. From the time the news was out that she was married, she was approached at least once a week by one of the principal's innocent female students or another with comments about their sex lives. Some of the things they imparted to June brought the blood rushing to her face and others sent her hurrying home and asking her husband what they were talking about.

～

The newlyweds happily received the news that their new home was ready for them to move into. That proved to be a minor task since the only possessions they had were their clothing, a few personal items, June's dressing table from her room when she'd lived on Lawrence Street, Dick's record player, and a radio June's dad had given her when she was eleven years old. Although they didn't own much, June knew there was no way they could transport it by bus to their new home. Dick solved the problem by asking his Uncle Raymond to help them. Barely topping five feet in height with light brown hair and blue eyes, nattily dressed as usual, Dick's young uncle showed up in his dark blue Pontiac to drive them across town to their first home at 27 Fulton Avenue. Once June greeted him with a cheery, "Hi!" she was unable to get another word in until they arrived at their destination. To say he loved to talk was an understatement. While June listened in awe, he talked about his work in his barbershop on East Main Street, about his new girlfriend, June Snelling, about his car, his money, and threw in some outrageous statements that June soon figured were flights of fancy.

After he helped bring their possessions into the house, he left for a date with "the other June" and the newlyweds started their tour of their new place. Their rooms were located inside a two-story yellow frame house. All the rooms were spacious and airy, with hardwood floors, and light painted walls. One of the first things June noticed was that every nook and cranny was immaculately clean.

Neva had greeted them at the door and escorted them to their bedroom at the top of the stairs. It contained a double bed, a bedside table on each side, and two bureaus. Centered on stiffly starched doilies on each table was a white shaded china lamp. The small rugs scattered across the gleaming floorboards matched the rose colored chenille bedspread. At the windows the sunlight was filtered through crisp white ruffled curtains.

Telling them to come to the kitchen when they'd put their belongings away, Neva left them alone. It only took a few minutes to place their clothes in the closet or bureau drawers, plug in the radio and record player and position the dressing table between the two windows. Then hand-in-hand they descended the stairs and made their way to the kitchen. Looking up from the potatoes she was peeling, Neva dried her hands on her apron and told them to follow her downstairs to their kitchen. After going down a flight of steps to the basement, she led them past her laundry room, the furnace, shelves of jewel-like mason jars filled with home-canned fruits and vegetables before they finally got to an open doorway. Ushering them into the room, Neva said, "This is it."

"This is great!" June exclaimed as she looked around the room. Against two walls was a long L-shaped counter top with a two-burner gas hot plate, and deep white sink. Against another wall was an open-shelved cabinet containing a number of dishes and pots and pans. In the middle of the room were two chairs and small wooden table. Neva had made a skirt for the counter and matching curtains for the small windows. Someone, probably Neva's husband, Kenny, had painted the walls and laid linoleum on the floor. Like the rest of the house, this room was sparkling clean. When they returned to the upstairs kitchen, Neva threw open the door to the refrigerator and pointed to an empty shelf. "I cleared this off for you," she said. June thanked her and grimaced before saying that she was a novice at cooking, so she probably wouldn't need much space. "You'll learn," Neva reassuringly told her.

As it turned out, June was soon to discover that her husband was an extremely picky eater, so learning to cook a variety of foods wasn't going to be necessary. Unfortunately, looming in the future were their first battles, and they were going to be food fights. Blissfully unaware then of what was to come, they were happily settling into a place of their own.

They soon established a routine. Each morning they'd walk the few steps to the corner of West Main Street and Fulton Avenue where they would board the city bus for June's day at high school and Dick's at work. In the evening, their room was their haven. They'd usually listen to music from Dick's record collection, or to a program on June's light green tabletop radio.

They'd discovered the first time they tried to listen to it in this room that without an antenna all they could hear was static. It didn't take long for them to solve that problem, though. They found that all they had to do was wrap the lead-in wire that was attached to the antenna, around June's big toe to bring the sound in clear and static free. Propped up in bed with the radio turned to one of the near-by stations, they'd listen to their favorite programs.

One evening when Dick reached over to turn the dial to the Jack Benny Show, he ran his hand along the long narrow crack that ran across the top and down one side of the green casing. "How'd you break this?" he asked. "Did you drop it?"

His question brought a smile to her lips that quickly spread to her eyes as she told him the story of the woman her father had been dating when he met Polly. "He had given her this radio as a present," she said. Then she laughed softly at the memory of what her dad had considered his narrow escape before she continued talking, "When he told this woman that he had fallen in love with Polly, she got mad and told him he could keep the radio.... Then she threw it at him."

"I hope your dad ducked!" Dick exclaimed.

"She narrowly missed him the first time, but when he saw her reach for it the second time, he scooped it up and beat a hasty retreat," she concluded, laughingly. This radio became a good conversation piece and the story was repeated anytime anyone asked about the crack.

FOOD FIGHTS

Another part of their routine was Saturday night dinner at her in-laws. Every Saturday after Dick got off work, they'd take the bus to the square, then walk the rest of the way to the house on Third Street. The menu never varied, and since it was so good they would have been disappointed if it had. As the newlyweds sat at the table with Dick's father, and his brothers, Gene and Kenny, his mother, Rowena, would heap their plates with mounds of garlic-laced spaghetti. Then she would hover over them, while she served creamy cottage cheese, deviled eggs, and home-baked dinner rolls.

She always brewed a pot of hot tea to go with the meal. In June's household, they'd always drunk coffee. In the summer they'd had iced tea flavored with lemon. June had never liked hot tea, but the first time she related this to her mother-in-law, she was emphatically told, "Yes, you do!" With those words, Rowena plopped the cup of steaming brew in front of her daughter-in-law. She didn't voice the words, "Now drink this!" but her expression dared June to refuse. Remembering both of her mothers' admonitions about not offending the hostess, June drank it, and though she didn't like it at the time, she could see that she had no choice. And after a short period, she did learn to enjoy it.

It bothered June that her mother-in-law never sat at the table with the family. She seemed to feel it was her job to wait on them. Although June volunteered to dish up the food and put it on the table so Rowena could join them, she couldn't talk her into changing her ways. One night, after they got home from one of these dinners, she broached the subject to Dick, but he nonchalantly replied that she'd always done it that way. "You mean, even when there's no one else there, she doesn't sit at the table with the family?" June asked.

Since he was accustomed to this behavior, he shrugged his shoulders, and said that was her way of doing things. Then he explained, "One reason she doesn't sit with us is if someone doesn't like what she's cooked, she can fix something else."

Although this was unheard of in June's young life, she didn't expect it to lurk as a major problem for her, or to lead to the first of many of the newlyweds fights over food. The first time she put a meal on the table, and Dick said, "I don't like this. You can fry me some eggs," she thought he was joking.

When she realized he wasn't, she informed him that in her family people ate what was put before them. "We wouldn't think of insulting the cook by asking for something else."

"You told Mom that you didn't like tea, didn't you?" he asked.

Hurt, June found herself flinging angry words at him, "Yes, but I drank it!" Then with her hands on hips, she cried, "You don't like any food! How am I ever going to learn to cook for you?"

Seeing the tears glistening in her eyes, Dick was beginning to feel sorry for hurting her feelings. Not sorry enough, though, for him to eat something he didn't like. "I'll just eat some of this bread and butter," he muttered between his teeth, but under his breath, he added, "What's the big deal about frying some eggs?"

Maybe if he'd known how June had struggled to try to fry the eggs that he had eaten Sunday for breakfast, he'd have been more understanding. He'd told her that he wouldn't eat a fried egg if the yoke was broken, and she couldn't manage to flip it over without turning it into a regular Humpty-Dumpty. She must have thrown away half a dozen eggs before she finally ran to Neva for help. After hearing her tale of woe, Neva had graciously volunteered to cook them for her.

A few days later, when they were waiting for the bus to arrive, June casually mentioned that she was going to cook one of her favorite dishes that night. "I hope you like macaroni and cheese," she said.

"Hate it," he replied. "I can't stand those mushy noodles." Before she had a chance to reply that she would cook something else for him, the bus pulled to a stop and they were greeted by several of her classmates. June didn't give it another thought until that night when she was ready to put dinner on the table. She'd baked the macaroni and cheese in Neva's oven, and on the two-burner hot plate she'd cooked one of Dick's favorite meals of liver and onions and mashed potatoes.

As she sat on the hard wooden chair and watched the gravy congeal and the liver turn to leather, she fearfully looked at her watch as the minutes turned into hours...without a word from her husband. When she realized he wasn't coming home for dinner, and if he'd met with an accident, she'd have been notified by now, she forced a few bites of the macaroni and cheese down her throat. Then she took another look at the unappetizing liver and onions, and dumped the entire dinner in the garbage pail. On the trek through the basement on her way to their bedroom, she was too upset to remember to duck. When she banged her head against the low hanging pipe, she could have sworn the basement was filled with stars.

Although it really hurt, she was glad of the excuse it gave her when she walked past the living room where Kenny, Neva, and the girls were seated next to the radio. When they looked up at the sound of her footsteps, she noticed Neva's startled expression and by way of explanation touched the lump that had already begun to appear. Then she said, "I bumped into the furnace pipe." Aware that the bridegroom was a couple hours late coming home from work, they had their suspicions about the real reason for the tear-stained eyes, but they were too polite to mention it.

When her husband slipped into the bedroom a few minutes later, she was in bed with the covers pulled up to her chin. As he opened the door and cheerily called out, "I'm home!" she turned her back and burrowed deeper into the covers. He seemed to be baffled by her cool reaction to his homecoming. Sounding like a hurt little boy, he asked, "What's wrong? Are you mad about something?"

Although June's intent had been to remain cool and calm, and literally give him the cold shoulder, she couldn't let that question go unanswered. Sitting up in bed, her eyes were blazing when she said, "You don't know why I should be angry. Try thinking about me cooking a big meal for you, and you not bothering to come home! Wouldn't that make you angry?"

He looked even more like a flustered little boy when he replied, "But I told you that I don't like macaroni and cheese. Since you were cooking it, I went to Mom's for dinner."

June's next words were spoken through clinched teeth, "I cooked macaroni and cheese for myself, but since you said you didn't like it, I cooked liver and onions and mashed potatoes for you." The picture of the congealed mess this meal had turned into flashed through June's mind as she fervently wished that she hadn't thrown it away. "If I'd saved it, he'd be wearing it," she grimly thought as she stared at her new husband in total amazement.

"But...but..." he stuttered. "You didn't say anything about cooking anything except macaroni and cheese. I'd have come home if I'd known you were cooking liver and onions!"

"I'm not any happier about being stood up now that we're married than I was before," June firmly announced.

While Dick honestly had not seen anything wrong with what he had done, he was sorry he'd upset her. Trying to get back in her good graces, he tried to put his arms around her, but she slipped out of bed and started pacing around the room. "I just don't understand why you would go to your mother's," she exclaimed. "Didn't you know that I'd fix something besides macaroni and cheese?"

By now he was passionately wishing that he'd come home even if it would have meant eating something he didn't like. "That would have been easier than having her mad at me," he thought. "I'm sorry, Honey," he said. "I thought you'd understand. Since you wouldn't fix me an egg the other day when I didn't like what you cooked, I thought it would be better not to try that again!"

While she was taking all this in, he added, "Mom would have...."

Before he had a chance to say anymore, June interrupted by reminding him that she wasn't his mother. He chuckled softly when he replied, "I've noticed that, and I'm glad of it."

He looked so remorseful that she couldn't stay angry any longer, so this time when he pulled her into his arms she didn't draw away. "The fun of fighting is making up!" he told her...and she soon discovered that he was right. Although later when he said he was looking forward to her warming up tonight's dinner for the next day, and she told him what she'd done with it, he wasn't very happy. This incident cured him of his dinnertime wandering. He never stayed away at dinnertime again.

When a few days later they went to Mansfield for the wedding reception that her mother was having for them, they didn't know that one of the brightly wrapped presents they would receive would prove to be the remedy for their mealtime problems.

PROBLEMS SOLVED

The day of the party when their bus pulled into the lot at the bus station, June's stepfather, Bill, and her younger brother, Dickie, were waiting for them. She could see the grin that spread from one ear to the other when Dickie walked toward them. June hugged him, and Dick shook his and Bill's outstretched hands before they piled into the car for the short ride to her mother's house.

When Bill eased the car to the curb, June was pleased to see the vehicles of her relatives parked on both sides of the street in front of the house on Arlington Avenue. "Who is here?" she asked her brother. Before he could reply, the front door was thrown open, and her mother stepped out onto the front porch.

"My daughter, the bride!" she called out as she wrapped her arms around June. Then standing back and smiling at her new son-in-law, she was as warm in her welcome to him, although she did tease him about making her a mother-in-law when she was barely thirty-six years old.

While they were talking, she led the way into the living room where several people were sitting on the couch and easy chairs. While June introduced him to her aunts, uncles, cousins, and friends of the family, Dick's head was swirling trying to remember all their names.

The table was laden with trays of meat, bowls heaped high with a variety of vegetables, and salads. While everyone loved all the food, the luscious coconut cake that Priscilla served with coffee and tea after the meal was definitely a hit. As an aside to June, Priscilla said, "I remember how you always loved coconut cake when you were a little girl."

"I still do, but the only coconut Dick will eat is fresh from the shell," June replied.

There was a soft knock on the door and Mrs. Shier, Priscilla's next door neighbor, who had narrowly escaped the holocaust in World War II, came in bearing a gift. "I just wanted to congratulate June's bridegroom and wish them both much happiness," she exclaimed. June was ecstatic to see her older friend from her growing up years, and happily made the introductions. Although Mrs.

Shier initially demurred when asked to stay for some cake, June was so anxious for Dick to get to know her friend better that she wouldn't take "no" for an answer.

In acknowledgment of the introduction, Dick said, "June has talked so much about you that I feel I know you."

Remembering their late night conversations during the past summer about the sailor and the soldier competing for June's affection, she and Mrs. Shier exchanged knowing looks before the older woman murmured for June's ears only, "I'd say you made the right choice."

While the two women smiled affectionately, Priscilla announced, "It's time to open the gifts!"

One of the first gifts they opened was a combination sandwich grill/waffle iron...the gift that was to put an end to their squabbles at mealtime. Everyone laughed when Dick exclaimed, "I love grilled cheese sandwiches! Now we'll have something to eat!"

"I don't think I have done a bad job cooking for you, considering that I just have a three burner hotplate to work with," June said.

Priscilla chimed in with, "When your dad took me back to West Virginia and we lived in the house at the cave, I would have welcomed a three burner hotplate. That wood burning cook stove was a lot of work and awful to cook on."

"I remember it. I wasn't old enough to realize how much work was involved for you, but I'll never forget the good meals you turned out," June mused.

They reminisced a few minutes more about the earlier days when the little family had lived at the cave house before they became aware of Priscilla's husband, Bill, taking in every word they were saying. Though he didn't say a word, the disapproving expression on his face showed his displeasure.

"Uh oh," June thought. "I forgot that Mom makes a point of never mentioning anything in front of Bill that would remind him of when she and Dad were married."

Trying to smooth her husband's ruffled feathers, Priscilla said, "This Westinghouse electric stove that Bill bought me is a cinch to use. Since Bill works at Westinghouse, he's not only gotten me the stove but the refrigerator, and the washer and dryer."

It was obvious that Priscilla's words had effectively unruffled Bill's feathers as he proudly proclaimed, "I want to make life as easy as possible for my wife." While he didn't say it, everyone in the room felt that his unspoken thought was that, unlike her first husband, he wouldn't expect his wife to cook on anything as primitive as a wood burning cook stove.

June didn't voice her thoughts but she wondered how, with Priscilla's three children in his wife's life, Bill could fool himself into pretending that he was her first love.

As June opened the other packages and found towels, sheets, table cloths, doilies, glasses, and cooking utensils, she knew these would have to be packed away until they had a house of their own. The last gift...a cookbook brought more teasing about June's cooking. "I'm learning!" she exclaimed laughingly. "You just wait! One of these days, I'll cook almost as well as Mom!"

She thought she heard her husband mutter under his breath, "That will be the day," as he and her brother, Dickie, exchanged grins. She was happy to see this exchange between the two of them. It was important to her for these two males in her life to be friends. From all appearances, Dickie had immediately accepted her husband as his second older brother, and Dick obviously felt the same.

The newlyweds were having so much fun at the party that they would willingly have stayed for hours longer, but a glance at her wristwatch showed June that they had less than a half hour to catch their bus. As the other guests started to leave, June wondered aloud how they were going to get all the gifts back to Newark. "Take what you can use now, and I'll bring the rest the next time we come down," Priscilla informed her.

"I'm taking this, and this!" June announced as she tucked the sandwich grill under one arm and the cookbook under the other. Telling her daughter that she wouldn't let her forget them, she motioned for her to follow her into the kitchen.

"I just wanted to have a minute to talk to you before you leave," June's mother said. "You look like you're happy. Are you?" she asked.

June assured her that she was very happy. In response, her mother said, "I was worried when you called and told me you were married. You know, I was your age when I married your dad, and you know how that turned out." June's eyes darkened, but she didn't voice her thought that she wasn't going to allow that to happen to her marriage, and that she wouldn't do that to her children.

Observing the stubborn thrust of her daughter's chin, Priscilla decided to move away from that subject by asking what June's father's reaction had been to the news. "I don't know," June moaned. "He hasn't answered my letter."

"He will," her mother assured her. Then after a second's hesitation, she added, "I'd suggest that you write to him again and give him Kenny and Neva's phone number so he can call you. You know how men are about writing!" June brightened as she realized the truth in what her mother had just said.

"I think I'll do that!" she announced. "That is, if I don't hear from him tomorrow." With that thought in mind, and words of best wishes ringing in their ears, they said their good-byes and went along with Bill to the bus station.

∼

As it turned out, she didn't have to write the second letter. When she returned from school the next day, the first thing she saw was a white envelope on the hall table addressed to her. When she picked it up, she realized that the handwriting was that of her stepmother, Polly, rather than her father's. Anxious to read it, she ran upstairs and into her room. She didn't even wait to remove her coat before she tore it open and eagerly began to read.

Polly started by expressing her surprise at the news of her marriage. Then she went on to say that the reason they hadn't written sooner was that neither she nor June's father had seen her letter when it first arrived. "Apparently, someone brought in the mail, and put it with some other papers in a basket on the buffet in the dining room. I don't know how long it was there before Mamma saw it. For some reason it was open, so she read it. Tonight at dinner she dropped the bombshell by asking what we thought of June getting married. I thought your dad was going to hit the ceiling. His first reaction was that he was going to come up there and have the marriage annulled, but I got him calmed down enough to at least read your letter."

June could feel a cold knot forming in the pit of her stomach when she visualized the scene. "Your dad was ready to jump in the car and come and give you the talking-to of your life about you getting married at such a young age until I reminded him that he'd been twenty-four when he'd married your mother, and being older hadn't made a difference then. I told him that the deed was done, and that I've never seen you set your mind to anything that you didn't find a way to make it work." She concluded by saying that he was warming up to the idea, but just needed a little time to think about it before he writes. She added a post script that said, "We love you, Baby. Be happy!"

The word of her father's reaction caused her a couple sleepless nights. Then, the long awaited letter arrived. As Polly had predicted, he had warmed up to the idea and even told her that if she were happy, he was happy for her. "Let me know the date when you'll be graduating," he wrote. "I'll be there!"

Waving the letter in front of Dick's eyes while he was finishing his grilled cheese with pimento sandwich, she joyfully exclaimed, "He can't be too upset or he wouldn't already be planning to come to my graduation!"

"That's good news," Dick quipped. "Now I won't have to worry about one of his notorious talking-tos!"

"You're lucky about that!" June matched his flippant manner as she plopped his second sandwich on his plate. "The only one I still haven't heard from is Cecil, but it might take a while for my letter to get to him since he's in Tsing Tao, China."

"He hasn't been there long has he?" Dick asked. "The last time I heard anything, he was still in the radar school in Florida." June explained that he'd graduated from the school in Banana River in October, and he and his crew had flown to China. "In his last letter, he said their mission was to set up a RADAR unit so they can bring pilots in during bad weather. He said they brought some in when they first got the unit set up with the visibility at around one hundred feet."

"Little too nerve racking for me!" Dick exclaimed. "Give me a field hospital anytime," he quipped in reference to his military service.

While she was finishing up the minimal clean-up this meal required, Dick mentioned that he'd seen an advertisement in the Advocate for a nineteen-thirty-seven Ford for sale for six hundred and fifty dollars. "I thought I might look into it," he said. "What do you think?"

With thoughts of not having to ride the bus anymore, she enthusiastically encouraged him to see if he could buy it. Her mother had always told her that she should be careful what she wished for, as she might get it. In this case, she should have listened to her mother. They were so anxious to have transportation that they chose to ignore the ninety-four thousand miles showing on the odometer, the balding tires, or the fact that it seemed to take a mile to bring it to a stop.

The farmer who owned the car knew that he didn't have to negotiate, and he didn't. "Well now," he had drawled. "The way I see it, you can take it or leave it. I've had several calls about it, and I'm sure it's going to be snapped up pretty fast."

Since this was the first car that he'd seen advertised since the war ended two years earlier, Dick decided to buy it before someone else beat him to it. Three weeks later after he'd replaced the battery and the generator, bought one new tire, and had a new thermostat installed in the radiator, they decided to take it for a spin to Mansfield. During the entire trip up and back, it sputtered and groaned and finally gasped its dying breath when they were still ten miles from home.

Fortunately, a few minutes later while Dick stood with his head buried underneath the hood, his father's sister, Bertha and her husband Fritz, drove by. Recognizing her nephew's backside, she told her husband to go back and see what was going on. After Fritz pulled over to the side of the road, he joined his nephew in studying the mysteries of the engine...tapping first one thing then another while he instructed Dick to give it another try. Finally they were able to revive it, and his aunt and uncle slowly followed along behind what Dick was now calling "the junker," until they had safely returned to the house where June and Dick lived.

The next day, Dick placed his own ad in the paper, and poorer but wiser, he sold it to someone who liked to tinker on cars. As the buyer counted out six one hundred dollar bills, he enthusiastically told Dick, "It won't take me long to get this car purring like a kitten!" When Dick told June what the buyer had said, he muttered, "From the sounds it was making when he drove away, that kitten sounded more like a sick lion."

June patted him on the shoulder and sighed, "It seemed like a good idea at the time."

"I've learned my lesson," he declared. "If it takes a year, I'm going to wait until my number comes up at one of the new car dealerships. No more pieces of junk for me!" He might not have been so emphatic if he'd realized that another year would come and go, and he still wouldn't be one of the lucky ones able to buy a new car. By the time the trees were budding and the grass was greening, though, he'd come up with another solution to their transportation problems.

Unfortunately, though, one that landed June in the protective custody of the police.

～

While the snow was still flying and the entire city was blanketed in white, June had finally received a letter from Cecil. As she read the first paragraph, she wasn't sure whether to be angry or amused. With the second reading, the latter emotion won. She was still smiling a few minutes later when she heard Dick's footsteps heading toward the open kitchen doorway, and his enthusiastic call of, "Honey, I'm home!"

Gathering her into a bear hug, he noted, "You look like the cat that ate the canary. What's going on?" In response, she reached into her apron pocket and pulled out her brother's letter. When he saw the familiar handwriting and the Fleet Post Office return address, he exclaimed, "The long awaited letter from China! I gather from your smile that he is happy about your news!"

"He didn't really say," she responded. "He just wanted to know if I was going to make an uncle out of him."

Dick let out a whoop of laughter that June was sure the family upstairs would be able to hear. "I wondered who'd be the first to ask that question!" he said.

"About becoming an uncle?" she teased.

"No!" he grimaced. "About whether or not you are pregnant!"

"I know what you meant," she saucily replied. "I guess I'd better write to him and let him know that I really don't want to disappoint him, but he's going to have to wait awhile to have the honor of being an uncle." After a slight hesitation, she continued, "I've noticed some of the kids at school looking me over to see if I'm gaining any weight. They're probably wondering the same thing."

"If anything, you look to me like you're losing. Are you?" he said.

"I guess I've lost about ten or fifteen pounds," she replied. "I get some kidding at school about marriage being rough on me, but I just ignore that. If they had to walk up and down all these steps, and bend over and duck all these furnace pipes several times a day like I do, they'd lose weight too."

Puzzled, he said, "We only have to come down here twice a day...once for breakfast then for dinner. Why would you have to make the trip several times?"

"Once I get myself organized and can remember to get everything from the refrigerator at once, I won't have to make so many trips. At this point, though, I always forget something and have to run upstairs for it. Then when we sit down at the table I find I've forgotten something else," she bemoaned. "It wouldn't be so bad if the refrigerator was in our kitchen," she exclaimed before adding, "I don't imagine this diet we have of grilled cheese sandwiches helps either."

He smiled mischievously when he told her that he liked the way she looked. "When we were at your Mom's on Christmas, Bill called us a couple of string-beans. I guess maybe he was right. I've always been skinny, though. You know that when I first got home from the service, I used to put handkerchiefs in my back pockets to make me look like I had a rear-end."

They bantered in this manner throughout the meal, but over coffee, Dick asked what else her brother had to say. Her response was to hand him the letter. As he read through it, he whistled in surprise. "What is it?" she asked.

"I just read about how the Chinese pilots seem to usually miss the runway and land in the grass, and about the time one of them mistook his gun trigger for the radio and shot out tires of several planes," he explained.

"Read on!" she said. "He wrote that another one accidentally shot out the windows of the control tower."

"I'd be putting up some steel armor," he exclaimed.

"Great minds work alike," she said. "That's just what they did."

June sighed when she added, "I thought the world was finally at peace. From what he says, that doesn't apply in China. The Chinese Communists have taken over the city of Tsingtao where he and his buddies have been going for R and R. He said none of the sailors are allowed off the base. They're confident, though, that the nationals will reclaim it. He says it isn't unusual to hear distant gunfire in the hills around them."

The word "communism" was beginning to make the headlines for the first time in their memory, especially in connection with China. They had no way of predicting that night in 1947 while they were talking over their coffee in their makeshift kitchen how much this "ism" was going to effect the next generations. For them, at that time, they were only wondering what effect this would have on her older brother.

~

Winter gave way to spring while June was excitedly looking forward to her graduation, and Dick was still trying to come up with a solution to their transportation problem. He'd been tossing around an idea for some time, but June had no inkling of what it was. She was to find out one evening while she was waiting in their room for him to come home, and she heard a sound like The Midland Theater's popcorn popper coming from the street outside. Running to the window and looking out she saw a slim man, his hair and face hidden behind an aviator style hat and goggles sitting astride a small motorcycle. When he looked up and motioned for her to come downstairs, she recognized the cocky grin. It was her husband!

Her soldier who had gone on a mission to buy a car, quipped, "Still not enough cars running off the assembly lines, but motorcycles are. This one sure is a doozie."

"It sure is," June replied. "Did you buy it?"

"Yep. We just joined the mobile society."

In a few minutes, her arms wrapped tightly around his waist, they barreled around the courthouse square. This was their introduction to their new two cylinder Czechoslovakian "Chek" motorcycle. Happily unaware that an incident involving the Chek would soon set the police on their tail, Dick suggested they show their new possession to his parents.

When they arrived at the house on Third Street, Kenny and Gene were excited and immediately had to be taken for a ride while Dick's mother wailed that they were going to be killed on it. His father called it, "That silly contraption." As they were to discover, with this small cycle, Dick had begun a love affair with motorcycles that was to last for years.

They were soon to find as time went by that there was an aggravating problem with this vehicle. The gasoline had to be mixed with the oil before being poured into the tank. If even a small speck of dirt or lint got into it, the motor would stop. Then Dick would have to clean the carburetor before it would start again.

The first time they rode it for any distance was when they went to Mansfield to see June's mother, brother, and stepfather. Up until this trip they'd found the Chek's little quirk to be inconvenient, but on this trip it went beyond that to something troubling. If they'd stuck to their original plan to go on Sunday morning and return that evening, they'd probably have been alright. Since June hadn't seen her Mansfield family for a long time, she didn't want to wait until the next day, so she convinced Dick to leave Saturday night when he got home from work.

About ten miles into their trip in the village of Utica, Dick stopped for gasoline and they were happily on their way again. By now though, total darkness had descended. This didn't bother them, though, as the headlight on the motorcycle cut a bright swatch through it. A couple miles north of Utica just as they were cruising up a slight grade to the railroad tracks, the light suddenly dimmed and the motor coughed, sputtered, and stopped. "Uh Oh!" Dick muttered as they found themselves sitting on a motionless vehicle. They both hopped off, and he pushed it to the side of the road. The flashlight that he took from the saddlebags provided just enough light for him to start the work on the carburetor. He'd no sooner gotten the words out of his mouth that he must have gotten some dirt in with the fuel when they saw a car approaching from the south.

"Good!" June exclaimed. "Maybe someone can give us a hand." What happened within the next few minutes showed her that she had been too optimistic.

First, they found themselves surrounded by a bright light and then they heard a deep, pugnacious male voice ask, "What are you doing out here at this time of night with a girl that young?"

At first they were too blinded by the spotlight to make out the speaker's face. When the light was doused, Dick could see the Utica police emblem on the car door, and the uniformed men in the front seat. Relief in his voice, he explained what had happened and concluded by saying, "If you would flash that spotlight over here, I could have this thing cleaned out in a few minutes, and we could be on our way."

Instead of helping him, they proceeded to lecture him for having June out on a deserted highway at that time of night. "Don't you know how dangerous that can be?" the tall, beefy looking one demanded.

Then his partner, turning to the frightened young woman snapped, "Does your mother know where you are?"

Intimidated by the officer's hand resting on his revolver, June's eyes widened as she weakly stammered, "No sir, not exactly." This seemed to bring more of their wrath down on Dick's head before the larger of the two men sternly ordered her to get into the cruiser.

Before they slammed the door after her, the driver told Dick, "We're taking her back into town. When you get this fixed you can come to the station." With June seated alone in the back seat, they drove away and left Dick stranded along the dark highway. She felt like a lost child when she looked out the back window and saw the pitiful light cast by her husband's flashlight disappear from her sight.

A few minutes later when the officers made their way into the small town of Utica, the burlier of the two asked, "Young lady, what were you doing out there?"

June's response, "My husband and I were on our way to my mother's house in Mansfield," dropped like a bomb in the darkened interior of the patrol car.

First there was a stunned silence from the front seat, before the questioner stammered, "Your...your husband! You...you...you're married?"

The second man seemed to mutter through clenched teeth, "We'll just leave you here at the restaurant where you can have a coke while you wait for your husband. I'm sure he'll be along soon." With those words still ringing in June's ears, they double-parked just long enough for her to scamper out of the back seat.

As June stood on the sidewalk and looked after them, she felt in her pocket for the nickel it would take for a coke. When her hands came out empty, she turned away from the restaurant and started walking toward where they had left her husband. As she walked along the deserted main street in Utica, she glanced right then left, as she thought of how much fun she and Dick had been having while riding their motorcycle until it had suddenly died on them. Then how unexpectedly she had been plucked away from Dick by the policemen, then as quickly dropped like a hot potato on this dark deserted street. Her thoughts were interrupted by the sound of a loud gunshot. Feeling her heart race in pure terror, she ducked into the safety of a store doorway.

The sound triggered a memory of a horrible night when she was a little girl and her family had lived at the cave house. As she cringed in the doorway her mind flashed back to that night and her father's cry of, "Help, Priscilla, I've been shot." She still had nightmares of the sight of her father's blood seeping through the white shirt and pants he was wearing when he'd stumbled into the kitchen.

Then as an old car drove by her and it backfired again, she realized the gunshot she had feared was just that car sputtering. She laughed nervously at her imagination and felt sorry for the car's owner who like she and Dick couldn't find a good car. Then as she thought about the junk car she and Dick had briefly owned, she saw the welcome sight of the one headlight traveling toward her. Anyone viewing their reunion would have thought they'd been separated for months rather than the brief period that June had been in protective custody. For the rest of the trip, she found herself wrapping her arms more tightly around her husband's waist. She hadn't liked the separation...brief though it was. As he was to tell her later, he hadn't liked it either.

Their experience was to make interesting conversation around her mother's dinner table the next day. While June suspected that her mother may have agreed with the officer's sentiments, she didn't voice them. Dickie, on the other hand, was angry when he heard the story of his sister's near incarceration. His anger subsided, though, when he went riding on the back of the "Chek" with his brother-in-law.

When they returned from their ride around the neighborhood, and the blond haired teen-ager trooped into the house with the dark haired young man, Dickie said, "Boy, you wouldn't believe how many people looked out the door as we went by. The kids waved, but some of the grown-ups gave us dirty looks!" June wasn't surprised since they'd already experienced this reaction in Newark.

"The darn thing sounds like a popcorn popper," Bill muttered. "No wonder people look!" The newlyweds exchanged smiles. He seemed to share Dick's father's opinion of their new method of transportation.

ACROSS THE THRESHOLD

In May of 1947 when the young couple moved into their first house, they didn't know at the time, but they were to find out later that some of their new neighbors were horrified when they first saw and heard them barrel down the tree lined street. Unaware that they had an audience or of the reaction of the onlookers, Dick had parked at the curb, taken June's hand and together they'd walked hand-in-hand up the wooden steps across the board floor of the porch to the front door. As he had done on their wedding night, he scooped her into his arms and carried her over the threshold. Still holding her, he bent to kiss her when they heard his father's commanding voice coming from the direction of the kitchen. "Put that woman down and come in here and help me!" Surprised, Dick sat June on her feet, and they both turned to face the older man.

To Dick's inquiry as to what he was doing there, he irritably replied, "I'm trying to fix this pipe in the bathroom. If you can leave that woman alone for a minute, you can give me a hand."

With an apologetic look at his bride, Dick sauntered after his father. Left to her own devices, June examined her surroundings. She was determined to make an effort to find something to like about the house. For the last few weeks she'd been heartsick at the prospect of living here. She'd had her heart set on another house, but her father-in-law had chosen this one for them...over June's objections.

For the last few months, the newlyweds had planned to buy a small cottage that Forest owned at 258 South Second Street. They had been ecstatic when he'd told them that his tenant had bought a house and would be moving in May. In June's mind, its small size was perfect for the two of them. She pictured it as their first home, one they'd live in for a couple years before buying the home of her dreams in the more fashionable North or West End of town. Since Forest had agreed to sell it to them, she'd daydreamed about how it would look with the furniture she planned to buy.

Her dreams had been shattered a few weeks ago when Dick had told her that his father had rented the cottage. "He has a bigger house on Oakwood Avenue that has unexpectedly become available. The tenant was killed in an automobile accident and his wife will be going home to Michigan to be closer to her own family," Dick explained.

As she felt her plans for the future slipping away, she felt like crying. Instead, she found herself saying, "Don't you think we should have had a choice in the matter?"

Dick had reminded her that when they had a family, the cottage wouldn't have been large enough. This conversation had been taking place as they sat at the table in their basement kitchen on Fulton Avenue. As she fought back tears that threatened to spill down her cheeks, June responded in a small, resigned voice, "I thought you knew I only wanted to stay in the cottage for a couple years until we could afford to buy a new house."

He felt sorry for what had happened, but at this point he knew there was nothing he could do about it. "Honey, the one on Oakwood is a nice house. It has six rooms...three up and three down. At first we need to just use the downstairs, but later we'll want to expand into the rest of the house. Once you see it, I'm sure you'll like it. Won't you at least try?"

Even though she'd told him she would give it her best try, as she looked at the reality of the large house where they were going to live, she could feel a cold knot form in the pit of her stomach. Mentally shaking herself, while looking around, she kept reminding herself that this was now her home. "I am going to find something to like about it!" she vowed. With this thought in mind, she walked through the large middle and front rooms. "That's good," she mused. "The rooms are big and airy."

The light that came through the large windows in the living and dining rooms was filtered through the branches of the two maple trees in the front yard. It cast shadows on the wide floor boards in the living and dining rooms. The living room walls were covered in a patterned paper. "Much too busy," June muttered. "Ugh!" was her only comment when she looked at the sofa her in-laws had given them. The cover was of a flower strewn cretonne and seemed to battle with the print on the walls. Suddenly feeling depressed, June sank down on the plump looking center cushion, only to immediately jump to her feet. "The darn spring is sprung," she grumbled before trying the other two cushions. They weren't any better. As they were to discover later, the only way to sit comfortably on this couch was to position your derriere between the cushions.

The room they had chosen as their living room was the middle room...the one they'd entered from the front porch. Off to the left was the room that was to be their bedroom. The area itself was spacious with a gas-fired fireplace in the corner of the room. The walls in this room were also papered in a flower design, and the floor was bare. The center of the room was dominated by a white iron bed. June noticed that the caster was missing on one of the legs, and it was propped up with a brick. Her familiar dressing table and stool sat next to a used chest of drawers.

This furniture was a far cry from the modern pieces June had dreamed of owning. When Dick had first told her that his dad had some furniture he wanted them to have, she had protested, but Dick had quoted his father. "You just need to wait until the prices come down. The prices now are too inflated by the war. You just watch," his dad had said. "There's going to be another depression. Then you'll be able to buy everything you need for a song!"

As June looked at the rag-tag collection, she murmured under her breath, "It had better be soon. I don't know how long I can put up with this junk!"

While she was standing in the middle of the room lost in thought, Dick called from the kitchen, "Come on out here. You haven't seen the kitchen yet!" She followed his voice through their living room, where she found him holding open the swinging oak door and exclaiming, "Well, what do you think of this?"

Wanting to please him, she was ready to assure him that she liked it, but instead, she was so surprised by what she saw...or, in this case didn't see, that she cried out, "There's no sink!"

He laughed at the astonished expression on her face before he replied, "Sure there is!" The words had barely spilled from his lips before he threw open one of the five doors that rimmed the room. "Here it is!"

Speechless, she walked into the tiny room that was hidden behind the floor to ceiling cabinet. Suspended from the pantry wall was a long, narrow sink. The only work space that she could find was about eight inches on each side of the sink. "This is certainly different," she concluded.

Not catching the sarcasm in her voice, her husband enthusiastically replied, " It sure is!" before leading her back into the kitchen. Other than the one cabinet, the room was barren of any storage or counter space. Dick looked admiringly around the room before he exclaimed, "Look at all these windows and doors! Have you ever seen so many in one room?"

"Five doors and two windows! It looks to me as if this house was built by someone who was going to be sure to have a quick exit no matter where he was in the room!" she joked.

Forest who had overheard this part of the conversation charged out of the bathroom, and defensively announced that there was a reason for every door. "One is to the back porch, the next one goes to the middle room, the one next to it is to the upstairs stairway." Then pointing to the one they'd just come through, he vehemently added, "That one, as you know, goes to the pantry, and this one is to the bathroom!"

"Uh, oh," June thought. "I just thought this man was quiet and good natured. I must have stepped on his toes." Deciding to keep additional comments for her husband's ears alone, she continued her study of the room. She almost broke her resolve to keep quiet when she saw the cook stove her father-in-law had gotten for them. It looked to her young eyes to have been manufactured around the time of her mother's birth. Light green, it sat on four long spindly legs. As she faced it, the four gas burners were on the right-hand side, and the box-like oven perched to the left side of them. She hated the stove and every other piece of furniture in the house. "So much for modern furniture!" she silently bemoaned. "Dick and I are the only modern things in this house!" Later that night when they were finally alone, she told her husband, "It's alright, I guess, but every since I was eight years old and first saw blond wood furniture in my friend Helen's bedroom, that's what I've always wanted."

"We'll have it someday!" he reassured her. "As Dad says, we just have to wait and see what's going on with the economy. You do understand, don't you?"

"It would make more sense to live like this if we couldn't afford anything better," she responded. "Besides, we did pay your dad for this stuff, didn't we?"

Nodding his head, he said, "Not too much. The stove was only twenty dollars. The rest of it was less than fifty." He brightened when he added that his parents hadn't charged anything for the couch. June laughingly added that at least the price was right.

～

After Forest left, it didn't take long for the new residents to begin the exploration of the rest of their domain. The first room they checked was the bathroom. June found that since the deep, claw-footed bathtub dominated the minuscule room, it barely left room for the rest of the necessary fixtures. They joked that the tub was large enough for both of them. "Even if the rest of the room isn't," Dick teased.

When they continued their tour and June threw open one of the dining room doors, she was surprised to discover that it led to the steps to the upstairs. Standing on the landing, to her right was the door leading to the kitchen. "As I said earlier," she reminded Dick, "I've never seen so many doors in my life."

They continued joking about some of the peculiarities of the architecture as they tromped up the stairs to look at the three empty rooms. The two front bedrooms were large and square with two large windows and only two doors in each room. One opened from the hall and the other ones hid the smallest closets she had ever seen. "The closets in our trailer were larger than these," June commented. She was referring to the vagabond years when she, her older brother, her father, and her new mother had lived in a trailer in order to keep the family together while her father followed the defense construction jobs around the country.

Deep in memories of that happy time in her life, she followed her husband into the third bedroom where she could see that that there was more floor space in this room, though the sloping ceiling made it appear smaller. As they concluded their tour and started down the stairs to their living quarters, June silently bemoaned the loss of her dreamed of honeymoon cottage. This bare house seemed too large now, but as her husband had reminded her earlier, it would be the right size when they had a family. Although that May day in 1947, she couldn't imagine it, in less than a decade his prediction would come true.

For now, though, this first night in their new home, they were happy to finally have a private place of their own. Standing beside the couch in the living room, Dick smiled as he crooked his finger and motioned for her to come to him. "Come over here and sit on the sofa with me," he murmured.

She grinned when she realized that he didn't yet know about the peculiarity of the couch. June couldn't resist introducing him to it. She rushed across the room, sat between the two cushions and patted the one to her right and urged him to join her. As he let himself drop onto the couch, his eyes told her that he was intent on some serious cuddling, but instead he sprang to his feet with a yell, "What in the world?" Rubbing the spot where the springs had stabbed him, at first he didn't find the situation as amusing as June did. After she could control her laughter long enough to tell him about her discovery earlier of what she thereafter referred to as the torture chamber, he began to see the humor of it.

"I guess it's funnier when it happens to someone else," June exclaimed. Dick nodded his agreement before he said, "This certainly is going to make quite a conversation piece when we have company!"

When they looked around the room at their motley collection of furniture, they both agreed that it was going to be difficult to wait for the prices to come down. As it turned out, a visit from someone Dick loved and respected was going to turn the tide and help him decide not to wait for the depression...that was never to come.

That was yet to be, and in the meantime there were a couple other important events looming in their future. June had two big red Xs on the calendar...the first was for the date when her father would be arriving for her graduation, and the second was for graduation day.

∽

Adjusting to her new home, finishing her finals, and trying to accustom herself to the well-meaning advice of her in-laws kept June busy while she was waiting for her father's arrival. It had not taken her long to discover that the time she and Dick had spent in their temporary home on Fulton Avenue had not only been a honeymoon period with her husband but with his parents as well. Since they had been living in someone else's home, her in-laws hadn't felt comfortable visiting, nor had they found anything that they felt needed their advice. Now that the newly-weds were ensconced in their own place, though, the floodgates had opened, and June found herself drowning in a torrent of advice. Some she received directly when Forest and Rowena visited, but most of it came via her husband. From then on, it seemed to her that every time Dick came home from the barber-shop where he worked with his father, the conversation would start with, "Dad said that you should...." One day he might be advising her to use a broom instead of a dust mop. Another time, it would have something to do with hanging curtains, or the right way to do the laundry, fry an egg, or shop for groceries. She tried to remind herself that they were only trying to be helpful, but for a girl who had made her own decisions before she was married and had prided herself on her independence, this proved to be very difficult.

When she complained to Dick about what she considered his parents' interference, he replied, "I guess it's because I'm the first one of their boys to get married, they're having a hard time letting go." Since her relationship with her parents had been so different, June had trouble understanding this concept, but she promised herself that she would try.

This was one of the first things she discussed with her father when he arrived for his visit. When she was bemoaning the deluge of unsolicited advice she was getting, he reminded her that he'd always told her there was something to be learned from everything that happened in your life. "You may have to look hard, but something will come out of this...someday," he said.

"Fat chance," she thought, but one day she was to learn that he was right. *It was to be more than two decades in the future when she found herself with her first son-in-law, and she remembered what her father had told her that day in the kitchen of the house on Oakwood Avenue. Because of that long-ago conversation, at that wedding and for each of her children's wedding day, they and their spouses received her silent pledge not to give unasked for advice.*

THE VISITOR

June had been disappointed that her father couldn't stay with them during his visit. He had laughingly demurred when Dick had jokingly offered to let him sleep on their couch. "You'd probably be more comfortable on a bed of nails!" June explained.

"I think I'll pass!" her father laughingly replied. "Mace and Mabel said they would put me up while I'm here. I've already told them that I'll take them up on it."

He'd been surprised when he first saw their furniture. Since he knew his son-in-law had a good job, he wondered what he did with his money. He didn't want to embarrass the young couple, though, so he kept his concerns to himself. As it turned out, June broached the subject to him the next day while Dick was at work. "Dick's dad picked out all this furniture," she said. She suppressed a giggle when she watched her dad try to find a comfortable spot between the cushions on the couch. "They gave us the torture chamber you're sitting on," she added. A more serious note crept into her voice when she continued, "We have the money set aside, but Forest wants us to wait. He's sure now the war is over that there will be another depression, and all the prices will come down!"

"Don't ever wish for a depression. I'll take the higher prices anytime!" her father vehemently declared. "A depression is something I hope you young people never have to face." She squeezed his hand when she told him that if they'd been poor when she was growing up, she'd never realized it.

She wondered if his thoughts were back at the cavern house where she'd spent the first years of her life with her parents and brothers when he mused, "I didn't either. I thought that I was the richest man in the world then. I had everything I wanted."

Young as she was, she knew what he meant. Even in this house with its meager furnishing, she was happy because she shared it with the man she loved. "Having you here for my graduation makes it perfect," she replied.

A few days after this conversation, June's graduation day dawned bright and clear. "Now everything would be perfect," she thought, "if only Mom would be here." She knew, though, that was not going to be. In fact, after June had written and told her mother when she expected her father, she received a note saying she wouldn't be able to make it.

As it turned out, on graduation day, her mother, stepfather and younger brother had come and gone. They'd visited the Sunday after June's senior prom, so she was able to model both her formal dress and cap and gown. Priscilla had taken pictures of June in each outfit. Then before she left, she'd hugged her daughter and said, "I'll have these for my memory book."

"I wish Mom had waited until today to come," the soon-to-be-graduate mused as she looked out across White's Field to the bleachers where her husband and father were sitting. Then when she heard the school principal call, "June Harman," proud of her accomplishment, she walked forward to receive her diploma. Unknown to June on this happy occasion, her mother had set a pattern she would always follow. Priscilla would never attend an event that her ex-husband attended.

～

After the graduation celebration was over, June and Dick were busy getting ready for their trip to Mississippi with her father. Burrel had hated every minute of his train trip from Mississippi. "I'd rather drive," he said. "It gives me something to do instead of just sitting there twiddling my thumbs!" Running his hand through his thick, dark blond hair, he added, "I probably would have driven, but I didn't want to leave Polly without a car."

Dick commiserated with his father-in-law since he wasn't looking forward to the long train ride either. "Before we have to leave, I'm going to check with the car agencies, and see if my name has come up for a car yet," Dick announced. It didn't take long for him to find that every one of his inquiries brought a resounding, "No!" Although some softened it with an apology, the result was the same. However, one salesman told him about a friend he had in Columbus who had a car for sale. "I don't know too much about it, but it might be worth your time to check it out," he said.

June's Uncle Mace volunteered to take the trio to see it, but their high hopes were dashed when the young owner ushered them to the garage and pointed out a shiny black Model A Ford, manufactured before June's birth. To her this car was ancient. As if they hoped for a miracle, the men walked around the box-like vehicle and peered into the interior before starting to ask questions. By the time they were through with their inquiries, they'd learned that the car was a nineteen twenty-nine model, had good tires, and could get the young owner anywhere he wanted to go. They soon discovered that his interpretation of anywhere differed greatly from theirs. Especially when he told them that he'd been driving it across town every day to Ohio State University, and proudly exclaimed that he had even driven it all the way to Buckeye Lake a couple of weeks earlier.

"That's twenty or twenty-five miles from here. We're looking for something we can drive one thousand miles to Mississippi," Dick explained.

With these words, the young man could see his prospect of making a sale vanish. His face seemed to crumble when he cried, "Good Lord! When you were talking about going on a trip, I had no idea you were going that far." Then in a voice that mirrored his disappointment, he mumbled, "I don't think it would make that long a trip."

Resigned that they were going to have to make the trip by train, the group returned to Newark where the following day they boarded the train. The last time June had been on a train was during the war years when she, Polly, and her brother Cecil had come from Mississippi to join her father in Newark. As the train chugged away from the station, June commented that the trip was going to be different from the last one. "Then," she said, "World War II was raging and the train was packed with servicemen either going home on leave or to a place of embarkation."

Dick joined in by telling them that he'd gone by troop train to Brownsville, Texas when he was transferred from White Sulphur Springs, West Virginia, then again when he went to a camp between New York and Boston to embark for Europe. "The last time I was on one was when I came home on leave," he reminisced. I wasn't feeling very well as I was just recovering from a severe allergic reaction to a spider bite I got on the ship. The doctors pumped me full of penicillin and by the time I got home I was beginning to feel better. Then with Mom's good nursing, I was good as new in no time. Then his grin seemed to spread to his eyes he continued, "Right after that, I met you!"

For most of the remainder of the trip, Dick's wild sense of humor kept them entertained and helped the miles whip by. Sitting in the seat facing the young couple, her father said to his son-in-law, "I think you missed your calling. You should have been a comedian." Over the years, June was to hear this assessment of her husband's humor many times. As time went by, she was to discover that he took the matter of entertaining friends, family, and strangers seriously...as if that were his special calling.

As the train rolled through one state after another and brought them closer to their destination, June found it difficult to contain her excitement. She could hardly wait to see Polly and Freddy again and to get her first glimpse of her baby brother, Billy. Full of anticipation, the last few miles seemed to take forever, but finally they heard the conductor call out, "Next stop...Meridian, Mississippi!" By the time they'd gotten their carry-on luggage from the overhead rack, the train was pulling into the station.

From Meridian, they boarded a bus for the final leg of their trip to Polly's parents' farm between Brandan and Jackson. When the driver braked to a stop beside the farm lane, June hopped out and impatiently waited for the driver to unload their luggage before she grabbed one of the suitcases and took off down the lane. Within seconds the familiar weather-beaten dwelling came into view, and she could see Polly's mother seated in a rocking chair on the wide porch. At play a few feet from her were Freddy and a chubby toddler that had to be Billy. "He's every bit as cute as his picture!" June thought as arms outstretched, she ran toward the dark haired boy. He took one look at this bright eyed stranger and let out a blood curdling scream. Then his plump little legs churned furiously while he headed for his grandmother. "Uh oh!" June thought as she watched the frightened child wrap his arms around his grandmother's legs and frantically cling to her. "That certainly wasn't very smart of me. I might be his sister, but he doesn't know it!"

She'd learned from the fiasco with the baby not to even attempt to approach Freddy. Having joined his brother at his grandmother's side, he was now staring suspiciously at June. When she looked into his wide blue eyes, she realized that since he'd been little more than a baby when he and his mother had left the house on Lawrence Street, she was as much a stranger to him as she was to his brown haired brother.

The sound of her baby's wails brought Polly to the screen door. Before she had a chance to ask the children's grandmother what was wrong, she saw her daughter looking longingly at the baby. "June!" she cried as she dashed onto the porch and enfolded her in her arms. When the little boys saw their mother's greeting of this stranger, they loosened their strangle hold of their grandmother and tentatively moved a short distance from her protection. The wariness in their eyes told June, though, that if she attempted anything threatening, they'd head for the safety of the older woman's presence.

By this time, Burrel and Dick had arrived at the porch, and were greeted heartily by Polly and Nanny (the children's name for their grandmother.) The new arrivals laughed at June's accounting of her reception by her little brothers. "Give them time," her father urged. "They'll warm up to you soon."

As it turned out, they did. Freddy was the first one, and this caused June to wonder if this was because of the early months of his life that they had spent together. While Freddy would bring a book for her to read to him, Billy would only let her hold him occasionally. It was obvious that he much preferred the more familiar lap of his grandmother.

Spending most of their days visiting with Polly, her mother, and the little boys while Burrel was working, and with the entire family in the evenings the time passed much too quickly. A couple times when they went into Jackson, Dick delighted in the soft southern accents of the people in the stores, and on the street. As June and Cecil had discovered during their brief stay in Jackson during the war, the natives were equally as fascinated by their "Damn Yankee" accents.

The main change June saw in the city was the absence of the airmen that she'd grown accustomed to during the months she'd lived here. While the little group strolled along the city streets, June wondered if the Dutch airmen who had fled their conquered land to serve with the American Air Corps had ever been reunited with their loved ones. Sighing deeply, she realized that this was something she would never know.

Some days when they went into town, they shopped and other times they explored, with June showing Dick where she had lived and where she had gone to school. During one of their excursions, Polly took them to see her sister, Ruby, and her husband, Paul. As soon as June stepped into the living room, and saw the pastel colors on their walls, the cool clean lines of their furniture and other interior decorations, she knew this was the way she wanted her own home to look...someday. By the time they were ready to return to the farm, she had garnered an equal number of ideas from the proud apartment dwellers and from her own observations.

June had found that the best part of this visit to Mississippi, though, was being with the family again. Most days, she and Polly had managed to find some time to talk and try to catch up on what had happened in each other's life. One day, while Dick went to the country store in the nearby village of Peelihatchie with Polly's father, Will Srite, June and Polly took their glasses of iced tea and sat in the rustic wooden lawn chairs under the sheltering branches of a large maple tree. While June relaxed and sipped her tea, she broached a subject that had been on her mind since they'd arrived. "Are you ever going to come home to Newark?"

Polly slowly moved her head from side-to-side before she replied, "This is my home. I'm happy here."

"How about Dad?" June asked. "Is he able to make a living here?"

"Since we live on the farm, he doesn't have to make much money," she replied. "Things are a lot better for your dad than they were when we came here with you and Cecil during the war. Then there weren't any jobs, but that's different now."

"I was just thinking how nice it would be if you lived close enough for the boys to get to know me as their sister," she said. "As little as they are, I'm sure they won't recognize me the next time they see me." Thinking of her own in-law problems, almost as an afterthought, she added, "I wonder if it's hard for Dad to live in someone else's house after he's had a home of his own for so long."

The sound of the farm truck rumbling up the lane interrupted whatever Polly's reply might have been and put a premature end to that conversation. The frantic look in Dick's eyes, as he bounded out of the pick-up truck, alarmed June and alerted her to the fact that the conversation she needed to have now was with her husband. Tucking her hand under his arm and leading him toward the back of the house, she was chanting, "What's wrong? What's wrong?"

Dick managed a chuckle as he mopped his brow and responded, "That grandfather of yours about killed us!"

The color seemed to drain from her face at his words. "What do you mean?" she cried.

When he saw how much his wild accusation had alarmed her, he was immediately contrite. "It's alright," he reassured her. Then he told her that it was the older man's driving. "It started when we got to the end of the lane and he started to turn onto the highway. It didn't look to me as if he even checked for traffic. He just swung onto the road like he owned it. When I said something to him about it, he just said that no one was ever on that road at that time of day." Even though she could tell that he had begun to relax he still sounded agitated when he continued, "That was just a preview of what the rest of the trip was like," he exclaimed. "Believe me it's good to be back on solid ground!"

For a minute June thought he was going to kneel and kiss the earth under his feet. She couldn't keep the laughter from her voice when she said, "You should have seen the look on your face when you stumbled out of that truck. I thought you'd seen a ghost!"

"It wasn't funny," he gulped. "I'd like to see your face after a ride like that!"

June's father had ambled into the back yard in time to hear Dick's last comment. "You rode with Will, did you?" he asked. At Dick's nod, he added, "It can be scary the first time, but he's a safer driver than you'd think. He's been driving these roads for close to forty years, and he seems to know them like the back of his hand." He paused for a moment before he added, "I don't think he's ever had an accident."

Dick was ready to respond when Polly called them to come in the house for dinner. As had happened every night since they'd been there, they sat down to a beautifully prepared meal. Nanny's cook, Lee, had prepared southern fried chicken, rice with gravy, collard greens, slaw, and applesauce. While the bowls heaped with food was being passed around the table, she placed a platter of her mouth-watering biscuits in front of June.

Dick grimaced when he saw his wife ladle gravy over her rice. Granddad Srite noticed his expression and urged him to try it, "We couldn't get your wife to eat it when she first came to Mississippi, but she tried it and found that it tasted pretty good."

"June likes rice, and I don't," Dick explained. "I will try some of that gravy on my biscuit, though."

The older man's only response was a shrug as he dipped his spoon into the baby food he was reduced to eating. Since he'd developed an ulcer a few years earlier, his diet had become almost identical to his baby grandson's. Dick had noticed that another staple of the man and boy's mealtime was crackers and milk. Over the years as the baby grew into manhood, he never got over his preference for this food. While the boy may have loved it, his grandfather looked enviously at the other diners, and couldn't imagine how June's new husband could turn down something that tasted as good as Lee's rice.

Although June was enjoying the food and the conversation, she was feeling sad. Since their return tickets were for tomorrow, this was the last night that they would be sitting around this table. As she looked at the beloved faces, she wondered when she would see them again. Inwardly she moaned at the thought that it would probably be at least another year. Even though she didn't know it at the time, something had happened in Newark during their absence that was going to make it possible for them to return much sooner. For now, though, she was storing up memories of her father's soft voice, Polly's grin, and the little boys' playful ways to take home with her.

Later that evening, she began to realize that might not be the only thing she was going to take back to Newark with her. First, she had noticed red spots on her arms and legs. Then, every one of the spots started to itch. The heat of the June night only seemed to make the itching worse. When she joined her parents on the front porch, where they had gone to escape the sweltering heat, she asked Polly if she knew what it might be.

Polly looked at the red dots and said one word, "Chiggers!"

"What's that?" June asked.

The redheaded woman shook her head sympathetically and explained that they were tiny mites that got on your skin and sucked out the blood. "Like leeches?" June cried.

"They're nothing like that," Polly replied. "All the damage they do is to cause some pretty bad itching. It will go away in a few days."

"Oh, no," June groaned. "It's going to be like this on the trip home."

Three pairs of eyes cast sympathetic glances at her before her father asked if she'd been in the woods that day. June and Dick exchanged glances at the thought that their pleasant exploration of the thicket behind the house earlier in the day could have resulted in her polka dotted skin.

Polly piped up with, "It could have been that, or it could have happened when the two of you were picking figs."

"Dick was with me, and he didn't get bitten," June wailed. "How did he manage to escape?" One glance at the difference in the way they were dressed gave them the answer. Dick had on his usual outfit of long pants, white shirt, shoes and socks while June was barely covered with her short-shorts, halter-top, and tennis shoes.

"I should have warned you," Polly lamented. As June tried to refrain from scratching, she found herself heartily agreeing.

Since they knew Burrel would be on his way to work before the sun had a chance to rise, they said goodbye to him before turning in. June was teary eyed when her father hugged her and told her he'd come to Ohio as soon as he could. As she planted a kiss on his cheek, she silently wished that Polly would change her mind and return to Newark.

The next day, Polly and the two little boys saw them off at the station in Meridian. As the train left the station, June watched the three figures who stood and waved until they had disappeared from her view. Her mind would always carry the picture of Polly balancing the dark haired baby on her hip while the sun seemed to set Freddy and her carrot-tops ablaze. "Dad sure got his little redhead," June thought.

"A penny for your thoughts," Dick murmured. As the miles clicked away, she talked about when Polly was pregnant for Freddy, she had wanted to have a blue-eyed blond girl, and her father had wanted a redhead...like Polly. When Dick commented that they both seemed to be pretty happy with what they had gotten, she nodded in agreement.

As the day ebbed into evening, June tried to divert her attention from the discomfort of the chigger bites. She found herself longing for the house on Oakwood Avenue and the luxury of their deep, roomy bathtub. That night, while she shifted uncomfortably in the train's reclining seat, her dreams were filled with images of herself covered to the chin with cool water leaning back in the tub where she could feel the itching disappear.

When they got home, without taking time to unpack, she made that dream come true. After she filled the tub to the brim and let her body slip into the water, she breathed a sigh of relief. For the first time since she'd first discovered the red spots, she felt comfortable. "That's the last time that I'll ever wear shorts in the woods," she vowed. Like so many lessons, she had learned this one the hard way.

As she relaxed, she talked to Dick in the kitchen through the open bathroom door. As she looked into the kitchen she saw through the window her neighbor's house so close. She could see her neighbor peering out his window into her kitchen window giving him a clear view of her soaking in the tub. Luckily with the deep tub, only her head was in view. From then on she kept the bathroom door shut even when she and Dick were alone in the house.

NUMBER ONE ON THE LIST

That evening, Dick's parents came over to see them. At first, the newlyweds thought this visit was so they could hear about the trip, but one look at the sparkle in Rowena's eyes, they knew there was something else. "What's up?" Dick asked. In response, his mother pointed through the window to the street. "Is that yours?" Dick yelled. Then, not waiting for an answer, he asked, "When did you get it?"

June moved to her husband's side so she could see what all the excitement was about. Parked at the curb in front of their house was a banana colored shiny new Ford. While she stared open-mouthed, Dick grabbed her by the hand and said, "Let's go see it!" The foursome exited so quickly that they left the front door wide-open while they all trooped to the curb to examine it.

The proud owners looked on as the young couple walked around it, ran their hands over the smooth shiny surface, and peered through the windows at the plush interior. "Hop in!" Forest ordered. "I'll take you for a drive." Not needing a second invitation, June and Dick stepped into the back seat where they reveled in the new car smell and the luxury of the comfortably padded seats.

Dick leaned forward as he plied his parents with questions. He wanted to know how, where, when, and from whom they'd gotten it. Then, when his father had answered all his questions, Dick asked the one question that had been running through June's mind. "Did the dealer say anything about my name coming up?"

When Forest acknowledged that he hadn't thought to ask, Dick said, "I guess I'd better look into it tomorrow. I've had my name in with that dealer since I got home." He didn't mention it, but he knew that he'd signed up with that dealership before his father had. While the young couple didn't begrudge his parents the new car, they couldn't help wonder what system the dealer used to determine who got one.

Later in the evening after their guests had gone home, Dick speculated aloud whether they'd missed out on a call from the dealer while they'd been gone. June smiled brightly and said, "I'm sure they'd hold it for a few days." He noticed, though, that her voice didn't quite match her optimistic sounding words.

As it turned out, Dick was to discover the next day that his name was no closer to the top of the list than it had been the last time he'd inquired. When he asked how his father's name had gotten ahead of his, the salesman only shrugged. June had an idea of her own on what might have happened, but before she had a chance to voice it, Dick said, "I wonder if Dad might have slipped some money under the table." June laughed as she responded that she'd wondered about that herself.

"I guess we'll just have to depend on the Chek to get us around a little longer," Dick asserted.

June gave him a quick hug as she told him that she liked their little motorcycle. "It gets us where we want to go," she said. "We'll be alright until this winter." Dick assured her they'd have a car by then. His prediction turned out to be true, but not in the way he expected.

∼

The young bride was soon to find that she was to personally profit from the fact that her mother-in-law was again mobile. Rowena was like a prisoner who'd been released from solitary confinement. For too long, she had been limited to going no further than her legs could carry her. When Forest had sold their car, he had in effect clipped her wings. Being without transportation had interfered with her established daily visits to members of the family. It didn't take long, though, for her to reestablish that routine.

During one of Rowena's afternoon calls on Forest's mother Eva, the older woman mentioned that she'd like to see Richard's house. Before the visit was over, she'd arranged to take her mother-in-law to the house on Oakwood Avenue that evening. When Forest heard about the upcoming visit, he decided to go along. He was anxious to show his mother the furniture he'd rounded up for Dick and June while at the same time, he'd be able to see how that girl his son had married was taking care of things.

If Forest had anticipated his mother's reaction and the subsequent results of this visit, he probably wouldn't have been so anxious to go along. On the other hand, June was delighted with Dick's grandmother. Dark-haired, with warm brown eyes, her high cheekbones hinted of an American Indian ancestry. Although later that night when June asked Dick about it, he responded, "Uncle Ray always says that she's full blooded Indian, but I think that's just another one of his tall tales. Her father's name was Tom Johnson and her mother's was Sarah Blamer. Neither name sounds Indian to me."

When they first arrived, Forest and his mother were in the midst of a good-natured argument about his birthday. June looked inquiringly at her husband when she heard Forest say, "I was born in nineteen hundred! I should know how old I am!"

His mother shot back with, "I think I should know a little better than you do that you were born in eighteen ninety-nine. After all, I am your mother."

Dick rolled his eyes and whispered to June that it was an ongoing argument. "Neither one will give an inch."

His grandmother greeted her grandson and his wife by asking, "Can you imagine a son who would disagree with his mother about when he was born?" After they shook their heads, she sighed and added, "He always has had a mind of his own. I'll never forget the time he cut off all his beautiful golden curls. I wouldn't let him get a haircut before he started to school, so he snitched my sewing shears, crawled under the bed and cut off all his curls."

While June tried to picture her dark haired father-in-law with blond hair, Forest fidgeted and muttered that he hadn't wanted the other kids to think he was a girl. When he noticed how uncomfortable his father was, Dick joked, "You must have been practicing to be a barber." June smiled, then quickly changed the subject by offering to show Grandma Eva around the house.

During the brief tour of the sparsely furnished rooms, the older woman hadn't commented. She did raise a quizzical brow when they returned to the living room and June told her she'd be more comfortable if she sat between the cushions on the couch.

While they were saying their good-nights, June noticed her husband's grandmother's gaze wander around the living room and bedroom before she quietly uttered the eleven words that were to delight June and cause her young husband to wonder just how wise he'd been to listen to his father's advice.

After she gave him a goodnight peck on the cheek, she had said, "Richard, can't you do any better than this for your wife?" Her question was followed by complete silence. For the first time since June had been in this family, she saw the father and son's gift of gab desert them. Finally, Dick managed to stammer, "D-d-dad said we should wait until the prices come down."

The older woman turned an inquiring eye on her son before she said, "Forest, do you really think that's going to happen?"

Her son stuttered that everything had been so cheap before the war, things were bound to come down. "I haven't seen any evidence of it!" she asserted. Then her voice took on a scolding tone when she added, "If the young people can't afford anything better than this, you should be able to help them out."

Forest hesitated for a second before he muttered, "I thought I was helping them when I got all this stuff." Before she could say any more, Dick came to his father's defense by saying that he had the money and could buy new furniture.

The older woman firmly replied, "If that's the case, then I suggest that you do so!"

June could see that the two men had completely capitulated and she could have hugged her new grandmother-in-law for making one of her dreams come true. Then while she was bidding her guests goodnight, she was mentally beginning her shopping spree. After they were again alone, Dick apologized to his wife for the condition of the furniture that had been foisted upon her. "I never really looked at how bad it all was until Grandma said what she did. We'll go shopping on Thursday when I'm off work, and we'll pick out something you like. Okay?"

June's face lit up like a kid at Christmas before she threw her arms around her husband and exclaimed, "That's more than okay! That's great."

∼

Thus began the first of their many steps of making the house on Oakwood Avenue the home of June's dreams. If they'd had an inkling of all the work and money that would go into this house over the years, they might have decided to go house hunting elsewhere. As it was, they took it one project at a time and when the final remodeling was completed twenty-five years in the future, they looked back on it all as a labor of love.

That summer of nineteen forty-seven, though, they sang and laughed as they removed the wild wallpaper, spread paint on the living room walls, and ran a rented sander over the wide boards of the bare floors. After they'd varnished and polished the floors, stretching his sore muscles, Dick exclaimed, "I'd say it looks pretty good. What do you think?"

"It's worth all the mess we've put up with and all the work we've done," June said as she looked at the pale pink wallpaper in the bedroom, the sparkling pale green paint on the living room walls and the high gloss shine of the floors. "Now, we can go shopping!" she announced.

"Now?" Dick moaned. "My muscles are so sore all I want to do is to take it easy the rest of the day."

June could sympathize with him since she was as sore as he was. "The stores are open Saturday and Monday nights until nine o'clock. I guess we can wait until then." To June, the next few days passed with the speed of a turtle, but the big night finally arrived. That evening when she heard the familiar sound of the Chek putt-putt its way down the street, she was ready to leave. She didn't even give Dick a chance to dismount before she hopped on behind him and said, "Let's go!"

Dick laughed at her excitement before saying, "What about dinner? Aren't we going to eat?"

"I thought we could have a cheeseburger and milk shake at The Busy Bee in the Arcade," she explained. He nodded and restarted the engine. As they barreled down the street, they were both too filled with their plans for the evening to notice the mixture of indulgent smiles and unfriendly glares they were receiving from some of their neighbors. They had been told shortly after they moved into the house on Oakwood that one neighbor had angrily said, "Those kids! I just don't know what's wrong with kids today!"

∼

Their first shopping trip downtown to Stewart and Alward's Furniture Store turned out to be successful. At first they cautiously eased themselves onto the soft-cushioned, upholstered couches on the showroom floor. Once they'd discovered that the springs in the cushions weren't going to attack them, they relaxed. The salesman was puzzled about the fearful way they'd approached each sofa until they told him about the one they had at home.

By the time they left the store, they'd bought a dove gray couch and a matching chair. They'd also purchased a moss green rug, a rose colored chair, and two blond wooden end tables with a matching glass topped coffee table. The entire shopping spree had cost them little more than three hundred dollars.

On their second furniture shopping trip they found a blond bedroom outfit that was a perfect match for the tables in their living room and an oak breakfast set for the kitchen.

After the deliverymen had brought the furniture and set it in place, June closed the door after them before she went about putting the finishing touches on the rooms. A few hours later, she stood back and surveyed her handiwork before she silently proclaimed, "That's more like it."

Her next thought was that she could hardly wait for Dick to come home so he could see the transformation. The soft pale colors on the walls, the shine of the wide floorboards that showed around the large area rugs, and the blond wood of the highly polished furniture served to accent the spaciousness of the room. For the first time since they'd lived in the house on Oakwood Avenue, she appreciated the beauty of the architecture, the high ceilings, the smooth plastered walls, and large windows and doorways. Although, she could still see things that needed to be done, such as installing a sink and cupboards in her kitchen, she was pleased with what they had accomplished.

When Dick got home, they reveled in the luxury of a comfortable couch, one in which they could sit side-by-side without any fear of retaliation from the cushions. "I can't wait for Grandma to see what we've done," he confided. "I want her to be the first one to come over once we get it finished." Since she didn't want to further embarrass him, she didn't voice her opinion, but she was sure his grandmother's criticism had really stung him.

~

Dick suggested that they invite friends and family over to see their new furniture. Thinking about how awful everything had been before, June was anxious to demonstrate to her friends that they weren't really as impoverished as they had first appeared. Thus began a series of informal get-togethers as family and friends responded to invitations to "drop in."

At Dick's request, his father's mother was invited first. She was closely followed by other family members and friends. The young couple had both enjoyed the compliments they received, but no one's meant as much to Dick as his grandmother's pat on the back as she exclaimed, "This is more like it!"

Her son, Forest, didn't quite share her enthusiasm as June was to discover a few days later when she overheard him telling Rowena that he thought Richard's wife was going crazy with her spending. The newlyweds exchanged grins as they heard him complain, "She's going to send that boy to the poor house."

When Priscilla, Bill, and Dickie next came from Mansfield, they brought another couple with them. Over dinner, Priscilla regaled them with an account of her experience during a previous visit. "The last time I came down, I spent the weekend. Dick graciously offered to let me sleep on the couch, but each cushion had a spring that jabbed me, so I decided I'd be more comfortable if I slept on the floor in one of the empty rooms upstairs." Mother and daughter exchanged grins at the prospect of what was coming next before Priscilla continued her story. "June came up with some blankets for a makeshift bed, but she didn't have any pillows. I'm used to sleeping with a couple of them under my head and just couldn't get to sleep without them. After tossing and turning for what seemed like hours, I decided to rummage around to see if I could find something."

Wondering what June and Priscilla found amusing about this story, Priscilla's woman friend asked if she'd found anything. "I did, but after what happened, I wish I hadn't!" Priscilla paused as she remembered how at the time she hadn't found anything funny about the situation, but looking back, it struck her as hilarious. Beginning to get impatient, Dickie urged his mother to tell them what had happened.

Priscilla continued, "I found some drapes that Dick's Aunt Bertha had given them. There was a nice thick stack of them and they worked out very well as a substitute pillow. Once I got comfortable, I slept like a log. When I came downstairs for breakfast the next morning, though, the top part of my body was covered with a rash, and I was itching like crazy." She smiled and added, "I think I offended June when I told her I'd been bitten by something and asked if they had bugs in the house."

"To me, she looked like she had chigger bites like I got in Mississippi, but I knew there wasn't anything like that around here," June asserted.

Priscilla smiled at her daughter and said, "Their reassurances that the house was bug free didn't make the itching go away though. Then after breakfast, June and I went upstairs to see if we could get to the bottom of this mystery. As soon as we walked into the room and June saw what I'd fashioned into a pillow, she knew what had happened. The drapes I'd slept on were made from a new material that Owens Corning is making."

"Once I saw that, I knew that the fiberglass in the drapes was the culprit," June confessed. That stuff is so scratchy that I couldn't even use the drapes. Bertha said that I wouldn't have any trouble as long as no one came into direct contact with them." June looked ruefully at her mother before she added, "Since I didn't want to have drapes that I'd have to put on protective gear to be able to hang, I decided not to use them. After I saw what had happened to Mom, I wished I'd thrown them away."

With a chuckle, Priscilla replied, "I wish you had too, but I can tell you one thing. I learned my lesson, and I'm going to stay away from fiberglass drapes in the future."

Clucking sympathetically, Priscilla's friend said, "Surely, they'll perfect it." *As they all nodded their agreement, they would have been surprised to know that summer day in nineteen forty-seven that chemists were already developing scratch-free draperies. Also that in the future people would be sailing in boats made of fiberglass, and using many other products fabricated from this "new material" without the repercussions Priscilla had encountered.*

"Anyway," Priscilla said, "I guess my son-in-law has forgiven me for thinking that they had bedbugs."

"This is one time," Dick said, "I was glad that when I told her goodnight, I didn't add, 'Don't let the bedbugs bite.' She'd really have doubted me then."

June smiled broadly at her Mom when she said, "You'll have a nice comfortable couch to sleep on the next time you spend the night. I even have some nice soft sofa pillows you can use."

"I noticed them. I like that rose color. It matches your chair," Priscilla commented. "Just the same, though, I think I'll bring my bed pillows the next time I come."

~

June and Dick invited Dickie to spend some time with them that summer. "We can go swimming every day," June promised, but much to her disappointment, her brother declined. "I'd like to come, but a couple weeks ago I teamed up with a couple guys to dig out a basement for a woman over by the Fischer Body Plant out toward Crestline."

"That sounds like a big job for three guys," Dick said.

"Three of us started, but one guy only lasted one day and the other one quit after a week," Dickie said. "I didn't want to let the woman down, so I am finishing it by myself. Once I start a job, I won't quit until I get it finished."

Those words were familiar to June because she'd said the same thing many times. "Sounds like a family characteristic!" she remarked. Priscilla nodded in satisfaction. She had instilled these values in her children when they'd lived in the cave house.

June was concerned about her young brother when she heard the rest of the story. Not only did he spend eight hours a day digging with a pick and shovel, but he either rode his bicycle or walked six or seven miles each way to and from his home on Arlington Avenue. June's remembrance of her husband telling her about having dug out the basement of the cottage on South Second Street for his dad when he was only thirteen started June thinking about how alike her husband and brother were in their work ethic. While the conversation twirled around her, June was lost in thought about the similarities in her brother and husband's experiences.

Both had started to work when they were eight or nine years old. Her husband had sold ice cream bars to the men who worked at the old Consumer's Brewery a few blocks from the square in Newark while Dickie had sold magazines. Both had been newspaper boys. Dickie had hawked them on a downtown street corner in Mansfield, and Dick delivered them door-to-door in the South-End of Newark. There the similarity in jobs ended but not in their determination to earn their own way. While as young teenagers, Dick had gone on to sell shoes in JC Penny's store, and to work as a gofer at the Aluminum Plant, Dickie had been a caddie and worked in a factory.

~

June had been too absorbed in her thoughts to realize that her mother had addressed her. A tap on the shoulder and a teasing remark offering a penny for her thoughts brought her back to the present. "What in the world were you thinking?" her mother asked.

"My thoughts were worth more than a penny," June retorted before beginning to relate some of the things she'd been thinking about. When she mentioned the paperboy job, her husband Dick was reminded of something he just had to tell them.

"I had this one house I delivered papers to here in town. It was a big house with a lot of young women living in it. I thought it was strange that these women came to the door in such skimpy outfits no matter how cold it was outside. Even in the winter, they wore really short shorts and halter tops." As his listeners were looking knowingly at him, he continued, "Sometimes, I'd get a peek inside and see women in fancy silk or satin robes or baby-doll pajamas. I also saw men going in or coming out. I would have thought they were salesmen except for the sneaky way they behaved. This one guy acted like a secret agent, in hiding, with his coat collar pulled up to conceal the lower part of his face and his hat pulled down so far over his eyes that he couldn't see. While he was trying to be invisible, he missed the step and tumbled off the porch and landed on his bottom." Dick chuckled mischievously before he added, "The noise brought several of the neighbors out on their porches. When the man saw them, he grabbed his hat, slammed it onto his head, and scampered away."

While everyone was still laughing at the verbal picture he had created, Priscilla wiped the tears from her eyes and asked, "Didn't you know what kind of a house it was?" When he replied that he'd been pretty young and naive, she could understand as she remembered the time she and her first husband, Burrel, had innocently spent a few nights in Washington D.C. in what they were to find out was a hotel filled with call girls. She blushed at the memory of being propositioned by one of "the Johns."

As she smiled ruefully at the memory, Dick added, "My mom wasn't very happy when she found out that I had a brothel on my paper route. I also had to take some teasing from the big boys in the neighborhood when they heard about it," he declared.

Still laughing about his experience, the group left with promises to return soon. "You come see us too," Priscilla urged. As the newlyweds assured them that they'd visit soon, their guests piled into Bill's car for the trip home.

After June and Dick again had the house to themselves, they made plans to make the trip in a couple weeks. Before they had a chance to go, though, Dick came up with a surprise that changed those plans. In a couple weeks, instead of going to Mansfield on the planned Sunday, they were driving down the highway in another state.

BELATED HONEYMOON

Although he'd been working on the surprise for awhile, he hadn't mentioned it to June because he didn't want to disappoint her if it didn't pan out. The idea had started shortly after they were married when June had told him that she'd always wanted to go to Niagara Falls for her honeymoon. While they still lived at Charlotte's, he'd promised to take her when they got a car.

After the last rejection by the automobile dealer, he'd decided not to wait any longer and had asked his father if he could borrow his. At first, Forest had refused, but today he had changed his mind. "I think that Mom changed it for him after I told her a couple days ago how disappointed I was," Dick told his flabbergasted wife. "Mom didn't say so, but I wonder if she's trying to make up for our wedding reception!"

"You mean your parents are going to let us use their new car to go on a honeymoon?" June asked. If she had been surprised at that announcement, she was almost speechless when he told her that they were going to let them have it for a week. "Your mother is going to give up her car for a whole week?" she breathlessly inquired before adding, "What a nice wedding present!"

As if fearful that their benefactors would change their minds, the young couple quickly prepared for the trip. By the next day they had stowed their bags in the trunk, and armed with a road map, they were excitedly on their way.

After ten hours on the road, they arrived at the United States side of the falls where they spent the night. The next day they drove across the border into Canada where they whiled away the morning browsing through the shops, exploring the surrounding area, and alternately taking pictures of each other with the falls as a background.

By early afternoon, Dick couldn't contain his urge to get back behind the wheel of the Ford and go somewhere else. They'd just finished their lunch at a restaurant overlooking the falls, and were making plans for the rest of the day when Dick said, "I've got an idea. Since we have the car for the week, let's go to Mississippi." June's squeal of delight caused nearby diners to turn and stare.

Within minutes le she was fumbling with the map, Dick was zooming across the bridge into the United States.

While in West Virginia, June noticed a sign for White Sulphur Springs. "Isn't that where you were stationed during the war?" she cried.

"It sure was!" he replied as he screeched to a halt. In response to her startled look, he said, "I want you to see it."

"Okay, but let's try to get there in one piece!" she admonished, but her smile took the sting out of her words. Like her husband, she thoroughly enjoyed being able to do whatever they wanted to...whenever they wanted.

A few minutes later when they drove past a sign that read "White Sulphur Springs," and onto the lush grounds of the Greenbriar Hotel, Dick eased into a parking place and sat gazing around him. "It looks so different without all the people in uniform," he reflected. "Before the war, this was a resort like it is now. The army turned the hotel into a military hospital," he said as he pointed toward the white pillared, redbrick building that was now and had been, before the war, the Greenbriar Hotel. "We took care of the men wounded in Africa in the battles with Rommel and some casualties from the fighting in Italy." Then he showed June a white building on the golf course and said, "That casino over there was the officers' club. I was recruited to be in the army band, having just graduated from Newark High School where I was first chair in their orchestra. I played saxophone, clarinet, and violin for non-commissioned officers on Friday night and commissioned officers on Saturday nights." Almost as an afterthought, he added, "The Ashford Generals."

When June looked puzzled at his last words, he explained that the name of the hospital had been The Ashford General and the band had been named after it. "I probably would have been here much longer, but the war was escalating in Europe. The allied forces had just landed in France for D-Day, and they were going to need more medics. I was transferred from here to the 414 Medical Collecting Company at Camp Bowie and then Camp Barkley in Texas so I could get some extra medic training before I was sent to the front."

Since he rarely talked about his war experiences, June took this opportunity to ask some questions. For once, he was apparently off guard enough to give her a few answers. As they strolled through the grounds of his former military base, he talked about some of the young wounded men he'd administered to on the battlefield or in the field hospital where he'd been assigned in Europe. He confided that the reason he'd become a medic was so he could help people who were hurt. "I'm a lover not a killer," he joked. In the same vein, June replied that she was glad.

When she urged him to tell her more about his war experience, the mental door he'd closed on that part of his life seemed to open and the words spilled out of his mouth. "When we left Texas, we traveled by troop train to New York City, then on to Boston. We had enough time in Boston for Russell Whitaker, a medic I became friends with in Texas, and I to go to a nightclub where we saw the great jazz trumpet player, Louie {Sachmo} Armstrong before we had to board the ship for England. When I walked up the gangplank with the other fifteen thousand or so soldiers to the deck of the USS United States and looked back at my country, I wondered if I'd ever see it again," he confided.

"Then after five days on the ship, we landed in Liverpool, England, took a train to South Hampton where we got on another ship. Then we spent three days anchored in the English Channel. I don't know if it's always so rough, but for those three days the current tossed the ship around like we were in a canoe." He groaned at the memory of what happened during those three days before he went on. "Almost everyone on that ship was so seasick that they were hanging over the rail on deck or the urinal in the john throwing up. I was one of the lucky ones. Although, I felt a little queasy at times, I managed to keep everything down. I don't know if there are any sharks in the channel, but if they were, we left such a trail of vomit that none followed us."

"When we landed, we were in St. Lowe in the Burgundy wine area of France. I'm sure it's beautiful in peacetime but there was destruction all around from the fighting that had taken place there. The army was now pushing through what they called the hedgerow country because of the beautiful hedges. As a medical company, we followed the army and collected the wounded. Since I was a litter bearer, my job was to give first aid treatment to the wounded on the battlefield and put them on a stretcher and carry them to an ambulance. There were four cots in most ambulances with two on the bottom and two on the top. I would ride with the driver in the ambulance to the field hospital which was usually set up in several tents. Then the doctors and nurses would take over and we'd get back in the ambulance to go back to the front for more wounded."

"When the front moved, the hospital would have to move too. Sometimes if we were lucky, the hospital would be set up in an abandoned building. The building couldn't be used, though, until the engineers went in and checked for booby traps that the retreating Germans usually set up in any building that would be useful to the Allies. The mine could be any size or shape but those guys who found and disarmed them really knew what they were doing. We never had one single one explode."

His eyes looked troubled as he looked back into the past but he continued. "The weather was awful that fall and winter during what they called The Battle of The Bulge as we went from Nancy France, into Belgium, Luxembourg, and into Lentz Austria. It rained all the time so we had to trudge through the mud under cloudy skies with a close hanging ground mist that made visibility poor for us on the ground and for aerial observation.

When we thought it couldn't get worse, the snows came. We were short of food, warm clothing and medical supplies. I either slept on a cot in one of the tents at the field hospital or if we were out on the battleground, I'd sleep in the ambulance." He grinned before he added, "I can tell you I sure missed my bedroom back home and the heat from Dad's old coal heating stove. Mom sent me some long underwear that sure helped."

His expression was more serious when he continued, "I had it a lot easier than the ones we treated. I saw an unbelievable amount of suffering and death. Some of the wounds were so serious that I figured they'd never get back home again or if they did their lives would never be the same. I just wanted the war to be over so no more people would have to suffer that way."

Then as if the memories were too painful to talk about, he changed the subject to say, "It was in Lentz that I saw an unusual sight. It was an experimental German plane without a propeller. The German Army, desperate to strike one last blow at the Allied Forces, had unleashed these rocket weapons. I found out later that the plane I saw was propelled by rocket fuel."

"The pure relief that the killing had ended was why Russ and I celebrated the way we did when it was finally over. We were in Lentz, Austria when we got the news. Everybody was drinking to celebrate the victory of the Allies. I'd never had a drink in my life but when someone gave us some wine, we both drank it. Then we found a supply of ammunition, and Russ got a rifle. First we used some fire extinguishers for target practice. I don't know why we did it except that we were so happy that we acted crazy. When Russ's bullets hit one, though, the foam sprayed out all over us, and we decided that was enough of that."

"Then we saw a herd of deer in the Forest, and Russ shot at them but he missed. He gave me the gun and told me to try it. I know I wouldn't have done it without the wine, but I fired into the herd. I hit a doe that turned out to have some little ones inside her. When I found that out, I was so ashamed of what I'd done that I didn't want to have anything to do with it. There was a camp for prisoners of war across the road. Their German captors had left, and they were starving so we decided to give it to them. Although they didn't speak English, we were able to let them know that we wanted them to have the meat. They really appreciated the food. Later after they cooked it, they brought a big platter over for us, but the memory of the way the doe's frightened eyes had looked at me right before she died made me sick. Russ didn't have any trouble eating the venison and he kept telling me how that one shot had provided so much food for those hungry prisoners, but I think I would have choked if I'd eaten a bite. That experience cured me of ever wanting to go hunting again."

"Didn't you carry a gun at all during the war?" June asked.

He looked a little embarrassed when he replied that he had once. "Even though I was a medic and not supposed to carry a gun, I was assigned to guard duty. I tried to protest, but I quickly learned that the superior officers weren't going to listen to what I as a lowly private had to say. Since we were right in the middle of some intense fighting, the sergeant cautioned me on some of the things that were going on around us. He said that some of the Germans had gotten hold of American and British tanks and uniforms and they were infiltrating our lines. He stressed that I couldn't allow anyone to pass me unless he gave the proper response to my part of the password."

In response to June's puzzled expression, Dick told her that he was to say "Charlie" and the other person was to respond "Horse." "Everything was quiet for the first few hours, and I felt stiff and sore from standing in one place so I decided to walk around and stretch my legs." He smiled ruefully before he added, "That wasn't the smartest thing I ever did! A few minutes later, I almost got myself killed."

When June gasped in shock, and asked if he'd encountered a Nazi soldier, he replied that it had been one of our own. "Everything was so quiet and I was bored so I did a little target practice by shooting at the windows of an abandoned house that was already half destroyed by the war. I didn't realize what a dangerous thing I'd done until I heard a gruff voice in the dark call out, "Charlie." Then a big corporal seemed to appear from nowhere, and I found myself staring into the barrel of a Thompson sub-machine gun...the kind that sprays bullets and could cut you in two. Since I didn't know whether or not he had a nervous trigger finger, I yelled out that I was the guard. He didn't lower the gun, though, until I said, "Horse."

They continued to talk about this incident as they walked around the quiet peaceful grounds of the resort. He told her that he'd expected to be in trouble for being outside his post, but he felt that the army probably didn't want it to get out that they'd forced a medic to carry a gun. Then he changed the subject and told her about his experiences in Europe after the fighting had ended.

"Once the war was over and there was no need for litter bearers, I was ordered to the 20th Corps Headquarters Building in a little village in Austria to work as a clerk typist. I was there from May when the war in Europe ended, until December when I finally got to go home. I also got to play music there for officers' clubs. I played fiddle with Homer Haines for Special Service Entertainment. Homer is now part of the Grand Ole Opry's musical comedy team of Homer and Jethro."

"Fortunately before I came home, I was allowed to take some of the extra leave I'd accumulated. A buddy and I took a train to the Riviera at Nice, France. It was wonderful to relax and enjoy ourselves for a change. We rented bicycles and rode them on the beach. One day someone pointed out to us that at one point we could actually see a tip of Italy across the water. Then the night before we had to leave, we went to a theater full of servicemen on leave and saw the comedian Morey Amsterdam and the Andrew sisters perform in person."

"We hitched a ride back to the base on a C47 twin engine transport plane. It had been used during the war to haul gasoline to the battlefield to fuel tanks. The inside of the plane was empty, but they did have wooden benches against the wall where we were able to sit. Not the height of luxury, but at least it was faster than the train."

"That was in November 1945. Then I got to come home in December. The trip home on a Liberty ship was awful. We were hit by five storms. Since the ship wasn't very big it was tossed all over the place. There were times before that trip was over that I thought it was going to break in two. As if that wasn't bad enough, I was bit by a spider and ended up with an allergic reaction and a terrible infection. That's when I had my first shot of the new drug, penicillin."

Even now, a couple years later, the relief sounded in his voice when he told her of his happiness when he saw the Statue of Liberty come into view. "I thought of all the suffering and death I'd seen, and felt as if God had given me a gift of the rest of my life. I feel that I owe it to the boys who didn't come back to appreciate every minute of my life."

When he saw the tears glistening in her eyes, he pulled her into his arms and gently kissed her. Then the serious minute was over, and the teasing glint was back in his eyes when he said, "I see a ground-keeper heading our way. They probably don't allow smooching in public around here."

Although the groundkeeper didn't come any closer, he kept his eyes on them while they lingered a few minutes and snapped pictures of each other. Before they returned to the car, Dick turned and gave the watching man a jaunty salute. Much to their surprise, the man stood at military attention and returned the salute.

~

"Seems like old times," Dick remarked as he shifted the car into gear and again turned south. "Mississippi, Here We Come!" he sang to the tune of a similar song about California. While June merrily sang off-key along with him, he stepped down on the accelerator and the miles seemed to whip away.

They made such good time that Dick decided to drive straight through. Since June hadn't learned to drive yet, he had to do all the driving himself. She couldn't relieve him at the wheel, but she did stay awake all night to keep him company, and to make sure he wouldn't fall asleep. Although they tried all the tricks they knew to keep awake, drinking coffee loaded with caffeine, keeping all the windows open, singing, talking, listening to the radio, by six in the morning, Dick could no longer keep his eyes open.

Although, they were less than fifty miles from their destination, he eased the car into the parking lot of a rest area and said, "If I don't sleep now, I'll fall asleep at the wheel, but if I can get a few winks, I'll be alright."

True to his word, he was awake and raring to get back on the road in a couple hours. Although they were hungry, June was too impatient to see the family to waste time on such a mundane thing as breakfast. When they arrived at Polly's doorstep that morning, June shouted out, "Surprise! We're on a road trip!" Polly was amazed to see them. Soon they were sitting at the table in Granddad Srite's dining room washing down Lee's melt-in-your-mouth biscuits and scrambled eggs with cups of hot coffee. June was glad they'd waited to eat.

"The last thing I ever expected was to have you two drop in," Polly marveled.

June laughed, "You should have seen your face when you opened the door. We didn't write because we didn't know we were coming until around noon yesterday."

"We're just glad you're here!" Polly exclaimed. "I can hardly wait to see your Dad's face when he comes home from work this evening!"

Later in the day, Freddy and Billy had gotten over their initial shyness and followed closely at the young couples' heels as they walked across the grounds to the new house that Granddad Srite was having built. Since the house had only been in the blueprint stage when they'd been here last, they were both surprised to see that the six-room brick house was already under roof.

While they were walking around the structure, they saw the familiar tan and brown Chevrolet slowly drive by. When the driver noticed that Polly had company, he turned around and drove into the construction area. Easing the lanky length of his body from behind the wheel, Burrel stepped out.

A broad grin spread across his face when he recognized the visitors. Before he had a chance to say anything, though, he found himself being hugged by his daughter, and his hand enthusiastically pumped by his son-in-law. Father and daughter were so happy at once again being together that their words of greeting seemed to tumble over each other.

The ensuing visit was a brief but enjoyable one. Their time was spent talking, laughing, and catching up on what had happened to each other since they'd last been together. Burrel was especially happy to hear about their new furniture and surprised to learn that Forest's name had come up for a car before Dick's had. "I would have thought a serviceman would have gotten one before a civilian," he said.

June grinned, "At least we have it for this one week. I don't think we'd have been able to go on much of a honeymoon without it."

This comment reminded Burrel of something that had been on his mind since they'd gotten here. Until now, he'd hesitated to mention it, but they were going to be leaving in another day, and he decided he'd better bite the bullet and come out with what was on his mind. "What you did on the way down here was dangerous! I don't want you kids to try to drive straight through on your way home," he declared. June waited for him to add, "That's all there are to it," but he didn't. Instead, he asked if they had enough money. "I will give you some, so you don't have to sleep in the car!" he promised.

Dick hastily assured him that they didn't need any money. "We were just trying to get here faster. Since we only have a week, we didn't want to waste any time." To his father-in-law's relief, Dick didn't seem to resent the advice. In fact, before they went to bed that night, Burrel had his promise that they definitely wouldn't sleep in the car. "We'll find a tourist court," Dick assured him.

That morning after June had again said goodbye to her family, she looked so gloomy that Dick felt sorry for her. As they drove north along the pine tree lined highway, he had been deep in thought. He wanted to come up with something that would erase that unhappy look. The idea of taking her to West Virginia occurred to him, but he didn't want to get her hopes up until he had a chance to study the map.

Later in a roadside diner, after he checked it out, he handed her the map and pointed out his planned destination. At first, when she noticed that his finger was on the state of West Virginia, she thought he wanted to go back to White Sulphur Springs. "Look closer!" he said.

As she realized what he had in mind, she readily agreed with his plan to visit her grandpap. "Aunt Gussie will really be surprised when she sees us!" June exclaimed. Then unmindful of the other diners, she leaned across the table and kissed him on the lips. Before he had a chance to respond, she jumped up and exclaimed, "Let's go!"

Several hours later, when they drove into the farmyard of the familiar white house, and June called out her aunt's name, not only her aunt, but her cousins, Hilda and Dale, came out to greet them. Once they'd been warmly welcomed, Aunt Gussie said, "You must be hungry. I'll just set out a bite." While she'd been speaking, she'd been loading the table with crocks, jars and bowls of food.

"If this is a bite, I can hardly wait to see one of her full fledged meals!" Dick had exclaimed.

While they'd been talking, Dale had run into his grandfather's room and told him about their arrival. When he ambled into the room, June had been proud to introduce her husband to this man who'd always been so important in her life. Much to her delight, the two men hit it off immediately.

It was wonderful to again sleep under the tin roof in the cozy farmhouse where she and her father had been born. Then the next morning when Dick and June followed the enticing aroma of sausage frying to its source in the sunny farm kitchen, the family was already seated around the table. They watched Dick's eyes widen at the sight of the platters of sausage, fried eggs, biscuits and gravy. Hilda couldn't resist teasing Dick about being a city slicker. "Don't feed you like this in the city, do they?" she kidded. Dick grinned as he plopped down beside Dale on one of the long benches that flanked the table. When June, dressed in her short-shorts started to sit beside him, she didn't notice the bee that had already staked its claim on the bench. She barely sat down when she let out a yell and jumped to her feet.

While she was trying to look behind her back to see what had stung her, her new husband chuckled, and she could see Grandpap's bushy mustache twitch as he tried to control his smile. Thinking that her husband was a bad influence on her grandfather, she resisted the temptation to dump the bowl of gravy on

Dick's head. Her haughty stare, though, quickly caused both men to contain their amusement.

In the meantime, Aunt Gussie had looked at June's reddening thigh and found the bee's stinger still attached. While her aunt clucked over her like a mother hen, Dick's comment, "I guess he won't do that again!" didn't endure him to his bride or her aunt. Mentally kicking himself for his weird sense of humor, he wiped the grin from his face and spent the rest of the meal being solicitous.

As June was to find out later while she was helping her aunt and cousin clear the table, that wasn't to be the end of the shenanigans with her husband and grandfather. Seconds earlier, she noticed the sly twinkle in Dick's eyes as he silently slipped through the door onto the wide front porch where Grandpap was sitting. Before the door had swung shut after him, they heard a shout and the sound of running feet. Fearful of what she was going to find, June rushed to the porch in time to see her usually sedate grandfather running around the side of the house with her husband armed with a toy water pistol in hot pursuit.

Her cry of, "Dick, stop that!" went unanswered. All she could do was to stare open-mouthed at this unbelievable scenario. Nowhere in her memory could she find any time anyone had treated her grandfather with anything but the utmost respect. Retired from teaching in one-room schoolhouses, and as the postmaster for the community of Key, West Virginia, he'd always been a quiet, reserved, dignified man. Never in her wildest dreams could she have pictured one of his grandchildren doing what her husband was now doing.

Not knowing what to expect, she circled the house from the other direction to head them off and come to Grandpap's rescue if he needed her. She didn't encounter either of them, but when she passed the open kitchen doorway, she slid to a stop at the sound of a commotion inside. Cautiously stepping into the kitchen, she saw the older man slumped against the wall with a big white handkerchief held up to his face. Her husband was standing in front of him with the dripping water pistol in his hand. "Got you!" he was shouting.

June could feel her heart thud in her chest as she rushed over to Grandpap. Fearful that he might be in the throes of a heart attack, she timorously asked the shaking man, "Are you alright?"

He finished wiping the water from his mustache before he removed the cloth, and she got a glimpse of his face. Much to her surprise, she discovered that he was shaking with laughter. "I haven't had that much exercise in years," he told his stunned granddaughter. "Everyone always treats me like such an old man," he announced. "That young man of yours makes me feel like a kid again!"

She breathed a sigh of relief when she realized he was alright. "That husband of mine is a practical joker!" June declared. Secretly she was wondering how her husband, the trickster, would respond to one played against him. While she was smiling sweetly at him, she was secretly plotting one of her own. "Just wait until I get him home," she silently vowed.

Although it didn't quite match the excitement of the morning, the rest of the visit was enjoyable. While Dick rode off in the pickup truck with Aunt Gussie's husband, Verde, to see some land Verde had just bought, June stayed behind with her aunt and cousins. Once the men had left, Aunt Gussie asked June if she remembered how much she and her brothers had liked the whipped cream pie she'd made for them as children.

"Do I?" June cried. "I've never tasted anything so good since then."

"I think I have enough cream here to whip up a couple of them. You girls can help me, and we'll have them ready when the men get back," she said. Three pair of busy hands made the work easy. By the time the men returned, the table was again laden with food...including the mouth-watering pies.

Before they were to get home that night, they were going to wish they had left earlier, but at the time they were enjoying themselves too much to think about their trip home. First, her uncle had hauled a chair out into the yard, and the two men swapped jokes while Dick cut Uncle Verde's hair. When Dick stood behind Uncle Verde, the uncle June had always thought of as the gentle giant, almost obscured her husband's thin frame. As the two men shook hands, June marveled at how Uncle Verde's huge hand was twice the size of her husband's.

Later, after they'd said goodbye to the family and started on their long journey home, they managed to make good time. One reason was because they didn't have to stop for food since Aunt Gussie had handed them a bag filled with sandwiches and cookies before they left. When she'd given it to Dick, she'd said, "I've got a poke of food here for you," he'd grinned at her choice of words.

"City slicker!" June had mouthed.

He'd chuckled, but when they'd gotten into the car he'd told her that although he'd lived in town all his life, his father had been a farm-boy. "Just like your dad!" he exclaimed. "Dad's mom and dad raised nine children on a farm on County Line Road at the Delaware/Licking County line near Johnstown. My Uncle Earl still lives on the farm. One of these days, I'll take you there and you can see that I'm not one hundred percent city slicker!"

Although their banter and the luxurious comfort of the new car made the time fly, they were more than two hundred miles from Newark when the sun went down. The night was moonless, and the only light that penetrated the darkness was the steady beam of the Ford's headlights. They were listening to a male vocalist crooning the words to, *Tenderly*, a song that had become popular that year, when the car came to a sharp curve then a steep hill. When Dick topped the hill, the headlights picked out a railroad track crossing the road. Too late to brake, the car which hit the tracks at too high a rate of speed, seemed to bounce in the air and land with a thud on the raised tracks.

While Dick was fighting to control the car, the road seemed to disappear. All he could see ahead of him was an empty field. "Where did the road go?" he yelled as he slammed on the brakes. Once he had brought the car to a screeching halt, they were able to see that the highway had taken a sharp curve to the right. They were both shaken by the experience, and even more so when they realized that they were still sitting on the railroad tracks.

Once Dick had eased the car off the tracks and around the curve, he pulled onto the berm so he could inspect for damages. "It drives all right, but we did bottom out back there on that track. I haven't driven far enough to be sure, but it seemed like it might be pulling to the right."

They piled out of the car, and June held the flashlight while Dick peered underneath. "Uh oh," he exclaimed. "I think the tie-rod is bent." As far as June was concerned, he could have been speaking Greek since all she knew about a car was what was on the surface.

"Does that mean you can't drive it?" she asked.

She was relieved when he replied, "Other than having it pull to the right, it will be alright. I'll just have to have it fixed when we get home." He didn't voice the rest of his thought, but he knew his father was going to be furious with him.

This prediction proved to be true. His father exploded in anger when Dick told him. His anger weakened slightly after Dick had the tie-rod repaired, but for weeks at work he reminded Dick of what he called his irresponsibility. "It's not a new car anymore," he grumbled. "I loan you a new car and you bring me back a wreck."

Dick tried to maintain his good humor, but at times it was difficult. Finally after hearing for the dozenth time that he'd ruined his dad's car, he declared, "Dad, I'll be glad to buy it from you." Although his father responded with an angry comeback, somewhere in the recesses of his mind, the idea was planted.

∽

As the trees took on the colors of autumn and the leaves began to fall, Forest had a reason to recall Dick's flippant comment. By some trick of fate, his name had again moved ahead of his son's for a new car. This time the letter had come from the local Nash dealer. It told him that they had a new Ambassador that had just come in. If he wanted it, he needed to let them know within a few days. Since he couldn't resist the lure of a new car and the chance to get rid of his "wrecked" one, he quickly took them up on the offer...and Dick on his. Instead of trading in the Ford, he offered to sell it to Dick and June for what he had paid for it.

"I love that car! Let's buy it," June coaxed. Dick readily agreed. Since he disagreed with his father about the car being damaged, he gladly counted out the seventeen hundred dollars Forest was asking for the car. With that simple act, they became part of the mobile society. Although they both liked their little motorcycle, it was nice to have four wheels and a roof over their heads the next time they rolled down the highway.

There was rejoicing behind many of the neighbors' doors on Oakwood Avenue when the little putt-putt was replaced by the sleek new bright yellow car. None was more heartfelt than the celebration that took place at Dick and June's house.

Late that night, though, before June drifted off to sleep, a thought nagged at her, "How did his name get ahead of Dick's again?" Still thinking about it the next morning when she slid into her chair beside her husband at the breakfast table, she asked him, "Are you listed as Richard or Forest at the car dealership?"

"Forest R.," he said. "You know that's the way I always sign my name!" He ladled two spoons of sugar and a swig of cream in his coffee before he inquired, "What made you ask that?"

After she buttered his toast and handed it to him, she answered his question with one of her own, "Do they have your address as Oakwood Avenue or South Third Street?"

"South Third Street," he replied. When she looked at him with raised eyebrows, he stammered, "You don't think…?"

"Why not?" she said. "Two men with the only difference in their names being the middle initial both living at the same address. Have you ever thought that maybe the letters were addressed to Forest, without the middle initial? Since it came to your dad's address, what would he think except that it was for him?"

"No! That couldn't have happened!" Dick cried.

"Probably not," June murmured, but for the rest of the day, she found herself thinking about it. "I wonder," she mused, but since Dick had removed his name from the list when he bought the Ford, she was never to know how long, if ever, it would have taken for him to get one of those most important letters.

SURPRISES

That evening when Dick came home from work, he called out, "Get ready, we're going to Cincinnati to see Aunt Thelma and Uncle Scottie."

She had wondered how long he could resist the temptation to get on the road. "Are those keys burning a hole in your pocket?" she teased.

He took them from his pocket and waved them in the air before he replied, "Come on, just throw a few thing in the suitcase, and we'll be on our way."

In a few minutes, they were packing the white trimmed maroon luggage, a wedding gift from her father and stepmother, into the trunk of the car and heading south. In little over three hours, they arrived at his aunt's house on Cardington Avenue in Oakley, a suburb of Cincinnati.

Before they'd had a chance to take their bags upstairs, Scottie told them that he'd made reservations at a nightclub in the city, "I thought you kids might enjoy the show," he explained.

Scottie had worked his way up to the rank of captain in the Cincinnati Police Department and knew the city like the inside of his own home. "The owner of the club is a friend of mine, and tonight we're to be his guests," he told them.

June had never been in a nightclub before and felt like a wide-eyed kid when Scottie pushed open the heavy wooden door and escorted them into the dim interior. The orchestra was softly playing *It's Almost Like Being In Love*, and couples were dancing. Almost immediately, a man dressed in a black tuxedo greeted Scottie by name and ushered them to a ringside seat only a few feet from the stage.

When the music stopped, the lights on the stage dimmed until all they could see in the soft glow of a rose colored spotlight was a beautiful young woman in an ice blue satin evening gown. While she moved graciously across the stage, the musicians played a soft melody in the background. The woman's long blond hair and wide blue eyes glowed with innocence as she started to sing softly.

While all eyes were upon her, she seemed to gravitate toward their table. June's first thought was how sweet she looked. A few seconds later, though, when the singer moved even closer to Dick and started to sing in his ear, she changed her mind. Thelma and Scottie laughed at Dick's reaction. With a frantic look at his wife, he was trying to back away from the singer.

The young couple breathed a sigh of relief when she turned her back to Dick. While he reached for June's hand to assure her that the woman meant nothing to him, simultaneously the dancer swung around and the orchestra began to play a rousing version of *Take It Off*. She began to peel off her long blue satin gloves, wave them in the air, and trail them sinuously across Dick's flushed face. Then while she undulated around the table, she slowly removed one item of clothing after the other, until all she was wearing was a pair of pasties and a g-string.

June and Dick both felt like babes-in-the-woods at how they'd originally been taken in by this strip-teaser. It hadn't taken June long to realize that Thelma and Scottie were amused at their reaction to the show. The stripper seemed to read something more into Scottie's expression though. Right in the middle of her bump and grind routine she came to an abrupt halt a few feet from them, and with her eyes wide with fright, she whispered, "Captain Scott, I didn't do anything wrong. Did I?"

After he assured her that her act was within the law, she looked relieved. The subdued nature of the rest of the acts made June wonder if the word that a police captain was in the audience had gotten around backstage. "Either that or I'm getting shock-proofed," she surmised.

Much to the young couple's relief, the rest of their visit didn't provide any surprises. Mostly, they visited with the family until in the afternoon when they took his pre-teenage cousin, Carol, to Norwood to see a movie, *The Bachelor and The Bobby Soxer,* starring a teen-aged Shirley Temple, Cary Grant, and Myrna Loy. While they were sitting in the darkened theater, June whispered in Dick's ear, "I like the entertainers on the screen better than what we saw last night." Dick agreed, but secretly he admitted to himself that he'd enjoyed the stripper's attention.

The day after they got home from their trip, June called Rose to tell her about her experience. While she was talking to her cousin, June had the feeling that she wasn't getting her full attention. Finally, June exclaimed, "What's going on? I thought you'd get a kick out of hearing about the stripper!"

"It is funny," Rose said, "but I have something I want to tell you."

"Did something happen while we were away?" June asked.

"Yes, something happened," Rose replied in a matter-of-fact tone. "Johnny and I got married."

"Married?" June squealed. "Why didn't you tell me?"

"How could I tell you?" Rose asked. "You weren't here!"

"Tell me all about it," June urged. Then before Rose had a chance to reply, she bombarded her with questions. "Where did you get married? Who went with you? Did your mom and dad know about it?"

"Hold on. Let me answer your questions before you ask anything else," Rose laughingly replied. "Inez and Bob took us to Green Up, Kentucky. We didn't tell anyone what we were going to do, but I think Mom might have suspected something." Before the conversation was over, June had discovered that her cousin had been married by a minister, and that they were going to stay at Uncle Mace and Aunt Mabel's until they found a place of their own.

June could hardly wait for Dick to get home that evening so she could break the news to him. Bursting with excitement, she met him at the door and after planting a hasty kiss on his lips, she blurted out her news. Dick's response was, "I'm glad but not surprised. Then he added, "I'm certainly glad to hear that you had something else on your mind. I thought for a minute after that little kiss that you were losing interest in me."

"Not a chance," she teased. "Didn't I tell you that when you said 'I do', it was going to be forever?" He didn't reply, but the kiss he gave her told her clearer than any words could that he whole-heartedly agreed.

Over dinner, they talked about Rose and Johnny's wedding and the other news June had received that day. Along with the electric bill, the mailman had delivered a letter from her mother, who wrote that Dickie was playing football and that the coach said he was a good player.

"I wish we could see him play," Dick stated. June's face brightened at the prospect until he added, "But by the time I get off work, the game would already have started."

Not for the first time, June silently lamented the long hours he worked. Many days, he didn't get home until six-thirty or seven o'clock, and for June the days seemed to stretch out forever. For that reason, a couple weeks earlier, she'd returned to work at the Auditorium Theater on a part time basis.

She'd been working less than two months when November arrived. June's mother had invited the young couple, and Forest and Rowena to their home in Mansfield for dinner on Thanksgiving Day. Since Forest hadn't driven his new car outside of Newark, he volunteered to drive. June was scheduled to report to work late in the afternoon on Thanksgiving Day. When she explained the situation to her mother, Priscilla still wanted them to come. June had also asked Dick to tell his parents about it. When they set off for Mansfeld, she was under the impression that everyone agreed that they would have to leave early.

As she was to find out a few hours later when they were finishing the delicious turkey dinner Priscilla had prepared, that was not the case. When June spooned the last morsel of the mince meat pie into her mouth, she looked at her watch and announced that they would have to leave soon. Everything might have been fine if she'd stopped there, but she added, "I have to be at work in a couple hours."

Her statement seemed to stun her mother-in-law, who cried, "No you don't!"

June almost dropped her fork and stared wide-eyed at the upset woman as she wondered what she had said that had brought on this reaction. She didn't have to wait long to find out, though. She'd barely had time to blink when Rowena stormily said, "You don't have to tell your family **that you have to work!** My son can support you!"

"I didn't mean that Dick couldn't support me," June explained. "I just meant that since I have a job, and I'm scheduled to work this afternoon, I don't want to be late."

Nothing June said would placate Rowena. In her mind, her daughter-in-law was embarrassing the family by working outside the home and although she didn't like to make a fuss in public, she hadn't been able to let June's assertion go unchallenged.

There had been dead silence from the rest of the diners while this drama was unfolding. While everyone was trying to pretend they hadn't heard the argument, Priscilla broke the silence by announcing that there was more mincemeat and pumpkin pie and plenty of coffee. Then with an aside to Rowena, she said, "And more tea."

As the minutes ticked away, June kept peering at her watch with a sinking heart. Although she wasn't worried about losing her job, she was concerned about making someone else work late to cover for her absence. After all, it was a holiday and the girl on duty would have a turkey dinner waiting at home for her.

When they finally got back to Newark, Forest dropped her off in front of the movie theater. When she threw open the door and ran into the lobby, she saw the assistant manager working in her popcorn booth. "Uh oh!" she inwardly moaned as she advanced toward him.

"I hope you have a good explanation!" he announced. A few minutes later after June had explained, his eyes softened and he replied, "I know what happened was hard on you, but it's harder for the older generation to accept change. My parents are like that too. They were raised in a time when very few women worked out of the home."

"My mom works," June said. "No one thinks anything about it."

"No two families are alike," he remarked before he told her that she could take over the booth. "I've got to get home for my turkey dinner." After he left, she reflected on the events of the day and on what he'd just said. She knew her mother-in-law was having trouble adjusting to having a daughter-in-law with such different ideas from her own. As these thoughts ran through her mind, she realized that she had a big job ahead of her if she were ever to get Rowena to accept some of her ways of doing things.

～

November arrived and June was occupied with thoughts of their upcoming wedding anniversary. For some time, she'd been mulling over an idea, and she'd decided that their first wedding anniversary would be the perfect time to talk to Dick about it.

When the big day finally arrived, they'd had dinner at the Sparta, then went to see the movie, *The Farmer's Daughter*, at the Midland Theater. A light romantic comedy, it perfectly suited their mood. Several of June's friends were working that night, and they swarmed around them on the way out to offer their congratulations. "One whole year!" Mary exclaimed. "And they said it wouldn't last!"

June grimaced as she replied, "I couldn't give the principal the satisfaction of being right, so I guess he's stuck with me."

"Suits me," Dick murmured as they made their way out of the lobby. Walking toward their car on the north side of the town square, they passed Galleher's Drug Store. Only a few people were sitting at the soda fountain counter and all the booths were empty. Dick held the door open, and steered her to one of the booths. "How about a banana split?" he asked.

He knew that had been her favorite since she'd been a little girl, so he wasn't surprised at her enthusiastic reply of, "I never turn down a banana split." Since they were practically the only customers, it was only a matter of minutes before they were digging into their gooey treats. Shortly, June considered telling Dick what she had on her mind, but the door opened and a group of young people surged in. A few stopped at the booth to talk to them and to offer their congratulations so she decided to wait until they got home. Since she wasn't sure how he'd take to her idea, she decided it would be better to be sure there was no danger of being interrupted.

That time came when they returned home and were able to close their front door and shut out the rest of the world. While they snuggled together on the couch and listened to the soft strains of a Glen Miller record, she decided that now was the time.

Without moving her head from his shoulder, she murmured, "I would like to have a baby."

He sat up so abruptly that she almost toppled over onto the other seat. "A baby!" he exclaimed. "You want a baby?"

He looked so startled that June found herself giggling when she replied. "Yes, a baby. You know one of those little people like Rose and Vonnie are expecting."

"I just didn't know you wanted one," he said. Then it was his turn to surprise her with his next words. "I'd love for us to have a baby if you're sure that's what you want," he said.

For the next hour, they talked about being parents. Dick's only concern was her youth, but she pooh-poohed that as of no importance. "I'll be almost nineteen when it's born," she reminded him. Then she asserted, "I'm mature for my age!"

"Relax," he said. "I'm not arguing with you. I told you that whenever you want to have a baby will be fine with me. I just want you to be sure."

"I'm sure!" she replied.

With that settled, Dick took her into his arms and murmured something in her ear. In response, she smiled and whispered, "That sounds good to me."

THE BEGETTING BEGINS

By Christmas, June was almost certain she was pregnant. When in January the doctor confirmed it and told her the baby was due on August twenty-fifth, she was ecstatic. She told Dick she wanted to treasure this little secret for awhile before they shared it with anyone else. "If that's what you want, it's alright with me," he replied as he patted her flat stomach.

"It won't be flat for long," she jested. "Soon, little Junior will be kicking your hand." Then she went on to tell him that Vonnie, whose baby was due in February, said hers felt like it was doing the jitterbug right under her ribs.

One day when she was four months pregnant, they had gone to the Arcade Theater to see Rita Hayworth and Glen Ford in the movie, *Gilda*. When Rita Hayworth began to dance across the screen and provocatively sing *Put The Blame On Mame*, June felt a feathery movement in her stomach. All the action on the screen was lost to her as she breathlessly waited to see if she had imagined it.

As she gently placed her hand on her thickening middle, she felt it again. Eyes shining, she took her husband's hand and positioned it so he could feel it too. A look of wonder crossed his face before he whispered, "It's the baby!" For the next few minutes, the scenes on the screen took second place as the prospective parents sat and smiled at each other.

Now that she'd felt life, they decided that it was time to let their families and friends know about it. June wrote to her father and stepmother so they would receive the news at about the time they told the other grandparents.

Since Priscilla was coming to visit the following weekend, they decided that would be the right time to make their announcement. June had planned to make a big production when she told her, but an opportune moment arrived the first afternoon of her mother's visit that made her change her mind.

Priscilla's older sister, Della Keller, had died during the summer, and Priscilla was still grieving over her loss. "She was only forty-eight years old," Priscilla said. Then she went on to lament, "She wouldn't have had to die so young if doctors could only do something to repair or replace a heart valve." As if the mention of her sister had opened a floodgate of memories, Priscilla began to talk about her.

"Did you know that your Aunt Della was the one who brought your dad and me together?" she asked. June replied that she'd heard something about it. "She was dating him first," her mother began. "Then she brought him to the house to meet Mom and Dad. He told me later that he saw my picture and fell in love with me that very night."

"Was Aunt Della mad at Dad?" June asked.

"I suppose she might have been hurt. I couldn't say whether she was angry... or not," she responded. She dabbed the tears from her eyes before she cried, "We have been so close since I moved to Mansfield, it's hard getting used to her not being there." A new stream of tears ran down her cheek when she moaned, "I don't know why God had to take her when she was so young!"

"We don't have the answer to that," June murmured sympathetically. "But sometimes, it seems that if God takes away one thing we love, he turns around and gives us something else." Then while her mother looked inquiringly at her, June put her arm around her shoulder and said, "I don't mean to say that anyone can replace Aunt Della in your heart, but I have some news for you that will give you something happy to look forward to."

Her mother looked doubtful, but when her daughter said, "Mom, you're going to be a grandmother!" a wide grin spread across her face. When June explained that the baby would be here in four and a half months, Priscilla exclaimed, "That soon! I've got to get to work if I'm going to get a couple of sweater sets and a shawl crocheted before then."

June laughed delightedly and said, "Mom, you have plenty of time!" Priscilla's only response was to wag her head from side to side and to insist that they go downtown so she could get some patterns and yarn.

Later that evening after Dick's return from work, Priscilla couldn't resist teasing him about making her such a young grandmother. "I'll only be thirty-eight when it is born!" she declared.

He studied his pretty young mother-in-law, with her pale skin, soft natural appearing make-up, and ash blond hair worn in a fashionable feather-cut, and honestly replied, "No one will ever believe you're a grandmother, Priscilla!" She blushed at the compliment, and expressed that she was too happy at the prospect to care what other people thought.

That night, they drove to the house on South Third Street and broke the news to Dick's parents. They were as pleased as Priscilla had been. "This calls for a celebration!" Rowena said. Then she brought out the fabulous cherry nut cake that she'd baked that afternoon and served it with steaming cups of tea. While they ate, she went into the downstairs bedroom and returned with photo albums filled with Dick's baby pictures. After he'd heard the tenth squeal of, "Wasn't he cute?" from the women, Forest shoved his chair back from the table and retreated into the other room. When Dick followed a few minutes later, June could hear the murmur of voices and make out an occasional word of advice on being a father from the older man intermingled with Dick's response of, "Yes, Dad." She grinned at the thought that Dick would have been better off if he'd stayed in the kitchen with the women.

Once they'd returned to the house on Oakwood Avenue, Priscilla murmured, "I know I've seen a picture of Dick as a little boy somewhere. If not of him then it was of a little boy who looked just like him. I remember remarking about the dark hair and eyes," she mused. It wasn't until later that night, just before she drifted off to sleep, that she recalled a time when she and her young first husband, June's father, had stopped at a confectionery on Mt. Vernon Road on their way home from a movie. She remembered a picture of a dark haired little boy prominently displayed on the counter. The dark haired woman who'd waited on them had proudly told them that he was her son. Although Priscilla tried to recollect the woman's name, with the passage of years, she'd forgotten. "I do remember that it was an unusual name." she thought before her eyelids became heavy and she fell asleep.

The next morning when she asked Dick if his mother had ever worked in a confectionery, he replied. "When I was little, we lived with my Grandfather Edward McNamee in his house on Mt. Vernon Road. He had a confectionery in the front, and Mom helped him out once in awhile."

"Then I was right!" she proclaimed triumphantly. "I had seen your baby picture before." Then she recounted the story to them.

Dick expressed surprise that she could remember it after all these years, to which she replied, "I wouldn't have if your mother hadn't shown me the same picture last night. I also remember Burrel and I talking about the name Rowena. He hadn't heard it before, but I'd read it in Ivanhoe."

"Mom hardly ever forgets anything!" June said.

"I'll have to remember that," Dick joked.

The day after her mother's visit was over, June walked over to Uncle Mace's and told her aunt and cousins her news. On the way home, she stopped at Vonnie's and told her. Everyone was pleased for her, especially Rose and Vonnie since that meant their children would get to grow up together.

⁓

A few days later a surprise announcement came from Mississippi. June's father, stepmother and Billy and Freddy were going to be visiting in June. Following close behind this letter was one from Cecil saying that he would be in Ohio on leave the same month. He planned to divide his time between his mother's house in Mansfield and Dick and June's in Newark.

After leaving China, he'd spent ten months in Guam and now he'd been assigned to Olathe, Kansas for additional training and reassignment. He'd complained in his last letter that the training in Kansas was unnecessary, as his group had already been operating the equipment, under less than ideal circumstances.

After a month on that base, he'd gotten his new assignment. He was going to be sent to a navy Air Reserve Station at Grosse Ile, Michigan where he would help provide radar training in assisted landings.

When Dick heard about the transfer, he announced, "I'll bet he won't find the scenery as interesting in Michigan as it was in Guam!"

"If you mean the Pan Am stewardesses, I'm sure the girls are as pretty there as any airline stewardess!" June retorted.

Dick pulled her onto his lap and told her that he was sure there wasn't one any prettier than his wife. Five months pregnant, his words were music to the expectant mother's ears.

When she'd received Polly's letter, June had put a big red X on the calendar that marked the first day of June nineteen forty-eight as the day of their arrival, and continued to mark off the days. Finally the big day came, and June anxiously waited to hear a car stop in front of the house. Every little sound in the neighborhood had brought her expectantly running to the front porch to scan the nearly empty street.

When they did arrive, she'd been in the kitchen and hadn't heard anything until there was a knock on the door and the sound of her name being called. "Dad, Mom," she cried as she ran to the door. This greeting was followed by hugs and kisses, while everyone excitedly greeted each other.

After the flurry of greetings was over, Polly said, "I thought you said you were five months pregnant. I don't see anything."

June laughed and rubbed her rounding stomach as she responded, "It's there...and it's an active little thing!"

"Another one of the advantages of being tall," Polly said. "When I was that far along, I looked as if I was carrying a pony."

While Polly had been talking, June felt a tug on her skirt and heard an insistent little voice say, "Dwink of wahwah!" When she looked down and saw Billy, she remembered his reaction the first time she'd seen him and resisted her impulse to scoop him into her arms. Instead, she half filled a glass with water and handed it to him, then repeated the action for Freddy.

"What beautiful children," she thought as she watched them down the water in large gulps. Both boys had blue eyes, but the resemblance stopped there. Three-year old Freddy's hair was the color of carrots, and two-year-old Billy's was a dark brown...almost black. She was pleased to see that each of the boys smiled warmly when she stooped down and talked to them. They didn't stay still long, though. Within seconds, the energy they'd stored up during the trip seemed to explode, and turned them into whirling dervishes. Then while they raced from room to room, their mother shouted, "Don't touch anything!" As June looked after these rambunctious boys, she was glad the house was childproof.

Midmorning the next day, Cecil and Dickie arrived in Priscilla and Bill's car. June was surprised when she saw the fantastic tan her older brother had acquired in Guam. When she complimented him on it, he told her that his uniform when he'd been stationed there had been shorts or a bathing suit. "And the only place we had to go was the beach." He grinned before he added, "That beach was a great place to go when the Pan Am flights landed and the stewardesses showed up in their bathing suits."

~

That afternoon Dick joined them when they went to a picnic at Uncle Mace and Aunt Mabel's house where the visitors from Mississippi were staying. Since Grandpap Harman was also in Newark for a short visit, the day turned into a wonderful three generation family reunion.

Before they left the house June drilled her husband, "You're not hiding a water pistol are you? I don't want another water attack on my Grandpap."

Dick innocently assured her he didn't have a squirt gun with him today.

Without a squirt gun available at the picnic, he came up with another idea. He walked up to June while she was chatting with her Grandpap, and quickly slipped an ice-cube down the back of her blouse. June let out a yelp, and began chasing Dick around the yard. Skip scooped up a cup of ice and called out to his brother, "Dickie, get this ice to June." Dickie quickly grabbed the cup of ice and ran toward June, handing it off to her in relay-fashion.

Her husband, Dick, thinking he was out of her reach, called back to her, "Bet you can't catch me."

Billy and Freddy, both laughing hysterically, ran toward Dick to join in the fun. Dick had to stop to avoid tripping over the two giggling boys, and June caught up, emptying the cup of ice down the front of his shirt.

"Gotcha," she laughed, "with the help of all my brothers."

June had slung her camera around her neck before she left for her uncle's house. Before the day was over, she'd taken several snapshots for her family album. When she handed the camera to her husband and asked him to take one of her with her four brothers, Cecil, Dickie, Billy, and Freddy, she had no idea that this would be a treasured picture. *Nor could she have guessed this would be the last time all five of them would be together again until after the little boys would both be over fifty years old.*

Although, June spent every waking minute with her parents either at her home or Uncle Mace's, the visit was much too brief. It had lasted long enough, though, for June to find out that Polly intended to stay in the South. On the other hand, her father had told her privately that he wasn't sure how long his job was going to last. "When it ends, I'll have to go wherever I can find a job," he said. When she asked if that meant, he might return to Newark, he replied, "There's not that much construction going on around here." He shrugged before repeating that he'd have to go wherever the work was.

June hugged him and murmured encouragingly that maybe by then, Polly would be willing to come with him. "I hope so," he said. He didn't say, but June still wondered if living in someone else's house was getting to him.

She was still thinking about this conversation the next day when she and Dick stood on her front porch and watched them leave for their trip home. She could see Freddy and Billy bouncing up and down in the back seat and Polly waving from the front seat until the car turned the corner onto Tuscarawas Street. "I'm going to miss them," she told Dick. He patted her tummy and told her that once the little one got here, they'd go to Mississippi for a visit. His words made the parting easier.

She didn't have much time to brood, though, as within a couple days, Cecil returned. This time, Priscilla came along. When she heard that Grandpap Harman was visiting, she told June that she missed him and had always been fond of her former father-in-law. "He told me when I was living with my aunt in West Virginia that he still loved you as a daughter," June said.

Before they had a chance to pursue the conversation, Cecil and Dick walked in from the kitchen with a tray of tall glasses filled with lemonade. The conversation took a different turn, and Grandpap wasn't mentioned again. Later while the others were chatting, June was deep in thought. She surprised everyone by breaking into their conversation with the announcement, "While you two are here, I'm going to invite Grandpap over for dinner." She quelled Priscilla's protest that he might not want to see her when she replied, "Why don't we let him decide?" Before her mother could object, June picked up the phone and called her grandfather. As she'd expected, he'd readily accepted. The next evening, the former in-laws had a happy reunion that was filled with pleasant remembrances and with no mention of the divorce. June had noticed earlier that when he came in, the older man looked a little leery of her husband, as if he expected him to whip out a water pistol at any moment. June was wary herself, but she soon found that her husband had something else on his mind that evening.

During the last few weeks when he'd been going to the hospital to cut his customers' hair, he'd become acquainted with a pretty red-haired nurse. In the course of a conversation, he'd told her about Cecil's visit. When he'd asked if she'd like to meet him, she'd enthusiastically replied, "You bet! Just have him call me."

When he related this to Cecil, he seemed reluctant to call, but Dick wouldn't take no for an answer. "You'll really like her," Dick insisted as he peered at a tiny piece of paper he'd taken from his wallet. While the rest of the family looked on, he picked up the phone and began to dial. Since they all expected to see him hand the phone to Cecil, they were surprised when they heard him say, "Hello. Is this Ginny?" After listening to her affirmative response, he said, "This is Cecil Harman, Dick's brother-in-law." Dick held the phone far enough from his ear that they could hear her respond that she'd been expecting his call.

It was obvious that he was enjoying himself when for the next few minutes, he lightheartedly bantered with her. While he arranged a date for the next night, June was interested in the reaction of his audience. She noticed that Grandpap's eyes were sparkling and his moustache twitching while Priscilla's expression flitted from amusement to disapproval, and Cecil seemed a little discomforted by the turn of events. Dick, however, was in his element anytime he was able to use his gift of gab.

After he hung up, he turned and triumphantly told Cecil, "You have a date for tomorrow night. You just have to pick her up at seven o'clock at the nurses' quarters," he explained.

While Dick filled Cecil in on the girl's side of the conversation, June brought out their new family bible. Sitting down between her mother and grandfather, she asked them to help her fill out the family tree. "All I have is my parents and grandparents names. I thought maybe you two could help me with the rest."

While June recorded the information in the bible, Grandpap, like the teacher he'd been in his younger years, gave her the information and told her how to record it. By the time he was through and Priscilla had added the information she had, June had traced the family back five generations on each side. She carefully wrote the information in their new family bible for herself and future generations.

Each had Civil War stories to tell. Priscilla's grandfather had been captured and held in Andersonville, the infamous Confederate prison of war camp. Grandpap's grandfather had fought bravely in a battle in Harman Hills near his home.

While she was doing this, the baby was moving around as if to gain its mother's attention. She cradled her hand around the small mound that was her unborn child, and silently reassured it that there was a place reserved for its name...and for the names of whatever brothers and sisters that might come along.

Later while Grandpap was saying goodbye, he turned to his grandson and said, "I'd like to hear how this blind date of yours turns out."

"Awh," Cecil muttered. "It's just a date." When they tried to quiz him the next night after he got back to the house on Oakwood Avenue, he didn't have much to add. "We had a nice time, but since I'm leaving tomorrow I probably won't see her again." Later he confided in June that the girl had told him she'd like to go out with him again, but she was surprised that he hadn't been as talkative as on the phone. "It would be hard to talk as much as Dick does," he uttered. "I think his Irish ancestors must have kissed the blarney stone." Priscilla who'd overheard his comment laughed and told him that she'd noticed that too.

~

After Cecil left to go to his base in Grosse Ile, Michigan, Dick and June settled into their normal routine. Then during the rest of the summer, the upcoming event of her child, Rowena's grandchild, seemed to draw the two women closer. June found herself spending more time with her and learning to appreciate the other woman's many fine qualities. She realized that it didn't matter whether or not they had the same taste in clothes or interior decorations and that where it really mattered, they had a great deal in common. They both loved Dick and his unborn child. It helped that she had learned to listen to the more experienced woman's advice, sift out what she wanted to keep and discard the rest. As she was to discover, this turned out to be a wise decision on her part.

While this strategy seemed to work with her mother-in-law, she and Dick soon found out that it was a different matter with her father-in-law. He had been upset with them since Dick had told him that they had been thinking about buying an automatic washing machine. He was opposed to the purchase and kept harping about how it wouldn't get their clothes clean like Rowena's wringer type.

Dick knew he'd never change his dad's mind so he decided to keep quiet about his intentions and to go ahead and buy what they wanted. This led to a situation that the young couple was to find hilarious, while on the other hand it was to leave Forest in the unusual situation of being left speechless.

It happened one day when he and Rowena came over to see them while June was sitting on the couch folding freshly laundered sheets. Forest took one look at them and triumphantly exclaimed, "See I told you. It doesn't get them clean! You'd never see yellow sheets like that come out of Rowena's old Maytag!"

Dick and June didn't succeed very well in containing their laughter when Dick exclaimed, "The sheets were yellow when we bought them, Dad." In response to his father's puzzled look, he explained, "Sheets don't only come in white anymore. You can get them in almost every color in the rainbow!"

Forest's only reaction was to mutter under his breath that he'd never heard of such a thing, and to no one's surprise, those were the last words they heard on the subject.

⁓

As the summer passed June took on the appearance of someone trying to hide a basketball under her dress. Her brother, Dickie, couldn't resist the temptation to sing the song *June Is Busting Out All Over* every time he saw her. She knew it would do no good to remind him that the song's lyrics referred to the month of June, since they could also refer to her widening waistline. Besides, she knew that teasing was part of a little brother's job, and he seemed to be taking that responsibility seriously.

During the rest of the summer, the days seemed to have taken wing until at last August twenty-fifth, her due date, arrived. Then they seemed to discard their wings and move with the speed of a turtle as she waited for the first sign of labor. "This is the longest part of my pregnancy," she moaned to Dick when she pointed to the eight days she'd marked off on the calendar since the twenty-fifth. "Mom is coming this Saturday for the weekend. I hope it comes then."

"I have a dance Saturday night at the Sunset Club. I hope it doesn't decide to come that night," he declared.

"If you had this baby kicking your ribs as hard as it is mine, you wouldn't say that! Except when I had the measles a couple months ago, I've felt great during this pregnancy until now," she asserted. Dick still hoped that since the baby had waited this long, it would wait until after he played the dance, but he decided it would be wise to keep that opinion to himself.

As babies have been doing since the beginning of time, this one didn't pay any attention to what the expectant father wanted, and June's labor started Saturday afternoon, September fourth a few hours after Priscilla's arrival. After June described her symptoms to her, Priscilla decided it was time to alert the doctor that June's labor had begun. Since this was a first child, the doctor assured them that it would be hours yet. He went on to tell Priscilla that he could be reached at the Country Club until around midnight, but not to call unless her pains got to be three or four minutes apart.

When Dick arrived home from work and found out what was going on, he called the band leader and asked him to get someone to fill in for him in the band that night. The leader was adamant that Dick was going to play. First the bandleader tried to bribe June with the promise of a new dress if she'd let her husband go. When that didn't work, he informed Dick that if he wanted to stay with the band he'd better show up.

The soon-to-be father was torn between whether he should go or stay. Priscilla again called the doctor who reiterated that it would be hours before June would have to go to the hospital.

With that assurance still in his ears, Dick decided that he'd go, but before he left, he said, "If you need me, just call the Sunset Club. I can be home in a half hour."

After he was gone, June's friend Vonnie called and when she heard that June was in labor, she hurried over. Although the two women kept up a steady stream of chatter to help June relax, nothing could distract her from the increased intensity of the pains. Finally, she told them that she thought it was time to take her to the hospital.

Priscilla, who had been more tense than she'd appeared, sprung into action and called Dick at the Sunset Club then the doctor at the Country Club. Dick replied that he'd be right home, and the doctor told Priscilla to get June to the hospital right away. Within twenty-five minutes, Dick arrived, but the doctor seemed to have dropped off the face of the earth. Although he'd given Priscilla the impression that he would meet them at the hospital, he wasn't there...nor could he be reached. Worried about June and frustrated with the doctor, Dick said, "This is ridiculous! I can't just sit here. June needs a doctor now. I'm going to go find him and bring him here where he belongs."

He'd no longer left, when it became obvious that the urge to push had taken over and the baby wasn't going to wait. With each contraction, June's mother told her to hold on to her hands and pull. June had pulled so hard that Priscilla ended up with a sprained wrist. Not wanting the baby to be born in the labor room before the doctor arrived, a nurse grabbed the front of June's bed and quickly wheeled it down the hall to the delivery room. This provided June with the only amusing note in the entire evening as she watched the roly-poly woman's buttocks bounce up and down. She told Dick later that they looked like two puppies in a sack trying to get out.

Only a few feet behind the bed, Priscilla and Vonnie arrived at the double doors of the delivery room seconds after they had swung shut. They moved near to the closed doors and waited expectantly for the sound of a baby's cry. Instead, the only sound that reached their ears was the hushed voices of the nurses. "I don't hear June," Priscilla whispered. Although they strained to hear, June's cries had stopped seconds after the doors had closed.

Worried, Priscilla stopped a nurse's aide who was on her way into the delivery room and asked if they'd had any word from the doctor. The woman cast a disdainful glance in their direction and said, "You know he does have other patients besides your daughter."

That was too much for the worried mother to take. She glared at the aide and impatiently said, "Two of his patients are here ready to deliver. Where else would he be?" Then when the woman smiled condescendingly, June's usually dignified, courteous mother snapped, "What did he do, pat you on the tush?"

Vonnie told June later that she'd managed to keep a straight face, but what she'd wanted to do was hug Priscilla. "She said just what I'd like to have said." *They weren't to find out until later that the aide was the mother-in-law of Dick's bandleader.*

A few minutes after this scene, Dick returned with the missing doctor. Following close behind was the doctor's harried looking nurse.

"I finally tracked the doctor down at his house. There was a light on in one of the upstairs rooms so I banged on the door until he finally opened it. As I stood in the open doorway, I saw a woman in a white nurse's uniform coming down the stairs. They both looked messed, like they'd just gotten out of bed. While I explained the urgency of the situation, he tried to tuck in his shirt and smooth down what little hair he had," Dick said.

Vonnie grinned and quipped, "With his wife out of town it looks like they're practicing the old saying, 'When the cats away the mice will play.' "

"If that's what they were up to it seems to me that with June and the other woman in labor, they could have put off their hanky-panky until later. I'd say they seem more like rats to me," Dick retorted.

Priscilla interjected, "Things aren't always what they seem. Maybe his nurse went over to the doctor's house to bring him to the hospital." Dick snorted his disagreement.

Within minutes after the delivery room doors swung shut behind the doctor and his nurse, they heard the baby's cry.

When Priscilla found out later that June had been given ether seconds after she went into the delivery room, and that the baby had been held back until the doctor got there, she was livid.

Before she could vent her anger, though, the nurse who'd wheeled June down the hallway came through the door with a blanket wrapped bundle. "The new mother is fine," she informed them. Then she lifted the corner of the blanket so they could see the tiny face and said, "It's a girl!"

They were happy at the news, but Priscilla's face carried a worried expression. Without telling anyone, she had been carrying around a secret fear for this baby. No longer able to contain it, she whispered the question, "Is she alright?"

"Of course, she's alright!" the nurse replied. "Why shouldn't she be?"

"I've been worried since the mother had the measles a few months ago," Priscilla replied. The nurse smiled reassuringly and explained to her that June's measles had been too late in her pregnancy to cause the baby any problems.

That settled, the new father, grandmother, and friend of the family spent the next few minutes admiring this beautiful infant. Despite their protests, a few seconds later, the nurse whisked the baby away and disappeared behind closed doors. She was no sooner out of their sight before another nurse stepped out of the delivery room and told them that June was fine. "She hasn't come out from under the anesthetic yet, but we will be taking her to her room anyway." While they nodded, she added, "You might as well go home, though, as you won't be allowed to see her until tomorrow. You can come back during visiting hours."

Although they protested, she was adamant that those were the rules, and that she couldn't make exceptions for anyone. Then without even allowing them to see the new mother, she unceremoniously ushered them out. Once they were in the car, Dick said, "I'll take you girls home in a minute, but first I'm going to swing by and let Mom and Dad know they're grandparents."

Vonnie's brief glance at her watch told her that she wasn't going to get any sleep anyway, since Dale would be getting up in less than an hour. "That's fine with me," she said.

Priscilla nodded her agreement, but reminded Dick that it wasn't quite five o'clock yet. "Won't they still be asleep?"

Dick shrugged and replied, "They always go to bed by seven-thirty. That makes it about time for them to get up now." While he'd been talking, Priscilla had noticed that theirs was the only car on the deserted streets. The lone light she'd seen burning in one of the houses they'd passed gave her the eerie feeling that, other than that unknown resident, she, Dick, and Vonnie were alone in this deserted town.

Rubbing her eyes and blinking, she thought that the events of the night were causing her to be fanciful. She'd barely gotten the words out of her mouth that she wouldn't want to have any trouble with the car this time of morning before the Ford rolled to a stop. "Dick, that isn't funny," she declared. June had told her about Dick's fondness for practical jokes so she naturally assumed this was one.

As he slipped out from behind the wheel and hurried around to the front of the car where he raised the hood, he said, "I don't think it's funny either." When he looked down at the intricacies of all the wires and hoses, he was forced to admit that he had no idea what was wrong. When Priscilla and Vonnie joined him, they were even more mystified.

"Where are we?" Priscilla asked. Dick pointed to the railroad overpass above their heads and told them that they were only five or six blocks from his parents' home. Asking them to stay in the car, he set off running toward the house on Third Street.

Within minutes he was back with his unshaven, uncombed father in tow. After they exchanged greetings, Forest and Priscilla congratulated each other on becoming grandparents. In response to his inquiry about the baby and the mother, Priscilla told him that June was sleeping when they left, then went on to rhapsodize about the baby's beauty until Dick interrupted her. "We'll take you two home then we'll see what we can do about the car."

By the time they discovered the problem was a water pump and Dick had a new one installed it was mid-morning. Without going home or to work, the new father decided that visiting hours or not, he was going to see his wife. Since he'd discovered the back entrance years ago when he had come in to cut the hair of his hospitalized customers, he headed for it now. Careful not to make any noise, he sneaked up the steps to the third floor and down the hall past the nurses' station. He looked through the open doors until he came to the third one and heard June's voice call his name.

It was a happy reunion between the new parents. The way they hugged and kissed each other, an onlooker would have thought they'd been separated much longer than the few hours it had been. Their words tumbled over each other's when June asked if he'd seen the baby while at the same time, he asked her how she was feeling.

June answered first, "I'm feeling like I just had a baby," She sighed, then added, "But they haven't let me see her yet."

He tutted in sympathy then said, "I saw her a few minutes after she was born and she's beautiful. I don't understand why you haven't gotten to see her."

Grimacing, she said that it was some dumb hospital rule. "I've waited so long, it's mean to make me wait any longer," she wailed. Then as if the thought had just occurred to her, she asked him how he'd managed to get in before visiting hours.

"I came in the back way. No one is going to keep me from seeing my wife... rules or not," he declared. The words were no sooner out of his mouth before they heard the rustling of starched skirts in the doorway, and a crisp voice say, "What are you doing in here?"

Dick flashed an impish grin, "I couldn't stay away from my beautiful wife any longer."

The nurse's pursed lips and stony glare told him what she thought of people who didn't obey rules. "You can't stay here. I'm going to bring the baby in." When June asked if he could stay so they could see her together, the nurse's expression only softened slightly as she reminded her that it was against the rules. The remark Dick muttered under his breath as he left the room clearly showed what he thought of **their rules.**

Since the nurse didn't trust him to leave, she stood in the doorway of June's room and kept her eyes on his retreating back until he got in the elevator. Then she watched the flashing floor numbers to be sure that he went all the way to the lobby. Once she'd assured herself that this brash young man was actually gone, she went to the nursery and picked up the baby wrapped in a pink blanket and carried her to June's room.

When she placed the bundle in the crook of June's arm, she actually smiled when she said, "Here you are, Little Mother. I'll leave the two of you alone to get acquainted."

After she was gone, June peeled back the blanket and looked down into the face of her sleeping daughter. As she studied the tiny features, the baby opened her eyes and seemed to study her mother's in return. June had never understood some of the things she'd read about how difficult it was for some women to adapt to motherhood. From the minute she looked at that tiny, beautiful face, she knew this was not going to be a problem for her.

Happier than she'd ever been in her life, she murmured softly to her new daughter, "I can't believe it. I've created a miracle."

Up until this minute, she'd thought that all babies looked alike...all red and wrinkled. That certainly wasn't true of this one. From her perfectly shaped head to her tiny toes, everything about this child was beautiful. "Sharlyn June," June murmured. "I hope you like your name." The baby stared somberly while her mother went on to explain that she had wanted to call her Sheryl Lynn, but that Dick had wanted to call her June. "I wasn't willing to give up the name I'd picked so we compromised. I just put Sheryl and Lynn together for your first name and added June for the middle one." While she'd been talking she'd let her finger trail across the soft cheek.

Before June had a chance to say all the things she wanted to say to her daughter, the nurse bustled back into the room to return the baby to the nursery. "Talking baby talk, are we?" she said.

Offended, June exclaimed, "I'm never going to talk baby talk to this child. Her father and I have decided that's silly. Why would we want to teach a child to talk that way? Then she'd just have to unlearn it!"

A knowing smile crossed the nurse's face, but she kept her thoughts to herself. She'd worked here long enough to be familiar with the feelings of first time mothers. It was amazing how strong their opinions were and how much some of them changed with the birth of each child. *That might have been true of some mothers and in June's case, she might change her mind on other matters as her family grew. Talking baby talk wasn't going to be one of them.*

The four days June and Sharlyn stayed in the hospital whizzed by with visitors' hours filled with the coming and going of friends and family. Forest and Rowena were the first to arrive. June heard Rowena's enthusiastic chatter before, arms laden with gaily wrapped packages, they bustled into the room. After briefly greeting June and asking how she was feeling, Rowena gushed, "The baby is beautiful!" She paused for a split second for breath before she added, "She has Grandma's little nose."

"Naw!" June protested. "The baby has a tiny nose. Dick's grandma's nose isn't big, but it's not a button one either!"

Rowena laughed and touched the tip of her own button nose. "Not that grandma! This one! You just made me the newest grandma on this side of the family."

The two women laughed at their misunderstanding while, ignored, Forest shifted from one foot to the other as he waited for his turn to compliment the mother on a job well done.

June asked Rowena if Grandma was what she wanted to be called. The older woman made a face and retorted, "I should say not! I'm not old enough to be called Grandma. When she's starts to talk, she can call me Rowie."

Before June had a chance to do more than nod, Rowena piled the packages on the bed and commanded June to open them. She had just unfolded the last tiny garment when she heard her mother and Dick's voices as they came down the hall.

Priscilla came in first and once she'd dropped a kiss on her daughter's forehead, she exclaimed, "She sure is a pretty little thing. I thought so last night when we first saw her, but now that they have her all spruced up, she's even more so."

One on each side of the bed, the two grandmothers chatted while Dick leaned over and kissed his wife. She was more interested in his presence than in their conversation until she heard Rowena say, "She has her father's little ears." June's hands immediately flew to her ears as if to reassure herself that they hadn't become basset hound-like during the night. Her mother noticed the gesture and smiled reassuringly while she mouthed the words, "Your ears are fine." Witnessing the little scene, Dick couldn't resist teasing his mother for her remark by saying that he'd lain awake many nights worrying that the baby might take after its mother. Rowena's reply was to stick out her tongue at her son.

They were still talking and joking when the nurse came in and scooted them out with the words, "Visiting hours are over. It's time for Mommy to rest." Since June was at least twenty-five years the woman's junior, she had to bite her tongue to keep from reminding her that she was hardly her Mommy. She was so happy, though, with her new state of motherhood that she let it pass.

Finally the big day arrived. She was going home! When the ambulance attendants arrived, mother and daughter were dressed for the big event. Sharlyn was wearing the white nylon dress that Rowie had brought for her, and the pale pink crocheted sweater, bonnet, and booties from Priscilla. Bundled in the pink satin bordered blanket Vonnie had brought, the baby was laid in a small wicker basket and placed on the gurney beside June as they were wheeled down the hall.

Priscilla and Dick were waiting at the door of the house on Oakwood Avenue when the ambulance purred to a stop at the curb. Dick almost tripped over his own feet when he rushed down the steps to welcome his family home. When he held out his hands to take the basket, the attendant sternly informed him that wasn't allowed. "We have to carry the baby into the house. Then we'll bring your wife in."

The new father and grandmother waited impatiently, until the attendants had June settled into her bed and the tiny basket had been placed on the fireplace ledge. "Now, you can put the baby in her bassinet if you want to," the attendant said.

While Priscilla chatted with the men, Dick was finally allowed to touch his first-born. The memory of her, sound asleep, as he lifted her from the tiny basket was one that was to stay in his heart forever. He was oblivious of the ambulance attendants' departure as he moved to the side of the bed and sat next to his wife. As June had been the first time she held their baby, he was awestruck.

While the new parents grinned at each other over their beautiful sleeping baby, Priscilla slipped into the room to observe this special event. When Dick became aware of her presence, he asked if she wanted to hold the baby. "In a minute," she said. "For now though, I'll leave you alone to get acquainted with your daughter." Although she was anxious to get her hands on her first grandchild, she felt after days of forced separation, the little family needed to be alone for these first few minutes.

Since June wasn't going to be allowed out of bed for the next week, Priscilla stayed and took care of her and the baby. It felt good to be pampered and the new mother couldn't have been happier. She hadn't spent this much time with her mother since her parents had separated shortly after June's eleventh birthday. Just having given birth herself made her feel closer to her mother. June discovered that this week was not only a time to bond with her tiny daughter but with her mother as well. As usual, they steered clear of any talk about the years of their separation. Instead, they talked about the here and now...about this new child and all their hopes and dreams for her.

When June was finally allowed out of bed and her mother had gone home, she found that she took to being a mother like a bird to the sky. The only thing she didn't like was being awakened at all times of the night. Even though it seemed forever, that period finally passed...and she enjoyed everything about being a mother.

~

About this time, she started to hear radio commentators refer to the post war population explosion as baby-boomers. Sharlyn and every other baby who had been born after the men came home from the war would always be referred to by that title. There were already several baby-boomers in Dick and June's family and circle of friends. Dale and Vonnie. Rose and Johnny, Dick's Uncle Ray and his wife June, and his Uncle John and his wife Jean had produced baby boomers of their own. It created quite a picture when all the new mothers brought their babies to June's house for a shower. Between June's gleeful cries over the gifts, the women's chatter, and plus one or another of the babies crying, Dick wasn't even noticed when he came home from work. His usual greeting of, "Honey, I'm home," went unanswered. After watching and listening for a while he found himself beating a hasty retreat, ending up at Dale's house where they commiserated with each other about being neglected husbands.

June was too keyed up by the excitement from the party and the beautiful gifts the baby had received to notice that his nose was out of joint. He gradually got over it, though, when he watched her add each tiny piece of clothing to the already lavish layette the three grandmothers had given her. "When Mom made the sweater sets and shawls, and your mom bought her all those dresses, added to the gowns and jackets Polly made, I thought Sharlyn was going to be dressed like a little princess." She waved her arm to indicate the shower gifts and exclaimed, "Now, look at all this!"

Dick grinned and hugged her, all thought of being neglected forgotten at her little girl excitement. "Looks like we might need to have another one, so none of this will go to waste," he teased.

June flippantly retorted, "That's fine with me, but for the next one, you get to be pregnant!"

"You're kidding, aren't you? You do want to have other children, don't you?" he asked.

She didn't answer for so long that he wondered whether she'd heard him. When she did reply, her tone was thoughtful and serious. "I'm not ready to even think about it yet. I'm sure that someday, I'll want more children, but for now I'm satisfied with Sharlyn," she said. She didn't confide in him, but she still remembered the absent doctor and the trauma she'd suffered that night and knew it would be awhile, if ever, before she allowed herself to be in that situation again.

He interrupted her thoughts when he exclaimed, "I didn't mean now! I was thinking about a couple years from now."

"We'll see," she mumbled as she folded the last of the gifts and laid them on top of the others and closed the bulging dresser drawer. Other than telling her that he was leaving the decision up to her as to when and if they had more children, that was the end of that conversation.

During the rest of the fall and winter, the young parents visited both sets of Ohio parents several times. No matter where they went, they ended up taking second place to the new addition. June couldn't resist reminding Dick that he'd said he didn't like to play second fiddle. His only response was to grumble that this was different. Since neither Dick nor June had a sister, there were no aunts to fawn over the baby, but all the uncles were pleased with their new position. Dick had teased twelve-year-old Uncle Kenny about no longer being the baby in the family only to be ignored as the new uncle tickled the baby under the chin and grinned proudly when she flailed her arms. When Uncle Gene first saw her, he promised to spoil her and in months to come, he did everything in his power to make good on his promise.

When her Uncle Dickie first lifted Sharlyn from her bassinet, his face was crinkled in a wide grin. Her large dark eyes seemed to study his features, then as if she were giving her mark of approval; her face lit up in a returning smile. Pleased, Dickie declared, "This kid is a good judge of character."

June had particularly enjoyed this visit to Mansfield. The first thing she had done once she'd discarded her coat was to run her hands over her flat middle and haughtily tell her brother that he could no longer sing that June was busting out all over. It was obvious that she had returned to her pre-baby figure when she slipped on the new dress her mother had made for her. During the last few months of her pregnancy, when she'd been feeling shapeless, she'd seen Teresa Wright wear a sharp looking black scoop-necked dress in the movie *The Best Years Of Our Lives*. Coveting it, she'd asked her mother to copy it for her, and during this first visit Priscilla had surprised her with it.

The last of the uncles to see his new niece was Cecil, but once he could get a three-day pass from the base in Grosse Ile, Michigan, he met them in Mansfield. When he bounded up the steps to the porch on Arlington Avenue, he had his duffel bag slung over one shoulder and the biggest stuffed elephant that June had ever seen tucked under his other arm.

Without stopping to greet the rest of the family, he made a beeline to the couch where Sharlyn was sleeping. When he sat the mammoth sized grey elephant beside her, she opened her eyes and stared at it. June held her breath expecting her to cry but instead, her eyes sparkled in delight. The proud uncle stood back and grinned when he saw her reaction, and June exclaimed, "That is big enough to make three of her!"

BERLIN AIRLIFT

While the family had been happily getting acquainted with the newest addition, events had been taking place half a world away that would curtail this kind of family get-together. At the end of World War II, Berlin had been split into two sections with the Americans, British, and French occupying the western zone and the Soviet Union occupying the eastern zone. The division of the city had become a major Cold War issue between the two factions. Then in the winter, the Soviets had set up a land and water blockade that effectively shut off the food supply to West Berlin.

Harry S. Truman, the feisty President of the United States, was a little man who wouldn't accept any nonsense, so he ordered an airlift of food and water to the isolated area. In order to do this, planes loaded with supplies had to take off from West German air bases every three minutes, day and night, for months.

The Air Force asked the navy to provide round-the-clock Ground Control Radar operators. The navy selected three units to carry out this mission, one being Cecil's unit at Grosse Ile. After a short leave and intensive training in the use of the Air Force's equipment, Cecil was sent to Rhein Main Air Force Base in Frankfort Germany.

June worried about her brother and anxiously awaited a letter from him. When one finally arrived, she quickly read it, then when Dick got home from work she read it to him.

Hi June,

We arrived on March twenty-first in Frankfort, and I was really shocked by the total devastation, and that so few of the damaged buildings had been repaired since World War II ended four years ago. The work we're doing here is so intense that we are given more than the usual amount of leave. Certain areas are still off limits and we're restricted to within a fifty-mile radius of the base. Even within that limited area I have gotten to see some beautiful countryside. We took the train to Heidelberg where we toured some castles and other historic buildings. This town had been spared the destruction we saw in other areas. On another trip we went to a vineyard where they had a humongous oak barrel that stood twenty feet high. We were told that it held hundreds of gallons of wine. You would have thought with that much wine they would have offered us a sample, wouldn't you? (Ha)

I have met some wonderful German people since I got here. Although Germany was our enemy in the war, I find myself feeling a kinship with this land and the people since our Harman ancestors came from here. One of these days I would like to do some research and find out more about those ancestors....where they came from and why they decided to leave Germany and come to the states.

The job here is the most stressful I've ever had since I got in the Navy. Our eight hour day consists of alternating with one hour on the radar scope and one hour off. As the tremendous pressure of assisting the pilots to a safe landing in all types of weather is nerve wracking, we need the time off. You can't take your eyes off the screen for a second as there are always at least three blips on the ten mile final scope at a time. Normally there would be only one. The controller (yours truly) only has one minute to properly align the aircraft as to direction and altitude. It is imperative that instructions be clear and precise. As soon as the plane is on the runway, the one minute cycle is repeated over and over for the rest of the hour. We can't afford to make any mistakes as a missed approach would leave the pilot with limited places to land as when one plane lands, another one takes off.

As the planes land empty, they immediately taxi to a location for refueling, reloading, minor maintenance and a new crew to return to Berlin with their valuable contents of food, medicine and coal. Usually the planes are airborne within the hour. This operation is well planned and carried out as planes are landing and taking off every three minutes.

I don't know how long I will be here but I'm sure it will be until the Russians allow food and other supplies to get through to West Berlin. I sure would like to be back at Grosse Ile where I could get to see the family. I bet that niece of mine is really growing. Tell Dick hello and keep the letters coming.

Your brother,
Cecil

When she finished reading the letter, Dick said, "His work does sound nerve wracking. He didn't tell you, but I bet he and his buddies relax over some German beer when they get off duty."

"Why not? He's of age !" June retorted. "If you're so curious, I'll write and ask him."

Dick couldn't resist teasing, "While you're writing, ask if he has met any beautiful frauleins."

She quickly responded, "As I said before, he is of age, but if you are so curious, I'll ask him."

～

The next day while Sharlyn was napping and Dick at work June wrote and asked her brother about his social life specifically about beer drinking and German girls.

His response was quick and to the point.

Dear June,

You can tell Dick that I have tried the German beer. I can't get used to the fact that the Germans serve it warm as they do all their drinks. I prefer my beer ice cold served in a frosted glass. As for the frauleins, I haven't actually met any but I have seen some beautiful ones.

Recently my buddy, Bob, and I spent a week in Garmish in the German Alps. Those snow covered peaks were the most beautiful sights I've ever seen. After our week in the snow, I can understand the fascination people have for the winter season. We enjoyed seeing the skaters on the ice and the skiers weaving and bobbing down the slopes, especially at night with their torches held high. Tell Dick that we also enjoyed relaxing with a good hot toddy by the fire as we watched the frauleins stroll by.

Your brother,
Cecil

Cecil turned out to be a prolific letter writer keeping his sister informed about his experience in Germany. Then early in July of 1949 he wrote:

Dear June

You have probably heard that after thirteen months of the airlift the Russians have lifted the blockade and food and other supplies are now getting through. We have been notified that our unit will be leaving here in July and I will be coming home soon. We're going to catch a ride home on one of the Navy planes to our station in Grosse Ile in Michigan. As soon as I get a few days off I'll go to Mansfield and will expect to see you there.

While this is a beautiful country, there is certainly truth to the saying that there is no place like home. I can hardly wait to plant my feet on good old American soil and see my family again.

Love from your brother,
Cecil

MEET YOUR FIRST GRANDCHILD

June and Dick weren't there to greet him, though, instead while he was in a naval plane winging across the ocean, they were in their car heading for Mississippi. When they arrived at the farm in Mississippi, Sharlyn was two months shy of her first birthday...old enough to relish the attention she received from this set of grandparents and great-grandparents. The little uncles, Freddy and Billy, took the attention she received in stride. After looking her over, they went back to their play as if this were an everyday occurrence.

Polly and Nanny were happy to show them around the new house that they'd so recently moved into. The visitors commented on the difference from their last visit when these spacious rooms were little more than a shell. The sun that was filtered through the sheer fabric that curtained the large windows cast soft shadows on the white walls. The country style furniture, the soft rugs scattered across the bare wooden floors and the splashes of color from the vases of wild flowers on every available surface created a welcoming atmosphere.

When Polly showed them to their quarters, they found that even though Billy's crib had been moved into this large airy guest room, the room was large enough to accommodate all three of them. While June unpacked the suitcase, the young grandmother hoisted Sharlyn on her hip, and told June how pretty she thought the baby looked in the pink eyelet embroidered pinafore she'd made for her. "When I was making it," Polly said, "I wondered if she'd look good in pink. Since I wasn't sure, I also made one in blue and another in white."

"I'm sure glad you did," June replied. "I brought all of them, so you'd get to see how pretty she looks in each one."

Polly switched Sharlyn to her other hip, and in a mock serious voice said to June, "When I first saw you run down that hill toward your daddy and me at your Aunt Calcie's house, I never thought you'd do this to me."

Puzzled, June asked, "What did I do?"

Polly's voice still held the somber tone when she proclaimed, "You made me a grandmother when I wasn't quite twenty-nine years old...that's what!"

June laughed and stuck out her tongue at this irrepressible woman before she retorted, "I'd be lying if I said that I was sorry. Besides, you're giving a good impression of enjoying it." Polly had to admit that she was pleased with her new station in life. She went on to bemoan the fact that she wouldn't be able to see the grandbaby more often.

June's reply of, "Well you know how to remedy that," was met with silence. Apparently, becoming a grandmother wasn't enough enticement to bring her back up north. Since June knew that there was nothing she could do to change this woman's mind, she decided it would be better to drop the subject.

The rest of the day went quickly, and soon after the mantle clock struck six, June heard the sound of a car braking to a stop behind the yellow Ford in the circular driveway. She barely felt her feet hit the porch steps as she propelled herself toward the long legged man as he stepped out of the car. "Dad," she yelled as he grabbed her in a bear hug.

Once they'd untangled themselves, father and daughter stood back and appraised each other. "You look great!" June said.

Burrel told her, "Motherhood seems to agree with you." Then before she could reply, he asked, "Where's that grandchild of mine?" For the next few minutes, it was June's turn to feel neglected as all the attention went to her child. The feeling didn't last long as she sat back and basked in her father's praise of her offspring. As June had when she first saw her daughter, the new grandfather commented that he thought his granddaughter was going to have the Harman's long fingers.

"And her father's little ears!" June quipped. When her remark was met with puzzled glances, she explained that it was a private joke between her and her husband.

Dick looked uncomfortable when he muttered under his breath, "Some joke."

The next day dawned bright and clear, so while Burrel was at work, Polly decided it was a perfect day to take them into Brandon for lunch at a small cafe on the main street. When she eased into a parking place in front of the low slung wooden building, she told them, "It's not fancy, but the food is good."

When the three adults were seated at the booth, the waitress brought a high chair for Sharlyn. It took them a few minutes to get her settled, and the boys took advantage of the distraction to wander off to explore their surroundings. When they ambled back to the table, Polly noticed their jaws move up and down in a chewing motion. "What are you boys eating?" she asked.

In response, four year old Freddy pulled a big wad out of his mouth, and proudly held it up for all to see before he said, "Chewing gum." His three-year old brother reached in his mouth and plucked an even bigger glob as he echoed his brother's words.

Polly leaned forward and addressed both boys. "Did the nice waitress give you each a stick of gum?"

Freddy's reply of, "Naw, she didn't give us none. We found it stuck under the tables!" brought a howl from his mother. Then while everyone stared at the gooey mess each boy held in his hand, Freddy turned to his sister and informed her that there was a lot more...if she wanted some, he'd get it.

Polly's exclamation of "Oh, no!" was almost lost in the uproar the boys raised when she grabbed the offending gum from their hands and tossed it in an ashtray. June and Dick tried to calm the boys' outrage, but they weren't to be comforted until a piping plate of French fries with a juicy hamburger on the side was set before each of them.

Gulping down their food kept them occupied while their mother explained about germs and instructed them to never do a thing like that again. "Do you understand?" she demanded. Although both boys angelically replied that they did, their sister thought she saw a glint in their eyes that made her wonder about the sincerity of that promise.

For the rest of the visit, though, the boys were as playful as a couple of puppies and all evidence indicated that they weren't going to try that trick again. If not that, Polly wondered, what would be next? These boys always managed to keep her on her toes.

The day before Dick and June headed for home, a letter arrived from Dickie. When Burrel slit it open and read it, a pleased expression crossed his face. "He sounds like he's fine. Working, as usual. Even though it's been two years since he spent six weeks here with us, he writes that he has good memories of the farm," Burrel said.

"That was a nice visit," Polly mused. "Burrel taught him to drive." With a chuckle she added, "I think he was a better student than I was when your dad taught me."

Her comment brought a flood of memories to June's mind of when they had lived in Maryland. The picture of her thirteen year old self and fifteen year old brother, Cecil, in the back seat of her father's Chevrolet with Polly at the wheel was as vivid as if it had only taken place yesterday. "I'll never forget that!" June cried. "When you almost went down that embankment, Cecil thought you were going to kill us all."

"Even though Dickie was only fifteen, he was a fast learner," Burrel chuckled at the memory before he went on with his story. "I'll never forget how proud he was when he passed the driver's test and got his license."

"How'd he get his license if he was only fifteen?" Dick asked. "He didn't fib about his age, did he?"

"No, nothing like that. You only have to be fifteen in Mississippi to get a license," Burrel explained. June noticed a faraway expression in her father's eyes as the conversation wafted around him. When he finally spoke, his voice was soft and pensive. "That was the longest Dickie and I have had a chance to be together since the divorce. He came down on the train to stay with us for six weeks, and even when Mace and Mabel arrived and offered to let him ride back with them, he turned them down. He said that he didn't want to miss any of the time he could be here."

June patted her father's hand and smiled in understanding. Before the conversation could continue, she heard the baby cry. The young grandmother jumped up and on her way to the bedroom, told June that she would get Sharlyn. A few minutes later she reappeared with the baby cradled in her arms. "Your MawMaw has you," she crooned. In response, Sharlyn flashed her spanking new baby teeth at her redheaded grandmother. "You want to be called MawMaw?" June asked.

"That's not what either of her other grandmothers want to be called?" she anxiously asked.

June chuckled, "No. That's a new one. Mom wants to be called Gram and Dick's mother, Rowie."

Burrel chimed in with, "She can call me plain ole granddad."

"You're not old!" June cried. "You're only forty-six."

"You'll be saying that when I'm a hundred," Burrel joked. To which June replied that she hoped so.

Burrel changed the subject when he said, "I hate to break this up, but you have a long trip ahead of you tomorrow. We'd better turn in."

Although they would have liked to stay up all night and talk, they knew that he was right. So they reluctantly said goodnight and traipsed off to their room. While they were getting ready for bed, Dick dropped a bombshell when he said, "Did your father tell you that he might be going to Pennsylvania to work?"

"No!" June exclaimed. "When did he tell you?"

"This evening when we walked down to the pond," he replied. "He said it wasn't definite yet, but he's been working with the union to see if they could set something up," he explained.

"Are Mom and the boys coming too?" June anxiously whispered.

"He said that they'd stay here. He'd just have to get back to see them whenever he could," Dick replied.

Her husband's words played in her mind as she tossed and turned while the sound of the crickets and bullfrogs wafted through the open windows. June was bleary eyed from lack of sleep when she stumbled to the breakfast table the next morning. Although she wanted to find a moment to talk to her father before he left early that morning for work, the opportunity never presented itself. The closest her father came to giving her the merest hint of his plans was when his lips brushed her cheek in a farewell kiss and he whispered, "I hope to see you soon."

～

Before they got on the road that morning, June pulled Dick aside and whispered, "I need to talk to Polly before we leave. Can you keep the others occupied so I can have a few minutes alone with her?"

"Are you kidding?" he asked. "I'll find something that will keep them glued to their seats." With a jaunty salute, he walked away to carry out his assigned mission.

Once June and Polly had settled in the rocking chairs on the front porch June said, "I was thinking about something this morning and I was wondering if you remembered it."

Polly smiled fondly at her daughter and said, "What were you thinking about?"

"I was remembering when Dad was working on the Seaplane Base at Great Mills in Maryland and the only place he could find for us to live was in a trailer in the middle of a junkyard."

Polly exclaimed, "How could I ever forget that place and those horrible people who owned it! Those terrible Overbys!"

"They sure were," June said. "I wasn't thinking so much of them as I was of the tavern they had on the bank above the junkyard. I remember how we could hear the music from the jukebox from our front patio. Ramon, the boy I liked at school, was always talking about his record collection and the different popular singers and bandleaders. I felt bad because since we didn't have a record player I didn't know any of them."

Polly let her gaze roam across the field of wildflowers beyond the porch. June could tell, though, that she wasn't seeing the flowers but in her mind's eye she was viewing that junkyard they called home and the tavern above it. "I remember how much you wanted to go up there to listen to the music so you would be familiar with the songs Ramon talked about."

June asked, "Do you remember that you talked Dad into taking you, me and Cecil to the tavern one Saturday for lunch and to listen to the jukebox? We not only heard the music but got an earful of the talk swirling around us." Polly nodded before June continued, "There were several men in there by themselves who confided in anyone who would listen that their wives thought it would be an embarrassment to live like vagabonds going from place to place in, of all things, a trailer."

June hoped that this woman who was so important in her life would remember and apply what she was about to say to the present situation before she added, "Since being together as a family was so important to us you couldn't contain yourself, you jumped up and very firmly told them that they should tell their wives there was nothing embarrassing about going with your man or living in a trailer if that was what it took to keep the family together. You told them you would be there with your man even if you had to live in a tent. Then if I recall correctly, you told them to invite their wives to come and you would show them how each of these women was making a home for her family." June sighed deeply before she added, "I didn't care where we lived, just that we could all be together as a family. I hate to see Billy and Freddy deprived of what we had. Didn't you think that it was good?"

Polly was quiet for so long that June was afraid she had gone too far, but when she spoke it was clear that her comments had given her young mother something to think about. Polly replied, "I do remember, and I felt the same way that you did at the time."

"If it was important for, you, me, Cecil and Dad to be together then, why wouldn't it be for you, Dad, Freddy and Billy to be now?" June asked.

Before Polly could reply, the screen door slammed open and Freddy and Billy hit the porch floor running. Dick who was only a few steps behind them said, "I couldn't keep these wildcats in the house any longer. I thought about tying them to their chairs with a rope but their grandmother wouldn't let me use her clothesline."

Hearing the ruckus, the rest of the household gathered on the porch to tell them goodbye and wish them a safe journey. June realized that there was no way she and Polly would be able to finish the conversation. With unanswered questions in her eyes, and with Sharlyn in her arms, she got into the car with her husband and joined in the chorus of good-byes that were coming from the people they were leaving behind. She and Sharlyn waved until Dick had maneuvered his way out of the circular drive and turned north for the trip home.

As the miles whipped away, June told Dick about her conversation with Polly. "I didn't have a chance to remind her of something else that we saw in that tavern," June said.

"What was that?' Dick asked.

"We observed the man that we'd heard complain the loudest about his wife refusing to join him. He was sitting in a back booth with a pretty young blond woman. They were being pretty lovey-dovey, if you know what I mean."

Dick grinned and quipped, "I get the picture."

"At first we thought his wife had changed her mind and joined him, but the gossips soon put us straight about that. Apparently, he got tired of waiting for her to change her mind and found someone else," June explained.

"Is your point that you think your dad would take up with another woman if Polly left him alone too long?" her husband asked. "Do you actually believe that?"

June sighed before she responded, "No I don't think that would happen, but I'd plant the idea in her head if I thought it would shake her up enough to get her and the boys to join Dad."

"I hate to say this but it really isn't up to you to interfere," Dick reminded her.

"You may be right," she said. "I'll think about it."

She kept her word and did give it some though before she made up her mind. Then she sat down and wrote Polly a letter. When it winged its way from Ohio to Mississippi, it contained the rest of the story of the lonely man in the tavern in Mississippi. With the letter on its way, June wondered if she might have gone too far. That night after a few hours of counting sheep while she worried about it, she decided, "I did what I thought was the right thing, but then, time will tell." With this thought in mind, she turned over and went to sleep.

LIFE DOES CHANGE

One of the first things they did when they returned to Ohio was to have a reunion with Cecil at their mother's house in Mansfield. When he arrived he had three of his navy buddies in tow. After being introduced to his friends, the tallest of the trio responded to the introduction by saying, "When Skip told us what a great cook his mother is, even the military police couldn't keep us away."

This was the first but not the last time the family was to hear Cecil's new nickname, and though it sounded strange to their ears, June found that she liked it. Before she, Dick, and Sharlyn left for Newark, she had a moment alone with her brother and asked him if he wanted the family to use his nickname. His response that he liked it and would like to be called Skip from now on decided the issue for June.

"You've been Cece or Cecil to me every since I can remember, but if that's what you want to be called I'll try," she promised. For the next year or two, he generally ended up being addressed as, "Cece...I mean Skip," by the entire family until it became natural to call him by his navy nickname.

While she was still adjusting to that change, Dick's brother Gene went to work at Jay King's Barber Shop in the Arcade downtown and his employer started to call him by his first name, Eddie. Soon afterwards, he let it be known that was what he wanted to be called from now on.

"I have to learn a new name for Cecil and now one for Gene!" June told Dickie on one of his visits. "You're not going to change yours are you?"

He wrinkled his forehead and raked his hands through his dark blond hair before asserting, "I am a little too old to be called Dickie! It's about time everyone started to call me Dick. That's what I'm called in school."

June threw up her hands in resignation, before she replied, "Why not? I guess this is as good a time as ever!"

Since within a couple weeks of this conversation, Dickie was to become a member of the Oakwood Avenue household, June found that the timing couldn't have been worse. Since it was too confusing having two people in one household with the same name, most of the time her younger brother still found himself being called Dickie.

～

A couple weeks into the school year, he'd had a problem with his coach that was going to keep him off the football team at Mansfield High School. A born athlete, he couldn't imagine not being able to play. This led to a family pow-wow, and with his approval, Priscilla and the young couple decided that he would come to Newark and stay with Dick and June for that school year. By the beginning of October, he was not so comfortably ensconced on their living room couch. June knew this wasn't the ideal sleeping arrangement but since a short time earlier, they'd turned the upper story of their house into an apartment that was currently rented, there was no other place for him to sleep. The first night when he prepared to bunk down, Dick reminded him that it could have been worse. "You can thank my grandmother for not being gouged by springs all night long."

As Dickie patted the soft cushions, he retorted, "Thank your grandma for me!"

The new addition to their household fit in well. Dick liked his young brother-in-law and was pleased to have him around. Since the brother and sister had not lived under the same roof since their parents' divorce, when he was eight and she was eleven, they both enjoyed being together.

One change they noticed immediately, though, was that the presence of a handsome teen-age boy in the house brought an influx of teen-age girls into the neighborhood. Hardly a morning passed, when he went out to get into his car for his drive to school, that he didn't find a mushy note stuck under his windshield wiper. He seemed to take this in stride although his sister teased him about his adoring fans.

Dickie doted on his little niece, and she thought her young uncle was wonderful. That winter, June would bundle her up in her little red snow suit, and he'd take her with him when he went to see his girlfriends. As he'd drive down the street, Sharlyn always stood on the seat close to him with her arm draped around his neck. "You'd be surprised at the girls' reaction when they see us together," he told June and Dick one evening after he'd brought Sharlyn back from a visit to a girl's house.

June teasingly commented that she understood now why he liked to take Sharlyn along. "You've got to be kidding," he flashed back. "I love to have her with me. We're buddies!" One look at his earnest face told her that he really meant it.

While he liked having his little niece around, he did despise one thing about living with them. It was the humungous cast-iron coal heating stove that occupied one entire corner of the kitchen. Not only did the monster devour buckets of coal on a daily basis, but it put out an equal amount of ashes that had to be scooped out and hauled to the trash barrel. Since Dick could manage to out wait Dickie, its care and feeding soon fell to the younger boy. Many a morning, Dick and June would awake to the sound of her brother vigorously shaking the ashes while giving the monstrosity a piece of his mind.

One morning as the sounds wafted into their bedroom, June told her husband, "I don't blame him one bit. Besides being so much work, it's an eyesore." Dick had gotten to know this woman he'd married pretty well, and he could anticipate her next words. She didn't disappoint him. "It's time we got rid of it, and put in an automatic furnace," she announced. "Now that we have the new sink in the kitchen and our nice table and chairs, the stove spoils the whole room!"

"I can just hear Dad's comments if I tell him that we're putting in a furnace. He thinks nothing can heat as well as a coal stove," Dick said.

"Just like he didn't think anything except a wringer style Maytag could get the clothes clean," June reminded him. He noticed her chin shoot forward, and he knew it would be futile to argue with her, especially when she added, "After all, this is nineteen fifty. We're going into the second half of the century and everyone has automatic heat."

"Next winter," he promised. While she would rather have had one installed immediately, she graciously accepted her victory in the form of a radiant smile and a big kiss to his lips.

~

When Dickie had first enrolled in Newark High School, he'd met the coach, Mack Douglas. When Mr. Douglas heard about the newcomer's experience in sports, he took an immediate interest in him. While it was too late in the season when Dickie enrolled for him to play football, he quickly recruited him for the basketball team. The day of his try out, he beat out a six-foot-three boy for the position of center.

The young couple encouraged him during pre-season practice, then once the season started, Dick attended every one of the home games while June stayed home with Sharlyn. During each game, she'd put Sharlyn to bed then curl up on the couch and listen to the play-by-play account on the radio. The announcer would get so excited that he would almost shout out each play. By the end of the game, though, his voice would be raspy.

At the beginning of the season while June listened to a game, she heard the announcer shout, "MACK DOUGLAS CALLS DICK HARMAN MANSFIELD'S GIFT TO NEWARK! THE WAY THAT BOY PLAYS, I CAN AGREE WITH MACK!" Later June smiled when she heard him rasp, "Dick Harman isn't very tall, only around six-foot-one, but look at him sink that basket."

Later when she related that comment to Dick and Dickie, they both told her that several of the players were even taller. Before the season was over, she was able to get a baby-sitter and to go with Dick to a game. She was forced to admit though grudgingly that a few, but not all, were possibly a smidgen taller.

For the rest of the school year, the new family of four enjoyed their life together especially during Sharlyn's second Christmas. This year she was old enough to be fascinated by the lights on the Christmas tree and the presents she found under it.

The only problem during Dickie's stay was his elderly car. A nineteen thirty-seven Ford, it snorted and wheezed as it chugged down Oakwood Avenue every weekday morning when he was on his way to the high school on West Main Street in downtown Newark. He'd stop on Lawrence Street for Annamae and then a few streets away for his friend, Wanda.

Since this vehicle had mechanical brakes that could only be adjusted manually from underneath the car, it wasn't unusual either in front of the house on Oakwood Avenue or anywhere along his destination, to see the car stopped and a pair of long legs with size twelve shoes peeking out from underneath while Dickie performed the manipulations.

He confided later that since the car was so unreliable he seldom drove it when he went to Mansfield to see his mother. Instead, he'd park it somewhere on the north side of Newark and hitch-hike the rest of the way.

~

When the month of June arrived, he surprised his sister and brother-in-law with the announcement that he had joined the navy. His father who had accepted the job in Pennsylvania and was now living close to Pittsburgh had signed for him to enlist. When June asked why their mother hadn't done it, he simply replied, "Dad is my legal guardian."

June told her little brother, "I don't want you to be in any danger."

He replied, "Gosh June, World War II has been over for four years."

Our country was at peace on June twenty-sixth when he was inducted into the navy, but the Korean War started the next day. This was on June and Dick's minds as they watched the young recruit board the train at Pennsylvania Station in downtown Newark for the trip to San Diego for thirteen weeks of boot camp. After they stood and waved until even the caboose was out of sight, Dick turned to his wife and muttered, "Rotten timing! Enlist right before a war starts!" June glumly nodded her head in agreement. As they walked back to the car, she worried about how this war was going to affect the people she loved. Skip (Cecil) who was already in the navy, would he be sent to Korea? Would Dickie? How about Dick's brother Eddie (Gene)? He was at draft age as were her own schoolmates.

Selfishly, she was glad that Dick had already served his time in the army. As it turned out, she discovered that might not make a difference in this crazy undeclared war. Several former service men had been recalled. She heard this news blared out of her green plastic radio one morning while she watched Sharlyn spoon cereal into her mouth.

As soon as she had her daughter tucked into her crib for a nap, she called Vonnie, then Rose. It turned out that they'd heard the same newscast and were as concerned about the situation as she was. They all shared the same opinion, though. If their husbands were called up, they would all become camp followers and go with their husbands wherever they were sent until they were shipped overseas.

June declared to Rose, "My family isn't going to be separated by orders from Uncle Sam!" Rose replied that she felt the same way. While she and her friends were making this vow, June was gazing around the room at the beauty she had spent so much time creating. She hated the thought that she might have to leave it. She knew that wouldn't be as bad, though, as being left behind.

When Dick came home that evening, he quickly put her fears to rest. "The only ones who are being called back are the ones who signed up for the reserves. Dale, Johnny, and I didn't do that. Although that monthly check I would have gotten was tempting, I'd had my share of the army life. I didn't even want to be a once a month soldier!"

She threw her arms around his neck and tearfully told him how happy she was. In typical male fashion, he asked, "If you're so happy, why are you crying?"

She dabbed her tear stained eyes, gave her long blond hair a toss and flippantly replied, "Being a man, you just wouldn't understand."

"Try me," he muttered, as he pulled her onto his lap.

At the sound of her father's voice, two-year-old Sharlyn had slipped out of the crib and ran into the living room. "Daddy," she yelled as she joined her mother on his lap. When she wrapped her arms around his neck and kissed him, she was rewarded with a kiss and hug from both of her parents.

June managed to disentangle herself and head for the kitchen to put the finishing touches on their dinner. Before she left the room, she turned and watched the tender scene of father and daughter sitting together on the couch, and breathed a silent prayer of thanks that their life wasn't going to be interrupted by this faraway war.

∼

In this fall of nineteen fifty, when Sharlyn turned two, all June's friends and cousins had already had their second child, or had one on the way. Rose's second baby was due in December. When June had remarked that it would be a wonderful Christmas present, Rose had asked June when she and Dick were going to have another one.

As she had told all the friends and relatives who had asked her that same question, she said she was happy with the one she had. While Dick hadn't pressured her to have any more children, his mother and grandmother Lula had. "It's selfish to raise a child alone. Sharlyn needs a brother or sister," they had chorused.

After a steady dose of these comments, June began to feel guilty. She wondered, "Am I actually depriving this child that I love so much? Am I really being selfish?" All she really wanted was what was best for her child.

Later when she talked to Dick about her uncertainty, he told her that she shouldn't let anyone rush her into anything. "I would like to have other children, but if you want to wait a while, that's alright with me," he informed her.

His comment, along with the urgings from her friends, his mother, and his grandmother helped change her mind. She announced to Dick, "If you really want more children, it might as well be now…so they won't be too far apart."

She was surprised at his enthusiastic reaction of, "Great, I'm so happy! Let's get started now!"

As she looked into his twinkling eyes and saw his big grin, she asked, "Why didn't you tell me you wanted other children that much?"

She was touched when he replied, "Since you're the one who has to carry it, I think it has to be your decision."

In over a month, she was able to tell him that they were going to be parents again. "I haven't been to the doctor yet, but according to my calculations, it should be here in July," she said.

While they'd been planning to increase their family, many of their friends were also adding to their households. This addition was not of the human variety, although it seemed to demand as much attention as a child. It was a television set, a new invention that had recently come on the market. This magic box had begun to crop up in appliance and furniture stores all over town. One afternoon on a walk around the square when June and Dick saw a crowd gathered in front of a store window, they strolled over to see what had caught everyone's attention. When they got close enough to see inside the store window, Dick said, "They're watching television."

June peered in the window and remarked, "I think that is Search for Tomorrow, the soap opera I listen to on the radio." They stood and watched for a few minutes then they sauntered away. "Good way to get people interested," June mused.

"Uh oh," Dick thought. "From the tone of her voice that ploy certainly worked on her." His wife was definitely interested. He wondered how long it would be until she told him.

∼

Joby, the leader of the band Dick played in, and his wife, Rachel, had bought one. One Saturday night, Rachel asked June and Sharlyn to come to her house on Cedar Street to watch television while the men played for a dance.

When June walked in, she noticed that the big walnut cabinet seemed to dominate one entire wall of the tiny living room. After the men left for their job, June and Rachel pulled their chairs close so they could see the tiny screen while

Sharlyn and Jody, Rachel's three year old son, sat at their feet with their eyes fixed on the shadowy figures on the screen.

Although the movie they watched appeared to have come from the deep recesses of an ancient movie vault, and that there seemed to be a blizzard between it and the audience, they were enthralled. Movies in your own living room! What would be next?

For the next few weeks, after Dick had listened to June's enthusiastic chatter about the television set, one day during his lunch hour he stopped at Airesman Appliance Store and talked to Dick Baker, the owner. While they talked, they wandered around the large showroom that was filled with television sets. There were a variety of cabinet styles and sizes, some had screens as small as seven inches while others were as large as ten. When Dick didn't quickly make up his mind on the make or model, Mr. Baker said, "Just pick one, and I'll set it in your house for you for a two week trial." When Dick hesitated, the other man added, "There won't be any obligation. In fact, if you don't like it, we'll let you try out others until you find one that you do like."

For the next few weeks, a regular parade of television sets made their way through the house on Oakwood Avenue. True to his word, Mr. Baker let them try out as many as they wanted, but none was exactly what they wanted. June had her heart set on one in blond wood to match their other furniture while Dick wanted one with a larger screen. So far, none fitting that description had materialized.

Surprisingly, the answer to their quandary came from Dick's Uncle Alvin when he stopped in for a visit. When he saw the television set of the week, he asked if they'd bought it. When Dick told him they hadn't found what they wanted, he steered them to a friend of his in Grove City who sold television sets from his front-room store. "My friend's slogan is if I don't have it I can get it," he pronounced before he got on the phone and called him. As it turned out, he had a blond Philco table model with a twelve-inch screen in stock.

Before Dick's uncle left that evening, they arranged to meet him the next night so he could take them to his friend's house. They found exactly what they wanted and at only three hundred and seventy-five dollars it was at least a hundred and twenty-five dollars less than the ones they'd been trying out. Although it was heavy and bulky, the three men managed to wrestle it into the car.

When June and Dick got to the house on Oakwood Avenue, it was a different matter. June found herself called upon to help Dick lift it out of the car, carry it up the porch steps, and into the living room. All the effort was worth it when they set it in place on the matching stand they'd also purchased.

They immediately turned it on, but at that time of night, all they got was the test pattern. "At least, it's pretty clear," June quipped before she flipped off the switch.

The next day, she and Sharlyn spent a great deal of their time before the set. This was only partly because of its newness. The main reason, though, was that June wasn't feeling well. The slight crampy feeling that had started during the night had continued throughout the day. By the time Dick came home from work, she was sure that she was going to miscarry this baby. By morning this was a reality.

She was feeling numb and a little weak from the shock of losing her baby just hours before, when the shrill ring of the telephone jolted her back to reality. Not being aware of June's sad news, Rose's happy voice announced, "June, I'm calling from my hospital room. I had a baby boy. We're going to call him Little Johnny."

Though sad for her own loss, she was still pleased that all had gone well for Rose, but thought how ironic it was that she had lost her baby on the same day her cousin had given birth.

Aside from suffering the physical effect, June was also feeling pangs of guilt. She knew that she hadn't been as enthusiastic about this pregnancy as she had been about the first one. On the other hand, Dick was blaming himself for letting her help with the television set. When she talked to the doctor, he assured her that neither one of them was at fault.

A few days later, while Sharlyn was napping June settled down in a comfortable chair in front of the television set to watch the characters she had gotten to know on the radio soap opera. Footsteps on the porch let her know that the mailman had left some mail in the box. The soap opera was forgotten when she opened the letter from Polly and read what she had written.

Dear June,

I have been thinking about what you said when you were here about how important it was to you when you were growing up for us to be a family. The more I thought about it, the more I realized that by staying with my parents instead of going with my husband, I was being unfair not only to Burrel, but to our sons. I got to thinking about our vagabond years when you and Cecil were at home, and how much we enjoyed being a family and our time together. I think that I owe as much to Freddy and Billy.

Your dad has gotten us a place to live near McKeyssport, Pennsylvania. It's in the country but close to where he'll be working in Pittsburgh. You remember how your dad was about not wanting you kids to live in the city. He's going to be the same with Freddy and Billy. We'll be there and settled in before Christmas. I hope you can all come and spend the holidays with us.

With love,
Mom

P.S. Thanks for reminding me of what is important!

June reread the letter to make sure she hadn't misread it the first time. There was no mistaking it. Polly had listened to what she had told her and had remembered.

As soon as Dick got in the door that evening, she showed him the letter and told him she would like to invite her dad, Polly and the boys to spend Christmas with them. "They'll just be getting settled in their new home. That's not the time to have guests. Besides I got a letter from Skip and one from Dickie. They're both going to be here on leave for Christmas. I'd like to invite them too."

"Are you sure you're up to it?" Dick asked. "I don't want you to overdo."

June assured him that she was fine. "It will cheer me up to be with my family. If I need any help, Mom will pitch in."

Though the entire family couldn't arrange to come at the same time, June was able to have separate visits to lift her spirits. Skip and Dickie had been able to come to Newark together a few days before Christmas for a quick visit to catch up with the family before heading back to their duties. They both looked very handsome in their naval uniforms.

Then a few days later, her parents and her two little brothers joined them at her house on Christmas Eve. June looked around the room at the brightly decorated tree, the gaily wrapped packages, the candles reflected in the mirror above the mantle, and was happy with the way everything looked. Nothing could compare, though, with the happiness she felt to see her dad, Polly, Freddy and Billy together as a family.

Later after the gifts were exchanged, the last drop of eggnog consumed, and good nights said, as June and Dick snuggled in their bed, she whispered, "I got what I wanted for Christmas this year."

"You mean me?" he teased.

"Of course you, but I was talking about Dad, Polly and the boys together at last." June was quiet for so long that her husband thought she had drifted off to sleep when she said, "I overheard Dickie and Skip talking the other night about reenlisting. Skip said he was seriously thinking about it, maybe even making it a career."

"How about Dickie? What does he plan to do?" Dick asked.

June laughed, "He said, though he hasn't been in for long, he can't wait to get out, and that he hates his job as a sonar operator. He can even hear that blasted sonar beep in his sleep."

"I know how Dickie feels. I didn't have to listen to the sonar like he does but when the war was over, I couldn't wait to become a civilian again," Dick murmured before he drifted off to sleep.

A PEN PAL BRIDE AND GROOM

When the new year got into full swing, a host of changes took place in the country and in the life of June and her family. The Korean War, still considered a police action, continued to rage with no sign of victory while Congress and President Truman argued the pros and cons of fighting an undeclared war.

In their family life, Dickie had been assigned as a sonar operator on a destroyer, the USS Hickox. Since the ship had been removed from mothballs for active duty, a great deal of work had to be done on it before it could be sent into the fray. After thirty days of quarantine, the ship started a zigzag journey that took all of that year.

Before they finally arrived in the war zone, the USS Hickox had gone to San Francisco to be fitted with new guns, then through the Panama Canal to Rhode Island and on to Newport, Virginia for more improvements. After that, they sailed back through the Panama Canal to San Diego, then on to Hawaii where they spent a week. Before the ship had reached the offshore waters of the Sea of Japan, they'd lost a day as they crossed the one hundred-degree meridian. They eventually arrived off shore of North Korea where they maintained a steady six month bombardment.

At the time this was going on in Dickie's life, Skip's unit was being sent to Atsuga, Japan to activate a Ground Control Approach Radar Unit. They were replacing a marine group that had been dispatched to active duty in Korea.

Shortly after Skip had gotten to Japan, his mother had given his name to a young redheaded co-worker, and the two young people had been keeping the postal service busy with their letters. Neither had expected to meet in person until after his three year stint in Japan was over. This changed though when he became ill and had to be returned to the states for surgery.

As it turned out, he was sent to the naval hospital at Great Lakes, Illinois, and it was close enough that he was able to get home on leave. After surgery and a six-week recuperation period, he was able to spend thirty days as he pleased. When he left the hospital, he made a beeline for Mansfield to spend the leave at his mother's house on Arlington Avenue. After briefly greeting his mother, he headed for the redhead's house. Since Skip and his pen pal, JoAnne Long, had already become interested in each other through their letters, they had a head start on love at first sight. In case there had been any doubt in either of their minds, there was none by the time his leave was over.

For the first time since he'd been in the navy, he spent all his leave time in Mansfield. "I guess if we're going to get to see him or meet this woman, we'll have to go to Mansfield," June told Dick.

"I think you're right," he replied. "It looks to me like you're going to have a sister-in-law before too long. If he won't bring her down here, then we'll just go up there so we can meet her."

June had some news that she was anxious to share with her mother and brother, but first she wanted to hear about Skip's romance and to meet his redheaded girl friend. She and her mother were sitting at the kitchen table sipping coffee and watching Sharlyn chase Shorty, Priscilla's tiny bulldog, around the room when June asked her mother what she thought about Skip's big romance.

"When I gave JoAnne his name and address, I never thought they'd get together. I just thought it would be nice for him to have someone to write to," Priscilla said.

"Don't you like her?" June asked.

"Sure I do. I wouldn't have given her his address unless I did," she replied. "In fact, I wouldn't be surprised if we have a wedding before he has to return." June grinned in delight, but in the back of her mind was the nagging thought that if that happened, she might not be able to be in the wedding party. Her mother gave her a quizzical glance when she murmured, "If they do it, I hope it's going to be soon."

Before Priscilla could voice her question, they heard the door open and the sound of Skip and a female's voice in the living room. By the time June and her mother had made their way into the other room, Dick and Bill had already greeted the young couple. This gave June time to observe what a very nice looking couple they made. The attractive young woman, who stood next to June's six-foot tall brother, had flaming red hair, and a sprinkling of freckles. She looked to be about five-foot tall with her head barely coming to Skip's shoulders.

June had been prepared to like her prospective sister-in-law because her brother did, and she soon found that was going to be easy. The girl was warm and friendly, and June was looking forward to having her in the family.

Before June, Dick, and Sharlyn left for home that evening, Skip told them that he had to return to the hospital in a few days. "I have to have the same surgery for the other arm that I had on this one," he said as he flexed his right arm. "I'll be back in the hospital for another six weeks, then I'll get another thirty day leave." While he was speaking, he and JoAnne exchanged knowing glances. June suspected that before the next leave was over an engagement would be announced.

As it turned out, the engagement was in the works even earlier than that. Before their announcement was made, though, June couldn't put off the one she had to make. She excitedly broke the news that Sharlyn was going to have a little brother or sister in February. During this pregnancy, she found that she was as anxious now as she had been reluctant earlier to have another child.

Once she was expecting, she confided in Dick that she felt strongly that she was meant to have this particular child. "Maybe that's why I wanted to wait as long as I did," she said.

All Dick could say in return was that he was happy about this baby too.

Shortly afterwards, when JoAnne asked her to be a bridesmaid, June told her that she would be five months pregnant by the time they got married, but the news didn't deter her future sister-in-law. "The bridesmaids gowns have full skirts so you'll be okay," JoAnne assured her.

The wedding was imminent when June had her fitting, and she felt confident that the full skirt would hide her condition. What she hadn't counted on, though, was that Skip wouldn't be released from the hospital in time for the scheduled wedding date. Unless they were to be married by proxy (which wasn't even a consideration), the wedding had to be postponed another week.

During that time, the baby seemed to have a growth spurt as was evident when the day before the wedding, June slipped into her gown. As soon as JoAnne's tyrannical wedding consultant noticed how difficult it was to fasten the zipper, she pulled herself up to her full four-foot eleven inches, puffed out her robin-like breast, and started to scold June. "You're eating too much! I can hardly get you zipped into this dress."

June and her mother exchanged amused glances over the little woman's head, but thought it would be wise to keep their mouths closed. The next day at the wedding, June noticed "Little Mrs. Hitler," her private name for the consultant, as she cast disapproving glances her way. Since she'd studied her reflection in the full-length mirror in the back room of the church, she knew that although she looked unusually buxom in the strapless green satin dress, no one would guess she was pregnant.

October twenty-seventh, Skip and JoAnne's wedding day, dawned cool and rainy, but the weather didn't dampen the joy in the occasion. It was a lovely wedding with the women looking lovely in green and gold satin gowns. Skip's navy buddies had come down from Grosse Ile to serve as ushers and his brother-in-law, Dick, was the best man. JoAnne's sister, Ada, was her maid of honor, and along with June, JoAnne's other sisters, Kate, Dorothy, and Patty were the bridesmaids.

Dick surprised everyone when he got his army uniform out of moth balls for the ceremony. The groom and his four groomsmen wore navy uniforms, while Dick, the best man, wore his army dress uniform. As she stood at the front of the church with the other bridesmaids, June looked first at her brother then at her husband. The sailor and the soldier looked especially handsome in uniform as they stood side-by-side to the right of the altar.

While Dick cast flirtatious glances at his wife, Skip's eyes never left his bride as she walked down the aisle with her father. Her head was covered with a gossamer veil, and she wore a white satin gown that hung in folds from the form fitted bodice.

It was obvious to his watching sister that once Mr. Long relinquished JoAnne's arm and the ceremony began, for Skip the rest of the people melted into the background as he and JoAnne exchanged their vows.

Before the ceremony, the ushers had attached a "Just Married" sign and some tin cans and old shoes to the back of Skip's car. When they left the church, the bride and groom got into the car for the traditional ride through the streets of Mansfield, and the entire wedding party began to pile into their cars to follow. As June settled into the front seat with her husband, Little Miss Hitler yanked open the door and announced, "You can't ride with the best man. He has to be with the maid-of-honor!" Despite Dick's protests, the bridal consultant ushered June out of their car and into one with a handsome, single usher while the equally single maid-of-honor was ordered to ride with Dick. As they drove away, June and Dick looked longingly at each other and their companions cast wistful glances at each other, but no one dared question this woman who looked so much like a robin and acted like a hawk.

When they joined the other guests at the home of JoAnne's parents for the reception, June and the rest of the wedding party looked around for Miss Hitler before they paired off. As Dick slipped his hand in hers, he whispered, "Do you think it's safe now?" Overhearing him, Skip chuckled as he informed him she was gone.

Everyone had such a great time that the celebration went on for hours. In fact, it continued even after the bride and groom left for their wedding night in Columbus. There were bets among some of the young guests that they would stop at one of the motels along the highway, but anyone who actually bet would have lost since, despite bad weather, they continued to the hotel where they had a reservation.

⁓

By the time the newlyweds returned from their honeymoon, which they spent in West Virginia and the Washington, D.C. area, June's pregnancy was really evident. They looked her over and told her how glad they were they hadn't had to postpone the wedding a second time. June agreed, "I don't think the consultant would have been too happy if she'd had to split the seams."

Eyeing her, Dick couldn't resist teasing her, "If your brother, Dickie, was here, he could honestly sing "June Is Busting Out all Over." Accustomed to her husband's teasing, she ignored his remark and pretended that she hadn't heard him.

Then Skip looked around for Sharlyn. When he didn't see her, he asked, "Where is that little niece of mine?"

June had to sadly admit that she wasn't home. "In fact," she confided woefully, "we haven't seen her since your wedding day. Polly asked if she could take her home with her for a visit. I didn't really want her to go, but the two of them were so insistent that they talked me into it."

In response to Skip's question as to when she would be back, June sighed and said, "We were going to Pennsylvania to pick her up over the weekend, but Polly called and asked if she could stay another week. I had her put Sharlyn on the phone so I could see whether or not she was homesick." June looked even more mournful when she told him that Sharlyn had been so excited at the prospect that she could stay that she'd forgotten Ma Ma Polly's name and had just squealed, "I want to stay with...with...with...HER!"

"I almost didn't let Polly take her, but when she told me that it would get Dad's mind off of having to miss the wedding, I couldn't say no!"

"I never did hear why Dad didn't come," Skip said. "I'd heard that neither of them could get there, and I was really surprised when I learned that Mom had come without him," he said.

"Dad had just gotten the news that his heart was enlarged, and the doctor wouldn't let him travel that far," June explained. "Polly said, though, that the closer it got to your wedding day, the worse she felt about not being there. She said that Dad got so tired of her moping around about missing her son's wedding that he told her to go without him."

"She didn't drive by herself, did she?" he asked. He was relieved when he heard that she had traveled by bus. At the mention of the bus, a picture formed in June's mind of her little daughter as she bounced up and down on the seat beside her grandmother on the bus. Her face had been wreathed in smiles when she waved at her mother and father, as the bus took her away from them. She shook her head as if to shake loose the memory before she changed the subject to ask about their trip.

A few days later, when June and Dick traveled to Pennsylvania to bring their daughter home, the newlyweds were on their way to his reassignment at the Patuxent River Naval Air Base. When June heard where he was going to be stationed, she was surprised to learn that this was the Sea-Plane Base at Cedar Point, Maryland that Burrel had helped build during the war...when the bridegroom had been a boy of fourteen. "I loved that place," June told Dick. "That's where we lived before we went to Mississippi." Her eyes took on a teasing glint before she added, "You should have seen the cute boyfriend I left behind! His name was Ramon and he loved playing records of big band music."

Dick bragged, "I love big band music too and I can play it for you on records or on my saxophone or clarinet."

June laughed and said, "That's true."

As it turned out, though, Skip and JoAnne didn't remain at that base long. After a few months, they were transferred to Brunswick, Maine. While they were settling into their new life, June was counting the days until her baby was due.

AT LONG LAST

The scheduled date arrived and departed as did several others with no sign that this child was ever going to be born. "I don't mind being pregnant for nine months," June groaned as she sat at her kitchen table with her mother-in-law. "But it looks like this one is going to take at least ten."

Rowena patted her on the shoulder consolingly and told her that she could remember the feeling. "Just think, though, how nice it's going to be when it gets here." She looked dreamily into space before she added, "Forest and I were talking the other night about how nice it's going to be to have two grandchildren!"

As June straightened in her chair to give the baby room to stretch its arms and legs, she smiled at her attractive mother-in-law and told her, "Our children are lucky to have such young grandparents."

June could see that her comment had pleased the other woman, and that talk of the baby had gotten her mind off her worries about her son Eddie (Gene) being drafted. Home from his basic training, he hadn't yet received his orders. Rowena had confided in June that she was afraid he might be sent to Korea. "I worried about Richard for the entire eighteen months that he was overseas in action. When that war was over, I never dreamed that I would have to send another son off to war," she'd said.

June had murmured words of encouragement, but she was concerned too. She knew that after almost two years into this war, thousands of fighting men had been wounded or killed. One of the casualties had been a popular World War II general named Douglas MacArthur. While he hadn't been killed, his career had been ruined when President Truman as Commander-in-Chief had fired him. The two powerful men had clashed over the way the war was being handled. For the first time in the history of war a line had been drawn and the general had been ordered to keep his forces behind that line.

When General McArthur wanted to cross that line, the thirty-eighth parallel, into enemy territory, and wage a full-fledged war, President Truman unceremoniously dismissed him despite an uproar from his countrymen, who considered him a hero. The President wouldn't back down, and a brilliant military man was put out to pasture.

~

June had other thoughts on her mind as she waited. Her beloved grandpap was ill and Polly had taken Billy and Freddy and gone to West Virginia to nurse him. June was not only worried about her grandfather's health, but whether Polly would get home in time to be with her when she got home from the hospital as they had planned.

Her mother, Priscilla, had originally agreed to come, but had become ill and was scheduled for abdominal surgery the eighth of March. June's friend Vonnie came up with a suggestion that they immediately acted upon, "I had a woman here who takes care of new mothers and babies when they get home from the hospital. She not only took care of me and Sherrie, but cooked the meals and did some light housekeeping."

Since Dale and Vonnie's third child was less than a year old, Vonnie was certain the "new mother's helper" was still in the business. After the woman came over to meet them and decided that they met her approval, she asked June when they would need her. After June explained that she was already a couple weeks overdue and all that the doctor could tell her was that it would be soon, the woman screwed up her face in a cross between a smile and a frown and stiffly replied, "I have another job lined up in three weeks. If you don't have yours within the next week and a half, I won't be able to take care of you." With that understanding in mind, Dick and June hired her on the spot.

At that moment, June was torn by conflicting emotions. While she was anxious for the baby to come, she hoped it might hold off a few more days until her doctor returned from an out-of-state seminar. "If it isn't born for a week, Mrs. Shore would still have time to take care of us before she had to go to her next job, and Doctor Avery would be back," she told her husband after she'd closed the door after the woman.

"I can't believe you would want to wait another week after the way you've been complaining that it was never going to get here. At least one thing you've learned from this experience is patience," Dick remarked.

"I don't know about that. I'm as impatient as ever, but I really like Doctor Avery. He's so kind and caring." She paused for a second before she added, "I don't know this Doctor Wells who is taking his patients while he's gone, and I don't want a repeat of the last time." As it turned out, June's wish only partially came true.

First though, in that next week the snow started to fall, and by March seventh, the stark branches of the maple trees in their front yard, and the telephone and electric lines were weighted down by the six inches of snow that covered everything in sight.

Unfortunately for June, Sharlyn picked this particular day to discover how to lock the front door, but not how to unlock it. That day June had not taken time to throw a coat over her bulging figure when she stepped out on the porch for the mail. While she ruffled through the envelopes she'd extracted from the mailbox, she heard a click as the lock fell into place.

"Sharlyn," she called. "Open the door and let Mommy in."

While little fingers fumbled with the mechanism, no reassuring sound of unlocking was heard. June brushed the whirling snow from her eyes and stamped her feet to try to keep warm as she patiently tried to tell her daughter what to do. After several frustratingly futile minutes of trying, Sharlyn admitted defeat. "I can't do it, Mommy," she cried. Then while June rattled the door as if she expected it to unlock magically on its own, Sharlyn skipped back into the living room and plopped down in front of the television set where she sat seemingly unaware of the racket at the door.

After seconds of frantic pleas went unanswered, June wrapped her arms tightly around her middle, took a deep breath, and marched down the porch steps. When she stepped off the last step onto the sidewalk, she sank into snow that came up over her sock clad ankles. By the time she'd trudged her way around the house to the unlocked back door, her shoes and stockings were soaked and every part of her exposed body was red and raw from the biting wind.

When brushing the snow from her hair and clothes and shivering violently, she walked into the living room, her "little darling" innocently looked up from her favorite television program, Miss Francis, and smiled sweetly at her frustrated mother. June gazed at her sparkling brown eyes, and soft brown braids, and thought, "Well at least I won't have to worry about her being able to let any strangers in."

After she changed her clothes, brewed hot tea and settled on the couch with piles of blankets pulled up to her chin, she reflected on what Dick had said earlier. She might develop some patience along the way. "Freezing is one learning experience I'd just as soon do without, though," she moaned, as the welcome effect of the hot tea and the mounds of covers started to bring some warmth back into her shivering body.

～

That night while Dick and Sharlyn slept, June spent a restless night. No matter how she tossed and turned, she couldn't get herself into a comfortable position. Besides that, she had a nagging backache. By around five-thirty on the morning of March eighth, she was hit by a sharp pain that consumed her. Despite her discomfort, she decided not to wake her sleeping husband until she was sure that this wasn't a false alarm. In less than five minutes, though, when the second one hit, all doubt was removed.

Still not waking Dick, she tiptoed to the phone and dialed Doctor Avery's number. As she waited for someone on the other end to answer, she glanced at the calendar. According to the big red X she had placed on it, today was the day the doctor was supposed to be back in his office.

She had expected him to answer the phone, but instead his wife came on the line. When June asked if the doctor had returned, Mrs. Avery replied, "He got back last night, but he has the flu. If you're in labor, you need to call Doctor Wells." Still speaking softly, she rattled off the phone number and said that she'd let her husband know what was going on.

Though June was disappointed, she had no choice but to make the best of it. She hurriedly jotted down the fill-in's phone number, and dialed it. Doctor Wells' wife answered on the first ring. When June told her that her pains were a couple minutes apart, Mrs. Wells frantically cried, "What are you waiting for? Get to the hospital...now! The doctor will be there by the time you are."

With memories of her experience with the doctor who'd delivered Sharlyn still fresh in her mind, June thought, "Oh, yeah. I bet he'll be there."

Now that the arrangements were made, June shook Dick to wake him. Since six-thirty was at least an hour earlier than he usually faced the day, he was having a hard time waking up. Her alarming announcement, "We have to get to the hospital. The baby is coming!" brought him out of the bed in a flash. Then while June bundled Sharlyn into her snowsuit to take her to Rowie's house, he scrambled into his clothes. He was so excited that he was in the car before he realized that he'd forgotten something crucial...his pregnant wife and three year old daughter.

He was laughing when he raced up the porch steps and took Sharlyn in his one arm and helped June down the steps with the other. "Are we doing a Laurel and Hardy routine?" June laughingly asked as he got his two girls in the car and turned on the ignition. They were fortunate that the streets were almost devoid of traffic, and there were no policemen in sight, since he broke every traffic law on the books while he sped to his parents' house, and then to the hospital.

When the woman at the desk heard how close June's pains were, she immediately called for an aide to take her to the labor room. "Your husband can stay here and take care of the paper work," she called after June as the aide grabbed the handles of the wheel chair in which the soon-to-be mother had been placed and hurriedly wheeled her down the hall.

When they arrived in the large airy room, June noticed a middle-aged woman turned from her task of washing the wide windows and smiled at the new arrival. Another woman, about June's age, was in the bed closest to the wall. The two women smiled and greeted each other.

As the aide got June settled into the other bed, a tall young man ambled into the room. With his horn-rimmed glasses and crew cut hair, he looked more like a college student than the doctor he turned out to be. "I'm Doctor Wells," he said. After a quick examination, he turned to the nurse who had followed him into the room and told her to get June into the delivery room.

Everything was happening so fast that she could feel her head reeling. This entire experience was totally different from the last time. She seemed to be the center of attention, instead of a nuisance. While this thought was flickering through her mind, the double doors of the delivery room opened, and she was wheeled inside. Then before she had a chance to become aware of her surroundings, a masked, white clad person clamped an object over her mouth and nose, and the pain disappeared as she sunk into unconsciousness.

When she awakened, she was in a room that contained two beds. She felt a little foolish when the nurse walked in and caught her in the midst of a conversation with the empty bed next to her. When the smiling woman asked who she was talking to, June replied that she thought she was still in the labor room, and that she was talking to the woman she'd met there.

"That's what Twilight Sleep will do for you," the nurse explained. "That's one of the things you were given in the delivery room. It will take about twelve hours for its effects to totally wear off."

"You mean I'll feel this goofy for that long?" June asked. The nurse responded by nodding her head up and down while she smiled and asked, "Aren't you even going to ask what you had?"

June tried to shake the fuzziness from her brain when she sheepishly replied, "I guess I didn't realize I'd had it."

"IT'S A GIRL!" the doctor said as he strolled into the room. "A really nice one, at that," he added. This news did more to wake June than anything else could have.

"A girl," she wondrously mused. "A little sister for Sharlyn to play with."

Fortunately, she wasn't made to wait quite as long to see this baby as she had with Sharlyn. A few hours later when the nurse put the tiny bundle in her arms, as she had done with her first-born, June peeled away the pink blanket and checked to make sure this one had the required number of fingers and toes. She was surprised at how well the little arms and legs were filled out.

As she studied the baby's tiny face, the guilt feelings she'd had about the baby that she'd miscarried a little over a year earlier disappeared. It was replaced by an overwhelming feeling that this baby girl was meant to be her daughter. If she hadn't had the miscarriage, this baby would never have been born. As her newborn slept quietly in her arms, June remembered the many times her mother had said, "God has a purpose for everything."

For the first time she understood what her mother meant. Snuggling her new daughter close, she mused, "God does work in mysterious ways."

~

Too soon a nurse whisked the baby back to the nursery, leaving June with her thoughts of how the nurses still acted as if the babies were the hospital's property. She was happy to see Dick who had slipped past the nurses' station and into her room. Since he hadn't seen their daughter yet, the proud mom filled him in on her appearance.

"She looks like she is a month old," she told Dick as he sat on the side of her bed. "She has some scratches on her cheek, and a big goose-egg on her forehead caused by the doctor using forceps. I think she must have had as hard a time as I did." Remembering the wide blue eyes that had seemed to observe everything June had said and done, the new mother added, "Even though she is banged up, she is still beautiful."

Before the nurse came in and chased the new father out of the room, Dick asked if she thought the new baby looked anything like Sharlyn. "Not a bit," June had replied. "This little one has eyes that look like they'll stay blue, and what little bit of hair she has is almost white." While Dick nodded his approval at her words, June mused, "Her coloring is a lot like the way Mom told me mine was when I was a newborn. Since I didn't go ten months like this baby, though, I'm sure I wasn't as filled out as she is."

Remembering that her mother's surgery was scheduled for today, June asked if he'd heard anything about her mother. "Has she had the surgery yet?"

Dick admitted that he hadn't left the hospital since he brought her in, so he didn't know. "I'll call Bill when I get home to let them know about the baby, and I'll find out then." Before he finally acceded to the nurses demand that he leave, he bent down and kissed his wife and whispered, "Good job!"

The nurse lingered for awhile in June's room as if she fully expected the aggressive young man to sneak back in. "I remember him from when you were in here before," she told June. "He certainly is persistent."

In reply, June grimaced and said, "That's a foolish rule anyway. It doesn't make sense that a man wouldn't be able to be with his wife at such a happy time...or that he can't even be in the room with his newborn child." An amused expression crossed the nurse's face as she cautioned the new mother not to get upset.

"Maybe if enough people got upset about it, the rules would be changed!" June flung back.

"Not in my lifetime," the nurse firmly replied before with a rustle of her starched uniform skirt, she turned and briskly walked out of the room. She'd no sooner left than June turned on her side and drifted off to sleep.

When she awoke, she looked up into the faces of her husband and his brother, Eddie (Gene). They were both wearing ear-splitting smiles. "She's beautiful!" Dick exclaimed as he tenderly kissed his wife.

"She is beautiful," Eddie echoed before he added, "Dick said she doesn't have a name yet."

"If she'd been a he, she'd have been called Richard Michael, but we didn't have a name picked out for a girl," the new mother said.

"Sounds like you were expecting a boy," Eddie noted.

June was quick to inform him that she'd had that name picked out for a boy even before Sharlyn had been born. "Any boy I have will be named after his father and his uncle Dickie," she said. Eddie made a face before he teasingly replied, "You mean you're not going to name one after me. After all, I'm an uncle too!"

"We'll talk about that the next time," she murmured. "That is, if there ever is a next time." She noticed the two brothers exchange glances, over her head, but had no idea what was on their mind.

She was to find out later, though, when Dick returned for the evening visiting hours. He could barely wait until after he kissed her before he blurted out that he and Eddie had come up with a name for the baby. Expecting to hear some outlandish name she would have to talk him out of, she was pleasantly surprised when he announced that they thought she should be called Janice Jean.

"I know you've always liked the name, Janice, but I hadn't heard you mention Jean before," June said.

"That was Eddie's idea," he exclaimed. "He told me that he really meant it when he said he'd like to have her named after him." A mischievous grin played across his lips and touched his eyes before he continued, "I didn't think you'd go for either Edward or Eugene, so we decided on Gene, but you can spell it J-e-a-n...if you like it, that is."

June didn't answer for so long that he thought she was unhappy with their choice and might veto it. During those few seconds of silence she had been letting the names roll around in her mind, liking it more each time she thought about it. "Janice Jean," she mused aloud. "I like it. In fact, Janice was one of the names we'd talked about that I really fancied."

Dick expelled his breath in relief before he said, "Eddie will be happy when he hears that you like it too." He stood smiling down at her and said, "Besides, I think it suits her."

Satisfied that their baby now had a name, it suddenly occurred to June that maybe Eddie was concerned that something might happen to him in Korea. She wondered if that was why he wanted to be sure someone carried his name before he left.

When she voiced this concern, Dick replied, "Good thinking, he was worried about his future but fortunately he just got his orders this morning, and he's not going to Korea." Before June could open her mouth to ask where he was going, he continued, "He's going to Germany!"

"Rowena must really be happy! A new grandchild and that good news...all in one day!"

"She's on cloud nine!" Dick replied.

"Who's on cloud nine?" a voice called from the doorway.

June looked up and saw the object of their conversation in the doorway. Dressed in a fire engine red coat with a matching hat perched on her black curls, she strode into the room with her arms loaded with pink ribbon tied packages. When she bent to place the boxes on June's bed, she dropped a kiss on her forehead, and said, "I saw her. She's a pretty little thing." While June was smiling her thanks, her mother-in-law added, "All my babies had a lot of dark hair when they were born. We don't have any blondes in the family...except you and Thelma's Carol. I didn't realize until now how cute bald babies could be."

June was quick to reply, "She has hair. You just can't see it because it's so light." Rowie laughed and went back to her original question, "Who did you say was on cloud nine?"

"You, Mom," Dick responded. "With the birth of Janice Jean, your second grandchild, and Eddie's news!"

Rowena perched on the side of June's bed while she fairly bubbled with excitement. "They say that when it rains it pours, but in this case we were showered with good news." Then she went on to tell them how happy Eddie had been with the prospect that the baby might possibly have his name. "When I left, he was on his way to Kelly's Ice Cream Parlor with Sharlyn. He was kidding her about having a date with his best girl. I think Sharlyn loves the attention she gets from her uncle as much as she does the ice cream."

A flash of homesickness surged through June at the mention of her little daughter. It was alleviated somewhat when Rowena seemed to anticipate June's unasked question and remarked, "Sharlyn is fine. She loves her Uncle Eddie and she's sticking close to him."

"What does she think about having a sister?" June asked.

"She's happy now, but she has the idea that she'll be able to play with her as soon as she gets home," Rowie replied.

Dick caught the worried look that sprang into June's eyes, and hurriedly reassured her that he would explain to their daughter that it would be awhile before she would be able to play with Janice. June sighed when she realized that Sharlyn was going to be disappointed when she discovered otherwise.

He'd no sooner uttered his reassuring words than they heard, "VISITING HOURS ARE OVER!" trumpeted over the loudspeaker. "Uh, oh," Dick muttered. "If we don't leave, the dragon lady will be in here to shoo us out."

While they said their good-byes, June hastened to remind Rowena to give Eddie (Gene) the word about the name. Rowena nodded and said, "Don't worry. I won't forget." Then she pointed to the packages and said, "Don't you forget to open those before you go back to sleep. I got her something she can wear home from the hospital."

〜

After they left, the excitement of the day began to catch up with her. She didn't fight it when her heavy eyelids started to close, and she began to drift into the welcome relief of sleep. Her slumber was interrupted, though, by the intrusion of a whiney female voice and a vaguely familiar male one.

She opened her eyes and squinted toward the sound of the voices and saw that a young woman had been moved into the next bed. She shuddered in distaste when she became aware that the other voice belonged to the doctor she'd had when Sharlyn was born.

Just the sight of his oily face, large brown cow-like eyes, receding hairline, and non-existent chin brought back all the unpleasant memories that she'd tried to suppress of the night she was in labor for Sharlyn, and he had been nowhere to be found. "Him!" June inwardly moaned before she turned her back on them. While she tried to ignore the conversation from the other side of the room, the woman's whining voice grated on her nerves, and it was impossible to do so for very long.

She couldn't escape the voices even though she pulled the cover up to her chin and buried her head in the pillow. The doctor's syrupy voice sounded so solicitous of his patient...just the opposite of how he'd been with June that it almost made her physically ill. While she choked back a wave of nausea, June heard the woman whimper, "I'm so hot."

Then to her distress, she heard the doctor reply, "We can't have that now, can we? I'll just open this window so you can get some fresh air."

June wanted to scream, "No! Don't do that! It's cold out there." Instead, she tried to burrow deeper under the skimpy covers as she felt the frigid air blow through the open window and the chill creep into her bones. "He didn't manage to kill me the first time I was in here," she grimly thought. "I guess he's going to give it another try."

June was shivering from the cold by the time he left, and the nurse came in and closed the window. Since her bed had been closer to the window than her roommate's, she had gotten the worst part of it, including some snow that had blown onto her covers. While she watched, the nurse silently brushed it away.

Since at that time in the medical profession, nurses were not allowed to question the actions of doctors, the white clad woman kept her opinion to herself. However, her tightened lips and flashing eyes told June that she wasn't any happier with what had happened than she was. June was sure she had correctly read the woman's feeling when seconds later the compassion showed in her voice when she leaned over and told June, "I'll warm a blanket for you, and bring you some hot tea. You'll be feeling nice and warm then when I bring in the baby."

By afternoon of the next day, June had such a bad cold that she had to wear a surgical mask every time the baby was brought into the room. This continued, even on the day she and the baby went home. "I hope having a masked mother doesn't prove traumatic for her," June quipped to the nurse as the two of them dressed the baby in her new finery for her first trip into the outside world.

Her helper assured June that this baby would take everything in stride. "Even having the masked lone ranger for a mother," she teased. While they had been talking, she'd slipped the pale green sweater, hat and booties over the white sheer dress, and wrapped Janice in the matching shawl that Priscilla had made.

"The dress is from your grandmother, Rowie," June whispered to the attentive baby. "The rest of your outfit is from your Gram, my mother."

Once they had her dressed, the nurse stood back and studied the baby. "She doesn't even look like a newborn. Just look at those round little arms and legs!" she exclaimed. When June told her that Janice Jean had been one whole month late, the nurse nodded and replied that she could believe it. "She looks like she could be a month old." While June cuddled her offspring in her arms, another nurse popped her head through the doorway and exclaimed, "She looks so pretty. If it's alright with you, I'd like to take her around the floor and show her off." The new mother beamed proudly as she gave her permission.

Minutes later, there was a flurry of activity in the room when Dick arrived to take June home and simultaneously the nurses returned with the baby, and an aide with a wheel chair to take mother and baby downstairs to the car. With mask in place, June held the baby on her lap while amid a chorus of farewells, she was whisked to the waiting elevator, across the lobby, out through the double doors to the yellow car. Once they were out of the confines of the hospital, Dick helped his wife out of the chair, and turned to the aide and firmly told her, "I can take over now."

After June had gotten herself settled in the front seat next to her husband, he leaned over and uncovered his daughter's face and took her tiny hand in his. While he studied the baby's face, her wide blue eyes seemed to peer seriously into his. "At last. I finally get to touch my own child," he plaintively announced.

"This is an improvement over the last time," June exclaimed. "Remember how I had to go home in an ambulance, and you couldn't even go near Sharlyn until after the attendants were gone?"

Dick chuckled and said, "Maybe someday, fathers won't be treated like second class citizens. Who knows, maybe we'll even be allowed in the room when the baby is brought in."

"In your dreams," June quipped. Then when she saw how hurt he seemed to be from his forced separation from his child, her voice softened when she added, "In my dreams too."

～

When Dick and June arrived at the house on Oakwood Avenue, the front door flew open and a tiny brown haired, brown eyed bundle of energy catapulted down the steps. "Mommy, Mommy!" Sharlyn yelled as she wrapped her arms around her mother's legs. While June laughingly disentangled herself, Rowena poked her head out the door and hustled them all inside.

"There's plenty of time for a reunion in here. If you stay out there any longer, you'll all catch your death of cold!" she scolded.

June's voice was muffled by the mask when she replied that her warning came too late, "I already have a cold," she croaked.

"That's what comes from having a baby in the hospital," Rowena bristled before she added, "You just crawl into bed and I'll make you a nice cup of tea. We'll have you better in no time." As she bustled out of the room, June could hear her mutter under her breath, "These young girls today just don't know how to take care of themselves."

As he watched his mother disappear through the door into the kitchen, Dick warned, "You're lucky that you're nursing or Mom would be giving you a big dose of castor oil for that cold of yours."

June wrinkled her nose in distaste before she replied, "The hospital already did that yesterday. They stir it up in some orange juice, put something in it to make it foam and make you take it before they'll let you go home."

The amusement was evident in his voice when he retorted, "I bet it took the threat that they'd keep you there to get you to drink it."

"Ugh!" June grimaced, "I don't think I'll be able to enjoy another glass of orange juice for a long time without remembering that awful stuff."

"The way Mom always made us boys take castor oil every time we were sick certainly cut down on our complaints …even when we felt awful," Dick confided.

"That is something your mother and I will never agree on," June stated. "Ever since Sharlyn was born, Rowena's tried to get me to give it to her every time the poor little thing didn't feel well. I couldn't do that to any child of mine."

While they'd been talking, Sharlyn had been standing looking adoringly down into the bassinet at the sleeping baby. "She's so little," she said. Then she asked if she was going to sleep all the time.

"Mostly during the day," June replied. "I have a feeling she'll be up a great deal at night."

The big sister didn't understand her mother's sarcasm and quickly told her that she didn't like that idea. "I want to see her with her eyes open."

Her parents laughed and explained that she would, and that if she could be patient a little longer, they would let her hold her little sister when she woke up. As Sharlyn's eyes sparkled with pleasure, Dick and June exchanged looks that seemed to say, "So far, so good." They'd been worried that she might be jealous.

As it turned out, though, their optimism was a little premature. They noticed that as the day wore on, and Sharlyn had to share her grandmother's attention with her new sister, her lower lip started to stick out. Even when she tried some of her attention-getting tricks that had always brought smiles to her precious Rowie's face, she couldn't budge her grandmother's attention away from the newcomer.

After Rowie went home, June moved over to the couch and Mrs. Shore, her hired helper, brought the baby to her. June patted a spot on the couch next to her, and told Sharlyn to join them. "After I've fed her, I'll let you hold her for a minute. Would you like that?" she asked.

The little girl's brown eyes sparkled as she snuggled close to her mother, impatiently squirmed, and repeatedly asked, "Is she through yet? Can I hold her?"

When her mother placed the baby in the big sister's arms, they both beamed with pride. "She's so pretty," Sharlyn breathed in wonder. "And so tiny."

"Both my girls are beautiful," June told her grinning daughter. When she'd seen Sharlyn's reaction to the attention Rowie had shown Janice Jean, she knew she would have to pay extra attention to her firstborn.

That night after observing Sharlyn's hurt reaction at a repeat of the same scenario by Dick's father, June confided her concern to Dick. "I think you need to talk to your parents," she informed him. "I know they're thrilled about the new baby, but they need to realize that Sharlyn has had all their attention all her life, and from the look on her face, I'd say she feels abandoned."

With his assurance that he'd talk to them fresh in her mind, she decided not to worry about it. She made up her mind, though, that if it continued, she'd have a little talk with her mother-in-law.

The next day, she had a new concern to face. Bill had called early in the day with the news that her mother, Priscilla, had developed serious complications from the surgery. By the time Dick got home, June was frantic with worry. She tried to contain it until after Sharlyn had been put to bed, and Mrs. Shore had gone to her room.

Once she was alone with her husband, though, she told him about her stepfather's call. "He said that there might be some kind of blockage. The doctor seems to think it's serious enough for Dickie to come home on emergency leave," she said.

June felt somewhat reassured when Dick reminded her that her mother's young age was in her favor. Janice's insistent cry to be fed interrupted their conversation, but not June's thoughts. While the baby nursed, she looked down into her tiny face and gathered comfort from this new life, praying that her mother would get a chance to know this baby too.

Before she fell asleep, though, she found herself remembering a movie, *Claudia and David*, she'd seen a few years earlier. The premise of the movie that starred Dorothy McGuire as the female lead and Robert Young as her husband, David, was that shortly after the birth of their first child, Claudia's mother died. As June had watched this movie when she was a girl of sixteen she had been moved by the way Claudia had reached the conclusion that God had sent her a child to make up for the loss of her mother.

Now as a woman of twenty-two with two children of her own, she realized it would be devastating to suffer the same fate as the noble movie character. She sent up a silent prayer, "I want my children…and my mother." They had been apart for too long after her parents' divorce, she didn't think she could handle another separation.

~

That afternoon when her father and Polly arrived to take over for Mrs. Shore, they brought good news about Grandpap's health. "He's doing fine," Burrel said.

"Thanks to Polly's good nursing!" While he'd been talking his eyes had been roving around the room. "Where are those granddaughters of mine?" he asked.

Before June could reply, half of his question was answered by Sharlyn's appearance and her squeal of, "Granddad! Ma Ma!" Both grandparents made over her while June talked to seven year old Freddy and six year old Billy.

During their brief conversation, she discovered that during their stay at Grandpap's, they'd gone to the one room schoolhouse in Germany Valley she had attended when she was their age. Their comments made it obvious it hadn't changed much since her early school days.

She sat back and waited until she felt that her firstborn had received sufficient attention before she said, "Sharlyn, why don't you take them into the other room and show them your little sister?" The little girl's brown curls bounced and her eyes shone proudly when she grabbed her Ma Ma by one hand and her Granddad by the other and pulled them into the next room where Janice Jean was just waking.

June watched when Polly picked up the baby and turned and remarked to Sharlyn, "I'll bet she'll be happy when she's older to have a big sister like you." Once she'd assured herself that her little sister wasn't going to usurp her place with this set of grandparents, Sharlyn trotted into the kitchen with her young uncles for the cookies and milk that Mrs. Shore had put out for them.

Once she'd washed and put away the children's plates and glasses, Mrs. Shore gathered the few belongings she'd brought with her, plopped her utilitarian hat on her gray streaked hair, collected her pay, and marched out the door to move on to another newborn.

While June had appreciated the woman's efficient service, she was much happier being surrounded by her own family. While her father could only stay for the weekend, Polly and the boys didn't have to leave for another week. Before Burrel left on Sunday evening, he hugged his daughter and with his eyes on the baby, he said, "Beautiful little girl you have there." When he saw his oldest granddaughter's hurt look, he stooped down to her level and repeated what he'd said, but this time he said, "Beautiful little girls."

Satisfied, she wrapped her little arms around his neck and planted a big kiss on his cheek. Then she and June watched from the living room while his wife and young sons walked to the car with him and helped him stow his luggage into the backseat before he drove away. June and Sharlyn stood by the large window in the living room and waved until his car was out of sight.

After he left, when Polly gave the baby a bath, she was appalled at the redness of her skin. "Uh, oh!" she cried. "She's got the Harman's sensitive skin. I'll have to do something about that." With those words she sent the new father to Larry's Drug Store on East Main Street to buy some over-the-counter ointment. Then for the next few days, her nursing skills came in handy, and Janice's skin became as clear as a summer's day.

As she observed the results of this care, June said, "You're such a good nurse. Look at how much you helped Grandpap, and now this with Janice. I don't understand why you gave up nursing to become a waitress."

The redheaded woman grinned and replied, "As a waitress, I didn't have to face the deaths of any of my customers." Her grin widened when she added, "Unless the cook was really lousy." Although Polly was flip with her answer, June remembered a conversation they'd had when she was eleven years old and Polly twenty-two. Polly had explained how difficult it had been for her when any of her patients died. As strong as her stepmother had always been, June knew that she also had a tender, sensitive side to her nature.

Then for the remainder of her stay while Sharlyn and the baby took their naps, and the boys sat at the kitchen table and worked on the tons of homework their teachers had given them, the two women talked...and talked...and talked. Since they hadn't spent this much time together since Polly, pregnant for Billy, had taken Freddy and gone to Mississippi to live, they had a lot of catching up to do.

During one of their talks, Polly confided in her that she was sorry she'd stayed in Mississippi as long as she had. "I think it was hard on Burrel when I didn't move to Pittsburgh with him," she admitted. "Your reminder of what we observed at the tavern above the junkyard and how much being together as a family always meant to you was what I needed to make me realize how unfair I was being to your dad and to the boys."

She took a sip of her cooling coffee before she softly added, "Since Daddy and Mamma's house was the only home Freddy remembers and the only one Billy has ever known, it's been hard on them to be uprooted. I think both boys miss their grandparents."

June replied that she was sure it would be alright. "They'll always remember their years with their grandparents as happy times, but it's good for the family to be together...like it was for you, Dad, Skip, and me."

On Saturday morning June's father came for the weekend. When it was over, he, Polly, and their sons left for Pittsburgh with promises to return soon. This left the little family on Oakwood Avenue alone for the first time since Janice's birth.

MIRACLES DO HAPPEN

Although she had enjoyed their visit and knew she would miss them, she had regained her strength and was anxious to take over her own household. Now that she was alone with the girls during the day she showered love and attention on them, but in the back of her mind was a nagging fear that her mother still wasn't quite out of danger.

She was frustrated that the doctor's one-month restriction on travel was keeping her from her mother's bedside. It was upsetting that Priscilla, who had been in the hospital for so many weeks, wasn't responding to treatment. When she called her stepfather that evening to inquire, he confided that he was worried too. "The doctor assures me that she'll be able to come home soon, but when I pressed him about it, he admitted that she still is a pretty sick woman," he said. June heard a deep sigh of frustration from her stepfather's end of the line before he again spoke. "When she had her gallbladder removed, she was up and around much sooner than this. I don't know what is taking so long this time."

Before she hung up, June explained to him that her doctor wouldn't let her travel to Mansfield until Janice was a month old. "It's driving me crazy that I can't come now," she lamented.

"I know that's hard on you, but try not to worry," he cautioned. "I'll keep you informed," he promised before he asked what Sharlyn thought of her little sister.

The mention of her little girls lightened her worry for a moment and there was a smile in her voice when she replied, "She loves her, but I think at times her nose is out of joint when people make over the baby before they pay any attention to her."

"That's only natural," Bill replied. "She's been the only grandchild on both sides for a long time. I can tell you, your mother is anxious to see her, and the baby."

"No more than we are to see her, I'm sure," June said. Then she told him to be sure to kiss her mother for her. "Tell her I love her, and that we'll be there as soon as the doctor will let me travel," she said before she returned the phone to its cradle.

Dick, who had been sitting on the couch listening to her end of the conversation, wanted to know what Bill had to say about her mother. After she had filled him in on Priscilla's condition, he put his arms around her and murmured that he was sure she'd be fine. "In little more than a week, we'll be able to go to Mansfield and see her," he promised.

The big day finally arrived and although Priscilla was still in the hospital, the doctor had given in to her pleas to allow June to bring Sharlyn and the baby into the hospital room. Leery of Sharlyn's reaction, both parents had tried to explain to their oldest daughter on their trip from Newark that Gram was sick and that she might not look the way she had the last time they'd seen her.

When they arrived at Madison Hospital, Priscilla looked lovely to June, although her suffering was still evident on her wan appearing face. Seconds later when Priscilla looked up and saw the little family, her eyes sparkled then started to mist over with the beginning of tears. Before they had a chance to spill down her cheeks, though, June walked over to the bed, and laid the sleeping baby next to her. "This should change those tears to smiles," she said.

The new grandmother looked lovingly into the baby's tiny face, and murmured, "I was so afraid I wasn't going to get to see you." Then she turned her attention to her other granddaughter and told her she'd missed her too.

Sharlyn brightened at Gram's attention, but her expression changed to resentment when she tried to join her little sister on the bed and was quickly stopped by the nurse's sharp cry. "You're too big a girl to get up there. Your grandmother can't be jarred!"

"I wasn't going to hurt her," Sharlyn sulked. "I was just going to give Gram a kiss!"

"A kiss!" her daddy said and scooped her up and held her upside down so that her head dangled over her grandmother's head. Amidst the little girl's squeals of laughter, he lowered her until she could plant a kiss on her grandmother's forehead without touching the bed. When he'd set the giggling girl on her feet, he'd turned and cast a mischievous glance at the nurse that seemed to say, "There's more than one way to skin a cat."

A kind woman, the nurse was sorry she'd spoken so sharply to the little girl and tried to make amends. She stooped down to the three-year-olds level, reached out her hand, and asked Sharlyn if she'd like to explore with her. "You're such a pretty little girl, I'd like the other nurses to have a chance to see you," she said. Sharlyn responded instantly by smiling brightly and happily trotting along with her.

Since Madison was a small private hospital slated to close in the near future, there were few patients and the nurses were glad of the diversion that Sharlyn's presence brought. Dick soon joined them and spent the afternoon entertaining everyone within earshot with his jokes and wisecracks.

Once June and her mother were alone, Priscilla said, "I think I'm going to be alright now, but for awhile I wasn't sure I was going to make it. I didn't want to give up and not get to see this baby or my future grandchildren," she said. Then she changed the subject to ask if she knew Dickie had been home. When June nodded her head, her mother added, "He got the one emergency leave to come home, and when he found out how sick I was, he requested an extension. When he hadn't heard by the time he had to return, he went back to the ship. I was pretty upset when he left and I thought that I might never get to see him again."

She had raised her head while she was talking, but exhausted she'd let it fall back onto the pillow before she went on, "A couple days after he left, I thought I was still dreaming when I woke up and found him sitting right where you are now."

"I heard about that," June said. "He went all the way back to his ship and when he got on board he was told he was going back. Bill told me that he'd gotten the emergency leave after all, and that he didn't even stop to sleep, but got the next train from Newport, Rhode Island."

"Just having him here helped," Priscilla said. "I couldn't face the fact that I possibly wouldn't be here when he came home."

"I know," June murmured. There were tears in her voice when she softly added, "I have been praying for you to get better, Mom."

"Prayer is what saved me," Priscilla said. "Even the doctor admitted that he'd done all he could do...that it was in God's hands. When he told me that, I remembered something my mother told me years ago. She said that when I was three years old, I had an insect bite on my leg that became badly infected. I got a high fever and almost died. She said that the doctor had done all he could and told her that my fate was now in God's hands."

"My Mom said that she fought his words and insisted that he had to do more. Since this was before penicillin or any of the wonder drugs had been discovered, he had little to work with. Anyway, Mom said that she finally accepted what the doctor had said, and dropped to her knees and cried and admitted defeat."

"She told me that she poured out all her frustration to God then finally put everything in His hands. She said that after praying for hours, she'd finally fallen asleep in exhaustion." Priscilla paused dramatically then continued, "When she woke a few hours later, my fever had broken, and I was on the mend."

June had seen the quarter size scar on her mother's leg from this long ago infection, but this was the first she'd heard of the miracle of her healing. "My God!" she whispered.

"That's right," Priscilla responded. "My God healed me when I was three years old and again this time." She was silent for a moment then in a barely audible voice, she continued, "I placed my care in God's hands...just like my mother did. I also promised God that if I got better, I would again walk in his ways."

June started to protest that she always had, but her mother shushed her. "I've gotten more involved in the ways of the world. When I get out of here, I'm going back to the church I grew up in." Janice's hungry cry interrupted their conversation. June immediately went to the baby, picked her up and fed her, and then she placed her in Priscilla's arms. While the baby studied her grandmother's face, Priscilla said, "She really does look like you did when you were this age." While she let the baby rest in the crook of her arm, she stroked her downy blond hair and murmured, "Your hair was this white color, your eyes were the same shade of blue, and your face a healthy red. Your Uncle Verde teased that you were our patriotic red, white, and blue baby."

Before June and her mother could return to their serious conversation, Dick, Sharlyn, and the nurse clamored into the room. Some of the starchiness was missing from the nurse's voice when she told them she was afraid that Priscilla was beginning to tire, and that they would have to leave soon.

Before they left, June handed the nurse her camera and asked if she'd take some pictures. For the next few minutes while the nurse clicked away, they posed together or with Priscilla. Finally, reluctantly, they said their good-byes and left for home. As they walked down the hall, June's mind was at ease. She was confident that her mother was going to get better soon.

As it turned out, when they returned to Mansfield in a few weeks, and visited her mother and Bill, Priscilla looked healthy, showing little physical evidence of her recent illness. Once the greetings were over, she asked June if she'd brought the snapshots from their last visit.

"I brought them, but some of them didn't turn out very well," she admitted. Priscilla noticed a strange glint in her daughter's eyes when she fished around in her purse for the packet of pictures. "Here they are. Let me know what you think," June said as she passed them to her mother.

"Nice...isn't that cute? Oh, look, she has her eyes open!" Priscilla commented while she looked from one picture to the next. Then suddenly she let out a snort of laughter when she came to the one of June, Dick, Sharlyn, and Janice. Curious, Bill walked over and looked over her shoulder at the picture she was holding. Once he saw it, he joined in the laughter.

"Your daughter didn't think it was very funny!" Dick told them.

"Aw, Mom!" June wailed. "I wanted that picture to be so nice. It was one of the first ones we've had taken of us as a family...and he had to put that stupid Blackjack gum on his front teeth. It makes him look like he's toothless!"

Priscilla murmured sympathetically, but she couldn't hide her amusement when she said, "We'll take some more pictures today."

June slipped a sideways glance at her husband's smug face and thought, "Practical joker! You like practical jokes! Well you just wait until I pay you back." The sweet smile on her lips did a good job of hiding her thoughts.

It was a few days later before she had a chance to carry out her revenge. She'd prepared a dinner of steak, baked potatoes, and tossed salad. With it she filled Dick's cup with freshly brewed coffee. "Everything looks good," Dick had announced when he started to eat. He quickly changed his mind, though, after he loaded his coffee with three teaspoons of sugar and a dollop of cream and took a big swig.

He made a rude noise and his mouthful of coffee went flying across the table. "What in the...?" he yelled. He downed one glass of water after another then demanded to know what she'd put in his coffee.

"Not a thing," she innocently replied. "You saw me pour it from the pot right before I poured mine." She took a swallow of her black coffee, licked her lips, and said, "Mine tastes fine."

"Then there must have been something in the cream or sugar!" he grimly proclaimed.

"Imagine that!" June murmured.

By then, Dick had cautiously tasted the contents of the sugar bowl and discovered that the bowl was filled with salt. "Did you think that was funny?" he demanded.

"The way you like practical jokes, I thought you might appreciate the humor in it," she guilelessly replied. "I thought it was every bit as funny as the Blackjack gum blacking out your teeth, didn't you?"

In return, he grumbled, "You have a strange sense of humor."

"I learned it from a master," she replied. "Now would you like some more coffee?"

"I'll pass," he mumbled, and as far as June could tell, he never did see the humor in that particular practical joke.

CALIFORNIA HERE WE COME

During the next few months while Janice was changing from a newborn to a toddler many changes took place in the family's life and that of the country. While Dick and June were delighting in their little daughters, June received news from Skip and JoAnne that in December of nineteen fifty-two, they were going to provide the girls with a cousin.

A few months later, Skip wrote that he was being transferred to Point Mugu, California. Although he had requested a base closer to Ohio, as is the case with most branches of the service, the navy decided to send him as far from home as possible.

He was given a month leave before he had to report for duty. After a brief stop in Ohio, they set off for the new base. Since the doctor had told JoAnne, whose baby was due in two months, that she couldn't travel more than two hundred and fifty miles a day, the trip would take three weeks of the leave. Skip kept them informed of their progress with almost daily letters or postcards.

The second week, he wrote, *"Things were going along fine until a couple days ago when we arrived in the desert. The heat was so bad that we thought we'd wandered into Hades. To make it worse we had to drive with the windows open and the unmerciful sun beating on the car. The hot, arid, sand-filled air that blew through the open windows was unbelievable. I heard that one of these days the car manufactures will put air conditioning in cars. We sure could have used it on this trip. When we stopped at a motel that first night, the woman who owned it took one look at JoAnne (who looked like she was ready to deliver) and very firmly told me that she needed to rest before she got back on the road. She said that we were like babes in the woods, or in this case in the desert. She couldn't believe that we didn't know that we should drive through the desert at night and sleep during the day. We stayed there a couple days then took her advice to drive during the cool night hours and get our sleep during the hot day. We're going to do that until we leave the desert behind us."*

The card that came a few days later read, *"We made it to beautiful California! I think we are going to love it here. Although parts of this trip were difficult, I believe the memory of the fun and adventure we experienced is something we will never forget. JoAnne says this trip gave us stories that someday we can share with our grandchildren. With this first child not here yet, she is really looking into the future."*

Once they arrived in California, though, they felt the full effect of being far from home without anyone to help JoAnne when the baby arrived. They solved the problem by not only inviting Priscilla to come and stay with them for a couple weeks, but making the invitation more tempting by sending her roundtrip train tickets to California.

This turned out to be a trip Priscilla would never forget. Not only did she get to fulfill a lifetime dream to see different parts of the country but to visit in her son's home and to help care for her first grandson, redheaded Michael Allen Harman. By the time she arrived on the twelfth of December, the baby was nine days old and JoAnne had just arrived home from the hospital. Since Michael had been delivered by caesarian delivery, she had been kept for a longer recuperation time. When she got home, her visiting mother-in-law was a welcome sight.

~

By Christmas, Priscilla was home again and had invited June, Dick, and the girls to come to her house for Christmas dinner. Christmas day in Mansfield was a Christmas tradition that had begun the first year the young couple was married.

This Christmas Eve of nineteen fifty-two, a new tradition was started at the house on Oakwood Avenue. That Christmas Eve and for years to come, June's father and his new family would arrive the day before Christmas with a trunk full of gifts for their own family and for June's. Then that evening, Forest, Rowena, Kenny, Eddie, and Lula would join them for refreshments and a gift exchange.

During the evening, they all gathered around the Christmas tree and exchanged gifts. This Christmas, Janice's first, was special for the entire family. As June sat back and watched these people she loved and listened to the conversation swirl around her, she was overwhelmed with happiness. Sometimes she was so happy that it frightened her.

As her little brothers, Billy and Freddy foraged under the tree for their gifts and those of their nieces, June observed the sparkle in the children's eyes as they opened them. She wished she could hold this moment in her heart forever. She mentally stored away the picture of her nine-month old blond baby girl with her blue eyes aglow while her little fingers tore at the bright paper. Then a smile played tenderly across the young mother's face when Sharlyn plopped down beside her sister and helped her unwrap her presents.

While Sharlyn leaned close to her sister and her brown hair mingled with Janice's blond, June again marveled at the contrast in their appearance. "I don't know why I should, though," she thought as she glanced from her blond father to Dick's dark haired parents.

The next day when they went to her mother and stepfather's house, June again found herself counting her blessings. After years of separation, her father and his family were again close enough that they could see each other often. In addition, her mother had miraculously recovered from her critical illness.

While they were exchanging gifts with each other she thought of her brothers, Dick and Skip, who couldn't be with them this year and Dick's brother, Eddie, who had just returned. She was thankful that although they were all in the military during the present police action, they were never-the-less safe. Last but certainly not least, she added the new babies, Janice and Michael to her list of blessings, and the fact that Sharlyn was now as happy as the rest of the family about her little sister.

As if her mother had read her mind, when they sat down to dinner and joined hands while Priscilla said the blessing, her mother's prayer echoed June's thoughts. June noticed though, that her mother hadn't mentioned Burrel and Polly's return when she offered thanks to God.

Although she had never understood why her mother didn't want their names mentioned, she had wisely decided not to tell her that she'd left her other set of parents at her house to fend for themselves on Christmas day. She soon found that even if she had wanted to talk about it, she wouldn't have been able to without interrupting her mother's enthusiastic report of her California trip. "Now I have a brunette, a blonde, and a redheaded grandchild."

Priscilla had loved everything about the train trip from the view from the wrap around windows in the observation car to eating in the dining car.

"What a difference your trip was from the time Cecil, Polly, and I came to Ohio from Mississippi during the war," June interjected. "Some of the people on that train had to stand or sit on their suitcases. I don't even know whether or not they even had a dining car." Dick picked up the conversation with some amusing anecdotes about his trip across the country on a troop train. While Priscilla admitted that traveling wouldn't have been much fun under the circumstances her son-in-law and daughter related, June was mentally reliving that trip and thinking that actually, being part of that time in history had been exhilarating. "I wouldn't have missed it for the world!" she thought.

While they'd been talking, June had been busy gathering their gifts and stashing them in a shopping bag and bundling Sharlyn into her blue velvet leggings, matching white fur trimmed coat, and bonnet. When Dick made one trip to the car with the shopping bag looped over one arm and Sharlyn tucked under the other, June slipped Janice into her one piece snowsuit, draped the corner of the blanket over her face, kissed her mother on the cheek, and made a dash through the swirling snow to the car.

She settled in the front seat with Janice on her lap while Dick shifted the car into gear, and Sharlyn excitedly bounced up and down in the back seat as she waved goodbye to her Gram and Grandpa Bill. While they traveled through the night, June noticed that the snow had brushed everything in its path with a pristine crystal beauty. Even when the wind surrounded them with a whirlwind of snow, she still marveled at its loveliness. Since both Dick and June were confident of his ability to get them through the worst driving conditions, they weren't concerned even as the weather continued to worsen.

They were to find that the same couldn't be said about the people who'd been waiting for them to return. When they arrived at the house on Oakwood Avenue, they found a set of worried parents waiting for them. Dick had no sooner stopped at the curb before the door of the house was thrown open, and Burrel strode out to the car. "Your mother was so worried about you," he muttered, but his face clearly showed that she hadn't been the only one.

While the family trooped into the house, Billy announced, "We've been watching the storm out the window. Wow, is the snow ever coming down! We never had snow like that in Mississippi."

Freddy yowled, "It looks like the North Pole out there! How'd you make it back without a sled and reindeer?"

Sharlyn giggled at her young uncle's remarks as the children gathered around the floor register to warm up from the bitter wind. Then as Polly called them all into the kitchen for Christmas cookies, they raced to the table to get first pick of the treats.

The rest of the visit was over much too soon. After Burrel, Polly, Freddy, and Billy had returned to Pennsylvania, the little family took a short breather. Then life became even more hectic.

PROJECT NIGHTMARE

For a long time June had been working on her husband to have cabinets built in the kitchen. While she had graduated from the sink in the pantry to a more modern one in the kitchen, she still had very little storage space and no workspace except the kitchen table.

Once she'd talked him into the modernization, they realized they had a problem. With all the windows plus five doors in the room, wall space was practically nonexistent. They had lived in this house for almost five years and for all that time she had dreamed of a modern kitchen. With this in mind, and speaking with more confidence than she felt, she told her husband, "Don't worry about it. I'll find a way!"

Once he'd downed his last drop of coffee, he kissed her soundly on the lips, dropped a kiss on the top of each of the girls' heads and with a quick look around the room, he wryly commented, "I wish you luck."

"I'm going to need it," she thought. She also reflected that it had taken her too long to talk her husband into the project to give up when she was so close to getting what she wanted. After she got Janice settled in the playpen with Sharlyn sprawled on the floor beside it, she turned the television dial to Captain Kangaroo, picked up her sketch pad, pencil, and ruler and headed back to the kitchen. While she stood in the middle of the floor, she turned the problem over in her mind.

After a few seconds of this, she could see that there was only one way she could possibly gain wall space. "That should do it," she muttered just before she settled herself at the kitchen table with her sketchpad. With a few strokes of her pencil, she had replaced the tall, vertical window, on the east wall with a horizontal one which stretched across the back of the sink, and rough drawn the refrigerator and the cabinets on each side of it.

Once she'd finished, she stared at her primitive art and realized she still had a problem. She hadn't left room for a stove against that wall. If she inserted it there, she wouldn't have much more counter space than she now had. Her wail of, "Oh, no!" as she glared at the unsuitability of the other walls brought Sharlyn on a run from the living room.

"What's wrong, Mommy?" she asked.

June laughingly assured her that everything was fine. "I'm just trying to figure out where to put the stove," she explained.

The little girl shrugged her shoulders as if the prospect of moving the stove were an everyday occurrence. "I'm going to watch Captain Kangaroo," she called over her shoulder as she turned and skipped back into the living room.

Sketchpad in hand, June followed her. Then, though her eyes were on the action on the screen, her mind raced. "Before Dick gets home for dinner, I'm going to have this problem solved," she determinedly decided. As it turned out, she did, but when she showed him her idea, he only laughed. Then in an incredulous sounding voice, he asked, "Who ever heard of putting a stove in the middle of the floor?"

Undaunted by his skepticism, she explained, "I saw a mock up of something similar in the gas company showroom. They had what they called an island with a sink in the middle of the floor and floor cabinets on either side. I adapted their idea to fit our needs." A wistful note had crept into her voice when she again spoke, "I don't see any reason why we can't do that with the stove. Then on the back of the island, we can add a breakfast bar."

She pointed to her rough sketch and added, "Instead of the bar being tall where we would have to use stools, I thought we could have it table height so we could use regular kitchen chairs."

Her anxious expression showed him how much this all meant to her, so he finally relented. "People are going to think we're crazy, but if that's what you want and we can find a carpenter who can do it, we'll go ahead!" he exclaimed.

He'd been right about one thing, people did think they'd lost their minds, when they explained what they wanted, but June didn't let that bother her. When the work was finally completed, the skeptics had to eat their words. Even if they hadn't, she wouldn't have let it bother her since she had a wonderfully workable kitchen. Her dream had come true and she had the satisfaction of knowing that she'd solved an almost insurmountable problem.

As she was to discover in years to come, she had created somewhat of a monster, though. Whenever the children were mischievous and wanted to get away from her, all they had to do was run circles around that island. Swift as their little legs were, she never managed to catch up with any of them...but then, she did get her exercise.

∼

Although, everything turned out well, the couple months it had taken for the work to be completed had been a nightmare. To begin with, they thought they'd found the perfect cabinet-maker for the job. Although he was in his early twenties he never-the-less had a wealth of experience and came well recommended by the adult son of one of their neighbors.

When they first talked to him, he promised that he would have the cabinets built in a couple weeks. June never found out what unit of time he operated with, but it certainly bore little resemblance to either the calendar or the clock she used.

While, before they signed the contract with him, he'd promised to show up every morning bright and early and put in a full eight hours, he'd actually only appear at the dinner hour, and would put in no more than two hours at a time. Some days, he wouldn't bother to come at all.

By the end of the first month when no apparent progress had been made, Dick talked to him about it only to be told that it was hard to work with June and the children under foot. "If that's it, I'll go over to Uncle Mace's during the day," June promised.

Since her grandpap was there for a visit, and she'd planned to spend some time with him before he returned to West Virginia, this would work out fine for her. When Dick explained this to the cabinetmaker, he replied, "All I need is a couple days without any distractions, and I'll have it all done!"

The two men talked for a few more minutes before the cabinet maker sidestepped the sawhorses he always left in the middle of the floor and shoved his tool box against the wall. Then in a strong sincere sounding voice he proclaimed, "I'll see you in the morning and if I have the house all to myself, I'll have the wall cabinets completed before supper-time."

June glanced at the framework that he'd built a couple weeks earlier, and breathed a sigh of relief at the prospect of real cabinets. Always an optimist and unaccustomed to being around people who fudged the truth, she believed every word he said.

When she returned from her visit with her grandpap late the next afternoon, though she had high hopes as she walked into the kitchen, those hopes were quickly dashed. Not only had he not completed what he'd promised, there was no evidence that he'd even shown up.

She was understandably upset not only about what had become such a fiasco with the remodeling, but because she'd become more aware that day that her grandfather's health was fast deteriorating.

Since she didn't want to upset the children, she waited until she had them tucked into bed before she unloaded all her problems on her husband. "I know I was the one who wanted this work done, but I don't know how much longer I can put up with the mess. It's not only hard to work around, but I have to worry that one of the girls might get hurt on the tools he leaves all over the place. Not only that," she cried, "but he doesn't even pick up the nails that he drops on the floor."

"With Janice crawling, we can't have that!" Dick vehemently exclaimed. It was evident that he was angry when he picked up the phone and dialed the number. While he was waiting for someone on the other end to answer, he told June that he was going to give the man an ultimatum. "Either he's going to get this work done, or we're going to get someone else. I'm not going to put up with anymore of this!"

From his end of the conversation, June could tell that the carpenter wasn't at home, but she was surprised when Dick hung up to find that the man's wife thought he'd been working on their cabinets all day. "In fact, she was upset that he was putting in so many hours on this job. Apparently, he tells her that he's been here every day."

"What do you think he's up to?" June asked.

"From the way his breath smells sometimes, I think he probably spends his days in a bar. Our neighbor's son is probably a drinking buddy of his," Dick said.

June replied that she thought that might be possible. "I know his parents don't drink, but we don't really know the son."

"Some reference!" Dick grimaced.

Within the next few weeks, June and Dick felt as if they were on a roller coaster ride with all the ups and downs they encountered. First, Dick tracked the cabinetmaker to a downtown bar, and convinced him that either he had to work on this job every day, or be replaced. Although the man didn't completely change his ways, this little talk did get him to put in just enough hours to keep from being fired.

Then, one evening after he'd hammered in a couple nails, he informed them that the job was going to cost much more than the estimate. "As I see it, I'm going to need more material than I figured," he asserted. "And look at all the time it's taking!"

This was too much for June to take. Up until this time, she'd managed to be polite, despite the chaos this man had brought into their lives. One look at the sawhorses in the middle of her kitchen, his banged up toolbox, and the bits and pieces of wood he'd left on the floor, she couldn't hold it back any longer. "Time it is taking! Did you say you've put more time in this job than you figured? Has it ever occurred to you that if you spent one third the time here that you do in the bar, you'd be through by now?"

After one glance at June's flashing eyes and the circles of color on her cheeks, the shiftless man grabbed his hat and beat a hasty retreat. Before he closed the door behind him, though, he muttered under his breath to Dick that he'd talk to him the next day at the barbershop.

When he was gone June reminded her husband that in less than a week the man they'd hired to install new tile in all three downstairs rooms would start that project. "Think what it will be like if we have both jobs going on at the same time. Try to impress upon him, if he does come in tomorrow, that he has to have the job finished by then."

Dick promised that he would, but added, "In case he doesn't, I think we'd better postpone the other job until he's out of here."

June grimaced and cynically replied, "The idea was to kid proof the house with the new floor. At the rate he's going, the girls will be grown and married before the job is finished."

She could hear the chuckle in his voice when he declared, "Can't you imagine how funny a movie maker could make this whole mess seem?"

"I thought it was hilarious when I was pregnant for Sharlyn and we saw that Cary Grant movie, Mr. Blandings Builds His Dream House, where everything went wrong," she replied. "Now that I've lived through it, I can't imagine why I ever thought that was funny! I guess it's a comedy if it happens to someone else, and a tragedy if it happens to you."

"It's been irritating, but I'd hardly call it a tragedy," Dick reminded her. While she wasn't sure she agreed with him, something was to happen soon that caused her to see his point of view and to put everything into perspective.

~

The onslaught of the real tragedy started a few days later with a phone call from Aunt Mabel. Grandpap was ill and had been admitted to the hospital. "The doctor says that it's his kidneys. He'll probably be there for a couple days. Mace wondered if Dick would go over and shave him," Aunt Mabel said.

June assured her that he would, and asked if Grandpap could have company. Her aunt replied that the doctor wanted him to rest for now. "Mace is going this evening. I think that if Dick goes over to shave him, that will probably be enough company for one day."

June reluctantly agreed to wait, but she knew she'd be worried until she saw him for herself. As it turned out, she didn't get to see him until he returned to her uncle's house on Lawrence Street. Instead of being reassured when she saw him, though, she was even more disturbed. Always before he'd worn his eighty-three years with a quiet dignity, now though, his face was ashen, and he looked frail and tired.

When she took Sharlyn and Janice and went to see him, he was ensconced in the downstairs bedroom with Aunt Mabel as his nurse. She spoke quietly to her aunt in the hallway before, with Janice in her arms and Sharlyn trotting along beside her, she tip-toed into his room and said, "Grandpap, it's me, June. How are you feeling?"

He opened his eyes and smiled wanly before he replied, "I guess, I'm just tired," he whispered.

"Are you too tired for us to be here?" she asked.

"I'm never too tired to see you," he softly replied. Then he spotted Sharlyn and Janice and added, "You brought the girls. They're pretty little things." June and Sharlyn beamed at the compliment. Then June noticed that the few words he'd said had tired him, and she asked if she should leave. He reached for her hand as if to restrain her, and whispered, "Don't go."

"Rest," she said. "I'll be right here." A few minutes later, when she heard sounds of children playing in the other room, she knew that Inez must have arrived with her little girls, Sandy and Cathy. "Do you want to go play?" she asked her older daughter. Sharlyn nodded eagerly and with a wave at Grandpap, she skipped out of the room.

After Sharlyn left, Janice wiggled around in her arms, and June sat her on her feet beside Grandpap's bed. Grandpap grinned and said, "She's an independent little thing...just like you were when you were little."

Grandpap had always had a soft voice, but in the last few years since his hearing had begun to deteriorate, his voice had become softer and lower. She'd long ago surmised that since he couldn't gauge how loud he sounded, he kept his voice low so he wouldn't offend his audience.

It seemed to June, though, that today she had to strain even harder than usual to hear him. Even so, while Janice held on to the bed and walked her way around it, she had what was to be her last conversation with her beloved grandfather.

"I am so tired," he murmured. "I'm ready to die." While she looked stricken at his words, he added, "I just wish I could die at home in my own bed, though."

The young woman could feel the tears burning at the back of her eyes when she listened to his words. She wanted to reassure him, but when she tried, her words rang hollow in her own ears. It didn't seem possible to her that this man who had always been such an inspiration to her could die, but deep within her heart, she knew he would...and soon.

As she sat by his bed, his thin dry hand in hers, memories echoed in her mind of him at the cavern house where she'd lived as a child; of the two of them on the back of his horse "Ole Don" while he comforted her about her parents' divorce. For all of her twenty-three years, he'd been there. The tears spilled down her cheeks at the thought that he would leave soon.

When he saw them, he squeezed her hand and softly said, "Don't cry. I've had a good long life, but I've missed your grandmother, Arletta. She's been gone for twenty-four years now. That is a long time for her to wait for me."

There was so much June wanted to say to him, but for now all she could do was to lightly squeeze his hand. As she sat in that chair in her uncle's house, she knew that no matter what happened, she'd always remember this scene, and this conversation with her grandfather while her eleven month old daughter with all the innocence of childhood played happily by his sickbed.

While she thought that both her past and her future were in this room, she heard Grandpap murmur something. "What did you say?" she asked.

When he again spoke, she had to place her ear within a couple inches of his mouth. Even then she wasn't sure, but she thought he said, "I want to go home."

At the time, she thought he meant his home in Germany Valley in West Virginia, but later she wondered if he might have meant his heavenly home.

Whichever it was, a few days later, on February thirteenth, nineteen-fifty-three, his wish came true. Ulysses S. Harman, at the age of eighty-three, beloved father of Olie, Calcie, Mace, Gussie, Burrel, and Nellie left them all behind and joined his beloved Arletta in their heavenly home.

His body was then returned to the place of his birth, and laid to rest in the Harman cemetery on top of one of the Harman Hills. Beside him on that windy hill lay his wife, his parents, and grandparents. When June said her final goodbye, it was with the thought that as long as she lived, his teachings would live with her. "I'll pass them on to my children too," she vowed. Although, they were not to know him, the life he'd lived was to be part of their avenue to the future.

⁓

At almost the same time that June lost her grandfather, the family suffered another loss. Her Uncle Fred's wife, her Aunt Lydy, died from an asthma attack. Twenty-five years older than June's mother, Priscilla had always thought of her as a second mother. June knew that this loss was a painful one for the family, especially her mother. Like her grandpap, Aunt Lydy had always been part of June's life. One of June's earliest memories was of this white-haired woman's visits to them at the cave house. She could also remember her aunt's amusement when she could get Cecil, June, or Dickie to say pie in their West Virginia accent. "Those children can make three syllables out of that one word," she'd laughingly tell their mother.

That was in the past, though, now the family was gathering for her funeral at the Church of God on Locust and Sixth Street. "Before we go to the church, we plan to stop at your house," Priscilla told June over the phone. "Lawrence, Betty, Velma, and Clarence and the boys have never seen it, and they want to while they're in Newark."

"Mom! Do you know what this place looks like?" June wailed. "All the downstairs furniture is piled in the dining room while the guy is laying the tile in the living room. I have two saw-horses, a tool box, and a couple sheets of plywood in the kitchen, as well as partly finished cupboards."

Her mother assured her that her cousins would understand. "I wouldn't want to tell them that you didn't want them to come," she said.

"She sure knows how to make me feel guilty," June thought as, against her better judgment, she gave in. After she hung up the phone, she talked to the workmen and explained what was going on and hesitantly asked if they could take a couple days off until after the funeral.

The cabinetmaker didn't bother to be polite with his response. From his words and his tone of voice, it was clear that he saw this as a chance to get even with them for making him work when he would rather be with his cronies at the bar. "First your husband gets after me to hurry this job up, now you're telling me to take off. It ain't convenient for me, and I ain't going to do it," he sneered.

The tile installer was more polite, but he also declined. "As I told your husband when he asked me to put off my starting date, I'm on a tight schedule and I have to get this job done."

Later that night when she relayed what they'd said to her husband, he just shook his head and grumbled, "If I ever decide I want to have a house built, just remind me of what we've gone through with what was to be a little job."

The two of them tried to bring a semblance of order to the chaos before their guests arrived, but the workmen could mess it up faster than they could straighten it. Finally Dick threw up his hands in defeat and said, "I agree with your mother, they'll understand."

As it turned out, they did, as did her father and his family, and his brothers and sisters who came to see them. Before both funerals were over, a steady stream of people had paraded through the house, and the workers had their turn to be frustrated. When June became aware of this, she smiled for the first time in days. "Bring in some more," she muttered under her breath to Dick. "Those two will wish they'd listened to me!"

Dick gave her the thumbs up sign as he opened the door to some more relatives and heartily exclaimed, "Come on in!"

IT CAME TO PASS

As Dick had reminded her, that time did finally pass, and the family was able to resume a semblance of normalcy in their lives. June knew that the passing of such important people would leave a void that could never be filled, but she had a husband and two little girls to care for. "Grandpap wouldn't want me to neglect any of them," she thought as she determined not to give in to her grief.

During that winter of nineteen fifty-three, new people came into their lives who were to make a big difference to the little family. First, Dick met a young man during lunch at the YMCA dining room. While they talked, Dick told him that he was a barber and invited his new acquaintance to the shop for a haircut.

The young man readily said that he would be glad to. Then in turn he invited Dick to drop in where he worked. "Just tell me when and where," Dick replied.

When the young man said, "Sunday morning at eleven," Dick was surprised at his response.

Since the Blue Law prohibiting businesses to operate on Sunday was in effect, Dick couldn't imagine what could possible defy that law. "Where in the world do you work that time of morning?" he exclaimed. The young man's answer brought a smile of understanding to Dick's face and a reply of, "Sounds good to me! You come to the shop between now and then, and my wife, little girls, and I will see you on Sunday!"

The two men sealed their deal with a handshake before they went their separate ways. That evening after Dick told June about his encounter and explained about the deal he'd made, she agreed to go along with it.

That next Sunday found the young couple sitting in a pew at the Plymouth Congregational Church listening to Dick's new acquaintance, the Reverend David Robinson, speaking from the pulpit. The young couple had been searching for a church to join, and from the beginning this one's creed that God is Love spoke to something deep in June's soul. She felt as if she had come home.

If she could have looked down through the years, she would have seen the love and laughter they'd experience within these walls. She would have seen the Sunday-School teachers that she and her husband would become...and her husband addressing the congregation as their superintendent...her children dressed as Mary, Joseph, a shepherd or an angel on that very platform for Christmas programs. For now though, she felt that God had a hand in bringing them to this particular church.

A few days later she received a letter from Polly with news about a job Burrel had accepted at the Atomic Energy Plant that was being built in Piketon, Ohio. June could feel the excitement leap from the page with each word her stepmother had written. "We're moving to Ohio! We'll be living in a little town called Jackson. Hilton got a job there too, so he, Bertie, Sharon, and Pat will still be our neighbors."

She was referring to close friends they'd made when they had moved from the Pittsburgh area to Charlaroi, Pennsylvania. Burrel and Hilton Tucker worked together, and the two families lived side-by-side a few miles from Charleroi. She concluded her letter by saying, "We love it here, but it will be wonderful if we can be closer to you and the family."

When Dick came home that evening, June didn't even wait for him to hang up his coat before she waved the letter in front of his face and burst out with her news. Since he knew that this move would make it possible for the two families to get together more often, he was as pleased as she was.

They would have been even more delighted if they'd realized the wonderful people they were to meet and the changes this move was going to have on their lives and the lives of many people they had never met.

June and Dick gave them a few days to get settled in their new location before they made their first trip to Jackson to see them. By the time they arrived, the entire town was wrapped in a cloak of darkness, but Burrel's directions were so good that they'd had no trouble finding the place. If there had been any doubt, it would have been erased when they saw the door fly open and Polly and Burrel rush out to greet them. In the excitement of the greeting, June at first didn't notice the different look in her father's eyes. Later though she realized that what she saw was pure joy.

"You really like it here?" she asked him.

"It is wonderful!" he replied. "We have met the nicest people at a little Southern Baptist Church we're going to." She wondered if new friends could account for the warm glow she could see. Deep inside though, she felt it was something more. The next day when the two families filled a pew in the small church, the mystery was solved. When the minister asked people to come forward and accept Christ as their personal savior, Burrel stood and proudly made his way to the front.

June knew now that her father the explorer, the adventurer, had found what he'd been searching for all his life...a personal relationship with Jesus Christ. He had always been a good man, a moral man, but now the love that shone from his eyes showed June his life was full. He'd filled in the one missing link in the chain of his life.

∼

After the services, June's father and the entire family were surrounded by members of the congregation. He drew June to his side and introduced her to many of them. "I'll never remember all their names," she murmured to her father. A young woman had moved to their side while June had been talking to the other couple. Her eyes sparkled and her blond curls fairly danced as she looked up at June, smiled and said, "I'm Dorothy Roberts. You won't forget us as you're going to come over to our house this afternoon."

Just then a big grinning man strode over and took hold of the young woman's hand. She immediately introduced him as her husband, Bill, and informed him of her invitation. "Great!" he boomed. Then he grabbed Burrel by the hand and while he enthusiastically pumped it, he told him how happy he was that he had gone forward. "That is the greatest thing that could ever happen to anyone!" he jubilantly exclaimed. While June watched this tableau, she noticed that this young couple had the same radiance, the same glow that she'd noticed in her father.

While they stood and talked, the congregation had thinned out. They found themselves alone with the Roberts, the Tucker family (Burrel and Polly's friends from Pennsylvania), and the minister and his wife, Bill and Ann Goodin. While she politely acknowledged the introductions, she had no idea that from now on, this little group of people would be so important in her parents' lives, or in that of her own family.

That afternoon, a caravan of three cars, the Harman's, the Tucker's, and Dick and June's family arrived at Bill and Dorothy's house. Within a few minutes Sharon Tucker, Sharlyn, and Janice were playing with their dolls, and Pat Tucker, Billy and Freddy, and the Roberts son, Mack had disappeared outside.

After the adults were left alone, Dorothy served iced tea, and she and Bill talked about the way they'd met Burrel and Polly. Dorothy fairly twinkled when she reminisced, "I feel as if I've known them forever, but it's only been two weeks since they first came to the church. I noticed Polly glancing my way when we sang the hymns, and I made up my mind that I was going to introduce myself after the services." She smiled at Polly before she continued, "Before I'd even gotten out of the pew, though, she'd rushed over to me."

Polly picked up the story at that point, "I'd heard Dorothy's beautiful alto voice, and I just had to tell her how much I enjoyed it."

Bill jumped in with, "Dorothy and Polly hit it off right away, and so did Burrel and I. We felt that we had to get to know them better so we asked them and the Tuckers over to our house for dinner, then afterwards, we all went mushroom hunting."

"I hadn't been mushroom hunting since I left West Virginia, and it was a real treat," Burrel beamed.

For the rest of the afternoon the conversation was light. "These people are fun," June mused. She was happy to see her parents have such good friends, and she found herself looking forward to spending time with them too. A few minutes later, though, she was sure that her husband had spoiled any chance for that to happen when he pulled one of his little jokes. He'd been standing by the aquarium watching the gold fish while the rest of them had been talking. Finally with his voice sounding serious, almost hurt, he interrupted by saying, "Dorothy, you didn't shake hands with me when I came in."

The young woman sprang from her seat and as words of apology spilled from her lips, she held out her hand. While Dick laughed, she drew her hand back and a goldfish flopped across the floor. The practical joker stooped down, scooped up the hapless creature, and dropped it back into the tank while the rest of the group looked on with mouths open wide.

While Dorothy grabbed a tissue and wiped her wet hand, June heard Bill mutter to her father, "Which one of us is going to get him?"

Later, when they were all in the cars ready to leave, Dick said that he'd forgotten something inside. While the girls fidgeted to get back to their grandfather's so they could play, June started to feel uneasy. "What could he be up to now?" she wondered.

A few minutes later, she had her answer when the door opened and a Hindu with a turban of toilet paper emerged. It was Dick, with the rest of the roll of toilet paper trailing behind him. Although everyone laughed, June wondered what these new acquaintances were thinking.

When she glanced into the rearview mirror as they drove away, she noticed Bill and Dorothy gathering up the trail of tissue. "Remember how much you enjoyed the salt in your coffee?" June quietly asked. When he made a face, she smiled sweetly and added, "You won't know where or when."

～

Several important events took place during the rest of that summer and fall, both in the nation and in the life of the people around Dick and June. In July a peace was negotiated in Korea and the men in the military returned home. "I told you that would happen as soon as we had a Republican in the White House!" Burrel informed them on one of their visits. "When General Eisenhower was elected, he promised he would bring our boys home, and he did!"

June had heard her father bemoan the Democrats in office for as long as she could remember. During her growing up years, she'd looked upon President Franklin D. Roosevelt as a hero. Most of the time she'd discreetly kept this from her father. Now, though, she found herself in agreement with him. In the few months since he'd taken office, President Eisenhower, a war hero from World War II, had kept his promise.

"I'm glad that the first time I was old enough to vote, I got to vote for Eisenhower," she told her father before she wailed, "I was twenty-two years old before I was allowed to vote. Here I'd been a mother for four years before the government considered me an adult."

Polly joined them where they were sitting under a shade tree in the yard. When Burrel stood up and took the tray holding glasses and a pitcher of lemonade from her, she joined in the conversation. "Unfortunately it's the law that you can't vote until you're twenty-one. What really bothers me about that is that a young man isn't considered too young to be dragged off to war when he's eighteen. Then if he's lucky enough to make it home, he still has to wait until he's twenty-one before he can vote."

"Whether he can vote or not, I'm glad it's over since that means Dickie will be able to come back to Ohio," Burrel added.

June said, "From what Mom told me, he's on his way home now. Instead of coming back the way he went over, they're going to make a swing around the world. Mom said that he's taking lots of pictures, and we'll get to see them and hear all about it when he gets home."

As it turned out, he was discharged on August tenth and immediately hitchhiked his way home from Newport, Rhode Island. "I had eleven rides the first twelve hours before I was picked up by an elderly priest and his young assistant. Then I got to ride the rest of the way with them."

He had taken several rolls of film, and he brought them all with him when he, his mother, and Bill came to visit June and her family. When June told Rowena and Lula that they were going to be looking at his slides that afternoon, they wanted to see them.

When they all arrived and were seated in the living room, June handed out bowls of popcorn and exclaimed, "Our own little movie-house!" Her brother turned out to be a good narrator as the images flashed on the screen, and he described each frame.

June found herself actually smelling the stench of burning flesh when he described a cremation scene in India. "A fire was built and they placed the body on it...right on the street where everyone could see it," he explained.

Other scenes were less gruesome and some downright funny as illustrated by Dick's grandmother Lula's cry of, "That woman is almost naked. Look at her bare titties! They're flopping all over the place!" June laughed along with everyone else, although she couldn't help remember how this earthy woman had embarrassed her on the day after their wedding, when she'd greeted the newly-weds teasingly by holding a cucumber in front of her in a risqué way. Now June knew that she was a wonderful person, and her choice of words and her antics served to add spice to their lives.

While her brother went through the rest of his slides, June glanced around the room at her family. Sharlyn was sitting on her Gram's lap and Janice on Rowie's as they munched popcorn and watched the pictures. June wondered if either of the girls was thinking what Sharlyn had voiced to her earlier. "Mommy, Rowie and Gram have softer laps than you do." Her little girl had seemed satisfied when she'd replied that by the time she was a grandmother, her lap would be as soft as theirs were.

Before they departed, though, the grandmothers had put in another pitch for June to have a boy. Although she didn't tell them, she had been thinking along the same lines herself. Not because of their urging, but because she wanted that boy they always talked about!

All through the last school year, she had watched the children as they walked by her front yard on their way home from Lincoln School. One little dark haired boy had caught her eye and she often found herself on the lookout for him. As her gaze followed him, she'd think, "I bet if Dick and I had a boy, he'd look like that." Finally, as she'd known with her other children, now was the time. If she got pregnant now, she mused, Sharlyn would be five and a half and Janice a little over two when it was born.

When she asked her husband if he'd like to have a son, he wouldn't give her a direct answer. Finally when she insisted, he replied, "Sure I would. We have our little girls, and a little brother would be perfect for them...and us."

June grinned mischievously and replied, "Won't our parents be happy? They'll think they talked us into it?"

"They don't know my wife if that's what they think," he replied.

"It's just that for the girls there was a right time, and now I feel this is the right time for our boy," she plaintively explained.

Within a couple weeks after Dick's brother Eddie had returned to civilian life from his stint in Germany, they were able to give him and the family the news that he was going to be an uncle again. "You don't get to name this one, though," June quipped. "I've already picked a name for my boy."

"What if you have a girl?" Eddie asked. "Do we get to name her?"

"You did a good job when you named Janice. If we need a girl's name we might call on you," June said. Then she turned her attention to the piece of apple pie her mother-in-law had set before her.

While she savored a bite of the flaky crust, she was happy to see the friendliness between the two brothers. That hadn't been the case in October of nineteen fifty-two when Dick had bought the barbershop from his father, and Forest had tried to force him to sell a half interest to his brother.

For the first time in Dick's life, he'd stood up to his father. Her husband's words still rang in her ears as she remembered what had happened that day two years ago in her in-laws' kitchen. "If that's what you wanted why didn't you tell me before I bought and paid for it?" Dick had demanded. "I told you I wanted to buy this shop so I could have a business of my own. I plan to put in another chair and hire two barbers to work for me. When I paid you more than you asked for the business, it was with the understanding that it would be mine, and I could operate it as I pleased. Nothing was said about me selling half interest to Eddie!" her husband had exclaimed.

"But your brother is coming home from the service, and you should let him have half the business!" Forest had shouted.

The argument had been unpleasant to hear, but June knew it had been more difficult for her husband since he had always practiced the commandment to honor his father and mother.

Never-the-less, Dick didn't give in, and his father finally capitulated, but not before he'd gotten Eddie involved. He'd apparently felt that if he couldn't talk this stubborn oldest son into it, his second son might be able to. June reflected on how her brother-in-law's original anger had at first softened then completely disappeared after he came over to the house on Oakwood Avenue, and he and Dick had put their heads together for a long conference. After their talk, Eddie told his father, "I'm going to work for Dick until I get a shop of my own. Right now, I have the choice of working for him or going back to work at King's Barber Shop in the Arcade." Then with a cocky grin, he added, "I'd rather work for my brother."

Forest had been cool to his older son for awhile, but Rowena had stepped in. She loved her family too much to allow a disagreement over business to drive a wedge between them. Although Dick and June never knew what she said or did, they recognized her fine hand in the change in Forest's attitude. He soon began to act as if no harsh words had ever been exchanged...in fact he eventually went to work for Dick himself.

Now that the baby was on the way, June was relieved that the family was again close. Although, after paying Forest cash for the shop and the house on Oakwood, they only had twenty dollars to their name, they weren't worried. To them, their future looked bright. They felt strong and confident, since Dick now owned his own business and they had their two little girls, and June crossed her fingers as she hopefully thought, "Our little Ricky is on the way."

When during the Harman's next visit, June jokingly told her father about only having twenty dollars left when they'd paid Forest, he opened his wallet and tried to give them some money. June pushed it away and cried, "No! We don't need it. With the three-chair shop and the dances Dick plays on weekends, we're getting along fine. It's just that ever since we got married, we've always had some savings."

Her dad patted her hand and assured her that he had a lot of confidence in Dick. "I'm sure you will be fine but if you ever need anything, I want you to know we'll help anyway we can."

June thanked him and told him that she would remember that when the baby was born. "I don't want money, but I want to borrow your wife then for a week or so when I get home from the hospital."

Polly, who until now, had sat beside them and listened piped up with, "You couldn't keep me away." Burrel nodded and said that he reckoned he could be a bachelor for that long.

THAT'S ONCE!

While the young couple waited for the blessed event, their families, friends (both old and new), neighbors, and the people they'd met at their church continued to weave bright threads through the tapestry they'd begun to make of their lives.

When they returned to Jackson for Burrel's baptism, they became better acquainted with their new friends, Bill and Dorothy Roberts. It didn't take June long to learn that the Harmans, Tuckers, and the Roberts had become one large family joined by their friendship and love. "The kids all think their last name is Roberts/Harman/Tucker," Bill laughingly informed them. The three sets of parents nodded agreement when he added, "They know that if any of us speak, they have to listen!"

"If there was ever any doubt they had to listen to Big Bill," Polly chuckled. "It didn't take them long to learn." Her eyes held a merry twinkle when she asked Bill to tell them about what happened in Sunday School.

When he heard those words, Mack nudged Pat Tucker, Fred, and Bill and muttered under his breath, "I think it's time we got out of here. Dad is getting ready to talk about <u>US!</u>" The boys nodded and casually sauntered along behind the older boy. "Gonna be outside," Mack called over his shoulder.

The adults watched as the screen door slammed behind the last of the quartet. "They don't want to hear what little hellions they were," Bill muttered.

Dorothy interrupted to ask if anyone needed a refill on coffee before Bill began his story. Once she'd refilled Dick and Burrel's cup and everyone was comfortably settled, she sat on the arm of her husband's chair, smiled, ruffled his hair and said, "I think everyone is taken care of now."

Bill returned his wife's smile and resumed his story. "There were about a dozen boys in the class and they were really wild! After they managed to drive out three Sunday School teachers, Bill Goodin, the preacher, asked me to take over the class."

"I talked to the other teachers to find out what the boys had been up to." He chuckled as he remembered those conversations. "Poor little Miss Turner turned pale and her hands began to shake when I mentioned the Sunday School Class. Then when I told her that I was going to be their new teacher, she just shook her head and skittered away."

Dorothy laughed as she picked up on the story. "After she left Bill, I heard her murmur, 'Oh, the poor man! He doesn't know what he's getting into.'"

"That's where she was wrong. I knew exactly what I was getting into. I'd already talked to the other two men who'd had the class, and I'd learned how rowdy the boys were, so I was prepared. I knew the boys weren't bad, just full of energy and mischief. I figured that what they needed was someone who wouldn't let them get away with any of their shenanigans. That's why I decided to tell them a little story I'd heard once."

"The first thing I did when I got into the class was to tell them to sit down... that I had a story I wanted to tell them. They jostled around for a few seconds for the seats. One of the boys, I think it was Little Bill, pulled the chair out from under Pat. Before Pat could retaliate, I gave them a look that managed to put a stop to their antics."

While he related the incident, he demonstrated his look. He appeared so fierce that June could understand why the boys had quieted. "Once I got them settled down, I was finally able to relate my story."

Everyone except June and Dick had heard this before, but that didn't prevent them from smiling expectantly.

"I told them about this rich young man who took his bride for a ride in his carriage. The horse that pulled the carriage was a beautiful creature, but it was stubborn as a mule. As they were riding along, the horse would occasionally bulk and refuse to move. The first time it happened was when they'd come to a little creek and the horse had come to a dead stop. The young man slowly stepped down from the carriage, looked the horse in the eye, stretched out his arm, pointed at the horses head, and sternly said, 'That's once!'"

"He got back into the carriage, and everything was fine for awhile. Then the horse bulked again. This time the bridegroom repeated the same procedure and said, 'That's twice!' The horse snorted and shook his head, but he took up his pace and again pulled the carriage through the beautiful countryside."

"The young bride was enjoying the pastoral scene and being with her new husband until they came to another little stream. This time when the horse refused to move, the young man didn't say a word. Instead, he just jumped to the ground, grabbed a wide board, and beat the horse over the head until it fell unconscious to the ground."

"This was more than the young woman could stand. She too clambered out of the carriage, kneeled over the still horse, and looked up at her husband and screamed, 'How could you do such a thing to such a beautiful animal?' The husband listened quietly while she continued to berate him. When she finally stopped for breath, he quietly said, 'That's once!'"

"When I finished my story, every one of the boys looked at me wide-eyed when I pointed at Little Bill and said, 'That's once!' Now anytime any of the boys act up, all I have to do is say, 'That's once!' " He chuckled when he added, "No one has made me say, 'That's twice!'"

June and Dick exchanged grins. While they knew that Bill was a kind man, and that his bark was worse than his bite, they could understand why a dozen little boys wouldn't want to challenge him. This was a story that was to be passed on from Bill and Fred and Dick and June to their children. In fact, in the future, Dick and June used this story behind the scenes to avert serious arguments. Anytime things looked as if they might get out of hand, one or the other would quip, "That's once!" Those two words usually eased the tension and averted a fight.

Usually it worked, but not always. Once, a few years down the road when Dick's teasing got out of hand, June tried to put a stop to it when she declared, "That's once!" Those words and her subsequent, "That's twice!" only seemed to egg him on. Something in June seemed to snap as she yelled, "That's it!" and grabbed a rolled up newspaper and took off after him. He scrambled for the safety of the kitchen island with his spouse in hot pursuit. Fire sparked from her eyes when she heard his taunting laughter.

As they circled the bar, she was determined to catch him, and he was just as determined to escape. "Hold still!" June shouted.

Dick didn't break his stride when he shouted over his shoulder, "And let you catch me?"

Just then, June heard a sound from the open doorway. When she turned she saw her little daughter, Janice, pale-faced, wide-eyed, and frozen in apparent fear and shock. Dick's teasing and her anger were forgotten at the sight. June immediately ran to her daughter, stooped down to her level and whispered, "What is it, Honey?"

Tears threatened to escape from Janice's blue eyes when she hesitantly whispered, "Are you going to get a divorce?" June was stunned by the question. Memories of her father telling her as an eleven-year-old that he and her mother were getting a divorce flooded her mind. "How could I ever do anything that would make any of my children think that?" June inwardly moaned.

With this thought echoing in her mind, she gathered her little girl in her arms and declared, "Your daddy and I will never get a divorce. We love each other." Janice's questioning stare demanded more of an explanation so June found herself stammering, "I wasn't going to hurt Daddy. He was just teasing Mommy, and Mommy lost her temper."

The little girl wiggled out of her mother's arms and looked her in the eye and matter-of-factly instructed, "Forgive him!"

Those two words brought back a memory of an incident that had taken place earlier when the children's redheaded Ma Ma Polly and the boys were on one of their frequent visits. Every day, Fred, Bill, Sharlyn, and Janice played next door with their good friend Betsy or she came over and played in their yard with them.

Several times each day Janice would come in the house with a complaint about something Betsy had said or done. Every time this happened MaMa Polly would give her a hug and tell her to forgive her. Janice would always hug Polly in return and trot outside. After the ninth time this happened, Janice finally asked, "What's forgive, MaMa?"

After her grandmother patiently explained, and Janice returned to her play, June asked Polly, "What do you think she's been doing every time you've told her to forgive?"

Polly shook her head and muttered, "I don't know, but I wouldn't be surprised if she thought it meant to clobber her!" As it turned out, they never did get the answer to that question.

～

Those events were to take place in the future. Now, though, that fall of nineteen fifty-three, Fred, Bill, and Mack were the first to go beyond, "That's twice!" and they found themselves in BIG TROUBLE, not only with Big Bill, but also with Granddad Srite.

It happened over the Thanksgiving holiday while the Roberts and the Harmans were on a visit to Polly's parents' home in Mississippi.

Mack, Fred, and Bill were restless after the two-day trip from Ohio. While Granddad Srite was in the back pasture, and the rest of the family lingered over a hearty breakfast, the boys silently crept through the front door, careful not to let the screen-door slam behind them. They managed to move from the front-porch to the first big tree without being seen. Then their actions became even more furtive as they dashed from tree to tree until they had distanced themselves from the view of the adults. Anyone watching them would have known that these boys were up to no good. Unfortunately though, no one actually saw them...at least not in time to avert disaster.

When the trio had determined that they were far enough from the house not to be seen, they stood straight and tall and strode to the edge of the pond where the grass was high enough to conceal their activities. When they stripped off their shirts and tied them around their waists, the morning sun beat mercilessly on their backs. They were too immersed in their task, though, to notice. "Are we far enough from the house that no one will see us?" Mack asked.

Fred peered toward the farmhouse and mumbled, "Yeah!" Then he dropped the heavy bag he'd carried hobo-fashion over his shoulder at Mack's feet. Within seconds, he stooped down and ruffled through its contents and asked the older boy which one he wanted to do first?

Mack dropped to his knees and peered into the satchel. "I like these!" he exclaimed as he pulled out a string of red, white, and blue star spangled cylinders from the satchel.

The freckles stood out on Bill's impish face when he flashed a grin and held out a handful of matches. "I got these from the kitchen when Nanny wasn't looking!" he boasted.

"Let's see how many we can set off at once!" Fred said. The two others nodded eagerly as they set about igniting them.

"One, two, three, go!" Mack yelled. At the sound of go, each boy let his fly into the tall grass. The sound of rat-a-tat-tat-boom and a few gasps was followed by shooting sparks that turned into flames that quickly shot as high as their heads.

The boys tore their shirts from around their waists and frantically started to beat at the flames. Then Fred ran to the pond and tried to scoop out water to throw on it, but this didn't help since the only container he had was his hands.

"Fire! Fire!" the boys screamed as they dashed for the house with the flames only yards from their feet. The adults in the house had smelled smoke a few seconds before they heard the boys' frantic cries. With brooms, mops, and water pails in hand Burrel, Polly, Bill, and Dorothy made a mad dash toward the spreading fire.

Granddad Srite and three farmhands joined the fight, but the grass and crops were so dry that everything in the raging fire's path was burned until all that was left was the scorched earth. Fortunately their heroic actions stopped the encroaching fire before it had a chance to reach the farmhouse.

Three very frightened boys stood repentant before the smoke smudged adults. Once their elders had ascertained that the boys had gone against their instructions not to light any of the fireworks that they had bought on the trip without an adult supervisor, Big Bill was ready to show them what happens to little boys when they go too far. Granddad Srite stepped in and said, "This is my field, and I think I should be the one to take care of these boys!" Bill and Fred exchanged cocky looks that clearly said, "That was a narrow escape." Since their grandfather had never laid an angry hand on either of them, they had no reason to believe otherwise this time. They were soon to find that they had gone too far even for their loving grandfather.

When years later, Little Bill as an adult related their trip to the woodshed to his sister, he'd rubbed his bottom at the memory of the impression his grandfather had made on him. "We didn't sit down very comfortably for awhile," he'd chuckled. "At least, though, Granddad saved us from finding out from Big Bill what going beyond, 'That's twice,' would have gotten us."

A NURSE AND A DOCTOR

Meanwhile, back in Ohio, on that Thanksgiving Day, the house on Oakwood Avenue was filled with anticipation. June's brother, Dick, was bringing a woman to meet them. The smells of the roasting turkey and dressing filled the kitchen while June finished dinner preparations, and her husband lingered over a cup of coffee. "Do you think it's serious?" June asked him.

Dick cautioned her not to read too much into her brother bringing a dinner guest. "As I recall, your mother said they've only known each other for a month."

June flashed an exasperated look at her husband before she replied, "I know that, but this is the first time he's ever brought a girl to our house. Doesn't that tell you something?"

"It just tells me that he's met someone he likes to spend time with." A teasing note crept into his voice when he said, "If you had your way, everyone you know would be married."

He'd laid himself open, and she couldn't resist saucily teasing, "I've always heard that misery loves company!"

Before he had a chance to respond, five-year-old Sharlyn shouted from the living room, "Uncle Dick is here!" June quickly glanced around the room to be sure that everything was in order, removed her apron and went to the front door. By the time she threw the door open in greeting, her brother and a tall, slender woman were walking up the steps. He looked dapper in his new dove gray wool suit. His companion was stylishly dressed in a coral two piece dress that complimented her ash blond hair and blue eyes.

Sharlyn happily greeted them while her twenty-month old sister, Janice, looked on. Once Dick disentangled himself from his niece, he introduced them to his friend. "This is Beverly Hunt," he proudly informed them. Something in his voice alerted June that this woman was special.

During dinner, when she asked how they'd met, they exchanged grins before Dick told her, "We met on a train."

"A train!" June exclaimed. "I didn't even know you'd been on a trip since you got home from the navy!"

Her brother chuckled, "I wouldn't exactly call it a trip. A couple guys and I took the train to a football game between Mansfield High School and Massillon. Bev and her roommate from nurse's training were on the train. Massillon is Mansfield's big football rival. So much so, that every year a few special cars are chartered on the train to take all the fans to the game."

"People of all ages go to that game, not just high school students," Bev interjected. "The car we were in was absolutely packed."

"Even though it was, I noticed Bev as soon as I walked down the aisle, and I stopped and started to talk to her," Dick said.

"I thought he was a little fresh when he asked me for a date," Bev explained. "Besides, I was a little leery since I knew the other man he was with, and he was married."

Dick chuckled at the memory, "She sure was suspicious and a little cheeky, I thought. She did let me sit beside her on the train and at the game, but when I asked her for a date, she turned detective." In response to his sister's raised eyebrow, he remarked, "She asked me if I were married. Even when I told her that I wasn't, she didn't believe me."

"I made him show me his hand," Bev said. "When he held it out for me to see, I checked to make sure that he wasn't wearing a wedding ring or a tell-tale white band in his tan to show that he'd taken one off," she declared. "I'm twenty-one years old, and I've met one or two married men who try to pass themselves off as single."

June smiled at Bev and said, "I can testify to his good character."

Her husband, Dick, flashed his mischievous grin and joked, "I can testify that he is a character too."

The entire day went well and before it was over and the visitors departed, they had taken several pictures to mark the occasion, and June had concluded that she had just met her future sister-in-law. Not only was she the first girl he had brought to meet them, but during the course of conversation, he let them know that this was the first holiday in her entire life that she had spent away from her own family.

The entire day passed pleasantly, and ended much too soon. Before their visitors left, June had told him as she had ever since she'd seen him in his new suit for the first time that when he was ready to get rid of it, she wanted him to give it to her. Her brother and husband had heard this before, but Bev looked at her as if she'd lost her mind.

"June has taught herself how to sew, and she plans to make herself a suit out of it someday," the wearer of the suit explained.

June added that there was enough fabric in one pant leg to make a skirt and that she could cut his jacket down to fit her. "He looks so good in it that I can't imagine him ever giving it up, though," June added in mock regret. *Months passed, but there did come a day when he decided it was out of style and he handed it over to her, and true to her word she turned it into a stylish suit for herself.*

∽

While those months went by, Dick and Bev's romance became more serious while June and Dick waited for the birth of their third child. As the delivery date drew nearer, June was beginning to feel certain that this baby was also going to be a girl. This feeling was strengthened by what she was told by her mother-in-law and her doctor.

One day when the little family was at the house on Third Street for a spaghetti dinner, Rowie had looked over June's increased girth and informed her that she could always tell the sex of the baby by the way an expectant mother showed. "You're showing in the front, and that means a girl," she seriously intoned. While June didn't believe in what she considered "old wives tales", her doctor lent some credence to what Rowie had said when he told her that the heartbeat sounded like it could be a girl.

That evening when she told Dick what the doctor had said, he spoofed, "What does that mean? It could be a girl...or it could be a boy? He does have a fifty-fifty chance of being right no matter what he tells you, but there is no sure way to tell until the baby gets here."

"Doctor Wells admitted as much today when I asked him if he'd been right about the heartbeat of his own four children," June explained. Her face flushed when she relayed what else he'd told her, "He said that he never even checked... that once he got his wife knocked up, he sent her on to another doctor."

Dick whooped and exclaimed, "Knocked up? He actually said knocked up?"

"Surprised me too!" June replied. "I guess I expected a doctor to use a more technical term."

Dick's grin was wicked when he said, "I guess doctors are human too."

At that time most people looked on doctors as God-like, even though June was no exception, she wasn't anxious to pursue the subject. She had something much more important on her mind. "If we have another girl, that will be fine," she said, but her voice sounded wistful when she murmured, "I would like to have a little brother for the girls." Dick squeezed her hand reassuringly before he moved across the room to switch on the television set.

Sharlyn and Janice had been sitting on the floor playing with their dolls until Sharlyn heard Tony Marvin, the announcer shout, "It's Arthur Godfrey Time!" With her doll clutched to her chest, she turned to her sister and said, "I-Forgot-free is on." Her pronunciation of the famous entertainer's name never failed to delight her parents as did Little Bill's, "Awful Godfrey." June knew that both children were old enough now to get the name right, but they didn't want to give up the attention their mispronunciation brought them.

During her pregnancy, June had spent hours poring over the writings of Doctor Spock. He'd published a book and wrote a magazine column on how to raise children. With memories of Sharlyn's reaction to a little sister in mind, an article she'd come across on how to prevent jealousy of a new sibling caught her eye.

The next time her mother came to visit, she showed it to her. "He recommends that when you bring the baby home from the hospital, you give a baby doll to each of the other children. I think it's a good idea...especially if I can find one that looks like a newborn."

Priscilla liked the idea, and that Saturday night the two of them left Dick to baby-sit while they went shopping. After Priscilla drove downtown and found a parking place, they made their way around the town-square to the stores. Although they stopped at every one that sold toys, nothing suited June's purpose until they entered the toy department at Sears and Roebuck's.

"Look, Mom!" she cried as her eyes settled on a display of dolls of all shapes and sizes. In the middle shelf was exactly what she was looking for. The clerk immediately noticed her interest and asked if she'd like to see it. As soon as the box was set on the counter before her, June lifted the tiny doll from its bed of tissue paper. Dressed in a christening dress, and a lace trimmed bonnet, it looked exactly like a newborn baby.

When June saw the downy wisp of blond hair that peaked from under the cap, she asked if it also came with brown hair. "I think it would be nice if each girl had one with her own color hair," June told her mother. The woman disappeared in a storage room only to return empty handed to tell them that it apparently only came with light hair. Seeing the young expectant mother's crest-fallen expression, she added a sincere, "I'm sorry."

"It looks like I'm going to have blond grandchildren," June announced.

"It won't make any difference to the girls," Priscilla assured her. "If you think they might get them mixed up, we can add a different color ribbon to each dress." June nodded and when they left the store a few minutes later, each woman had a shopping bag containing a doll looped over her arm. "I'm sorry I won't be there when they see these," Priscilla said. "I think it's a great idea, though! I wish we'd been able to afford to do something like that for you when Dickie was born, but it was during the depression and things were different then."

"Was I jealous?" June asked. "I certainly don't remember."

Priscilla laughed, "The problem I had with you was just the opposite. You were only two and a half years older than he was, and you looked at him as your own doll baby. Your dad and I used to laugh about you being Mama's little helper...whether I wanted you to be or not."

This conversation seemed to put Priscilla in a nostalgic mood. On the way back to the car she began to reminisce about her own childhood. "The activities around the square haven't changed since I was a little girl," she said as she looked around at the throng of people rushing in and out of the stores, waiting in line at the movie theaters, or the spectators sitting in the cars watching.

"I remember when Mom, Dad, and I used to bring our produce in to the farmers' market on the square. Mom would pack a basket of food and we'd stay all day...then sit here like these people are doing and watch the world go by." She laughed softly and added, "At least to my little girl eyes, it looked like the entire world."

"The more things change, the more they seem to stay the same," June mused when her gaze wandered from the bustling activities to the seated on-lookers.

"You're right," Priscilla agreed. "The cars may be more modern and the clothes and hair styles are different, but people's habits are the same."

Priscilla's nostalgia was contagious, and June soon found her mind flooded with the thoughts of her own childhood. As she felt her unborn child stretch and move, she felt a strong connection with the past and the future. "All these people who are here now and have gone before are part of us," she silently mused. "I hope my own children will feel the way I do about family."

A PREMONITION

By May 1954, June's due date was only four days away. There was an air of expectancy in the house on Oakwood Avenue as they waited. June's bag was packed, and she and Dick had discussed the procedure they would follow when she went into labor. Sharlyn was looking forward to spending time with Rowie and Toots (the children's pet name for Forest). Janice was already in Jackson with her Ma Ma and Granddad.

That evening, Sharlyn and Betsy had their paper dolls spread over the living room floor, Dick's eyes were glued to the television set, and June idly flipped through the pages of a magazine when the quiet was shattered by the shrill ring of the telephone. It was Polly calling so Janice could talk to her mother, but in actuality she wanted to check on June.

After June chatted briefly with her little daughter and heard how much fun it was to be with **"them,"** and that she wasn't the least bit homesick, Polly took over the phone. Then Polly laughed and said, "You should have seen Janice before I gave her a bath this evening. As usual, she couldn't wait for dinner, so I sat her on the counter and let her feed herself a bowl of mashed potatoes. She had them in her hair, all over her face, and her clothes. I think she got more on herself than in her mouth!"

June chuckled and said, "I've seen how you set her on the counter and feed her potatoes. You know that you spoil both of the girls. Polly responded that it would be difficult not to, before she asked, "How are you feeling?"

"Fine," June responded. "I'm getting a little anxious, but the baby isn't due for four more days. If it's anything like the girls, it will be late."

Polly was persistent. "Are you sure you're feeling alright? No pains or anything?"

"I just miss Janice," June replied. Polly still seemed dubious, but June's assurance that she would call her at the first pain seemed to satisfy her.

"Just be sure you do!" Polly said before she hung up.

She and Dick discussed the conversation and watched a couple hours of television before they turned in for the night. When she finally fell asleep, her sleep was filled with dreams. The most realistic one was of Sharlyn as a three-year old. As the little girl had done so many times when she was that age, in June's dream she'd bounced into her parents' bedroom and chirped, "Time to get up, Kids! It's ten-furty!" Even in her dream, June knew that Sharlyn hadn't done that for at least two years...maybe three.

The child's voice in her dream sounded so real that she found herself struggling to awake. She managed to open her eyes in time to see the door fling open and the light stream in from the hall. Seconds later, a tiny blond whirlwind threw herself onto the bed and shouted, "Mommy! Mommy!"

"I must still be dreaming," June thought...only now Janice was in her dream. The feel of little arms around her neck brought her completely awake. Her daughter who was supposed to be miles away in Jackson was actually here in her room.

The patch of darkness at the window proved that it was not yet daylight, and a glance at the clock told her that it was one-thirty. Voices from downstairs confirmed that Janice had not magically appeared.

June flung back the covers, grabbed her robe, ran a comb through her hair and said, "Come on. Let's go downstairs and see what's going on."

She fully expected to see her father and stepmother. When she stepped into the kitchen, she discovered that she was only partly right. Polly was there and with her were her next door neighbors.

Astonished, June could only stammer, "W-w-why?"

Her stepmother looked a little sheepish when she replied, "After I hung up from talking to you, I had a premonition that the baby was going to be born tonight. Your dad thought I was crazy, but I was absolutely certain." She smiled apologetically at her neighbors before she continued. "Your dad couldn't bring me, but Harry volunteered. So here we are!"

June studied the flushed face of her stepmother and said, "I can't understand why you'd think that. I told you I hadn't even had a twinge." At the sight of the other woman's crest-fallen look, she added, "I'm glad you're here anyway. We'll have a nice visit."

When she offered to make some coffee, they all declined. "Everyone is tired," Polly said. "I think it's time we call it a night."

After they'd all trooped up the stairs and settled in, June said to her husband, "I must have been out like a log. I didn't hear anyone at the door or you get up to let them in."

"You sure were sleeping soundly!" Dick declared. "Now we'd better get back to sleep. The girls will be awake before we know it."

"Yep, it's ten-furty, kids," June sleepily mumbled.

To Dick's, "What?" she sleepily replied that she'd tell him in the morning.

In the morning though, she had other things on her mind. The hands on the bedside clock showed that it was barely six o'clock when she was awakened by a stabbing pain. Her first thought was that it wasn't the twenty-third yet. This couldn't possibly be labor. All her children had been late.

The next pain was persistent enough to make her change her mind. She nudged Dick and told him that she thought her pains had started. At first he sleepily buried his head in the pillow, but her cry of, "I don't think we have any time to waste," brought him awake.

"I'll wake Polly," he shouted as he raced down the hall.

"Don't wake the girls," June called after him.

June felt less frightened when Polly appeared and took over. She started by timing the contractions and telling June she'd better get ready to go to the hospital. "I'll call the doctor while you get dressed," she instructed. With a look at Dick, she said, "You, too."

It only took the expectant mother a few minutes to be ready, but once she got downstairs, her husband seemed to have disappeared. Before she could fret too much, though, she heard his footsteps on the stairs. "Finally," she breathed as she felt the urgency of another pain consume her.

When Dick appeared in the room, she gasped in surprise. He was wearing a new suit she'd never seen. "Where did you get that?" she asked.

"I got it at Sherman's. I wanted to be dressed up for such an important occasion!"

Despite her anxiety, she was pleased. "You look handsome!" she told him. "But I think we'd better get this show on the road unless you want to deliver it yourself." That statement got his attention, and she found herself hurried into the car and sped to the hospital.

The next couple hours were de ja vu. Everything was an exact repeat of what had happened when Janice was born. As they had done before, they arrived at the hospital at seven o'clock. The same housekeeper was washing the windows in the labor room. Doctor Wells arrived a few minutes after she did. June was given twilight sleep and ether, and the baby was delivered a little over two hours after they got to the hospital. While Janice had been born at 9:20 a.m., this baby made its entrance into the world at 9:15 a.m.

When the new mother awoke, she found her husband anxiously waiting to tell her of the one major difference. He kissed her soundly then he announced, "We have a little boy!"

"No we don't," she protested. Despite his assurance and that of the doctor, she had been too indoctrinated into expecting a girl to believe she really had a boy until she was able to see for herself.

Holding him, she was euphoric. By some miracle, she had what she wanted... first the girls and now her son. "Life couldn't be much better than this," she thought as she studied his tiny features. His nose was a little tip-tilted, his eyes were a dark blue as Sharlyn's had been. Since his oldest sister's had turned brown, June surmised that his would too. The nurse told her that he weighed in at eight pounds and nine ounces and was twenty-three inches long. "Perfect," the new mother thought.

Fortunately, she had no idea that this tiny creature might be in danger as she looked tenderly into his eyes. The first inkling she had was when her stepmother visited that afternoon. After she had properly admired the baby in the nursery, she came into June's room. She hugged June and exclaimed, "You got your boy! I'm so glad!"

June's smile was radiant when she talked about the baby. After several minutes of happy chatter, she said, "I was going to call him Richard Michael, but after Skip and JoAnne named theirs Michael, I figured I was going to have to come up with another name."

"Have you picked one?"

"I decided to name him after Dad," June explained.

"You're going to call him Oscar!" Polly cried.

June laughingly responded, "No, I'm not going to call him Oscar, and I'm not going to call him Burrel. His middle name is going to be Harman. I've given it a lot of thought, and came to the conclusion that with that name he'll not only be named after Dad, but also Grandpap, and Skip. Maybe it's because we just lost grandpap, but recently the connection of the past, present, and future has been on my mind. Since I don't carry the Harman name anymore, this is the only way I can pass it down."

"As we've always planned, his first name will be Richard, and we'll call him Ricky," June explained.

"Dick probably likes that," Polly said. "I think all fathers like to have their sons named after them, but if you call him Ricky that should cut out the confusion of having a junior in the family."

June nodded and added, "The Richard is for Dick and Dickie."

Polly reiterated that she thought June's choice of names was good and told her that she was sure her dad would be pleased, and Grandpap would have been if he'd known. Then she changed the subject by asking if June had heard Janice's cough.

"Yes, I heard it last night. When did it start?"

Polly explained that it had been going on for awhile. "I thought that I'd take her to the doctor when I get back to Jackson. I'd take her here to Doctor Petersilge, but I know Nada and Harry are anxious to get home. Besides our doctor is pretty good."

"You're not still going to the one that believes in treating everything with a little whisky and sugar in water, are you?" June asked.

"Heavens no! That was when we lived in Pittsburgh." Polly laughed before she continued, "She really did believe in doing that. She had me give the boys whiskey, sugar, and water to cure colds and sore throats. I remember how she gave it to Bill to make his measles come out."

"I do too," June teased. "It's probably a good thing you moved from there or you all might have become alcoholics."

The nurse poked her head through the open door and announced that visiting hours were over. Polly leaned over and kissed her daughter and whispered, "What do you think of my premonition now?"

All the excitement of the day had temporarily wiped the strange occurrence of the night before from her mind. "How did you know I was going into labor?" she breathed.

"Maybe I didn't give birth to you, but I've always thought that we were connected at the heart," she quietly replied. "Why wouldn't I know when you need me?"

Before June could reply, she heard the stern voice of the nurse repeat, "Visiting hours are over!" Polly nodded, informed June that she would be back from Jackson in time to take care of the two of them when they got home from the hospital.

"Let Dick know about Janice's cough," the new mother called after Polly's retreating back.

The redhead turned, gave a jaunty wave, and called out, "Will do!" before she headed for the elevator.

~

June was surprised that so much had changed in the way new mothers were treated in the two short years since Janice had been born. She thought of how when Sharlyn was born she'd been taken home from the hospital in an ambulance and had to stay in bed for ten days. Now Dick could take her home in the car and she wouldn't even be confined to bed. While she was still going to have to take it easy for at least ten days, she would be allowed to help a little with the care of the baby.

When Dick came to the hospital to take her home, she was disappointed that the girls weren't with him. "They're waiting at home with Polly to give you a big welcome. Polly and I have the dolls you got for them out of hiding and ready for you to give to them."

Her welcome couldn't have been warmer if she'd been away for months instead of the three days. By the time the car stopped at the curb, both girls ran down the porch steps onto the brick sidewalk to greet her. They tried to peek at the baby's face, but June had it hidden by the blanket. "When we get inside," she promised.

When she stepped into the dining room, she saw that the fold down couch had been made up with fresh linens so she and Dick could sleep downstairs. Polly winked and gestured toward the bassinet that was standing a few feet from the makeshift bed. Although a fleecy, pastel green baby blanket was casually thrown over it, June knew what she'd find hidden there. She turned to Dick and handed him the baby. While he seated himself on the couch, the girls sat one on each side of him. All three of them looked tenderly at this new addition to the family while June reached under the blanket for Sharlyn and Janice's newborn baby dolls.

Since Polly had wrapped each one in a receiving blanket, the appearance of having their own baby seemed even more realistic. Both girls smiled happily when their mother placed the dolls in their arms. "Now you have your own baby to take care of," she beamed. "You'll have to watch me take care of little Ricky, so you'll know how to take care of your own baby," she added.

After June and the baby were settled in for a nap, the girls ran out to show off their babies to their friend, Betsy. June observed that they took this mothering job seriously, and that there was no sign of jealously toward the baby. "Thank heavens for Doctor Spock!" she told Polly.

"Speaking of doctors, I did take Janice to our doctor and he said she was just getting over the whooping cough," Polly announced. At June's look of alarm and cry of, "The baby!" Polly explained that he'd assured her that Janice was no longer contagious.

June's sigh of relief was replaced by pure terror when her stepmother added, "He did say that Sharlyn has been exposed and could come down with it in the next few days. What he suggested we do is separate Sharlyn from the baby until she either has the whooping cough or we're sure she's not going to catch it."

June shot a panicky look at her sleeping son before she asked if there was any danger now. When her stepmother assured her that there wasn't, June said, "Both Mom and Rowie will be here sometime today. I'm sure one or the other would be glad to take her. The only problem I can see with Mom is that she'd have to take off from work. It might be better if she stayed with Rowie."

THEIR GUARDIAN ANGELS

When both grandmothers arrived, June waited until they each had a chance to hold Ricky before she broached the subject. To her shock and dismay, neither grandmother was able to help her. "Kenny has never had the whooping cough," Rowena said. "I don't think it would be right to deliberately expose him to it."

June's heart sank when her mother said, "Bill hasn't had it either. I think it might be dangerous for a man his age to catch the whooping cough." June found herself biting her tongue to keep from retorting that it would be even more dangerous for a baby. She'd always been aware that her mother was careful not to let her children interfere in her life with her second husband, and although Bill had always treated her well, she didn't want to cause problems, real or imagined for her mother.

Polly had been staying in the background while the other grandmothers were visiting, but once she heard their responses, and saw June's stricken look, she jumped in with both feet. Her voice was dangerously low when she said, "Don't worry, June. We'll work something out. I'm not going to let anything happen to this baby!"

Before anything else could be said, the baby cried to be fed. Although he wasn't happy, he was awake, and his Gram and Rowie got their first look at his eyes. While they made over him, and June fed him, she couldn't quite rid herself of the fear. In the midst of all the chatter, she silently prayed that God would protect her baby. Oblivious of everyone around her, she made all kinds of promises to Him if He'd save her son's life. She'd go to church every Sunday. She'd never say another harsh word to anyone as long as she lived. She'd be the best mother in the whole world. In His wisdom, God probably knew she couldn't keep all these promises, but He smiled on her anyway. God had some earthly help, though, in the shape of a young redheaded grandmother and June's doctor.

Once the stream of visitors had left, the new mother and the grandmother began to talk about ways to solve their problem. "I could take the girls home with me, but then you wouldn't have anyone to take care of you and the baby," Polly said.

"I can manage," June insisted. "I'll do anything to keep him from being exposed!"

"Nothing doing!" Polly exclaimed. "Just look at you. You're exhausted!'

"That's different!" June protested. Then less vehemently, she added, "I think everyone I know stopped in today. I have to admit that although I loved to show off the baby, I did get pretty tired."

Immediately concerned, Polly insisted that the new mother rest. "Take a nap, and I'll have dinner ready for you when you wake up. We'll talk some more then. Okay?"

"Okay," June replied. "I just want to check on the baby first to be sure he's alright. Then I'll lie down for awhile."

When Polly noticed June's brow wrinkled in worry as she watched the infant's steady breathing, she reminded her that Ricky had not been exposed. "Janice is no longer contagious, and it hasn't been long enough since Sharlyn was exposed for her to have caught it."

June nodded in understanding, and replied, "I know he's safe for now...but for how much longer? You know yourself that if he gets the whooping cough, he wouldn't be able to cough up the phlegm!"

June recognized the determined glint in Polly's eye when the older woman declared, "We won't let him catch it! This house is big enough that we can keep Sharlyn away from him until the danger is over." When she saw the conflicting emotions of hope and doubt battle on June's face, the older woman added, "I'm sure that will work but if it will make you feel any better, you can check with the doctor tomorrow."

The next morning, June impatiently waited for the clock to strike nine to dial Doctor Wells' number. When the nurse heard the panic in the new mother's voice, she immediately put her through to the doctor.

Once he heard June's story, he said, "Babies generally have a six month immunity from their mothers for most childhood diseases." She felt her heart sink when after a brief hesitation he went on. "Unfortunately, this doesn't always work with whooping cough."

"What can we do?" June asked.

The line was silent for so long that she at first thought they had been disconnected. Finally he replied, "I've never done this for a baby this young. Usually, I wait until at least three months to start, but I'm going to make an exception with your baby."

June was so tense that she wanted to scream, "What? What are you talking about?" Instead, she waited for him to go on.

Abruptly, the doctor broke the silence. "Bring him in. I will start his inoculations now. Between that and keeping the infected child away from him, he should be safe. I'll tell the nurse to bring you in as soon as you get here."

When she tried to express her appreciation, he brusquely dismissed her with a reminder that he had patients to see. June laughed when she related this to her stepmother, "No one would ever accuse him of having a gracious bedside manner," she quipped.

"Who cares about that?" Polly asked. "All I care about is whether he knows what he's talking about." June nodded in agreement as she started to get ready for her trip to the doctor's office.

Less than an hour later, June, with Ricky in her arms, and Polly with the girls in tow showed up at the doctor's office. Within a few minutes, Ricky was screaming his protest when the needle pierced his flesh. June's feeling of sympathy for her son's pain was mixed with relief when she saw the life-saving fluid enter his body.

The next few days might have been more difficult if Polly hadn't been able to enlist the girls' help. As June had always known, her daughter was willing to do anything this young grandmother suggested. This was no exception. Once she explained to Sharlyn the importance of separating her from the baby the little girl readily agreed to stay upstairs, and when she did come downstairs to stay in the kitchen or in the yard. "I'll close the door into the front part of the house...where your mom and Ricky will be. You can go out on the porch and look through the window at them. If he's awake, we'll hold the baby up so you can see him."

Sharlyn seemed to enjoy this different game of hide-and-seek, and her little sister tagged along with her. It wasn't unusual for the new mother to look up and see the two little faces pressed against the glass of the front window. Many times their friend Betsy and other neighborhood children would be peering over their shoulders.

On one such occasion, June murmured to the tiny baby she'd laid on the bed beside her, "This must be how the monkeys feel in the zoo."

After all their worry and protective action, neither woman could be sure if Sharlyn ever really had the whooping cough. If she did, it was an extremely mild case. At one point, they heard her cough and make a sound that sounded like a whoop, but neither the cough nor the whoop was ever repeated.

"This isn't unusual," June explained to Polly. "When the girls had the chicken pox, Janice was peppered, and Sharlyn only had four."

Both women agreed that the little girl must have had the whooping cough and that no matter how mild the case, it had still been contagious, and that their precautions had been worthwhile.

"Now that we can relax," June said. "I want to talk to you about my experience with de ja vu at the hospital."

"Let me get us a cup of coffee first," Polly said as she headed for the kitchen. When she returned a few minutes later, she not only brought two cups filled with the steaming brew, but a plate of cookies. She settled in an easy chair beside the couch, placed the tray on the table between them and said, "Tell me all about it."

Once June had related how this birth had appeared like a repeat performance of Janice's, she added, "That wasn't all, though. When I was in the hospital when Janice was born, I had a whiny roommate that almost drove me wild. One day, she complained so much about being hot that her doctor opened the window between our beds." June sipped her coffee before she continued. "All I have to do is close my eyes to see all the snow that blew onto my blanket. It really felt like a trip back in time when I heard that same voice across the hall this time. I knew that there couldn't be two voices like that…and I was right!"

"The second day I was there she popped into my room. She'd had a little girl the day I had Ricky." In response to her mother's unasked question, she said, "When I had Janice, she had a little boy." June grinned and quipped, "How's that for coincidence?"

"You must have felt that you were dreaming," Polly commented.

While they'd been talking, Dick had returned from work and joined the conversation. "Did you tell June what Dad did that first Sunday when all our company was here?"

Polly threw back her head and laughed, "No. I saved that for you to tell her."

June sighed and asked, "What now?'

The smile on Dick's lips had spread to his eyes when he said, "You know that chip on the lid of the washing machine?" June nodded quizzically. "Dad tried to rub it off when he was over here."

"He tried to rub it off! What in the world are you talking about?" June asked.

"You know how picky he can be?" Dick said.

"Your dad? Picky?" June teased. "You must be kidding me."

He ignored her smart retort and continued, "No matter how many times I told him that the enamel was off and that all the cleaning in the world wouldn't help, he wouldn't listen." He stopped, expecting to hear a sarcastic remark from his spouse. When she held her tongue, he said. "He used so much Ajax cleanser on it that it turned white. You should have seen how proud he was of himself when he hauled me into the kitchen and showed me. When I tried to tell him that once the cleanser came off, the bare metal would show, he wouldn't believe me."

Polly interjected to say that she thought she'd stumbled into an episode of the I Love Lucy comedy show when she walked into the kitchen just in time to see Dick scrub off the cleanser. "For once in his life, Forest was speechless," she chuckled.

"Reminds me of the yellow sheets," June quipped. Then she sighed and added, "I'm sure he meant well." Then as an afterthought, she asked. "While he was in a cleaning mood, did you get him to scour any more of the appliances?"

"I'm afraid he lost interest after that disaster," her husband chuckled.

Her tongue was firmly lodged in her cheek when she replied, "That's too bad."

Her stepmother patted her on the shoulder as she started for the door to call the girls in for dinner. "After all the stress of the last couple weeks, it's good to be able to laugh," she said.

June nodded her head and lifted the stirring child from the bassinet. While she looked tenderly into his tiny face and held him close, she sent a silent prayer of thanks heavenward. Then she turned to Polly and said, "I thank you too. You may have saved Ricky's life." Polly looked puzzled at the change in the conversation but pleased at the praise.

Her response of, "Anytime," was almost lost in the noise made by the little girls as they clamored into the room. June heard her, though, and smiled.

Then she made room for her husband and girls on the couch beside her. "It's good to be together as a family," she murmured.

She grinned happily when she heard Dick say, "The Five Musketeers, that's us!" She didn't have to say a word. Her radiant smile said it all.

⁓

Before the summer of nineteen fifty-four came to an end, and months before the sixth musketeer was added to the family, they found themselves caught up in an adventure that could have been disastrous.

The eventful day dawned bright and clear. A gentle, almost imperceptible breeze ruffled the trees. That morning, June had kept the car so she could take the children to visit Rowie. Later, when it was time to pick up her husband at work, Ricky was asleep in his bassinet. Not wanting to wake him, she got Betsy's older sister, Patti, to stay with him and the girls.

On the way home, they stopped at the Natoma, a restaurant on the square, for a cup of coffee. As they got out of the car, Dick looked around and commented on the stillness of the air. Now that he mentioned it, June noticed that not a leaf moved on the stately trees that stood sentinel around the courthouse. They'd no sooner gotten to the restaurant and eased into a booth, ready to place their order, when they heard one of the men who stood by the front door exclaim, "Will you look at that!"

Something between fright and bewilderment sounded in his companion's voice when he replied, "We're in for it now!"

June and Dick joined other patrons who'd overheard the remarks in time to see the trees that only seconds before had been so still begin to violently sway from the force of the winds. She was barely conscious of the bits and pieces of conversation that swirled around her as one patron cried, "It looks like a hurricane."

While another one said, "Hurricanes don't happen in Ohio."

Hurricane or not, the young parents knew they had to get home to their children. Dick grabbed June's hand, and together they ran to the car and scrambled inside. The wind was so strong by now that it had threatened to sweep them along with it.

As Dick turned the corner onto East Main Street, they heard a loud shattering noise behind them. "A tree fell on a car!" June cried.

"Was anyone in it?" Dick asked.

She had to shout her response that it had been empty in order to be heard over the roar of the wind. Once they'd gotten away from the square, the next couple blocks were void of trees so they were safe from that danger. That rapidly changed when they crossed the bridge and entered a residential section where the hundred year old trees that lined both sides of the street almost touched as the force of the wind bent them to its will. June felt as though they were driving through a dark tunnel. Then as they continued down East Main Street, they could see and hear trees being uprooted all around them. When June glanced at her husband's face, not a trace of fear or worry showed on it. He seemed to feel her gaze and smiled reassuringly and said, "Don't worry. We'll get there. I've driven through worse than this on the battlefield. At least here, no one is shooting at us."

Her breathing quickened when they turned the familiar corner onto Oakwood Avenue. She was even more frightened when he pulled to a stop in front of their house, and she could see that a humongous part of their maple tree had broken off. It was so large that it covered one half of their front yard between their house and the Eis's.

Before Dick had switched off the engine, June flung open the car door only to have it wrenched from her hand. Then she fought the wind to make it to the safety of the house. When she opened the door and called the children's names, she was met by silence...and darkness. Although it was still evening, the storm had brought on an early night. Then along with the trees, the wind had also blown power lines down, and the entire city was without electricity.

The clamor of her loudly pounding heart almost drowned out the sound of her own voice in her ears when she told her husband, "They're not here."

"They're probably next door at the Eis's," Dick assured her.

"Of course," she thought. With this realization, the worried parents dashed next door. As they knocked on the front door of their neighbor's house, the sound of children's laughter could be heard over the howl of the wind. Betsy's mother, Ginny, threw the door open and called, "Come in and join the hurricane party." The first thing they saw when they walked into the room was Sharlyn and Janice seated on the floor with Betsy. Then in the candlelight, they could make out Patti, with Ricky in her arms; her older sister, Vickie; and their father, Bus, seated on the couch and easy chairs. Although the light was muted, an air of gaiety pervaded the room and the young couple could see the gleam of excitement in their daughters' eyes.

"We're having fun!" Sharlyn announced. "Ginny gave us some cookies and we've been playing games."

For the first time since they'd left the Natoma, June managed to relax. The children were safe! That was all that mattered.

Before they took the children and went home, Ginny explained that when the storm first started, she'd called Patti and told her to bring the children over. "By the time I got outside, the wind was fierce and I was afraid it was too much for the little ones to make it on their own so I had Patti hurriedly toss them across the hedge to me. I quickly passed the girls on to Vickie and Bus who took them inside. Then I brought the baby in myself. They were a little frightened, so we played games with them. I think that after awhile, they thought it was fun."

With her hand on the door, ready to leave, June remembered the huge part of the tree that had fallen into their yard and asked Ginny when it had happened. "Right after Patti tossed Ricky over the hedge," Ginny declared. "It landed right where the children had been standing." The slight tremor of Ginny's hand showed June that her neighbor hadn't been quite as calm as she'd wanted the children to think she was. Before they said goodnight, Ginny murmured for June's ears only, "A guardian angel was with us all tonight."

"I think our guardian angel had some help from you and your family," June proclaimed in gratitude.

When they returned next door to the safety of their own home, June realized the experience had been a wild one for her children, Sharlyn excitedly told her that the wind was so strong that they could hardly stand up. Little Janice piped in with, "Mommy, Patti threw me over the hedge! Bus caught me!" This exciting day was etched into their memories forever.

∽

From her kitchen radio the next day, June heard a news report that labeled the storm as hurricane-force winds and rain. The paper was filled with pictures of downed trees and power lines. Aside from the tree they'd seen fall on the parked car, several others had been uprooted on the courthouse lawn. No section of town had escaped the savagery of the storm. From the look of the pictures, city crews would be working night and day to remove the trees that were clogging the streets.

They appeared to have escaped the ravages of the storm, except for the split tree, many smaller branches, paper and other debris that had blown into their yard. While June was picking up the remnants of the storm, she momentarily turned her back on the girls who had followed her outside. She turned when she heard the frantic call of, "Mommy, Mommy," from behind her.

She raced to her two-year-old daughter, Janice, who was standing knee deep in the rain water in the plastic swimming pool with blood dripping from her outstretched hand while her frightened sister tried to help her. "I hurt it," she said. Her big blue eyes were so full of confidence that her mother could make it better that June could feel her heart sink. The extent of her knowledge of first aid was how to apply a Band-Aid.

After she tried that and saw that blood still seeped from the wound, she knew she needed help. Through the open front door, she could see her neighbor, Hazel Loughman, on her porch across the street. All June had to do to bring Hazel on the run was to call across to her that Janice was hurt.

After one look at June's pale face, and Janice's bloody hand and blood splattered play-suit, the middle-aged neighbor sent the frightened mother four doors up the street to Cannazarro's little grocery store for some adhesive tape and gauze. By the time June returned with her purchases, Hazel was sitting at the breakfast table with the little girl on her lap. The wound had been cleaned, the bleeding had been stopped and Janice wore a carefully applied bandage. This life-saving neighbor had even soaked the blood from Janice's playsuit.

"Janice was calm through this entire thing," Hazel told June. She didn't add, but June figured she probably thought, "Much more so than her mother."

When she related the incident to Dick that evening, she said, "She didn't really need to have me go to the store. I think she just wanted to get me out of her way. She probably thought I was going to faint or something."

Dick laughed and replied, "Smart woman. She didn't want two patients on her hands."

June made a face in response. Then she went on to tell him that after the excitement was over, she'd checked to see what had caused the cut. "I found a broken beer bottle in the bottom of the pool. The wind must have blown it from someone's trash barrel."

"No kidding? Here we were dodging fallen trees and a beer bottle caused all that trouble," he exclaimed. "Did you find anything else in the pool?"

"Just some sticks and leaves. Nothing else serious. I did clean it out and empty it, though." She was silent for awhile before she told him, "I think we are lucky to have such good neighbors. Since they're old enough to be our parents, they seem to have taken us under their wings. Have you ever noticed that?"

Dick nodded and chuckled softly before he added, "When we first moved in with our motorcycle, I thought they were never going to accept us!" On a more serious note, he said, "I'm glad they have. When I'm working or playing for a dance, it's nice to know there is someone you could call on if you needed something."

"That's the good thing about living in an older neighborhood like this," June replied.

During the next couple days when June thought about these events, she concluded that her neighbors were indeed the helping hands of the guardian angels Ginny had mentioned. The thought left her with a good feeling as she looked out the window at her children and Betsy at play.

BUGS, ROBBERS, AND SIRENS

June found herself passing on to her young children all the things her mother and father had taught her and her brothers while they were children at the cave house. Years later a man named Robert Fulghum wrote a book called, "All I Ever Needed to Know I Learned In Kindergarten." It contained most of the things that June and her mother had taught for years about sharing, caring, not taking what doesn't belong to you, and living by the Golden Rule. June had also stressed the importance of loving and taking care of each other in the family, not repeating what was heard in the privacy of their home, and being gracious and polite to guests.

She was proud of the way the children seemed to take her teaching to heart. She found that Janice was so impressed with what her mother told her that with all the wisdom of her not-quite-three years she put to use these teachings about graciousness to guests. This created a moment that the family never quite forgot. It was during one of June's father and his family's visits. June and Polly had come down with flu-like symptoms...coughing, wheezing, barely able to talk. Too miserable to do more than sit on the couch and commiserate with each other, they'd turned the care of the children over to the men of the family. When Janice had asked what was wrong with them, Polly had told her they had bugs.

The little girl nodded sagely and stored this bit of knowledge away in case she ever needed it. Much to the women's chagrin and amusement, the time came that very morning after they heard a knock on the door; "Will you see who's there?" June had croaked.

With all the graciousness she'd been taught, the little girl opened the door to an encyclopedia salesman and said, "My name is Jonnie Jean. Won't you come in?" While the young man looked uncertainly at the two red-nosed wheezing, coughing women in the living room, Janice gazed at him through serious blue eyes and added solemnly, "We've got bugs!"

That statement and the appearance of Burrel at the bottom of the steps holding his grandson at arms length and saying, "I think he needs changing," was all that the salesman needed to hear. While Janice looked on in surprise, he backed away until his foot encountered the top porch step. Then he turned and scurried down the stairs and to his car as fast as his feet would carry him.

"I don't know whether it was the bugs or your comment," June laughingly told her puzzled father.

A smile was in Burrel's voice when he replied, "He either expected to have cockroaches crawl all over him, or be asked to change the diaper."

June nodded, then waited until Janice left the room before she stated, "So much for not repeating anything heard in the privacy of your home."

"That might be right, but she gets an A+ on being gracious," Polly pronounced.

~

During the beginning months of nineteen fifty-four and into the next year, television news was filled with stories about a groundbreaking case in Topeka, Kansas called Brown Versus The Board of Education. This case challenged the School Board's policy of separate but equal schools for Negro children. "I can remember Lee's granddaughter when I lived in Mississippi," June told Dick. "She went to one of those so called equal schools. I never saw it, but I do know that even though she lived out in the country, the school board didn't even provide a bus for her or other colored children."

Since Dick had always lived in Newark where the schools were integrated, he'd never given segregation much thought. "I don't understand what the big deal is," he commented. "I think it would be much easier for the board of education to have everyone go to school together."

When they heard Walter Cronkite report that the Supreme Court had determined that the policy was unconstitutional, they had no idea how much an impact this would have on their country, or that it was to be the fore-runner of the civil rights movement.

This and the so-called "Cold War" with the Soviet Union filled the news reports, but the young family had other things on their minds. Ricky, who had just taken his first toddling steps, was about to celebrate his first birthday. Sharlyn was finishing the first grade. Janice was now three and a great help to her mother around the house.

Skip and JoAnne were still stationed in California, and their second redheaded son, Christopher Lee, was now seven months old. June's brother, Dick, would graduate from barber school in June, and he and Beverly Hunt were in the midst of plans for a November wedding. Burrel and Polly were planning an upcoming change in their lives.

It was at this time that the little family on Oakwood Avenue added the newest family member...their sixth musketeer. Another male, he was sweet and gentle with soft brown eyes that would melt the hardest heart. When June looked into them, it was love at first sight. "He'll make a wonderful companion for Ricky," she told Dick.

Janice piped up with, "Me too!"

"I didn't mean to leave anyone out," June said. "Being so close to Ricky's age, I just naturally thought of the two of them together. I'm sure he'll love all of us."

"What are we going to call him?" Sharlyn asked. "Can we pick out a name?"

"I've had a name picked out since I was a little girl," she said as she stroked his honey-brown hair. "We're going to call him Toy."

"What kind of a name is that?" Dick demanded.

June defended her choice by recounting the story of the little Pekinese named Toy she'd had when she was barely in her teens, and how its previous owner had taken it away while she was in school. I'd only had it for a couple days. I was crushed," she explained. "I vowed then that if I ever had another dog, I would call it Toy." As if she thought they needed more convincing, she added, "What better name could anyone pick for such a beautiful toy collie?"

They all laughed when the puppy wagged his tail as if to say, "I like it!"

～

A few weeks later, June's mother and stepfather came to the house on Oakwood Avenue for Sunday dinner. Halfway through the meal, Bill mentioned that he was thinking about buying a country store.

"A country store?" June parroted. "Where?" Then with a sidewise glance at their mother she added, "Why?"

"It's close to Miflin at a little place called Widowville. I'd say, it's probably about ten or twelve miles from Mansfield," he explained. "We could sell our house and move into the attached living quarters. Priscilla could take care of it while I'm at work, and I could take over in the evening. Then when I retire in a couple years, we could run it together," he concluded.

June noticed that while he was enthused about the project, Priscilla was unnaturally quiet. After dinner was over and the two women were alone in the kitchen, June asked her how she felt about it. "I hate to give up our life as it is. We have our house and yard the way we want it. My bookkeeping and sales clerk job at the dress shop is going well. We have our weekends free to come spend time with you and the grandchildren or to go to Indian or Chippewa Lake with our friends." She shrugged as if to dismiss her doubts before she said, "Bill has his heart set on it. He says that since he's eleven years older than I am, he'll go before I do. He thinks that if we have the store, I'll have some security."

"Have you told him how you feel?" June asked.

"I sure have," she replied. "He hasn't made up his mind definitely. He respects Dick as a businessman and plans to ask his advice today."

June nodded, then asked, "He couldn't sell the house and buy it without your signature, could he?"

"Of course not, but if he has his heart set on it, I won't fight him," Priscilla concluded.

She gave her daughter a warning look when the men and children trooped in from the back yard. June reluctantly dropped the subject, but later that evening she asked Dick what advice he'd given Bill.

"I told him that I wouldn't recommend it. It's a Mom and Pop type business that will need to be kept open seven days a week, twelve hours a day in order to make a living. I tried to explain to him the disadvantages of being self-employed, but I don't think he really listened," he explained.

June tut-tutted, and responded that apparently people didn't want advice even when they asked for it.

"Unless you tell them what they want to hear," Dick quipped.

As they suspected, Bill did buy the store and before the summer was over they'd sold their house on Vernon Avenue and moved into the living quarters behind the store. Before the move, they showed it off to June and her family.

Surrounded by rolling hills, it was located in a lovely setting three miles outside of Miflin at the intersection of two country roads. To the left of the store was a small white clapboard church and century old cemetery. On a hill to the right of the store was a small white house and across the road was another. This and a few scattered homes in the distance made up the community of Widowville (named for the many women of the community who had been widowed during the Civil War). In front of the building were two Sohio gas pumps. When they stepped inside they found themselves in a large shelf lined room, with a marble topped counter to their right and a glass case stocked mostly with deli-type meat and cheese straight ahead. A glass candy case atop the counter immediately caught the children's eyes as did the refrigerated Coca-Cola cooler. June could picture the wheels turning in their heads repeating, "Our own candy store!"

In response to their unspoken words, June reminded them that they would be paying for their candy here the same as they did at the neighborhood store. Priscilla smiled indulgently and said, "Not all the time. If it's alright with your mother you can each have a candy bar and bottle of pop now."

June nodded her approval and while the girls seriously studied the contents of the case, she held Ricky up so he could pick something for himself. He reached in and grabbed as much candy as his little hand would hold. Once she'd taken all except one piece away from him, she stood aside and waited for the girls to make their selection. The decision was finally made, and Priscilla led the way into their living quarters. The openness of the living room, dining area, and kitchen created the illusion of space. Priscilla gestured toward some work in progress and explained, "Since I like a little privacy when I'm in the kitchen, we're having a shoulder high bookshelf built to separate the kitchen from the dining room."

As June almost tripped over some tools the workman had left behind, her mother said. "Mr. Hicks isn't too good about picking up after himself, but hopefully, he'll be out of here pretty soon."

"I sure hope he doesn't take as long as the guy we had do our kitchen," June quipped.

"Me too," her mother responded as she led the way into the bedroom and bath. "That completes the tour," she grinned. "As you can see, it's not very big, but it's big enough for the two of us." By the next time the little family visited Widowville, not only was Mister Hicks finished, but Bill had painted all the walls, ceilings and woodwork. With the addition of crisp white curtains in the kitchen, colorful draperies in the other rooms and Priscilla's crocheted and embroidered handiwork, the place was attractive and homey. Those two visits were the beginning of many the young family would make over the years.

~

One day Priscilla was alone when she heard a car stop in front of the store. Two men got out of a late model green car, peered intensively at the empty churchyard and the nearby houses and glanced furtively up and down the converging roads before they came into the store. After they ordered pop and candy bars, the driver asked Priscilla, "Are you alone here?"

After her response of, "My husband will be home soon," they were friendly and pleasant as they continued to ask questions and make small talk.

Their manner quickly changed, though, when she went outside with them to fill their near empty gas tank, and asked the driver, "What kind of a car is this?"

The driver's eyes were cold and his voice hard when he demanded, "Why would you ask that?"

Both men visibly relaxed when she explained, "I always have to be careful with a certain model of car since it always splashes gasoline out on me."

The driver smiled then and joked with her while she put the gas in the car. They paid their bill, again checked the empty highways, and sped away.

Less than a half-hour later the sheriff showed up and said, "The bank in Lucas was held up this morning by two men in a late model green Plymouth. Did you happen to notice if they drove by here?" Priscilla could feel the hair rise on the back of her neck when she heard his words and realized the danger she'd been in. When she told him what had happened, he exclaimed, "You're one lucky lady. Those men are armed and dangerous. They must have thought you'd heard a newscast about the robbery and knew what kind of a car they were driving. It's a good thing you had a good reason for asking!"

She told the sheriff which direction they'd gone when they left the store. To her relief, they were picked up in a very short time.

When she related this happening to her family, they were understandably frightened and cautioned her to be careful in the future. In response, she reached behind the counter and pulled out a Billy club and said, "The sheriff left this here for me, and I will definitely use it if I have to."

All her children talked so much about her need to be careful that she finally promised that she would watch out for desperadoes. The story of Gram and the clumsy robbers who hadn't bothered to fill their gas tanks until after they'd robbed a bank became a frequently told part of family lore.

∽

A few weeks after June's mother and stepfather had settled into their new home, June received news that Burrel, Polly, and the boys would be moving to Newark. One evening when Dick returned from work, his wife met him at the door and excitedly proclaimed, "Dad and Polly are moving to Newark!"

"To Newark?" he parroted. "What are you talking about?"

"Sit down for a minute before dinner is ready, and I'll tell you," she replied. Once he was seated, she handed him a letter from Polly and said, "Read this!" She was too excited about the news, though, to give him a chance to finish before she said. "They've been planning this move for awhile, but they didn't want to say anything until they were sure. She wrote that the job outside Newark just came through and that they plan to move here in a couple weeks! She wants me to see if I can find them a place to live. She particularly likes the mobile home park on the east side of route seventy nine. I'm going there tomorrow to see if they have any vacancies."

Dick was as pleased as she was to know that the Harman family would be back in Newark. "That's a nice place, but if you can't get a lot there, check out the one close to the Orchard Street bridge. Since it's in the country, your dad would really like it."

Although June was optimist at the beginning of her search, she was discouraged by late afternoon. Most of her inquiries had been met with an emphatic, "Sorry, no vacancy." She was hoping this wouldn't be the case when she drove into the tree shaded park on Orchard Street that Dick had recommended. When the middle-aged owner ushered her into the old-fashioned living room of the comfortable farmhouse, she'd already made her decision to reserve a space here. The proprietor was businesslike until she introduced herself. Then his face creased into a smile as he said, "I knew a girl who married someone with that name. Her name was Rowena McNamee. Do you know her?"

When June replied that Rowena was her mother-in-law, he said, "She was one of the most beautiful girls I've ever seen. She and her sister Thelma both were. I used to go to their father's confectionery on Mt. Vernon road just so I could see them." June noticed the wistful look in his eye when he added, "I had my eye on Rowena, but once she met Forest, she wouldn't even give me a second glance."

Before he would discuss business, he wanted to know all about Rowena and Thelma. When he'd extracted all the information he could from June, he regretfully told her that he didn't have an opening in the park but if one became available, he would contact her immediately. She managed to swallow her disappointment when she drove away as his hearty instructions to remember him to Rowena and Thelma rang in her ears.

That evening she finally located a spot for them in a park next to a fire station and across the street from a school on the west side of route 79. They brought their trailer to Heath and settled in quickly. While its proximity to the school was convenient for the boys, the nearness to the fire station was a different matter. Everyday at the stroke of twelve, and anytime day or night when there was a fire or other emergency, the siren would cut loose with a lengthy, ear-splitting sound. When June visited for the first time and almost jumped out of her seat when she heard the blast, Burrel told her that the siren had to be loud and last that long to summon all the volunteer firefighters. He chuckled before he continued, "Unfortunately, when it happens at night, it wakes everyone else…especially those unfortunate enough to live next door."

Although he seemed to be taking the situation lightly, June apologized profusely. "I never would have picked this place if I'd realized that."

"I don't think you had any other choice," her father said. "Besides, this is just temporary. We plan to buy a house and settle down here. Next to back home in West Virginia, I've always liked Newark better than any other place I've lived. Besides, I'd like to raise the boys close to the rest of the family."

June patted her father's hand and told him how glad she was to hear that. "This way, you won't be taking off for some distant place. Do you think there will be enough work around here for you?" she asked.

He shook his head from side to side, and replied, "Probably not, but Polly and I have discussed it and feel that it's time to give the boys some roots. I might have to work away from here, but hopefully I'll be able to be home on weekends." June smiled happily at the thought that for the first time since she'd been sixteen, she and her father would be living in the same town. She could hardly wait to get home and tell Dick and the children that this move would be permanent.

MILDRED TOOTHPICK

The next major event to take place for the family in nineteen fifty-five was the wedding of Dick Harman to Beverly Hunt. Bev asked June to be a bridesmaid, but since they only had one car and Dick worked evenings, she couldn't get to Mansfield for fittings and the rehearsal. When June told her husband that she hoped Dick and Bev would understand, he teased, "They're going to be too interested in each other to notice whether you're even there or not!"

That settled, June relaxed and enjoyed everything about the wedding. She had never seen her brother look happier or more handsome, and the bride was lovely in her long white gown and veil. As Dick had predicted, the happy couple did only have eyes for each other. "It's better that I'm not a bridesmaid with the way my makeup is smearing," June thought as she felt the tears of happiness roll down her cheeks. As she dabbed her eyes, she became aware that her mother was sobbing at losing her youngest son.

As was the custom of the times, a reception followed the ceremony in the social rooms of the church. Then throughout the afternoon, flashbulbs popped as the bride and groom cut the cake and opened their gifts. The wedding had started in the early afternoon and the reception continued into the evening. Like the rest of the guests, June, Dick, and the girls were enjoying the party too much to think about the time.

The sound of excited voices directed their attention toward the front of the room just in time to see Bev throw her wedding bouquet. Amidst the ensuing excitement the newlyweds ran hand-in-hand for the outside door with the guests following them.

While the young couple darted through a shower of rice to the car, June's cousin, Annamae, nudged June, pointed toward the street, and asked, "Isn't that your car?"

June looked in time to see their car with its front end suspended from the back of a tow truck being hauled away. Dick saw it at the same time she did. He waved his arms in the air and ran after it. His shout of, "Stop!" got the attention of the bride and groom and their guests, but the tow-truck driver either didn't hear him or if he did, he completely ignored the plea.

While June and Dick woefully looked on, Dick and Bev drove away from the church closely behind the tow-truck, with Dick and June's car dangling from its rear. As she watched them disappear from sight, June moaned, "What do we do now?"

Priscilla consolingly replied, "Bill and I will take you to the police station. They can help us." A few minutes later, as the little group tromped into the station, the desk sergeant looked up. His eyes scanned their wedding finery before he asked what he could do for them. Once he'd heard Dick's tale of woe, he asked where they'd been parked.

"Across the street from the Lutheran Church on Park Avenue," Dick responded.

Understanding dawned in the officer's eyes before he asked, "In front of the theater?"

"Not directly in front of it, but in that general vicinity," Dick replied.

The sergeant's inquiry as to whether they'd seen the No Parking sign brought blank stares from all of them. He went on to explain that no parking was allowed by the theater after four o'clock. He pointed toward the wall-clock and said, "You can see it's after five now."

While he'd been talking, he'd reached into the drawer and pulled out a form. Then he asked Dick a few questions and noted the answers on the paper before he shoved it across the desk and said, "I need your signature and eighteen dollars for the fine and the impounding fee. You can pay the fine here, and I'll call ahead to be sure they release your car to you."

When they again had the car in their possession and were on their way home, Dick grinned and said, "I don't think Dick and Bev were even aware of what happened to our car."

"If you didn't think they'd know who was there, what makes you think they'd notice one car...more or less?" June quipped. Her tone softened when she added, "They looked so happy, so much in love. Despite what happened to the car, it was a beautiful wedding."

〜

Shortly after the wedding, Dick played one of his practical jokes that not only backfired on him but also got him into trouble with his wife. Before the honeymooners had returned home, June had started to buy Christmas toys for the children. Sharlyn had her heart set on an expensive ballerina doll she'd seen advertised on television. Mindful of her limited Christmas budget, June looked around until she found a similar one in a catalogue for half the price. That evening when she showed it to her husband, nothing in his manner warned her not to let him fill out the order form. His offer to help with something so humdrum was unusual, but she didn't give it a second thought, not even when he said, "So Sharlyn won't see it when it comes in, I'm going to have it mailed to Mom's address."

He volunteered to mail the order on his way to work the next morning. Once it was on the way, June expected to receive it in a week to ten days. Ten days, then two weeks, then four weeks came and went without any sign of the package.

"I can't imagine what happened to the doll Dick ordered," June told Rowie and Dick's grandmother, Lula, one day when they'd stopped at her house for afternoon tea. "Dick mailed it almost a month ago. Christmas is less than two weeks away. Since Sharlyn has her heart set on a ballerina doll, I guess I'll have to buy one downtown if it doesn't get here within the next couple days."

She sighed and said, "Are you sure that nothing has come from them? No letter or anything?"

"A package did arrive a couple weeks ago," Lula said. "It was addressed to someone named Mildred Toothpick, though. I told the mailman that no one lived here by that name and sent it back."

"Oh, no!" June moaned. "Dick thinks it's funny to call me Mildred Toothpick sometimes. I guess he thought he'd get a rise out of me when I saw it." The tone of her voice showed that the humor was completely lost on her. "This is one time his sense of humor has backfired on him...and unfortunately on Sharlyn."

After her company had gone, she called every place in town where toys were sold. When she asked if they had any ballerina dolls, one salesclerk after another said, "Sorry. We sold out of those by the first of December."

The last store on her list was The Moore's Store on the square. When the clerk responded with, "Yes, we do have one left," she immediately told her to hold it for her. When the clerk quoted a price almost three times that of the one she'd ordered, she almost had second thoughts, but the picture of the disappointment on her little girl's face if Santa didn't bring the coveted doll helped her make up her mind. With an audible gulp she told the clerk that she would pick it up that evening.

After she put the phone back into the cradle, she considered another dose of salt in her prankster husband's coffee, but on second thought she decided he was going to pay enough for this little joke...through his pocketbook.

When he heard what had happened, he was unusually silent...even when June told him the price of the doll. Then when he was unsuccessful in tracing his order or in getting his money back, he never mentioned the incident again. June hoped he had learned his lesson.

Christmas morning June saw how happy Sharlyn was with the doll Santa had brought her. This happiness erased any bad feeling June might have felt for her husband. While Sharlyn put her ballerina through its pirouettes, Janice cradled her baby doll, and Ricky pushed his toy truck around the tree, the young couple smiled in satisfaction as they looked back over the blessings of the last year. Dick and Bev had gotten married. June's father and his family were now living nearby and last but not least, Toy, their sixth musketeer, had joined their family.

A couple hours later, they sang, "Over The River and Through The Woods to Grandmother's House We Go," as they traveled to June's mother's house for Christmas dinner. As the last chorus died down, June quietly mused, "Do you realize that this is the first time in years that we haven't had to leave Dad, Polly, and the boys at our house on Christmas Day when we came up here?"

"That's another good reason for having them live so close. I'm sure the boys appreciate being able to stay at home Christmas Day and play with their toys," her husband responded.

Contentment was in their voices and in their smiles as they quietly talked during the rest of the journey. "This is indeed a wonderful holiday!" June thought when they reached their destination and were greeted by the familiar sights, sounds and smells, of Christmas when Priscilla opened the door and welcomed them with a heartfelt, "Merry Christmas!"

As the rest of the family responded with Christmas wishes, to be different Dick called out, "Happy New Year!" Priscilla pensively replied that she wondered what this new year might have in store for them. At the sound of her mother's words, June wondered too. *As they were to discover, the upcoming year was to bring many changes into their lives…some welcome and others the very opposite.*

DOING GOD'S WORK

While June's father and stepmother's move to Newark was great for her, it would also have an unexpected impact on the community. It started with their disappointment when they were unable to find a Southern Baptist church in Newark or Heath. Although they attended other denominations, there were enough differences in their beliefs to leave them frustrated.

Later on a return visit to the church in Jackson, they explained the situation to the pastor, Bill Goodin. After he'd listened to his former parishioners' outpouring, the young minister remained deep in thought for a few seconds before he said, "If you think you can get some people together and find a place for it, I'll come up once a week for a bible study meeting."

While Polly enthusiastically nodded her head, Burrel assured him, "If you agree to come, we'll have a meeting place and people there." Before they left, they'd set a date ten days hence for the first meeting.

When her father returned to Newark, he enlisted his daughter's help. After she heard his plan she instantly told him, "We can have it here, and I'll invite some people to come."

The next day, though, the plan changed when she mentioned it to her next door neighbor, Ginny. "I'd love to have everyone come to my house," Ginny responded. As an additional enticement, she added, "Patti can take care of the children at your place." Although, June protested that she didn't want to impose, Ginny insisted and June finally agreed. As it turned out, only Burrel, Polly, Dick, June, Ginny, Bus and their wandering daughter, Vickie, were at the first meeting.

The day before when Vickie had returned from her job at the National Airport in Washington, D.C. for a short visit, she had created quite a stir on Oakwood Avenue. Her neighbors, eyes agog, had watched from their porches or peeked from behind lace curtains when she first stepped from her father's car with a humungous boxer dog half her size on a leash. As she and the animal pranced from the car to the front door of her parents' house, she had looked like a movie star with her blond hair in a sophisticated upswept style and her blue eyes hidden behind enormous dark glasses.

That night when June talked to her, it didn't take long to discover that although Vickie had taken on the appearance of a big city woman, she was still the warm, friendly girl who'd grown up next door. As the evening progressed, Vicki was a welcome addition to the study group, but her canine companion almost broke up the meeting. At that first gathering, he'd occupied a prominent spot in the middle of the floor at Bill Goodin's feet. Ever so often, he would get up, turn around, sniff the air, cast an accusing glance at the people, and haughtily walk out of the room only to return a few minutes later. After the second time this happened, Bill announced, "He must not like my message."

Dick fanned the air in front of his face and exclaimed, "I don't think that's it!" The ensuing laughter was hollow as everyone tried to ignore the pungent odor. After this scenario had been repeated three or four times, Ginny asked Vickie to put the dog in her room.

In a voice as lady-like as it would have been if she had been inviting the queen to tea, she said, "I think he has a slight problem with flatulence."

"Either that or you have a serious problem with your sewer," Dick joked.

Once the culprit had been banished, Bill began the bible study portion of the evening and instructed them to open their bibles to Genesis. "As God did," he said, "let's start at the beginning."

As June watched and listened as he taught his little flock, a thought nagged at the back of her mind that he reminded her of another preacher she'd heard recently. "But who?" she silently mused.

A few minutes later, she remembered the young minister she and Dick had watched on a televised crusade a few weeks earlier. Recently he'd been making a name for himself throughout the country for his inspirational preaching and for the number of converts he was bringing to Christ. Before the evening was over, after Ginny served refreshments and the little group chatted casually while they ate, June managed to talk to her father about her comparison. He appeared to study their guest speaker for a few seconds then he slowly replied, "Now that you mention it, Bill does remind me of the Reverend Billy Graham. Not so much for the way they look as the way they teach or preach. In both cases their love of the Lord and their desire to share the message with everyone comes through loud and clear." While the little group dallied over their coffee, Bill brought them back together when he called for questions. This led to a lively discussion that kept them there for another ninety minutes. Fortunately he was going to spend the night with Dick and June so he didn't have to worry about the lateness of the hour.

After the group finally dispersed and the threesome crossed the yard to their house next door, June went to bed, and left Dick and Bill to continue the discussion well into the night. For this one night, it didn't bother her that she had to go to bed alone since she knew how much her husband enjoyed the opportunity to discuss the bible with someone as knowledgeable as their guest. She was also pleased to see the friendship that had begun to develop between the two men.

When she awakened at two a.m., she found Dick's side of the bed was still empty, and she could still hear the rumble of male voices from the living room. The next morning she noticed that although their lack of sleep showed in their reddened eyes, both men were in good humor as Dick walked their departing guest to his car.

While they stood next to Bill's ancient vehicle, Dick glanced down and shocked, exclaimed, "Look at your tires! They're bald!" As if to illustrate his point, he drew back his foot and gave the front one a resounding kick.

Horrified, Bill yelled, "Don't do that!"

Dick couldn't believe his eyes and ears. This young preacher had driven up here to spread the gospel, and his tires were so bad that he was afraid the one he'd kicked would go flat.

"Man, you can't drive around on those things. You need new tires!" Dick said.

"I need a lot of things, but preachers in small town churches don't make much money. The truth is, I can't afford new tires," Bill confessed.

Dick was deep in thought after his friend left and later he spent hours lamenting Bill's situation. "I can't believe a congregation would let their minister ride around on something that dangerous," he bemoaned.

Before the next bible study meeting, June's father informed her that an anonymous donor had contributed money to the church in Jackson. "It was designated for the purchase of new tires for Bill Goodin," he reported.

June looked questionably at her husband, but couldn't quite catch his eye. After her father went home, though, she asked him point-blank if he knew anything about it. "I'll never tell," was all he would say.

When she pressed him for an answer, he finally said, "I'd say that if the donor wanted to be known, he wouldn't have asked to remain anonymous."

"Even from his wife?" she demanded.

"Even from his wife!" he replied.

*

The anonymous gift and the incident with the dog became part of the folklore of everyone associated with the beginning of the church. This was evident ten years later when Dick and June visited Bill and Anne at their new church home in Whitley City, Kentucky. Anne's eyes sparkled with amusement when she asked, "Do you still have the dog with the...er...ah...problem with gas?"

Dick chuckled and explained that luckily he'd never owned that particular dog.

"Bill loves to talk about that time when the church was just getting started," she said. "I don't know which is his favorite story...the one about the Good Samaritan who bought him the new tires, or about the dog."

Dick quickly passed over the mention of the tires to add, "The dog story doesn't quite match the baptismal one."

"I haven't heard that one," June said.

Bill's good-natured face creased into a grin as he leaned forward in his chair and began to relate what had happened. "It was shortly after we came here," he began. "One Saturday afternoon, I had started to fill the baptistery for the next day's baptisms when Anne sent one of the boys to tell me that dinner was ready."

"I figured that I'd only be gone for a few minutes so I left the water on when I crossed the yard to the parsonage. Then after dinner a couple of the deacons stopped in to discuss some church business. The discussion went on for hours. After they left, I worked on my sermon for awhile before we went to bed."

"About three o'clock in the morning, I awoke to the sound of running water. At first I thought we must have a burst pipe. Then I remembered the baptistery."

"I recall yelling that I forgot to turn off the water as I jumped out of bed and ran for the church. Anne was only a few feet behind me when I threw open the church door. When I turned on the lights, neither of us could believe our eyes! We were met by a regular Niagara Falls. The tank was full, and the water was gushing over the sides and splashing down the walls onto the pulpit."

"After we got the water turned off, we grabbed every towel in the house and started to sop up the water. By then, the carpet was so wet that we couldn't begin to get it all out."

Anne and Bill exchanged amused glances at what was to come before Bill again took up the story, "When we'd heard the water running, we'd been in such a hurry that we'd dashed over in our nightclothes. Then for the next few hours, we were too busy to think about getting dressed."

"It hadn't mattered when we left the house since it had been dark, but by the time we were through, it was daylight. Anne was in her nightgown, and I was wearing boxer shorts and a tee-shirt," he sheepishly admitted. "Before we left the church we felt like criminals the way we had to scan the area to make sure no one was out and about. Since we didn't see anyone, we made a dash across the churchyard for the house. As it turned out, we'd barely closed the parsonage doors behind us and glanced out the window just in time to see the first early bird parishioners arrive at the church for Sunday morning services. We wondered if they had glimpsed our mad dash across the lawn."

June grinned at the mental picture of the preacher and his wife in their wet nightwear with their arms loaded with wet towels and wondered what some of the more staid parishioners might have though if they'd stumbled onto the scene.

Before she could voice this thought, Anne chimed in with, "We threw on some clothes and got back to the church before the organist started the first hymn." June noticed the impish grin she cast in her husband's direction before she added, "You should have seen the look of bewilderment on the faces of the choir members when they squish-squashed across the carpet to the choir loft. When they turned and looked inquiringly at Bill, he had such an angelically innocent look on his face that I half expected to see a halo over his head."

Dick and June laughed at the vision that her words conjured up before June asked, "Did he ever tell them what happened?"

"Not for awhile," Anne replied. "But it was too good a story for him to keep to himself for very long."

～

That conversation was to take place in the future. Meanwhile back in nineteen fifty-six, as Dwight D. Eisenhower was beginning his second term as president of the United States, the meetings of the bible study group were coming to an end, but not Burrel and Polly's interest in bringing a Southern Baptist Church to the Newark area.

When June had first met Pastor Bill Goodin, she had discovered that next to his love of God, his wife Anne, his children, his congregation, and his fellowman, he loved peanut butter ice cream. With this knowledge in mind, June saw to it that the freezer was always stocked with Velvet peanut butter ice cream every time the young minister was to be in town.

After the final bible study class, June, Dick, Burrel, Polly, and Bill Goodin were sitting in the kitchen of the house on Oakwood Avenue eating peanut butter ice cream and drinking mugs of steaming coffee. June told Bill, "This Velvet Ice Cream is made locally near Utica at Ye Old Mill. The historical building also had a skating rink upstairs where Dick and I went on a few dates when we first met." The group laughed when Dick demonstrated how clumsy he was on skates.

Then Bill said, "I really love this area…the people and the ice cream." Before his bowl was empty, he stopped eating long enough to say, "I'm sorry I can't keep up these meetings any longer. The deacons are starting to complain about me spending so much time away from my job at the church in Jackson."

They all nodded in understanding, and Burrel replied, "We knew it couldn't last forever. We're just grateful for the times you were able to come." A deep sigh escaped from his lips when he added, "We sure do miss the church in Jackson and the good old Southern Baptist preaching."

Bill allowed June to refill his bowl, ate a third of it and washed it down with coffee while he quietly mulled over what his former parishioner had just said. Finally, he spoke, "If you feel strong enough about it, and you're willing to work hard, you can get a small Southern Baptist Church started here."

Since this idea had been lurking in the back of Burrel's mind for some time, all he needed was Bill's encouragement for it to take wing.

"I'm not afraid of work," Burrel said. "And I really do want to do it. Just tell me how to get started."

Without a thought of the early hour when they'd all have to start the next day, the five people, three Baptists and two Congregationalists, sat in the kitchen and talked into the wee hours. Before Burrel and Polly went home and the others went to bed, the rudiments of a plan had been made. Burrel and Polly were on the way to making their dream of a Southern Baptist Church come true.

According to their plan, the first step was to contact the Southern Baptist Conference in Columbus to enlist its help in getting started. When they got through to the Columbus office, the voice on the other end of the line told them that it would take more than one interested family for the conference to consider the establishment of a new church. The deep male voice was kind and filled with encouragement when he said, "You'll need to find others to join in your efforts."

Neither Burrel nor Polly was daunted by this information. "If that's what they need, then we'll just have to find some more people." Burrel exclaimed. "There's nothing that you and I can't do if we have the Lord helping us." Then for emphasis, he chuckled and added, "And that's all there are to it!"

Polly agreed, and together they bowed their heads and prayed that He would show them the way. That night after they'd gone to bed, Burrel lie awake and wondered how they were going to go about this business of starting a church. After he'd tossed and turned for awhile, he decided that he needed to put this in God's hands. Once this decision was made, he felt such a feeling of peace that he knew; it was going to work. Someday there would be a small Southern Baptist Church in Newark or Heath, and it was his job to start on God's work tomorrow.

That tomorrow and many other tomorrows, the determined couple could be seen as they knocked on doors and invited the inhabitants to join them in their venture. Burrel tackled this task with the same fervor as he had when he'd cleared and opened Seneca Caverns a quarter of a century earlier. While he hadn't given up on that challenge until he'd successfully completed it, he stayed with this one despite the many doors that were closed in his and Polly's faces.

One day despite Burrel's warning that it wasn't safe for her to canvass without him, Polly set out alone to knock on the doors of several houses in a quiet, charming west-end neighborhood. Although she was met by polite refusal at the first three houses, she was confidant her luck would change. As she determinedly strode up the three steps to the front door of the fourth house, she cast a glance heavenward, took a deep breath and rang the doorbell. As the sound of its musical notes rang out in the empty house, she heard the threatening barking of a dog from the backyard. As she turned and started toward her car, a large black dog appeared. As the snarling, angry animal rushed toward her, Polly felt its hot breath and wet mouth against the back of her leg, and anticipated its sharp teeth sinking into her flesh. Her dignity was forgotten as she hiked her skirt above her knees and high-tailed it to the car as fast as her short, chubby legs would take her before the dog had a chance to complete his attack.

Once she'd reached the safety of the inside of the car, she eyed the still barking dog and muttered, "Alright, you nasty beast, I've learned my lesson. No more knocking on doors without Burrel." Later when she told him about the dog incident, much to her annoyance he first teased then reminded her that he'd warned her not to go out alone. She responded by telling him that if he'd been along the only difference would have been that his long legs would have gotten him to the car faster than her short ones. Although he wanted her to think he was amused by her misadventure, none-the-less, before they turned in for the night he made her promise not to canvass without him. The memory of the hot breath and the touch of that dog's mouth against the back of her leg made it easy for her to promise.

The next time they went out, they knocked on one door and were invited in. Then another and another until three families had joined them in their effort to start a new church. Once this information was conveyed to the offices of the Southern Baptist conference, the same friendly voice told them that a tent meeting would be held in the area. "We'll send someone to preach if you find us a location. You will need a field large enough for us to pitch a tent big enough to hold at least one hundred people. It also has to be near a highway and have enough parking spaces to accommodate everyone," the representative told them.

"That looks like a pretty big order," Burrel commented on their way home.

"Don't worry, Honey," Polly replied. "We've come this far, and I'm sure we're not going to be stopped now."

He was to find out the very next evening just how right she was when he happened to notice a field with a large weathered barn along route 79 south of Newark. He hadn't paid particular attention over the years when he'd passed this building many times when he'd worked on the construction of the aluminum plant. Today, though, as he drove by, his pulse quickened at the sight.

"I've found the perfect spot," he excitedly told his wife a few minutes later when he arrived at home. "Come on!" he commanded. "It's just down the road a piece. I want you to see it and tell me what you think."

"I have supper ready. Don't you want to eat first?" she asked.

"We'll eat when we get back," he said. "Let's go now."

His insistence had aroused her curiosity, so she followed him to the car. "Come on boys," she called to Fred and Bill who were in the yard next door. When Fred asked where they were going she shrugged and replied, "I don't know. Your daddy won't tell me." When the boys piled into the back seat, they noticed the exhilaration in their father's eyes and wondered what the mystery was all about. A few minutes later the car came to a stop in front of a humungous gray barn, and their father exclaimed, "Well, what do you think?"

Fred and Bill exchanged puzzled glances. They still had no idea what the big deal was, but their mother knew. She seemed to be as excited about the place as their father had been. She enthusiastically clapped her hands together and rhapsodized, "Perfect! There's plenty of room here for the tent and for parking too!"

"Mystery solved!" Bill muttered.

"Yeah, Buddy, they want it for the tent meeting!" Fred said.

Burrel noticed the boys eye the hay mow, and charged, "Don't even think about it!" Even though Bill was primed to argue, his father's look and utterance of, "And that's all there are to it!" put a stop to any plans to explore...at least for now.

Burrel and Polly had been too engrossed in their find to notice the farmer who had ambled over from the farmhouse until he asked, "How can I help you folks?"

Burrel turned and extended his hand in greeting. After he'd introduced himself and his family, he explained their mission. The farmer had been nodding while Burrel was speaking, leading them to think he was going along with their request. Instead, he furrowed his brow, ran his work roughened hand through his graying hair and slowly replied, "That's something I'd have to think about... and of course I'd want to talk to the Missus."

"If you're worried that we'd damage the field, I can assure you that if we did, we would take care of any damage," Burrel explained. Then he studied the other man's face before he added, "We'd also pay you for the use of the property." Then he mentioned the amount they'd been authorized to spend.

The farmer smiled, nodded, and reiterated, "I'll think about it, and I'll let you know."

Before they left, Polly added her plea to her husband's. "This is your chance to help with the Lord's work. I'm sure it's not every day that you're given such an opportunity!"

The farmer nodded and again repeated that he'd let them know. On the drive home, Burrel was disappointed but not discouraged. "It's such a perfect spot," he told Polly later that night while they sat on their patio and talked about all the advantages of the location. "It will be easy to find. It's so close to the Aluminum Plant and everyone knows where that is."

"Besides that, there's drive-by traffic," Polly enthused.

Burrel looked toward the star-filled sky and commented that he hoped the weather would hold out. Then he reached over, took his wife's hand in his and asked, "Do you want to pray with me that God will help us get this spot? Or if not this one, then another just as good." She nodded and together they bowed their heads and prayed. Within a few days, they learned that their prayers had been answered. The farmer had agreed to let them rent the field between the highway and the barn. When he added that the barn was off limits, Bill and

Fred stole glances at each other, and Fred mumbled under his breath, "Is he a mind reader?"

The younger boy rolled his eyes, shrugged his shoulders, and grumbled, "Either that, or Mom and Dad have been talking to him."

～

The next couple weeks the Harman's job was to get the word out to the community about the tent meeting. The experience that Burrel had earlier when he'd opened the caverns in West Virginia came in handy now.

First he enlisted the aid of the three families he and Polly had recruited. Then with all the enthusiasm of the early disciples, the little flock set about spreading the word. Soon many of the telephone poles throughout the city and surrounding area wore bright green signs that invited all the people of the community to come to the big tent meeting on route 79 to hear some old fashioned preaching.

When the big night finally arrived, the Reverend Darty Stowe stood in the pulpit and looked out at the near empty tent. Undaunted, he preached a rousing, but moving sermon. Before the evening was over and the call to the altar was given, a couple people moved forward to profess their acceptance of Christ as their personal Savior.

After all the cars except Burrel and Polly's and Reverend Stowe's had left the parking area, Burrel sat dejectedly on one of the folding chairs near the pulpit. When the Reverend Stowe noticed, he hurriedly stuffed his sermon notes into his briefcase and came over and sat beside him. He smiled warmly, put his hand on his shoulder, and in a soft caring voice said, "There is nothing to be disappointed about. I know you were expecting multitudes, but that doesn't happen overnight. Tomorrow night there will be more and even more the next night."

At the sound of his words, Burrel's shoulders straightened and he returned the ministers smile. He found himself beaming at the preacher's next words, "Tonight two more people accepted Christ and you now have two more families in what will be the new church."

Burrel looked the other man in the eye and responded, "With God's help, there will be more before this revival is over."

As it turned out, he was right. The next night, more people came. Some had been enticed by the signs; others had simply driven by and seen the big tent and heard the sound of old-time gospel music, while still others were there because of "word-of-mouth" advertising. Before the revival was over, the once near-empty tent was full, and six families had been added to the new flock.

June and Dick, had gone every night. The last night, they brought Sharlyn, Janice, and Ricky with them. While June held two-year-old Ricky on her lap, Dick held Janice, and Sharlyn sat demurely between them. Once the singing started, June noticed that her oldest daughter's feet were tapping and the younger ones were clapping their hands in time to the music.

The songs were ones her mother had sung to her and her brothers when they were children at the cave house. June's favorite hymn that night, though, was "When The Roll Was Called Up Yonder." The many voices raised in that particular song took her back to the vagabond years when she, her brother, Skip, and her new stepmother, Polly, had followed her father's jobs around the country.

She could remember how many nights while the others had slept, she'd kept her father company while he drove into the night. The rumble of her father's voice as he'd sung along with her off-key rendition of what he always referred to as his favorite hymn echoed in her mind as she opened the hymn book and joined the congregation in song. Her father turned and smiled at her as if he too remembered.

In the next few weeks as the tiny flock continued to grow, they met in each other's homes until even the most spacious would no longer hold them. Then they moved to a room in the YMCA. June, Dick, and the children attended the Sunday service when Reverend Stowe baptized the new members in the swimming pool. This body of water that hours earlier had held splashing children seemed to June to be spiritually transformed into the Sea of Galilee. Then before her eyes, as the waters flowed over the new converts, they emerged aglow with the spirit of a new-birth.

Although June and her family frequently went to Sunday evening services at the new church, they remained active in the Plymouth Congregational Church. One Sunday, in a hopeful sounding voice June's father tentatively said, "You've been so much a part of this church from the beginning. Have you ever thought of joining us?"

Since June had anticipated this question, it didn't take her long to reply. "I've thought about it, Dad," she said. A pleased look flicked across his face, but quickly vanished when she continued. "Although we have a large church building, our congregation is small and struggling. They need us too. You know that Dick is Sunday-School superintendent, and I teach the five year olds." With a sigh, she added, "I wouldn't want to leave them in the lurch."

To her relief, her dad smiled, patted her hand, and assured her that he understood. "You've been like that since you were a little girl. I remember your mother saying that you were never one to quit in the middle of anything."

"She can blame herself for that," June quipped. "She sure drummed a sense of responsibility into all three of us kids!"

With a grin, he replied, "I wouldn't want you any other way." Then anxiously, he added, "You'll still visit the church though, won't you?"

"You couldn't keep me away," she replied. "Even though we're not members, I'll always feel as if we're a part of it."

SURPRISES AND MYSTERIES

A few days later when the Harman family stopped in unexpectedly at the house on Oakwood Avenue, her father's eyes sparkled with excitement and the same look shone from Polly, Fred, and Bill's.

"You four look like the cats that swallowed the canary!" June joked. "What's going on?"

Burrel's only reply was, "Get your husband and children and follow us. We have something to show you."

No matter how much she coaxed, none of the four would tell her where they were going. "Just get in your car and follow us," her father urged.

"Now what are they up to?" Dick quizzed as June and the children piled into their car.

As he turned the ignition on the late model blue Nash Ambassador, and started on their mysterious journey, June shook her head and replied, "Your guess is as good as mine!"

June watched her little brothers in the car in front of them waggle their fingers in their ears and stick out their tongues as she fiddled with the radio knob until the cloyingly sweet sounds of, "Love Me Tender," filled the car. "Mommy, leave it there," Sharlyn coaxed. "It's Elvis Presley!"

Dick laughed and muttered, "Move over Frank Sinatra. You've got some competition!"

June turned and glanced into the back seat. As usual, Sharlyn and Janice had the window seats, and Ricky was perched on the fold-down armrest in the middle. As she watched, three pair of little feet moved in time to the music while her oldest daughter sang along with Elvis.

As if the music were contagious, June and Dick soon joined in. "I'm so glad we are young enough to enjoy the same kind of music our children do," June murmured. Although she and her children would remain Elvis fans as they were that summer day in nineteen fifty-six, she was happily oblivious of the changes about to take place on the music scene that would forever create a conflict in the two generations' taste in music.

By the time the song had ended, they had left the traffic of the city square, and the less congested area of the south end of Newark behind and were driving up a tree dotted hill in a much less populated area. Finally, her father turned onto a side road and eased the car to a stop in front of a small white house.

As June's family scrambled from their car, they turned questioning eyes upon Burrel who beamed in pleasure. Still puzzled, June looked around at the country-like atmosphere of the half-acre of ground with its grapevines and apple trees before she asked, "Is this for the church?"

Polly clapped her hands in glee and cried, "It's for us. It's going to be our new home!"

June expressed surprise by saying that she wasn't aware they planned to buy a house. In response Polly said, "We hadn't, but we happened to see this advertised and it sounded perfect for us."

"The grounds certainly have potential," June said. "How about the house?"

In response, Polly opened the front door and motioned for them to come inside. June looked around at the small compact kitchen they had just entered. The same description fit the next two rooms. The only large rooms in the house were the bedrooms. June's first thought was to wonder if the advertisement had called this a dollhouse and a fixer-upper, since both descriptions would be appropriate.

As June had said, although the grounds were overgrown they still had potential. The house, though, was a different matter. "Too small," she thought. "No room for furniture. It's been neglected and needs a great deal of work to get it in shape." It was obvious when she stole a glance at her husband that he shared her misgivings about this house. From their own experience with the house on Oakwood Avenue, they could foresee the work that would need to be done to make this house a home.

Her stepmother was so enthusiastic that June was reluctant to say anything to burst her bubble. On the other hand, Dick jumped in with both feet. "If you buy this, you may be biting off more than you can chew. It has a lot of possibilities, but you need to be aware there will be a lot of work involved and expense too."

"It will be fun!" Polly enthused. "We can do a lot of the work ourselves." She went on to say that while Burrel was at work, she and the boys could get the yard in shape. "Then in the evening and on Saturday, we can all help Burrel with the inside work."

Apparently she felt that her daughter needed more convincing, so she added something she knew the younger woman would be unable to resist. "You know how much your father has always wanted to go back to his West Virginia roots. We both know that will never be possible, but with the hills and woods around here and the garden to putter in, this is like a little bit of country for him."

June looked inquiringly at her father who nodded his agreement and said, "I agree with you, though, that there will be a great deal of work, but I think we can handle it." From the corner of her eye, June noticed Bill and Fred exchange doubtful looks. Until now they had only paid attention to the woods around them and the sight of all the other boys their age in the neighborhood. Now all the adults in the family had mentioned that nasty four-letter word, "Work." When Bill and Fred sauntered outside a few seconds later, June was sure she heard Bill mutter, "Yuck!"

June was sorry if they had dampened the little family's enthusiasm, but she knew they faced a major challenge. Later her father told her that he'd felt the same way when he first saw the house, but had been caught up in Polly's excitement. "Besides, she has been really homesick for the friends we left behind in Jackson. I thought this project might be good for her."

June had also noticed Polly's depression at being separated from Bill and Dorothy and the Tuckers. She had thought the work on the church had alleviated it, but apparently she'd been wrong.

"I hope this helps," she murmured.

He looked at the smiling face of his wife and replied, "I think it will."

~

During the rest of the summer months, the Harman family tackled the task with vigor, but as June had feared, they soon found that the job required more than enthusiasm. "I'm afraid Polly has seen too many nineteen forties movies," June confided to her husband one evening in late summer. "You know those where all you had to do was think you could do it and gee whiz, you could!"

"You mean the Judy Garland and Mickey Rooney ones?" Dick asked.

June nodded glumly before she replied, "I think Polly thought that all it was going to take was some wallpaper and paint, but when they started, they found it would take more work than they could handle. In fact, Polly said the entire house seemed to be held together with chewing gum. You know they had to get a carpenter and drywall-man to take care of the structural changes.

"They'll find that's going to be better in the long run," Dick said. "They'll have enough to do once those changes are made," Dick said.

"I told Polly today how glad I was that they decided to have the wall taken out between the living room and dining room. The room is really large now. While I was there today, Stewart and Alward delivered the new round maple dining room table and chairs and a matching hutch. She's going to put them in one end of the room and use the rest as a living room."

In response to Dick's question as to whether she was going to get maple furniture for the living room too, June replied, "What else? She said she was going to try to find some like we had on Lawrence Street." With a teasing grin, she added, "Do you know what else she said?" Before Dick could shake his head, she went on. "She said that maybe some of the grandchildren might do what Fred did and learn to walk by pushing one of the chairs around."

With a quick glance at their off-springs who were flopped on the floor engulfed in the new television show, "Leave It to Beaver," he asked, "Doesn't she know that we're through?"

"We are and I guess Skip and JoAnne are, but Dick and Bev haven't even started," she replied.

"Give them time. They're just newlyweds," he joked.

~

When June picked up the phone later that evening, she was surprised to hear her brother, Dick's, voice on the line. He didn't waste time on pleasantries, but immediately got to the point, "Mom is in the hospital. The doctor said she has to have her gallbladder out, and she wants you to come up."

"Her gallbladder!" June cried. "She had her gallbladder out years ago!"

She heard her brother's soft chuckle wing its way across the wire before he replied, "That's what she told them, but they said it showed up on the x-ray, and that it has to come out. Mom is mad as a hornet. She said there is no way she is going to let them cut her open again."

"I would think not," June replied before she thought to ask, "What happened? Why is she in the hospital in the first place?"

"She's having strong abdominal pains that sound suspiciously like gallstones," he told her before he asked if she would be able to come to Mansfield.

"Dick will have to drop me off but then I won't have a car to get to the hospital," she replied.

"No problem!" he assured her. "You can stay at our apartment. We're only a couple blocks from the hospital. You can walk from here."

June asked him to tell their mother that she would see her the next day before she rested the phone in the cradle and turned to her husband with the news.

"Can't the hospital just check with the surgeon?" Dick asked.

"Afraid not," June replied. "Doctor Warthen died a couple years ago."

Dick's usually cheerful face looked serious when he asked, "If it was removed, how could it show up on an x-ray? Hospitals don't make mistakes like that, do they?"

"In this case they have!" June fumed. "I certainly never will forget that surgery. That's when I went to see her right after she came out of the operating room, and the ether was so strong that I started to pass out while I stood beside her bed. Bill was on the other side and when he saw me start to fall on Mom, he ran around the bed and caught me before I landed."

"I remember that! Bill said he had never moved so fast in his life," Dick exclaimed.

"That day I was wearing a black coat," she reflected. Bill said the whole thing was like a blur of black and white, me in the black coat and Mom covered in a white sheet with the two ready to converge when he grabbed me. The last thing I remember was Bill's shocked face as I started to sway toward Mom there in the bed. If he hadn't caught me, I would have fallen right on her and I'm sure it would have torn her incision loose. I still don't know how Bill got there so fast."

"Maybe he jumped," Dick speculated.

They both laughed at the picture of her usually slow moving stepfather as a pole-vaulter before June brought up the question of baby-sitting.

"With the mess Dad and Polly are in with the house, I don't want to ask Polly to watch the kids. Do you think your mom will take care of them while I'm gone?"

"I'm sure she will," he replied. With a look at the clock on the wall above the kitchen sink, he added, "Too late to call tonight. It's almost eight-thirty. They've been in bed for at least an hour and a half."

"If the kids are there overnight, they won't like going to bed that early," June commented. "Do you think your mom would stay up a little later?"

"Are you kidding? I had to go to bed that early until I went in the army. I never even saw the moon until I was in basic training!" he quipped.

June poked him in the ribs and cried, "You lie!"

In mock seriousness, he replied, "When I was at White Sulphur Springs and saw that big white ball in the sky, I asked one of the other soldiers what it was."

"Sure you did!" she exclaimed.

"Would I lie about a thing like that?" he teased.

She laughed and nodded before she got back to the subject at hand. "I think they'd really hate to go to bed that early. Maybe I'd better make other arrangements," she concluded.

"Don't worry about it. I'll pick them up after work and bring them home for the night and take them back the next morning," he assured her.

The girls were excited when they heard that Rowie wanted them to stay with her, but Ricky was a different matter. While the girls would pack their suitcases and visit any of the grandparents at a minute's notice, two-year old Ricky was a homebody who didn't like to be away from his mother for very long.

June knew that as she had done with her children during their childhood, Rowie would lavish so much attention on her grandchildren while their mother was out of town that even Ricky would enjoy the visit.

Fortunately for June, Dick was off in the afternoon, and they were able to leave shortly after lunch for the hour and a half drive to be at the hospital in Mansfield before visiting hours were over. As they hurried down the hushed hall of the hospital, June noticed a tall slender woman in a stiffly starched white uniform with a white cap perched atop her curls disappear into her mother's room. When they followed closely behind her, June was surprised to see that the official looking nurse was her sister-in-law, Bev.

"This isn't my floor, but I've been checking on your mother any time I can get away," Bev said in the way of greeting.

June kissed her mother and asked how she was feeling. Her mother's smile didn't quite hide her anxiety when she replied, "I've got some pain in here," she said as she placed her hand on her abdomen. "But I'm not going to let them open me up again. I should know whether I had my gall-bladder out or not!"

June leaned back and took a good look at her mother. Her blue eyes showed her determination as did her firm chin and compressed lips. "Don't worry, Mom" June pleaded. "No one is going to operate on you. We won't let them. I don't know how, but the x-ray was in error." She then turned to Bev and asked, "Don't they keep records of surgeries performed in this hospital?"

Her sister-in-law assured her that they did. "Anything that many years ago has been put on film, and they're going to have to go through the film library until they find it."

Just then, a metallic sounding voice filled the room with the announcement that visiting hours would end in five minutes. June leaned over, kissed her mother, and whispered, "You rest now. We'll do battle for you if we have to."

Priscilla squeezed her hand and whispered, "I'm so afraid that I have cancer." June wanted to stay and reassure her mother, but the visiting hours were strictly enforced. With her mother's words ringing in her ears, she found herself joining the other visitors in the short trek to the elevators.

Later that evening when June returned to the hospital she was met with good news. A clerk had dug into the dusty recesses of the film library and retrieved proof that Priscilla had indeed had her gall bladder removed ten years earlier. Priscilla was relieved that she no longer had to do battle with the powers-that-be, but she and the doctors were mystified by the pain she still experienced.

"It's cancer. I know it is!" Priscilla wailed. "My mother died of cancer of the colon when I was pregnant for you," she added.

"Oh, Mom," June said. "Just because that happened to your mother doesn't mean it's going to happen to you." To further reassure her, she told her that she had read about a very simple test the doctor could perform that would prove whether or not she had that kind of cancer. "You have to trust your doctor to do the right thing."

As soon as she uttered these words, her mother reminded her that he hadn't been able to tell the difference between a shadow and a diseased gallbladder. "He wanted to take out my gallbladder that had already been taken out!"

Before they could continue this conversation, Bill ambled into the room with a bouquet of vivid red roses from the bush he'd planted beside the store. Priscilla smiled when she saw her husband and quickly blurted out her news.

"Now they can find out what is really wrong," her husband informed her, "and you can come home."

June looked from her mother to her stepfather and decided to give them some time alone. Before she left, she kissed her mother and assured her that she'd be back the next day. She glanced over her shoulder as she walked out of the room in time to see her stepfather tenderly kiss her mother. Since he was such a quiet undemonstrative man, this was the first time she'd ever seen him express affection. She was surprised to find, as she walked the short distance from the hospital to her brother and sister-in-law's apartment, how happy that little scene had made her feel.

～

At the apartment she told Dick and Bev about her conversation with her mother. "Why is she so worried that she might have cancer?" Bev asked.

June explained that her mother's mother had died of cancer a few days before Priscilla's nineteenth birthday. "Mom spent weeks taking care of her, and the shock of her suffering left her with a horror of the disease."

"That isn't unusual," Bev said, "for someone as young as she was to be traumatized by that kind of experience. You were right to tell her there is a very simple test that can find that kind of cancer. We need to assure her that she doesn't have any of the symptoms, though."

The brother and sister exchanged relieved glances as Bev added, "Her doctor is one of the best in the hospital. He was the one who insisted that the film library find that report. He'll find out the cause of her pain."

June respected Bev's judgment, and for the first time since she arrived, she relaxed. Then despite her effort to hide it, she yawned. Her brother noticed and asked if she was ready for bed.

She grinned sheepishly and replied, "I am more tired than I realized." With a glance at the comfortable looking couch, she added, "I guess that must be my bed for tonight."

"We have another bed for you," Dick said.

Puzzled she replied, "I thought this was a three room apartment."

"It is, but we do have an extra bed," Bev said.

When her brother grinned impishly and informed her that there was another one in this room, she was even more puzzled. To her eyes the room held the couch, a couple chairs, end tables and a coffee table. She could see a door that led to the kitchen, one to the bedroom and tall double doors that apparently led to a closet.

"I give up," she admitted. "Where is it?"

"I don't know how you could have missed it," he teased as he opened the double doors to expose the underside of a bed that appeared to lean against the inside wall. While she watched, he grabbed one side and Bev the other and a full sized bed plopped to the floor.

"A Murphy bed!" June explained in delight. "I've never seen one of these, let alone slept in one." Then she changed her story to say, "I actually saw one in a movie that starred the Marx Brothers. As I recall, it closed on them and they ended upside down between the bed and the wall."

"You're safe," her brother assured her. "That only happens in the movies."

In this case he was wrong. His sister wrestled with the bed the whole night through. More than once she found herself plastered between the bed and the wall…in her dreams. The next morning when Bev asked how she'd slept, she lied when she said, "Fine."

Over breakfast, though, the three of them had a good laugh when the humor of the night before won out, and she admitted that she'd relived scenes from the old movies as she'd dreamed of herself as the victim of the wild uncontrollable bed.

⁓

When she arrived at the hospital, she found her mother rested and pain-free. As soon as she poked her head through the doorway, her mother told her, "The doctor has been here. They're going to do the test for colon cancer, but he assures me it's going to be negative. He says the pain was caused from adhesions from my earlier surgery." She grimaced before she added, "And from nerves. It seems to me that if a doctor doesn't know what is wrong, and if his patient is a woman, he always says it's nerves." She angrily added, "I've never heard a doctor tell a man that."

Her daughter could sympathize as she'd encountered the same treatment from doctors herself. "Things will be different when we have more women doctors," she assured her mother. *As it turned out, though, when that time did come, a new word had been coined to replace the hated, "nerves," and both men and women were legitimately diagnosed as suffering from "stress."*

The day passed quickly with June constantly being scooted out of her mother's room while the older woman was being poked and prodded and wheeled into the recesses of the hospital for tests. After hours of waiting for the results, the doctor officially reported that the tests had revealed adhesions caused by her earlier operations. He assured her that surgery wasn't warranted at this time, but if the problem persisted, he might have to rethink his options.

Priscilla tried a feeble attempt at humor when she said, "I think the next time I'm operated on, I'll just have you install a zipper."

The doctor managed a faint smile before he started toward the door, but Priscilla's next question brought him back to her bedside, "What about cancer? Did you find any sign of it?"

He came back, pulled a chair to the bed, and sat beside his patient before he said, "I can assure you that you do not have cancer. Your chance of getting it may be higher because of your mother but not much higher. Believe me that is not something for you to have to worry about."

Priscilla smiled weakly, but when he left she told her daughter that if she or anyone else in her family ever had cancer, she didn't want to know. "I don't think I could live with the knowledge."

Just then, the nurse came into the room and told them that the doctor wanted to keep her for a couple more days for observation. "He just wants to be sure that the pain doesn't return, and he also wants to keep an eye on that blood pressure and make sure that the dosage is right on your medication."

Priscilla had been too worried about the possibility of the other diagnosis to mention that her blood pressure was sky-high. *As it turned out high blood pressure, not cancer, was to be the plague she was going to live with for the rest of her life, but when cancer did strike someone in the family, she didn't handle it well.*

Now that June knew her mother was on the mend, she was anxious to return to her husband and children. When she told her mother that Dick was picking her up early so they wouldn't keep Forest and Rowena up past their bedtime, she took the news much better than June had anticipated.

～

As it turned out, Dick had arranged for the children to spend the night with their grandparents. "How did that happen?" June asked on their drive home. "Did your mother agree to stay up later?"

Dick laughed at that suggestion before he said, "It would take an act of God to make Mom or Dad do that, but the kids had so much fun that they agreed to go to bed early just to get to stay longer."

June tried to hide her disappointment when she replied, "I thought they would be anxious to see me."

Her husband squeezed her hand and told her that he was sure they were. "It's just that staying with the grandparents is a real treat."

"Even for Ricky?" she asked.

He had to admit that their son was pretty anxious to have her come back. "As I'm sure the girls are," he lamely added.

She was to find out the next morning just how anxious they were when she walked into her in-laws' house on South Third Street and found herself almost bowled over as she felt three sets of little arms wrapped around her and heard their squeals of, "Mommy, you're back!"

She thoroughly enjoyed the welcome and was reluctant to disentangle herself, but Rowie's words that they'd better finish their rice before it got cold brought all three of them back to their interrupted breakfast.

For the next few minutes, June sipped from the steaming cup of tea her mother-in-law had set before her, watched them spoon the sweet concoction into their mouths and listened to their reports about their visit.

"We've had rice every morning," Janice reported as she handed her bowl to her grandmother for a refill. While June idly watched, Rowie dipped hot rice from the pan, added a smidgen of Carnation milk, a couple spoons full of sugar, a little bit of butter, and a dash of cinnamon and nutmeg before she placed the bowl in front of the little girl.

"Lula let us sit in her little room and drink tea!" Sharlyn reported.

As June's glance automatically went to the sunny breakfast nook off the kitchen where the children's great-grandmother usually sat, Janice piped up with, "Yesterday Rowie made homemade noodles for lunch!"

"And a strawberry rhubarb pie!" Sharlyn added.

June smiled at Rowie and Great-grandmother Lula. They obviously had prepared every one of the children's favorites. June knew that, both women delighted in doing for their grandchildren. Neither knew it at the time, but as it turned out, every time the children came for a visit, memories were being built that would stay with these children for the rest of their lives.

These short, plump women with their black curls, red lips, and pink cheeks, dressed in their favorite bright sunny colors saw to it that every morsel of their grandchildren's favorite foods was filled with love. "Our little grandmothers," is what all three of the children called these two women and Polly.

June smiled at the memory of how when Polly first heard this, she'd quipped, "It must be because we're short since we're all at least two ax-handles wide."

When the children overheard this remark, although they didn't know how wide an ax-handle was, they protested that their grandmothers were just right. When June watched these two pleasingly plump women bustling about the kitchen, seeing to it that June's teacup was always full and the children had enough to eat, she found herself agreeing.

At different times, all three of the children confided in their mother that all four of their grandmothers had soft laps. Even though no one would say that about June, Ricky didn't seem to notice as he climbed onto his mother's lap as if to make sure she didn't leave without him. Even after they got home, he stuck to her like paper to the wall for awhile. In fact, it took a couple days before he felt secure enough to go outside to play with the other children.

~

The first night June was home, she and her husband talked about the children's visit with their grandparents. "Sharlyn told me that she couldn't get over the way Rowie waits on your father hand and foot. She said that she tried to get your mother to sit down with them at the table, but she was told that she couldn't because someone might want something."

"Sharlyn might as well save her breath. We've all tried that, but she won't change her ways. She likes to serve her family," Dick responded. June could tell by the mischievous glint in his eye that he was going to say something outrageous... and he didn't disappoint her. "After all," he intoned, "that is a woman's role."

In mock sincerity, she exclaimed, "You poor boy! You married the wrong woman." He pulled her close and murmured, "Not on your life!"

She abruptly sat up as she remembered something else Sharlyn had told her. "Did you know that your mother even takes the seeds out of watermelon for them?"

"Didn't I tell you that I didn't know watermelons had seeds until I went into the army?" he joked.

"Just like you had never seen the moon?" she quipped. "Sounds good, but I don't believe a word of it!"

She fell silent for a few seconds as she reflected on the complexities of this woman, her mother-in-law. June was aware that although all the things they'd just said were true, there was another side to her. She knew Rowena could be assertive, and many sales clerks had discovered this when they tried to tell her an advertised item was out of stock, and she'd have to return to the store. June had heard her inform more than one hapless manager, "I'm here now. Your ad said you'd have it today, and I want it now!" Rather than stand up to her determination, the manager would always find a suitable substitute.

June broke the silence when she said, "Besides, I think your father makes the noise, but your mother makes most of the important decisions in the family."

Dick smilingly agreed. "You'd better not tell Dad, though!"

"I don't want you to think that I don't appreciate the way your mother and Lula treat the kids," June exclaimed. "If anything, it just makes me sorry that I didn't know either of my grandmothers. I guess though, my aunts kind of made up for it. Aunt Calcie with her sugar cookies, Aunt Nellie and her cakes." She licked her lips before she added, "And Aunt Gussie's whipped cream pies!"

At the mention of Aunt Gussie, Dick snapped his fingers and said, "I almost forgot to tell you. Aunt Gussie is in town."

"At Uncle Mace's?" she asked.

"Aunt Mabel called last evening. They were coming to see you, but I told them you were out of town," he explained.

June checked her watch to be sure it wasn't too late to call before she dialed her uncle's number. Her Aunt Mabel answered and immediately called Aunt Gussie to the phone. After a brief greeting, she asked June if she'd talked to Polly since she gotten home. When she admitted that she hadn't, her aunt chuckled and told her. "We have a project for you tomorrow. Polly got some wallpaper for her big room and I told her I'd help her hang it. We need your help!"

Astonished, June replied, "I don't know a thing about wallpapering!"

"Then it's about time you learned!" her aunt informed her.

∽

It didn't take long the next day for June to find out that she was more of a gofer than wallpaper hanger. While the children and Toy played in the yard, she slapped the paste on the paper, handed it to the two women who put it on the wall. They also had her go for ice water, go for sandwiches, and go for iced tea. She would go for anything they needed.

By the end of the day, although she hadn't hung one strip, she felt that they couldn't have done it without her. Besides the work, she found that she enjoyed the visit with her aunt. She particularly enjoyed the news about her cousins.

Aunt Gussie told her Hilda and Avanelle both lived outside Washington, and coincidentally were both married to meat-cutters. She said that Dale had followed in his brother, Clyde's, footsteps to become an electrician, and that Merlin's trucking company was beginning to grow.

When June asked about her Uncle Verde, she was told that he was busy with the farm. "You know we bought more land up on the ridge, and that takes a lot of time," her aunt replied. Familiar with the duties of a farmer from her brief stay with her Aunt Calcie and Uncle Gordon following her parents divorce, June nodded in understanding before her aunt glanced at the clock and asked June if she was ready to take her home.

Before she gathered the children and dog into the car, June surveyed the results of their labor. The green wallpaper with its hint of a design caused the large room to take on the look of a cool peaceful glen. A second glance made her think of the willow pond of her childhood. Nothing about this lovely room forewarned her, though, that it would soon be the scene of almost devastating humiliation for their beloved dog, Toy.

What happened might not have been as embarrassing for a dog with a different personality, but Toy was an animal with impeccable manners and all the reserve and dignity of an elder statesman. Even when he was a pup, he never crawled onto the furniture, or jumped on visitors, or conducted himself in any but the most gentlemanly fashion.

Even though now he was little more than a pup, he took his job as the children's protector seriously. Wherever they went, he was never far behind. Anytime June needed to find the children; all she had to do was check the front porches of their friends for their faithful companion. "He's always by the door waiting for them to come out. Then he walks home with them," she told Polly one afternoon as they sipped iced-tea on the front porch. She motioned toward a familiar sight at the house next door. Betsy's father was sitting on the porch swing, reading the newspaper and idly stroking Toy's head. "Even Bus loves him!"

"Probably because Toy is reserved like he is," Polly commented.

Toy's humiliation took place a few days after this conversation when June, Dick, and the children went to dinner at June's dad and Polly's house on the hill. As usual, they took Toy along with them. Since Dick hadn't seen the new wallpaper, they all trooped into the living room to see his reaction to all their efforts.

Toy who had trailed along with them looked around at all the walls encased in greenery. He must have thought, "Wow, look at all those bushes!" since before their astonished eyes, he lifted his leg and relieved himself on the new wallpaper. Then and only then did he realize what he had done. While they looked at him in surprise, he hung his head in embarrassment and with his tail between his legs slunk away.

As June and Polly tried to sponge off the paper, Burrel was the first to speak. "I believe he was overwhelmed by the sight of all this green. He must have thought he was outside."

June was as embarrassed as her dog had been when she stammered, "He never goes in the house. He'll hold it no matter how long we're gone."

Her dad chuckled and replied, "I think poor Toy was as surprised as we were." Then with a sympathetic pat of her hand, he added, "Don't worry about it. It's not going to leave a stain, but someone probably needs to let Toy know we're not mad at him."

"I tried to talk to him, but he's under the bush in the yard," Sharlyn said. "And he won't come out."

"He's ashamed," June told her.

They tried to put the incident behind them during dinner and afterwards when some of the people from the new church dropped in. June did notice that as one of the parishioners played the guitar while they all sang old-fashioned gospel songs, Toy managed to keep his distance.

It was months later before Toy again went back into the house on the hill. By then Polly had tired of the green paper and the walls had been painted a sunshine yellow. If a dog could look relieved, though, Toy did when he noticed the change. "Temptation has been removed," Burrel stated as he noticed the animal's reaction.

JAPANESE/AMERICAN RELATIONS

By the time the New Year rolled around, the incident with Toy faded into the background as more momentous events began to take place in their lives and in the world. The airwaves were filled with reports of a space capsule called Sputnik being launched by the Soviet Union. Animal rights activists were up in arms when within a short time a second one was propelled into space with the dog, Laika, inside.

"I think it's cruel too," June bemoaned to her husband as she idly stroked Toy who was curled at her feet. "I was listening to the news this morning and I heard one of the commentators say this was the beginning of the space age, and that this country was going to have to get on the ball or the Russians were going to leave us behind."

"You should hear some of my customers at the barber shop. One of the teachers complained that our students didn't have the math and science education that the Russians do. He said this may be a wake-up call for our educators," Dick announced.

"Do you think they'll ever send a man into space?" June asked.

"Sounds like the old Buck Rogers comic strip, but I suspect it will happen," Dick replied.

June changed the conversation to tell him that his mother had received a letter from Kenny that day. "She called and said that she wanted to talk to us about it. She sounded upset, but when I tried to get her to tell me about it, she just said that she wanted us to stop in this evening after dinner."

"It's after dinner now," Dick observed. "Don't you think we'd better leave now or they'll be in bed?"

"Shall we take the kids or do you want me to see if Patti can come over and stay with them?" June asked.

"Maybe you'd better get Patti," he replied. "This sounds serious."

On the trip to his parents' home, they speculated about the situation. "Maybe Kenny has signed up to stay longer in Japan. He's due to come home in a few months. I know your mom has been counting the days."

"I don't think she's ever gotten over the fact that he enlisted in the Air Force when he first got out of high school," Dick said.

"It might not have been so hard on her if he hadn't been sent overseas quite so soon," June speculated. "He'd hardly finished basic training before he was on his way to Japan."

"I've often wondered if he just enlisted because of the car incident with Dad," Dick wondered aloud. "Do you remember when he asked if he could borrow his car and Dad turned him down flat?"

"He was pretty mad when your dad told him to save his money and buy himself one, but I don't think that was the only reason he enlisted."

Dick braked to a stop in front of the house on South Third Street before he asked, "What other reason could he have had?"

June shrugged and replied, "Maybe he wanted to follow in his older brothers' footsteps."

"Eddie and I didn't have a choice. I don't think either of us would have been in the service if we hadn't been drafted," Dick exclaimed.

"You have to remember that Kenny was just a little boy when you came home. The things you and Eddie told him about your experiences probably made a big impression."

Before they could pursue the subject, Rowie threw open the door and announced, "Your dad is upset, and I don't know what to do!"

Dick put his arm around his mother and assured her that whatever it was, it couldn't be as bad as all that. She drew away and informed him that he'd better wait until he heard about it.

⁓

He and June exchanged puzzled glances over his mother's head before they traipsed along behind her into the kitchen. Forest looked up from his place at the table and without a word of greeting waved a letter in front of his son's eyes. "Read this!" he commanded. "That fool brother of yours doesn't know what he is doing!"

Dick obligingly read the letter, then handed it to his wife before he turned to his father and said, "So Kenny wants to get married! Is that why you're so upset?"

"Can't you read?" Forest snorted. "He not only wants to marry a Japanese, he wants us to sign a paper that we will be responsible for her when she comes to this country! We don't know this girl. How can the government expect us to take care of her?"

June read the letter then silently listened as the conversation raged around her. After several minutes, Dick was finally able to get them to calm down enough to look at the situation more calmly. "Kenny is almost twenty-one years old. From what I see from this letter, you will only have to be the responsible party until he turns twenty-one. The girl is past twenty-one. Kenny will still be in the service, so he will have a steady income. Once he gets married, he'll receive an allotment for his wife...probably extra money for housing too," he said.

"That well may be, Boy!" Forest announced. "But that doesn't change the fact that she is Japanese."

"That's right," Rowie added. "How will people treat her? Will she have a hard time in this country? How about their children? Will people give them a rough time?"

June could understand her mother-in-law's concern. The twelve years since the war with Japan had ended hadn't erased the bitterness some Americans still felt toward this young woman's country. Was it possible anyone would take it out on a woman, who like June, had been a child during the entire conflict?

"Had Kenny ever written about her before this letter?" June asked.

"He mentioned a Japanese girl once, but he didn't say anything about being serious about her," Rowie replied. Then she pursed her lips and proclaimed, "I'm going to write my son in the morning and tell him that before we sign anything, we need to have some answers to a lot of questions."

That signaled the end of the conversation and her glance at the clock on the wall shouted as loudly as words that it was time for her son and his wife to go home. Once Dick was settled behind the wheel and June comfortably seated next to him, she quipped, "At least she didn't tell us to go home."

"Ouch!" he exclaimed. "It embarrasses me when she tells me that she's tired and it's time we take the kids and go home."

June was immediately contrite. "It shocked me the first time she said it, but it really doesn't bother me at all," she said. "I know how much she loves the children and likes to have them around, but I guess it's a grandparent's privilege to spoil them and then send them home."

"I'm glad you feel that way. I'm used to Mom being outspoken, but I didn't know whether or not you were offended," he murmured before he asked what she thought about Kenny's letter.

"I can understand your parents' concern, but I think if they love each other they should get married," she replied.

"Me too," he agreed. "I also know that if Kenny loves her, Mom will too." His voice was a little less sure when he added, "Dad probably will...eventually."

∽

As it turned out, Forest and Rowena did sign the papers, and once Kenny arrived home with his new bride, it was only a matter of minutes before Forest was charmed by his new daughter-in-law...as was the rest of the family. That afternoon of November twenty-fourth, Rowena had telephoned June and in a low voice announced, "They're here. They got here this afternoon while I was watching *As The World Turns*. I heard someone at the door, but before I could even stand up, there they were!"

"Where are they now?" June asked before she added, "What is she like?"

"They're upstairs getting unpacked now," Rowena replied. "She's even prettier than her picture. I expected her to be wearing a kimono, but she has on American clothes. When I asked her about it, she told me that she only wears that on special occasions," Rowena said. Then she added, "I have some spaghetti sauce on the stove, and made deviled eggs, and apple pie. When Richard gets home from work, bring the kids and come for dinner. You can see for yourself."

When a few hours later, the little family arrived at the house on South Third Street, June found herself agreeing with her mother-in-law. This new member of the family was indeed even more attractive than her picture. Poised and beautiful with her shiny black hair, golden skin, full pouty lips, and almond shaped black eyes, she was also warm and friendly. June noticed that her three-year-old son, Ricky, and five-year-old daughter, Janice, had seated themselves on the couch next to her and that their older sister, Sharlyn, couldn't keep her eyes off of her new aunt.

The newlyweds had brought gifts for the family, a Japanese baby doll for Janice, and a young lady doll for Sharlyn. Ricky was fascinated by the stuffed teddy bear they brought him. While the black and gray embroidered picture of a Japanese scene they gave to Dick and June contrasted with the boldly colorful one they had chosen for Forest and Rowena, both were stunning. The bride explained that Kenny had said his mother loved bright colors and that June liked things more subdued.

To the children's delight, Rowena had opened the parlor for this occasion and had already hung the picture in a place of honor over the mantel. Since they had seldom been allowed in this room, they knew tonight had to be very special. June couldn't tell which fascinated her little son more, the colorful stripes and bold flowers of the wallpaper, or the pretty Japanese woman next to him. She liked the young bride even more when she noticed her tender smile when Ricky gingerly touched her bronze colored arm.

While they went about the process of getting to know her, she patiently answered her new relatives' questions. Her name, Yoko, meant "sunshine" in Japan. She and Kenny had met when she brought her employer's dog to the vet. Kenny had been the veterinarian's assistant and had taken care of the dog for her. "Before I left, Kee-ny asked me for a date," Yoko informed them in her accented English.

Before anyone had a chance to ask why an Air Force vet would treat a civilian's dog, Kenny explained that Yoko had worked for an American officer and his family. "I am trained as a dress-maker," she informed them. Then with a shrug, she added, "Hard to get job in Japan even twelve years after the war was over. I went to work for the major."

"She took care of the major's children and helped around the house," Kenny explained.

"Lucky for you, she also took care of the dog," Dick quipped.

Yoko had cheerfully answered all the family's questions until Rowena mentioned that she'd read that Japanese women were known for the way they waited on their husbands. With a look at her first daughter-in-law, she'd added, "Men really like that."

The new bride bristled and her dark eyes flashed when she quickly shot back with, "That my mother. That not me!"

Rowena looked disappointed. She'd hoped that at least one of her sons would have a wife who would carry on her and Lula's tradition of serving the men in the family. Instead she had two independent daughters-in-law.

~

During the next month before they had to leave for Kenny's new assignment in Austin, Texas, the family's admiration for this newcomer increased. She seemed perfectly at home in her new surroundings and took it in stride when Rowena invited twenty of Forest's relatives to meet her over the Thanksgiving holiday. Rowena had been worried about her reception by the aunts, uncles, and cousins, but before the day was over she had made friends with all of them.

During the waning days of nineteen fifty-seven, a winter wonderland was created in Newark when large flakes of snow fell on the city. While the children built snowmen, the stores did a bang-up business in the sale of snow tires while people of all ages bundled up like Eskimos as they went about their preparations for Christmas.

Within the snug walls of the house on Third Street, Yoko taught June, Rowie, and Lula how to cook shrimp tempura, and they dined on this often during the newly-weds' visit. While the women cooked, they talked.

June learned that although Yoko was Japanese, she was raised in Manchuria. "I was fourteen when the war was over, and the Russian soldiers came to our town," she said. "My mother cut my hair and dressed me as a boy so I would be safe. Since we were Japanese, we were considered the enemy. My mother heard stories about other young girls who had been raped. Since I looked like boy, I was safe."

June looked at the tall, well developed young woman and commented, "I don't think that you could pass for a boy now."

Yoko laughed and said, "Lucky for me, my father moved his business to Japan before I started to fill out."

After some quick arithmetic, June commented, "If you're twenty-seven now, you'd have been more than fourteen when the war was over, wouldn't you?"

"I adopted the American way of counting birthdays when I married Kee-ny," she replied.

Although June had learned a little about the difference in the Japanese and the American cultures, this statement had left her puzzled. Yoko noticed and laughingly explained, "In Japan, everyone is counted as one year old the day they're born. I was born on December the twentieth. Then the first of the year, everyone has a birthday." She held up two fingers as she said, "I wasn't even two weeks old when I became two years old. I no like that, so now I go by my real age."

"Then you're twenty-five, not twenty-seven?" June mused aloud.

"That's right," Yoko said as she stirred the pan of fried rice. While the young women were talking, Rowie bustled into the room with her grandchildren trailing behind her.

"These kids are ready to eat," she announced. "Is it ready?"

Yoko set a platter piled high with golden shrimp on the table, and June sent Sharlyn into the living room to call the men to the table. After they'd settled into their chairs, June reminded them that everyone was to come to her house on Christmas Eve. "It's a family tradition that Dick's family and my dad, step-mother and little brothers come to our house for Christmas Eve. My brother, Dick, and his wife, Bev, come on the Sunday before Christmas, then on Christmas Day we go to my mother's house in Mansfield."

June had earlier offended Rowie when she'd asked if Yoko were a Christian, and if she celebrated Christmas. Her mother-in-law had come back with, "I'm sure she's as good as anyone else!"

Immediately aware of how her question had been misinterpreted, June only dug the hole she'd gotten herself into deeper when she tried to explain that she knew there were different religions in Japan and that she'd thought Yoko might belong to one of them. The toss of Rowie's dark curls and the frost in her voice when she replied that Yoko was a Baptist like Kenny showed that she was still upset at June's question.

Whether Yoko heard about the conversation or not, she later explained to June that her mother practiced the Shinto religion, but that she didn't. After having suffered her mother-in-law's wrath, June decided not to pursue the subject any further. "I certainly didn't mean anything by it," June explained to her husband when they were alone.

He just grinned and said, "I know you didn't, but you sure did stir up a hornet's nest with Mom. I don't think she's aware of all the different religions in the world."

June spent the day of Christmas Eve on preparations for the family get-together. Then she stood back and surveyed her work. The star she'd placed on the brightly decorated tree in the corner of the living room brushed the ceiling. Plates of sandwiches, cookies, trays of cheese and crackers and a punch bowl filled with eggnog covered the tabletop. The smell of pine, lighted candles, and freshly baked cookies greeted the guests when they entered the house.

Burrel and Polly were the first to arrive and their gaily wrapped gifts had already been added to the ones June had placed under the tree earlier. When June heard her in-laws' car stop in front of the house, she opened the door and though the air was frigid, she stepped onto the front porch to greet them. She was surprised to see that Yoko was dressed in a traditional Japanese kimono. Although there was still snow on the ground, she wore Japanese wooden sandals and socks. Her hair was fashioned into a style June had seen the actresses Miiko Taka and Mioyoshi Umeki wear in the new movie, Sayonara. June was honored when she remembered Yoko's comment that she only wore her Japanese garb on special occasions.

She and Dick, who had just joined her, were surprised to see that Yoko had her arm under Forest's elbow, and that she helped him out of the car and into the house where she guided him to a chair and settled him into it. When Dick followed them into the house, in an aside to his mother he asked if his dad were sick. "No," she whispered. "He just likes the attention. I think Yoko misses her father, and that's one reason she's concentrating on Forest."

This comment caused June to look at the young woman with different eyes. She couldn't imagine what it must be like to be that far away from your father. Burrel was surprised at the warm smile she turned on him and the enthusiasm in her voice when she said, "Dad, I'm so glad you're here."

His grin didn't quite hide his puzzlement when he replied, "Where else would I be on Christmas Eve?" *She wouldn't have been as happy if she'd foreseen how few Christmas Eves they were going to have together.*

This Christmas Eve of nineteen fifty-seven was perfect, though, as the merry group ate, drank eggnog, opened presents, and sang Christmas carols. While everyone's eyes were on Yoko's beautiful outfit, the coral colored dress June had just made for herself didn't escape attention. Lula's question, "Are you in style or are you pregnant?" brought some snickers, especially from the little boys.

June defended her taste with the comment that this was a sack-dress. "It's the newest style, and I like it!"

Eddie couldn't resist asking Dick what he thought of it. "Whatever I say, I'm going to be in trouble," Dick joked. "I think it looks good on her, but I must confess it's well named." He cast a glance at his wife before he added, "I don't know why she wants to hide her figure in it!" Then as if he'd just remembered the other part of Lula's question he said, "She's in style not expecting! We've done our part in that department. Now it's up to Kenny or Eddie."

While everyone laughed when Eddie protested, "Don't look at me!" June noticed the confidential look the newly-weds exchanged.

She could hardly wait until the door had closed behind the last of her guests before she asked Dick, "Did you see the way Kenny and Yoko looked at each other when you said it was their turn?" Without giving him a chance to reply, she blurted out her suspicions. "I think they're going to have a baby!"

As it turned out, June guessed it before the young couple had been sure themselves. In less than eight months, Alan Dale was born. From then on, Dick teased his brother about the newest off-spring being stamped on the bottom with the logo, "Made In Japan," as all products from that country were marked that year of Alan's birth.

DICK'S NOSE AND JUNE'S TOE

June had been involved with Girl Scouts since two years earlier when Sharlyn had excitedly run into the house and announced that she wanted to be a Brownie. "I just talked to Mrs. Evans' granddaughter, Ellen," she said. "She's a Brownie and she said I could be one too." In a coaxing voice, she added, "Please say I can."

June glanced at the house across the alley from Hazel and Lester's and waved at their neighbor, Mrs. Evans and her granddaughter Ellen before she replied, "We didn't have Girl Scouts where I lived when I was growing up, but I think it would be fun for you to belong. Ask Ellen when the next meeting is and you can go along with her."

Sharlyn raced across the street with her news and returned in a few minutes to tell her mother that it was after school the next day. "I'll send a note along with you to let the leader know that you have my permission," June told her radiant daughter.

The next day, though, the smile had turned upside down when the little girl returned with a note from the leader clasped in her hand. "They wouldn't let me stay," she wailed. "The leader said their troop was for third graders, and I'm only in the second."

"That's alright," June cooed as she pulled her daughter onto her lap. "I'll find out when the troop meets for girls in your class, and you can join that."

She soon found that remark was one that would join the ranks of famous last words when she unfolded and read the note Sharlyn had handed her. The leader not only informed her that Sharlyn couldn't join her troop, but that there was no troop for second graders because they couldn't find a leader. The last sentence was the one that was to lead June not only into twenty years of volunteer work but to a seventeen year career with the organization. "We would like to talk to you about being the leader," the note read. As a P.S. she had scribbled her phone number and the two words, "Call me!"

June had mulled over the idea for a few days before she broached the subject to her husband. His reply was his usual one, "Whatever you want to do is alright with me." Then he asked, "But what do you know about being a Girl Scout leader?"

"I don't have any trouble being a Sunday-School teacher. I'm sure that leading a Brownie troop wouldn't be much different," she confidently informed him. She was to eat those words and to find in years to come that her agreement to be a leader was going to provide her with a wealth of education and experience, some heart-warming and other heart-breaking.

Looming big in the picture, though, was training. First she had to be trained in order to work with a troop. That went well but she soon found that the training to take a troop camping wasn't as easy. She had to be trained in fire building, tent pitching, and the rules of the out-of-doors. She discovered, when she and her co-leader, Joyce Stalling, showed up for this particular session how woefully ignorant she was about the out-of-doors. While the trainers were dressed in their hiking boots and layers of outer clothing, June and most of the other trainees wore a single layer that the wind whipped through. "I might as well be naked for all the good this does me," June thought as she stood and shivered along with the other trainees.

She remedied that at lunch when she made a quick trip up the hill to her dad's and borrowed his heavy woolen red and black plaid jacket, a knit cap, and some heavy socks and gloves. When she returned, she looked more like a lumberjack than a fledgling leader. Later that day when she was asked to evaluate the training and list the most important thing she had learned, she penned the words in large letters, "TO DRESS FOR THE WEATHER!"

She and Joyce tested their newfound knowledge a few months later when they took the troop on a campout at Girl Scout Camp Wakatomika. Her mother-in-law couldn't believe she planned to take fourteen little girls out into the woods and tried to talk her out of it. When June told her they were going to sleep in a lodge and cook most of their meals inside, she was somewhat mollified. When she bid June good-bye, though, she predicted dire happenings.

Actually, the worst thing that happened was that June and Joyce were to learn that underwear does get damp when it's hoisted up the flagpole as theirs had been. While all the girls looked as innocent as if they had just sprouted wings, the two leaders decided to avoid a repeat of this incident. "From now on, our underwear will be in our sleeping bags with us," Joyce whispered to June.

Rowie was relieved when her daughter-in-law and granddaughters returned safely from the weekend. Later, though, when June took the entire family with her to Wakatomika when she directed a family camp, her reaction was totally different.

June was to find that she should have listened when her husband told her that he really didn't want to go since his hay fever was bothering him, but to their regret, June talked him into going. She knew she'd made a mistake when they started to stow their gear in the director's tent and his eyes started to water and he began to sneeze non-stop. Much to the other campers amusement, before the day was over, he'd found the only place in the camp where he could find relief... the walk-in cooler in the lodge. "It's the only place I can breathe easily and stop sneezing," he explained. For the rest of the time, although he had to put up with being teased, he spent most of his time in this safe-haven. As if that wasn't bad enough, the next morning, he stepped out of the tent and was stung on the top of his foot by a bee. By the time they returned to the house on Oakwood Avenue his foot had swollen to double its normal size, and he had to make a quick trip to the doctor. When Rowena saw her son's blood-shot eyes, runny nose, and swollen foot, she gave June a look that seemed to scream out, "What have you done to my poor boy?"

Having learned her lesson and being properly repentant, she never asked Dick to go with her to any other outdoor Girl Scout activity. He did go along with her a couple times to dinners for the Girl Scouts and their parents in the neighborhood. This also proved to be disastrous. At the first one, June had been told before the event that the main course was to be chicken and noodles and she had pictured fried chicken with a side dish of noodles. When the plate of noodles and shredded chicken mixed together was set before him, Dick, who didn't like noodles, looked as if he'd been served a mess of squiggly worms. As she ate her dinner June found herself also digesting some dirty looks Dick cast her way as Dick mouthed the words, "Why didn't you tell me?" She shrugged and threw him a sympathetic look when she saw him dine on bread, butter, and a salad.

Since the second one he attended was a potluck, he was sure there would be enough food there that he'd find something he liked. When they saw the tables laden with all kind of covered dishes, neither suspected that they were wrong again! As it turned out, there was enough for three hundred ninety-eight people, but June and Dick happened to be the three hundred ninety-ninth and four hundredth. This time they dined on Jello and baked beans. "The next time," Dick muttered under his breath, "I'll come for the program, but I'll eat somewhere else."

⁓

All three children grew up in Girl Scouting with Sharlyn being eight, Janice five, and Ricky three when June started. Since June had happy memories of the years she'd lived in the country as a child, this was one way she could still give her town children the same kind of experiences.

While the girls attended the day camps their mother directed, Ricky went along first in the "Cookie Jar" a unit for younger children of camp workers. Then when he was older, he and the other boys would play in the woods or wade in the creek while their mothers were with the girls.

Once when several troops in the neighborhood went camping at the farmhouse at Camp Wakatomika, one of the leaders, Inga Martin, brought her son, Chuckie, with her. One year older than Ricky, Chuckie came loaded down with a tent of his own for the boys to use. Much to the amusement of all the leaders, the boys posted a sign outside that read, "NO GRILS ALOUD!" (*This was a good twenty years before Chuckie became an editor at The Times Recorder newspaper in Zanesville. By then, his spelling would improve.*)

When Sharlyn and other girls in her troop went to summer resident camp, they learned a truth about June that she'd tried to conceal from them. This woman they'd thought could do no wrong couldn't carry a tune. They'd discovered this when they sang around the campfire, and they were the only ones singing it June's way. From that day on, their shame-faced leader happily bestowed the job of song leader on the girls to spare them from future embarrassment. A few years later, Janice joined their ranks when she was old enough to be in a troop with her friends and to go to resident camp. Both girls had pleasant singing voices as did their brother. Fortunately they inherited their father's musical ability.

Some of the girls' most pleasant memories were of their years in Girl Scouting.

Bill and Fred had quite an adventure the first time they went to the Boy Scout Camp. Work for their father had run out in Newark, and he had been sent on a job in New York City. While she went to New York to spend a week with her husband, Polly sent the boys to Boy Scout Camp. She'd given June's name to the camp director as the contact person in case of an emergency while she was gone. When Polly had first mentioned it, June had replied with a casual, "Sure. Don't worry. I'll hold down the fort here."

When Polly asked if she were sure, June replied, "Nothing is going to happen while you're gone. Don't worry." As had happened so many times before, this turned out to be another example of words June was going to have to eat.

On the day she saw Polly off at the train-station, the boys were already at camp, and the state was in the midst of a hot, dry, sweltering summer. There's an old saying in Ohio that if you don't like the weather, stick around, and it will change. And change it did! With a vengeance!

A couple days after Polly left, June had been awakened in the middle of the night by the sound of rain pelting against the windowpanes. "I wouldn't want to be out in this," she thought before she turned over and went back to sleep. The next morning, though, when she saw that it hadn't slackened, she started to worry about her little brothers.

"I think, I'll call the camp and be sure Bill and Fred are alright," she told Dick as she handed him his first cup of morning coffee.

"I'm sure they're fine," he'd replied, but he looked worried when he walked over to the window and looked out at the rain as it splashed from the gutters. "It really must be coming down hard if the spouting won't handle it," he said.

"I'm calling the camp," June told him and headed for the phone.

Before she could dial out, though, the phone rang. "We have your name as an emergency contact for Fred and Bill Harman," a male voice told her. June shot an alarmed look in her husband's direction before she asked if the boys were okay.

"They're fine," he quickly informed her. "We've been flooded out here, and we're sending all the campers home. Can you come and get them?"

"How bad is the flooding," June wanted to know. "Are the roads washed out?"

"Water rushed through their tents last night. Everything any of the boys had with them is soaked," he said. "It's safe to drive to the entrance, though, and we'll have the boys and their gear out there by the time you get here," he said before he hung up.

Dick, who had been listening to her end of the conversation, was heading out of the door within seconds after she was off the phone. An hour later, he returned with two very wet boys and two duffel bags filled with extremely soggy belongings. "I can see what I'm going to be doing today," she thought as she motioned for the boys to put everything on the floor of the utility room.

Fred and Bill were understandably upset that their camp-out had come to such an abrupt end, but they compensated in a fashion when every night of their stay at the house on Oakwood Avenue, they rolled out their sleeping bags and camped out on the living room floor.

The first night after their return, June listened to their tale of woe. After excitedly sharing their flood experience, they listened intently while she told them about a flash flood that had come up at one of the day camps she'd been overseeing. "We were having a day camp at Agape, a church camp north of town. Barbara Tatum, one of the council staff members, and I had gone out in the afternoon to see the two international Girl Guides who were visiting the camp. To get there, we had to drive down a long lane to a shallow creek at the entrance to the camp. While I usually parked in the lane and stepped on the stones to cross the creek, this day Barbara wanted to drive across. When I checked and saw that the creek bed was almost dry, I agreed."

"We parked and walked to the top of the hill where we spent the afternoon watching the two Girl Guides from Ceylon, dressed in native costumes, as they entertained the girls with songs and dances from their native country. This went on until the end of the camp day. Then Barbara and I walked down the hill with the leaders and girls to where the parents waited on the other side of the creek for their daughters."

"A sprinkling of rain was falling, but certainly not enough to prepare us for what met us at the bottom of the hill. On the way down we heard an unfamiliar roaring sound. Then as the girls ran ahead to cross to their parents, we saw that what had been a shallow stream had turned into a raging river filled with humongous logs and other debris. I don't think I've ever seen anything as pitiful as the stranded campers who stood on one side while their parents called across to them from the other side."

"What did you do?" Fred asked.

"Fortunately, the caretaker knew of a back way out of the camp. He shouted the directions across to the parents before we walked all the girls back up the hill, through the woods, and a couple cornfields before we reached the road. To keep up the girls' spirits, we sang Girl Scout songs all the way. Some of the parents told me that they'd never heard anything as welcome as the sound of all those Girl Scout songs."

Sharlyn couldn't resist teasing her mother with the remark that she must not have been leading the songs. June made a face at her daughter before she continued. "We had to leave the car and bum a ride from one of the leaders to the Girl Scout office in Newark." When we told the people in the office that we were late because of the flood, they thought we were putting them on since it hadn't even sprinkled in town. We found out later that the flash flood came from a storm north of the camp." With a grin, she added, "We made the national news that night."

The boys nodded then Bill said, "We had all that water running through our tent. We'd have been alright, if our tents had been on platforms, but we all had to pitch our troop tents right on the ground."

Fred grumbled, "I guess we were lucky we didn't lose any of our stuff."

"Or float away," Bill added.

Polly returned from New York a few days later with several exciting stories to share, but none topped the boys' tale of being flooded out of their tent. She also brought the good news that their father would be coming home soon.

As it turned out, he was able to return to Newark that summer of 1958 in time to vote on the new constitution of the church and to welcome the new minister, Brother Jack Walker.

∼

In the future, comedians on television would make fun of the nineteen-fifties as a time of innocence. The shows that June and Dick, and the children watched such as Leave it To Beaver, The Donna Reed Show, Father Knows Best, and The Dick Van Dyke Show would be ridiculed as too "goody-goody." To June, though, these shows represented her own life and the values she had been taught by her parents and had passed on to her own children.

Like all the mothers and fathers on these shows, June stayed home and raised the children, and Dick made the living. For Dick, this involved working five long ten to twelve-hour days at the barber shop and playing for dances a couple nights a week. Dick made up for the time away from the family by spending all his free time with them. In the summer, they picnicked, swam, visited friends, and family. As the seasons changed, so did the activities, but the church, their extended families, their friends, and neighbors were always a part of it.

The very core of their lives, though, was their love for each other and for their children. June saw her job, as her mother had seen hers, as a mentor to all three of her children, a teacher of morals, values, and the Golden Rule. The fact that she didn't believe in the old adage that "they should do as she said not as she did" kept her on her toes more than once.

The very thought of "toes" always brought a vivid picture to June's mind of the time she thought she must have slipped out of reality into the Twilight Zone. The day had started like many other summer days with the children and Toy playing in the front yard with Betsy. A few lazy clouds were drifting across the clear blue sky, and the sun was shining brightly through the sheer curtains and casting shadows on the living room floor.

On closer observation, June realized that the shadows were actually scuffed spots on the tile floor. "Time to get out the old floor polisher," she decided. After she'd dragged the bulky machine and all the other paraphernalia out of the utility room, she stepped out on the porch to check on the children. When she saw that Betsy's mother, Ginny, was talking to them across the hedge that separated the two houses, she quickly explained what she was going to do. Once Ginny assured her that she would keep an eye on the children, June went back inside, slipped off her shoes and started on the task at hand.

When she next glanced out the window, she saw that another neighbor, Joyce Stalling, and her two daughters had joined the little group in the yard. Satisfied that the children were fine, she concentrated on the polishing. As the machine whirled across the floor, she started to sing the words to a Harry Belafonte song. She no sooner got the words, "Day O," out of her mouth when she simultaneously felt a sharp pain in her toe and the polisher came to an abrupt halt.

In astonishment, she looked down at the source of her pain and saw that her big toe was firmly lodged between the brush and the inside frame of the machine. She reached down and tried to dislodge it, but all she got for her effort was more pain. "I've got to have help," she thought as she tried to hobble over to the window. This proved to be no easy task with the polisher as a seemingly permanent appendage, but she finally made it.

This is where the feeling that she was in the Twilight Zone began. Where only moments before, the yard had been filled with people, now it was completely barren of any form of life. While June frantically scanned the front porches of her neighbors for help, the only sign that she wasn't completely alone in the world was the gentle movement of Hazel and Lester's porch swing. As she started to knock on the window and shout for help, she became aware that the swing was also empty.

It didn't take her long to realize that she was on her own now. "I certainly can't wait until someone shows up to help me," she grumbled as she sat on the floor and began to tug at her toe. When that didn't work, she tried to pull out the brush...also to no avail. Determinedly, she glared at the offending machine and muttered, "You just think you're going to beat me. If I got that toe in there, I'm sure I can get it out." Finally, as she yanked on her toe and yowled in pain, the machine gave up its vise-like grip on her toe, and it was free. As June watched in horror, the toe doubled in size. At the same time, the children came trooping into the house with Toy at their heels. "Where did you all go?" June wailed.

At first, Sharlyn, Janice, and Ricky stared wide-eyed at the strange sight that greeted them, but then they crowded around her and offered their help. "We were in Betsy's house," Sharlyn explained. "Ginny made us some Kool-Aid,"

"I'm alright now," June assured her frightened children. "I just did a dumb thing. I got my toe caught in the floor polisher." To their credit, none of the three laughed.

～

This wasn't the case, though, with June's friends who thought the story was hilarious. At the Girl Scout Day Camp that June directed that summer, Norma McCune, her business manager, teased her unmercifully when she saw June hobble around the grounds of the camp at Moundbuilder's Park with a hole cut out of her tennis shoes to allow space for her throbbing toe. "I don't know if I'd trust someone who can't keep her toe out of a floor polisher with my daughter for two weeks," she joked.

June looked at the hundred and twenty-five girls who stood in horseshoe formation around the flagpole and answered in return, "Someone must trust me."

In a low, teasing voice, Norma replied, "They don't know about your floor polishing skills."

During that camp session, second-grader Janice got her first taste of politics when she was nominated by her unit to run for camp council. The unit leader had assigned two of the older Girl Scouts to act as her campaign managers. Apparently having watched some real life campaigning on TV, they patterned their campaign after some of the more unsavory practitioners of the political game. "Promise them everything," one of her campaign managers told Janice. "A television in every shelter-house." When Janice heard this, she thought, "How could I buy TV sets?"

The second manager said, "A new Barbie doll for each camper." At this suggestion, Janice's eyes widened in surprise.

Then the first manager piped in with, "No more brown bag lunches, she'll provide pizza every day!" Janice gulped at the thought of all the money she would need. She looked on wide-eyed as the older girls began to print these promises on poster-board for the younger girls to carry throughout the camp. The little girl was torn between not wanting to offend the older girls and her discomfort at the thought of lying to her fellow campers. Then one of the older girls squealed, "No more milk and juice for lunch, Janice will buy them all pop!"

The worried little Brownie couldn't contain herself, "I can't promise to do all those things. How can I give them televisions, Barbie dolls, pizzas, and pop?" Knowing that would be lying to her fellow campers, Janice told the girls she wouldn't feel right campaigning that way. "I couldn't do any of those things, so why should I say so?"

The girls replied that everyone did it that way. "No one really expects you to keep your promises. That's what politics is about. You promise them everything, but you don't have to deliver anything," campaign manager number one said while her co-manager parroted her sentiments.

Still full of inner turmoil, Janice talked to her adult leader who at first seemed to agree with the older girls that no one took it seriously. "Don't worry about it," she echoed. When she saw that her light approach to the problem was only making the little girl feel worse, she sat down beside her and asked what she'd like to promise her fellow campers. Janice replied that her mom had told her that her job would be to let the camp council know what the girls in her unit liked and didn't like about camp, and what else they'd like to do. "I know the Girl Scout Promise says: On my honor I will try to do my duty to God and My Country, to help other people at all times, and to obey the Girl Scout Laws." She added, "One of those laws says I promise to be honest. So I want to tell the other campers that I want to promise to honestly help them any way I can."

When the leader told the older Girl Scouts that they had to change their entire approach and promise only what Janice could actually deliver, they moaned in unison, "Brownies!" To their surprise, though, honesty won out, and Janice was elected. June was proud of her little daughter when she heard what had happened. When she related this to her business manager, they agreed that the little Brownie had taught the older girls a valuable lesson, one they wished their leaders in Washington would learn. Overhearing their conversation, Janice's leader quipped, "We've finally found an honest politician, but unfortunately she's not old enough to go to Washington."

THE LAST MAN OUT

On the national scene, the launch of Explorer I from Cape Canaveral shared the headlines with the news that Elvis Presley was drafted, and that school desegregation had been ordered. The desegregation order didn't affect Newark, though, as blacks and whites already went to school together. During the day, June kept her radio turned to WCLT-FM where they played the newest hit songs such as *Splish-Splash* by Bobby Darren or *Volare* by Dean Martin. The television show, *Gunsmoke*, made its debut that year, and she and Dick quickly became avid fans.

When the New Year arrived, the ground was covered with snow and the air felt as if someone had left the back door open in the arctic, and the frigid temperature had found its way to Newark. At first the children had excitedly retrieved their sleds from the basement and pulled them to the hilly street that had been blocked off from traffic for the neighborhood children to sled on its slopes. Then when the temperature dipped below zero with the chill factor even lower, they came home, thawed themselves out by standing over the big floor register, gulped down mugs of hot chocolate, and stayed within the snug walls of the house on Oakwood.

The only time Sharlyn and Janice ventured outside was to trek the couple blocks to Lincoln School. While Sharlyn muffled her head and face in a long woolen scarf, yanked her hat down to cover her ears, buttoned her coat to her chin, slipped long pants on under her skirt, and slipped her feet into fur-lined boots, June did the same for Janice. She'd check to make sure they had their gloves on before she'd let them out the front door. As they joined their friends who waited for them by the white fence in the front-yard, June noticed that within seconds, her daughters' noses were as red as their friends' who had been out longer.

Everyone was jubilant the morning halfway into the month when they awoke to warmer temperature. "Finally, the January thaw," Dick commented.

"I won't have to wear all these clothes!" Sharlyn gloated.

Their elation quickly turned to alarm as the rain started to fall. At first no one realized what a disastrous combination the two were to become. June first became aware of the potential problem when she heard the news on WCLT that the ground was frozen too deep to absorb the melting snow and rain. By evening the rain still fell, the top layer of snow had melted, and the rivers and creeks were ready to overflow.

June listened to the radio all afternoon and was horrified to hear that all residents north of the river in the South-End of town, where her in-laws lived, were being asked to leave their homes and go to higher ground.

She called her mother-in-law, told her what she'd heard, and invited them to stay with them until the danger was over. At first Rowena refused to abandon her home but later when Dick called her, she reluctantly agreed. She was worried though because Forest still refused to leave.

While June stayed home with the children, Dick drove to the house on Third Street for his mother. Before he left, he told June he was going to try to convince his father to come home with him.

Dick was even more determined to get his dad to leave the house when he saw the rising water in the streets. He had to drive through the alley across the street from his parents' home since it was on higher ground than Third Street. Even so, he still had to go through about a foot of water. The brief time he was inside his parents' house he helped his father drag some of the furniture to the second floor. Then although they could see the water rising higher and higher he still couldn't convince his father to leave the house. Finally he said, "Dad, I've got to get Mom out of here while I can still drive through this water," and he reluctantly left. When he brought his mother out to the partially submerged car, he had problems starting the engine. By the time he managed to get the car started and had driven under the railroad underpass, the water had risen another foot. He breathed a sigh of relief when he got on higher, dryer ground, and the only thing he had to contend with was the frozen ruts in the street where the snow had melted and refrozen.

They were all worried about Forest, and called him several times, but he was adamant that he wasn't going to leave his home unprotected. Around nine o'clock that night, public officials were warning residents in the South-End of the danger of gas-line explosions, and urging people to leave their homes if they hadn't already. He concluded by saying that the National Guard was out in boats to pick up anyone who still hadn't evacuated. When Dick tried to call his father with this news, the phone went unanswered.

"Maybe that means he's been picked up by one of those boats," Rowena said.

"I'm going to go back downtown to see if I can find him," Dick announced. "If he's been brought out, he'll need a ride home."

June grabbed her coat from the closet and hurried after him as he started down the porch steps. "I don't want you out here by yourself. It might be dangerous down there," she said.

He grinned and said, "You're going to protect me?"

"Maybe not, but there is safety in numbers," she reminded him.

When they got downtown, there was no sign of Dick's father. When the national guardsman saw their headlights, he marched over to their car and asked where they thought they were going. When Dick explained about his father, the young man asked, "Does he live on the corner of Third and Gilbert Streets?"

When Dick nodded his head up and down, the uniformed man looked grim when he said, "We've been by there a couple times, but he refuses to come with us. The last time anyone stopped, he said he was going upstairs to bed, and that he didn't want to be bothered anymore."

"No one's going back?" June asked.

"No one's going back tonight." He took one look at the worried young couple and added, "The water is so deep now that the only way to get in is by boat. Don't worry, we'll get him out tomorrow."

"Is the water in the house?" Dick asked.

"I'd say, it's in almost every house in this part of the South End," he informed them before he went back to his patrol duty.

When they returned to the house on Oakwood Avenue and told Rowena what they'd learned, she just shook her head and muttered, "He's so stubborn." Although her words were critical, her eyes betrayed her fear for her husband's safety. The children seemed to sense this and they lavished her with love and attention until their mother scooted them off to bed. Before she left the room, Janice put her arm around her beloved Rowie and whispered, "Toots will be alright."

Tears sparkled in their grandmother's eyes as she watched her three grandchildren traipse up the stairs to their bedrooms.

∽

The first thing June did the next morning when she awoke was to turn on the radio. She heard the newscaster announce that school was canceled because the water was contaminated. "Everyone is to boil their drinking water or any water used for cooking," the announcer informed his audience before he went on to say that the National Guardsmen were going back into the flooded area to evacuate anyone who still remained. "The electricity and gas are both off in the section of the South End between the railroad tracks and the river," he reported.

June poured a piping hot cup of tea for her mother-in-law who had joined her in the kitchen in time to hear the end of this report. While Rowena sipped it, June told Dick that if he was going to work, she would drop him off and take the car and wait for Forest to be brought out. Once her mother-in-law had agreed to stay with the children, Dick whispered in his mother's ear, "Don't worry. If I know my wife, she won't come home until she has Dad with her."

Rowie laughed at that and joked, "That could take a while. June, if you don't get back in a few days, I'll take care of the children." June hugged her and assured her that she would be back soon.

Then she dropped her husband off at the shop and drove to South Third Street, parked in the Big Bear Grocery Store lot, and walked toward the underpass where she was stopped by what looked like a brown murky lake that the darkness had hidden from their view the night before. Familiar front porches and yards had disappeared beneath the water. She strained her eyes to try to see any sign of life in this unfamiliar scene. As she looked toward her in-laws house, a rowboat with a National Guardsman rowing and a lone man sitting hunched over covered by an army blanket came into view. It was hard to tell if this man was Forest until the boat pulled up to dry ground and he stood up and faced June. Still clutching the blanket around him and holding Lula's birdcage containing her canary, Dickie Bird, in his right hand, he stepped out of the boat onto solid ground.

He managed a faint smile when he saw his daughter-in-law and muttered, "I am about frozen. I didn't have any heat in the house after ten o'clock last night. It must have gotten down to zero before the night was over. I took Dickie Bird upstairs with me, and covered us with all the blankets I could find, but that didn't help much."

By the time he'd wound down, they had reached the car. "We'll be home in a few minutes, and you can have a cup of coffee, and I'll fix you some breakfast. First let me run into the shop and let Dick know that you're alright. Okay?" June said.

She only stayed at the shop long enough to reassure Dick that his father was safe before she headed for the house on Oakwood Avenue. When she stopped at the curb in front of the house, the door burst open and Sharlyn, Janice, and Ricky flew through the door as they called out, "Toots, Toots!"

Only the relieved look in Rowie's eyes told Forest that his wife was glad he was safe since her words of greeting were, "You are indeed a stubborn man!" She had warm words though for Dickie Bird who had burst into song when the warmth of the kitchen had finally penetrated his feathers.

Her father and Polly arrived shortly afterwards with jugs of fresh water from their well. "Since we're on such high ground and we're not on the Newark Water system, our water is safe. We'll keep you supplied until yours is pure," Burrel told his daughter as he sat the jugs on the countertop.

When June asked how they'd gotten through all the water, Burrel had informed her that they'd by-passed the flooded area. "We took Orchard Street to Licking View Drive, then came through Heath into Newark."

"Leave it to your father to find a way," Polly told her grateful stepdaughter. "As soon as he heard the news on the radio this morning, he started to fill these bottles."

When Bill heard Janice refer to her grandparents as Rowie and Toots, he teasingly sang his own version of Row, Row, Row Your Boat, "Rowie, Rowie, Rowie your boat, Toots, Toots!"

Janice responded with, "Bill, you're a nut!" before she started giggling at his cleverness. Before the day was over, she and Ricky had all their friends in the neighborhood singing Bill's revised version.

In days to come, since her in-laws were to be with them until the house on Third street was once again habitable, June was grateful for the many times her father showed up with fresh water for the family.

~

Once the water finally receded, and they were able to get into the house on Third Street, they found that the water had been three feet high in the downstairs. The floors were covered with mud and sludge, the wallpaper, carpets, and all upholstered furniture was ruined as were the washer, dryer, and refrigerator. The stove was the only appliance that could be repaired.

Although it was difficult for Rowie to lose so many of her furnishings, the hardest loss of all was of her irreplaceable photographs. The only ones salvaged were ones she'd stored on closet shelves.

Forest, Dick, and Eddie worked for days shoveling out debris, sweeping, cleaning and removing the wallpaper, and scrubbing the floors before Rowena went shopping for replacement furnishings, and new wallpaper.

Unfortunately, they discovered that the recent insurance they had taken out would not cover flood damage. Forest fussed, fumed, and canceled the policy. "What good is insurance anyway if it won't cover a disaster like this one?" he grumbled.

Although June and Dick's house was not touched by the flood, they did not escape the disaster unscathed. They were to discover that their car's motor had been ruined when Dick had driven through the water to bring his mother out. Like Forest and Rowena, their insurance would not cover it. They'd only had the car for a few months, and when they tried to trade it in, they found it was almost worthless. Like so many other people in Newark, the flood had been costly for them. This was one time, though, when they learned that things weren't as important as the people they loved. "At least everyone is safe," Dick told himself as he shelled the money out for a different automobile.

FOIBLES AND FABLES

Once this traumatic experience was behind them, everything settled down into a normal routine. Everything about the family's life was again going well, and they had no reason to expect that it would ever be different. Rowie occasionally complained to June that she wished her middle son, Eddie, would get married.

June replied that she thought Eddie would make a good husband and father. He loved being around Sharlyn, Janice and Ricky, always lavishing them with attention, playing and jitterbugging with them. Since they'd been old enough to go with him, he'd taken them for rides in his car and brought them back with their hands and stomachs full of candy, soda pop, or ice cream. She grinned at the memory of the New Year's Day when he'd arrived with a bag full of noisemakers he'd brought home from a party he'd gone to the night before. She remembered Dick's remark when he had been blasted out of bed by the ruckus the children had made with them. "Just wait until you have children! I'll buy each of them an entire set of drums!" Eddie had laughed at his brother's threat before he joined his nieces and nephews in the noise-making.

June recalled the day the previous year when Rowie had called and excitedly said, "Eddie told me last night that he'd met a girl, and that she invited him to go with her and another couple to Virginia Beach in a couple weeks. She's going to call back with the details."

"Is he going?" June had asked.

"He's really excited about it. He's already dug my old suitcase out of storage and is ready to pack as soon as he hears when they're going to go," Rowena had replied.

While Eddie had waited for the call that never came, they'd shared his disappointment. They would have felt differently if they'd foreseen the unhappiness the return of this young woman would eventually bring into their lives. After awhile, though, they'd dismissed her from their minds until a few weeks short of a year later in the summer of nineteen fifty-nine she'd shown up at Eddie's shop. Although Dick had met her when Eddie brought her to the Natoma to have lunch with them, June still hadn't when she heard that they were going to be married in a few days.

The date was set for the wedding to take place in July in the home of the bride's brother in her hometown of Mt. Vernon twenty-five miles north of Newark. Eddie had asked Dick to be his best man, and her brother's wife was to be her matron-of-honor. Rowie had told June that it was going to be a small wedding and that she, Forest, Dick, and June were the only ones in Eddie's family who were invited.

When the wedding day arrived, June called her mother-in-law to find out when they were to be in Mt. Vernon. Rowie's voice sounded strained when she replied that she wasn't sure there was going to be a wedding.

"What do you mean?" June asked. "Dick told me they were getting married today. Have they changed their minds?"

June could hear the regret in the older woman's voice when she replied, "They're not sure whether they want to get married or not." June recalled a conversation she'd had a few days earlier with her mother-in-law when Rowie had told her that Eddie's girlfriend was a lot of fun, and that she liked her. "Besides, it's about time he got a place of his own. I've been ironing his shirts for too long as it is. He needs a wife to do them for him." June had refrained from reminding her mother-in-law that the Licking Laundry did all Dick's shirts.

In years to come, Rowie was to realize that this was a case of needing to be careful of what you wanted as you might get it. As much as she loved her son, if she had known what the future held for him, she would have done everything in her power to talk him out of this marriage.

Throughout the rest of that day, the wedding was first off, then on, then off again. When Dick and June concluded that the wedding wasn't going to take place, they decided to take advantage of the fact that Sharlyn was at Girl Scout Camp and Janice and Ricky were going to spend the night at Dick's Uncle Ray's house by going to the movies. Then Eddie called and told them the wedding would be in an hour and a half. He'd laughed happily and said, "Don't be late!" before he hung up.

During the day, June had felt a sense of forewarning about this marriage. That feeling only increased when during the ceremony the minister called Eddie by the wrong name. "Will you, Jim, take this woman, Joy, as your lawful wedded wife?" the preacher had intoned.

Although the groom replied, "I, EDDIE, take this woman, Joy, as my lawful wedded wife," the minister continued to call him Jim throughout the rest of the ceremony.

During the festivities that followed the service, June tried to forget her misgivings, but she couldn't quite shake the ominous feeling of impending disaster. "Oh, how I hope I'm wrong," she thought as she watched the beaming couple.

Later she was to wonder how all their lives might have been different if this wedding hadn't taken place. As it turned out, the young couple's decision to go ahead with the wedding turned out to be the perfect example of the wrong road taken.

―

When a few weeks later the newlyweds bought a two bedroom house at 118 Leonard Avenue in Newark, and settled in, June put her misgivings aside while she became acquainted with her new sister-in-law. Of medium height and stocky build, Eddie's wife had short attractively styled dark hair, a sallow complexion, and dark circles under her protruding gray eyes. June was soon to discover that she was a complex young woman subject to pronounced mood swings.

She did have a sense of humor, but her talk was punctuated with language straight from the gutter. Although June had overcome her original shock from this vulgar language, she was embarrassed when Joy and Rowena came over for a visit when Sharlyn and her new friends, Connie and Bonnie Taylor, were in the living room. When Joy cut loose with a few choice words that would have embarrassed a ship full of pirates, and June noticed the shocked looks on Sharlyn's friends' faces and the embarrassed look in her daughter's eyes, she hurried her guests into the kitchen for a cup of tea.

That wasn't nearly as embarrassing, though, as what happened a few days later at Joy and Eddie's house. June related the incident to Dick that evening after the children had gone to bed. "I took Ricky and the girls to see Joy today. She had some new records she wanted us to hear. When she put on "Mac The Knife", she told us that dancing was all in the hips. Then she demonstrated with a few bumps and grinds that would have put any stripper to shame." June paused while she tried to control the twitching of her lips before she continued. "You won't believe what happened next."

Dick ventured a guess, "She split her tight pants."

June couldn't control the laughter any longer, "Worse than that. Ricky stuck a pin in her bottom!"

"Good Lord!" Dick gasped. "Why did he do that?"

June shook her head from side to side and said, "I don't know. Why do you think he would do such a thing?"

June noticed that the shock in his eyes had been replaced by a wicked gleam before he said, "Well I've noticed that her pants are stretched so tight across her hips that they look like a couple of big balloons. Maybe he just wanted to let some of the air out."

"Men!" June exclaimed as she let the sofa pillow fly at her husband's head.

"Good shot!" he laughed as he returned it. Then he calmed down and asked what Joy had said.

"Nothing I'd care to repeat, but she got over it. I gave Ricky a talking too. He said he didn't know why he did it, but he promised it would never happen again."

"I just have one more question," Dick said. "Did he let any air out?"

"I give up," June said. "You're worse than he is." She was smiling, though, when she walked over to the television set and turned it to her favorite new show, Perry Mason.

A couple weeks later, they discovered another facet of Joy's character when Dick, June, Sharlyn, Janice, and Ricky were invited to dinner at the house on Leonard Avenue. The meal was good, but the crowning touch was the large melt in your mouth dinner rolls. As if she needed assurance that she was a good cook, several times during the meal, she would ask what they thought of the biscuits she'd made. Everyone's praise and the fact that every roll was devoured seemed to satisfy her that she'd done a good job.

While they were still at the table, Forest and Rowena stopped in. The first words out of Rowie's mouth were, "How did you like the rolls I baked for Joy?" The new bride didn't blush or bat an eye to be caught in a lie. She just calmly replied that everyone liked them.

Much to June's relief, Joy apparently forgot all about the episode with Ricky and the pin. In fact, a few days later she and Eddie took the little boy into Kline's department store on the square and bought him a stuffed toy Dalmatian he'd wanted since June had taken him and his sisters to see the Disney movie, *101 Dalmatians*, at the Midland Theater. Earlier that day, Joy and Eddie had come over to take him and his sisters out for an ice-cream cone, but since the girls were at friends' houses, Ricky was the only one to go with them. When they brought him home, he was beaming and clutching the toy to his chest. Joy apparently read their surprised looks and commented that she wasn't mad at him. "I like mischievous little boys," she said. "You know, snakes and snails and puppy dog tails, that's what little boys are made of," she quoted.

Before they went home, Sharlyn and Janice returned, and Joy taught all three of the children her brand of dancing to June's record of, Kookie, Kookie. "It's all in the hips!" she again told them as she demonstrated how to gyrate in time with the music. When June thought back to this scene years later she realized that her sister-in-law had her own brand of rock-and-roll dancing before Chubby Checker ever hit the scene.

～

During that eventful year of 1959, there was a split in the new Baptist church. When June asked her stepmother what had happened, she was told that she didn't want to talk about it. All she'd say was that they just needed to move forward. June did know that part of the tiny congregation had stayed at the Grange Hall while Burrel and Polly, the Story's, and several others had moved to the Union Hall in Heath. "Since there is no church in Heath now, we thought there was a need for us here," Polly explained. "This village is bound to grow. Already more homes are being built and more people are moving into the area."

About this time, the congregation changed the church name to the Heath Baptist Church then shortly afterwards they bought two acres between Liberty Drive and route 79 where they enthusiastically made plans to build the new church building. For the time being, the old house on the property was used for a parsonage by the first minister, the Reverend J.D. Walters.

One Sunday afternoon as they sat around the maple table at the house on the hill, Burrel told his daughter and her family that the congregation was ready to start to build the church. He turned his glance on his sons seated on either side of him and said, "Bill and Fred and I are going to work on it along with the other men and boys in the congregation."

"Bill and Dorothy are moving to Newark next week, and they are going to park their travel trailer in our side yard for a few months. I'm sure Big Bill will help too," Polly said.

June had noticed a suppressed excitement in her stepmother throughout the meal that she had attributed to the prospect of the new church building. Now she understood that it had another source. She was ecstatic because she would again be close to her friend, Dorothy.

Later that night when she was alone with her husband, June confided in him, "I'm so glad that Bill and Dorothy are coming here. I think it will help Polly get over the depression she still sometimes has. I've always felt that she never quite got over leaving her friends behind in Jackson, Ohio."

"I'm sure that all the problems they encountered when they had to remodel their house didn't help either. They weren't expecting it to be such a big project." Dick said. "She's so much better now, though, than she was the day I saw her downtown. The doctor had her on so much medication then that she couldn't even find her car."

"I think that doctor gave her too much. Once she quit going to him, she got better," June asserted. "As far as I could see, she was dealing with a bad case of homesickness. The end of that is in sight. It would be hard for anyone to be depressed with Bill and Dorothy here. I know that it makes me feel good just to be around them."

∼

During the six months that the Roberts' travel trailer was parked beside the apple tree in the Harman's yard, the little family had plenty of chances to be around them. June particularly liked to listen to her father, Polly, Bill, and Dorothy talk about some of their experiences either in Jackson or at the restaurant Bill and Dorothy operated at Lake White. One evening, as they all sat outside, when the conversation started with, "Do you remember," June perked up her ears ready to be entertained by all their stories. The first, "Remember when", conversation yielded a wealth of material when Dorothy started with, "Do you remember when I shocked all my customers when I told the three young men who stopped in one day dressed in business clothes that I didn't recognize them with their clothes on?"

Polly chuckled when she replied, "I remember. They were the water skiers we'd only seen in their bathing suits."

"How about the time the priest came in and a woman and little girls were right behind him, and you asked if they were his wife and children?" Polly asked.

"I didn't notice his clerical collar until after I said it!" Dorothy protested.

"How about the time we cooked the hamburgers with everything on it for the men who were working on the lines?" Polly asked.

Dorothy giggled, "You mean when we put everything on the bun, but we forgot the hamburger?"

"Do you remember how mad you got at us when you left your dog, Ripple, with us when you went to Mississippi, and we gave her so many ham-bones that she was a regular little porker when you got home?" Bill asked Polly.

"How could I forget that? We'd named her Ripple because she wasn't big enough to make a wave. When I picked her up at your house, she looked like an entire ocean," Polly lamented.

"She was one mighty happy dog, though," Bill chuckled.

Burrel directed at Dorothy, "How about the time you and I went shopping for a Christmas present for Polly? We were walking arm in arm in downtown Jackson when we ran into that gossipy woman from the church, and she asked what we were up to. When you told her what we were doing, she stuck her nose up in the air and sniffed like she'd just gotten a whiff of a barnyard."

"She didn't believe a word I said," Dorothy asserted.

"I'll never forget the way she looked at us the next Sunday in church," Burrel added.

"I was pretty happy when the gossip got back to me. I knew for sure then that Burrel hadn't forgotten to get me a present," Polly teased.

"Yeah. Like you and Dick forgot my birthday," June quipped.

Dorothy hadn't heard that story so she ignored Dick and Polly's sheepish expressions and protests that no one wanted to hear about it when she turned to June and said, "I'd like to hear it."

That was all the encouragement June needed to launch into her tale of woe. "In this family, we always make a big deal out of everyone's birthday. Mine was coming up, but everyone was really mum about it. Since I had made up my mind that Dick and Polly were planning a surprise party for me, I played it cool and kept my mouth shut. I didn't give them even a little hint that I suspected."

June grimaced as she went on, "They surprised me, alright. They both forgot my birthday!" she added.

"And she's never let us forget it!" Dick said.

"Well I don't blame her," Dorothy murmured sympathetically.

June smiled gratefully at Dorothy and cast a haughty glance at her shame-faced stepmother and husband before she laughed self-deprecatingly, and said, "I wasn't angry, but I did learn that if I wanted my birthday to be celebrated in the future, I'd better drop some hints along the way."

Sharlyn and Janice had been sitting quietly listening to the adults talk but when they heard this story, they couldn't keep quiet any longer. "Tell them what we did for your wedding anniversary," Janice pleaded.

Sharlyn piped up with, "Let me tell them!"

"Go ahead," June smiled encouragingly at her older daughter before she added, "This was the best wedding anniversary we ever had. We usually went out for dinner and to a movie to celebrate, but this year the kids said they had something special planned. I can tell you their surprise more than made up for the forgotten birthday party!"

Dick reached for his wife's hand and the rest of the adults smiled lovingly at the children as Sharlyn related the story. "We got the idea to put on a party for Mommy and Daddy from *The Parent Trap*, a movie we'd seen. First we made up the invitation for them for a special celebration. Then we set up the card table in the living room. We put a bottle of Seven Up and ice in Ricky's sand bucket for them to use to drink a toast," she explained.

Janice interrupted with, "Ricky poured the drinks into Champaign glasses, and we served them soup and sandwiches that we made ourselves."

"They each had a white napkin draped over their arm when they served us... just like the waiters in a fancy restaurant. The food was not only beautifully served but delicious too," June announced.

"All the time, we played a Dean Martin record that Mommy likes," Sharlyn added.

"I remember that one of the songs was *Volare*. What we liked the best, though, was the show they put on for us," Dick told the attentive audience. "They sang and danced and told jokes. It was the best show we've ever seen."

"That wasn't all," June said. "They wouldn't let me lift a finger to clean up. They did it all." She hugged both girls then grabbed Ricky as he and Toy ran past in hot pursuit of an elusive lightning bug.

"What was that for?" Ricky asked as he disentangled himself.

"That was to thank you for the anniversary party," June said.

"You're welcome," he politely replied as if the party had happened only yesterday. While the adults took up their conversation, the little boy and his dog took off again in search of fireflies.

While Polly refilled the lemonade glasses, the "Do you remembers?" continued when Bill asked, if anyone remembered the time Polly had gone to pick up a license for the trailer when they lived in Beaver.

Burrel and Polly smiled and nodded, but June, Dick, and the girls said they hadn't.

"That was a good one," Bill said. "Burrel was at work and Polly went to the bureau to get the license renewed. The man behind the desk glanced at the title, shoved it across the counter to her, and said that he couldn't issue it without both her signature and Burrel's. Polly didn't take to that idea very well because that meant another trip into town. Even though she tried to explain that her husband had asked her to get the license, he looked down his nose at her and pronounced that he couldn't bend the rules for her or anyone else."

Bill took a long swallow of his lemonade, and they noticed that there was a chuckle in his voice when he continued, "Polly came up with a pretty good answer that got him to change his mind, though."

"I've never had any luck with people like that," Dick said. "How did she manage that?"

"It was simple," Bill said. "She just asked him if he agreed that she owned half of the trailer, and that Burrel owned the other half. When he said that was right, then she said that it only made sense that if she tried to move her half, Burrel's was sure to follow."

Polly piped up with, "So he issued me the license!"

While June and Dick laughed at Bill's story, June said, "That reminds me of the time when we were on the way to Mississippi when I was growing up and had all the flat tires and how Polly managed to get ration stamps when Dad couldn't."

"I learned then that a pretty red-headed woman can accomplish a lot more than a mere man can," Burrel quipped.

Seconds later, as they arose from their lawn chairs, the fragrant mixture of Polly's flowers in the garden, the scent of the apples that still clung to the tree, and the sweet purple grapes that hung in clusters from the vines caressed their senses. Then with glances at their watches and murmured words about the next day being a workday, the little group dispersed for the night.

The tales told, though, were filed safely in June's mind, like a mental notebook, she had recorded all their stories today. That night in those seconds before sleep overtook her, she spoke into the darkness, "Someday, I do want to write a book."

"Sure, Honey," Dick murmured. Before she could pursue the subject further his even breathing signaled to her that he had fallen asleep. She turned her back and in a few minutes joined him in slumber.

ON THE ROAD AGAIN

Later that fall during a visit with her mother and stepfather at Widowsville, June found that her mother was excited about Dick and Bev expecting their first child. While she and June walked around the grounds and admired the late blooming flowers, Priscilla said, "Just think, my baby is going to be a father."

"Your baby will be twenty-seven years old when that happens! You'd better not let him hear you call him that," June said.

"I know, but you just wait and see, no matter how old your youngest gets, he'll always be your baby," Priscilla replied somewhat defensively.

"I'm just teasing you," June said. "I know you're excited at the prospect. I am, too."

They talked for awhile about the baby that was due the early part of December. June heard that Bev planned to work until a few weeks before it was born. Priscilla's eyes were aglow when she showed June the sweater set she was crocheting for her newest grandchild.

"Now that Skip and JoAnne and the boys have finished their stint in Japan and are back in this country, maybe all my children can get together here sometime soon," Priscilla said.

"Isn't it a coincidence that Skip is stationed in Maryland at the base Dad helped build during the war?" June asked. She didn't even wait for a reply before she reminisced, "We had some good times there. Dick and I plan to take the children to visit next summer. I hope Skip and I can find the woods we used to play in and the haunted house we found in those woods. I'd like to show them to the kids."

June had noticed before how uncomfortable her mother appeared any time she talked about the years when the family had been separated following the divorce and how quickly she changed the subject. Today was no exception.

"What's new in Newark?" Priscilla asked.

June talked a little about Eddie's marriage, news from Kenny in Sacramento, about how earlier in the summer Sharlyn, Janice, Ricky, and Betsy had gone to

Bible School at a neighborhood church. "Is that the church where they went a couple years ago and learned the song, "The Devil Is A Sly Old Fox?" Priscilla asked.

June laughed at the memory before she replied, "That's the one. I'll never forget how during the program, the little ones couldn't say converted so they sang 'I'm glad I am con-turniped.' The congregation enjoyed it, and I'm sure when God heard it, He did too."

The mention of church reminded June of what was going on in Heath with the Baptist church. While she told her mother about the land the congregation had bought and how they had already started to dig the basement, her mother listened quietly. "They're going to hold services there until they get the rest of the building completed," June told her. "Dad, Fred, Bill, Big Bill and a lot of the men and boys of the church are all working on it now."

Her mother remained silent for a few seconds when June finished talking before she finally spoke. June noticed the far away look in her eyes and the pensive note in her voice when she said, "If your father had done this while we were married, we would still be together. When we were first married, he always went to church with me. He even talked about wanting to be a preacher some day. Then when we went to West Virginia, he never stepped foot into another church." Unshed tears glistened in her eyes when she added, "He knew how much that meant to me, but he just quit going."

"If only! If only!" June felt like screaming as she thought of how she and her brothers would have been spared the pain of the divorce and the long separation if only her father had done things differently or if only her mother had reacted in a different way. Her mother's words had reminded her of something that had been in the back of her mind recently...how we all have the choice of so many different roads to take, and the road taken can make such a difference in a person's life.

When later that evening, June confided this conversation to her husband, he reminded her that if her parents had stayed together, Polly and the boys would never have been in their life. "You know, Honey, when you're not picking and teasing, you make sense," she informed him. "You can also thank Mom for me being a good wife and mother. I would never put my kids through a divorce," she confided.

"You were smart enough to choose me," he murmured teasingly as he pulled her onto his lap and gave her a heartfelt kiss.

∽

June was sitting at the kitchen table making her Christmas list on the evening of December sixth when the phone rang. She tucked the list in her pocket so the children couldn't sneak a peek when she went into the living room to answer it. She was pleased to hear her mother's voice on the line. Priscilla hardly bothered with a greeting before she said, "Dick just called from the hospital. He said the baby was born a few minutes ago and that Bev is doing fine."

"Are you going to keep me in suspense or are you going to tell me whether I have a niece or nephew?" June asked.

June could hear the happiness in her mother's voice when she replied, "They have a little girl. I can hardly wait to see her."

"Me either," June replied On the following weekend when they made the trip to Mansfield, she and Dick were delighted with their first niece, Janet Kay, with her fair skin, big blue eyes, and fringe of light colored hair. Sharlyn, Janice, and Ricky were old enough to be totally captivated.

A few weeks later, after June listened to the church bells ring in the New Year with Sharlyn, Janice, and Ricky, she waited up for her husband to return. Although the girls wanted to stay up until their father got home from the New Year's Eve dance he was playing, June sent them along to bed with their sleepy eyed brother. "Your dad won't be home for a couple hours yet," June told them as she scooted them up the stairs. "I'm sure I'll be asleep on the couch before he gets here." She knew it was probably silly but she had never been able to make herself go upstairs to their bed until she knew that her husband was safely home.

Although she laid down on the couch to wait, sleep eluded her this night as her mind reflected on the events of the past year. Although it had started disastrously for the family with the flood, it had ended happily with the birth of Janet Kay.

Her mind strayed to what had happened in the country, and she smiled to herself at the thought that with the addition of Alaska and Hawaii as states, her children would have to learn the names of fifty states instead of the forty-eight she and Dick had to memorize.

Her last thought before she went to sleep that night was how glad she was that everyone in the family was safe, healthy and happy. *She might not have slept quite so well if she'd known that only one more New Year's Eve would pass before that would no longer be true.*

When New Year's Day of 1960 arrived, Bill and Dorothy moved from their spot in Burrel and Polly's yard to Washington D.C. While living in Newark, Bill had been working as a printer at The Newark Advocate, but now he was moving on to bigger and better things to the Washington Post. Shortly before they moved, they received word that they were grandparents. Their son, Mack, and his wife, Bernice, had a little girl they'd named Linda.

One of the last things Dorothy said before she left was to be sure to come to Washington and visit them. That summer June, Dick, and the children took her up on the invitation on their way to visit Skip, JoAnne, and the boys nearby in Maryland.

Sharlyn, Janice, and Ricky were as excited about the trip to the national capital as June and Skip had been on their first visit nineteen years earlier. When Big Bill asked his guests what they wanted to see first, they had no trouble deciding that they wanted to go to the top of the Washington Monument.

When they arrived at the grassy mall, they found a long line of people that snaked a couple times around the base of the monument. "There will be a long wait for the elevator," Bill said. Much to the children's delight, he added, "We could walk up the steps."

June tilted her head backwards and looked toward the tip of the monument five hundred fifty-five feet, five and one half inches above her. "I don't know about that," she demurred as she thought about all the steps involved.

"It's not bad at all," Bill assured her.

"We've walked it before," Dorothy said.

June gave in but she still had misgivings. "I just hope it's not too hard for the kids," she said as they started up the stairs.

As it turned out, though, the adults panted and perspired, while they trudged up the steps, stopped at each landing to catch their breath and read the inscriptions, while the children ran to the top and back down the stairs several times to ask, "What is taking you so long?"

When they finally joined Sharlyn, Janice, and Ricky at the lookout area at the top of the stairs, June observed their excited faces as they peered through the peepholes at the panorama spread below them. She was happy to see that her children were as awed as she and her brother had been when they'd first looked through these same openings.

Meanwhile Ricky had found a new interest. He was as fascinated by their host's new camera as he snapped pictures of them and of the view below. Almost like magic, the slip of paper Bill pulled from the slot in the front of the camera slowly turned into the picture he'd just taken. "It's a Polaroid," Bill told his curious visitors as he demonstrated how this new invention worked. Ricky still asked questions as they rode the elevator to the ground level and Big Bill continued to take more shots. *June wondered years later when her son studied photography in college and later became a professional photographer if his interest might have stemmed from the first time he saw such an unusual camera that summer day in 1960.*

∽

The next day the little family set off, bright and early, for Skip and JoAnne's house. June's mind was flooded with memories of late 1942 and early 1943 when she, Skip, her father, and Polly had lived in the area while her father worked on the construction of the base where Skip was now stationed. "It was called Cedar Point when we lived here," June said. "Now it's the Putuxant River Naval Air Base," she added. A faraway look appeared in her eyes as if she had mentally journeyed back in time before she continued. "I remember how shocked we were when Dad took us to the park where we were going to live. It looked like a junk-yard!"

Sharlyn's voice sounded incredulous when she said, "You lived in a junkyard?"

"Not exactly," June replied. "It was during the war, and when all the families of the men who worked on the base moved into the area, there were few places for them to live. The only way a man could keep his family together was to buy a trailer. With the influx of mobile homes, people around here rented out any space they had for them to park. The first place we lived was bad with junk cars on the grounds. The people who owned it were horrible." She shivered at the memory before she went on, "After awhile, Dad moved us to a farmer's yard that was really nice." She turned in her seat and smiled at her children before she told them, "While we're here, we'll see if we can find it and the woods across the road where your Uncle Skip and I used to play."

While June answered questions about what it was like in the "olden days," Dick had to stop at a guardhouse where a lowered gate barred his way into the neighborhood. A young white-gloved sailor stepped over to the car and asked, "What is your business here?"

When Dick explained that they were going to visit Chief Cecil Harman who lived on the base, the guard told him to pull over to the side and wait. Then he went into the guardhouse and returned in a few minutes with a pass, verbal directions to the non-commissioned officers' housing, raised the gate, and waved them onto the base. The children were amazed that they hadn't been allowed to drive directly to their uncle's house. June explained that these security measures had to be taken on all military bases. During their visit, they would notice other differences between civilian and military life.

A few minutes later when June and her family arrived at the two story redbrick town-house, it was to be the first time she had been in her older brother's home since his marriage nine years earlier. June realized it had been a long time when she saw the sleeping accommodations JoAnne had set up for Ricky. The six-year-old boy's eyes widened when he saw the baby-crib. "Mom, I won't sleep in a baby bed," he announced. Sharlyn and Janice thought it was hilarious and couldn't control their laughter. After Sharlyn reminded Ricky that he was the baby in the family, he became so angry that she quickly regretted teasing him. June calmed him down when she told him that he could camp-out on the floor during their visit. It all became an adventure and the injury to his pride was soon forgotten. During the next few days, both families made up for lost time with the children playing and the adults visiting.

The children weren't the only ones confused by the happenings on the base. The first night there, June was startled awake by the sound of a jet plane that sounded as if it were right over their heads. While she listened, the sound of the engine grew even louder. Then it abruptly quit. In the ensuing seconds, the silence was deafening as she waited to hear the sound of a plane crash. Terrified, she could hardly breathe, but the only sound that penetrated the silence was the pounding of her own heart. Mystified, she finally went back to sleep only to again be awakened as the scenario was repeated.

The next morning, when she mentioned the near crashes she'd heard to JoAnne, her sister-in-law grinned knowingly before she replied, "They were testing the engines. I should have warned you about it. If you don't know what is going on, it can be scary." June sighed in relief when she realized the planes she'd envisioned losing their power while in flight had never left the ground.

The first few days of their visit, a smartly uniformed Skip would leave for the air control tower where he supervised several radar operators. While he was gone, JoAnne would pack a picnic lunch, then she, Dick, June, and the children would get into their bathing suits and head for the beach where they would spend the day. Although the Harman family's years stationed in California and later in Japan had separated the cousins, that forced time apart didn't keep them from having a good time now. Six year old Ricky and Chris, a few months younger, dug holes and built castles in the sand while the eight year old duo of Mike and Janice talked and played. Sharlyn who was approaching twelve spent more time with the adults than with the children.

While they watched the children on the beach, JoAnne asked June, "What is this with Janice and the sailor hat? I don't think she's taken it off since she got here."

June glanced quickly at her husband. When she determined that he wasn't listening to their conversation, she explained that Janice had always had long hair but she'd talked her into a short cut for the summer. "After I had Dick cut it, she was so unhappy without her long hair that she said she vowed to wear the hat until it grows out, and she has worn it every day!" *As it turned out, she didn't remove it until later that summer when Grampy Eis, from next door, whispered to her, "If you keep wearing that hat every day, your hair will fall out."*

To the visitors' surprise, they discovered during the visit that JoAnne didn't like the water. Consequently she and the redheaded boys spent most of their time on shore or at the very edge of the water even when June and Dick splashed around in the bay with Ricky and the girls.

A few days into the visit, they all piled into the cars and set out to try to find familiar places from June and Skip's earlier years in the area. They had no trouble finding the school they'd attended, but June was disappointed to discover that the other places had changed too much to be recognizable. This was to be the first, but not the last time, the young woman was to learn that you can never really go back except through the memories that forever seem to live as echoes in your mind.

On Skip's day off, they drove into Washington and took the children to the Smithsonian where the adult brother and sister again retraced the steps of the eleven and thirteen-year-olds they had been when they'd last explored these buildings together. Girls and boys alike were fascinated by the dinosaur skeletons, the Spirit of St. Louis, and other examples of early flight, but when they moved on to see the gowns worn by the First ladies, Mike, Chris, and Ricky fidgeted in boredom while the females thoroughly enjoyed the exhibit. Although she didn't tell her mother, Janice secretly agreed with the boys. She'd much rather spend her time seeing the flight or cavemen exhibits.

Hours later when nine very tired people returned to the house on the base, they all agreed that they'd enjoyed the day. "I think the kids all liked the museums but the Lincoln and Jefferson Memorials made a hit too," Skip observed.

June added, "Skip, do you remember that they were in the midst of building the Jefferson Memorial when we moved away from here as kids?"

After Skip agreed, Dick said, "That must have been exciting for you to see it today for the first time. Even though, I'm not a kid anymore, I was pretty impressed by all of it myself. The feeling doesn't change no matter how many times I see Washington D.C."

June replied, "I might argue with the kid part, but I agree with the rest. This has been a wonderful vacation. I hope it is one the children will remember."

"It's not over yet," he reminded her. "Tomorrow we're going to see your Aunt Calcie and Uncle Gordon on the farm in Pennsylvania."

"As if I could forget. I've been telling the kids how great they are, and how nice they were to me when I lived with them," June murmured. "Even though they don't live where they did then, the atmosphere in their farmhouse will be the same."

~

Their last night at Skip and JoAnne's as the kids played a noisy card game of War, June asked about the slot machines that had been added to the area since she'd lived here. When she expressed her amazement that they were everywhere except in churches, schools, and the post office, Skip told horror stories of young sailors who'd gotten the gambling bug and lost their entire paycheck as soon as it was cashed. "One robbed a bank out of desperation, and I heard that another committed suicide when he got too far in debt to borrow or beg his way out," he grimly reported.

"Skip won't even put a nickel in one," JoAnne related.

"It might be alright for a visitor, but I live here and it's too easy to get hooked," Skip replied.

"Like we did in Zanesville?" June asked. "We had to lose all of our allowance before we finally got smart," June reminded her brother. "Polly sure did set us straight!"

Skip cast a side-wise glance in his sons' direction to see if they'd overheard this conversation before he nodded and replied, "I remember, and I guess I learned my lesson then."

The next day when they resumed their trip, June had a chance to test how well she'd learned hers when they pulled into a roadside restaurant shaped like a giant tee-pee. Sharlyn, Janice, and Ricky had noticed it on the way down and pleaded with their parents to stop, but June, anxious to see her brother, had put them off with a promise to stop there on the way home.

When they entered, they had two surprises...the lack of Indian decor and the presence of rows of slot machines. Dick, who liked to play the one-armed bandits, got a couple rolls of nickels, handed one to his wife and headed for the machines with an entourage of three young followers. "Remember, it's illegal for the kids to gamble," June hissed after him.

Within minutes she saw the downward motion of three small arms and calls of, "Oh, no!" when the machine failed to deliver. "We're all going to end up in jail," June thought as she rushed over to remind her husband.

"I'm putting the money in. I'm just letting them pull the lever," he responded but his eyes didn't stray from the machines. When she started back to the booth and her now cold coffee, he called after her, "Why don't you play the nickels I gave you?"

A half hour and three cups of coffee later, completely bored with the wait, she finally succumbed and started to drop her nickels into first one machine then the other until she had parlayed her two dollars into five dollars and forty-five cents. Then she returned to her seat.

"You won!" Dick reminded her. "Aren't you going to play anymore?"

"Nope," she replied. "I'm going to buy the new blouse I saw at the Betty Gay with this money." No amount of coaxing would change her mind while she waited for them to win or lose. Finally, a few dollars poorer, the lure of Aunt Calcie's house won, and the family piled into the car and headed for Palmyra, Pennsylvania.

∼

The children soon discovered that what their mother had told them about this woman was true the minute Aunt Calcie opened the side door to her kitchen and called, "Come on in!" To June's eyes, this woman who had been so much like a mother to her after her parents' divorce hadn't changed. Maybe her hair had a few strands of gray, but her cheeks were still smooth and unlined. The combination of kindness and the hint of the laughter that had always filled any house where she and Uncle Gordon lived still shone from her eyes.

The smell of freshly baked cookies tantalized their noses as they walked into the room. June soon found herself wrapped in her aunt's soft arms as the older woman said she was glad to see them. While Aunt Calcie told Janice how much she reminded her of June when she'd been that age, Ricky had his eye on the fresh batch of cookies she'd placed on the counter by the stove. "I'll pour you some milk, and you can have some while they're still warm," she said as she motioned for them to pull up some chairs and sit at the kitchen table.

While they munched on the cookies and downed the milk, she studied Sharlyn's face and said, "Your coloring is different from your mother's but you look like her too."

Seconds later, they all turned at the sound of footsteps on the porch as Uncle Gordon opened the screen-door and strode into the room. His well chiseled face lit up in a smile as he saw his niece and her family. "It's been too long since we've seen you," he said.

"I know," June sighed. "Since Dick is self-employed, it's almost impossible for us to take any vacation. It's been years since we've been able to get any time away from the shop."

Uncle Gordon nodded in understanding. As a farmer, he had the same problem. "How's your dad and Polly?" Aunt Calcie asked. "Are Freddy and Billy as rambunctious as ever?" June and Dick exchanged smiles at the thought of just how rambunctious her little brothers were before she replied that her parents were fine and that the boys kept their mother and father on their toes.

Uncle Gordon wiped away his milk moustache and brushed a few crumbs from his shirtfront before he pushed his chair away from the table and said, "If you're through with your snack you can come out into the barn. I have something to show you."

June told the rest of the family to go with her uncle. "I'm going to stay and help Aunt Calcie clean up the dishes."

"Oh, shush," Aunt Calcie said. "I can do this! You just trot along with your family. You'll want to see them too." The word "them" had conjured up pictures of little animals, maybe kittens or puppies, in everyone's minds. Once they reached the barn, those mental pictures were quickly replaced by the reality of a half dozen stalls...each containing a beautiful, sleek race horse.

When he brought one out into the barnyard, June felt dwarfed by it, and for a second felt a flicker of fear. This was not the case with Sharlyn, Janice, or Ricky. They were fascinated by the first one, and the others he led out. Within minutes, he'd offered to take each of them on a ride. "Ricky, you're first," he told the excited little boy. For the next hour, he put one child then another on the horse with him and rode around the farm while their mother snapped pictures.

As June observed this delightful scene, she remembered the times she and Grandpap Harman had spent riding around his farm in West Virginia. Then as Uncle Gordon and Janice rode by, she heard the murmur of his deep voice and saw her young daughter's eyes light up; June wondered what he'd told her. If she'd have been a fly on the horse's back she would have heard the older man say, "Consider this horse yours, but I'll have to keep him here for you." When she heard this story later, it reaffirmed her belief that her uncle was a kind man. He'd certainly brought joy to her young daughter.

"I didn't know you had race horses," June told her aunt when she joined them a little later.

"They're not ours. We board them here," she explained.

Before Sharlyn, Janice, and Ricky left the barn, they watched the young, handsome farmhand milk the cows. He was young enough to enjoy flirting with the girls and showing off his milking skills by squirting milk in the cat's mouth. Later that evening at the dinner table as he was seated between June and Sharlyn his face twisted and contorted into a strange expression. Little Janice and Ricky thought he was making faces at them so they laughed accordingly. Suddenly while the visitors looked on in horror, his face crumbled and he fell into Sharlyn's lap.

Frightened and confused, Sharlyn let out a small whimper as she looked from her parents to her uncle as if to ask what was going on and what she should do.

As if in response to her unvoiced question, Uncle Gordon's voice was calm and reassuring when he said, "He's an epileptic, and he's having a slight seizure. When it's over, he won't remember it. We don't want to embarrass him when this happens, so we don't mention it when he comes out of it."

"Doesn't he remember anything?" Dick asked.

"Not usually. I think he's coming out of it now. Just watch and don't say anything," Uncle Gordon cautioned. While they looked on, the young man sat up, picked up his fork and his conversation as if there had been no interruption.

The rest of the visit was not quite as dramatic, but fun, never-the-less. June got to see all her cousins except Bea and Maxine who were still in the Washington, D.C. area, and Bonnie who was now married and living in King of Prussia, Pennsylvania. In the course of conversation, her cousin Ruby mentioned that her husband, John, was one of the Hershey boys.

Astonished, June exclaimed, "Milton Hershey who owns the candy factory is your father-in-law?"

Ruby laughed before she replied, "No, he's not my father-in-law. Mr. and Mrs. Hershey don't have any children of their own. So they take groups of boys who are orphans and set them up as small families on farms. Each group of Hershey Boys has a married couple act as their parents. Like any other farm family, the boys have chores working on the farm. Mr. Hershey wants to instill the work ethic in them. Which he certainly did in John. Then when the boys graduate from high school, he sends them on to college."

"It sounds like Mr. Hershey is more than a candy maker," June said. "He is also a philanthropist."

Then June and her cousins reminisced about the time June had lived with them after her parents' divorce. They laughed about their skinny-dipping adventures in the river that ran through the farm.

"What's skinny-dipping?" Ricky asked.

After June explained, he said, "That sounds like fun, Daddy. Can we do it sometime?"

Dick laughingly responded, "I'm afraid we'd get in trouble if we tried to do that back home in the Licking River."

Confused, Janice asked, "Why didn't you get in trouble when you did it, Mommy?"

June's cousin's explanation that they had lived in the country and that the river they'd skinny-dipped in ran through their farm seemed to satisfy the children's curiosity. Aunt Calcie's entrance with a plate full of freshly baked sugar cookies brought an end to their questions.

∼

Much too soon it was time to leave. Before the children got into the car, Aunt Calcie handed each of them a brown paper bag to take with them. "Just some Hershey candy from the plant where I work," she said. As soon as the children had looked into their sacks and expressed their appreciation, Aunt Calcie told Dick he really should go through the town of Hershey on the way home. "It's the only place in the world that smells like chocolate and where you'll find street lights shaped like Hershey kisses," she said.

After they'd said their good-byes and traveled a short distance, their noses told them they were close to the town before they saw the sign. "Aunt Calcie is lucky to get to work here," Ricky enthused as he breathed the chocolaty smell.

"It would be nice to bring home samples," Dick quipped. Less than an hour after they had left behind the sights and smells of Hershey, the question, "Are we almost home?" from the backseat made Dick and June realize that the vacation was over. The children were now anxious to see their friends and their grandparents.

They might not have been as anxious if they'd known what waited in store for them upon their arrival and in the months to come.

NINETEEN SIXTY

When they got home, they found bad news waiting for them. Lula, Dick's feisty dark-haired grandmother, was ill and the doctor didn't know what was wrong with her. "She feels so tired and weak all the time," Rowie told Dick. "When she didn't want to go next door to Ag's to play cards in the afternoon anymore, I knew something was wrong."

Every since his Grandfather McNamee had died in 1944 when Dick had first gone into the service, and Lula had started to divide her time between Rowie's house in Newark and Thelma's in Oakley, near Cincinnati, she had never missed an afternoon when she was with Rowie to head next door to her friend Ag's house for their daily game of cards. Dick grinned when he added that she always left the house with a brown paper bag containing two cigarettes and a cold beer for herself and one for her friend. They played one hand of High, Low, Jack, and the Game, each drank her beer and smoked her cigarette. Then Lula would come home for her "before dinner nap."

June could tell by her husband's worried expression that the fact that she had given up this routine alarmed him. Another thing he told her he'd noticed was how much she had started to dwell on the past. "When I stopped there after work tonight, she talked about when she, Mom, and Kenny came home from shopping and found her husband, my grandfather, dead in his big easy chair."

In response to June's horrified look, he added, "He apparently had a heart attack while they were gone."

"Not only must that have been awful for Lula but for Kenny and your mother," June cried. She could feel the sting of tears in the back of her eyes at the thought, "I can't imagine anything worse then to find your father or grandfather like that."

"What about a husband?' Dick asked.

She squeezed his hand before she replied, "That would be horrible too, but you're so young, I can't really identify with that."

A few weeks later, when June's mother came for a visit, she was saddened to hear of Lula's illness. "If you think she's up to company, I want to go see her," Priscilla told her daughter and son-in-law the first night of her visit.

"She still likes company," Dick told her before he turned to his wife and said, "Why don't you and your mother visit her tomorrow?" As if he thought his wife needed a further enticement, he added, "Mom had just put an apple pie in the oven when I left this evening."

June dropped Sharlyn, Betsy, Janice and Ricky at the Midland Theater on the square for the afternoon matinee before she headed to the house on Third Street. When Rowie led them into the kitchen, Lula was seated at the kitchen table with a cup of tea, a box of photographs, and a rectangular wooden box on the table in front of her.

"I see, you did manage to salvage some of your photographs from the flood," Priscilla commented.

"Rowena saved some of hers, but these are mine...some I had with me at Thelma's," Lula responded.

As Lula flipped through the photos, she chuckled when she pulled one from the stack. She handed Priscilla a photo of her and her sisters. While the rest wore the feminine fashions of the day, their sister Addie was dressed in a man's suit and surprisingly was smoking a cigar. At Priscilla's puzzled expression, Lula said, "Addie thought it would be funny to dress up in her husband's clothes for the picture. She would do anything for a laugh. She was the character in our family."

Remembering some of Lula's antics, June remarked, "Must run in the family."

Rowena motioned her guests to chairs on either side of Lula, and offered them each a cup of tea and slice of apple pie which they readily accepted. Then while they savored the steaming liquid and delicious dessert, Lula held up a picture of a small elderly man dressed in the uniform of a union soldier with a taller distinguished looking middle-aged man. "The soldier is my poppa, Jacob Stoner, with Congressman Ashbrook. Poppa enlisted to fight in the Civil War. He was captured in his first battle and was sent to Andersonville, that awful prison camp in Georgia," she told Priscilla.

"Andersonville!" Priscilla cried. My grandfather, Josiah Glancy, was in Andersonville, but he died shortly after he got home because of the bad treatment he'd received when he was a prisoner."

Lula opened the varnished wooden box and showed June and Priscilla its contents. "Poppa said he carried this with him while he was in the army. It has his papers in it from the war including the one he signed when he promised never again to fight against the confederacy in exchange for his release from prison."

Lula pulled out some paper money with the words, "Ten Cents," printed on it, a few receipts, and a recipe for a tonic for the treatment of catarrh.

"What's catarrh?" June asked.

"That's an old fashioned word for an inflammation in your throat or respiratory system," Priscilla explained.

The visitors were both interested in Lula's pictures and the contents of the box, and before they left they'd concluded that Lula's father and Priscilla's grandfather must have been captured in the same battle and been in the prison camp at the same time. Even though Priscilla wanted to pursue the subject, the older woman looked tired so they decided to cut their visit short.

They realized they'd been right when before they had even gotten to the door, they heard the sound of Lula's shuffling feet as she made her way across the floor on the way to her bedroom for her afternoon nap.

"I hope she doesn't have cancer," Priscilla whispered as they made their way to the car.

"Mom thinks that if someone has a hang-nail, it's cancer, and Rowie thinks every sneeze is menopause," June thought. She felt sad when it occurred to her that this time her mother could be right.

A couple weeks later when Lula returned to Thelma's house in Oakley, and to her doctor there, and was diagnosed as anemic, everyone breathed a sigh of relief. "The doctor says that it is curable. She just needs to take iron supplements and eat liver to get her blood built up again," Rowie happily reported to Dick after she received this information in a long letter from her sister. After awhile, though, when there was no improvement in their mother's condition, both sisters began to wonder if the doctor had made the wrong diagnosis.

∽

While this was going on in Dick's side of the family, June still saw her father as often as possible. He, Bill, and Fred had been working on Saturdays to finish the church building. Since the congregation had grown to almost seventy with the Sunday School attendance almost double that, they had out-grown the basement where they had met for the last few months.

At the time, while the trio worked alongside the other men and boys in the church, they didn't realize that they not only were building a church but building memories that the boys, especially Fred, would never forget. Fred loved working with his father. This was the most time they'd ever spent together. While they worked, he taught both Fred and Bill so many things they would use later in life. Maybe that time might not have been as special to them if the future had taken a different turn.

Bill's most outstanding memory of the time he worked on the church was when someone had yelled, "Look out," and he'd only heard the word, "Look." When he turned to see what he was to look at, he was hit in the chest by a two-by-four one of the men carried. Since he didn't have much meat on his chest to cushion the blow, a couple ribs were broken.

During the years they lived in the little white house on the hill, both boys had built other kinds of memories. Of course, they never thought of what was going on in that way. They were just having fun...being boys. More than once after one of their pranks, Burrel was heard to mutter under his breath, "No wonder parents get gray."

Once unbeknownst to Burrel or Polly, Fred and Bill souped up the riding mower so they could ride through the woods with the other boys on their accelerated machines. The next time Burrel tried to mow the grass, he found himself careening wildly down the hill. When he finally brought it to a halt, and looked back to where his wild ride had started, he found he'd mowed a path through the apples that had fallen under the tree. Two boys got a good talking too that night. "No one messes with my apples!" Burrel told his repentant sons. "Just think of the good applesauce, dumplings or pies your mom could have made with these apples." Before he left the room he gave them a stern look and pronounced, "That mower had better be back to normal tomorrow...and that's all there are to it!" Although they had to work late into the night, the next day it was!

As June had told Aunt Calcie, the boys managed to keep both parents on their toes. One time Bill helped plant the garden, but he planted the sweet corn in with the popping corn. They had no way to distinguish the two, until they tried to pop it. No matter how hard you tried, the sweet corn wouldn't pop.

Halloween found Bill and Fred and the rest of the Huck Finn\Tom Sawyer act-a-like boys on the hill out in full force. The next day many neighbors found their windows soaped and lawn furniture perched dangerously high in branches of trees. One year they moved the one outhouse that still existed in the neighborhood. Unfortunately, Jay, one of their friends was in it. When they pushed it over, the hapless boy landed in the hole. His friends saw him begin to sink. Then they grabbed him by the arms and pulled and pulled until the gunk loosened its hold. As they got splattered by the smelly mess, they just thought that was the worse of their troubles. When Jay looked down at his feet, he found that the suction had pulled his shoes off, and they still rested under the accumulation of months of goop in the hole. When Jay's father found out what had happened, he made the boys go back and fish them out. That was a prank they never repeated.

While most of the neighbors were tolerant of the boys' antics, the one across the road and another behind them were exceptions. Over a period of time both houses found themselves toilet papered and the one had a cherry bomb thrown into the swimming pool. No boy on the hill ever took credit for that prank.

This time in the sixties, an underlying fear gripped much of the country... the fear of the atomic bomb. Movies, radio, and television programs were filled with warnings of what could happen if an atomic bomb were dropped on this country. The message was loud and clear that the only way to be safe was to build a bomb shelter and keep it stocked with food and water.

These neighbors with the pool were the only ones the family knew who actually built one. Unfortunately, they dug it too close to the pool, and the pool sprung a leak and completely flooded the shelter. Burrel and Polly breathed a sigh of relief when they realized the flooding was the direct result of frozen pipes from a deep-freeze winter and not from any prank pulled by their sons.

June had inadvertently added to the misery of the neighbors on the hill when a stray cat decided to make its home on her front porch on Oakwood Avenue. The animal was like none she had ever seen. The missing fur, torn ear, and half closed eye were trophies from the many battles it had fought. Beyond a doubt, it was the meanest, ugliest cat she had ever seen.

Sharlyn, Ricky, and Janice already had their cat, Honey Sugar, and her kittens, so their mother didn't even consider keeping this stray. Since it was obvious that it was hungry she couldn't turn it away without food. When Dick saw Sharlyn putting out food and water for it, he declared, "This can't go on. We have to find a home for it." Their problem was solved when Bill first laid eyes on it. It was love at first sight. Polly's reaction was different when she saw Frankenstein, as it had now been named, but Bill won her over.

Frankenstein took his job as the attack cat seriously. He wouldn't bother anything, though, unless it was threatening his family or his territory. For months, one particularly vicious dog had been terrorizing people and animals within a three mile radius. He met his match one summer day when he tangled with Frankenstein. June was a witness when she parked beside her father's house in time to see a yellow dog streak past her with a snarling Frankenstein's claws dug into the mongrel's back. As she heard the dog's anguished howls in the distance, she felt certain that Frankenstein had rid the neighborhood of that particular menace. Weeks later, Bill confirmed this when he told her that the boy who owned it wondered why his pet never left its yard. "I could tell him," Bill chuckled, "but I won't!" From that day forward, Frankenstein ruled the neighborhood.

~

Before the year was over, a rising star in the political scene dominated the television screens as John F. Kennedy, dubbed JFK by the media, ran against the current vice president, Richard Nixon, for president of the United States.

June and Dick were no different from millions of other Americans as they avidly sat mesmerized by the television screen as they followed the presidential debates between the two fierce competitors. It was obvious that Vice President Nixon was in trouble before the debate was over. JFK was handsome, self assured, and exuded charisma with every word, smile, and gesture. Since he had agreed to wear makeup, he looked healthy and vibrant under the bright lights. Nixon, who had refused, looked white and ghostly. As the camera moved in for a close-up of the Vice President's pale perspiring face, June said, "I'm afraid Nixon has his work cut out for him, if he hopes to win this election."

"This is just the beginning of the debates. Maybe he will do better in the next two," Dick responded. As it turned out, he'd lost his advantage and never quite regained it. It became apparent during the campaign that Nixon was being overshadowed by this charming competitor. In the weeks to come, it was impossible to turn on the television or open a newspaper without seeing Kennedy's smiling face.

Not all the comments by the media were favorable, though. During the weeks preceding the election, many news programs explored the issue of JFK's religion. "I don't know what the big deal is," June said one night after a particularly venomous attack on Kennedy's Catholicism by a news panel. "I've never heard anyone else's religion questioned," she asserted.

"I heard someone say that they were afraid he'd take his orders from the Pope," Dick told her.

"That's nonsense," June said. "He doesn't seem like the kind of man who would take orders from anyone if he becomes president," June replied as she turned the television set to a new program, Father Knows Best, that the entire family liked to watch together. While they watched Robert Young as the father on the show and Jane Wyatt as the mother so calmly and lovingly deal with life with their three offspring, June glanced at her three children sprawled about the room. Although her children were younger, her family was so much like the one on the show that when she watched it, she felt as if friends had dropped in for a visit. She had to admit, though, that no matter how hard she tried, she didn't always stay as calm as her television counterpart.

～

During that year, television continued to play an integral part in everyone's life. That's where they first saw Chubby Checker introduce the new dance called The Twist. Children took to this dance immediately while the adults took a little longer. Dick Clark's American Bandstand became as important to the younger members of the family as the Mickey Mouse Club had been before. As June sat with the children and watched this new show, she knew the jitterbug she'd grown up with was as outdated as the Charleston. As one show followed another, they watched and listened as the big band sound was replaced by a new one called Rock and Roll. Over the next few years, dances with funny sounding names like the Mashed Potato and the Monkey were added to the Twist.

That September, though, June's thoughts were not only on world events but on her little son who, with one year of kindergarten behind him at Kettering School, would be joining the girls at Lincoln School which would take them from the first to the ninth grade. "It hardly seems anytime at all since Sharlyn started school. Now she's in the seventh grade, Janice's in the third and Ricky is starting the first," June lamented. "Time is going too fast."

Dick just laughed and asked if she thought she could keep them young forever. "Now for the first time since you were eighteen, you won't have a child at home during the day. You'll have some time for yourself. Don't tell me that you're not looking forward to it," he teased.

She flippantly replied as she glanced toward the row of unread books in the bookshelf, "Once I get the cleaning, washing, ironing, cooking and sewing done, I might find something else to do just for myself. Her eyes were misty, though, the next morning as she watched her youngest child walk along with his sisters and their friends toward the big brick school at the end of their street.

She found out later that he had as vivid an imagination as she did when he told her what he'd expected from his teacher. "Mrs. Armstrong isn't anything like the Mrs. Armstrong on TV," he told his bewildered mother. "She didn't do one single flip."

"Flip?" June asked. "Why would you think your school teacher, Mrs. Armstrong, would do a flip?"

"The one I saw on TV did!" Ricky announced.

This answer only served to confuse his mother more. Dick, who until now had been quiet, got the connection. "He's seen that commercial for Armstrong linoleum where the woman gets so excited about her new floor that she does all kinds of flips all over the place," he says.

With the mystery solved, June felt her lips begin to twitch, but she contained her smile as she assured her little son, "I can see why you expected to see some acrobatics, but your teacher isn't **that** Mrs. Armstrong."

June was pleased as she thought about the healthy experiences her children were having while attending this friendly neighborhood school. Black and white children were friends, growing up together, not separated in different schools as in her early childhood. Janice confided that her first and second grade teachers had been sweet, loving, grandmotherly types who were unmarried and dedicated to their students. Miss Bishop had begun each day with the children reciting the twenty third Psalm by memory. "The Lord is my shepherd, I shall not want…" What a way to start the day!

June found that three children in school meant more time spent as a room mother and with the PTA. During the year she baked dozens of cupcakes for each holiday, glued and painted Santa Claus faces on an equal number of brown paper bags filled with goodies at Christmas time, and attended every school function.

At one PTA meeting, she was shocked to hear the handsome new science teacher, who had recently immigrated from Greece, say that the children in Sharlyn's class had thrown fruit at him. A picture flashed in June's mind of a hapless performer being booed off the stage and pelted by over-ripe tomatoes. Her shocked expression and stern glance at her daughter brought a quick explanation from a teacher who had overheard the comment.

"They didn't throw it. They rolled it," he quickly explained. As understanding dawned, June could feel her expression turn from alarm to comprehension. She'd heard of this custom before. As it had been explained to her, each student would take a piece of fruit to class and as a show of appreciation for a teacher at a given signal, they would roll the fruit from their seats toward the teacher's desk at the front of the room.

"He's so good-looking, I don't blame you for having a fruit roll for him," June told her daughter that night as they walked toward the house on Oakwood Avenue.

Sharlyn wrinkled her nose and threw her mother a cryptic look before she replied, "That's not why we did it. Science is hard enough but with his accent, we're all having a terrible time understanding him. Besides, he's a tough teacher. We thought a fruit roll might make him ease up a little."

"Butter up the teacher, huh?" June murmured.

Sharlyn didn't respond but her grin told her mother all she needed to know.

November came and with it, the election. That day for the third time in her life June cast her vote for President of the United States. That night she and Dick sat with their eyes glued to the television screen until they learned that their candidate had lost. Before the votes were even cast in the western part of the country, television commentators had declared John F. Kennedy the new president.

"Maybe it will change when all the votes are counted," Dick said as they traipsed up the stairs to their bedroom. When June flipped on the radio the next morning, though, she heard that the results hadn't changed. When she filled her husband's mug with coffee, she wryly commented, "Now I know how Dad felt all those years when Roosevelt won." In months to come, they were to find that though it wasn't easy to have their candidate lose, like almost half of the voters in that election, they had no choice but to grin and bear it.

During the next one thousand-plus days while President Kennedy was in office, the American people were charmed by this man and his lovely wife, Jacqueline, their small daughter, Caroline, and son, John Junior, who had been born a few days after the election. This was to be the beginning of what was later to be known as the years of Camelot. Unfortunately these years were to end much too soon.

Although she hadn't voted for this charismatic man and didn't always agree with his politics, it was difficult not to be interested in this new president, his trend setting wife, and their winsome children. During those thousand days, the First Lady received media attention for her devotion to her family and for her sense of style, and like many other young American women, June found herself wearing Jackie style pillbox hats, low heeled shoes, and softly feminine suits like the new first lady.

During the holiday season, downtown Newark resembled a scene from a Christmas card. Crisp snow crunched under everyone's feet as with their arms loaded with packages they bustled around the square. The sparkling lights from the brightly decorated Courthouse twinkled and glistened as they reflected the surrounding field of pristine white. As June had noticed every year since she'd moved to Newark, people had smiled at friends and strangers alike as they called out holiday greetings. The sound of Christmas music was all around them, outside as carols were broadcast from atop the courthouse and inside every crowded store.

The spirit of the holidays spilled over into the house on Oakwood Avenue. The Christmas Eve guests were met by the familiar sights and sounds of Christmas; Bing Crosby, singing White Christmas, lights and ornaments sparkling on the tree, and colorfully wrapped packages resting under its branches.

Unfortunately, that year Dick's grandmother, Lula, was missing from the little Christmas Eve gathering. Since her health hadn't improved, she'd decided to stay in Oakley with Thelma. Although she was missed, the tradition continued with June's father and his family, Dick's mother, father, Eddie and Joy gathered around the Christmas tree.

After they exchanged gifts, Rowie and Forest went home, and the children went to bed. Then Dick and Burrel started to assemble all the children's toys. They had no problems with anything until they came to a box labeled Space Station. "Ricky really had his heart set on that toy," June explained as her husband dumped the pieces onto the carpet, and he and Burrel set about their task of turning this confusion of parts into a little boy's dream of a spaceship.

An hour later, the two men eased up from their place on the floor, stretched weary muscles, and looked down in satisfaction at their handiwork. Then only seconds after Burrel announced to Polly, "We can go home now, it's all done," June hesitantly pointed to an extra piece on the floor and asked, "Where does that go?"

Dick rubbed his sleepy eyes and muttered, "The instructions said that even a child could put it together." Waving the instruction sheet in the air, he read, "Put piece A into piece B, piece C into piece G, piece H into piece Y. I've never seen such a mess! It would take someone with a degree in engineering to do it." That said, he plopped the extra piece beside the toy space station and announced to one and all that he was going to bed.

The next morning, Sharlyn, Janice, and Ricky awakened their parents, before they ran down the stairs, where they found their gifts displayed under the tree. The little boy immediately picked up the extra piece and promptly placed it where it belonged. June wisely refrained from reminding her husband or father that the instructions had been right, even a child could do it.

The children were excited to find that the adults in the family had taped Santa's visit on their Daddy's new-fangled reel-to-reel tape recording machine. Ricky and Janice knew it was really Santa Claus's voice because at one time or the other, they could pick out each of the adults voices in the background. That recording put all doubt aside and proved, for one more year, that Santa really did exist.

Later in the day when the family arrived at Priscilla and Bill's house in Widowville, Janice and Ricky excitedly told Gram, Grandpa Bill, their Uncle Dick, and Aunt Bev about their jolly visitor of the night before. "That was wonderful of Santa Claus," Priscilla said. "We didn't have any recording machines when your Mom and uncles were little." As she talked about Christmas in the past, and how the children had been excited to receive an orange, although no one voiced it, more than one of the children thought of how rough it must have been in the, "Olden Days."

In the house on Oakwood Avenue after the Christmas cookies had all been eaten, the eggnog had been consumed, the tree taken down, and the gifts put away, June smiled at the thought that this had been another great Christmas. "Next year will be perfect if Lula is better and able to be with us," she told her husband as she brushed the last piece of tinsel from the carpet.

"She's too full of pep and vinegar to let anything get her down," Dick said with a little more confidence than he felt. "Once the doctor gets her blood built up again, she'll be alright, and we'll have a full house again."

LIFE IS CHANGING

On April seventeenth of nineteen sixty-one, when June came out of the church where she had conducted a Girl Scout Leader's Training Course, she flipped on the radio as soon as she got into the car. At first she couldn't make any sense out of the newscaster's words. She had obviously tuned into the middle of a special news bulletin. The first words she heard were that President Kennedy had ordered Air Force planes in Florida to be on the alert. The excited voice then urged people to prepare for attack. "No one is to panic, but everyone is urged to stock up on canned food, and a supply of drinking water and find an air tight place where the fallout couldn't get to you." June's confusion was complete when he concluded his broadcast with the rather cryptic words, "Cuba is only ninety miles from the Florida coast."

On her way home, she stopped at the barbershop to ask her husband what had happened while she'd been behind closed doors in the church. "Some Cuban exiles from Florida launched an attack on Cuba today. Apparently it was a fiasco, and most of them were either killed or captured," he told her. "The Cuban government blames the United States. I can't imagine that Cuba would attack the United States, but it looks like they have Russia behind them. I guess, just to be on the safe side, it wouldn't hurt to have some supplies in the basement in case an atomic bomb is dropped."

At school, fire drills were replaced with air raid drills where the students had to go into the hall and crouch down with their hands behind their heads while they leaned against their lockers. Though this would have provided little protection against an atomic bomb it was something the government thought would help in case of attack.

Although they prepared for the worst, as they either watched the news on television or listened to it on the radio, after a few frightening days they heard that the crisis was over. Everyone breathed a sigh of relief when the disaster known as The Bay of Pigs was put behind them.

This incident only served to fuel the fear the American people had of the possibility of an atomic attack. Although, more and more bomb shelters were put in the ground, no one in June or Dick's family ever built one. Fortunately for them, none was ever needed.

More national history was made that spring, and Sharlyn and June got to watch it on television. May 5, one day after they'd celebrated Rowie's fifty-fifth birthday, Sharlyn was home from school with a cold. For that reason, she was the only one of the children who got to watch live on television what the country had worked to accomplish. The mother and daughter watched as Alan Shepard became the first American to be launched into space. Although his actual time in space was only fifteen minutes, he reached an altitude of one hundred-fifteen miles. The suspense became intense as they wondered if the force of gravity would allow him to return from this dangerous trip. When his space capsule, Freedom 7, splashed into the ocean, they held their breath while they waited to see it hoisted onto the waiting ship, the door pried open, and a smiling astronaut emerge.

"I wish I'd had Janice and Ricky stay home to see this," June told Sharlyn. "They'd have learned more from this than from any textbook."

"Good thing I had a cold, wasn't it?" Sharlyn joked.

"I wouldn't say that, but I am glad you got to see it," her mother replied before, in a more reflective voice, she mused, "Just think how much things have changed. When I was a little girl, we would run outside and look up at the sky every time a plane went over. I used to read Flash Gordon comic books, but I never thought I would see anyone actually launched into space."

Since the sonic boom of jet planes from Wright Patterson Air Force Base in Dayton that flew over the house on Oakwood Avenue was a part of her everyday life it was difficult for Sharlyn to imagine what it had been like when her mother had been a child. In her mind, anytime before she was on this earth was, "the olden days." With this thought in mind, she smiled politely at her mother and murmured, "Sure, Mom."

A few weeks later, when June's brother, Dick, and his growing family came to Newark for a Sunday afternoon, June invited her father and his family to join them for dinner. While the women were putting the finishing touches on the meal preparations and plying Bev with questions about her second pregnancy, the men mysteriously disappeared. June didn't realize this until Fred wandered into the kitchen and asked, "Do we have to wait until Dad comes back before we eat?"

Surprised, Polly asked, "What do you mean? Where did he go?"

"He didn't say. He, Dick and Dickie left awhile ago," Fred replied as he stuffed half of a roll in his mouth and sauntered out of the room.

"I guess dinner can keep until they return," June said. "If they're not gone too long." After a quick peek in the oven at the ham, she refilled her stepmother and sister-in-law's coffee mug and said to Bev, "Has the doctor said why you're having so much trouble with this pregnancy?"

Bev's expression was grave when she replied that he didn't really know. "You know how it is, the doctors don't have all the answers. Things were fine when I was expecting Janet, but this one has been a problem from the very beginning. At first, he thought I might lose it. Since I'm almost six months along now, he says things will probably be alright."

After the question, "When do we eat?" had been asked by every child in the house except Janet Kay who hadn't mastered the sentence yet, the men wandered back into the house to be met by the question, "Where have you been?"

June's father looked a little sheepish when he replied, "We went to the store. I saw something the other day that I wanted to buy for Dickie...so I took him out and got it for him."

In answer to everyone's questioning look, Dickie, as his father still called him, brought his right hand from behind his back and held up a brightly colored yo-yo. Then like a kid at heart, he proceeded to put it through its paces.

Polly asked what everyone was thinking, "Why would you buy a grown man a yo-yo?"

Burrel's smile was for this day's gathering, but his eyes had the look of being in another time and another place when he softly replied, "When Dickie was about five years old, and we lived at the house by the cave, he saw a red and white yo-yo pretty much like this one in a store in Franklin. I remember how he cried when I told him we couldn't afford it." Then as if after all these years he had to explain to that little boy Dickie had been, he added, "It was during the depression, and we just didn't have money for little extras. I hope you never know how awful it makes a father feel to have to refuse his child something like that."

He glanced at his listening audience before he concluded his story. "When I saw this one in the Seaway, I decided to take Dickie out when he came down and buy it for him."

A little later when they were all seated around the harvest table June had bought with her Girl Scout Day Camp Director's salary, the conversation shifted to other topics, but her thoughts were on what her father had said. She wondered if this simple gesture was his way to say he was not only sorry about the yo-yo but for all the other things he hadn't been able to do for his son during the years of their forced separation.

∽

That gathering and another that was to take place later that summer were to be ones June would never forget. They became especially significant in her mind because of what was to happen in the near future.

The second one was like any other time June and her family had dinner at her father's house on the hill. After they finished the dinner and while they polished off the apple pie Polly had baked that afternoon, someone asked what they would like if they could have anything they wanted. Most people listed material things, a one-story house was June's response, teen-aged Fred and Bill each wanted a car, Sharlyn wanted a new bicycle since the one her Grandfather Forest had given her was old and hard to pedal. Ricky and Janice wanted toys, Polly a new washing machine, and Dick dittoed Fred and Bill's request for a new car. Burrel who had waited until last to speak looked around at his family and with the happiest expression June had ever seen on his face, he said, "If I could have anything I wanted in the world, I would like to see our Savior, Jesus Christ. Someday, I hope to see Him in heaven."

A few seconds of silence followed this statement then as if to lighten the solemnity of the moment, Dick said, "We know you'll make it, but don't get in any hurry!"

"I didn't mean to put a damper on the evening, but I am ready any time He calls me," Burrel responded.

June felt a chill run up her spine at the thought of what his words meant before he completely changed the subject to say, "You know that there hasn't been much construction around here. I haven't worked in Newark for quite awhile, but until now I have been able to find work in other parts of the state." He sighed deeply and added, "This has meant that I have to be away from home all week." June had an inkling of what his next words would be, and she didn't want to hear them.

He looked into his daughter's anxious eyes before he continued, "You know how it was when you and Cecil were children. Polly and I thought we all needed to be together. It's the same now with Bill and Fred. They need more than a weekend father. The only way that can happen is if we move from here."

Although, she wanted to say, "Don't go," June understood. Her father's new family had as much right to a full time father as she and Cecil had. In her heart, she knew they had been able to stay here longer than she could have hoped.

"Where are you going?" she asked.

"Baltimore," he replied. "The union can get me on a big job there...one that should last a couple years. Maybe when that job is over, we can come back here."

"Are you going to sell the house?" Dick asked.

"Since we plan to come back someday, we'll rent it," Polly said. "We were going to ask you if we could just have the rent sent to you, and you could make our house payment for us," she told June.

"A landlady is the last thing in the world I'd ever want to be," June quipped. "But I guess if you twist my arm I could give it a try." Then a few days after the advertisement appeared in the newspaper, a young couple named Paul and Ethel Large rented it. *At that time Janice was nine years old, none of them had heard the last name of Large before or knew that in eleven years the name would be hers and that this redheaded young man would become her uncle.*

∽

By the time the house was rented, Burrel had already left to start his new job and find a house for the family. When he returned a few weeks later, Polly was packed, and ready to load their furniture and other belongings into a U-Haul and set off for their new adventure. June stood in the yard of the house on the hill and waved as her father maneuvered the vehicle onto Franklin Avenue on the first leg of their journey. Fred and Bill's faces looking back at her brought back memories of the many times during her growing up years when she'd watched her friends through the rear window of the car as she rode away with her family. Now she knew what it felt like to be the one left behind.

The birth of Dick and Bev's son on September the sixth helped to take June's mind off of the family's departure. Although David Richard Harman had arrived prematurely and weighed in at a little over five pounds, he was a healthy baby. A couple weeks later, when the little family went to Mansfield to see him, they were amazed at how tiny he was. *They would never have believed that someday he would be six feet five inches tall.*

The new parents were disappointed that Dick's father hadn't been able to come to Mansfield to see the new baby. "Dad only had enough time off from work to come home, get the van packed and drive back to Baltimore in time to get the boys in school. He said to tell you that he wanted to come, but he would have to wait until he came to Ohio for Christmas to see him."

Unfortunately when that holiday arrived, a winter storm kept the family in Baltimore. When June bemoaned the fact that it wouldn't seem like Christmas without them, Dick reminded her that if they tried to come, they might have an accident. "You wouldn't want that to happen, would you?"

"Of course not!" she exclaimed, but in her heart she still wanted the weather to miraculously clear and for the family from Baltimore to appear in Newark before Christmas Eve. Since this didn't happen, the family carried on as well as they could with their traditional holiday. Although the adults tried to make this a good Christmas for the children, the empty seats around the large harvest table made everyone feel sad. No one was as unhappy, though, as Dick's brother, Eddie, whose wife had evicted him from his own home a few weeks earlier when an old friend came back into her life. The strain of losing his wife and his home showed on Eddie's usually smiling face as he tried to get into the holiday spirit.

"This Christmas was pretty rough," June bemoaned after the last guest had departed and the children had gone to bed. Her voice took on a wistful tone when she added, "Next year, it will be different."

As they were to discover, she was right. The next year would bring more change, but it wouldn't be the kind she wanted.

HEART AND SOUL

As they entered the new year, Dick and June were concerned about Eddie's depression over the upcoming divorce. "I had lunch with Eddie today at the Natoma," Dick explained to his wife one evening in early January. "He just can't believe what has happened."

"I can't say that I blame him," June replied. "As far as I could tell, they were getting along fine. In fact the last time we saw them together before she kicked him out, I remember thinking that I must have been wrong to be worried when they got married."

"Eddie has been upset for awhile because she was gone so much, and she wouldn't tell him where she was going," Dick said. "I guess that one day, she put almost three hundred miles on the car."

"Was Eddie checking up on her?" June asked.

"No! You know Eddie, he always keeps the tank filled for her. He started keeping track of his mileage way before he'd even met Joy," he said. "Since she usually just goes to Columbus to go shopping or to Mount Vernon to see her family, it was pretty obvious when she started going farther."

"When did her friend come on the scene?" June asked.

Dick responded, "Apparently she's been seeing Terry for awhile. When Eddie questioned her about it, she told him that Terry was an old friend who needed help. You know how good hearted Eddie is, he let Terry stay at their house. After awhile, it became evident that Terry was disrupting their lives. Eddie began to feel like an intruder in his own home. Then when he gave Joy an ultimatum that she choose between him and her friend, she kicked him out. He said he couldn't believe it when he came home from work, and found the locks changed and the drapes pulled tight so he couldn't see inside."

"Is that when he banged on the door, and she called the police and got a restraining order against him?" June asked.

Dick nodded. "It's really killing him that the court can keep him out of a house he saved all his life to buy. What was even harder for him was when Joy finally let him in to get his clothes, and he discovered that Joy's friend had moved into their bedroom with her. He said that he hit the ceiling and ordered Terry out of his house, but Joy just laughed and waved the court order in his face," Dick explained. "When he told his attorney what he suspected, he was told he wouldn't even be allowed to mention his suspicions unless he had concrete evidence." Dick threw his hands in the air in frustration when he muttered, "It would take Superman's X ray vision to see into that house. She even has something hung over the tiny windows in the front door so no one could peek inside."

"Dick!" his wife exclaimed. "You didn't try, did you?"

"I'll never tell," he chuckled. Then in a more serious vein, he pronounced, "I'd do anything I could to help my brother."

"I think just being there is the most important thing you can do," June concluded.

"I hope you don't mind all the time this has taken, but he really needs me to go with him to the lawyer's office. When we were there today, I thought I was helping Eddie when I told the attorney that Joy's friend had been discharged from the army because of improper sexual activities, but he just shrugged his shoulders and said that didn't prove anything," Dick said.

"I'm wondering if we recommended the wrong attorney to him," June said.

Dick replied, "My feelings exactly. I thought he'd really fight for Eddie since he was so gung-ho last year when he got that woman off for murder. I can't see that he's done much for Eddie!"

June sighed dejectedly before she said, "It looks like Eddie can't win for losing."

"It might not be quite that bad," Dick reassured her. "Today the lawyer brought a proposal from Joy's attorney. She will give up any claim on the house, Eddie's earnings, his savings, the furniture, car or anything else he owns in exchange for a cash settlement of four thousand dollars."

"What was Eddie's reaction?" June asked.

"About what you would think. He said he wasn't going to give her a penny. Then when we talked to Mom and Dad about it, Dad blew his stack and told Eddie that he shouldn't give her one thin dime!"

Her husband's words caused chills to skitter up and down June's spine as she felt the return of the ominous feeling she'd had when Eddie had married Joy. When he finished talking, she surprised him when she said, "I don't agree with your dad. I think he should pay her off and get out of this marriage. As long as he's married to her, he'll be responsible for her legally and financially. She could run up a lot of bills."

As she was to learn, although she was the only one in the family with that opinion, Eddie did eventually come around to her way of thinking. Then once Joy learned of his willingness to settle, she and her friend moved to Mount Vernon and Eddie regained possession of his house...and his life.

June, who for the last three years had directed a day camp for the local Girl Scout council, had been promoted to coordinate all the day camps in the four county area. She was looking forward to attending a four-day seminar in Columbus. She had already explained to her family that since she would be away from home on her birthday, they could celebrate when she returned.

Unfortunately, a week before she was to leave, she became ill. Suspecting an over-active thyroid the doctor ordered that blood be drawn immediately. When the lab called him with the results, he discovered the error in his diagnosis and sent June directly to the hospital for blood transfusions. When the nurse notified Dick, he hurried to the hospital where he found his wife in bed, with the life giving red fluid flowing into her arm. When she saw him leaning over her bed she smiled wanly and joked, "I guess I'm a quart low."

For once, he didn't smile at her feeble joke. Instead, his brow was furrowed with worry when he asked what had happened. I guess I've lost almost half the blood in my body," she replied. "I didn't realize how shaky I was until the doctor asked me to hold out my hands and though I tried to hold them steady, they shook like leaves in a storm.

Before Dick could reply, the doctor walked in. For the first time in her life she saw this grandfatherly-like man angry. "How could you allow her to get into this condition?" he demanded of her husband.

Dick's usually smiling eyes flashed when he retorted, "How could I let her get in this condition? I tried for three days to get an appointment, but your nurse said you didn't have any openings!"

The doctor's expression had changed from anger to concern when he responded, "I didn't know that. Did you tell her June was bleeding?"

Dick wasn't quite ready to let the doctor off the hook when he replied, "I certainly did, but the dragon lady wouldn't listen."

"She will from now on," the doctor assured them. They never knew what he'd said to his nurse but that was to be the last time June ever had to wait for an appointment.

Disaster almost struck after a surgeon performed minor surgery to stop the bleeding, and she was given a second transfusion. While the first one had been life giving, something went wrong during the second one. First, she felt as if her blood had turned to ice, then she started to shake violently. Alarmed, the patient in the other bed rang for the nurse who promptly removed the IV from June's arm, almost smothered her in blankets, and forced hot tea through her shivering lips.

The woman in the starched white uniform looked bewildered when, thinking of Rowena's love of tea, her patient stammered, "Y-y-you r-r-remind m-m-me of my m-m-m-mother-in-law."

The warmth finally returned to June's body, but that was the end of the blood transfusions. No matter how hard she tried to find out what had happened, she was never told what had caused such a violent reaction. At first, when June asked the doctor if she could go to the seminar, he replied with an emphatic, "No!" but before she left the hospital, he relented. "If you promise that you will just go to your sessions then return to your room to rest, I'll let you go," he reluctantly told her. Since June knew how important this training was if she were to be successful at her new job, she readily agreed to take it easy.

When they arrived in downtown Columbus at the Deshler Hotel where the seminar would take place, June told her husband, "He doesn't have to worry about me gallivanting around. I'm still pretty tired."

"You be sure to follow the doctor's orders," her husband told her as he said goodbye to her in her hotel room. Dick didn't let the fact that the day camp director she was to share the room with was already there keep him from pulling his wife into his arms and fervently kissing her goodbye. June's redheaded roommate discreetly turned her head, but when they heard Dick whistle as he walked down the hall to the elevator, she laughed and told June, "You just missed my big scene with my husband."

~

June enjoyed the seminar but as her birthday approached she began to miss her family. She concluded that her husband must have felt the same way when on the big day she looked up from her notes and saw him in the doorway to the classroom. Her happiness quickly turned to alarm after she saw the expression on his face as he talked to the instructor, who in turn walked over to her and said, "Your husband needs to see you right away."

With pounding heart, June walked over to her husband. As she approached, she noticed that Eddie was with him. She hid her fear behind a bright smile when she greeted them. "Did you come to take me out for my birthday?"

She became even more alarmed, though, when she saw that neither man returned her smile. Instead, Dick led her to a secluded spot in the lobby and told her to sit down. "What's wrong?" she whispered fearfully. "Has something happened to one of the children?"

He quickly assured her that everyone at home was fine. "It's your dad," he said. "Polly called and said that he had a heart attack this morning."

She couldn't find the words to voice what was in her mind, but Dick's next sentence answered her unasked question. "He's in the hospital in Baltimore. Polly said that it's a good hospital and that he has a wonderful doctor."

Dick proceeded to tell her that her stepmother had said that when Burrel had gone out this morning to scrape the ice from the windshield, she happened to look out the window in time to see him grab his chest and collapse in the snow. "She called the emergency squad, and they got him into the hospital right away."

June had sat quietly and listened but as soon as he finished, she jumped up and exclaimed, "I'll go upstairs and pack so I can leave for Baltimore."

Her husband who had anticipated her reaction replied, "You've only been out of the hospital for a few days. I'm sure the doctor won't allow it. Besides how would it help your father to have you get sick too?"

Before the words were out of his mouth, he noticed the stubborn thrust of her jaw, but he had decided that this was one time it wasn't going to faze him. "You're not up to the trip, and, as your dad would say that's all there are to it," he said.

Eddie who until now had kept quiet added his words of advice to his brother's. "Dick is right. Your dad wouldn't want you to jeopardize your health."

If their words hadn't convinced her, the wave of weakness that caused her to sink into her chair would have. When the two men observed her shaking hand wipe the beads of perspiration from her face, Dick said, "I'm taking you home now. I shouldn't have let you come in the first place."

The young woman didn't protest as they took her upstairs to her room and stuffed her clothes into her suitcase. After she scribbled a note to her roommate and another that she gave to the bellboy to give to her instructor, she left with her husband and brother-in-law for the return trip to Newark. Once there, she never strayed more than a few feet from the telephone and the news she feared might come.

With each call she received from Polly, the news became better and better. After a couple weeks, her father called and said, "I am home, and I feel fine!"

While they chatted, she learned that he wouldn't be able to go back to work for a couple more weeks and that he would be on medication for the rest of his life. He concluded by saying, "Believe me I'm going to listen to the doctor. I don't want to have to go through something like that again."

Relief had flooded June at the sound of her father's voice. She hadn't realized until then just how frightened she'd been that she might lose him. Although this was the case she felt almost overwhelmed by the need to see for herself that he was really alright.

When she mentioned this to her husband that evening, he quickly said, "It's February now. If you can hold off until school is out, we'll all go to Baltimore for a few days."

With the knowledge that the two families would soon be together, she decided she needed to focus her attention on her husband, children, and new job.

~

In the last few months, changes had taken place on Oakwood Avenue that had affected her family. First, she was concerned about Sharlyn who seemed lost without her two best friends, Connie and Bonnie Taylor. Their parents had bought a new house north of town and moved the family into a different school district. Shortly before that, Betsy's parents had bought a farm in that area, and the Eis's were spending some time away from the Oakwood Avenue neighborhood.

"That's fine for them. They're all going to school together, but we have to stay here," Sharlyn complained. "I don't know why we don't move too."

June had thought of this many times but Dick was solidly anchored to the house on Oakwood Avenue. "This is our home. We've put too much into it to move now," he would reply every time she mentioned the possibility. Like him, she loved the house, although at times she yearned for a one floor plan. If she mentioned this, Dick would respond, "All those steps help you keep your youthful figure."

One of the things she liked about the older neighborhood was the front porches. During the afternoon, women and small children would sit and watch the passing parade. In the evening, while children played in their yards, the parents could be seen sitting on their porch furniture, as they visited their neighbors. From their vantage point, everyone watched out for everyone else. Even after dark, the red glow of a cigarette, or the scent of pipe tobacco would signal that one or another porch was still occupied. Crime, at that time, was almost unheard of on this quiet tree lined street. "No wonder," June mused. "This little stretch around us must have one thousand eyes."

To observe Janice walk up the street to her new friends, Janet and Marsha Ford's house was quite an experience. Since she was a sunny, friendly girl who loved all the neighbors, as they loved her, it might take her fifteen or twenty minutes to walk the short block. June could hear her call out, "Hello, Grampy. Hello, Ginny. Hello, Who Who. Hello, Mr. Lake. Hello, Mrs. Knot," before she crossed the street to talk to Hazel and Lester or Mrs. Evans who were relaxing on their front porches. Observing this, June would wonder why they should change this stable neighborhood for an unknown one. As she remembered how difficult it had been for her to be yanked out of someplace she loved when she was a kid, the urge to move would disappear.

For months now, the airways had been filled with news of the next space accomplishment. A young man named John Glenn was not only going to leave the earth's atmosphere, but he was going to orbit the earth. His bright friendly face smiled at them from the covers of magazines, the front page of the local paper, and from most news broadcasts as speculation ran wild as to whether this could actually happen.

Being an astronaut had replaced cowboy or fireman as the choice of what little boys wanted to be when they grew up. Ricky was no exception. As the big event drew near, June stressed the fact to Sharlyn, Janice and Ricky that John Glenn had grown up in New Concord, less than fifty miles from Newark. "He grew up in a town smaller than Newark. That just goes to show that Ohio has its heroes too," she told them.

On February twentieth, most things in Newark came to a halt while people watched this historic event on television...June in her living room, Sharlyn, Janice, and Ricky in their classrooms, and Dick with his customers at the barber shop. Many prayers joined the cheers as John Glenn in his space capsule, Friendship Seven, blasted off to orbit the earth three times.

"The teacher kept the television on until after he splashed down," Sharlyn remarked that night at dinner. "It was pretty exciting there for awhile."

Dick added, "Everyone in the shop cheered when they plucked the capsule out of the ocean."

"It was pretty suspenseful when they opened the hatch, and we had to wait for him to step out," Janice said.

June looked from her husband to her little son and softly said, "I was thinking about his wife and mother and what it must have been like for them." She didn't voice the rest of her thought, that she'd rather have her son choose a safer profession.

~

A few months later on May 13th, Dick had been invited to bring June and the children for a dual celebration at his parents' house to celebrate his father's birthday and Mother's Day. "Since this is Mother's Day, and we're celebrating your dad's birthday too, I got them each a present," June told Dick as she showed him the dress shirt she had bought for his father and the red nightgown for his mother. While Dick watched, she wrapped the gifts. "Put your finger on this ribbon so I can tie a bow," she ordered before she asked, "Did your dad turn sixty-two or sixty-three yesterday?"

His customary sparkle appeared in his eye and he grinned from ear-to-ear as he replied, "That battle raged as long as his mother lived, and to this day he insists that he was born in nineteen hundred, not eighteen ninety-nine." Dick grinned before he admitted, "I wouldn't tell him, unless I wanted to start World War III, but I believe his mother should know when her son was born."

"Do you think that since she had so many children, she could have gotten his birthday mixed up?" June asked.

"That's pretty much what Dad says," Dick informed her. "I wouldn't mention it, though. It's still a sore point with him."

June put her finger to her lips and whispered, "Mum's the word," before she called to the children to let them know it was time to leave for their grandparent's house.

The mystery wouldn't be solved for years to come, until little Janice became a grandmother herself. Searching the nineteen-hundred census records, she found that Forest had been one year old in the year nineteen-hundred. This proved his mother to be the winner of this battle of the century, since Forest had actually been born in the nineteenth century, not the twentieth century as he had insisted. However, this was years later, and his claim had already been carved in stone.

Then a few minutes later when they walked into the kitchen of the house on South Third Street, they were shocked when they saw the expression on everyone's faces. Although sunshine was coming through the windows, it was obviously lost on the sad gathering. Slumped in her chair, Rowena's face was crumbled in pain, and tears spilled from her eyes and ran unchecked down her cheeks. June noticed that while Eddie sat beside his mother, trying to get her to drink her tea as if that would make her feel better, Forest was uncharacteristically quiet. June had sadly realized what had happened so she scooted Sharlyn, Janice, and Ricky into the living room as she heard her husband's alarmed voice ask, "What is it, Mom? What happened?"

She didn't have to hear the answer to know that Rowena's beloved mother, Dick's Grandmother Lula, had died. As she was to hear after she left the children in front of the television set and returned to the kitchen, Thelma had just called and given Rowena the news. At the age of eighty-two, this woman Dick had said was full of pep and vinegar had passed away in a hospital in Cincinnati. Her tiredness had been from more than anemia. It wasn't until the doctor issued a death certificate that they were to know that she had died of leukemia. They always wondered if the doctor knew this, and if so, why he had never told the family.

June noticed the pans bubbling away on the stove burners, and checked to make sure that nothing had burned. As women have done since the beginning of time, she dished up the food and set it before her loved ones to make them feel better. Then for the first time since June had known her mother-in-law, Rowena sat at the table and let someone else take care of the dinner.

Everyone, even Lula's great-grandchildren who had been told by the time the food was on the table, picked at the food but they did manage to get through the day. As June and the girls cleaned up after the meal, Lula's presence was all around them, laughing, telling her jokes, or sitting at her chair in the breakfast room puffing on a cigarette. June felt a smile flicker across her mind at the picture of this feisty, dark-haired woman with her red cheeks and bright lipstick teasing her and her new husband the morning after their wedding night. "There will never be another Lula," she thought as she looked around the kitchen to be sure all the work was done. "We don't want to leave anything for Rowie to do," June told Sharlyn and Janice. The girls agreed and between the three of them, the kitchen was left spotless.

The next day, Lula made her last trip between Cincinnati and Newark in a long black hearse to be laid to rest in the Cedar Hill cemetery beside her husband who had died seventeen years earlier. On this bright, sunny day in May, Lula and Edward McNamee's three children, Roland, Rowena, and Thelma stood at the graveside with all the descendants of this couple and watched their mother take her place beside their father.

While everyone thought about this woman who'd brought so much happiness to their lives, Sharlyn was remembering the day Lula had whispered in her ear,

"You are my favorite great-granddaughter." At the same time, Janice was also treasuring the special secret Lula had shared with her that she, Janice, was her favorite great-granddaughter. Although she didn't know what was going on in her daughters' minds, June knew, as she watched this scenario, that as long as even one of these people lived, Lula and her husband would forever be alive in their memory.

As June glanced at the gravestone of Lula's husband, and read, "Edward Everett McNamee born June 13, 1871, died January 8, 1944," she realized he had died just after New Year's Day when she was only thirteen years old and Dick was a young eighteen year old soldier serving in the army in World War II.

She felt an unusually strong connection to this man she had never met. Her thoughts were, "It must be because I've heard so many wonderful stories about his love of writing poems, stories, Christian songs, and his knack for having fun."

She felt an overwhelming need to send up a prayer, "Thank you, God, for giving Dick this special grandfather and grandmother. And thank you for bringing Dick to me."

Unknown to June, she was the answer to this old man's last prayer, for his grandson Richard to find a young woman to love. Every day she and Dick were living out his final wishes.

June looked at her husband and thought, "I know that the fun loving antics of Grandpa McNamee and Lula will live on through Dick and through generations to come in this family."

Dick had one arm around June's shoulder and the other arm comforting his mother as they said their final goodbye.

For the next few months, Dick made a practice of stopping to see his mother everyday either during his lunch hour or on the way home from work. June didn't resent this time spent away from his family since she knew that if anyone could help Rowena through this difficult time, Dick could. She knew that his mother loved him and encouraged his nonsense. Rowena enjoyed the frustrated comedian's antics as much as he enjoyed having such an appreciative audience.

BALTIMORE AT LAST

As the days of summer passed, the family was looking forward to their upcoming trip to Baltimore. A letter from June's brother caused them to postpone it for a couple weeks, though. "Before we start to watch the Beverly Hillbillies, I want to tell you my news," June informed the family as they gathered in front of the television set for their evening ritual. "Skip is being sent back to Atsugi, Japan," she announced. "Before they go, they are going to stop and see Dad. Then they're coming to Ohio. We'll just wait until after their visit before we go on our trip."

No one wanted to miss the visit with Skip's family, so the date of the trip was pushed forward a couple weeks. When the little family went to Mansfield to see the travelers, Skip told June about his family's visit to Baltimore. "I'm concerned about Dad. He looks great, but I thought he seemed to tire pretty fast," he said. This conversation only served to make June more anxious than ever to see her father.

This worry was put aside while Skip, Dick, and June and their families enjoyed a reunion at their mother's house in Widowville. The cousins were excited when Priscilla took them into her country store and said, "You can each have either a candy bar or bottle of pop."

Chris exclaimed, "You guys are lucky to live in Ohio. You can get all the candy you want."

Ricky explained, "We do come up once a month and when we are here Gram lets us pick out one thing."

Priscilla smiled and teased, "One candy bar is enough. I wouldn't want your parents to be mad at me for ruining your teeth."

While they were contemplating their choices, a customer came in to pay her bill. When Priscilla quoted the amount due, the woman was shocked at the figure and practically shouted, "It can't be that much! You know that I usually only buy bread and milk!"

Priscilla calmly replied, "Your husband told me that Ralphie could put candy and pop on the bill any time. Ralphie has been taking his dad up on the offer every day."

The mother sputtered, "My husband didn't bother to tell me about that idiotic idea!"

Priscilla controlled the laughter she could feel threatening to escape when she replied, "Apparently Big Ralph had never heard the expression, 'Like a kid in a candy store'."

The words were barely out of her mouth when the woman went to the door and screeched, "Ralphie, get in here!"

The cousins watched wide eyed as Ralphie sauntered in and made a beeline to the candy case and asked, "Mom, can I have a Hershey Bar and an all day sucker?"

Mom's voice raised to an ear splitting level when she said, "Young man, you have had the last candy bar you or your dad are ever going to put on this tab!"

As the mother dragged Ralphie out to the car, Janice said, "I was always surprised when I heard kids come in and say to put it on their parents' bill. I thought they were so lucky to be able to get all the candy they wanted without having to pay for it."

Her cousin Mike laughed and said, "From the look on his mother's face I think Ralphie will be paying for it when he gets home. I wouldn't want to be in his shoes."

～

The older cousins hadn't lost their enthusiasm for the War card game that Mike and Chris had taught them. The girls were equally interested in mothering the newest cousins, Janet Kay and David. "You could never tell from looking at him now, that David was ever premature," June said as she watched the healthy looking infant squirm in Sharlyn's lap.

Skip, JoAnne, and the boys were excited about the upcoming trip. They were going to fly to San Francisco, then take a ship to Japan. "A sailor finally gets on a ship," Dick teased.

"I've been on a ship before," Skip protested.

"Another luxury liner?" Dick asked.

"You'll never hear us complain about him being land-based," JoAnne stated. "A lot of the women I've met spend most of their time alone while their husbands are at sea."

As usually happened, the visit ended much too soon, and the brothers and sister again went their separate ways.

～

"Are we almost there?" thirteen-year-old Sharlyn teased as a couple weeks later they left Newark behind on their trip to Baltimore.

June and Dick exchanged grins at this familiar phrase before June replied, "We should be there in about ten hours." The ten hours seemed to last for twenty, but before dark they pulled into a driveway in Baltimore beside the small house Burrel had rented. Polly and Burrel both stepped onto the porch at the sound of the car's motor. While the children and grandparents exchanged hugs, June watched her father. He did look tired, but his gentle smile was the same and his hug felt as strong as ever.

"I'm going to enjoy this visit," June told herself. For once, she was going to go by her husband's philosophy that there was only today, that yesterday was gone and tomorrow never really came. This decided, she let herself relax and enjoy the moment.

Since the house was small, Sharlyn and Janice spent the nights next door at the home of the landlady who had a daughter Sharlyn's age. The next morning they joined the family for breakfast before they went out on the bay with Fred, Bill, Ricky, and Liz, the landlady's daughter. The boys taught Ricky and Janice how to catch crabs. They were catching so many crabs that they were out for the day. Then when they finally got home, they had enough for a cookout for the family with some extra for the neighbors.

While the foursome was in the boat, Sharlyn and Liz decided to cool off by wading in the bay. The water felt wonderful on such a hot humid day and since it was barely up to her knees, Sharlyn decided to wade out toward what looked like a barge with an opening in the side. Liz, who hadn't kept up with her, started to scream for her to stop and come back when she saw where she was going. The slight breeze seemed to blow the words back into her mouth making her sound even more frantic when she finally got Sharlyn to hear her screams. Although Liz kept yelling for her to come back, the water was so inviting that Sharlyn was tempted to go on. When her new friend got close enough for Sharlyn to see her clearly, the look of pure terror on Liz's face finally got through to her and she turned back When she was close enough to hear, a shaken Liz said, "Oh, my gosh! You were heading for the channel, and there's about a hundred feet drop off!"

While Sharlyn thought this was probably an exaggeration, she knew that any sudden drop off would have startled her, and not being a strong swimmer, she could have drowned. Frightened by her close call, and aware of how worried her mother was about her grandfather, she decided to keep her close call to herself.

Janice, Ricky, Fred, and Bill had already returned to the house by the bay when Liz and Sharlyn got back. As a result of their sunny day on the bay, Janice's fair skin had turned bright red from her severe sunburn, and she was in excruciating pain by then. Although Janice protested vigorously, the landlady took her home with her, slathered vinegar over her reddened skin, and put her to bed. Unfortunately, she felt too ill to even help eat the steamed crabs that she had helped catch. From the window, Janice looked out into her grandparents' yard next door as the crab bake party took place. Amidst the family's happy talk and laughter she heard Granddad exclaim, "These crabs are delicious! You kids made my day!" Her granddad's enjoyment took her mind off her sunburn pain for a little while.

The rest of their stay was spent savoring again being together as a family. Every moment of their visit took on a special significance to June as she listened to her father talk, smile his gentle smile, and enjoy having his grandchildren with him. Then the last morning of their visit when June walked by her father and stepmother's room, she saw her dad lying back against the pillows with Ricky sitting on the bed beside him. A memory flashed through her mind of her father and son, one fall night, when the Harman family had lived in southern Ohio. She and Polly had gone out for the evening and left Burrel to baby-sit with all five children. When they'd returned, everyone was asleep except Burrel and Ricky, who were watching a wrestling match on TV. She'd never forgotten the sight that greeted them of her father propped up in bed with his grandson comfortably seated on his tummy. She smiled inwardly when she remembered how her father's eyes had gleamed with excitement while he'd alternately booed and cheered the wrestlers as they slammed and grunted their way across the screen. His enthusiasm had been reflected in Ricky's eyes as he'd laughed and clapped his hands.

The memory disappeared from her mind as she observed the now eight year old Ricky lean over and kiss his grandfather goodbye. As June watched, her father hugged her son, and rubbed his rough cheek against Ricky's smooth one. As Ricky climbed off the bed, she heard him say, "I'll see you later, Granddad." Then when he came out of the room and saw his mother, he rubbed his reddening cheek and said, "Granddad's cheek is really scratchy." In years to come, Ricky didn't remember June's explanation that her father hadn't had time to shave yet that morning, but he never forgot the feel of his grandfather's cheek against his as they said their private goodbye.

The older man had been smoothly shaven when, an hour later, he'd hugged and kissed his daughter and granddaughters goodbye and shook his son-in-law's hand. Their last sight of him was as he and Polly stood on the porch and waved as they drove away. As they left the sights and sounds of Baltimore behind, they all felt that the visit had ended much too soon. They might have found a way to stay longer if they'd realized how different the circumstances would be the next time they would all be together.

THE PARTING

Before the year came to a close, Eddie's divorce was granted, and he tried to pick up the pieces as best he could. This meant spending most of his time with his family. Mostly, though, when he was off work, he could be found at the house on Oakwood Avenue. Almost every time when Dick and June went out to dinner or to a movie, they would invite the lonely young man to go along. For weeks the young couple served as a sounding board while he tried to sort out what had happened. "I'll never understand," he lamented. "I gave her everything. I thought that we were happy." Then he'd end every conversation with a deep sigh and the words, "I can't believe she let her friend break up our home."

June noticed that his good humor returned when he was around Sharlyn, Janice, and Ricky. He'd always played with them, filled them with ice cream and candy, and lavished the attention on them he would have on children of his own. All their lives, they'd loved being around him. He hadn't realized when he got married how hurt Sharlyn had been that she hadn't been invited to his wedding. At the time, she'd complained to her mother that he should have waited until she got home from camp. Now, though, his oldest niece felt very sad for her young uncle. As they watched him with his nieces and nephew, Dick and June hoped that since he was only thirty-three years old, he would eventually marry again and have a family of his own.

Her worry about her brother-in-law receded into the background when the word arrived that Burrel had another heart attack followed closely by yet another. Then shortly before Thanksgiving, Polly called with the news that he was back in the hospital. This time, he had pneumonia. According to Polly, they were on a visit at Bill and Dorothy's in Arlington, Virginia when he became ill. At first, they'd thought he'd had another heart attack, so they'd rushed him to a nearby hospital where a young intern took charge of his care. Once he'd diagnosed the problem as pneumonia, he'd treated him with an antibiotic without first identifying the strain. Unfortunately, this made it almost impossible for the doctor to get rid of the pneumonia.

Then three weeks before Christmas, June received a letter with the sad news that Polly's father, Will Srite, had been killed in an automobile accident. On his way home from Brandon, less than five miles from the farm, when he'd tried to pass a slow-moving vehicle, a car had pulled out in front of him. In trying to avoid a collision, he'd gone off the road into a field. Before he could bring the truck to a stop, he'd slammed into a tree and had died instantly.

June's eyes were moist when she slowly folded the letter and returned it to the envelope. As she sat alone at the table, she let the tears roll down her cheeks as she cried for her stepmother and younger brothers' loss...and for her own as she remembered his many kindnesses to her. As she tried to express these thoughts in a letter to Polly, she felt the weight of the world settle on her shoulders. This had been the worst year of her adult life, Lula and Granddad Srite's deaths, Eddie's divorce, and her father's deteriorating health. Certainly, during the next year their luck would change.

∼

As the year neared an end, there was no chance of the Harmans coming to Ohio for Christmas. On Christmas Eve, June's mind churned with disappointment as she got ready to go to the candlelight services at the church. Although everyone else in the family was ready to go out the door, she lagged behind. This year, despite all the trappings of Christmas throughout the house, she couldn't get into the holiday spirit. As she finally slipped into her coat, she remembered how she'd thought things had been bad this time last year. "I never realized how much worse it could be," she reflected as she reluctantly followed the family through the door into the frigid night.

Just as Dick closed the door behind him, they heard the muffled ringing of the telephone. He quickly unlocked the door, and June ran to answer it. The words from the other end of the line, "Hello, June. It's Dad," brought tears of joy mingled with cries of happiness from her. When she heard that he was home from the hospital, and felt fine, the gladness of the season again flooded through her.

When she hung up, she beamed at her waiting family, "That was the best Christmas present I could ever get. Granddad is home. The pneumonia is gone. Now let's celebrate Christmas!"

∼

The family went into the New Year with hopeful hearts. This hopeful state lasted until January thirteenth when the call came June had dreaded. In a surprisingly calm voice, Polly told her, "You need to come. Your father is back in the hospital with another heart attack." This was the first time her stepmother had ever asked this of her. Alarmed, she could barely manage to ask if the doctor thought he'd make it. "He's not holding out much hope," Polly replied before she added, "I think you should get here as soon as possible."

"I'll take a flight out of here either tonight or tomorrow. Let me call the airline, then I'll call back."

After the first call she discovered that there would be no flights out that night. The entire country was blanketed in fog, but it took the same message from three more airlines, though, before June would accept it. Disappointed, she called her stepmother and gave her the bad news. "Each airline told me to try again in the morning. By then the travel agency will be open. I'll call, and if there's even one airline flying, I'll be on it," she promised.

She was to discover the next morning, though, when she called Wilson Travel Agency that all airlines were grounded. "It might be days before the fog lifts, so if you really need to get there soon, I'd recommend you go by bus," the voice at the other end of the line informed her. A little later that day June was on a bus heading for Baltimore. The bus driver seemed oblivious of the fog as he barreled through it. During the thirteen-hour trip, June couldn't even watch the scenery since everything within a foot of the bus window seemed to be enveloped in a gauzy mist. As they passed through one small town after another, June felt as though she was caught in a nightmare. This was undoubtedly the worst trip of her life. Despite the treacherous conditions, she wasn't worried about her own safety. The worst part was that she didn't know whether she'd ever see her father alive again. She was frightened at what she might find at the end of this journey.

When the driver finally lumbered to a stop at the bus station in Baltimore, she searched the waiting crowd and saw her brother Fred as he walked toward her. She breathed a sigh of relief when he greeted her with the news that their father was still in intensive care. As he stowed her gear in the trunk of the family's green Nash, June asked, "When did you start to drive?"

"I've been driving quite a bit since Dad got sick. Mom says it helps her out... like now when she's at the hospital," he replied. As he maneuvered through the traffic on the way to the hospital, they passed a drive-in hamburger place. She noticed the marquee above the golden arches proclaimed that over one million hamburgers had been sold. "They're building one of those in Newark, but I didn't know it was a chain," she remarked.

As they got closer to the hospital, June realized that their conversation about the fifteen cent hamburgers sold at McDonald's was their way to avoid what was on both their minds...their father's condition.

When they arrived at the hospital, Polly was in conversation with a white clad man whom she introduced as Burrel's doctor. To June's shock, he didn't make an effort to be civil when she sought reassurance from him. Instead, he'd leveled cold eyes on her and brutally pronounced, "No, he's not going to make it. His old ticker is worn out." On June's part, it was hate at first sight.

When June repeated this conversation to Polly, her stepmother replied, "He's like that with me too, but he is wonderful with your father, and your father loves him."

"I guess he flunked bedside manners with patients' families," June grimaced.

A nurse came to the door of the waiting room and announced each patient was allowed a ten-minute visit. "Only one visitor for each patient," she said before she returned to her desk.

Polly nodded for June to go in. "He's been anxious to see you," she said. June hid her alarm when she saw him in the hospital bed by a window at the end of the room.

When he looked up and saw her, he welcomed her with a warm, though weak, smile and said, "There's my girl. I was worried about you being out on the road in this fog."

She leaned over and kissed him, careful not to disentangle the spider-web of tubes that enveloped him before she responded, "A little fog wouldn't keep me away."

While they visited, the ten minutes ticked away, and much too soon, the nurse came in and told June it was time to leave. She turned as she started to leave the room and said, "I love you, Dad."

He weakly mouthed the words, "I love you too."

When she returned to the waiting room, she felt strangely comforted. When she mentioned this to her stepmother, Polly replied, "You've always been like that with your daddy. You're good for each other."

⁓

Shortly afterwards they returned to the house by the bay where Bill waited for them. He was obviously discouraged when he heard there had been no change, but he swallowed his disappointment and visited with his sister for a few minutes before he went to bed. While June got ready to turn in, she could hear Polly talking on the telephone to her brother, Fred, in Texas. She returned to the room in time to hear her stepmother say, "I'm afraid Burrel's not going to make it this time."

Big Fred's combination Mississippi accent and Texas drawl came over the line as he asked, "Do you need me?" When Polly replied that they all did, he replied, "I'll get a flight out as soon as I can."

When Polly turned from the phone, she explained that Big Fred would be here soon. With the knowledge in mind that they would soon have a strong shoulder to lean on, they called it a night so they could get up at daybreak to return to the hospital. When they arose, they found that the fog still hadn't lifted and that the temperature remained below zero. On their trip to the hospital, the traffic seemed to move at a snail's pace, but when they finally arrived, to their relief, they found Burrel feeling better.

June was upset, though, when she went in to see her father and felt the frigid January air from the open window, beside his bed, seep through her heavy clothing. When she saw him shiver, she pulled the covers more tightly around him and piled her coat on top of the blankets before she headed for the nurses' station. Appalled when June told her about the open window, the white-clad woman rushed over to it and hurriedly brought it down. Her gentle tone of voice belied the spark of anger June saw in her eyes as she asked Burrel if he knew who had opened it.

Burrel pointed to an orderly who was bustling around the room and said, "He said that with all the moving around he has to do, he was hot." Still shivering, he added, "It's been open for a long time, and I'm chilled to the bone."

"It won't happen again," the nurse assured him before she returned to her station. When June left the room a few minutes later, she noticed the woman in earnest conversation with the orderly and overhead the words, "Keep in mind that the patients' comfort is more important than yours."

Polly went in during the next visiting hour, and when she came out her eyes sparkled and her grin spread across her face when she reported to June that he had gotten over his chill, felt better, and would be sent to a regular room within an hour. "I think your visit has really been good for him."

After he was in a regular hospital room, June and Polly were allowed to be with him for the entire day. While Polly returned for the rest of her shift as a nurse at a nearby hospital, June stayed at her father's side. While she stood at the head of his bed, she held his hand and they talked away the hours. The words they spoke that day were ones that she would forever treasure and hold close to her heart.

"I had a good visit with Cecil, JoAnne and the boys this summer before they left for Japan," he told her. "I really enjoyed it when they lived here in Maryland." Then he went on to talk about how much he hated to see them leave. "This is the first time I've wondered if I'd still be here when they returned." June started to protest but was stopped by his murmured, "Hursh." A sad expression flickered in his eyes when he went on. "I only have a few regrets," he said. "What happened with your mother and the fact that I didn't get to spend as much time with Dickie while he was growing up." He sighed before he continued, "And I hardly got to see his son." When his head sank deeper in the pillow and his eyelids closed, June thought he'd gone to sleep until he quietly said, "I never expected this to happen when I left Newark."

June patted his hand and assured him that Dickie understood. "I was so happy when Dickie and Bev came to Baltimore to see me this summer. We had a real nice visit," he said.

"They told me they enjoyed it," June replied. "When you're better you can come back to Newark and see Baby David and all your Ohio grandchildren," she explained. "Sharlyn, Janice, and Ricky sent their love," she added.

"They're all good kids," he replied.

June didn't show her alarm when he abruptly changed the subject to say, "I've been thinking that if anything should happen to me, I'd like to be buried at Wilson's cemetery...up by Saint Louisville. Do you know where it is?"

"That's where Aunt Lidy is buried, isn't it?" she replied.

He nodded before he went on, "Your mother and I lived around there when Cecil was a baby, and I always loved it." When he continued to talk, his eyes held a far away look, "We were young and happy then."

"I know," June replied. "Mom showed me her father's store where you worked in Saint Louisville, and the house where you lived."

Burrel smiled faintly and murmured, "I didn't think she remembered."

"She remembered," June assured him.

As if the conversation about his first wife made him feel disloyal to Polly, he said, "Polly has been a good wife and mother. You know how much I love her. She has taken good care of me since I got sick, and she had to become both wife and breadwinner. She's really a good, strong woman, but it would be hard on her if anything happened to me." Then he grasped his daughter's hand and desperately held on to it when he pleaded, "I want you to promise me that if she ever needs you that you'll be there for her."

She felt him release his grip when she assured him that she would. Then she tried to lighten the conversation with talk about days gone by. "Do you remember all that paste she used to serve us in Zanesville before she learned to make gravy?" she asked.

Burrel chuckled and replied, "I'll never forget that."

Polly returned in time to overhear them talk about some of her other early culinary disasters. Hands on hips in mock anger, she teased, "Fine thing! I can't leave the room without being talked about."

A few minutes later, June cringed when the hated doctor strode into the room, but she relaxed when she heard him say that he was pleased with Burrel's progress. She noticed that the harsh tone he'd used when he'd talked to her had been replaced by a gentle, caring voice when he told the sick man that if he continued to improve at the same rate he'd get to go home in about a week.

When June smiled in relief, the doctor only scowled at her. "Not too good with families, are you?" June muttered under her breath. Polly grinned but made a shushing motion as the white coated figure stalked from the room. It was two very elated women who left the hospital a short time later.

When they walked through the door of the house Burrel had rented, Bill and Fred looked up from their homework and asked in unison, "How's Dad?" They were visibly relieved when their mother reported what the doctor had said.

Their conversation was interrupted by the ring of the telephone. Bill answered it and after a few words handed it to his sister. It was June's husband with news that he, the children, and her brother, Dickie, were coming to Baltimore the next day to see her father.

June explained what the doctor had said and encouraged them to wait a few days until after he was dismissed from the hospital. Dick's voice sounded incredulous when he said, "The doctor actually said that he was doing better and would be home that soon?"

"That's what he said!" she replied.

"If you're sure, then we'll wait," Dick said before he hung up.

When June placed the phone back in the cradle, she had no idea how much she would regret that conversation or the guilt she would carry for years because of it.

~

The next morning when they left for the hospital, the women were feeling optimistic. When they stopped at a little cafe for breakfast, they merrily hummed along with the jukebox as Nancy Sinatra sang, "These Boots Are Made For Walking." As they paid their checks, Polly quipped, "These boots we've got on had better head for the hospital. Your father will wonder what happened to us."

They soon knew his condition had worsened when they stepped off the elevator. Even though they were at least twenty-five feet from Burrel's room, they could hear the chain-stoke breathing…first a loud, harsh, rasping sound that was followed by complete silence as if the breathing had stopped. Then when they thought it wouldn't happen, it started over again. As they walked toward her father's room, June thought it was the most disturbing sound she had ever heard.

"It's your father," Polly said. "He sounds worse."

When they entered Burrel's room, a young resident raised his stethoscope from Burrel's chest and turned to look at them. "We hadn't quite gotten rid of his pneumonia, and it seems to have returned," he said. "We're going to have to get him in an oxygen tent right away." As he spoke, the picture of the open window in intensive care flashed in June's mind as she looked at her father's flushed face. Surely getting so chilled must have contributed to it.

The oxygen tent helped at first. Then things seemed to go from bad to worse as his condition continued to worsen throughout the day. Worried, neither Polly nor June went more than a few feet from his bedside. At one point he looked June in the eye and told her that he thought he was going to die. She added another layer of guilt to what she already felt from the advice she'd given her husband the night before when she cried, "No, Dad. You're not going to die." Even as the words left her lips, she knew that for the first time in her life she had knowingly lied to her father.

He wasn't fooled by her falsehood as was evident by his next statement. In a surprisingly strong voice, he said, "I think it's time to call the family together." When June heard these words, she felt even worse that her husband and brother wouldn't be here. Maybe if they'd left this morning, as planned, they could have made it in time. After one look at his face, followed by a glance at the mist that clung like white curtains to the outside of the window, she knew it was too late to call them now.

When Polly heard him ask to see his family, she rushed from the room in tears. June stayed with him until he told her, "Polly needs you. You'd better go to her."

When she saw her daughter come out into the hall, Polly waved her back into the room. "Stay with him while I pull myself together," she instructed her. "While I'm out here, I'm going to call Bill and Fred and Big Bill and Dorothy and tell them to come right away. You can call your Aunt Nellie. She's at her daughter, Violet's, house here in Baltimore."

Polly tossed the words, "I wonder when my brother Fred will get here," over her shoulder as she started down the hall. June had wondered the same thing. It had been thirty-six hours since he'd told them he would take the first available flight out of Houston. She wondered as she again glanced out the window at the fog engulfed city if he'd even been able to leave the airport in Texas.

~

By the time Fred, Little Bill, Big Bill, Dorothy, and Burrel's sister, Nellie arrived, Burrel's breathing had become more labored. After they had been in the room for a few minutes, the boys became so disturbed by what they saw that Big Bill took them with him to the waiting room. Also upset, Nellie trailed along behind them. As things got worse within the four walls of his hospital room, Polly left briefly to comfort her sons. While they consoled each other, Fred noticed a nurse enter the room with restraints dangling from her right hand. Alarmed, he told his mother who immediately rushed back into the room and stopped her before she could tie him down. This was to be the only small victory the family would have during the long night that lay ahead of them. The three women, his wife, his daughter, and his dear friend, Dorothy, stayed in his room where they continued to stand by his bed to comfort him. While Polly held one hand, Dorothy held the other, and June stood at the head of his bed, he seemed to smile gently at each of them. Then June could see his eyes look up toward the ceiling, and his soul quietly slip from his body. The horrible sound of the tortured breathing had stopped, and the room was silent.

When they went into the waiting room, and Polly told the others that it was over, they were too involved in their grief to notice the young resident who entered the room seconds after they'd left. As they tried to deal with their loss, they were shocked to hear the harsh anguished breathing begin again.

At the sound, Polly rushed into the room and confronted the resident with, "What have you done? Did you actually bring him back? Hasn't he suffered enough?" Before she could physically vent her rage at this young man, someone in the group led her back into the waiting room while June and Dorothy resumed their vigil at Burrel's bedside. As they stood, one on each side of his bed, and held his hands, June wanted to hold him back from that other world he'd so briefly entered...not to the world of pain he was now in, but to the way he'd been before his illness.

Finally, his hand grew slack in hers, and she knew it was over. This time there was no young eager beaver resident to interrupt his journey. June knew from the serene look she'd seen on his face the first time he'd died that he'd been on the threshold of heaven's gate when he'd so rudely been yanked back. For now, her grief was intermingled with anger at the extra hours of pain her father had been forced to endure.

An hour later, when they left the hospital, it was difficult to imagine the high hopes they'd shared less then eighteen hours earlier when they'd entered these doors. When in the wee hours of the morning, they returned to the house by the bay, a light shone through the windows, and they were met at the door by Polly's brother, Fred. Although he looked cold and exhausted, he was a most welcome sight. One look at their pale, drawn, faces told him what had happened. June could see how weary he was when he raised himself from his chair and went to his sister. It was obvious at that moment that his only thought was to console her and her children.

His soft southern voice comforted them when he drawled, "I'm sorry I didn't get here in time to be with you." Then he explained that it had taken him four days to get from Houston to Baltimore. "At first, I couldn't get out of the airport at Houston," he explained. "When I finally did, we couldn't land in Baltimore. I've crisscrossed the country a few times and have landed in more places than you could possibly imagine." He rubbed his tired eyes and added, "But not in Baltimore."

"If you didn't land, how did you get here?" Little Fred asked.

"We touched down in New York City late this morning. I waited there until I found out that it might be another day before a plane could land in Baltimore or Washington. The only way I could get here was by bus. Fortunately the driver was good enough to let me off near here, and your landlady was kind enough to let me in."

∽

The next morning, when the tragic news winged its way across the miles of telephone lines, June's husband in Newark and her brother in Mansfield were stunned when they heard. This realization only served to make June's guilt deepen. Her feelings came across the line as she wailed to her husband, "If only I hadn't told you not to come." Her guilt lessened somewhat, though, when Dick told her that it might have been too dangerous for them to try to drive through the fog.

When Dick broke the news to the children of their grandfather's death, he was so visibly upset that even in her own grief, ten-year-old Janice wanted to do something to make him feel better. Many times she'd observed when he came home tired from work, her mother would massage his back. So while the other children dealt with their grief in their own way, the little blonde haired girl had her father lie on the couch and with compassionate hands tried to ease his pain away with a back rub.

Back in Baltimore, before June left with Polly and her brother, Fred, to make arrangements for a local service, and to have the body transported to Newark for the funeral and burial, June called the Red Cross to have them notify Skip in Japan. Polly had asked her to be sure they told Skip that it would be too dangerous for him to try to come home. Although they all wanted him to be with them, they had to think of his safety. "The way things are now, he might not be able to land in time for the funeral anyway," Polly said.

After Dick received the news, he called June's Uncle Mace and then Mace and his sister, Nellie, contacted the rest of the family. She felt comforted when her Aunt Calcie and Uncle Gordon, Uncle Olie and Aunt Josie, and most of the cousins from Pennsylvania, West Virginia, and the D.C. area arrived for the services in Baltimore. Her cousins Maxine, Bea, Avanelle, Hilda, Wanda, and Violet had driven to Baltimore several times since they'd gotten the news. Not for the first time, she realized how important it was to have family around.

During the calling hours June's eye caught the familiar face of a young woman near the casket. She recognized her as a neighbor girl who had lived across the road from them when they'd lived in West Virginia in the house above Seneca Caverns. As Maudie hugged her and told her how much June's dad had meant to her, at first neither woman said a word about the horrific incident they had lived through together when Maudie's mother had held a gun on eight year old June and her brothers. Or that Maudie's father was the one suspected of trying to kill Burrel. June cringed at the thought that her father's body still contained some of the pellets from the shotgun blast.

When Maudie gave her a final hug before she moved away to talk to some of the other mourners, June spoke softly so only Maudie could hear her, "I don't think I ever thanked you for saving my life that day. If you hadn't grabbed your mother's arm and deflected the shot, I'm sure that my mother, brothers and I would all have been killed. So thank you."

Maudie squeezed June's hand and said, "Mom was out of her head that day. It took every inch of courage I had to sneak across the porch and fling her arm with the gun in it toward the ceiling before the gun went off. You don't need to thank me. You and your family always meant a lot to me."

~

Then on the day of the service in Baltimore, something happened that made them all feel better. When Burrel and Polly's twenty-five year old neighbor came into the chapel, he confided that he had been inspired to dedicate his life to Christ because of the faith Burrel had demonstrated during his long illness. "Burrel really lived his beliefs," he told Polly. Polly treasured these words as well as the many floral offerings that filled the front of the chapel. Each represented someone whose life Burrel had touched. Tears glistened in her eyes when she whispered to June, "I wish Burrel knew."

June whispered in return, "How do you know he doesn't?"

After the service, June sat in the tiny office at the back of the chapel and listened to the hushed tones of her stepmother and the funeral director discuss her father's final train ride to Ohio. Her thoughts wandered to the time her father had taken the long train ride from Mississippi to Newark for her high school graduation. She remembered how she and Dick, as newlyweds, had gone back to Mississippi with him and how the three of them had talked for hours as the wheels of the train click-clacked away the miles. She mentally stored the echoes of that with other pleasant memories of her life with her father as she noticed that the earnest conversation had ended, and her stepmother was ready to leave.

When they returned to the house by the bay, they were greeted by the smell of freshly brewed coffee and the concerned faces of several of their neighbors. One woman June had met at the cookout during her family's summer visit gently ordered them to sit down and eat. "There's enough here to get you through today and for you to take along on your trip to Ohio tomorrow."

By the time they had eaten and the neighbors had washed and put away the last dish, darkness had descended. The family knew that this was not going to be the last physically and emotionally exhausting day they had to face. In the morning, they would have to leave for Newark. As it would turn out, they would only arrive one day before the funeral. With what was ahead in mind, Polly said, "Fog or not, we're leaving early. We'd better turn in now or we'll never make it." No one argued with her statement and within an hour they had all gone to bed...some to quickly fall asleep while others lie awake only to wrestle with their thoughts.

The next morning when Polly woke them at five o'clock, everyone was glad they had followed her advice. At first they all seemed to move in slow motion as they made their way through the fog to stow their bags in the trunk of the green Nash. By the time they'd fortified themselves with hot coffee, toast and oatmeal they felt ready to face the long trip.

During the snail's pace through the city traffic, they hoped that once they left Baltimore behind, the fog would have lifted. Although this was not to be, Little and Big Fred managed to steer them safely through the mountains and get them to Newark. It turned out that their arrival was much later than expected by those who anxiously awaited their return.

One reason they had been so late was because they'd interrupted their stressful journey to stop in Pennsylvania to see Burrel and Polly's friends, Bertie and Hilton Tucker. By the time they left, the travelers' bodies had been sustained by the hot food Bertie had prepared for them and their souls by the outpouring of love from their hosts. Fred and Bill had been disappointed that their friend Patrick wasn't there, but when they asked about him, they were told he was in the army stationed in a place called Vietnam. Since this was the first time the visitors had heard of this country, June voiced what was on everyone's mind when she asked, "Where's that?" Bertie replied that it was somewhere in South East Asia. "Our servicemen are over there to help train their army."

The name Vietnam conjured pictures of exotic places to all their minds. No one in the room that sad day in nineteen sixty-three could possibly imagine the turmoil this country would soon face because of what was about to take place in that far-away unknown land.

∽

Later that night when the five tired travelers arrived in Newark, they went directly to the funeral home only to find the parking lot empty and the windows as dark as the cold night around them. As Fred turned the car toward June's home, she glanced toward the clock at the top of the courthouse and exclaimed, "No wonder they've all gone home. It's after ten o'clock."

Things were different though when they arrived at the house on Oakwood Avenue. All the lights were ablaze when June's young brother stopped at the curb in front of the house. Dick, who had spent the last hours worried for their safety, opened the front door and hurried to the car to meet them. The children were not far behind. When she stepped out of the car, Dick grabbed her and held her so tightly that it was difficult for her to make her way up the steps to their front porch.

Once inside, she and her children clung to each other. Their nearness comforted her as hers did them. Then while they helped themselves to some of the food the Oakwood Avenue neighbors had brought in, Dick caught them up on the day's events in Newark. "Calling hours were from two to four this afternoon and seven to nine tonight. Your Uncle Mace and Dick and Bev were there all day. I've never seen so many people in one day in my entire life. They started to arrive when we first got there and kept coming until we were finally able to leave."

"By the time we left, we were all worried that maybe you'd had an accident," he added. Then as if that had reminded him of something, he reached into his pocket and pulled out a sheet of paper and said, "This is a list of the people who have called or stopped to find out if you're alright. You'd better call and let them know you made it home."

When June scanned the messages, she was relieved to see that several were from her Girl Scout friends and co-workers while others were from neighbors or friends at church. Since she was much too tired to call everyone, she called one from each group, explained, and asked that person to call the others. That done, she told everyone where they were to sleep, and within a short time they'd all trooped up the stairs to bed.

∽

The services the next day were held at the Heath Baptist Church where Burrel had put so much of his heart and soul. The little building was packed with people who had known and loved him. June was happy to see her father's sister, Gussie, in one row with her son Clyde, his wife June, Burrel's brother Mace, and his wife, Mable and behind them her cousins, Rose, Inez, and Annamae with their husbands and children.

June sat between her brother, Dick, and her husband while Sharlyn, Janice, and Ricky sat with their grandmother, Rowie, and their grandfather, Forest, while the minister talked about her father's life. At one point she heard a sound of grief escape from her brother, and she quietly reached over and squeezed his hand. Then when the choir marched in for a closing song, she held her breath until she heard them start to sing. She slowly expelled it when she discovered it wasn't the song she'd dreaded hearing. Just this morning, Polly had told her that they planned to sing her father's favorite hymn, "When The Roll Is Called Up Yonder." Without thought, she'd cried out, "No. They can't do that! It's going to take every bit of strength I have to get through this service. I don't think I can handle that...too many memories."

"The memories are good, though," her husband reminded her.

"They are very good, and I'll enjoy them later, but not today." Polly understood, and had somehow managed to get to the choir in time for them to substitute another hymn.

When the song and final prayer were over, and the people began to file from the church, June's neighbor, Ginny Eis, and her husband, Bus, came up to her, and Ginny said, "I know you shouldn't say you enjoyed a funeral, but this was beautiful. The church was filled with so much love that you could actually feel it."

A few minutes later, as she got into the car with her husband and children, the thought flickered through June's mind that her father would have enjoyed it. The same thought she'd voiced to Polly in Baltimore returned as the long procession made its way from the little church in Heath to Wilson Cemetery. "How do I know he didn't?" She liked the thought that his spirit was here with them.

No one lingered long at the cemetery, as the temperature had dropped to below zero the night before. Everyone's nose immediately turned red, the women's nylon-clad legs turned numb, and the few floral arrangements they'd brought from the church froze as soon as the air hit them. June's husband discovered this when he pulled a long stemmed flower from a bouquet and tapped it against a stone only to have it shatter like a piece of glass. When Dick walked away from the gravesite, he commented, "It's January the twenty second and it is twenty-two degrees below zero. It seems unbelievable. I don't think I will ever forget that."

∼

A couple days later when Polly, her brother, Big Fred, Little Fred, and Bill left for Baltimore, the fog had finally lifted only to be replaced by a blizzard. Since Dick was at the barbershop and the children at school when they departed, June was alone for the first time since her father's death. She couldn't stand the silence of the empty house when she went into the kitchen to refill her coffee mug, so she turned to the kitchen radio for the sound of a human voice. A few seconds later when she went into the living room, she added the babble from the television set to that of the radio. As she sank into her husband's large comfortable recliner, she felt too depleted to move.

The name of a new Broadway play, "Stop the World I Want To Get Off," ran through her mind as she stared unseeingly at the familiar objects around her. "I do want to get off," she thought but even as the thought surfaced, she knew that for the sake of her family, she had to pull herself together. For the next few minutes while she let the warmth from her steaming cup of coffee warm her hands, she gave herself a talking-to like the ones her father had given her when she was a child. In the midst of that she could almost hear him remind her that his daughter wasn't a quitter.

Before she was through with her mental pep talk, she heard the scrunch of tires in the snow in front of the house. This was followed by the slamming of car doors, and a voice calling, "We're back."

When she opened the door she saw Polly, Big Fred, and the two boys on the front porch. While they stomped the snow from their feet, they told her that the highway was closed in Zanesville. "There were so many cars off the road that a state of emergency was called, and no one can get through. We went into a restaurant for awhile, but it was standing room only, so we decided to come back," Polly said.

June watched them as they stood over the register to warm their cold hands and feet and felt a flood of relief that they'd been forced to return. "I just wasn't ready to be alone," she thought as she heated some hot soup to warm their insides.

∼

When Dick and the children came home that evening, they were pleasantly surprised at the return of their guests. Later that night, Dick confided to his wife that he'd been worried about their lack of snow driving experience. "You know Little Fred hasn't driven for long, and Big Fred, being from Texas, has never driven in the snow. It's hard enough for an experienced driver to get around in this weather, let alone a boy and someone who's never seen snow before."

By noon of the next day, they had another reason to be glad the family hadn't left earlier. Polly's brother had awakened with a terrible cold. Possibly he'd been exposed to something on the airplanes, plus the result of the Maryland and Ohio weather and the fact that he'd gone around these last few days without a coat. "Don't even own a top coat. No need for one in Texas," he'd drawled when people asked why he didn't wear something heavier than a suit jacket. When Dick had offered to loan him one of his, the older man soon found that he'd eaten a few too many good southern meals to be able to button his niece's skinny husband's coat.

"I don't know how you all can stand to live in this deep-freeze," he sputtered between bouts of coughing that afternoon while he and Dick sat in the doctor's waiting room.

"We're used to it," Dick replied.

Several hours later, after the doctor had worked his way through all the patients ahead of them in his crowded waiting room, the two men tired and hungry returned home. By then, Fred was full of penicillin and on the way to recovery. The next day the blizzard was over, the roads were cleared, and the travelers again left for Baltimore. This time, there was no reason for them to return. The extra time they had been with her, though, had helped to strengthen June. Now, she felt better prepared to begin to face the grieving process.

One night her husband asked if she remembered her father's answer when they'd been at his house on the hill a year or so earlier, and someone had asked what they'd like if they could have anything they wanted.

"Of course I remember," she replied. "He said he wanted to go to heaven."

"Don't you think that's where he is?" he asked.

June was indignant when she exclaimed, "Of course!"

"Doesn't it make you happy to know that?" he asked.

"It does, but I'm selfish enough to want him back!"

"No you don't. Honey," he said. "You wouldn't want him to suffer like that again, would you?"

Like a child, she wailed, "You don't understand. I want him back the way he was before he got sick."

Her husband's voice was quiet and consoling when he replied, "He is the way he was before he got sick, but he's with his Father in heaven." June didn't doubt for a minute that was true, but she missed him.

As the years were to pass and she went about her daily life, she was the only one who knew that before she could think of her father's death without pain, her young children would be adults.

⁓

Shortly after the funeral, June had received a comforting letter from her mother in which she wrote that she had wanted to be with her daughter and grandchildren at this time, but hadn't wanted to intrude on Polly's grief. She'd gone on to mention the good times she and June's father had when they'd lived in Saint Louisville and Newark. After she'd read it, June folded the letter and placed it in the family bible where it was handy whenever she wanted to reread it.

Then three days after her father was buried, she turned thirty-three. Although she was in no mood for a celebration, she put on a bright smile for the sake of the family as she opened the presents and blew out the candles on the cake the girls had baked. As she looked around at the expectant faces of her children, she felt almost overwhelmed by the love she saw there.

At that moment, she knew it was time to take care of today and to set her sights toward tomorrow. She had a neglected family to attend, a house to put in order, an instructional manual to write for the Girl Scout Day Camp directors, and four new directors to train. During the cold days of winter, with her good memories of her father tucked snugly in her heart, she set about these tasks.

EDDIE

When she'd taken stock of her family, she was surprised to see that while her back had been turned her oldest daughter had changed from her familiar loving little girl into a teenager. From the beginning, June and Dick found that living with an adolescent was much different than living with younger children.

Conversations with their daughter began to sound like this: "Where are you going?"

"No place."

"Who are you going with."

"Nobody."

"When will you be home?"

"I don't know."

On the other hand when their teenager asked questions, she never seemed to like their answers, and they'd hear, "Oh Mom, or oh Dad, everyone else's parents let them do it."

To which they'd give the answer parents have given since the beginning of time, "But we're not everyone else's parents."

One day in Sunday school, while the class talked about a story in the local paper about the birth in another state of a set of quintuplets, June's friend, Inga Martin, expressed June's thoughts perfectly when she'd sighed and said, "Those poor parents! Just think, those little babies will all become teenagers at the same time." While everyone laughed, June recognized the background moan, "Oh, no!" from the mother of a new teen.

Later when June related this comment to her husband, she pensively added, "Sharlyn used to think I knew everything. Now even though some of her friends seem to think I'm pretty sharp, she doesn't think I have enough sense to come in out of the rain."

"This too will pass," Dick assured her. "Remember Mark Twain said that when he was seventeen his father didn't know anything, and that he was surprised at how smart his father had become by the time he himself became twenty-one?"

"Don't tell me I have to wait seven years?" June cried in mock seriousness.

Dick refrained from reminding her that before Sharlyn reached that milestone, Janice and Ricky would also become teenagers. *Fortunately for the parents' sanity, one of the two would sail through those difficult years with her sunny disposition intact.*

∽

Meanwhile, they began to notice a subtle change in Dick's brother, Eddie. His eyes had regained their sparkle; he was talking less about his former wife, and was again kidding around with his nieces and nephew. One evening in March, after Dick had his usual lunch with him, he enthusiastically reported to June, "Eddie said today that he and his new buddy, Russ, were going to Southwinds Night Club tonight. Russ said he wanted to introduce him to a girl who loves to dance as much as Eddie does."

This was good news to June. "I'm so glad he's going to try to move on with his life," she commented. "All this brooding has been hard on him."

"And us!" Dick quipped.

The next day, Dick told June that Eddie had told him that Russ had introduced him to more than one girl. "He said he had a ball! When I asked if he thought any one of them might become special, he just laughed and said he didn't want to get in that trap again." Then that weekend when Eddie stopped to see them, he was behind the wheel of a new nineteen sixty-three gray Oldsmobile. Rowie, who'd ridden over with him, chided him about the color. "You need something brighter," she exclaimed. Her comment, "I like a little bit of color!" brought teasing laughter from her sons.

Eddie looked at the bright red dress and matching shoes his mother wore and joked, "A little bit of color! I bet you want me to pick out any color as long as it is red, huh?"

She tossed her curls and made a rude noise before she replied, "I just thought if you are going to spend that much money, you'd want one of the prettier colors that are out now." It was obvious the next time they saw him that he'd taken his mother's comments seriously. The gray car had been replaced by a beautiful pink one with gray trim. His brother, sister-in-law, and nieces and nephew luxuriated in the plush interior and the new car smell when he took them for a spin through the streets of Newark and out into the countryside.

When they got back to the house, he informed them that he'd ordered seat belts, the optional safety features that had just come on the market. It would take awhile for them to be delivered and installed. "I told you that you should do that. I certainly plan to the next time I get a new car," Dick emphatically stated.

June was to wonder later how different things might have been if the car had come equipped with seat belts.

～

Then a few weeks later on Easter Sunday, June's mother, stepfather, Dick's parents, and Eddie came to the house on Oakwood Avenue for dinner. When Eddie arrived he clutched a bottle of sassafras tea in his hand which he plopped on the kitchen counter, as he exclaimed, "I made this." Then he uncapped it and passed it around for everyone to sniff. With a wide grin on his face, he said, "Smells great doesn't it? I read that it's good for you, and from now on, it's the only thing I'm going to drink."

Dick teased him about giving up Southern Comfort, but the younger brother just laughed and replied, "No hangovers with this." Throughout the day, he was back to his old self...the laughing, teasing man the children knew and loved. At one point, though, when June mentioned that she had a plant to put on her father's grave and asked if anyone wanted to go with her, Eddie joked, "That's the last place I want to go!"

His words fell like slivers of ice on June's mind, and she found herself crying out, "Don't say that! That's nothing to joke about!"

Someone at the table gave a nervous laugh while someone else said, "That's the last place any of us want to go."

June remembered these words when, before another Sunday rolled around, this little group stood huddled together as they watched while a casket was slowly lowered into a freshly dug grave.

～

Two days after Easter, Dick and Eddie again ate lunch together at the Natoma. Dick told his wife that night as they got ready for bed, "Eddie mentioned that tomorrow is the first anniversary of his divorce from Joy."

"Is he brooding about it?" June asked.

"Doesn't seem to be," Dick said. "I really think he is almost over her."

"That's good," June said as she crawled under the covers.

They talked some more about his brother before they both fell asleep only to be awakened by the insistent ringing of the telephone. Startled that the phone would ring at one thirty in the morning, June jumped out of bed and ran downstairs to answer it before the children were roused. She didn't recognize the deep male voice at the other end of the line when he asked to speak to her husband. In response to her question, "Who's calling?" he informed her that he was from the Newark Police Department.

By now, Dick had joined her and anxiously asked, "Who is it?"

"He said he's a policeman," she replied as she handed him the phone.

"I must have left the barbershop door unlocked," Dick said. "You know the police check the doors of all the businesses downtown and call the owner if it isn't locked."

While she watched her husband's smile turn to a look of alarm, she realized that whatever the officer had just told him was more serious than an unlocked door. When he dropped the phone back in the cradle, he told her that the policeman said that he was at Forest and Rowena's and that they needed him to come down there right away. "He wouldn't tell me what was wrong, but he sounded pretty serious."

They quickly dressed, and Dick broke every traffic law as they careened through the deserted streets of early morning. When they arrived at the house on Third Street, they saw Dick's parents in the open doorway. Rowena's face was ashen and her eyes red as she grabbed her son and clung to him. June looked at her father-in-law whose expression was one of total bewilderment.

"What's wrong?" June asked one of the officers.

He waited until Rowena had released Dick before he said to him, "I hate to tell you this but your brother, Edward, is deceased."

"What do you mean...deceased?" Dick asked.

"There was an automobile accident. He was killed instantly!"

When June heard a strangled cry from Forest, "Does he mean Eddie's dead?" she went to the older man and led him to the nearest chair before he could collapse on the floor. "I didn't know why they were here," he murmured. "I thought they said he was diseased, and that didn't make sense."

When he dropped his face into his cupped hands, June's heart went out to this grieving father. Then she looked across the room at her husband whose face reflected his grief, as he tried to console his mother who had understood from the start what the officers had said.

The thought suddenly occurred to June to ask about the people in the other car. To her question as to whether anyone else was hurt, the officer responded that it was a single car accident. "It happened at the top of the hill right before you get to the Sunset Club on the way to Mt. Vernon. We don't know what caused it. It could have been that a deer ran out in front of him." As he raked his hands through his hair and wrinkled his forehead, it was obvious to everyone in the room that this was a part of his job the policeman hated. "Since there are driveways on each side of the road as you crest that hill, someone could have pulled out in front of him, or as he came over the hill there could have been a couple of cars passing. Skid-marks indicated he'd slammed on his breaks. His car apparently became airborne before it struck an embankment," he said.

Before the officer left, they'd learned that no witnesses had come forward. The person who had discovered the accident had gone to the Sunset Club and called the State Highway Patrol, but he hadn't given his name nor stayed until they'd arrived. Everyone in the room wondered if the caller might have been the person who caused the accident, but they were never to know.

"How do we know it was really Eddie who was killed? Even policemen make mistakes," Dick said as soon as the door closed behind the two officers. "They said he was at a funeral home in Mt. Vernon. I'm going to go see for myself!"

Hope sprang into Forest's eyes when he heard his son's words. "I'm going with you," he said as he grabbed his hat and jacket and followed his son to the car.

June tried to console her mother-in-law while the two women sat and waited for the men's return. One look at Dick and Forest's faces when they walked through the door told them that there had been no mistake. Forest's voice sounded hollow with undertones of anger when he intoned, "He was on his way to Mt. Vernon to see that woman." They all agreed with his statement, but they were never to know why he was going to see her. They sincerely hoped that it had been to let the woman who had caused him so much grief know that he was over her and ready to go on with his life.

⁓

Before they left the house, June had promised Rowena that she would call the Red Cross and have them contact Dick's brother, Kenny, in Japan. She would also phone Rowena's sister and brother, and Forest's sister, Bertha or Annabelle, to ask them to notify the rest of his family. After she made these calls, the sun was peeking over the horizon and she knew she had to phone the mother of her oldest daughter's friend, Bev Culver, where Sharlyn had spent the night, and let her know what had happened. She had to be sure Sharlyn didn't listen to the radio that morning. June didn't want her to hear about her uncle's death on the news.

A short time later when the confused teenager slipped into the seat beside her mother, she angrily demanded to know why she had to come home so early. "You told me that I could spend the day with Bev," she complained. "After all, this is spring vacation!" June pulled over to the curb, turned off the ignition, and faced her daughter. It took every bit of control she could muster to explain what had happened. Her goal had always been to shield her children from pain and the harsh realities of life. This time she knew she had no choice.

Earlier that morning, Dick and his mother had insisted that June go with them today to the funeral home and cemetery to help make arrangements. This put her in a quandary. She didn't want to tell the younger children then leave them to deal with their grief without her. When she mentioned her concern to Dick, Sharlyn overheard her and said, "You go with Dad. I'll stay here and answer the phone if someone calls. I won't let Janice and Ricky find out until you have a chance to tell them."

June and Dick were both proud of her. Although, she wasn't quite fifteen, she was acting like an adult. This didn't keep the young mother from feeling guilty, though, about putting so much responsibility on such young shoulders.

When they got home after a day of making the arrangements, Janice and Ricky rushed to meet them at the door. Their mother's unusual absence when they'd awakened that morning, Sharlyn unexpectedly being in charge, all the phone calls, and the apparent mystery had caused Janice and Ricky's imagination to take wing. June's heart sank when she realized that her children expected good news.

June and Dick had decided before they got home that she would talk to Ricky while Dick told Janice. "This is going to be difficult for both of them. Each one needs some individual attention," June had rationalized to her husband.

Then she took her son by the hand and led him upstairs to her bedroom while Dick stayed downstairs with Janice. She stooped down so she could look her eight-year-old son in the eye when she told him. At her words, the excitement and anticipation in his eyes quickly faded as he turned his back on his mother and sobbed out his grief for his young uncle.

June's futile words of comfort were almost drowned by the pounding of feet on the steps. She turned in time to see Janice run past her open door on the way to her own bedroom. Close behind her was Sharlyn. While June was torn between staying with her son or going to her daughter, Ricky turned his face to the wall and stammered between sobs, "I want to be by myself."

When June slipped down the hallway and looked through the open doorway, she was greeted by the scene of her younger daughter lying across her bed and crying heart-brokenly. Sitting on the bed with her arm around her sister, Sharlyn was mumbling comfortingly, "Don't cry. Uncle Eddie wouldn't want you to cry."

Janice's face was buried in her pillow but although her words were muffled, there was no mistaking her reply as she cried out, "Yes he would want me to cry! Uncle Eddie would expect me to cry!" Tears ran down the young mother's cheeks as she watched the sad scene. Then she tiptoed down the hall and looked in on her son who still stood ramrod stiff with his back to the door. She wanted to go to him but his posture told her that he still needed to be alone.

When she got downstairs, she found her husband slumped on the couch with his head cradled in his hands. He looked up at the sound of her footsteps. "She thought I had a good surprise for her!" he wailed. "When I told her that I had something to tell her about Uncle Eddie, the way she looked at me made me think that she knew what I was going to say."

"How could she know?" June asked.

"She didn't know but I didn't find that out until too late," he exclaimed. He went on to explain that he'd said, "You know, don't you?" and Janice had nodded. His voice broke as he revealed that he'd blurted out something about

Eddie's death. "She looked like I'd hit her in the stomach. Before she ran upstairs, she yelled that she thought he'd gotten married." Later Janice told her mother she'd overheard them say that her Uncle Eddie had started to date again, and she remembered the mysterious way everyone had acted when he'd gotten married to Joy. She'd then put two and two together and decided that must be what all this mystery was about.

As she looked into the clear blue eyes of her eleven year old daughter, June felt overwhelmed by guilt as she wondered how much grief she might have spared her children if she'd been able to stay with them that day.

∼

For the next three days the family hardly had time to think as Eddie's customers, friends, and loved ones streamed into the funeral home during the three days of visitation, and crowded the chapel during the services. On the way home from the funeral, Dick commented, "Eddie wouldn't have believed the number of people who cared about him."

"That's true," June replied. "It's too bad he didn't know."

Sharlyn sounded miffed when she asserted, "He knew we all loved him."

Ricky and Janice echoed her sentiments from the back seat where they were safely strapped into the new seatbelts their father had had installed before the funeral. "I'm convinced that Eddie would still be alive if he'd been buckled up," Dick said in a low voice to his wife. "If you'd only seen his car, you'd agree with me. It was hardly damaged at all. If he hadn't been thrown out, he'd have been bruised, but he'd have survived." He raised his voice so Sharlyn, Janice, and Ricky could hear him when he said, "I want you kids to realize how important it is to always wear your seat belts!" The realization that wearing this simple little belt could have kept their beloved uncle with them for many more years made an indelible impression on them. They never had to be told again to buckle up.

Within minutes they were at the house on Oakwood Avenue. As they walked up the steps to the porch, they became aware of a high pitched sound from inside their house. "What in the world is that?" Dick asked as he opened the door.

Inside now, the sound was eerie, like nothing they'd ever heard before! When the little group cautiously followed the strange noise into the kitchen, their eyes went to a spot on the wall above the sink. "It's Uncle Eddie's clock!" Janice cried.

She was right. The hands of the kitchen clock Eddie had given them four months earlier for Christmas were spinning so wildly that it looked like it might take flight. Huddled together, they stared and listened as the whirling, wailing sound continued. Although they tried to hide their feelings, everyone was shaken by this strange phenomenon. While the baffled family stood momentarily rooted to the floor, the words to an old song about a clock that quit running when an old man died flashed into June's mind. Those words and the memory of what Rowie had told her about her first visit to Eddie's house after the accident when she'd been greeted by the persistent ringing of his alarm clock were in her mind as she looked at her wide-eyed family.

She thought that occurrence had been strange, but this was even stranger. She suspected that if they had been superstitious people, these strange happenings could have caused them to wonder if this was Eddie's way of trying to contact them.

"Nonsense!" June thought as the whirling hands took their final spin as Dick unplugged the clock.

When he stated, "The clock must have been defective," a little voice in the back of her mind nagged at her with the thought of, "We never had any trouble with it before. Why today?" In days to come, they learned that the repairman wouldn't be able to repair it, nor could he explain what had happened. Like the clock in the old song, this one was never to work again…in this case, though, after the "young" man died.

When Dick started to put the clock in the waste-paper basket, Ricky protested since it was from his Uncle Eddie. Dick nodded at his little son, retrieved the clock, placed it in its original carton and started up the stairs with it.

"I'll make room for it on a shelf," June called after her husband as she followed him up the stairs.

She realized he had shared her thoughts when she saw him place the box in the far corner of the closet and heard him say, "I wonder if…" but before he finished his sentence he vigorously shook his head as if to rid himself of an unwanted thought and muttered, "Nah, couldn't be." A pensive look crept into his eyes as he mused aloud, "But you know Eddie always was a stickler for time."

The entire family missed him, but they never forgot him. In the days, months and years that followed, they found they didn't need a clock to remind them. Since he'd always been so special to them, they only had to look into their own bank of memories to bring him back to life. Then later as an adult, these feelings would spill out of Janice in a poem she wrote called, "IT'S TIME."

IT'S TIME

By Eddie's niece, Janice Large 3/94

That great uncle of mine
Was fun all the time
Good at the jitterbug
Or giving me a hug.

He played a wild horn
From the day I was born
I had a special friend
Never thought it would end.

In love he did believe
From him on Christmas Eve
A wall clock was our gift
The time away did sift.

His sports car was his pride
He gave us such a ride
What a One and Only
Though, at times, so lonely.

At Easter, family fun
But clouds shaded our sun
There was a bad car crash
How could God be so rash?

Lay on my bed and cried
Sissy said by my side,
"Though everything seems wrong.
He'd want you to be strong."

His Mom went to his room
Should be a quiet tomb
His alarm rang out loud
His pillow now a cloud.

Our lives had come unwound
We put him in the ground
Back at our house we found
Wild clock hands swinging round.

It was as if to show,
"It was my time to go
I left against my will
Time just will not stand still."

"Life is fragile like a time piece
We share such a small piece of time
Just wipe that frown off your brow
I'm dancing with the angels now."

YOU'RE IN THE JAILHOUSE NOW

Eddie might have hesitated when he'd signed his name to a will with his parents as beneficiaries if he'd known it was going to bring on a fierce battle between them. As executor, Dick started the first round when he asked what they wanted to do about Eddie's house. "Do you want to sell it, rent it, or what?" he'd asked.

"We're going to move into it ourselves," his mother had quickly replied. Her words were almost drowned out by Forest's assertion that they were going to sell it.

"Are you crazy? I'd never sell Eddie's house!" Rowena exclaimed. "I know that he'd want us to live in it. He knows how much I've wanted a one floor plan ever since the kids moved out."

Forest almost cried when he replied, "I love this house. This has been our home for thirty-one years. How could you even consider selling it?"

When later that evening, Dick related this conversation to June, she said, "If I were a betting woman, my money would be on Rowena."

"I don't know about that," Dick replied. "Dad's pretty stubborn."

June laughed and muttered, "Tell me about it!"

"Want to bet the usual?" Dick asked.

With a grin, June had replied, "Why not?" They had their own reward to the winner of their little wagers. Only the two of them knew what it was. Dick chuckled at her words because he knew that with their bets the winner wouldn't be the only one who enjoyed the collection of the reward.

It would be weeks before they knew who would win the bet as the battle raged on. Forest pleaded his case with anyone who would listen. Every time June and Dick saw them, he'd add another reason to his list of complaints. At one time he said, "It's on a side street. I couldn't sit on the porch and watch the cars go by." Another time he complained, "It's too small. Our furniture wouldn't fit in it."

June wasn't surprised that Rowena had an answer for all his objections. She could tell that her mother-in-law had made up her mind to move, and nothing her husband said would change it. "I think we have an irresistible force against an immovable object," she told her husband at the end of the first month when he brought her up to date on the stalemate.

Then five weeks after the argument had begun, Dick reported to June that when he'd stopped at his parents' home after work that evening, his father was furious. Dick told her that he'd no sooner stepped through the door when Forest had practically shouted, "Boy, do you know what that woman told me today?" Before Dick could reply, his father had pointed an accusing finger at Rowena and added, "She's going to move into Eddie's house whether I do or not!" When Dick reported to his wife that his mother had seemed calm but determined, June grinned and reminded her husband that she'd told him so.

"It looks like we may both be right. Dad says she can go but he's not going," Dick sighed.

"We'll see," June replied. "If your mother moves, he'll go with her."

"She wants to move this Thursday when I'm off work. I told her we'd help her. I have to get a truck and someone to help me with the heavy stuff." Almost as an afterthought, he added, "I think I'll ask Raymond."

When Thursday rolled around, June, Dick, Sharlyn, Janice, and Ricky joined Raymond at the house on Third Street ready to roll up their sleeves and get to work. It only took a second for June to know that she'd won the bet. Although he was still grumbling about it, Forest was packing his belongings too and moving to the house on Leonard Avenue.

The first time they visited Dick's parents in their new home for one of Rowena's wonderful spaghetti dinners, Forest insisted they come out in the yard after they ate. He pointed at the willow tree at the side of the house, and the row of sycamores at the back of the large lot and said, "Look at this place! Smell the air! It's like being in the country. Everything is cleaner and fresher up here!"

June and Dick exchanged amused glances and the girls giggled but no one said a word. It was as if the move had been his idea. Rowie had won that battle but they were soon to be embroiled in another one. No one had anticipated it but when it started, June again bet on her mother-in-law.

∼

Before this happened though, June and Dick were involved in another project. Since school was out, Polly, Fred, and Bill were leaving Baltimore and moving back to the house on the hill and the family had planned a surprise for their homecoming. June, Dick, Sharlyn, Janice, and Ricky had worked for several days and had completely repainted the entire interior of the house and all of the outside trim. Then they had someone come in and replace the linoleum in the kitchen.

Although the tenants had left the house in good condition, June had wanted to do something special for Polly and the boys. She didn't even tell her husband but she knew that she was also doing this for her dad.

The homecoming was bittersweet for those who returned and the ones there to greet them. They were all glad to see each other but they all felt an empty place in their hearts at Burrel's absence. June noticed that once Bill and Fred had unpacked, they'd shot out of the house like a bolt of lightning to find their friends. By the time Fred returned, Polly and June had dinner on the table.

"Where's Bill" Polly asked.

"Don't know," Fred mumbled as he plopped down at his place at the dining room table.

"I saw him go down in the basement awhile ago," Ricky said.

June sent the little boy to tell him that dinner was ready. A little later when Bill joined the rest of the family, he told them how he felt about that old cellar. "You know that Dad, Fred, and I dug that basement. I wasn't much taller than the shovel I used to throw the dirt out of the hole when we started. I loved the smell of the earthen floor in that little room, and of the apples Dad always stored there for the winter. I even liked the smell of the potatoes."

Later Bill would go there when he needed to be alone to think, to work his way through a problem, or to escape from trouble. He always felt close to his father when he was in that special place.

⁓

For all the years of their lives, June and Dick had been law abiding and their contact with the law had been almost non-existent but before the year was over, they or their family would become familiar with the workings of the sheriff and police department.

The first time was on the Fourth of July when June received a frantic phone call from Polly. "The boys and their friend, Mike, are in jail! Mike's father is on his way to the jailhouse to bail them out. Can you meet me there?"

"J-j-jail?" June stammered. "What are they doing in jail?"

"I'll tell you when you get here," Polly replied.

June called over her shoulder to her astonished husband that she was on the way to jail to bail out her brothers. Puzzled, her husband watched as she sped away from the curb. She'd managed to calm down before she reached the fortress-like jailhouse where her stepmother waited impatiently.

"Mike's dad is inside. He going to try to keep the deputy from filing charges against them," she nervously reported.

"What in the world did they do?" June demanded.

"They were cruising around in my Volkswagen. They thought it was funny to throw cherry bombs out the sunroof when they saw a man working in his yard." Polly grimaced before she went on. "Unfortunately, it landed at the feet of the man who happened to be a deputy sheriff! Apparently he jumped in his car and chased after them. When he caught them, he placed all three of them under arrest."

Almost speechless, all June could say was, "Good heavens," as she followed the redheaded woman into the jailhouse. Both women felt out of place in this dark, dingy, dungeon-like building as they hesitantly approached an officer seated at a humongous desk. "I'm Fred and Bill Harman's mother," Polly squeaked. She cleared her throat and added in her normal voice. "What do I have to do now?"

They thought they saw a smile tug at the corner of the man's mouth as he told them to take a seat in one of the wooden chairs that was lined up against the far wall. Polly and June exchanged relieved glances as they followed his instructions. "This might not be as bad as we thought," June whispered.

A few minutes later, Mike's father strode into the room with three very repentant boys close behind him. "It's all taken care of," he informed Polly. "You can take them home now."

Fred and Bill withered under their mother's sharp glare as she directed them to the car and announced, "I'll drive. In fact it might be a year before either of you get behind the wheel of this car again!" June knew that her stepmother would relent, but for the moment Fred and Bill looked like they believed her.

∽

Before Dick and June again encountered the law, Forest and Rowena were involved in their second battle of wills. This time Dick and June didn't bet on the outcome. They knew Forest didn't have a chance. The problem had started when Rowena had a new color television set brought to the house on a trial basis. Up until now they had watched their favorite shows on a small screened black and white model. Now, though, since color television had been developed, Rowena decided that they needed to replace their old set.

June and Dick's family became aware of the squabble on a Saturday night when they arrived at the house on Leonard Avenue for their weekly spaghetti dinner. Janice was the first to notice the patch her grandfather wore over one eye. Concerned, she asked how he'd hurt his eye. "It's that new television set your grandmother wants to buy. The color is so bright that it hurts my eyes," he replied.

Janice looked puzzled but she didn't say anything. Dick couldn't resist teasing his father, though, by asking why he didn't cover both eyes if it hurt him to watch. "Doesn't it hurt the other eye?"

Forest snorted and replied, "You don't know anything, Boy! Your mother is trying to blind me!"

"It's not the color that hurts him. It's the thought of the seven hundred dollars it's going to cost," Rowena quipped.

One look at the determined glint in Rowie's eyes convinced everyone in the room, except Forest, that she was going to win this battle too. Not ready to give up the fight, though, Forest wore the patch for a few more weeks. When his wife realized that he wouldn't give in, she simply took seven hundred dollars from the rent money they'd collected that month and paid for it. Then when she informed her husband that it was bought and paid for, he took the patch off, and he never again complained that the color hurt his eyes. Rowena was the victor of the Great Color Television Set Battle.

∽

A few weeks later, on a Friday evening, as Dick walked into the living-room wearing his new fancy plaid dinner jacket that the band members had chosen, Ricky exclaimed, "Hey, Daddy, do you ever look snazzy! The Dynatones will all be decked out tonight."

Just then, Janice walked into the room carrying her bag packed for her overnight at Betsy's house next door, "Daddy, where is your band playing tonight?"

Dick answered, "We'll be at a club in Mount Vernon."

As Janice hugged him goodbye, she thought about how proud she was of his musical talent. He played the saxophone, clarinet, and fiddle. Being so musically inclined, he could read music, or play by ear. Ricky and Janice helped carry his instrument cases to the car, then Ricky headed back into the house with his Mom, while Janice went to Betsy's.

After a fun evening, the girls got up early and walked to Betsy's piano lesson, which was about a mile away. On the way home, they were happily chatting and avoiding the cracks in the sidewalk while chanting, "Step on a crack, and you'll break your mother's back."

As they walked by a porch full of three women and many children of all ages, one of the women called out to Janice, "Aren't you that barber's daughter?"

Puzzled, Janice answered, "Yes, I am."

The lady blurted out, "I heard on the radio that your Dad was killed in a car accident outside of Mount Vernon."

Janice stared wide-eyed at Betsy, who stared back as her mouth dropped open. Suddenly, the shocked little girl turned and began running toward home. As she furiously ran, she was hurting inside with the thoughts, "Daddy is dead. How could this happen? It can't be true."

As she bounded up the steps of the front porch and burst into the house, everything seemed quiet, with her Mom in the kitchen busily preparing breakfast.

"Mommy, where is Daddy?" she asked breathlessly.

June, surprised by Janice's outburst, replied, "He is still in bed. He got home late last night, so he is sleeping in."

Letting out a sigh of relief, Janice plopped down on her chair at the kitchen bar, and relayed the whole terrible ordeal to her mother.

June hugged her daughter and comforted her with, "Oh, Honey, those women were talking about hearing about Uncle Eddie's accident. It was a very thoughtless thing for them to say to you. Some people are so insensitive."

Just then, Dick came downstairs, his hair tousled, and his eyes still sleepy. Janice jumped up and gave him a hug.

He looked at her in surprise and said, "What did I do to deserve that?"

Her answer was, "Just being here. I love you, Daddy."

With a big smile, he looked at June, who gave him a wink. He knew she'd explain later.

For now, she asked, "Who's ready for breakfast?" In unison, Janice and Dick answered, "We are!"

～

One morning of the next week, when June answered a loud knocking at her front door, she was alarmed to see a uniformed policeman standing there. The officer didn't return her tentative smile when she opened the door. Instead he demanded to know if she were Ricky's mother.

Her heart pounded so hard that she was afraid it would leap out of her chest, "What is it? Has something happened to Ricky?"

His tone sounded ominous when he answered her question with one of his own. "Are you his mother?"

"Yes I am. Now will you tell me what is going on?" June asked.

He continued with his probe as if she hadn't spoken. "Do you know where your son is?" he asked.

June relaxed at this question. At least if this stern faced man had to ask such a question, he hadn't come to tell her that her son lie injured or dead. With this understanding, her fright had begun to turn to irritation when she returned this stranger's stern look and stated, "Of course I know where my son is. He's at his friend Joey's house. Now I want to know what this is all about."

"I didn't mean to alarm you, but we had a call from Joey's mother an hour ago. I just came from her house. She says that her son and yours ran away from home this morning," he reported.

"That's ridiculous!" June replied. "My son wouldn't run away from home. What ever made her think such a thing?"

"She said that Joey told her they were going outside to play but when she looked in the yard they weren't there. Then later when she noticed that food and some of Joey's clothes were missing, she became alarmed and called us," he said.

Aware of the curious stares of neighbors at the sight of a policeman at her door, she finally invited him in and offered him a cup of coffee while they continued to talk. "I'll try to answer your questions but I can assure you that no matter what Joey did, my son wouldn't run away from home," she asserted.

The policeman's face relaxed into a smile before he asked, "How can you be so sure?"

"Of all my children, Ricky is the homebody. Since my girls were little, they've packed their suitcases and gone to visit their grandparents at the drop of a hat, but my son loves his home. He'd never run away," June firmly informed the officer.

When the officer asked if Ricky had ever said anything that would indicate what his friend was up to, June replied, "He did tell me the last time he was at Joey's house he'd found him sitting on the ground digging around the foundation of the house with a tablespoon. When Ricky asked him what he was doing, he told him that he hated where they lived, and that he was going to dig up his house and move it."

The policeman looked up from his note-taking to ask if Joey had said anything else. "I don't remember exactly what he said, but apparently Joey is unhappy about his parents' divorce," she informed him. "Has anyone checked with his father?" she asked.

"We did that when we first got the report. He's out looking for his son now," he replied.

Throughout the long day, despite return visits from the officer, and frantic calls from Joey's mother, June's faith in her son wasn't shaken. Janice and Sharlyn shared her opinion. "If he's with Joey he's probably trying to get him to come home," Sharlyn assured her.

After the word had gotten around the neighborhood about the missing boys, Janice's friends, Janet, Marsha, Diane, and Joey's sister, Linnie, came over to see if they could help. "Let's get our bikes and go see if we can find them," Janice said. Within minutes they were off on the search. At first, they rode up and down the streets and alleys in the neighborhood and yelled, "Ricky...Joey!" Although they scoured the neighborhood, they couldn't find them. The boys seemed to have completely disappeared.

Looming above their heads were the new mounds of raw earth where the route sixteen expressway was being built. Janice knew that Ricky loved to play in an area the neighborhood boys called "Dirt Hill." Less than a mile from the house on Oakwood, dirt had been brought in to raise the level where the highway was being built. This fill dirt formed hills and gullies the boys scampered over and culverts they crawled through.

While the girls headed in that direction, they saw two figures in the distance. Janice cried, "That looks like them!"

"They're heading this way. They must be coming home," Janet said.

As they pedaled closer, there was no doubt that they'd found the two very bedraggled looking boys. Ricky looked glad to see them while the other boy appeared decidedly unhappy. "You'd better get home!" Janice told her brother. "You're going to be in trouble!"

"No I won't!" Ricky asserted. "Not when I tell Mom what happened." Then Ricky gave his sister a pleading look before he added, "I didn't do anything wrong. Let me get home first, okay?"

Janice and her younger brother were very close, friends as well as siblings, and she'd always been able to tell if he told a lie. Without a doubt, this time she believed him. "Okay!" she responded. "I'll be right behind you."

~

Dick had gotten home from work about the time this conversation took place. He'd just assured June that he agreed that their son wouldn't run away when they heard footsteps on the front-porch and saw a tired, grimy faced boy walk through the front door with his sister, Janice, behind him. Before they could even ask what had happened, Ricky spilled out the story of his misadventure. "I didn't know Joey was running away from home until about an hour ago," he explained. "When we left his house, he wanted to play this game where we would pretend that we were the good guys and that everyone else was the bad guys. He said he'd taken food and clothes so we could pretend that we had to camp out while we hid from the bad guys."

While his parents and sisters listened, he explained, "We saw a lot of police cars, but every time we saw one, Joey would play that they were the people who were after us in disguise. We'd duck behind a tree or jump in a ditch every time we saw anyone." June interrupted his story long enough to set a plate of cookies and a glass of milk in front of him. He took a long swig of the milk and stuffed a couple cookies in his mouth before he went on. "We spent a lot of time at Dirt Hill. Once a plane went over and Joey said they'd taken to the air so we ducked into a culvert and hid."

"We got all the way to the pond up past the shopping center before I found out what Joey was doing," he explained. "When I told him that I was tired of the game, he got upset and confessed that he was going to run away from home, and he wanted me to go with him." Ricky polished off the last cookie before he added, "He got more upset when I told him that I didn't want to, and he yelled at me that if I didn't go he'd just go without me. I told him that my mom would miss me if I left, and I bet his would miss him too."

Dick interrupted to say, "We'd all miss you."

Ricky grinned at his father before he continued, "It seemed like hours before Joey said he'd come back with me. We were almost home when we saw Janice and her friends. I wasn't afraid, but Joey was almost too scared to go in when he saw a police car in front of his house. Before he did go in, he told me that we were both in trouble," Ricky said. The little boy looked at his mother for assurance that she believed him, and that she wasn't angry. He quickly received all the reassurance he needed in the form of a big hug.

June smiled warmly and said, "I told the police that you liked your home too much to run away." She hugged him even tighter when she added, "I never for a minute believed you'd do such a thing." He managed to free himself enough to look around at the brightly lighted kitchen, sniff the aroma of the food in the pans on the stove, and grin at his family before he said, "You're right! I'm never going to leave home!"

June and Dick exchanged knowing looks over their son's head. They knew this was the talk of a nine-year old boy. They also knew that someday he and his sisters would all leave home. It would have surprised them to know that he'd be the one that went the farthest and would be away the longest of any of their children.

Later that evening after the rest of the family had gone to bed, June and Dick sat on the porch and talked about the events of the day. "That was quite an adventure Ricky had today," Dick said. "Weren't you worried?"

"Sure, I was concerned that he was gone so long, but like I told the policeman, Ricky likes his home too much to run away," she replied.

"And his family," Dick said.

"I've always wanted to give our children a more secure home than I had. It looks like we succeeded," she stated. Since he knew how much stability in her children's life meant to her, he was glad not only for the children but for himself that she felt that way. Before he could voice this thought, though, she changed the subject to ask, "Isn't it incredible that we've had so much contact with the law lately. I certainly hope this is the last of it."

Unfortunately this was not to be the case. As it turned out, before too many more weeks passed, there would be another incident with the police.

TO GRANDMOTHER'S HOUSE WE GO

The accidental run-away was put behind them as they got ready for Janice's visit to Gram's house in Widowville. The eleven year old girl was excited with the prospect of being able to help in the store as her grandmother had promised in her invitation. "She's going to teach me how to pump gas," Janice had bragged to her best friend, Janet Ford, as she packed her bag for the trip.

On the ride to Mansfield they were all having a great time together in the car, talking, laughing, and singing. As they neared the spot where Uncle Eddie had been killed, they grew quiet; each lost in their own thoughts about him. As they drove by, they could actually see the scar in the embankment where his car had hit. After they crested the hill and started down the other side, Janice asked, "Daddy, do you think we'll ever know what caused Uncle Eddie to wreck his car?"

Dick replied, "I don't think we'll ever know exactly what happened. We just know that something caused him to swerve off the road. It could have been a dog or a deer, or two cars drag racing toward him, or one car passing another at the top of the hill in the no passing zone."

At that point, they came to the top of the next hill, and coming straight at them in their lane was a speeding car as it passed another in a no passing zone. Ricky and Janice screamed as Sharlyn yelled, "We're going to be killed," but Dick swerved over onto the berm with only seconds to spare before they would have collided.

As they saw the driver in the other car continue without a backward glance, Sharlyn exclaimed, "That might be what happened to Uncle Eddie!"

"That's right. Only it was night, and Eddie wouldn't have been able to see how narrow the berm was," her father agreed as he eased the car to a stop along the highway. Like the rest of the family, this experience had shaken him and he needed a minute to compose himself.

Deep in thought, Janice felt that this had been God's way of answering her question of what had happened to Uncle Eddie that terrible night. She knew God had watched over them and kept them safe during those last few seconds as He sent them the message.

When they arrived in Mansfield, June told her mother about their near car accident. "We can thank Dick for his quick action! He saved our lives with the way he handled the car!"

Dick grinned and quipped, "Must be from driving an ambulance on the battlefield in World War II." Now that the crisis was over, he could joke about it, but for the next few trips, he traveled the back way to Mansfield.

∼

Before they left Janice for her two weeks stay, June took her mother aside and said, "Go ahead and let Janice help at the gas pumps, and in the store, but don't let her operate the lunch-meat slicer. I don't even want her to touch it!" An evil looking machine, June hated to use it herself, and had visions of her little daughter coming home with some of her fingers missing. Janice didn't mind the restriction since she was much more interested in the large glass candy case that sat atop the marble counter. Her eyes always widened when she peered through the glass at all the wonders it contained. One entire shelf was filled with boxes and jars of all kinds of penny candy such as tootsie-rolls, jawbreakers, and peppermint sticks. Another shelf held the nickel candy bars.

Whenever they had visited as a family, Priscilla and Bill had allowed each child to select one candy bar or five pieces of penny candy. It had always been hard for them to choose from such an array of goodies since everything looked so good. They wanted it all! Now as Gram and Bill's guest, she was given what could be every child's dream. "As my little helper, you can have whatever you want," Priscilla had told her the day of her arrival, while Bill beamed his approval.

During this visit, Janice got to know another side of Bill. It seemed to her that every time they'd visited before, he'd spent all his time either sitting silently in his recliner or waiting on customers. He'd hardly talked to her at all. Now he was warm and friendly, talking, laughing, and joking with her. The change was so complete that, by the time she left for home, she had started to call him Grandpa Bill instead of the plain Bill she'd always called him before.

As she waited on customers, she continued to hear the phrase, "Put it on my bill." Even though Janice remembered the incident with Ralphie and his angry mother when he had followed his father's advice to get whatever he wanted and put it on the bill, she was never-the-less astonished when children her age or younger came in and got candy and blithely instructed her to charge it to their parents' account. When she laughingly mentioned Ralphie at the dinner table, Gram said, "I sometimes wonder how closely the adults check their statements at the end of the month. Either they just spoil their children or they don't pay any attention to their purchases."

Janice grinned at Gram's choice of the word, "Spoiled." While she thought that just maybe Gram and Grandpa Bill weren't exactly spoiling her, they certainly were treating her like a very special little girl during this visit. They had even sat down with her the evening before and let her select a new school dress for them to order from the Spiegel catalogue. Janice didn't voice her thought, but she wondered if she reminded them of her mother at eleven, and if they were trying to make up through her for the time they'd missed with June when she was that age.

During her stay with this set of grandparents, several other things fascinated her. One was that any time her grandmother needed anything, she would just tell Janice to go into the store and get it. Another was being able to play with and feed the puppies. The furry little creatures belonged to Lady, Gram and Bill's German Shepherd and a neighbor's collie.

The grandparents had decided to keep a good-natured male they called Laddie. Although, he was to become as large as his mother, he had the loving nature of a lap dog as his owners were to discover when he grew up. In months to come, it was amusing, when he was allowed into the house, to see him make a dash for Priscilla or Bill and jump onto their laps. Priscilla had been heard to grumble, "This animal thinks he's a Pekinese."

While Lady and Laddie were outdoor dogs, Gram had an indoor one too, a Boston Bulldog she called Pepper. Although, he had a face that only a mother could love, and he snorted and snored, Priscilla adored him. During her visit, Janice was allowed to feed him. Since she had been raised with Toy, who had never bothered anything in the wastepaper basket, it didn't occur to her that Pepper would retrieve the empty dog food can she tossed in the trash.

As it turned out, he fished it out of the basket and tried to lick the inside of the can. Janice was horrified when she heard his yelp of pain and saw the blood gush from his mouth. When Gram pried the dog's mouth open and looked inside, she found that he'd cut his tongue. Although the horrified little girl didn't think the bleeding would ever stop, it finally did. Gram wasn't angry, but she did gently remind the frightened child that in the future she should put cans outside in the big barrel.

That evening while Janice washed the dishes and Priscilla dried them, Priscilla exclaimed, "I don't know why your Mom and Dad bought that new-fangled automatic dishwasher. You still have to rinse the dishes, so why not just wash them by hand? It also seems like a lot of trouble to go through to roll that dishwasher over to the sink each time and hook it up to the faucet."

The little girl had been very pleased when her family had been the first on the block to have a dishwasher. Janet, Marsha, and Diane had all commented on how lucky she was. She shared her views with her grandmother, "Even though we still rinse off the dishes, it does save time, because we don't have to wash them after breakfast, lunch, and dinner. We just load them after each meal and run it when it is full."

Priscilla replied, "I still like to do dishes the old-fashioned way." Janice smiled as she handed her grandmother another plate. Then Priscilla changed the subject when she asked, "How are Polly and the boys doing?"

Janice replied, "They have moved back to Newark to their little house on the hill." She refrained from adding that Fred and Bill had practically become convicts after throwing that cherry bomb at the feet of a deputy. She didn't want Gram to think less of her uncles, though she knew that they could be pretty ornery.

Priscilla stated, "You know that Polly isn't your real grandmother. You aren't really related by blood at all."

Janice's unspoken thoughts were, "MaMa Polly and I aren't related by the blood in our veins, but by the love in our hearts." She knew that her grandmother was very jealous of Polly, but couldn't understand why. Gram had been the one who had left Granddad, and this had happened long before he ever met Polly.

After finishing the last pan, realizing that she still had a great deal to learn about the adult world, Janice filed this conversation in the back of her mind to think about later. Then she gave Gram a hug and told her, "I love you, and I'm really glad you and Grandpa Bill have had me stay with you. I've really enjoyed it."

They continued to cover other subjects, before they said goodnight, and Janice snuggled under the covers of the sofa bed in the living room. Before she went to sleep, she thought about how Gram seemed to think of love as a pie that had to be cut into pieces and shared with others. A large piece for one meant less for someone else. Even as a eleven year-old, Janice thought of love as never ending possibilities, where if you loved one person a lot, you could still love another without taking away from the first person. She knew that she had plenty of love for all three of her grandmothers and extra for other people in her life.

She started thinking about how Priscilla had left when June was about her age and hadn't seen her daughter until she was close to fifteen-years-old. She had missed the entire time when June grew from a child to a young lady. Janice felt sadness for her own mother who hadn't had her mom around during that time. Then she thought about how glad she was that Polly had come along to fill the gap. Janice knew her own mom was always there when she needed her, and always would be.

As she did every night, she silently prayed the Lord's Prayer, then on to Now I Lay Me Down To Sleep, followed by God Bless Mommy, Daddy, Sissy, Ricky, followed by all the names of people she loved, until she dropped off into a peaceful sleep.

ATTACK ON INNOCENCE

Soon after Janice returned from Mansfield, school started. The evening they next encountered the law was unseasonably mild for September, a perfect evening for the chili supper at the schoolhouse. This was an annual fund-raiser for the school, and the family never missed it. After they ate, Dick handed Janice and Ricky some money to play the carnival type games, and they rushed off to join their friends. Sharlyn was already with her friend, Bev, and a girl named Barb. June noticed how pretty her older daughter looked in her new red and white ruffled crop-top blouse and blue jeans. Her brown curls bounced about her shoulders as she and her friends headed toward the dance in the gymnasium.

Sharlyn loved to dance, and she knew all the popular ones: the Twist, the Jerk, the Monkey, the Mashed Potato, and never missed a chance to do them. As she strolled by her parents, she gave them a little wave. June returned the wave then grinned at her husband and said, "Did you see that? She actually acknowledged us in public?" To her parents' distress, there had been little of that since she'd become a teen.

"Don't let it go to your head," Dick joked. "She'll be back to normal tomorrow. One of my customers told me that his teen daughter only recognized him if she needed money from the time she was thirteen until she turned twenty. Don't let it bother you, when she's older, she'll be glad to have you around." As it turned out, June was to be a very welcome sight to her daughter a few hours later.

When the dance was over, the teen-ager had called from the schoolhouse to tell her mother that she, Barb, and a couple boys were going to walk Bev home. "Will you pick us up at Bev's in about twenty minutes?" she'd asked.

Fifteen minutes later, as June drove onto East Main Street, she saw a crowd of people in front of The Cascade, a neighborhood grocery store. When she saw two black and white police cars parked by the doorway, she had a sinking feeling in the pit of her stomach that something had happened to her daughter. With this thought in mind, she made an illegal U-turn and braked to a stop next to the patrol cars.

As she ran into the building, the proprietor met her at the door and exclaimed, "She's alright, but some man just attacked Sharlyn! The boys she was with and some of the kids from the Children's Home pulled him off of her."

June was almost speechless with alarm, but she managed to gasp, "Where is she?"

He pointed toward the parking lot and said, "The police are talking to her."

June didn't wait to hear any more in her rush to get to her daughter. Even in the dim light, she could see a cluster of teenagers at the far end of the parking lot in earnest conversation with a police officer. When Sharlyn broke away from the group and ran toward her mother, June was shocked at the change in her appearance. Buttons and ruffles had been ripped from her blouse, her hair was tousled, and her face was tear stained and smudged with dirt. June hugged her and asked if he'd hurt her. Then once Sharlyn had assured her that he hadn't, June asked what had happened.

"We stopped here so Barb could go to the rest room," Sharlyn explained. "I waited in the parking lot with the rest of the kids. When Barb came out, she'd no sooner told us that she wanted to get out of here because some man in the store had acted really strange when he came running out yelling like a madman."

"Before I could move, he grabbed me, tore my clothes, and held my arms behind me so I couldn't get away," she declared. "I tried to kick him but the way he held me, I couldn't even move." She shuddered before she continued, "He had his face right up to mine and kept muttering something that I couldn't understand. His breath was awful, and he was drunk!"

By now the policeman had joined them. Once he'd found out that June was the victim's mother, he'd assured her that Sharlyn hadn't been injured. "Thanks to these young people who pulled him away," he nodded toward the group of teenagers before he went on. "I don't know what would have happened if they hadn't been around."

When June asked who he was, he pointed to a man in the back seat of one of the cruisers. The officer's words oozed with contempt when he said, "His name is Larry, and we've had trouble with him before. He gets mean when he's drunk."

June could see a young man, probably in his twenties, muscular but with the beginning of a beer paunch, seated not five feet from where she stood. For a moment, she had a primal urge to pound the leering look from his face, but she managed to control herself with the thought that the law would take care of him.

As the family was soon to discover, the facts would become so twisted by the behind the scene maneuvers of Larry's family and their minister that by the time the trial took place, the justice system would see him as a pathetic victim and Sharlyn as the aggressor. A few days after the man was arrested, June and Dick started to notice a coolness in the officer's manner, evasive responses to their questions or a failure to return their calls.

A few days after the attack, they began to receive phone calls at all hours of the day or night, but there was never anyone on the line if anyone except Sharlyn answered. When she answered, though, she could hear heavy breathing and words whispered too low for her to understand. After the second week of this, Sharlyn had become jumpy and afraid to leave the house alone. "I'm sure it's him," June told her husband. "I think I'll call and tell that nice detective who came over and questioned Sharlyn. He was really sympathetic and so concerned about her when he confided that this wasn't the first time the police had trouble with Larry because of his drunkenness and bad temper. He also said he thought he was a menace because he has VD."

It didn't take her long to discover that "the nice detective" had done a complete about face. She hardly recognized the man's almost hostile voice when he answered the phone with a curt, "What is it?"

Taken aback by his abrupt tone, June said, "If I'm calling at a bad time I can call you back. Something has come up I wanted to talk to you about, but it can wait if you don't have time to talk."

None of the previous warmth or concern was evident in his voice when he barked out the words, "Now is as good a time as ever." Then he repeated, "Whadda you want?"

Once June had told him about the phone calls, he asked, "How do you know it's Larry?"

Disappointed by his response, she replied, "I don't need to be much of a detective to put two and two together and come up with Larry. The calls didn't start until after Sharlyn was attacked. The heavy breathing and whispering only happens when she answers. Who else can it be?"

"It could be anyone," he snapped back. "You can't go around making accusations without proof."

The officer was surprised by June's next question. "What's happened since the last time I talked to you?"

He stammered, "N-n-noth-ing has happened."

June didn't believe him, but she could see no reason to continue this frustrating conversation. After a quick, "Good-bye," she hung up.

When she told Dick what had happened, he wanted to go to the station and talk to the officer but she convinced him not to go. They soon realized that Sharlyn had overheard their conversation and seemed disturbed by what she'd heard. After dinner, she went upstairs to listen to some music then went to bed early.

"Did you notice, Sharlyn didn't even talk on the phone once tonight?" Dick asked. "This whole thing must really be getting her down."

They were to find out a few hours later just how much when they were awakened by ear-piercing screams. June shrieked, "He's gotten into the house!"

as she jumped out of bed and ran toward her daughters' room, with her husband only a few feet behind her.

When they got in the room they found Sharlyn sitting up in her bed, her eyes wide with terror as she sobbed, "He's at the window! He's trying to get in!"

Dick went to the window and looked out onto the empty porch roof. From what he could see, the street appeared to be deserted. "I don't see anyone, but I'll go downstairs and look around," he told the frightened girl. The screams had awakened Ricky and Janice so the entire family waited in the girls' room until he returned. "No sign of anyone!" he informed them.

Sharlyn was still frightened, but she'd begun to think that she could have had a nightmare. "It was so real," she exclaimed. "I could almost smell his stinking breath."

"I didn't hear anything until Sis started to scream, but I was sound asleep," Janice told her mother.

Nine year old Ricky looked fierce when he said, "He doesn't know that Dad lifts weights, and I have my ball bat. We'd take care of him if he got in here!"

June smiled at her little boy and said, "I'm sure the two men in our family could protect us. Now I think we'd all better try to get some sleep. It's almost time to get up."

Whether it was a nightmare or not, there was no repeat of the incident either that night or any other.

～

The day of the trial was filled with surprises. The first one was the changed appearance of the attacker. The dirty, smelly person had been replaced by the clean-cut, well-groomed young man at the defense table. He was barely recognizable as Larry. The second one was the almost fawning respect shown by the police and the judge to the attacker's well-to-do uncle who appeared in court with him.

After Sharlyn told her story, the minister of a neighborhood church testified to the attacker's good character while Sharlyn, June, and Dick listened in astonishment. Then Larry apologized and the judge accepted his apology, and told him to go no closer than twenty-five feet from Sharlyn. "If you see her on the same side of the street as you are, you're to cross to the other side," the judge cautioned Larry in a tone reserved for a favorite child. Then he nodded coolly to Sharlyn and her parents and stood up as if to leave.

Angry, Dick stood up too and almost shouted, "Don't you know what this man did to our daughter? He grabbed her on the street, twisted her arms behind her back, and practically tore her blouse off of her. The Lord only knows what else he might have done if her friends hadn't pulled him off of her."

The judge's patronizing reply showed his total lack of understanding for the young girl's ordeal. "I'm sure Larry will be glad to pay for a new blouse for her," he said, before he turned to the defendant's uncle and said, "That's right, isn't it, Sir?"

"Absolutely!" the uncle replied. "We'd be glad to buy the little lady a new blouse."

June could feel her stomach churn at the condescending look the older man cast in their direction. The look on her daughter's face showed that she felt the same way, while Dick just looked angry. On the way out the door while the policemen, the uncle, Larry, and the minister chatted casually, Dick walked up to them and declared, "I can see why the statue of justice is blindfolded. In this case it certainly was blind!" Then without a backward look, he strode away to join his wife and daughter.

∼

It wasn't until a week later that June discovered what had gone on behind the scenes. When she confronted the minister and asked how he could possibly vouch for Larry's good behavior. Apparently, when Larry's uncle had found out his nephew was in trouble, he'd immediately turned to the family's minister. The minister solemnly announced, "When they told me how your daughter taunted and teased Larry for being drunk, until he couldn't stand it any longer, I told them I'd go into court for the poor boy. It's my opinion and that of the police who worked on the case that she brought it on herself," he announced. June was almost speechless with shock and anger, but at least now she knew why the police had changed so much.

She took a deep breath to get herself under control before she emphatically responded, "That's a lie! I can't believe all of you were taken in by it!" The minister looked less sure of himself when she continued, "Did it ever occur to you that was a story Larry made up to help get himself off?"

If the minister believed her he didn't admit it. Instead he said, "The poor boy has had a rough time this year. His grandmother died a few months ago, and he hasn't gotten over it."

To June's ears, this sounded like a poor excuse, and she let him know exactly how she felt. "Let me tell you a few things about my daughter. One, she is afraid of drunks and would cross the street to avoid one. Two, she is too tenderhearted to do such a thing. Three, she not only lost a grandmother this year, but an uncle and her grandfather, and now she can add being attacked on the street and that fiasco that took place in court to the bad things that have happened to her. To me, grief is no excuse for his actions! If everyone who lost a loved one was allowed to break the law, we would have a pretty lawless society," June asserted.

The minister tried to ease out the door with the excuse that he had an appointment in a few minutes. June wasn't quite through, though. She'd made up her mind that if she had to follow him to his meeting she was going to finish what she had to say. "I don't expect to change your mind but I think what you did is almost as bad as what he did. You don't really know Larry...just his uncle.

Yet you were ready to go into court and testify under oath to his good character. Don't you realize that most of the young people in the neighborhood look up to you? Or at least they did! Sharlyn has heard you speak at Girl Scout gatherings and she always respected you and your opinion. I think you have a responsibility toward the youth in this neighborhood as much as to your parishioners."

He looked surprised at her last statement, but he wasn't willing to admit that he could have been wrong. Instead, he looked at his watch and said, "I really do have to go." As she watched his clerical clad figure retreat, she wondered if he'd think twice before he testified to another's stranger's good character.

Dick was as angry as she was when she relayed this conversation to him. "That boy's family must be big contributors to the church, if you ask me!" he said. "I guess money talks, even to a preacher."

"Maybe so, but I think his intent was good. He just didn't bother to get all his facts straight. We shouldn't tar all preachers with the same brush," she said. "I don't think our minister or Bill Goodin would do such a thing, do you?"

"No I don't," he admitted. "I can see a preacher being fooled by that story, but you'd think the police would know better." His usually cheerful face looked grim when he added, "I think I'll have a little talk with a couple of those officers."

Although June tried to discourage him, he did talk to them. "I don't know if it did any good...or changed any minds, but I told them the same thing you told the minister. I also let them know how I felt about them going behind our backs and smearing Sharlyn's reputation," he told June when he returned from the station.

"Did anyone apologize?" June asked.

"Not a one. Although the detective you thought, at first, was so nice did look a little sheepish," he replied.

June grinned and joked, "Let's hope neither of us gets stopped for a traffic violation!"

"I'm sure the judge wouldn't be quite so kind to us. We'd probably end up under the jail," he quipped.

"Seriously though, my concern now is how this whole thing is going to affect Sharlyn," June said.

"As far as I can tell, she seems to be alright," Dick replied. "What do you think?"

"I've noticed that she isn't afraid to answer the phone anymore," June said.

"Any more of those calls?" he asked.

"Not since the day before the trial," she responded.

A few days after this conversation, Sharlyn came home from a movie and told them that she'd seen her attacker downtown. "When he saw me, he looked like he'd seen a ghost. Then he turned and ran across the street," she reported.

"Sounds like he must have paid attention to what the judge said after all," June mused before she asked, "Do you feel better about it now?"

"I'm fine!" she said as she plopped down on the couch with Janice and Ricky to see the end of an episode of Ozzie and Harriet. "If you'd seen the way he ran, you wouldn't worry about it either!" she laughingly told her mother.

As it turned out, that was the last any of them saw or heard of the man who'd caused so much turmoil in their lives. *Ironically, twenty-three years later, a much more serious incident happened to Sharlyn's teenaged daughter, Debbie, a little over a mile from where Sharlyn was attacked that fall of nineteen sixty-three. This time, though, the police would come through like knights in shining armor.*

A SHOT RANG OUT

As November twenty-third approached, Dick and June prepared for their sixteenth wedding anniversary. On the big night, Sharlyn had agreed to stay home with Janice and Ricky while her parents went to Columbus for dinner at Jong Mea's, their favorite Chinese restaurant and a movie at the Palace Theater. The day before the anniversary as she and Polly walked around the square and shopped in all the men's stores for Dick's gift, the air was pleasantly brisk as a hint of winter mingled with the last trace of fall. While they chatted with the clerks, or smiled at passers-by, they had no premonition of what was to come.

Oblivious of this, June finished her shopping, tucked Dick's gift, a wine colored robe, in the trunk of the car before she drove to the shop to get him to go with them for lunch at the Natoma. They were in such a festive mood when they walked into their favorite downtown restaurant that at first they didn't notice the solemn faces of the other patrons. They did observe, though, when the waitress took their order that she seemed close to tears. "I wonder what's going on?" Dick muttered. "All those guys at the bar look like they've lost their best friend."

June turned to scan the men and women's faces. Their expressions ranged from sadness, to fear, to anger as they watched a program on television. She couldn't see the screen from the booth but heard the commentator mention the name Kennedy and say something about him being near death. "Did you hear that?" June asked Polly and Dick. "President Kennedy's father hasn't been well. Maybe he had another stroke," she surmised.

They nodded their agreement just as the waitress sat their food on the table. "Are they talking about the President's father?" Dick asked the distressed looking woman.

"Didn't you know?" she asked. "Someone shot President Kennedy in Dallas." The lone gunman crouched in an upstairs window in a large Texas city had changed their smiles into tears.

The three in the booth could only gasp in shock as she turned and hurriedly returned to her place behind the bar. The salmon cakes they'd ordered sat untouched as they turned their attention to the newscast in time to hear Walter Cronkite announce that the President had died at Parkland Hospital in Dallas from head injuries. Everyone listened in stunned silence while he went on to announce that Vice President Johnson would be sworn in as the new president.

Although his death was a great loss to the country, June and Dick felt that it was a personal loss as well. As they left their food untouched, paid their bill, and silently walked out of the restaurant, they felt overwhelmed with grief for the young president, his beautiful first lady, and two small children. From then on when they talked about that horrible year of nineteen sixty-three, they remembered it as the year they lost June's father, Dick's brother, and President Kennedy.

They were too stunned to speak as June took Dick back to work and Polly home before she hurried home to her children. A white faced Ricky met her at the door with the question, "Have you heard?" June noticed the same expression on Janice's pale face when she walked into the room from the kitchen.

When June asked who told them, Janice responded that the principal had announced it over the intercom at school. "He told us what happened, then he dismissed school early," Janice said. While Ricky nodded in agreement, Janice went on to say most of the kids and some of the teachers cried. "Everyone was upset except Craig," she said as she referred to a particularly nasty boy in her class. "When we got outside the school he yelled, 'President Kennedy is as dead as a door-nail!'" She wrinkled her face in disgust when she added, "The only thing that mattered to him was that he got out of school early."

"You remember him," Ricky said. "He's the one who stopped in here to use the phone one day and stole Dad's shoes."

June grinned at the memory of how the boy had bragged at school about how easy it was to steal from them and how quickly, once he'd heard about it, Dick had confronted Craig in front of his father and had gotten an apology and his shoes back.

"Troy and I walked home together today," Ricky said. "He said that now that we didn't have a president that we probably didn't have any laws anymore. Is that true, Mom?"

He looked relieved when she explained that the vice president, Lyndon Johnson, would take over as president. "He'll be sworn in sometime today. That's the way the constitution is set up," she explained.

When Sharlyn got home, she told them she'd heard it from other kids while she waited for the school bus. Someone had heard it on the radio and passed it on. "Everyone talked about it on the bus." While they'd been talking, June had been setting out a snack of cookies and milk. While they munched on the cookies, Sharlyn told her mother that she and Bev were going to a dance that night.

"Not tonight," June said. "I don't think it's right to go dancing when the President was just murdered, do you?"

"Oh, Mom!" Sharlyn exclaimed. "I don't see how me staying home from a dance is going to help the President!"

"I know it won't, but I don't want you to go!" June replied.

Sharlyn left the room to call her friend on the phone to let her know what a stick-in-the-mud her mother was. When she returned, she had a counter proposal. "If I can't go to the dance, may I at least go with Bev to baby-sit for her sister in St. Louisville?" she asked.

"I thought Bev was going to the dance," June said.

"Not if I can't go," was the reply.

Although, June would have preferred to have her entire family together that night, she relented and let her baby-sit with her friend. When June relayed this to her husband that evening, he said, "Don't let it bother you. Someday she'll see things your way. Now though, she's a teenager."

Her only response was a deep sigh, and a murmured, "I've noticed."

The next day, instead of celebrating their wedding anniversary, they sat before the television set and listened to the reports of the happenings in Dallas and in Washington. They saw the President's coffin being loaded onto the plane for his return trip to Washington and the new president sworn in. They heard statements from doctors and from police officers. Before the day was over, it was announced that a man, Lee Harvey Oswald had been captured in a movie theater. First, though, he'd shot and killed a policeman who tried to apprehend him.

Dick reported in the evenings after work that several of his customers were afraid that Oswald had been sent by Cuba in retaliation for the blockade. The fact that the suspect had lived in Russia for awhile, had married a Russian woman, and had recently returned from Cuba added fuel to that suspicion. "They're afraid if that's the case, we'll be at war with Cuba and a lot of our boys will be killed," he said.

"He hasn't confessed yet, but I'm sure he will soon. They have too much evidence against him for him to keep saying he didn't do it. The bullet was from his gun. His co-workers saw him carry something the size and shape of a rifle wrapped in a blanket into the building, and his fingerprints were all over the windowsill. I don't know how he can deny it," Dick declared.

The next day, June was alone in the house when her mother-in-law called, as she did daily. "Did you see it?" she asked by way of greeting. Before June could ask what she meant, the older woman went on, "Someone just shot Lee Harvey Oswald! Sharlyn and I were watching TV, and we saw it. Dick just got here with Janice and Ricky to pick up Sharlyn seconds after it happened. They're watching a replay of it now." Then before June could ask any questions, Rowie said, "Gotta get back to the TV!" and hung up the phone.

June flipped on the television set in time to hear a report and to see a replay of the shooting. At first she saw an arrogant looking young man she knew to be Oswald, hand-cuffed and surrounded by several large official looking men, as he was brought into the building. The scene was one of confusion as around them, flashbulbs popped as photographers competed for a close-up of the suspect and a gaggle of reporters shouted questions. Into all this confusion, a nattily dressed, portly, balding, middle-aged man had suddenly stepped forward, and fired at the accused assassin. While blood colored the young man's clothing, the officers tackled and restrained the shooter.

In later reports, they heard that the killer's name was Jack Ruby, and that he owned a local nightclub. When asked how he'd gotten close to the suspect, it came out that he regularly hung out at the station to the extent that no one even noticed his presence that day. There was speculation that he had shot Oswald to silence him from revealing that others were involved in this conspiracy, either Castro or the mob. When questioned, he said he'd killed Oswald to spare Mrs. Kennedy the ordeal of a trial.

Jackie Kennedy remained mum on this matter as she went about the business of comforting her children and planning her husband's funeral. Vivid pictures of this brave woman were etched in June and her family's minds as the heart-rending scenario continued to unfold. They would never forget the pink suit stained with her husband's blood that Jackie Kennedy still wore during the swearing in of the new president. Nor would they forget, her black-clad figure a few days later when she and her little daughter, Caroline, knelt and kissed her husband's casket, or the sight of her as she stood beside her children as three year old John-John stood at attention and saluted.

They would always remember the day of the funeral when Mrs. Kennedy, and the family walked behind the black, riderless horse and the caisson that carried the coffin from the capital building to Arlington National Cemetery where the young President was laid to rest. During the long funeral procession, the solemn beating of the drums continued. The beat of the drums seemed to express a nation's collective grief. Even when they stopped, the mournful sound seemed to remain in everyone's mind.

For the next few days, this scene was replayed over-and-over on the nightly news. June's brother Dick didn't mean to be disrespectful when they visited a few days later when he said, "I don't think anyone will assassinate a president anytime soon."

In response to their quizzical looks, he added, "If everyone is like me, they'll never again want to hear the sound of those awful drums."

"Or lose another president," June replied as she thought about the country's loss of what the media had dubbed "Camelot."

NOT THE JOURNEY'S END

Less than a month later, Polly took a bus to Virginia to spend a few days with Bill and Dorothy to gather the furniture she had left behind when they'd moved back to Newark. "They're going to Dayton to visit their family for Christmas," she'd told June. "If I rent a U-haul, they'll bring my stuff back and I can ride home with them."

The December day she'd left for the bus ride to Arlington had been cold and clear, but the day of the return trip was a different matter. Polly shivered when she heard the forecast was for snow as she remembered the trip she, Burrel, June, and Cecil had made along the same route the winter June had been twelve. When she mentioned it to Bill, he pooh-poohed her concern. "You said yourself that Burrel's' car was old and the heater was bad on that trip." He patted her hand and added reassuringly, "The DeSota drives like a tank. We'll be fine."

They got a late start since they couldn't leave until Bill and Dorothy got off work. Then a few miles from home, they drove through a snowstorm. Fortunately the snowplows seemed to keep ahead of it although it did slow them down a little. Around three in the morning, they saw a little restaurant just before they got into Uniontown, Pennsylvania. That's when their trouble began.

When the women urged Bill to stop, he teased them by saying, "You two can't see a sign that says food without wanting to eat."

Polly jokingly replied, "You're the one who's always hungry." As they were finishing their meal, a trucker came in, stomped the snow from his feet, and announced that the weather was getting worse. Bill had reason to believe him as he pulled out of the parking lot and found that the road was covered in a thin sheet of ice. As he saw what lay ahead of them, he had a sinking feeling that they were in big trouble. He hadn't realized until they started down that they were at the very top of the mountain. Through his rapidly icing windshield, he could see that there wasn't even a hint of a curve to slow their descent. To make matters worse, the weight of the U-Haul seemed to be pushing the car wildly down the mountain.

As Bill fought for control, Dorothy cried, 'We're flying! Can't you do something?" Bill yelled for them to lean the other way, as if he thought their weight would keep them on the road. No matter what Bill did, though, the car continued its uncontrolled careening down the mountain. At one point they felt the car scrape the guardrail before it bounced back and forth from lane to lane. Thankfully no cars were coming toward them. As they reached the bottom of the mountain, it was warmer and ice hadn't yet formed there, and he again regained control and was able to bring the car to a stop. As they breathed a sigh of relief, they concluded that nothing in an amusement park could ever match their wild ride.

Then the next day, at the house on the hill, Bill related their close call to June. "You won't believe this, but for once in Dorothy and Polly's lives, they didn't speak a word."

"We were too scared to say anything!" Dorothy exclaimed.

"If I know these two," June thought, "if they were quiet, they were praying." They talked some more about the incident before June and her family left. Now that the danger was over, they had begun to look at it as fun...scary, but exciting.

As she headed for the car, June told Bill how much the entire family appreciated the thick copy of the Washington Post that he'd sent about President Kennedy's death. "The kids had never seen anything like it. You know our paper doesn't have color pictures yet. Janice was even more impressed when she learned you had sent it and that you'd helped print it."

"I thought they might appreciate it," he murmured as she slid behind the wheel of her car. Then on her drive home, her thoughts were filled with images of Bill, Dorothy, and Polly's narrow escape.

As she thought about these three people whom her entire family loved so dearly, she had a feeling that the previous night their guardian angel had been in the car with them. Certainly, their prayers had been answered.

∽

The visitors had left for Dayton by the time the family gathered at the house on Oakwood Avenue for their first Christmas Eve without Burrel and Eddie. Although the lights on the tree shone as brightly as they had every other year and the house was filled with the sights and sounds of Christmas, it wasn't the same. This was most evident when they gathered in the living room to hand out the presents. Three seats were vacant as was the place at June's feet where Toy usually sat. As if God had felt that Burrel, Lula, and Eddie needed his company in heaven, their beloved toy collie had gone to join them just before the first snow of winter.

When the gifts were opened and thank yous said, they chatted briefly about their plans for the next day. "You're going to your mother's for Christmas Day as always, aren't you?" Rowie asked.

"Not this year. Mom changed the plans. She wants us to come on Sunday instead. That way we can spend the day with Dick and Bev and their family too," June replied. "We're staying home. I'm going to cook a ham with raisin sauce, and you're all invited to join us for dinner," she told them. Polly readily accepted the invitation for herself and the boys.

"We'll be here, and I'll bring a cherry nut cake," Rowie said. Then with a glance at her watch, she added that it was past their bedtime.

"Good heavens, yes!" Dick teased. "The moon is out." Rowie laughed and gave him a peck on the cheek before she joined Forest who was already in the car. Like his wife, he preferred being home once the sun had gone down.

After they left, Polly followed her daughter into the kitchen to help with the clean up. Once they'd finished, she poured them each a cup of coffee and said, "Sit down. I want to talk to you." They both took a seat at the kitchen bar before Polly continued. "This is a bad time for all of us. We have to think of the children and how our sadness affects them," she said.

Dick ambled into the kitchen just then, emptied the remains of the coffee into his cup and joined them at the bar before he said, "Polly is right. This has been an awful year for them too. I'm sure your dad and Eddie would both want them to have a good Christmas!"

June sighed and murmured, "I know. They both loved this holiday so much. Janice said something to me the other day about last Christmas when Eddie got us the clock. She also reminded me of the year when you got your tape recorder, and we made a tape of Santa Claus. She said she was at the age where she had started to doubt his existence. Then when they listened to the tape, though, she told me she wasn't sure. At first, she said, she thought it was her Uncle Eddie being Santa, but then she'd hear his voice in the background. Then she thought it was you, then Dad, then Forest, but at one time or another, she could hear all of you talking to Santa. She said that recording made her believe in him for one more year."

"I remember that," Polly said. "We recorded some Christmas carols too. Do you still have the tape?"

Dick shook his head regretfully and replied that he'd looked for it earlier but couldn't find it. "That shouldn't keep us from singing some now though, should it?" he asked.

"If you think you can stand my singing, I'd love to," June said.

"That's okay," her husband teased. "We'll be loud enough to drown you out." That said, they joined the young people in the living room, and for the next hour they sang carols while visions of past Christmas gatherings with Burrel, Lula, and Eddie flickered in all their minds.

As if his images were too real to contain, Fred asked his mother, "Do you remember the time, you and Dad got us the guns that shot out ping pong balls?"

"How could I forget? Your dad thought it was funny to shoot me in the rear with one of them!" she replied.

"Yeah, I remember those guns. I seem to remember that they disappeared not too long after that!" Bill muttered. Polly looked extremely innocent, but June recognized that look and wondered where the guns were hidden.

Then Bill, with a glint in his eye, piped up with, "Let's sing another song. We didn't sing Jingle Bells."

Their voices joined together as they all sang the familiar words to Jingle Bells. Bill's voice got louder and louder as he sang the new version of the song, "Jingle Bells, Batman smells, Robin layed an egg."

This struck Ricky as so hilarious that he dropped to the floor laughing. Bill jumped right in and started poking Ricky, causing him to laugh even more. Everyone smiled at their antics, as Polly said, "Okay, you ornery boys, calm down and let's sing a real Christmas song."

Bill innocently volunteered, "How about Rudolph The Red Nosed Reindeer?"

They all light heartedly sang, "Rudolph The Red Nosed Reindeer had a very shiny nose..." Then loudly, in union, all five kids shouted, "LIKE A LIGHT BULB!'

The adults smiled at each other, and June thought, "Life goes on, and there sure is a lot of life in this group."

∼

The next day, as they'd done since they were toddlers, the children woke her before they ran downstairs to find their gifts under the tree. At first, she felt a twinge of sadness but then, she remembered what her stepmother had told her. She shouldn't let missing her father on this day ruin Christmas for the family. With this thought, she could almost hear her father say, "And that's all there are to it!" By afternoon, when the family gathered around the harvest table, she let her eyes roam to the chair where her father usually sat, then to Eddie's, then to Lula's. She didn't have to close her eyes to picture the three of them in their usual place. In her mind, they were there as they'd always been. As he had at other Christmas dinners, her dad would have them join hands while he said a blessing on the food and the hands that prepared it.

As she had in the past, Lula, with her black curls dancing and red lips curving into a smile would be telling a joke while Eddie would be talking and laughing with Sharlyn, Janice, and Ricky.

With the conversation swirling around her, she was enjoying the tableau that was taking place in her imagination. As she listened to these echoes in her mind, she realized that these three were alive in the memory of everyone in this room, and as long as anyone who knew and loved them lived, they always would be. Somewhere in the back of her mind the thought again surfaced... someday she would write a book and in it her father, Dick's brother, and Lula would come alive for future generations. "If I ever write one, it will be about all the people I know and love," she mused.

"A penny for your thoughts," her husband said.

"My thoughts are worth more than that," June said. "Wait until I put them on paper. Then you can read them."

"A plain Merry Christmas would do," he replied.

The love she felt for everyone at this table and the happiness that they were all together was evident in her heartfelt reply of, "Merry Christmas."

She could almost hear her father's deep bass voice mingled with the voices of the people seated around the harvest table as they replied, "Merry Christmas to you!"

MOVING ON

June tucked her plan to write a book into the back of her mind as the family moved into the year of nineteen sixty-four. While the news media talked about President Johnson sending more troops to Vietnam, a different type of take-over was going on in this country. Known as the British Invasion, it started with a singing group called the Beatles who soon took the country by storm. When the long-haired foursome burst onto the stage of the Sunday night Ed Sullivan Television Show, Dick, June, and their family sat in Dick and Bev's living room at their house in Mansfield. At first, they couldn't hear the beginning of the first song for the wild roar of the studio audience. "Sounds like the way girls reacted to Frank Sinatra when he first started," June murmured seconds before the sound died down enough for the Beatles to be heard. The children were enjoying the music, but the two men, being barbers, were focusing on the performers' long hair.

A frown wrinkled her husband, Dick's, brow as he muttered, "They look like girls. I've cut a lot of hair in my time, but that's the first time I've ever seen a boy wear bangs or hair over his ears!" June's brother, Dick, agreed that he'd never seen anything like it.

"It'll never catch on here!" June predicted. "I know that neither of my guys would wear their hair that way!"

Bev declared, "That might be the way they wear their hair in England, but I can't imagine any boy walking down the street in Mansfield with a haircut like that!"

As June looked at Ricky and her nephew, David's, flat-tops, she would have been stunned if she'd been able to foresee the future when both boys would wear their hair much longer than anything they'd seen on the screen that night. Almost from that night on, only adults would wear short hair while teen-agers would let theirs grow... first over their ears, then below their shoulders. While this created friction between fathers and sons in many homes, it had a more devastating impact on Dick and his barber business. For now, they were all blissfully unaware of the effect these young men's appearance would have on their lives.

Soon, on the streets in Newark, only new military recruits were wearing crew cuts. Dick began to notice that customers who had gotten a haircut every week or two now waited for at least a month. Then to his amazement, he discovered that all his customers under the age of twenty wanted to look like the Beatles. He found himself in a dilemma. Since he had a growing family to support, he either had to change with the times or go into another line of work. One evening on their way to Columbus for a night out, he told June, "I have decided to take hairstyling courses." He grinned and quipped, "I guess I can do it, but I feel as if I'll be learning how to cut women's hair."

She realized that, as usual, he'd used a light tone to cover his true feelings. Although, he'd never admit it, she knew how badly he felt at having to start over at the age of thirty-nine when he'd thought he was set for life. With this in mind, she matched his tone when she replied. "Good! Just think how much money you can save me at the beauty shop!"

When later he told his father of his plans, Forest grumbled, "I'm sure glad I retired before I had to get into something like that!" He made a rude noise and groaned, "Pretty soon, you won't be able to tell the boys from the girls. What's this world coming to?" While his voice didn't say, "Bah, humbug!" his expression did.

He would have been even more shocked if he could have seen in years to come that many barbershops, haircuts, and clothes would become uni-sex. As time moved on, the entire family found, as generations before theirs had, that nothing ever stays the same, and they changed with the times.

∼

Sharlyn had always been very pretty. Now that she was a teen-ager, she had become even more beautiful. Of medium height, she had inherited her mother's long legs and some of Rowie's genes for feminine curves. This combined, with her dark hair and gold flecked brown eyes created quite a picture. Her beauty had not escaped the notice of a neighborhood teenage boy named Larry. He was one of several boys who called or came to see her, but for a few months, he was special. Tall, with brown curly hair, his eyes usually danced with the joy of living.

While June and Dick couldn't say it about all their older daughter's friends, they did like this boy. He was one of a few they would let visit when she babysat her brother and sister. The first time this happened, Sharlyn and Larry sat together on the couch while Janice sat in her favorite chair ready to watch television. Ricky had crawled behind the couch, and in typical little boy fashion began to make kissing sounds. When Sharlyn grabbed his arm to forcibly remove him, he slipped right through her hands. This happened every time she tried to get hold of him. Then, frustrated, she demanded to know why he was so slippery. He laughingly replied that he'd poured the entire bottle of his mother's bath oil in his bath water. After a few more aggravating minutes of trying to remove the slippery squirming little boy, Sharlyn finally admitted defeat. Then for the next few minutes, while she and Larry sat and watched television, Ricky peeked over the top of the couch to see if they were kissing. Since they weren't, he lost interest in teasing them, and slipped out of his spot and settled himself on the floor in front of the television set to watch Batman.

Sharlyn tolerated her younger siblings' presence for a few minutes before she banished them to the upstairs. They begged her to unlock the door at the bottom of the stairs to let them out. After awhile, when they realized she wasn't going to give in, they found a way to amuse themselves that was even more irritating to the young couple. Janice told Ricky, "Hey follow me into the bedroom. I have an idea."

In each of the bedrooms, there was a register that when opened gave them a perfect view of the rooms downstairs. Unaware of this building feature, Larry was noticeably surprised the first time he heard a voice apparently coming through the ceiling telling him, "Go ahead and kiss her." Then when he did, he heard cheering...or more kissing sounds.

For the next few weeks a battle of wills took place between Sharlyn and her younger siblings. She continued to send them upstairs, and they continued to watch and kibitz. At one point, Janice became so frustrated when her sister wouldn't let her come downstairs that she pounded on the upstairs window that faced Ginny's house next door and yelled, "Help! I'm being held prisoner by my baby-sitter." Since the television set at the house next door was turned up so Wilbur's seventy-eight year old father, Grampy, could hear the news, Janice's plea for help went unheard. If it had been heard, Ginny would certainly have passed the news on to June, and the baby-sitter might have found herself the one banished to the upstairs.

∾

June and Dick didn't usually let Sharlyn go out on school nights, but they didn't object if Larry came to the house...if he left early. Unfortunately, one night, to their regret, they broke their own rule when he stopped by and asked if Sharlyn could go to the laundromat with him. He explained, "My mother's washing machine is broken, and she wants me to do some laundry." Sharlyn cast a beseeching look at her mother who relented and let her go if she'd be back in an hour.

After Larry explained that his mother had told him the same thing, she watched from the doorway as hand in hand, they ran down the porch steps and slid into the front seat of Larry's father's car. She was pleased when she saw the teenaged boy drive away as sedately as a middle-aged father on his way to church with his family in tow.

After they left, she and Dick watched television while Janice and Ricky finished their homework. It wasn't until after the younger children had gone to bed that she started to worry. Finally when the couple had been gone over two hours, she voiced her concern to Dick, "They should have been home an hour ago!" she exclaimed.

Dick pooh-poohed her concern by saying they might have gone to the Dairy Isle. She made a face at his remark and informed him it had closed a long time ago. Seconds later, she jumped when the phone rang. "Something has happened to them. I know it!" she cried as she scrambled to the phone. It was Larry's mother wanting to know if Larry was at their house. When June explained that she hadn't heard from them, the other woman replied, "I'll send his dad down to the laundromat to check. Call you back."

The sound of June's frantic heartbeats almost drowned out the monotonous drone of the dial tone as she realized that Larry's mother had hung up. After she related the conversation to her husband she thought she saw a flicker of worry cross his face, but he hid it with a wisecrack that did nothing to allay her fear.

Minutes later, they heard the sound of a car coming to a stop in front of the house, footsteps coming up the walk, and knuckles pounding against the front door. When June threw open the door, she expected to be confronted by a policeman with bad news. Instead, they were met by Larry's frantic mother. Without a word of greeting she charged into the house and launched into her tale, "No one is at the laundromat! My wet clothes are still in the washing machine! The car is gone!" She dramatically added, "They've vanished!"

Larry's father's voice sounded reassuring when he stepped from the shadows and put his arm around his wife and said, "I'm sure there's a logical explanation for this."

Between her sobs, as her husband led her back to her car, the woman incongruously cried out, "There had better be, or I'll kill him when he gets home!"

Despite their worry, Dick and June smiled at the contradiction of this woman's statement. "After I saw her butt his bike with her car that time they were in the ally across the street, I'd be worried if I were Larry," Dick said.

June remembered the incident too. She and Dick had been raking leaves in the front yard when they'd heard a ruckus across the street. Larry was on his bike and his mother in the car behind him. As he pedaled toward them, they could hear her yell as she would nudge his bicycle with her car. As they came closer, her words had reached their ears. "I told you to be home an hour ago!" she shouted as she gave his bike another nudge. She seemed oblivious of the gathering crowd her spectacle had drawn as they continued their journey down the alley with every one of her shouts punctuated by a bump of the bicycle with her car.

Since Larry hadn't been hurt, the spectators had been amused by the incident. Some of that amusement still sparked in Dick's eyes at the memory, but June wasn't amused tonight. "That's why I think something must have happened to them. Larry wouldn't deliberately defy his mother! She might not kill him, but he wouldn't want to risk her temper."

Her statement had erased the amused look from her husband's face. She knew that he was as worried as she was when he suggested she call the police. "I'm calling the hospital too!" she cried as she dialed the number. All they knew after she'd made the calls was that no accidents had been reported, and no accident victims had been brought into the hospital.

"All that means is that no one has found them!" she cried. "Something has happened…something so bad that they can't call us!" The memory of what had happened to Dick's brother, Eddie, was too raw for them to pretend that such things couldn't happen. Dick was also thinking of his brother when he nodded his agreement.

After several agonizing hours, they heard a car stop in front of their house and seconds later recognized the sound of Sharlyn's footsteps on the front porch. When the cold, shivering girl came through the door, she announced, "You'll never believe what happened tonight!"

Relieved, but not quite ready to let her off the hook, June replied, "Try us!"

When Sharlyn stood over the register to warm herself, June draped a warm robe over her daughter's shivering shoulders. Then as Sharlyn snuggled into the robe and wrapped an afghan around her, she sipped the hot chocolate her mother had made for her and began to tell them what had happened since she'd left the house five hours earlier.

"After we put the clothes in the washer, Larry wanted to go for a drive. He said we'd be back in time to put them in the dryer. We drove around on Waterworks Road for awhile. Then decided we'd better get back. We'd have made it too, but when Larry pulled into a turn-around along the road, he couldn't back up!" Sharlyn made a face before she went on. "I didn't believe him at first. I thought it was a line like running out of gas, but it was the truth. The car wouldn't go in reverse."

"Why didn't he just go forward and turn around?" Dick asked.

"He couldn't go any further because his front tires were up against a railroad tie. The only way to get out would have been to back up," she said. "We thought about walking home, but it was so cold that we decided to stay in the car and flag down the first car that went by. The first one went on, but the second one stopped. Larry gave him his parents' phone number and yours and asked him to call. He said he would before he left."

"What time was this?" June asked.

When she heard it had been hours earlier she replied, "Well, he didn't!"

"We figured that out after awhile when no one came to help us." She shivered at the memory as she added, "I hadn't realized how deserted that road was that time of night until we sat there for hours and no other cars went by. The man who finally came along was such a welcome sight. Although he wouldn't bring us home, he did promise to call Larry's parents, and he did! When Larry's dad came to pick us up, he said he'd recently been having some trouble with the transmission, but he hadn't said anything to Larry about it."

"Might have saved us all from a pretty bad night if he'd had it fixed," June muttered.

Dick nodded. Then as if the last few hours hadn't been hard on him too, he said, "Your mother was really worried!" Sharlyn, who hadn't hugged her mother since she'd become a teen, put her arms around her and kissed her on the cheek before she went upstairs to bed.

"That one was an ulcer maker," June murmured as she felt the familiar pain in her stomach. "Do you think we're going to be able to survive these teen years?"

Dick quipped that he was sure they were tough enough to make it. He squeezed his wife's hand and added, "The main thing is that she is alright."

"I know," June replied. "I just can't get over expecting something else bad to happen in this family. Every time the phone rings, I think it will be bad news."

"No wonder," he said. "With everything that's happened in the last couple years, I sometimes feel that God must think we're modern day Jobs!"

June thought about his comment, but her last thought before she fell asleep that night was that at least for tonight, her family was tucked safely into bed.

～

The entire family enjoyed Larry's company as Sharlyn continued to see him for a few months after this incident, but as time passed, he wanted to go steady, and she didn't want to be tied down. She didn't tell her parents what she planned to do until after she'd broken up with him. Poor Janice, though, found herself in the middle of a very uncomfortable situation when it happened.

Sharlyn had waited until a night when her parents and Ricky were out of the house before she broke the news to him. She and Janice were in the living room listening to records when he arrived. As soon as the record ended, Sharlyn played Leslie Gore's "You Don't Own Me." At first, Larry didn't realize the message was for him. When he did, he tried to talk her out of breaking up.

While Janice looked on, wide-eyed, Sharlyn tried to get him to go home. When he wouldn't give up, she went upstairs and locked the door at the bottom of the steps. Janice felt sorry for Larry as the words of the song played over-and-over and he pounded on the door and tried to get Sharlyn to come down. "Please, Sharlyn open the door. You know I love you." The little sister felt that she should do something to help Larry, but only being eleven years old, she didn't know what to do.

Then when Larry started to cry, Janice cried along with him. She wanted her mother to be home, but since she wasn't, she went next door to Ginny for help. When she ran into the house and poured out her tale of woe, Ginny told her, "You have to let your sister handle this the way she wants." Although Ginny's words had lifted a big weight from the little girl's shoulders, she had been even more relieved when she returned home to find that Larry was gone.

They all missed the young teenager, but Dick reminded June that she wouldn't want their daughter to get too serious about any one boy at her age. June grinned and replied, "Do as I say, not as I did, right?"

~

The summer of nineteen sixty-four, June was upset because Polly, Fred, and Bill were going to move to Arlington, Virginia as soon as Fred and Bill graduated from high school. They had wanted to stay in Newark, but Polly's nursing license hadn't been recognized in Ohio, and she had to work at a lower paying job as a technician at Newark Hospital. In addition, the employment prospects weren't good in this area for either of the boys.

The move had been cinched when Big Bill Roberts had found both Bill and Fred a job with the Chesapeake and Potomac phone Company in Virginia. Polly explained to June that this was too good an opportunity to turn down. "I have to do this for them," she explained to her daughter. "Once they get their training they can work for Bell Telephone anyplace in the country! Now that your father is gone, I couldn't send them to college even if they wanted to go. This is my way of giving them a start toward a good future."

"Don't think that just because you're moving, you're going to get away from us! We'll come to see you wherever you go!" June promised. As she looked at this woman who had made such an impact in her life, she realized that even though the man who had bound their lives together was gone, the ties they still had were as strong as blood, and would remain as long as they lived.

In weeks to come, there were some memorable moments before the Harman family left the house on the hill. The first one took place during Bill's graduation ceremony. While the families in the audience sweltered in the ninety degree heat, they could see rivulets of sweat run down the faces of the graduates and soak through the gowns they wore over suits or summer dresses. As if oblivious to this, the speaker had spent interminable moments telling them that they had a choice of spending the rest of their lives using either their heads or their tails. He made the point that if they used their heads, they would be successful, and if they used their tails, they'd be failures. Then, in conclusion he demonstrated that he couldn't successfully use either when he proclaimed, "Heads, you win! Tails, you lose!" He then sat down, tilted his chair back against a non-existent wall and fell off the back of the stage. Fortunately, he wasn't injured, but he certainly got the attention of the graduates. They were sent out into the world with quite a bang!

The participants were more comfortable during Fred's ceremony since it was held outside at White's Field where June had graduated seventeen years earlier, but it was equally as dramatic. While the graduates lined up for the procession onto the field, a scream rang out from the bleachers, and a woman yelled, "My baby! I dropped my baby." All eyes quickly turned to a gathering crowd underneath the steps where the baby had landed.

A call went out over the speakers for a doctor, and a couple men ran toward the gathering crowd. As the audience held its collective breath, the same voice again came over the speaker to announce that the baby wasn't injured. The audience breathed a collective sigh of relief, then the band again struck up the processional, and the rest of the ceremony proceeded without further incident.

Polly's prediction, though, that now that both boys were out of school, she could relax proved to be wishful thinking...as she would soon discover.

While Fred had worked at Sandy's, a McDonald's style drive-in restaurant, during his senior year, he had saved enough money to buy a nineteen fifty-four Nash Rambler automobile. He'd reluctantly let Bill drive it a couple of times. However, the night his younger brother brought his car home looking like it had been in a demolition derby, Fred had angrily grabbed the keys from Bill's hand and yelled, "That's it! That's the last time you'll ever drive my car!" Fred was too upset with his brother to listen to his explanation that he had lost control and slammed into the fence in front of the animal shelter. As he told his mother later, the fence looked even worse than the car.

A short time later, Bill might have been trying to get back in his older brother's good graces when he offered to change the oil for him. As it turned out, Fred soon discovered that he would have been better off if he'd just let him drive the car. After Bill finished, Fred should have been suspicious when Bill told him that he'd only had to use two quarts of oil. Instead he had his mind on an upcoming date with his girlfriend, Judy Marquis. Once he started down the hill toward town, though, it didn't take long to find that he had a problem. As he went around the first curve, the car came to a dead stop, and no amount of pumping the accelerator would get it to restart. When the befuddled driver checked under the hood, he found oil all over the motor. After he pushed the car onto the berm of the narrow road, he hurriedly hiked back to the house and confronted his younger brother. "What the devil did you do to my car?" he yelled.

"I just drained the oil and replaced it!" Bill shouted. "What do you think I did?"

All the yelling in the world was not going to change the fact that Fred's car had been fine an hour ago, and now it wouldn't start. Just then their friends, Mike and Dave, sauntered into the yard to find out what the ruckus was about. Once Fred explained, they swaggered a little as they let him know they'd help get it going.

When they got to Fred's car, he raised the hood and poked his head under it, and insisted that his brother show him exactly what he'd done. When he explained that he'd drained the oil in one spot and poured the new oil in another place, Fred roared, "You idiot, you didn't drain the motor oil! You drained the transmission fluid! No wonder you spilled it all over everything when you tried to pour the oil in!"

While they went with their friends to buy transmission fluid and returned to get the car on the move again, they had no idea that this would be one of their last arguments. Their lives would soon move in different directions, and the two incidents with the Rambler would become amusing stories to relate in the future.

～

A week before school started, Dick, June and the family went with Ed and Marilyn Bevard and their two sons to a cottage on a lake in Michigan. They'd had a fabulous time boat riding and learning to water-ski. The younger members of the family took to the skiing like ducks to water, but Dick did it his own way...underwater with the fish. No matter how many times he tried, he couldn't stand up. He finally announced, "I'm tired of imitating a submerged submarine." Although, his friend Ed teased him about having a lead bottom, he couldn't be coaxed into another try. "I'll just ride in the boat while the kids do the skiing!" he announced. That was fine with them as that gave them even more time on the skis.

Since the lake was small, the water-skiers could be seen from either the beach or cottage. June and Marilyn anxiously kept their eyes on them, but the only one they could definitely identify from a distance was Janice because of the two foot long pony tail that swung out behind her as she whizzed around the lake. June and Marilyn would point out to each other, "There goes Janice again. That ponytail is a dead give-away." (June almost cried when they got home, and Janice decided to have her hair cut shoulder length.)

On the trip to Michigan, they had followed the Bevard's car. Since Marilyn drove miles beyond the speed limit, Dick did too, in order to keep up with her. Sharlyn who was terrified of fast driving called out, "Dad, slow down slow down." She had been in a panic until they'd safely arrived at the cottage.

On the way home, though, she urged her father to hurry as she wanted to be back that night in time to go to the Gene Fullen dance with her friends. Sharlyn had met the television host several times during that summer at the dance parties held for young people at the Crystal Ballroom at Buckeye Lake. Although the big bands had been replaced by rock'n'roll, the enthusiasm of the young people for the ballroom by the lake hadn't changed since their parents had danced there as teenagers. Although she loved to dance, that wasn't the only reason she wanted to be there that night. She didn't want to miss the end of the season drawing for a very coveted prize. The year before, David Clary, a boy she'd known since they were both young children had won.

"This is my birthday," she told her friend, Bev, that night as she dropped her twelfth entry for the season into the large drum by the door. "That would make a wonderful sixteenth birthday present!"

"Look at all those entries," Bev muttered as she watched her own ticket flutter to the top of the pile. "Don't get your hopes up. I don't think we have much of a chance," she cautioned her friend.

As the soft summer breeze floated over the lake and through the open windows, there was a feeling of excitement in the air. Everyone wanted to win the prize! For the entire evening, Sharlyn and her friends alternately danced and eyed the grand prize, a bright red Honda motor-scooter, that was displayed on a platform by the bandstand. The baby of the Honda family, it was never-the-less coveted by every teenaged boy and girl in the room.

"Mom told me that if I wanted a car of my own, I'd have to buy it. This would be the next best thing!" Sharlyn told Bev as Gene Fullen, the master-of-ceremonies, called for their attention as he gave the round wire drum a spin. Every eye was on it as the entries tumbled around and around as if stirred by a giant's invisible hand. As the pink tickets settled into a loose pile in the bottom of the drum, the entire room was silent as Mr. Fullen buried his hand in the heap and came out with one ticket. The winner was too surprised to notice the crest-fallen expressions on the faces of the one hundred ninety-one other people in the room when the name was called. About an hour later, Sharlyn burst into the bedroom of her sleeping parents and excitedly exclaimed, "Guess who won the Honda!"

While Dick pulled the covers over his head, June sat up in bed and sleepily asked, "What's going on? Is something wrong?"

"Didn't you hear me, Mom? I want you to guess who won the Honda!"

June had to struggle to come awake enough to make sense of what her daughter had just said. "I'm too sleepy to guess anything," June muttered as she glanced at the bedside clock and saw that it was one thirty in the morning. When she realized that her daughter wasn't going to go away and let her go back to sleep, though, she sighed deeply and said, "I remember how excited you were when David won last year. Did one of your friends win tonight?"

"Not exactly," the excited girl replied. "It was me! I won the Honda!" That last statement brought Dick's head out from under the covers. "You won a motorcycle?" he asked. When he heard that it was a Honda fifty, more like a scooter than a motorcycle, his voice sounded relieved when he said, "That's better. That's more your size. I wouldn't want you to try to handle a big cycle."

∼

After Dick taught her how to handle it, Sharlyn got her motorcycle operating license. In months to come, she had a great time as she proudly rode around the town. Within an hour, the first time she drove it to school, she was called into the school nurse's office where she was lectured about how unladylike it was for a girl to ride such a machine. When she told her mother that evening what the school nurse had said, June was quiet for a few seconds, but when she did speak, Sharlyn could hear a hint of steel in her mother's soft voice. "Don't let it bother you. I'll take care of it."

"Can I drive it tomorrow?" Sharlyn asked.

"Day after tomorrow," June replied. Sharlyn never knew what her mother had done, but from then on, she rode her cycle to school several times, and she never heard another word from the nurse.

Dick had been adamant that if she ever let anyone ride with her, she would have to instruct the rider to hang on to her. Only one person ever refused, and he paid the consequence.

Sharlyn had met Dean, a young country western singer, at a dance and had dated him a few times. At first she was impressed with his talk about being a singer with one recording to his credit. After awhile, though, his bragging began to get on her nerves. One evening when he came to the house on Oakwood Avenue, he presented her with one of his records as if he were offering her the Hope Diamond. The entire family sat in the living room and listened when he played it for them on their stereo.

They were impressed with his voice, but as Sharlyn had already discovered, no one was as impressed with it as he was. After the record ended, he bragged for an interminable time about the stars he'd met when he was in Nashville to make his recording. June and Dick exchanged amused glances as he arose from the couch, unfolded his six foot frame, which was incased in tight white pants and a western style shirt, ran a comb through his slick hair, and placed his cowboy hat squarely on his head. Then when he and Sharlyn went outside, Dick murmured, "I was surprised that he could find a hat big enough for that big head of his."

June knew he didn't refer to the actual size of the young man's head as she laughed and teased, "I thought only women were supposed to be catty." Then as she watched Sharlyn's date prance over to the Honda and look down his nose at it, she added, "I don't know what she sees in anyone that pompous."

Sharlyn had already come to the same conclusion. The condescending way Dean's expression belittled her prized possession certainly hadn't endeared him to her, and she had to make a conscious effort to hold back the searing things she wanted to say to him. The words, "Arrogant, self centered, stuck-up," were the mildest ones, but she bit her tongue and offered to take him for a ride. He rolled his eyes skyward as if such a conveyance was beneath his position in life, before he finally accepted.

When he climbed on the seat behind her, she told him he'd have to hang onto her before she would start the engine, but he refused. He'd no sooner informed Sharlyn that he didn't need to hold on, that he certainly wouldn't fall off of such a tiny scooter, then she proved him wrong. While her surprised parents watched from the front porch, she floored the accelerator, which caused the front wheel to rear up like a bucking bronco. A surprised look flashed onto the face of the city cowboy as he flipped off the back, and his white-clad rear hit the pavement.

The entire family had been on the front porch and had witnessed this scenario. Once they'd discovered that only his considerable pride was injured, they watched in amusement as Dean scrambled for his hat, tried unsuccessfully to wipe the dirt from his trousers, and gave Sharlyn a scathing look before he strode away. Even though the sight of the humongous black spot on his white pants as he high-tailed it down the street was to be the last they saw of him, they enjoyed the record he'd given Sharlyn for months to come.

DANGER IN THE HOUSE

One day when June was alone in the house, she had just settled herself into Dick's easy chair with a good book and a steaming mug of coffee when she heard a strange sound from somewhere above her. Alarmed, she listened and looked around, but she didn't see or hear anything. "Must have been my imagination," she thought as she reopened her book and started to read. She became so engrossed in the book's plot of things that go bump in the night that it was at least forty minutes later before she realized that she wasn't alone. Something was making scratching and bumping noises upstairs in her daughters' room.

June's first thought was to get out, to go next door and call Dick at the barber shop. On second thought, though, she decided to handle whatever was up there herself. With this in mind, she placed her book on the table by her chair, tip-toed into the kitchen, grabbed her broom as a weapon and crept up the stairs. When her foot touched the fifth step, it let out its usual squeak. She stood stock still, barely daring to breathe, while she waited to see if her intruder had heard her. When no one or thing appeared in the upstairs hall, she cautiously made her way up the rest of the stairs and down the hall to the girls' bedroom.

When she slowly opened the door and looked into the room, it appeared as it had an hour ago when its occupants had left for school. While she held the broom like a sword ready to defend herself, she heard it again. This time, though, a sound like the cry of a newborn baby or animal had been added.

When she realized that she wouldn't have to do battle with a burglar, she was relieved. This feeling only lasted a moment as she ruled out the thought that she'd find a baby behind the closed door of the closet. Then, her imagination took over. It had to be an animal, but what? Once she'd rationalized that it made too much noise to be a mouse, she was really spooked. Although she'd never heard of rats in the neighborhood, she was sure that when she opened the door, one would lunge at her.

Her hands trembled violently as she gripped the broom in one and slid the door open with the other. Seconds later, she dropped to the floor and stared at the whimpering creature that greeted her. Its big brown eyes looked as frightened as June's blue ones had until she reached out and patted his white hair and murmured, "Where did you come from?" In response, it wagged its tail and yipped. Her first reaction was relief to see this tiny white and black puppy in a towel lined cardboard box instead of the long toothed rodent she'd expected. Her second was anger. After Toy had died, she'd emphatically told her children and husband, "NO MORE DOGS!" So much for doing as she said! Someone had deliberately gone against her wishes! As she relived the last few anxious minutes, she could only mutter, "Just wait until I find out who did this!"

Oblivious of the turmoil he'd caused, the newcomer continued to wag his tail and try to get out of his cardboard prison. Her anger dissolved when she lifted him from the box and cuddled him in her arms. She couldn't be angry with him... not even when he licked her face, yipped, and peed all over her jeans.

Then he continued to wiggle and look at her with his soulful brown eyes, as she carried the box downstairs, changed her clothes and waited for her family to come home. "Don't give me that look," she told him. "I said we weren't going to have any more dogs and I meant it! Just wait until I find out who smuggled you into this house. That person is going to be in big trouble." He just barked and wagged his tail.

It didn't take long for June to discover the culprit once the children came home from school. When Ricky sauntered in, his eyes lit up at the sight of the little white and black bundle of fur. While he lifted the wiggly animal and held him, he exclaimed, "You got us a puppy!"

"One down and three to go," June thought as she watched her son play with the animal. Janice's surprise was also evident when she saw their little guest. That left either Dick or Sharlyn as the guilty party. By now, as June watched her younger children with the puppy she could feel herself begin to weaken. He was such a cute little thing, and he reminded her of Rex, the dog she and Skip had during their vagabond years with their father and Polly.

Since Sharlyn always stayed downtown after school with her friends, she was the last one to get home. Walking into the room, she was met by the sight of Ricky, Janice, and the puppy playing on the floor of the living room. Her face flushed as she realized she'd been caught before she'd had a chance to break the news to her mother that one of her friends had given the puppy to her.

At first, her mother was angry with her for going against her wishes. "You'll have to take him back!" June announced.

"I can't!" Sharlyn wailed. "When Joanie's mother gave him to me, she said she wouldn't take him back!"

Dick, Janice, Ricky, and the little puppy had been anxiously listening to this exchange between mother and daughter. It was obvious the little creature had worked his charms on them when they added their plaintive pleas to Sharlyn's to let her keep him. At first, June ignored them and told Sharlyn that if she didn't take him back, she would. Her husband was no help when he said, "I don't know why you won't let them have another dog. Don't you remember how much company Toy was for you?"

"Sure, I remember, but Toy was a dog in a million. He was like one of the family. We could never find another dog like him," she replied as she let her eyes rest on the intruder.

Something in the tone of her voice revealed the chink in her armor, and the children took advantage of it to coax her even more persistently. As if he realized his fate was in her hands, the puppy loped over to June and tried to jump onto her lap. When his little legs would only take him as high as her ankle, everyone laughed, and June conceded defeat. "He is awfully cute," she said as she reached down to help him. Then she added what mothers have said since the beginning of time, "You can keep him if you'll promise to take care of him."

Then the children replied as countless generations of children before them had, "We will! We promise!" June sighed, since she knew that although they meant it now, she would be the one who was home during the day and the task of training this animal would be hers.

Dick made the same wisecrack he always did when she complained about being too busy, "At least he'll keep you out of the bars!"

June laughed and retorted, "Since I haven't been in a bar since the time Polly took Skip and I as kids to a honky-tonk, that's a pretty safe statement."

June soon discovered that the new member of their family had a personality of his own. He was mischievous, hard to train, and completely adorable. Although he was officially Sharlyn's dog, he soon ingratiated himself into all their hearts. Sharlyn, Janice, and Ricky waited until he'd been part of the family for a couple days before they came up with a name for him. They briefly flirted with their mother's suggestion to name him after Rex, but decided he needed a name of his own. After much discussion and a few arguments, they finally decided that since he was so small they'd call him Squirt. In days to come, as their mother wiped up one more puddle from the kitchen floor, she was heard to mutter, "I can think of another reason to call you Squirt."

As if Squirt didn't want to slight any of the children, he seemed to divide his time equally between them. While he liked to play with the younger ones, he took on a different role as Sharlyn's confidant when she needed one. Many an evening, she'd carry him up the stairs to her parents' room where she'd play her records and dance with him in front of their full-length mirror.

Then she'd sit on her parents' bed, hold him on her lap while she poured out the ills of her teenaged world to him. While she talked about a teacher who'd been mean to her that day, or a certain boy she wanted to ask her for a date, or the new sweater she wanted but her mother wouldn't buy, Squirt would listen as if he understood. This little animal became her father confessor and her psychologist. Sometimes, as she went through her difficult teen years, she felt he was the only one who understood. Deep in her heart, she knew that he was such a loyal friend that even if he could talk, her secrets would have been safe.

Early that fall, Sharlyn shared confidences about a young sailor named Dave with her four legged friend. While stopping downtown after school one evening for a cherry coke with her friends, Dave had come into the snack bar, spotted Sharlyn, and talked one of her friends into introducing them. Only a few inches taller than Sharlyn, he had dark wavy hair, brown eyes, and his snug fitting uniform showed off his slim, fit build. When he noticed her go-go boots tapping to the music of the jukebox, he asked if she liked the Beatles. In response to her enthusiastic nod, he said, "I just got a forty-five record of their new song, I Want To Hold Your Hand. If you'll let me come over some evening, I'll bring it, and we can listen to it." His smile was warm and friendly with just a hint of flirtatiousness when he added, "That is, if it's alright with you." While trying to decide how to respond, Sharlyn caught her friend, Cathy's, encouraging eye, and to her surprise found herself inviting him to come over that evening.

At her house, he and Sharlyn had already listened to the record and were ready to go out for a walk when Janice and Ricky came into the room. When he realized that Janice was a Beatles fan and saw how disappointed she was to have missed their newest song, he jauntily said, "I'll leave it here tonight so you can play it. I have a date with your sister tomorrow night. I'll pick it up then." Ricky and Janice watched this light-hearted young man as he stopped in the doorway and gave them a snappy salute before he and Sharlyn walked out into the starlit night.

The next day, Sharlyn, Janice, and Ricky danced to the record as Janice played it over-and-over. Then leaving the music to the rest of the family, Sharlyn went upstairs to start getting ready for her date by putting large bristly curlers the size of Campbell's soup cans in her hair. She ignored the ringing of the telephone until she heard Janice yell, "Sis! It's for you!"

With her head covered with metal cylinders, she looked like a girl from outer space when she put the receiver to her ear. Thinking it was Dave on the phone, Ricky teasingly said, "It's a good thing he can't see you, or he wouldn't show up tonight."

Hearing her son's remark, June came into the room and motioned for Ricky to come into the kitchen with her and for Janice to turn the sound down on the stereo. Before they left the room, though, they heard Sharlyn say, "Hi, Bev. I'm getting ready for my date with Dave tonight. He only has a short leave, and he says he wants to spend as much time with me as possible." Then they heard Sharlyn say, "No, I've been too busy to listen to the radio. Why?" There was something about Sharlyn's silence and the way all the color drained from her face at Bev's reply that stopped June, Janice, and Ricky in their tracks.

Then when she slowly put the telephone back on the cradle, her voice sounded hollow and filled with disbelief when she said, "He's dead. Dave is dead. Bev said that she heard on the radio that he was killed last night when he went off the road and slammed into a tree. It was about an hour after he left here."

While her mother, sister, and brother were too shocked to react immediately, Sharlyn scooped Squirt into her arms and ran up the stairs to her parents' room where they could hear her sobs mingled with her words as she poured out her feelings to her silent companion.

The entire family felt sad at the loss of this happy-go-lucky young man they'd barely had time to know. They felt even worse when the rumors started to make the rounds that he had committed suicide. With the memory alive of his enthusiasm at meeting and starting to date Sharlyn and his final words to her about picking the record up the next night still ringing in her ear, no one could convince Janice that he'd wanted to die. Nor could they convince Sharlyn who had spent several of his final hours with him.

TIME FLIES

In January of nineteen sixty-five, Fred married his high school sweetheart, Judy Marquis. While Fred had returned to Newark many times to see his fiancée, the wedding marked Polly and Bill's first visit since they'd moved to Virginia The solemn ceremony was performed by Judy's brother, a Catholic priest. Then the reception afterwards was quite festive. After the newlyweds left with the wedding party honking their horns as they rode around the square, and the parking lot of Sandy's, the hamburger joint where Fred had worked his senior year in high school, the rest of the family returned to the house on Oakwood Avenue.

That night after everyone else had gone to bed, June and Polly sat in the living room and talked about the day's events. "I don't think I've ever missed your daddy so much as I did today," Polly said. "When they seated me in the parents of the groom aisle all alone, I almost cried. I couldn't help think how much Burrel would have loved seeing his son get married."

"I thought about him too. I could almost feel him in the church with us," June replied. "Dad never got to attend any of his children's weddings, but I'll never forget the wonderful wedding day we shared when Skip and I, as children, stood with you and Dad when you got married."

The two women talked into the wee hours of the morning. At one point Polly mentioned that she had gone out on some dates with a man she'd met through some friends. June was surprised at her own reaction. It was almost as if she had lost her father all over again. She didn't feel any better when Polly explained that it wasn't serious. "Just dinner and dancing," she said. June tried to smile and hide her true feelings as her stepmother continued to talk about it. These feelings were with her the next day when they waved good-bye to their visitors. The uneasiness stayed with her all day as she went about her routine.

That night after they'd gone to bed, she was so restless that she couldn't begin to fall asleep. Finally, Dick sat up in bed, flicked on the light, and said, "I don't know what is wrong with you, but we're neither one going to get any sleep unless you talk about it."

She told him about her conversation with Polly the night before and her unexpected reaction. After she finished, he took a few seconds to mull over what she'd said before he replied, "I know this is hard for you, but you have to realize that while you lost a father, she lost a husband. Even with the boys around, she's probably been lonely. After all, she is only forty-five years old. You have to face the fact that she's bound to date and probably will remarry one of these days."

June opened her mouth to speak, but her husband shushed her. "Fred got married yesterday and Bill is going into the navy soon. Then she'll be all alone. Don't you think it will be natural for her to want some companionship?"

"I know all that!" she replied. "I guess it's hard for me to think about her with someone besides Dad."

Dick pulled her into his arms and held her while she cried one more time for her father. "It's not fair that Dad didn't get to live out his life!" she cried.

Dick took a tissue and wiped her eyes, and said, "I agree, but I think your dad packed a couple lifetimes into the one he had."

By now, June's common sense was taking over. With her husband's arms around her, she realized what her life would be like if she lost him. "I was just thinking of my feelings. It will take time, but I know I will get used to her having a life of her own." She sighed deeply before she added, "I don't want her to spend the rest of her life alone."

June wouldn't have believed it that night, but in less than three years, she would be the one who would encourage Polly to marry a fishing boat captain she had met and fallen in love with in Florida.

∼

Meanwhile, that year of nineteen sixty-five, Janice, a student in junior high school, had a close group of friends who lived in the neighborhood, referring to themselves as The Gang. It included Janet and Marsha Ford, Diane Sunkle, Linnie Williams, Jackie Griffith, Charlene (Charlie) Brooks, Debbie and Bobby West, Ronnie Smith, Dennis Conley, Danny Hughes, Cliff Wise, Dave and Bill Arnold, Bob Pfeiffer and a few others. While they spent most of their free time together, they rode bikes, hung out at each other's houses (especially the basement of the house on Oakwood Avenue), and had boy and girl parties.

After one party, Bobby was so upset that Janice had slow danced with Dave more than she had with him that he played a telephone prank on her. It wouldn't have worked if Bobby and Debbie's family and Janice's hadn't been on the same party line. Until now, Janice had liked this arrangement since it meant she could call any of the girls, and Debbie could just pick up her phone and they'd have three-way-calling years before it became an official telephone feature.

That night Bobby had Bill call Janice and get her to talk about her feelings for Dave. He'd already invited Dave to his house so he could listen. Once Bill and Janice were on the phone, Bobby picked up his and handed it to Dave so he could secretly listen to the conversation.

"Don't you like me better than Dave?" Bill asked Janice.

Her response was, "I have brotherly love for you, and love for your brother."

Dave was so shy and embarrassed to hear this that he hung up and blurted out everything he'd heard to Bobby. Later Bobby teased Janice unmercifully, "You're so poetic, you should write poems."

Her wide blue eyes flashed as she retorted, "Maybe I will. Here's one for you. BOBBY WEST THINKS HE'S THE BEST. REALLY BOBBY IS PRETTY SLOBBY! Now what do you think of that poem?" Bobby's face turned red as she smiled smugly and with a toss of her head turned and left the room. "Got you back, didn't I?" she thought as she sauntered away.

This episode didn't prevent them from remaining friends and having good times together. In the back of his mind, Bobby always thought that someday she would become his wife. *In fact, a couple years later, he made plans for them to be married. His target date was June nineteen seventy-four, when Janice would graduate from college. He was partially right. Janice did graduate that year, and she would be married, but Bobby wasn't the one to become her husband.*

In the summer of nineteen sixty-six, a boy named Sonny Fisher joined their gang. His mother and Janice's had been friends as teenagers. Coincidentally, his family now lived in the house on Lawrence Street where June had lived during her teen years. In the bedroom where June had dreamed of her future husband, Sonny now dreamed of Janice.

One day, when June picked up the girls who were visiting at Sonny's house, his mother, Mary, took her for a tour of her old homestead. When they went into her former bedroom, she felt as though she had stepped into the past. She could almost envision the room as it had been. When she looked out the window at the house across the street, she almost expected to see her cousin, Rose, at the window. (Instead, Rose now lived across town and like June, she was the mother of three.) Standing in that familiar room, it didn't seem possible to June that so much time could have passed.

In weeks to come, Sonny was very persistent with all his gifts of candy and jewelry. He even carved Janice's initials in his arm. At first it turned a bright red. Then a dark scab formed before it became a white scar. He couldn't accept it when Janice went out with anyone else. When Dave wrote JANICE AND DAVE on the expressway wall, Sonny crossed out DAVE and wrote in SONNY. When she later discovered that he'd tried to pay Dave off not to date her, Janice told Sonny, "Cool it! No bribes allowed." Sonny was so persistent that she agreed to go to her ninth grade prom with him.

Sonny's younger brother, David Christopher, whom the kids had dubbed D.C., became a close friend of Ricky as did Sonny. Even when Janice wasn't dating him, Sonny would come to her house with D.C. and hang out with the rest of the family. He seemed to like Ricky and Janice's parents, and they liked him. He soon become one of Dick's favorite visitors because of the great backrubs he gave him. One night, he confided that he hated school and wanted to quit.

This earned him one of what June's father had always called a talking to. He seemed to listen as she talked to him about the importance of education, but he didn't tell her until after he'd graduated from high school that their little talk had kept him in school.

Years later when a tragic automobile accident took his life, June went to see his mother. The grieving woman took her upstairs and showed her the walk-in closets that June remembered so well. JANICE had been written all over the walls. "Janice meant so much to Sonny," Mary told June. "I'm never going to paint over it!"

~

While Dick Clark's American Bandstand Television Show was still popular with the young people, a television dance party hosted by Gene Fullen on a Columbus station soon gave it some competition locally. This was primarily because he sponsored a dance contest on the show. Since Ricky had inherited his Uncle Eddie's love to dance, he and a neighbor girl named Gay Orr decided to enter the contest. For weeks they practiced either at his house or Gay's.

Once they had sent in an application to enter the contest, Ricky waited anxiously for an answer. Every evening, when he got home from school before he'd take time to make his favorite after school snack, a four layer mayonnaise sandwich, he'd try to keep his voice casual when he'd ask if he'd gotten any mail. This scenario was repeated every day until the long envelope, with the television logo splashed across the top, finally arrived. He and Gay had been invited to appear on the show in a couple weeks.

When the big day arrived, Gay's mother took them to Columbus to the television station while June stayed home and watched it in her own living room with his and Janice's friends. While the contestants moved across the twelve-inch screen in time with the rock 'n' roll music, June thought that even though the competition was stiff, her son and his partner were the best. It never occurred to her that she might be prejudiced. While she waited for the winners to be announced, though, she planned what she would say to her son to help him get over his disappointment...just in case they lost.

She was so engrossed in what she planned to say to comfort him that she almost missed the announcement of the winners. "The winners are...," Mr. Fullen said. Then he looked at the faces of the expectant dancers, paused to build up the suspense before he boomed, "Ricky and Gay!" June didn't hear him when he announced the runners up and awarded the prizes because of the resounding cheers of Ricky and Janice's friends.

Even though, later that evening when he came home with his prize, a Beatles album, tucked under his arm, only the family remained at the house on Oakwood

Avenue, the celebration couldn't have been more festive if the entire neighborhood had been there.

~

Janice had lots of fun with her gang of neighborhood friends. One of their favorite activities was to have sleepovers at each others homes. They all missed Linnie Williams who had moved with her mother to a mobile home park at Wilkins Corners near Rocky Fork where Priscilla had been raised. One night Linnie invited all the girls in the gang to a slumber party at her home.

Since Linnie's mother was out on a date, they had the place to themselves. While they'd made pizza and munched on it, the girls were taking turns telling scary stories. Janice exclaimed, "I've got a good story for you, and it's true!" They were all a little spooked as Janice began to speak, "There was this couple parked on a secluded road. As they were kissing, the boy and girl heard a noise outside the car. The boy said, 'I heard about a man with a hook for a hand who has been attacking teenaged couples.'" Janice raised her voice when she continued, "The girl screamed, 'Let's get out of here!' So the boy floored the accelerator and sped from the scene. Later, when he arrived at his girlfriend's house, and got out to open the door for her, he found…," Janice hesitated for effect before she shrieked, "a hook hanging from the handle of the car door!"

As Debbie and Diane cried out, "Oh that's terrible!" Janet went into the kitchen to get a drink of water. As she let the water run to get colder, she looked up into the face of a strange man who was staring at her through the kitchen window. She let out a shriek, dropped the glass in the sink, ran into the bedroom, as she screamed, "There's a man looking in the window!"

"Oh, sure!" Janice announced. "You're just trying to scare us!" At that moment the man's face appeared in the bedroom window. Screaming, they all jumped onto the bed causing it to collapse under their weight. While the rest of the girls stayed a safe distance from the window, Janice and Janet rushed over and closed the draperies. Then while they huddled together in fright, scratching bumping noises started from under the trailer. Debbie, Diane, and Marsha were so scared that one of them wet her pants. (We won't mention names to avoid embarrassment). Equally frightened, Linnie, Janice, and Janet tried to calm them.

Once they'd settled down, Linnie, with all the other girls close behind, crept into the living room and called her mother. Mrs. Williams told her daughter that it would take awhile for her to get home. She instructed Linnie, in the meantime, to call the owner who lived in the mobile home park. When the frightened girl telephoned him, although she got him out of bed, he promised to be there in a few minutes. The minutes seemed like hours as the girls could still hear the noises from beneath their feet. When the owner arrived, he crawled under the trailer and drug out the young man who had terrorized the girls.

While they listened, the intruder kept repeating, "I'm so sorry. I just couldn't help himself." Then the owner gave him a stern look and made him apologize to the still terrified girls. Linnie's Mom came home while they were still standing outside, and she sent them back inside while she talked to the owner.

When she came in, she told the girls, "The man is a Peeping Tom who lives with his parents two trailers from us. According to the owner, he feels compelled to look into other people's windows. The couple who live in the trailer between us usually leave their curtains open and he watches them, but the accommodating neighbors were away tonight so he decided to spy on you girls."

After all the excitement, the girls settled down and enjoyed the rest of their slumber party. When they left for home the next morning, they all agreed that it had been a memorable night since they had actually lived through one of those scary stories.

～

Later that summer, a neighbor had welded two bicycles together, one on top of the other to make a double-decker and had given it to Ricky. When he dragged it home, it lacked a chain or tires, but Ricky and his dad thought it had possibilities. Once they'd come to that conclusion, they took it to the bicycle shop to see if the proprietor could make it usable. After the man studied it from every angle he pronounced, "I can do it, but you need to know that the seat will be almost six feet from the ground."

His statement hadn't changed Ricky's mind, but his father was having second thoughts. "It might not be safe," he told his son.

"I'll be careful," Ricky promised him.

"How will you get on it if it's that high?" Dick asked.

"I'll figure out a way," Ricky responded. The two conferred for a few minutes before Dick gave the man the go-ahead. A few days later, when Dick brought it home, Ricky quickly mastered it and became the envy of the boys in the neighborhood. The first few times he rode it, a crowd of boys and girls gathered around him, while he leaned the double-decker against the porch, stood on the top step, swung his leg over it and rode away. Then he pedaled around the neighborhood with his friends on their bikes close behind.

Once his mother was assured that he wouldn't be hurt, she appreciated the advantage of such a tall bicycle. No matter where he was on the street, she could see him. One afternoon while she and Ginny stood in their front yards talking over the hedges, they smiled in amusement when they saw Ricky on his double-decker pedaling toward them with one of his friends on a twenty inch bicycle beside him. "Reminds me of a Great Dane and a Chihuahua," Ginny commented. June laughed and nodded in agreement.

Ricky had been given orders not to allow anyone else to ride it, but occasionally a few of the neighborhood boys would take it upon themselves to "borrow" it. Most of the times it would be gone for a few days, then mysteriously reappear in the backyard of the house on Oakwood Avenue. The last time, though, when it had been missing for several days, everyone in the family except Dick thought that this time it must be gone for good.

After several days of seeing his unhappy son mope around the house, Dick decided to do something about it. Like Sherlock Holmes, he started a search of the neighborhood. As he walked down the alley, he peered into back yards, onto back porches, and through the windows of people's garages until he found it. There had been no doubt in June's mind that if it was anywhere in the neighborhood, her husband would come home with it. He was too persistent to give up until he did. When an hour later, he wheeled it into the back yard, all the reward he needed was the sight of his son's happy face and the big grin that spread from ear-to-ear as he ran toward his double-decker and found that it was all in one piece. "Where'd you find it?" he asked his father.

When Dick explained that he'd seen it through the window of the garage of one of the boys who lived down the street. Ricky said, "I wondered if it was him. Ever since you got it fixed up, he's been telling me that it's half his."

June had heard her son's excited voice and had come out in time to hear his comment. "Why would he say that?" she asked.

"The guy who gave it to me offered it to him first, but he didn't want it. He thought it was a piece of junk until Dad got it fixed for me. Then he told me that it was half his."

"I talked to his father when I found the bike," Dick explained. "He said that his son told him that Ricky loaned it to him. When I told him that Ricky thought it was stolen, he was pretty mad at his boy. I don't think I'd want to be in his shoes," Dick said before he and June went into the house, and Ricky took off down the street on his double-decker.

When June's brother, Dick, and his family came down the following Sunday, June and Dick made an exception to their rule, and allowed Ricky to let his younger cousin, David, try to ride it. When Ricky sat the younger boy on the high seat, Bev watched anxiously. She didn't have to worry for long since once little David looked down at the ground so far below him, he quickly decided that he didn't want anything to do with it. Although Ricky tried to assure him that he wouldn't let him fall, no amount of coaxing could make him change his mind. Their rule about no riders hadn't been broken after all.

BATTLE OF WILLS

Sharlyn, Janice, and Ricky had always kept June on her toes, but she'd hoped that since the girls were now teenagers and Ricky was fast approaching his teens, she would be able to relax. As she was to discover, she had just exchanged one set of challenges for another. Her teenagers and near teen certainly kept her life from being boring. Sometimes, though, she would have settled for a little boredom.

One of those times was when she and Sharlyn became locked in a battle of wills. Every morning, as June tried to make her get up in time to catch the city bus to school, Sharlyn resisted. The harder June tried to make her get out of bed, the more her daughter would burrow under the covers and plead for a few minutes more. Although no one else in the family had to get up that early, none could sleep once the daily battle began.

One morning after this had gone on for weeks, Dick decided he'd had enough. So when June started to jump up for the sixth time to go into Sharlyn's room to try to rouse her, he held his wife in bed. When she struggled, and argued that if she didn't get their daughter out of bed she'd miss her bus, her words didn't faze him. Instead he calmly replied, "Let her."

June's frantic explanation that if Sharlyn missed the bus, she'd be tardy still didn't convince him. He'd already decided that he wasn't going to put up with the same ruckus every morning, and as his wife knew, once he made up his mind, it would almost take an act-of-God to change it. She finally accepted that he was right when he declared, "She's never going to take responsibility for getting herself out of bed as long as she knows you won't let her be late. If she's tardy and has to go to the principal's office, she'll learn to get up by herself. She's a pretty smart girl, so I think once will be enough!"

Sharlyn was angry when she finally got up and discovered that she'd missed the bus. She was even more upset a short time later when she left the principal's office with a fistful of tardy slips she had to take to the teacher of each of the classes she'd missed. As it turned out, her father's prediction had been right. Once was enough! From then on Sharlyn got out of bed without prompting from her mother. (*In the future, Sharlyn would get a taste of her own medicine when two of her four offspring would refuse to get up in the morning.*)

Dick and June barely had time to congratulate themselves on how well that problem had been resolved before they were barraged with something potentially more serious.

∼

It happened a few days after the Christmas of Sharlyn's senior year in high school. Dick and June had been savoring a quiet evening at home, while Janice and Ricky were at a youth meeting at the Methodist Church when Sharlyn and a boy they'd never met returned from a date. June noticed an air of suppressed excitement from the young couple when they joined them in the living room. At first, Sharlyn and her date exchanged anxious glances as they sat side-by-side on the couch while the young man clutched Sharlyn's hand as if he fully expected her to leave him alone with these strangers.

Seconds later, all interest in the Dean Martin television show they had been watching flew out the window when Sharlyn dropped her bombshell on her unsuspecting parents. Their first reaction was disbelief, and for seconds they were too shocked to respond. Not to be put off, though, Sharlyn repeated, "We want to get married."

Although she was shocked, upset, and violently opposed to the idea, when she looked into the happy faces of this young couple, she knew she had to be careful with her response. If she were too quick to condemn, she would make them even more determined to get married. What she wanted was for them to wait and get to know each other better before they rushed into anything as serious as marriage.

While she struggled for the right words, Dick jumped in with both feet and announced that he thought they were too young to even think about getting married. Sharlyn's small determined chin shot out before she cried out, "I'm seventeen! I'm older than Mom was when she married you!"

June was afraid her husband had used the wrong tactics with this determined young woman when he made the anticipated reply, "That was different!"

As could be expected, Sharlyn demanded to know just how that had been different. Undaunted, Dick had the perfect answer. "You're right. Your mother was younger, but she'd been on her own for awhile when we got married. Also, I had finished my schooling, had a good job and money in the bank." He hesitated dramatically before he went on. "Now, if you can tell me that your young man can say the same thing, then you and your mother can start to plan your wedding tonight."

Sharlyn and her boyfriend, Skeet, exchanged uncomfortable glances before they admitted that they couldn't meet any of her father's requirements. While Skeet was no longer in school, he didn't have a job, but he assured Dick that he'd go out the very next day and find one. "That's a start, but before I will give my permission, you also have to have money in the bank," Dick responded.

They were noticeably disappointed, but they reluctantly agreed. If they'd thought they could get by with a hundred dollars in the bank, Dick quickly dashed their hopes when he continued, "I had four thousand dollars saved when your mother and I got married, but I won't ask you to have that much." Their smiles of relief quickly vanished at his next words, "Two thousand will do."

Although they agreed to abide by his terms, it was obvious that some of the happiness had left their faces by the time Sharlyn walked Skeet to the door. As her mother's eyes followed the attractive young couple, she wondered if her daughter might be infatuated with the way this young man looked. Decidedly handsome, he was tall, tanned, blond, blue-eyed, with broad shoulders, and slim hips. Shirtless, he wore a light blue cardigan, his Christmas gift from Sharlyn, unbuttoned almost to his waist. June had always told her children that there were two important decisions they would have to make that would determine their happiness. One was whom they married, the other was what they did for a living. She was afraid her daughter hadn't known this boy long enough to be sure she'd made the right decision on the first one and if she got married now, the second one would probably fall by the wayside.

Since her own marriage was good, she'd always wanted the same for each of her children. She also knew that she'd been one of the lucky ones. Of the five girls in her graduating class who'd gotten married when she had, only three were still together, and two had divorced in the first year. With this in mind, in days to come, she found herself trying to talk her daughter into waiting a few years before she took such a big step and to give herself time to grow up. After listening to this for a couple weeks, Sharlyn blurted out that the sister of a friend of hers had gotten pregnant when her parents had refused to let her get married. "They had to let her then!" she cried.

This was too much for her worried mother to let pass. "That sure was smart!" she snapped. "Just think how much fun it would be to spend your wedding night with your head over the toilet! I can't think of anything more romantic than while your bridegroom looks on, you vomit up your guts! I would certainly hope you have more sense than that!"

"I didn't mean that I'd do it!" Sharlyn hastily explained. "I wouldn't get married until I had your permission."

June laughed and reminded her daughter, "I wouldn't have liked to do it, but if you'd kept up that kind of talk, I'd have been forced to give you one of my Dad's talking tos."

Sharlyn grinned and replied, "Anything but that!" Then in a more serious vein she added, "You probably don't believe this, but I wouldn't do anything to let you and Dad down."

June was relieved, but deep in her heart, she was afraid of what the future might hold for her headstrong daughter. Later that evening as she put away the last of the Christmas decorations, Dick sat on the couch and supervised. As she unwrapped the last strand of tinsel from around the tree, she said, "Doesn't it seem to you that Sharlyn's rushing too fast toward tomorrow?"

"Toward tomorrow? I have enough trouble taking care of today. I don't want to even think about tomorrow," he replied. As he'd told her many times, he again said, "I feel that I only have one time, and it's now. Yesterday's gone, and tomorrow never comes." This kind of talk always upset her since she liked to dream, to plan, and to talk about the future. She'd always known exactly what she wanted tomorrow to hold for her children; a college education, good jobs, good marriages, and happiness. For herself, she dreamed that someday she'd own a spacious ranch style house in an area off Granville Road in the west-end of town. She knew a secret about her husband that he didn't realize she knew. Although he didn't want to talk about it, the reason he worked two jobs was to save money to ensure that their children could have all the things she wanted for them. However, since there was a conflict between what his mother had always told him (not to plan for the future because you might be disappointed) and his wife's beliefs, he never uttered a word, but quietly went about preparing for the tomorrow that he'd told his wife would never come.

As it turned out, she needn't have worried about her daughter's tomorrows with Skeet. Sharlyn's own teenaged inclination to be free and have a good time soon helped her get over any thought of tying herself down to one person. There was never a dramatic announcement that she'd changed her mind, but as other young men came to call, it soon became evident to her parents that they could now put that worry behind them. Sometimes in that second between wakefulness and sleep, June wondered if just maybe, Dick's tactics or some of her words of wisdom had gotten through to their daughter. Whether it had or hadn't was one of those questions that would always remain unanswered.

∼

Sharlyn lacked three months of being eighteen when she graduated from high school. A few nights before graduation, she learned a valuable lesson she might not have learned if she'd been on time for a friend's party. At that time in her school, the drug of choice was alcohol, and like many of her friends, she'd tried it but it made her throw up. In spite of this, she had planned to have a few drinks at her friend's pre-graduation party.

That night, the party was in full swing when she and Bev arrived. As she looked around, she realized that everyone there was intoxicated. Obviously, they all thought they were adult and cool, but as she later confided to her mother, in her sober state she saw them as they really looked...stupid and immature. She had already observed the unhappiness and poverty level in the home of one relative and several of her friends with drinking fathers. This, combined with her friends' behavior tonight, had made a strong impression on her.

Over the years, she'd found that these homes with the shouting adults were so different from her own. With this in mind, she decided that night that alcohol wasn't for her. To her friends' surprise, throughout the party she stayed away from the spiked punch and no amount of coaxing would make her change her mind.

After graduation, her parents encouraged her to go to college, but she wanted to strike out on her own. The year before, she had switched from a college preparatory course to a business one and had done very well. Now she was ready to put those skills to use to make herself independent. Although this wasn't what they wanted for their oldest daughter, they could see, determined as she was, they had no choice except to let her go. As she helped her find a job, June consoled herself with the thought that once Sharlyn had a taste of the business world, she would decide to continue her education. For days she and Sharlyn scoured the want ads in the Columbus Dispatch for a job. Despite stiff competition from more mature applicants, she got the job at the Byer and Bowman Advertising Agency in Columbus. After checking several places, June decided to rent a room for Sharlyn at the Columbus YWCA.

They decided to wait until Sunday to move so Sharlyn could spend Saturday evening with her friends in Newark. As Ricky and Dick stowed her suitcases in the car, and Sharlyn talked on the phone to her friend Bev, June felt a twinge of sadness at the thought that her first child would no longer live in the house on Oakwood. She knew that while Sharlyn was in a hurry to grow up, she still saw her as a little girl.

She had been so deep in thought that she hadn't realized the bags were all in the trunk, Sharlyn was off the phone, and they were waiting for her to join them in the car. When she heard Dick say, "Time to go," her mind was saying, "Time to let go." As she slid into the front seat next to her husband, she thought, "I've always known that the only way to hold onto your children is to let them go. I'll try to remember that."

As they drove away, Sharlyn didn't look back. Her thoughts were on tomorrow while her mother's were still on yesterday. As if reading her mind, Dick reminded her, that Columbus was less than forty miles away. "It's not as if, she's going to New York or someplace else that far. We'll probably see more of her now than before." As it turned out, he was right. Once she was on her own, her parents became as important in her life as they'd been in her pre-teen years.

Once they arrived at the YMCA and got Sharlyn's belongings unpacked and put away, Sharlyn had a rude awakening. She discovered that toilet paper doesn't automatically grow on the roll, nor does soap in the dish. Since she'd so emphatically declared her independence, her mother had left it up to her to pack for her new home. Since those two items were missing, the foursome had to drive around downtown Columbus in search of a store. They finally found a small neighborhood grocery where they were able to buy the necessary items. With the brown paper bag in hand, Sharlyn said goodnight to her family at the door of her new home, and turned and walked toward the stairs and her new life as an independent woman.

While Dick, June, and Ricky had been part of the move, it was different for Janice who returned home from camp after her sister was gone. It felt strange when she walked into the bedroom she'd always shared with her sister to find half of the closet empty and to know that Sharlyn would no longer sleep in the other twin bed. To her surprise, she'd already begun to miss her. Although she'd always wanted a bedroom of her own, now that she had it, it felt too empty and lonely.

Sharlyn continued to surprise them when within a couple months, she took over her supervisor's job. As the new Traffic Coordinator, she was a liaison between the agency and Lazarus Department Stores, their largest account. When Sharlyn told her parents that the head of the department had been impressed with her performance, and by her habit of always arriving early for work, Dick couldn't resist a little teasing. "Now aren't you glad I made you learn to get up on your own?" Her response had been a big grin.

As it turned out, twenty years in the future, Sharlyn would meet and exceed her mother's hopes and dreams for her daughter when she received her first college degree. Proudly, the family would sit in the audience and watch Sharlyn, as valedictorian, deliver the commencement address.

THE MUSIC GOES ON

After a three-year tour of duty in Japan, Skip and his family were finally back in the states, stationed at Quonset Point, Rhode Island. Skip had written that they'd purchased their first home and that he'd like all of his family to come for a visit. June and Dick had immediately taken him up on the invitation. As Sharlyn had barely started her new job, she wasn't able to go with them.

With a vacant place in the back seat, and knowing how anxious Priscilla was to see her son and his family after so many years, Dick and June invited her to go with them. Since most of Priscilla's traveling had been between the pages of books, the trip was a dream come true for her. "I've always wanted to see this part of the country," she commented several times as they drove through New York State and into the New England states. Both days of the drive, Ricky and Janice were caught up in their grandmother's enthusiasm, equally thrilled with her presence and the prospect of again seeing their cousins.

When they arrived at the brick ranch house near Quonset Point, they were met at the door by a very trim JoAnne. When they commented on how fit she and the boys looked, she led them to the back yard where she pointed out a fieldstone patio, flower borders, and fence. While they expressed their admiration, she explained that she and the boys, with help from Skip when he was off duty, had transplanted all the stones from various parts of the yard. "We call the place Harman Achers," she said. She went on to explain that the name had nothing to do with the size of the lot. "Just all the sore muscles and aches and pains we've suffered in order to get our yard to look so nice."

That evening, after an enthusiastic reunion with Skip, he told them he'd taken a few days off work so he could show them around the area. Then when he spread out a fistful of brochures on the table, he asked, "What do you want to see?"

Priscilla said, "I want to see everything!" For the next few days, her oldest son made every effort to see that they did.

Like hundreds of tourists before them, they posed in front of The Plymouth Plantation, The Mayflower, and Plymouth Rock. Ricky and Chris had a great time playing sailor as they manned the big guns on the battleship, the USS Massachusetts. Of all the places they visited, though, Priscilla and June's favorite was the Coast Guard Station with its lighthouse that sat atop a craggy cliff. To the mother and daughter, it was soul satisfying to sit on the rocks and watch the white waves as they churned and splashed against the rocky shore below.

During the visit, Janice was surprised by the attentions of her cousin, Mike, who seemed to have developed a crush on her. Since they hadn't seen each other for three years, and only a few times before that, she didn't seem to him so much like a cousin as the new girl on the block. As they went from site to site, Mike would call out, "Janice, wait up!" Then he would catch up to her and put his arm around her as they walked. Being at the age where girls are taller than boys, Mike was a head shorter.

One evening after one of their sight-seeing trips, Janice confided in her mother, "Mom, it's so embarrassing!"

Then that night, Janice was mortified when Mike sat beside her on the bench, put his arm around her, and asked their grandmother Priscilla, "Can cousins get married?" Although Gram thought her grandson's crush was amusing, Skip didn't see the humor in it. Although he reminded Mike several times that they were related, it didn't seem to change anything during the visit.

Mike continued to court Janice, even walking her to the car and opening the door for her as the family left for Ohio. Ricky teased Janice as they drove away, "Mike wants to be kissing cousins with you!"

Janice punched his arm, "If you want to talk about kissing, let's talk about you and Debbie West. I heard you gave Debbie her first kiss last week." As Ricky smiled broadly, Janice turned to Priscilla and asked, "Gram what should I do about Mike?"

Priscilla answered, "Oh, he's just going through a phase. He'll meet other girls and soon just look at you as a pal again." *Her words came true when his father retired the following year and they moved to Mansfield. Mike again looked at Janice as a cousin, and they became good friends.*

When the travelers left Harman Achers, they spent a day and night sightseeing at Niagara Falls. Although June and Dick had been there before, this was the first time for Janice, Ricky, and Priscilla. June realized as she watched them enjoy all the sights that her mother's presence had helped her get through this first vacation without her oldest daughter being along.

As it happened, those were to be the last truly happy days her mother would have for a long time. Within a few days after their return, she'd received news of something that would hang heavily over her head for years to come. What Priscilla had feared since she was a young woman of nineteen had happened. Someone close to her had been diagnosed with "the big C." Bill had bladder cancer. The urologist offered a glimmer of hope when he had assured them that this was one kind of cancer that could be controlled if closely monitored. When Priscilla told her daughter about Bill's illness, June put a comforting arm around her mother and said, "Bill has the best doctors in town. Believe them when they tell you it's controllable. Medicine has come a long way in the last thirty-five years when your mother had it." Priscilla appeared to believe her, but as it turned out, Bill handled the problem much better than his wife. While there would continue to be some good days along with the bad, nothing would ever be quite the same for Priscilla.

As the days passed and they continued their journey toward tomorrow, Sharlyn wasn't the only one of their daughters who had become a beautiful teenager. Janice's blond ponytail had been replaced by a fashionable flip. With her vivid blue eyes, and light complexion, Janice had always been pretty, but now as she approached womanhood, she had become truly lovely. From her earliest years, she had been a warm friendly girl with many friends.

During the late nineteen sixties, schools were generally safe havens. While most of the boys and girls at Newark High School were well behaved, the school contained a small element of rough students. Unfortunately, Janice was to become one of their targets.

When Ronnie, one of her neighborhood group of friends, became her boyfriend, neither suspected the problems this would cause her. One weekend when Ronnie came to see her, Janice helped him change the headlight on his car out in front of her house on Oakwood Avenue. Later that night, as they cruised down East Main Street, the beam of the headlight shone up in the air, lighting the second floor of all the buildings. As they laughed at their lack of mechanical ability, Ronnie pointed to one of the houses and told Janice that a tough acting girl named Ava lived there and had been calling him. He assured Janice that he wasn't interested in anyone except her.

Later that week, Libby, one of Ava's rowdy friends, cornered Janice by the sink in the school restroom and told her to stay away from Ronnie. When Janice told her that she and Ronnie had been friends for a long time, Libby attacked her, pulling her hair and shouting obscenities. Never having been in a fight before, Janice defended herself as best she could. Later that day, she became alarmed when her hair continued to fall out. She went to the school nurse who assured her that was normal after all the hair-pulling, and that fortunately she had plenty of hair to spare.

Since Newark High School was spread out in a college campus style, when the students changed classes they had to walk from building to building. The day after the attack on Janice, the rumor was all over school that Ava and her friend were going to beat up on her when they caught her between the buildings. Janice had heard the rumor, and couldn't believe the nightmare of being hassled by such tough girls.

Then before she could get to her next class, Ava and her friend jumped in front of her, and started yelling for Janice to leave Ronnie alone. Anticipating a fight, a crowd had gathered in the area. Before either girl had a chance to strike Janice, though, Ronnie rushed up behind them, ran to Janice's side, put a protective arm around her, and said, "You leave Janice alone. She's my girl!" That said, he turned and walked her away, leaving Ava and her friend with their mouths open, as the crowd cheered.

As Ronnie escorted her to her next class, Janice told him, "I've never been so glad to see you! Thanks for coming to my rescue."

"I felt like we were in a movie," Ronnie replied. Then with a grin, he added, "At least this time the good guys won!" Needless to say, the threats stopped and life returned to a more normal pace.

~

The year before Ricky had experienced a growth spurt. When he'd gone into the seventh grade he'd looked like a little boy. By the time the year was half over he looked like a teen-ager. "Three of them, at once," Dick teased. "Do you think you can survive it?"

"So far, Janice seems to have escaped the turmoil. As far as I can tell, she still likes me," June quipped. "Things are looking up! Now that Sharlyn is a working woman, she doesn't seem like a teen-ager." She held up her crossed fingers before she added, "This is for Ricky. We can only hope."

For now, he and Janice were active in the youth group at church and most of Ricky's activities took place either there or at school. His and Janice's friends still spent a great deal of time at the house on Oakwood Avenue. One day when June and some of the other mothers were putting on a party for their sons' class at school, one of the other mothers came up to her and inquired, "What was going on at your house the other day?" Puzzled, June asked what she meant. "I drove by and there must have been fifteen kids in your front yard. I just took it for granted that something was wrong," the woman replied.

June grinned and told her that was just a normal day at the house on Oakwood Avenue. "That was just some of Ricky and Janice's friends," she explained to the astonished woman. "They were probably ready to go down in the basement to listen to some music."

Then one Sunday afternoon, Ricky, his friends Steve Ford, and Rodney Guisinger were in the basement playing rock 'n' roll music on the stereo while June and Dick were in the living room directly above them. The music was so loud, they could feel it pound against their chests. The vibration massaged their feet as it came through the floorboards, bounced around inside the registers, and reverberated through the very walls. While the music itself was something they liked, it was so loud that it was actually painful to their ears. After the third time Dick tried to say something to his wife only to be greeted by, "What did you say?" he pounded on the floor for Ricky to turn it down.

It appeared that he did, but when that record ended and they put on a different one, Ricky played his dad's maracas to the beat of the music, and the noise level was more than Dick wanted to put up with. "They only have one volume, and it's loud!" Dick shouted. "I can't stand much more of this. Let's go see Ed and Marilyn." Since June felt that her pounding headache might subside if she got away, she readily agreed. If escape from the music was their goal, they would have been smart to turn around and leave before they crossed their friends' threshold, but by the time Ed opened the door, and invited them in, it was too late. They immediately realized they'd gone from the frying pan into the fire. If they'd thought Ricky's records were loud, it had been as soft as chamber music in comparison with the sound that came from Ed and Marilyn's basement.

While Dick looked around for the nearest exit, Ed shouted, "Bob and Bill are practicing with their new group. Come on downstairs and listen." Being a musician, Dick couldn't turn down the offer, so he and Ed traipsed downstairs. A few minutes later, June and Marilyn noticed an increase in the volume. By now, June's head throbbed worse with every beat of the drums. Looking around for an escape, she noticed a new flower garden toward the back of the lawn. Marilyn was surprised when June sprang from her chair and expressed a sudden interest in her landscaping, but gladly took her for a tour of the grounds. June managed to prolong it by expressing interest in every tree, shrub, and blade of grass until she heard her husband shout that they needed to leave. "Remember, we promised Ricky we'd be home by four," he announced.

When they made their escape, June murmured, "I think Ricky would have been surprised to know that you were so anxious to get home to his music."

Dick grinned and said, "After being in the basement with all those electronic instruments, I'll never complain about his stereo again!" Then he asked if she'd noticed when the volume got louder. She replied it would have been impossible not to. "When we got downstairs, they were concerned because one of the guitars was being drowned out by the others. When I suggested they adjust the speakers so he could be heard, I meant to turn them down. Instead, they turned his up," he explained. "At some point the decibel level has been so high that it has actually cracked the plaster on the basement walls and ceiling!"

When that evening at the dinner table, they told Ricky and Janice what had happened, Ricky grinned like the Cheshire cat when he saw his dad put his hand to his head and mutter, "Unbelievable! Let me tell you, I discovered this afternoon that there's no place like home...your records and all!"

⁓

As the months turned into years, Dick and June's brothers were on the move. While Skip and JoAnne had moved back to Mansfield and built a spacious A-Frame house only a few miles from Dick and Bev's new home on Woodcrest Avenue, Kenny and Yoko had returned to the states. They were now living in Austin, Texas.

For the first time since Skip left his father's home on Lawrence Street to spend twenty-two years in the navy, he lived close enough to spend time with the family. Dick, June, and the family attended many picnics and cookouts at the country-like setting of his and JoAnne's new home. At one of their get-togethers, June made an announcement, "We're going to San Antonio, Texas to visit Kenny and Yoko and go to the Hemisfair. We'd love to have you go with us." They readily accepted the invitation and within a couple weeks, in a two car caravan the brother and sister with their spouses and children in tow traveled together for the first time in over twenty years.

After the Hemisfair, their hosts took them to see The Alamo. While inside the fort, Ricky and Janice's vivid imaginations transported them back to eighteen thirty-six when heroes, Davie Crockett and Jim Bowie had fought. They could almost hear the noise of battle as the one hundred eighty-two brave men heroically fought and died for Texas's independence from Mexico. The slogan, "Remember The Alamo," took on new meaning to them as they stood inside this memorial to fallen heroes and realized that these brave men had held off thousands of attacking Mexicans for twelve days.

Before they left for home, since Kenny and Yoko knew June had lived around caverns during her early years, they took them to see one...Texas-style. When they began to walk through the stone passage, they were immediately aware that it was completely devoid of formations. When June asked about it, the guide announced that this was part of a fault caused centuries ago by an underground tremor. Then halfway through their tour, he turned off all the lights to demonstrate the total darkness. To his surprise and that of his audience, a disembodied pair of lips seemed to be suspended in midair. While they moved and smiled, Kenny's daughter, Anita, giggled when she recognized them, "That's Mommy's lips!" To Yoko's surprise, her lipstick actually glowed in the dark! As it turned out, next to the Alamo, the glittering lips were remembered more vividly than anything else they saw during their Texas trip.

ROMANCE IN THE AIR

After a few months living at the YWCA, Sharlyn had moved into an apartment with a couple girls she'd met there. While living at the Y, she'd been able to walk to work, but now that she was miles from the office, she had to ride the bus. It didn't take long for her to decide she wanted a car. Once her friends and her parents taught her to drive, her father shopped around until he found a small four-cylinder Pontiac Tempest. She honored her promise to pay him back if he'd buy it for her. In fact, she repaid it even sooner than he'd expected.

Now that she had her own car, the next step was to get her driver's license. The first time she took the test she failed. "Mom, it was terrible!" she wailed. "When I tried to maneuver into that awful little parking place, the steering wheel just froze up." The second try a few days later, she and the car performed perfectly and with new license in hand, she set off for her first solo drive to Columbus. Although the car was small, Sharlyn looked so tiny behind the wheel that her watching mother wanted to shout after her that she was still a child, that she was again rushing much too quickly toward tomorrow.

When she confided her thought to her husband, he reminded her of how responsible this girl had become. She could only agree, but she couldn't resist teasing, "Maybe I should remove my curse that she have a half a dozen just like she was in high school."

Since their oldest daughter had left home, her mother had learned to adjust to the facts that she was not yet ready to continue her education, that she lived away from home, and drove her own car around the city. None of these quite prepared her, though, for her daughter's next announcement.

∿

Janice's sixteenth birthday was fast approaching, and her mother wanted to make it special. She had given her a choice between a party with her friends or dinner with her parents, brother, and sister at a Polynesian Restaurant called the Kaheki in Columbus. To her parents' surprise, she had chosen the restaurant.

It was not only famous for its good food, but also for its tropical decor. With this in mind, the foursome had left the house on Oakwood Avenue in plenty of time to be able to explore the simulated Polynesian surroundings, and to take pictures in front of the indoor waterfalls and the statues of the Tiki gods that appeared to guard the entrance. As they walked to their table, they were mesmerized by all the beautiful tropical fish that swam through the walls in built-in aquariums. When they were finally seated at a table inside what looked like a native hut, Sharlyn rushed in to join them. For the next hour the family divided their attention between the food and the birthday girl. As they lifted their fruit laden drinks in a toast for this special occasion, Ricky teased, "Sweet sixteen, and never been kissed." Dick and Sharlyn joined in the teasing, but though June laughed along with them, Ricky's comment had reminded her that her younger daughter was also growing up.

Sharlyn waited until dinner was over, the toasts had been made, the presents opened, and her parents had taken the last sip of their after dinner coffee, before she dropped her bombshell. "I think I've met the man I'm going to marry," she announced.

While Ricky and Janice wanted to hear all about him, June was too surprised at first to respond. She knew that her daughter had dated, but hadn't been aware there was anyone special in her life. Ricky and Janice had plenty to say, though, when they learned the man's name was Charlie Brown. "Does he have a dog named Snoopy?" Ricky teased.

"If you marry Charlie Brown, do you have to change your name to Lucy?" Janice asked.

"I've read about him in the funny papers," Dick added.

While they teased, her firstborn's expression told her mother that this was no joking matter. She had made up her mind. Without another word being spoken, Sharlyn's determined brown eyes, made June realize that all her efforts to slow the approach of tomorrow, or Dick's beliefs that tomorrow never comes, had just gone out the window.

~

Shortly after the March birthday party, Sharlyn informed her parents that she and Charlie wanted to be married in June. All June and Dick's protests that it was too soon fell on deaf ears. The more she and Dick tried to talk Sharlyn into having a longer engagement, the more determined she and Charlie were to be married in June. Once June realized that the young couple really loved each other, she wholeheartedly threw herself into the wedding preparations. As she thought about her own wedding and the unpleasant reception that greeted them upon their return, she remembered the promise she'd made that long-ago night to provide wonderful weddings for all her children. With that in mind she set about making this a wedding Sharlyn would always remember. Unfortunately, she only had six weeks to accomplish this.

With the help of every friend she knew who had planned a wedding, she managed to pull it off. First she and Sharlyn found a white lace, hoop-skirted wedding gown reminiscent of the days of Scarlet O'Hara in Gone With The Wind. Then while Sharlyn worked, June set about looking for gowns for the two attendants. She almost panicked when clerks in one store after another informed her that they were out of formal gowns because of the high school proms. Finally, when she was ready to admit defeat, she found a pink lace gown for Janice, the maid-of-honor, and a matching blue one for bridesmaid, Cathy Rhodes.

Once this hurdle was surmounted, everything seemed to fall into place. The flowers were ordered, the bridal portraits taken, and the sanctuary decorated. All the rosebushes that belonged to any of the churchwomen had been stripped of their blooms to decorate the small white-clothed tables in the church social rooms where the reception was to be held. Then on June sixteenth nineteen-hundred sixty-eight, from her vantage point in the first row, June watched Cathy and Janice each make their way down the aisle, and a frightened looking Charlie and his best-man, his brother-in-law, George Burton, and usher, Ricky, take their place at the front of the church. (Charlie confided later that he hadn't expected so many people). Then seconds later when the organist began to play "The Wedding March," June stood and turned with the rest of the congregation and watched Dick escort the bride down the aisle. June suppressed a smile when she realized the width of Sharlyn's skirt barely left room for him to walk beside her.

Sharlyn turned and smiled at her father when he answered, "Her mother and I," to the minister, Keith Herreman's, question as to who gives this woman. Then she turned her attention to her bridegroom. She realized just how nervous Charlie was, when she saw his jacket visibly shaking. At first he was so shook up, that he began repeating his vows while looking straight ahead at the minister. As Sharlyn began to repeat her vows, Charlie finally turned toward his bride. She tilted her head to look up at him and the love in her eyes was reflected in his.

During the reception, before Sharlyn and Charlie left for their honeymoon at Niagara Falls, Priscilla held the beautiful keepsake napkin engraved with the newlyweds' names and wedding date and reflected, "Your dad and I got married on this same date, June sixteenth, forty-one years ago."

Romance was in the air and another wedding took place later that summer, but June and her family didn't hear about it until after the elopement. As her sister-in-law Linda was to tell her later, she had just moved to Virginia, a few miles outside of Washington D.C. Along with two other girls, Sandy and Jodi, she had rented a room in the home of a middle-aged woman named Pauline while she and her young housemates worked as hairdressers at The Hecht Department Store in Arlington.

Then one fateful night, Sandi had gone home at the regular time but Jodi and Linda had to work late. A few minutes before they were scheduled to leave,

Sandi called and told them not to get a taxi as a young male friend of the landlady was coming to pick them up. Jodi was excited but Linda didn't like the idea of getting into the car with a stranger although her landlady did know the man's mother. Then when he stopped in front of the store, Sandi was already in the front seat with the good-looking blue-eyed dark haired sailor she introduced as Bill. When Jodi hopped in beside her, Linda got in the back. While the other girls flirted with him, and he bragged about how fast his souped up fire engine red 1964 Ford Falcon would go, all she wanted to do was get home safe and sound. Much to her relief, this happened a few minutes later.

As she told June later, "When we got home, he asked if we wanted to go for a joy ride. Jodi and Sandi, sitting in the front couldn't get out fast enough to change their clothes and go with him. Me, of course, sitting in the back jumped out, said, 'NO,' and slammed the door. I guess he liked rude girls. When I got inside I was properly introduced to Polly, the young man's redheaded mother."

Right from the start, the brash young man, who was in the navy stationed at Newport News, Virginia aboard the USS Wright, was interested in the peppy little Italian girl who'd stayed in the back seat and had more-or-less ignored him. He soon began to burn up the miles between his ship and her home. As she later laughingly told the family, "He had a heavy foot and the car could really go, and he had the speeding tickets to prove it."

Before too long, with her landlady's daughter and son-in-law as witnesses, they eloped to North Carolina. After a brief ceremony, instead of the elaborate reception she knew her mother would have had if they'd had a church wedding, the foursome celebrated the marriage over sandwiches at Hardy's. Now the difficult time came as Linda had to break the news to her family that she had married a man who not only wasn't Italian but wasn't even a Catholic. She put off this dreaded task as long as possible but when she became pregnant, she knew she couldn't put it off any longer.

Bill, who kept pushing her to call them, finally said, "If you don't tell them soon, the three of us will be showing up at their doorstep one of these days. I don't think they'll take too well to that, do you?" She had to admit he was right and made the call. As she'd suspected, her news wasn't well received.

Then to make it worse, the setting for the first meeting between Bill and her father and brother took place in jail. She'd had to call her father to drive the three hours from his home to a West Virginia jail to pick them up. She and Bill weren't inmates, but the victim of an automobile accident on a rain slicked road in the fog encased mountains of West Virginia. Fortunately, they weren't hurt, but their car was completely totaled.

Her father's reception of Bill was polite but decidedly cool, but when they arrived at Linda's childhood home, both of her grandmothers took him to heart immediately. Her mother reserved judgment until she knew him better. Their next trip, however, was different and Bill was wholeheartedly accepted, and he and her father soon became close bowling and hunting buddies. Linda Piconi

Harman knew that her husband had been accepted into this wild, crazy, Italian, Catholic family when her father made him an honorary Italian by bestowing the Italian name of Bill Harmondo on him.

~

Shortly after Sharlyn and Charlie returned from their honeymoon at Niagara Falls, Janice had one of her first dates with someone outside her circle of neighborhood friends. Diane and her boyfriend, Al, had arranged a double date for her with Gary, a boy from the neighboring town of Heath. Since she and Diane and their other girlfriends were going to spend the night at the house of their friends, Janet and Marsha Ford, the girls were hanging out on the Ford's front porch waiting for Janice and Diane to return. While Diane and Al were saying goodnight in the car, Gary walked Janice to the porch where they had their first kiss. While Janice's friends looked on, he jumped off the side of the porch and shouted, "I think I've died and gone to heaven!" Then he ran down the sloped yard, jumped into Al's car, and they sped away.

The girls all laughed at his dramatic display. Diane joked, "You sure made an impression on him!" They all teased Janice unmercifully for the rest of the evening and for weeks to come.

That summer, Janice and her friends left for a four-week stint as Counselors-In-Training at Girl Scout Camp Wakatomika. Gary had gotten a car while Janice was away, but since he only had his learner's permit, he had to have a licensed driver with him. If he'd known what this would lead to, he might have selected someone else to come with him. As it happened, he brought along a friend from Heath who worked with him at McDonalds. As Janice sat in the front between Gary and his seventeen-year old friend, Mike Large, Mike said something to her that she didn't quite catch. "Excuse me?" she asked.

As he repeated, "Wie geht es ihnen?" she realized he'd spoken in German, and laughed. He then translated for her, "How are you?"

Mike told her that he'd been born in Germany to a German woman and an American serviceman. He had lived back and forth between the United States and Germany all his life. Now his family was living in Heath because his father had retired from the army and was working at the Newark Air Force Base. The three of them had fun that evening riding around in Gary's car. As she looked out of the corner of her eye at Mike, she couldn't help notice the contrast between Gary, who was blond and freckle faced, and Mike, who was tanned and handsome. When Gary walked her to the door and kissed her goodnight, she was aware of Mike watching from the car. Then when her date returned to the car with a happy smile, she was relieved that he hadn't jumped off the porch with another wild declaration.

The next day when Janice returned to camp she told a fellow camper, Marsha (Chip) Runyon, "I met a guy from your school last night." When Chip raised her brows questioningly, Janice said, "Mike Large came over with Gary, since Gary only has his driver's permit."

Chip's face lit up, "Wow! Mike Large is really nice looking. Do you think maybe you could fix us up? Maybe we could double date with you and Gary."

Janice replied, "Well, I'll see about that." As it turned out, that was one double date that never happened.

Later that summer, other young men came into her life. After her friends, Debbie and Bobby West had moved to the small town of Somerset, they'd introduced her to a young man named Rick. Rick, who visited her often, took her to a drive-in movie in Lancaster to celebrate his eighteenth birthday. Also, a boy named Mike Spangler, who lived in the neighborhood, had been coming to the house on Oakwood and taking her for walks. One October evening when she returned from the Methodist Youth Fellowship meeting, her mother told her that she'd had a call from Mike. "I wrote the phone number down so you can call him," her mother said. Janice assumed the call was from Mike Spangler, and since he had just left her at the front door, she didn't return the call.

On Tuesday, when her mother answered the phone and told Janice that it was Mike, she again thought it was Mike Spangler. As they began to talk, she was pleasantly surprised to learn that the person on the other end of the line was Mike Large, Gary's friend. When he told her that he had called on Sunday and had been waiting for her return call, she realized her mistake. As the words flowed easily between them, she slipped under the family's large harvest table and stretched out, while they talked for over an hour. Before the conversation was over, Mike explained that he had to work the next day, Wednesday, but wanted to come over when he was off on Thursday. With plans made, Janice happily went to bed. With her thoughts on Mike, she was glad that she hadn't fixed him up with Chip.

On Thursday when June and Dick met him, they were impressed with his friendly polite manner. He talked to her parents for a few minutes before he drove Janice in his '62 Mercury to a cozy restaurant where they drank hot chocolate, talked, and enjoyed each other's company.

Mike told her about his years in Boy Scouts in Germany where they had camped in tents during the winter. "During one of those winter campouts, it was so cold that I got frostbite."

"Wow! That sounds intense!" Janice declared. "I prefer my campouts during the summer. Last summer our Girl Scout troop went to the New England coast. The Atlantic waters were so cold, that when we waded into the waves, our legs turned so red that it looked like we were wearing red knee socks."

When she visibly shivered, Mike smiled and reached across the table to take her hands in his. She liked the feel of his hands on hers. As she gazed into his green eyes, she sensed a special connection, and felt a tingle of joy.

She laughed, as she added, "A funny thing happened in Cape Cod on that trip. The streets of Cape Cod were full of lounging hippies. We got out our cameras and took pictures of the hippies in their bell bottoms and colorful shirts. Then they took out their cameras and took pictures of us Girl Scouts in our green uniforms. I guess they looked strange to us and we looked strange to them." As Mike laughed, Janice added, "Well, enough about me. How do you spend your free time?"

"I spend a lot of time working at McDonalds flipping hamburgers to support my car payments, car repairs, and car insurance," he explained.

"Was that your first job?" she asked.

"No, I worked at Wells Department Store and for Howard Johnson's Motel, driving guests to and from the Columbus Airport." When he told her about other jobs he'd had as a baby-sitter, a carryout at a grocery store, and an usher in a movie theater, Janice realized this boy didn't have a lazy bone in his body.

When he mentioned his usher job, Janice told him, "My parents met in the Midland Theatre when my mom was an usherette. My dad had walked into the theatre, wearing his army uniform, with a girl on each arm. Mom sold him three boxes of popcorn, and he came back and asked her for a date right at the popcorn counter. Isn't it funny how couples meet?"

Mike added, "Well, I sure am glad that Gary didn't have his driver's license, or maybe we wouldn't have met yet. But I'm sure we would have eventually, because I have a good feeling about us." While Janice didn't tell him that evening, she felt the same.

After they talked for awhile, he drove around Heath High School, showing her the school building and the track where he ran in the track meets. As he paused at a stop sign in the school lot, he put his arm around her and tried for their first kiss. She pulled away and said, "I've never kissed on a first date before." He accepted her decision, but appeared disappointed.

When they left the school grounds, he asked, "Do you want to see where I live?" Then when she nodded in agreement, he drove by a big two-story farmhouse on Licking View Drive not far from the school.

On the way home, words just spilled out until they arrived at the house on Oakwood Avenue. Mike opened the car door for her and walked her to the front door and said, "Why don't we pretend this is our second date?" When he gently tried for a goodnight kiss, he was pleasantly surprised when Janice put her hands on his shoulders and kissed him.

He smiled and said, "See you Saturday night." He was so happy when he walked down the steps, he wished he didn't have to work the next night. As he drove home, he thought, "It sure was better being with Janice on her front porch than watching from the car."

The next night, Janice and her friends were at White's Field for the Newark High School football game. Although, she was with Rick, her thoughts were with Mike who was working only a few blocks away at McDonalds. Each time Janice spoke to Rick, she would accidentally call him Mike. After the sixth time of being called by the wrong name, Rick said, "You've met someone else, haven't you?"

Janice answered, "Yes, I have. Maybe you and I should just be friends." She felt badly about letting him down, but Mike was the one on her mind now, as was obvious by all her slips with his name that evening.

Later at the game, Janice said to her friends, Janet, Marsha, and Diane, "This has been such a crazy week. Tuesday Mike called, Wednesday Rick came over, Thursday Mike and I went for a ride, Friday Rick and I came to the game. Now Saturday night Mike and I are going out." When Diane asked if that meant that Sunday night was Rick's turn, Janice quickly replied, "No! Rick is out of the picture. From now on, I want to spend my time with Mike."

Then on Saturday, Janice and Mike went bowling. Since Mike had bowled on several teams while his Dad was in the service, and Janice had only bowled a few times, she welcomed his tips on improving her game. When he told her about his grandmother who lived in Somerset by an old covered bridge, Janice exclaimed, "Oh, yes, that's the small town with a statute of General Phil Sheridan in the middle of the town square." Mike was astonished that she was aware of this small town. Then she asked, "Have you ever been to that small cemetery in the woods outside of town?"

A small smile tugged at the corner of Mike's mouth when he expressed surprise that she knew about the place. Unknown to Janice, that cemetery was a popular parking place for local couples. Janice went on to tell him that she and her friends liked to go there and read the names, dates, and epitaphs from the old tombstones. Mike jumped at the chance to go there that night, but when they arrived at the old cemetery, he was surprised when she actually got out of the car and started to check out the markers.

Her enthusiasm was contagious and within seconds with his flashlight and their imagination they discovered people who had lived and loved long ago. The search through the past was fun, and the fall night was beautiful. Then standing in this quiet place, near the woods, Mike kissed Janice and told her, "Someday, I want to marry you." Being only sixteen, "someday" seemed far away to Janice.

During the weeks and months to come, they spent lots of time together. During her first visit to the farmhouse of Mike's Granny (Nellie Large), everyone was friendly and made her feel welcome. Janice thoroughly enjoyed visiting in this house and meeting Mike's relatives. The house was warmed by a pot-bellied stove like the one Janice remembered in the house of her grandparents, Forest and Rowena, when she was younger. During this visit, they all sat in the kitchen while Mike's uncles played their guitars and sang country and gospel songs. The kitchen was warm and cozy and filled with the wonderful aroma of Granny's good cooking and baking.

After Granny waved goodbye from the front porch, Mike drove around the bend and stopped by the covered bridge. When she saw it, Janice exclaimed, "Wow, it's so close to Granny's house. Near Camp Wakatomika my friends and

I visit an old covered bridge. We always make a wish, hold our breath, and run across it. If you can run all the way through without taking a breath, your wish will come true."

Mike smiled at Janice before he drove into the covered bridge and stopped halfway through. Then he pulled her close and murmured, "This bridge also has a tradition. If you kiss inside the bridge, it will bring you good luck." So not wanting to break with tradition, they kissed under the sheltering roof of this magical structure. This was a tradition that continued for years to come. *All that kissing must have helped, as their future was filled with good-luck and happiness.*

In weeks to come as Mike became a constant visitor in their home, it became apparent to her parents that this boy was special to their daughter. Usually around eleven o'clock, Dick would find himself calling down to the basement recreation room, "Mike, it's time to close up shop!" and Mike would reluctantly say goodnight to Janice and trudge off toward his car.

One night he told Dick, "My car won't start. I need a push. Can you help me out?"

Dick was aware of the problem Mike was having with his Ford Falcon's engine. The compression was so poor that it was hard to get the car started. Whenever possible, Mike would park on a downhill slope to give the car a running start so he could get up enough speed to pop the clutch and the engine would have enough torque to start. Since Janice's house on Oakwood Avenue wasn't on a hill, Dick would sometimes give Mike a push with his 1966 Catalina Pontiac.

That night, Mike got into his Falcon with Dick behind him-bumper to bumper ready to get Mike's car moving. Dick accelerated quickly and the two cars sped past all the houses on Oakwood Avenue, under the expressway overpass, and over the railroad tracks. As Mike's Falcon flew over the tracks, he caught a glimpse of Dick's smiling face in the rearview mirror. Mike thought, "Janice's Dad is enjoying this much too much!" He then popped the clutch and the engine came to life and he left Dick's car behind as he drove to his home in Heath.

When Dick walked back into the house, June asked, "Did you give Mike a good start?"

He grinned, "Oh, I gave him a good start alright. He was airborne when he went over those railroad tracks."

"You didn't, did you?" she warned.

He replied with, "Just ask Mike tomorrow. I'm sure he will give you the details of our wild ride."

While she and Dick were getting ready for bed, June told her husband what had been on her mind for awhile. "I think Janice is like me. At sixteen, she's met someone she's pretty serious about. Unlike me, though, I think she'll still go to college before she gets married. She has her mind set on it."

"Don't worry about Janice," Dick said. "She's not going to rush into anything."

"Like I did!" June teased. Her husband tossed a pillow at her head, but he missed. When she returned it to him, though, she hit the target. As they laughed and teased, thoughts of what tomorrow had in store were forgotten. As her husband often said, there were times to live for today.

EXCITEMENT IN THE AIR

Dick and June had gotten in the habit of going to Columbus on Thursday, Dick's day off from the barbershop, and taking Sharlyn out for lunch. On one visit, June was reminded of her own early married life when she and Dick had so many disagreements over food. It was evident that Sharlyn and Charlie had carried their food fights a step further by the mustard and bits of ham that clung to the back of Sharlyn's blouse and the sandwich with all the fixings that was sliding down the kitchen wall.

When they saw the furious glint in their daughter's eyes and became aware that Charlie was nowhere in sight, Dick and June decided this was no time to be interfering in-laws. Without batting an eye, Dick said, "We're going to Jong Mea's for Chinese food. Get ready and come with us!"

While Sharlyn slipped into the bedroom to change her clothes, June cleaned the mess from the wall. When Dick raised a quizzical eyebrow as if to ask what was going on, June whispered, "Don't ask. She'll tell us if she wants us to know."

When they were seated at the restaurant, Sharlyn spilled out her tale of woe. "Charlie came home for lunch and I told him I was going to make him some scalloped potatoes, but he said it wouldn't do any good since he didn't like them and wouldn't eat them. The more I tried to change his mind, the madder he got. Finally I gave up and fixed him a hot ham and cheese sandwich. He took one bite and said the bread was stale. The next thing I knew, it came flying across the room and hit me in the back. I felt like turning around and smashing my sandwich in his face, but I refrained myself. I guess I just saw red, so I let mine fly too and as you saw, it landed against the wall." She grinned ruefully as she added, "After Charlie left, I felt pretty foolish about what I'd done when I saw the mess I'd made and realized I would have to clean it off the walls." Then she turned and smiled at her mother, "Thanks for taking care of it for me."

June told her about some of their early fights about food. "I don't know who trained who, but after awhile I learned to cook what he liked, and he learned that once a meal was on the table I wouldn't jump up from the table like his mother had done and fix something else for him. I'm sure you and Charlie will work things out too." The prospect looked promising when they returned to the apartment to find a very apologetic looking young husband. Dick and June left shortly afterwards so the young couple could be alone and have a chance to make up.

On the way home, Dick said, "As I recall, the best thing about fighting is making up."

To which his wife replied, "That was the only good thing about fighting!"

When the newlyweds came over in a couple weeks for Sunday dinner, Dick teasingly suggested that she prepare Charlie's favorite, scalloped potatoes and ham, but June decided a nice pot-roast might be safer. Although June joked about it with her husband she had been worried that the fight might have serious consequences. It didn't take long after the young couple arrived for her to realize that the making up had worked, and that Sharlyn and Charlie seemed happier than ever.

Shortly after the newlyweds arrived, Mike came over to spend the afternoon with Janice. As June had predicted earlier, in Mike, Janice had found the man she planned to marry. Although she was still in her teens, like her mother had earlier, she had known when she was very young that she'd met the man she wanted to spend her life with. For now, she still had another year of high school to complete and four years of college. Marriage would have to wait.

~

Fourteen year old Ricky had changed a great deal in the last year or more. One evening at the dinner table, he'd announced, "I'm too old to be called Ricky. From now on I want to be called Ric." That change hadn't surprised them as much, though, as what had happened with his hair. Since his father and Uncle Eddie had proudly given him his first haircut, it had always been cut short, generally in a flattop or a burr. However, he'd decided he wanted to wear his hair long like most of his friends. Although his father disapproved, he'd reluctantly agreed. To everyone's surprise, when it grew out, it was a mass of curls. Then for weeks they'd had to answer questions like, "Does Ricky have a perm?" or "Who has curly hair in the family?"

To the first question, they could reply, "No perm." Forest came up with the answer to the second when he reminded them that he'd had curly hair until it was time for him to start to school. "I hated those curls and being asked if I was a girl. So when my mother wouldn't have my hair cut, I got hold of her sewing shears, crawled under the bed, and did it myself!" he exclaimed.

"His mother has told that story a lot of times," Rowie chuckled. "She was really mad at him when his hair came back in straight! That must have been when he decided to become a barber."

Unlike his grandfather, though, Ric's were there to stay. Although he wanted straight hair, he soon found an advantage to having curls. Since girls liked them, he became increasingly more popular with the opposite sex. The constant ringing of the telephone and the sound of a feminine voice asking to speak to Ric reminded June of the months her brother Dick had spent with them and the girls who'd chased after him.

A pretty girl named Judy, who had come from Mississippi to live with her aunt and uncle at the top of the hill on Oakwood Avenue, had caught his eye. Ric, who spent many summer evenings visiting with her and her aunt and uncle, was fascinated by Judy's soft southern drawl. Sometimes because of her tendency to turn a one-syllable word into two or three syllables, Ric had trouble understanding her. This was especially true one evening when they were alone in her kitchen. She had just set a glass and a bottle of Pepsi Cola on the table in front of him before she turned to the refrigerator and in her soft southern drawl casually asked, "Do you want some ass?"

Startled, Ric's face turned a deep red as he asked what she'd said. When she calmly repeated her question, he sputtered, "What do you mean?"

Exasperated, she opened the refrigerator door, yanked out a tray of ice-cubes, waved it in front of his face, and asked, "Do you want some i-c-e for your Pepsi?" Hearing ice spelled out, the shock wore off. Needless to say, Ric never told her what he thought she'd asked him.

That spring, one of Janice and Ric's new friends, Gib, invited Ric and Judy, Janice and Mike, and some of their neighborhood friends to go on a canoe trip on the Mohican River. The gang asked June and Dick to come with them. The man who rented the canoes to them mentioned that the water was up, as he provided lifejackets to them. Before they got into the canoes, Dick and June made sure all the teenagers were safely buckled in their jackets. The trip started with a lot of excitement, as they loaded by twos into the canoes. They were all laughing and joking as they learned to control the boats. Later, when they were out of the view of the adults, Jackie and Janet removed their lifejackets because they thought they were too bulky.

Janice and Mike had gotten a good paddling rhythm going, and as their canoe cut through the water, they enjoyed the peaceful scenery along the river. After awhile, the water was flowing more swiftly and it didn't take much effort to paddle the canoe. Then they hit some rapids and had trouble controlling the boat, almost hitting some protruding rocks and overturned trees. Looking back, no other canoes were in sight, so they pulled over to the shore to wait for the rest of the gang.

Suddenly, a picnic basket of food came rushing by. Janice started to laugh at this sight until she saw two bodies come into view. Janet and Jackie had capsized and were being rushed along in the water yelling, "Help! Help!" Mike immediately jumped in and swam to them. Janice watched in terror as thoughts flashed through her mind of the four people she knew who had drowned; the neighbor boy she'd baby-sat, one of Ric's classmates, and a friend's father who'd drowned during the unsuccessful rescue of a drowning child.

Janice breathed a sigh of relief when she saw Jackie hit shore and grab onto an overturned tree. Mike rescued Janet as she swallowed another mouthful of water. Janet and Jackie were both gasping for air and coughing as Mike brought them onto the dry land. Janet gasped, "I kept going underwater as I was being pulled along. I thought for sure that I was a goner!" Since both girls were happy to have escaped with their lives, they planted their feet firmly on the ground and decided to stay there until someone came for them in an automobile.

~

Meanwhile upstream, the rest of the group was having their own frightening experience as Gib and his younger sister had also capsized. Although, Gib had tried to grab her as she was washed downstream, the force of the water had pulled her from his grasp. When Dick and June came around the bend in the river and saw what was happening, Dick dived in and swam toward the screaming teenager and managed to get her safely to the shore. Like Janet and Jackie, this girl had also removed her life jacket. "This is it!" Dick exclaimed. "We are going to go ashore at the nearest pickup point and have our lunch. By the time we're through, the trucks should be here to get us."

When they reached the next clearing, they found Janice, Mike, Janet, and Jackie waiting. After she and Dick got out of their canoe and pulled it onto dry land, June watched as Ric and his friend Judy brought their boat in. The girl was so pretty and well dressed with perfect makeup and every hair in place. She could easily pass as a fashion model in a teenage magazine. Ric had told his mother that Judy had stayed up half the night finishing the pretty pedal pushers and matching top she was wearing today. Then as she stood up in the canoe and started to step onto shore, the swiftly rushing water rocked the canoe and before anyone could get to her, the canoe tilted, and she fell into the water. In a flash, Ric jumped in and helped her to shore before she was pulled downstream. It was obvious, at first, that the young girl was embarrassed at her bedraggled appearance after she'd tried so hard to look her best for Ric. When she looked around at the rest of the group, who with the exception of Janice and June, were as soaked as she was, she relaxed and smiled flirtatiously at Ric whose grin clearly showed that in his eyes, she still looked lovely.

Once they'd gotten all the canoes onto shore, Dick said that he was hungry enough to eat a horse. Gib grumbled that he might have to. Then when June asked who had the food, Janice told them about seeing the picnic basket floating down the river a few feet ahead of Janet and Jackie. June then asked, "Who has the Tupperware container full of the sandwiches I brought?"

In response, Gib looked glum before he explained that half had been in Janet and Jackie's and the other half had been in his canoe. "Since both canoes capsized, I guess the fish must be having a feast," he moaned. As the little group sat around the picnic table and munched on the potato chips June had stashed in their canoe, they may have envied the fish, but they were eternally grateful that the food was all they'd lost.

A few weeks later, Skip and JoAnne's son, Mike, went on a canoe trip on the same river. His canoe also capsized and unable to swim, his lungs were filling with water before he was pulled from the Mohican River, and one of his companions saved his life by administering artificial resuscitation. This news was enough to earn Ric and Janice a talking to from their mother about the importance of wearing lifejackets. Janice and Ric seemed to understand that her fear that something terrible might have happened to them was delivering the lecture, so they didn't remind her they hadn't been the ones who'd removed their lifejackets.

~

That summer of nineteen-sixty-nine was a thrilling time for June and her family as Sharlyn and Charlie were expecting their first child in August. As June spent hours making maternity clothes for the expectant mother and buying clothes for the little one, she was in seventh heaven. Dick, Janice, and Ric also got caught up in the excitement during the family's weekly visits to Sharlyn.

Then on August fifteenth, Sharlyn called and told them that she had gone into labor, and that Charlie was going to take her to the hospital. Dick and June rushed over to Columbus to St. Anne's hospital, but the guard on duty wouldn't let them go anywhere near their daughter. While they waited in the lobby, Charlie would occasionally come downstairs and give them a progress report. After hours of sipping cold coffee and pacing the floor, the phone finally rang. The guard took his time answering it. Then as they waited anxiously to find out if he had news for them, he slowly sauntered over and told them that it was a girl. They had thought they would get to at least see Sharlyn, if not the baby, but the guard wouldn't let them go beyond the lobby.

Then on the way home, Dick was so caught up in the excitement of being a grandfather that he didn't watch the speedometer, and they were stopped for speeding. Much to their surprise, when Dick told the officer about the baby, he didn't give him a ticket. As it turned out, he was a new grandfather too.

The next day, Mike and his brother, Andy, went to the hospital with the family to see Sharlyn and the new baby. Before they left, Janice asked her mother if she knew that when Andy had come over from Germany last month, and she'd been fixing him up with her friends, that when he saw Sharlyn's picture, he had wanted to meet her. "I told him he was too late. She was already taken," Janice said.

That was a special night. They got to see the baby for the first time, and saw how thrilled Sharlyn and Charlie were. Janice whispered to her mother, "The baby is so tiny...so petite with such angelic features. She is the most beautiful baby I've ever seen!"

While Sharlyn had been pregnant, she'd said if she had a girl, she wanted to call her Tracie, but she had changed her mind. Before the family left the hospital that night, she told them that she and Charlie had decided to call the baby Sherrie. Then the next day when they returned, she told them they'd named her Deborah Elizabeth. When June expressed surprise, Sharlyn said, "She seemed more like a Debbie than a Sherrie to me. Besides, Charlie and I like the way her initials spell out DEB." Although June liked the name, her special one for her first granddaughter was Debbie Liz.

∽

An idyllic time followed as the whole family reveled in the joy of the new life. Rowie was particularly happy about the birth of her firstborn's first grandchild. She had bought a peach colored sleeper and a pink blanket for Debbie. While she gave Sharlyn the sleeper when she went along with Dick and June on one of their frequent visits, she put away the blanket to give her for a Christmas present. The look of complete joy on the face of the new great-grandmother was evident as she cuddled the little one and cooed baby talk in her ear. As June and Sharlyn watched this tender scene, June was happy with the knowledge that although she'd never known either of her grandmothers, this child was blessed with two generations of them. If anyone in the room had known what was going to happen in a few short weeks, they would have tried to hold on tightly to this precious moment. As it was, they took it for granted as they happily looked forward to many tomorrows just like this day.

The next visitor was Priscilla. She hadn't visited June and her family as much since Bill had been diagnosed with cancer, but she did make the trip to Dick and June's, then on to Columbus with them to see her first great-grandchild. When Sharlyn placed the infant in Priscilla's outstretched arms, Debbie went to sleep as soon as she was settled on Priscilla's soft lap. "I'm only fifty-eight and I'm already a great-grandmother," Priscilla quipped before she turned her glance on June and said, "I was only thirty-eight when you made me a grandmother. Now Sharlyn has done the same thing to you. How does it feel?"

June responded that she was older than her mother had been. "I'm already thirty-nine," she quipped. "I think it's wonderful, though. This way I'll be around to see her grow up."

Priscilla turned to Sharlyn and said, "Holding my first great-grandchild is one of the happiest moments I've had since I got the news about Bill. It's right up there with the twenty-fifth wedding anniversary you all helped me and Bill celebrate a couple years ago."

While Sharlyn joined in the lighthearted bantering, June was relieved to see the worry leave her mother's eyes. Although Bill had survived several surgeries to keep his cancer in check, Priscilla lived in fear of the time when he would be taken from her. Although he felt fine and was able to live a normal life, the weight of the diagnosis hung like a guillotine over her head. Although it had been almost forty years since she'd watched her mother dying of the dreaded disease, she couldn't erase those pictures from her mind. No matter how much her children tried to convince her to appreciate the day and not worry about tomorrow, she couldn't do it. June was happy to see that for these few minutes, though, the feel of little Debbie in her arms had provided solace for her mother.

A few days later when Rose was talking to June on the phone, she mentioned the coincidence of June having her first granddaughter the same summer that her little brothers Bill and Fred's wives had daughters. June agreed that it was indeed a coincidence but a nice one. After they got off the phone, June thought about this summer and how Bill had brought his wife and their beautiful dark-haired, pink cheeked baby girl, Beth, to Ohio to meet his side of the family. It had been almost midnight by the time the little family arrived. After the excitement of meeting Linda and holding her cuddly little niece for the first time, June had rustled around the kitchen to set some food on the table. June had heard from Polly that Linda was a tiny, vivacious, dark-haired Italian girl. She was indeed tiny and her hair was dark, but her first night at the house on Oakwood Avenue, she was quiet as she sat on the stool at the kitchen bar and watched Dick demonstrate his own brand of humor. *After she got to know June better she confided that on that first visit, she'd thought June was really nice but that she was married to a crazy man. She said she knew she became a part of the family when she was able to come back at Dick with "his little funnies." During a subsequent visit to Bill and Linda's home in Sterling Park, Virginia, when they all went to the grocery store, Dick and Linda did an exaggerated impression of the southern accent of Gomer Pyle, a television character. While Bill and June pretended that these two characters were complete strangers, they strolled, wide-eyed around the store saying, "Look at all them lights! I've never seen so many lights. We don't have them lights back home." June and Bill exchanged grins as they realized that Dick had indeed met his match.*

A month after Beth's birth, June and Dick had been at Sharlyn's house when Fred had called and excitedly told them that his little boys, Chucky, and Jimmy had a little sister. He had stumbled over his words when he said, "She has blond hair and blue eyes, and looks like the boys. She's going to look like a Harman."

After hearing the news, Sharlyn had rubbed her hand over her tummy and when her baby moved in response, Sharlyn had said, "I can hardly wait."

When brown haired Debbie's birth had followed in August, June marveled at how thoroughly different these girls were. She also wished her father had lived to see and enjoy them. She smiled inwardly when she thought about Fred's little boys who were close in age as Fred and Bill had been, and who were as cute and full of fun and mischief as their father and uncle had been. As she thought about them a couple stories popped into her mind. The first was the time when Chucky and Jimmy spent the night with her while their parents went out-of-town. Jimmy had still been in diapers and Chucky was a couple years old. Fred and Judy had brought the playpen for a bed, but neither boy wanted to sleep in it. Both boys missed their parents and didn't want to have anything to do with this substitute bed. The only way June could get them to go to sleep was to sleep on the couch with Chucky beside her and Jimmy on her stomach.

The next morning when she woke up, her shirt was wet where Jimmy's diaper had leaked around the edges, and Chucky was standing beside them stuffing chocolate candy into Jimmy's mouth while Jimmy tried, but failed, to eat it as fast as Chucky put it in his mouth. She'd been so busy getting the candy from Chucky and changing Jimmy to do anything for herself when she heard a knock at the front door. Holding the squirming Jimmy in her arms she'd opened the door to Rowena and Thelma. If she hadn't known how awful she looked in her rumpled wet shirt and her hair as yet uncombed, Thelma's comment would have reminded her. While June motioned them in, Thelma asked Rowena, "Why does she look like that?"

All thought of replying was wiped from June's mind when Chucky sauntered up to them with what looked like a skinny brown stick in his hand and kept repeating, "Cigar, cigar," until June snatched it away from him. She didn't tell her guests, but she knew this inquisitive little boy had crawled behind the couch and found a couple little deposits their as yet un-housebroken puppy had left behind.

Another time, June and Dick stopped in to see Fred and Judy at their two story townhouse in Columbus. A few minutes after they arrived, Dick had gone upstairs to the bathroom. When he came down, June heard him ask Fred what was going on. "I see that you have found a new use for your ties." When June looked puzzled, he explained that he'd peeked in on the boys and saw that Fred used them to tie the boys in their beds. Startled, June reminded him that he'd better watch it or someone will accuse him of child abuse.

Fred chuckled and said, "They wouldn't consider it child abuse if they'd had as much trouble as we've had keeping them from taking the screen out of the window and climbing out on the porch roof. We've tried everything, but no matter what we say or do, we keep finding them perched out there. I'd had enough worrying about them, so I finally decided to put some of my old ties to good use. It's not as if I have them bound and gagged or anything like that. They only have one leg tied to the bedpost. The ties are long and loose enough for the boys to move around in their bunks." Judy added that it might look strange to someone who didn't know what was behind it, but at least this way she knew her boys were safe.

After June went upstairs to see for herself, she chuckled when she rejoined the group before she said to Fred, "If Dad could look down and see these boys, he'd say they were just like you and Bill."

You know what else he'd say, don't you?" Dick asked. In unison, June and Fred chanted, "THAT'S ALL THERE ARE TO IT!"

ROWIE AND TOOTS

Six weeks later, as the smell of burning leaves was in the air and the stores in downtown Newark were filled with Halloween decorations, Janice and Ric went to a costume party with their youth group at church. While they were gone, Dick and June visited Forest and Rowena. While Forest sat in his maroon leather recliner, Rowie rocked in her brown chair while Dick and June sat together on the couch. After talking about Christmas plans, Rowie told them about kids in the neighborhood who had thrown eggs against the side of the house, and a pumpkin on her new red Pontiac Grand Prix. Forest also told them about the damage the tenants had done to the house on South Second Street. "They lived in that house for years and I never thought they'd smash doors and windows or put big holes in the plaster, but they did," he grumbled. June and Dick sympathized and offered to help any way they could, but the older couple said they could handle it.

Then Rowie jumped up, went into the kitchen where she bustled around for awhile before she called them to come in for a cup of tea and a slice of the apple pie she'd baked that afternoon. While June was finishing her pie, Forest motioned for Dick to follow him down the steps to the basement. "He's going to show him the wine we just made. Someone gave him some grapes and we decided to try our hand at it," Rowie told June.

The women could hear Dick's teasing voice as he came up the stairs. "I can't believe you filled gallon jugs with the wine. Just don't drink it all at once," he said. Rowie commented that it would last them a long time before she changed the subject to ask what everyone wanted for Christmas. As they got ready to leave, June told her she'd see what she could find out and call her.

Although they talked a couple times on the phone over the next two days, June still hadn't gotten a Christmas list together when at one-thirty the morning of October twenty-ninth, they were awakened by a frantic call from Forest. His voice was hoarse with emotion when he told Dick that Rowie was having chest pains and he didn't know what to do. "We have to get dressed and we'll be right there," Dick said, "In the meantime, call the emergency squad." When Forest protested that it was the middle of the night, Dick repeated his instructions before he and June hurriedly dressed and ran to the car.

When they arrived at the house on Leonard Avenue, they found that Forest had been too alarmed to make the call so Dick made it for him. Pale faced and obviously in pain, Rowie asked June to help her get into the pretty new nightgown she'd saved since the previous Christmas. When June tried to help her, though, the effort of trying to raise her arms was too much for Rowena. "You look beautiful as you are," June whispered seconds before two strong husky paramedics came into the bedroom. One scooped the ill woman into his arms and tenderly placed her onto the gurney. As they sped away into the night, Dick, June and Forest followed in Dick's car.

That night and the next week were filled with pain and heartbreak. Then a short time later, Janice handed her mother something she had written that expressed her feelings. "I want you to read it, Mom," she said. I call it "You Are The Source Of My Creation."

YOU ARE THE SOURCE OF MY CREATION

The shrill ringing of the telephone downstairs woke me in the middle of the night on October 29, 1969. I could hear the voices of my parents, so I jumped out of bed and pressed my ear to the floor register to hear their words. They were saying that my grandmother, Rowena, had suffered a heart attack and was being taken to the hospital. Mom said, "Let's not wake Janice and Ric. They will just worry." Little did she know that I was already awake and would worry for hours before their return.

In my mind the words formed, "YOU ARE THE SOURCE OF MY CREATION. NOW I HEAR YOU MAY GO AWAY." I thought of my loving grandmother, Rowie…short, soft, round, cuddly, with dark hair, red cheeks. She reminded me of the littlest of the three good fairies in Disney's Sleeping Beauty (Merryweather who always dressed in blue). Except Rowie's favorite color was red, which showed in her clothes, her coat, her car, and even in her living-room carpet.

Only living a few miles away, she was an important part of my life. I began to think about her great cooking. Her specialties were homemade noodles, apple pie, rhubarb pie, and spaghetti with homemade rolls. Her breakfast rice with nutmeg, cinnamon, and cream would tempt anyone's palate. To let her know she was appreciated, whenever she was tired we'd have her lay down on the bed and we'd give her a backrub.

I just saw her a few days ago as I left for one of my college visitations to a nursing school. I had given her a big hug and she had slipped a quarter into my hand before saying goodbye. As I sat in my room, waiting, I silently pleaded, "Oh, please, don't let that be our last goodbye. I'm not ready yet. It's not time."

When my parents returned and I saw their faces, I realized that my Rowie was gone. We were crushed. My grandfather, Forest loved her so much and depended on her so much, that in a few days, he died of a broken heart. A massive coronary took him instantly. He joined Rowie in Heaven where they were together again.

One week ago, our lives had been normal, but that had all changed. Now we stood in their empty house, in shock about their sudden departures. They were suddenly gone, but wonderful memories filled my soul. Rowie and Forest will forever be remembered in my heart. You are a source of my creation.

Rowie
Rowena Jane
May 4, 1905-Oct 29, 1969

Toots
Forest Dale
May 12, 1899-Nov 3, 1969

~

Rowie had died a couple hours after she'd gotten to the hospital. The Red Cross had been contacted and arranged to have Kenny and his family flown home from Alaska. Two days after their beloved Rowie had been laid to rest at Cedar Hill cemetery in Newark, while Dick and Forest were in the car on the way to pick out a marker for her grave, the family suffered another tragedy. June, Yoko, Kenny, Alan, and Anita had watched as they drove away from the house on Leonard Avenue, but seconds later when ten year old Alan saw his Uncle Dick's car return, he ran into the kitchen and said, "Uncle Dick is back, but Granddad isn't in the car with him," the entire family rushed to the carport to see what had happened. They found Dick in the driver's seat with Forest slumped over beside him. Forest's face looked purple, and they could not find a pulse. While Kenny and Dick tried to revive him, June called the emergency squad. Then when the squad arrived and whisked him away to the hospital, with Dick and Kenny in the seats beside her, June drove. As she careened wildly behind the emergency vehicle, Dick and Kenny were sorry they'd asked her to drive.

Then a few minutes later at the hospital, a middle-aged doctor came out of the emergency room to tell them that Forest had been dead when he arrived at the hospital. Although the doctor told them that he'd died of a heart attack, his family was convinced that inconsolable as he'd been at the loss of Rowena, he hadn't been able to live without her.

The loss was almost more than the family could bear. An especially poignant moment occurred while June and Janice were going through Forest and Rowena's belongings. Janice found and showed her mother the blanket Rowena had bought for Debbie's first Christmas. They silently exchanged sad looks as they remembered Rowena's joy when she had bought it. Shortly after the funerals, Janice actually became physically ill. Worried that she might have mono, June took her to the doctor only to be informed that her illness was caused by her grief. For the next few weeks, Mike's love helped her handle her loss. As time passed, their family, friends, and church helped them deal with the unthinkable that two such vibrant people had been taken so quickly. The absence of the older couple left a deep hole in their lives, but after the first raw grief lessened, they were gradually able to fill that hole with never-ending memories.

COLORFUL CHARACTERS

The death of Dick's parents completely changed Dick and June's lives. With Kenny stationed in Alaska, Dick and June were thrust into the position of being landlords. June remembered her earlier remark that a landlady was the last thing she ever wanted to be. Although her opinion hadn't changed, she now found herself with that title. The job taught them both a great deal about human nature. They met some wonderful people and some that in retrospect seemed to have crawled out from under a rock. When that particular kind of tenant vacated the property, they left filth and destruction in their wake.

There were also some light moments. Once when Ric answered the phone he was told by one of the tenants that her Aunt Tina had fallen off the roof. June had been in the kitchen when she'd heard him exclaim, "Your Aunt Tina fell off the roof! What was she doing up there?"

After the woman had shouted, "Not my Aunt Tina! My Aunt Tina!" Ric had called his mother to the phone and said, "This woman says she rents from you and that her Aunt Tina fell off the roof. Then she said it wasn't her Aunt Tina, it was her Aunt Tina. I don't know what in the world she's talking about. Maybe you can make some sense out of it!"

Once she'd gotten on the phone, June was as confused as her son had been. For a few seconds she felt as if she were in the middle of an Abbott and Costello routine like "Who's On First?" as the tenant frantically shouted that her Aunt Tina had fallen from the main roof and landed on the lower kitchen roof. When June had tried to find out what the woman's aunt had been doing on the roof and if she'd been hurt when she fell, the tenant became hysterical as she repeated, "I'm trying to tell you that it ain't my Aunt Tina! It's my Aunt Tina!"

Finally, intrigued by his wife's end of the conversation, Dick ambled into the room and asked who was on the other end of the line. When she put her hand over the mouthpiece and explained, he threw back his head and laughed, before he said, "That's the way she pronounces antenna!" Once the mystery was solved, Dick left for the rental unit to take care of the baffled woman's Aunt Tina.

As fall turned to winter, the family balanced their time between taking care of their new responsibilities, and going with Janice to check out several schools in the state. Janice had always been a strong, independent girl so her parents weren't worried about her striking out on her own, but they knew they would miss her sweet loving ways when she went away to school.

At Christmas time, they received a letter from Polly, who was now living in Florida with a surprise announcement and an invitation to visit her during Janice and Ric's spring break to meet the newest member of the family.

∼

Soon Dick, June, Janice, and Ric were in their blue Pontiac Catalina laughing, talking and singing their way across five states. Within one hundred miles of their destination when they saw a sign that proclaimed, "EVERYTHING YOU CAME TO FLORIDA TO SEE," Ric quipped, "I don't think so! Not unless MaMa Polly has moved up here!" A few hours later when Dick halted the car in the driveway of a small yellow cottage, the door flew open and Polly rushed through it with her arms spread wide as if to gather them all to her.

After the excited greetings were over, June asked, "Where is that new husband of yours? We're all anxious to meet your Captain Bob!"

Polly replied that he was out on his boat, the Florida Belle. "He had some work done on the engine and he took it on a trial run to check it out. He might not get in until later tonight."

They were all disappointed, but with all the catching up they had to do, the afternoon and evening passed quickly. They turned in for the night before they had a chance to meet Polly's commercial fishing boat captain. A few hours later, June was only half asleep when she heard the murmur of the voices of her stepmother and her husband. Anxious but reluctant to meet this man who had taken her father's place in Polly's life, June thought, "I'll face that tomorrow," before she rolled over and went to sleep.

Breakfast came and went with no sign of the bridegroom. Then while they were finishing the last bites of the pancakes Polly had prepared for them, they heard a male voice call out, "Mommy, I'm ready for breakfast."

June noticed the puzzlement she felt mirrored in her family's eyes when she said, "I didn't know his mother was here. Does she live with you?"

Polly giggled and coyly replied, "He's not talking to his mother. He calls me Mommy and I call him Daddy." The family absorbed this information without comment although the glances that Dick and June exchanged spoke volumes. In their twenty-three years of marriage, they'd had a few terms of endearment for each other, but Mommy and Daddy had been reserved for their parents.

June almost choked on her next sip of coffee when Captain Bob boomed, "You can bring my breakfast to me in bed," and Polly jumped up from the table, hastily prepared a tray and carried it into the bedroom. June reached back into her memories to try to recollect a time when her father had been served breakfast in bed. Only one time came to mind and that was once when he'd had an allergic reaction to penicillin and was too sick to come to the table.

As if he could read her mind, Dick whispered, "Wait until you meet him. It's not fair to compare him to your father."

When he finally joined them in the bright sunny kitchen, the entire family was won over by his warm, friendly ways. With his salt and pepper colored hair and whiskers, chiseled features, and bright flashing smile, he reminded them of a smaller version of June's Uncle Gordon. "Mommy has fixed a basket of food for you, so you'd better get into your suits so we can be on our way. First we're going to the dock, and I'll take you out on the Florida Belle before you go to the beach. You can have a picnic lunch there, then this evening we'll take you to a seafood restaurant on the beach."

As Dick drove to the dock, like typical tourists, they were fascinated by the pastel colored houses with tiled roofs, and by every palm tree, seagull and pelican they saw along the way. Polly teased that all northerners who came to Florida stopped alongside the road and had their picture taken by a palm tree. Not to be different, they found a particularly nice one and posed by it. Then when they got to the boat, they had a regular photo shoot of all the pelicans that crowded around hoping for a handout. When Captain Bob gave Ric some fish to toss to them, Janice grabbed the movie camera and filmed her brother as he held the fish as a conductor would a baton. The onlookers laughed as they watched as the pelicans swayed their heads back and forth in time to his direction.

After Captain Bob gave them a quick tour of the forty-foot fishing boat, he showed them the large deep icebox where the catch of the night before was ready to be weighed and sold. Then he described a life threatening experience he'd had. "Icebox doors like these saved my life when I was shipwrecked during a hurricane." He had his guests rapt attention as he related the story of his ordeal and rescue. "When the boat I was on broke up during the storm, I was lucky enough to find one of the doors floating among the debris so I grabbed onto it and pulled myself up on top of it. While I clung to it, the door rode the waves during the worst of the storm, until I landed in the calm of the eye of the storm. I didn't see a single soul for three days, until a Coast Guard Cutter found me. They said, they'd about given up hope of finding any survivors when one of the seamen spotted the door. One member of the crew said when they pulled up beside me, I looked so bad that they thought they would be pulling a corpse onboard. Lucky for me, I didn't suffer anything worse than dehydration and a bad sunburn. A few days in the hospital, and I was ready to go back to sea."

∽

Polly interjected, "Speaking of adventures at sea, Bob and I had a pretty scary one a few weeks ago. Usually everything is quiet on the Gulf of Mexico with nothing more exciting than watching the dolphins swimming and playing alongside the boat. Sometimes we'll snag a shark or a barracuda in our lines that we'll quickly send to its maker. Then in the evening when we're finished with our work, we like to sit in lounge chairs on the deck and watch the sunset. We've seen some really fantastic ones, where the sky seems to be on fire and the waves have been turned into red and gold. One night when the sun had gone down and it had gotten dark, we'd dropped anchor and turned in for the night. A couple hours later, we were awakened by an angry sounding Spanish speaking male voice. We were both groggy from having been so rudely awakened and alarmed by the strange voice making demands that my limited memory of my high school Spanish could not translate. Then when we got dressed and on deck, Bob recognized the ship as a Cuban military vessel, and he was able to figure out that they wanted to come aboard and search the ship for drugs, contraband, or people we might be smuggling into or out of Cuba."

Bob interrupted to add, "We didn't know it, but we had wandered into Cuban waters and were at their mercy. Fortunately between one of the crewmember's limited English, and with my little bit of Spanish, I was able to introduce myself as the captain and Mommy as my first mate. Even though I showed our catch of fish to demonstrate to them that we were fishermen and had no intention to smuggle anything, they still conducted a thorough search."

Polly grinned as she added, "It probably only took an hour for them to finish, but it seemed much longer as we sat on deck guarded by uniformed men with guns and wondered whether we'd be spending the rest of the night, or of our lives in a Cuban jail. The officer who had led the search looked disappointed when he came on deck and told us that we could leave. Then they stayed close by while we hauled up the anchor and headed back to American waters. We didn't feel safe though until we saw them turn around and head back toward Cuba."

After telling this story, Captain Bob asked if they were ready to go out on the Florida Belle. "Only if you promise to stay in American waters," Dick joked.

"We're just going to cruise along the shore. That will give you a chance to see the town and the beaches from a different view," Captain Bob explained. Then while they stood on deck, he maneuvered the boat past the other fishing and shrimp boats that lined the shore, and took them for a cruise out into the Gulf and back along the shore. Along the way, they could see sun worshipers baking themselves on the sandy beaches, fishermen standing knee deep in the water, and women and children stooped over to gather the plentiful shells that littered the golden beaches.

Polly pointed out a secluded cove and told them that they would picnic there after they got back to shore. Then before they went back to the dock, Captain Bob motioned toward beachside houses built on tall stilts, with their decks and wide expanse of windows facing the water. Polly explained, "We'll take you over and show you the house we've rented and plan to move into after we get the inside painted and ready. It's not on the Gulf but on the river that runs into it. We'll go see it tomorrow."

For the rest of the day, Polly and her visitors felt as relaxed and free as natives on a South Sea island as they explored the cove, soaked up the sun and gathered shells on the beach. While they filled bags with their collection, Polly said, "You'll never believe it, but I got your Aunt Mabel to wear slacks or shorts while we shelled. I think what finally convinced her was when she got some wolf whistles when she stooped over and the back of her dress blew up over her head. I think she decided that no matter what her minister said about women wearing pants, she'd be more modest in shorts or slacks." While she looked at their cache of shells, she told them about her little business of making and selling jewelry and crafts from her collection. "I'll send some home with you for yourselves and Sharlyn. I'm sorry she couldn't come with you. I'm really anxious to see the baby. I bet she's a living doll baby!"

"She's perfect, MaMa, but you need to come up and see for yourself," Janice said, "I'm going to graduate in June and go away to college this fall. I hope you can come up before I have to go." Polly promised that she would. Then they stowed their gear in the car and returned to the yellow house.

The next morning, they awoke to the sound of rain pounding on the roof and pummeling against the windows. "I've never seen rain like this!" Ric moaned as he dejectedly watched the puddles form in the yard. "I guess this means we won't get to go to the beach today."

Polly explained that the rain could stop and the sun could come out. "We get these sudden showers, but they don't usually last very long. If it stops by noon, we could be on the beach in a couple hours." Several hours and several inches of rain later, the downpour continued until around eight inches had fallen on the little house at Fort Myers Beach where the little group watched and waited for it to let up. Unfortunately it didn't stop until they were ready for bed. The sun peaked through the clouds enough the next morning to dry the ground, but in a few hours a less ferocious rain began to fall.

Having only been on the beach long enough to become sunburned, Ric and Janice were disappointed that they had to stay inside until their dad came up with a proposal, "Why don't we paint Polly and the captain's new place? We have painted so many of the houses Mom and Dad left to me and Kenny that we have a pretty good system going," Dick explained.

Polly protested, "That's no way for you to spend your vacation!"

The family overrode her objections and within minutes they'd loaded paint, roller and brushes into the car and were on their way to the house overlooking the river. "This looks like a Polly size house," June quipped as they wandered through the kitchen, living room, two bedrooms and bath. Then with five people working, singing, and laughing, the drab looking rooms soon took on the soft glow of the pastel colors Polly had selected. While they hammed it up, Janice took movies of the workers. She captured MaMa sticking out her tongue at the camera then she filmed her from the rear, wiggling her fanny. Unfortunately there was no sound track to capture the ring of her mischievous laughter.

Dick teased that June held a record for rolling the paint on a room in twenty minutes. "Wait until you see this movie. It will look as if the camera has been speeded up." Then Janice captured her father pretending to take the roller away from her mother only to have his wife purloin his brush and paint his nose.

While they worked, Polly asked Ric and Janice how they'd learned to paint and Janice replied, "Ric and I have helped Mom and Dad on the houses."

Ric teased his sister by saying, "It must be real love. Mike still comes back to see Janice even though Dad has put him to work high up on a ladder painting the outside of some of the places."

Dick joked, "I couldn't chase him away."

To which, in a more serious vein, Janice informed her grandmother that her dad wouldn't chase him away even if he could. "Mom and Dad like Mike."

Polly replied, "I'd say you like Mike too. Are we going to hear wedding bells soon?"

Janice hid her secret behind a smile. She and Mike had been excitedly making plans for their future together. They were going to have her great grandmother Lula's diamond mounted into a modern setting for their engagement ring. They'd also talked about getting matching wedding bands. Mike wanted to present the ring to her on New Year's Eve at their favorite Chinese restaurant, Jong Mea's, in Columbus. With her smile spreading to her eyes, Janice dreamily told her grandmother, "Oh, I more than like Mike." Then she picked up her paintbrush, and spread some bright yellow paint on the kitchen walls as she began singing, "Happy Together." Painting along with her, they all joined her in the chorus, "I can see me lovin' nobody but you for all my life." June caught Dick's eye and they smiled at each other, pleased that Janice and Mike were happy together.

After the last drop of paint had been spread on the kitchen walls, Polly called out, "Break time! I brought some sandwiches, fruit, chips, and drinks. We have some lawn furniture out there so we can be comfortable while we eat and watch the boats go by."

While they relaxed on the porch, they heard the sound of someone in the house and seconds later one of the most beautiful women they'd ever seen poked her head through the open doorway and said, "Captain Bob said I'd find you over here. Hope you don't mind if I join you." Then like a bee to honey, she buzzed over to the empty chair between Dick and Ric and began to turn her considerable charm on Dick. He looked particularly handsome with a lock of his dark hair falling onto his forehead, his brown eyes sparkling, and his bright flashing smile. While the family looked on in astonishment, Polly's friend, Ruby, made a big play for him. Dick, who was a natural flirt, played along with her until something in his wife's eyes told him if he continued he was going to be in big trouble. When Ruby realized that he'd only been kidding her, she turned her attention on fifteen year old Ric. While June hadn't liked this young woman flirting with her husband, her Mother Lion protecting her cub persona took over when Ruby started on Ric.

As Dick told her later that night, "I hadn't met too many women like her, and I don't think Ric had met any. I know you didn't like it when she made a play for me, but when she went after Ric, I thought you were going to shove her off the porch."

June retorted, "Remember that sign we saw on the way down here that advertised Ruby Falls? If she had kept it up, we wouldn't have had to go to Tennessee to see Ruby Fall! We'd have seen it happen before we finished our lunch." With an exasperated sigh she said, "I don't know why Polly even has a friend like her. Since she always has a soft spot for anyone with a sad story, I'm sure Ruby must have one."

The next day in the car on the way to Fort Lauderdale, Polly explained, "Ruby and her little boy moved here a few months ago. The way she gathers men and boys around her, I thought she was just man-crazy, but there is more to it than that. Right before she moved here, her husband, who was a heavy drinker, shot and killed himself in front of her and their eight-year-old son. She told me that when he did that, she felt it was her fault and that she wasn't desirable enough as a woman for him to want to live. I think that after such an experience she feels she has to prove herself with every man she meets." June nodded, but although she sympathized with her, June hadn't changed her mind. As far as she was concerned, her husband and son were still off limits. This young woman would have to prove herself with someone else.

When they reached Fort Lauderdale, they found the waves too high and rough for swimming, but they enjoyed combing the beach for shells and escaping from their painting holiday. At one point on the beach, Janice relinquished her camera to her mother so she could actually be in one of the home movies. As she handed it to her, she said, "Anyone looking at these films won't believe I was on this vacation." As it turned out, given her mother's lack of skill as a photographer, when June had filmed several feet of her scarf blowing in front of the lens and her own face when she turned the camera to see what was wrong, Janice still wasn't in the movie.

Despite the weather and the filming disaster, the little group had a wonderful time. Then when they returned to Fort Myers Beach they found that Captain Bob and his cronies had moved everything into the river house while they'd been in Fort Lauderdale. That night as they all stayed in Polly and Captain Bob's new place on the waterfront, they could smell the fresh scent of paint when they crawled into bed. They were awakened to the smell of coffee perking and bacon sizzling in the skillet and Polly's voice calling to them, "Wake up you sleepy heads, it's time to rise and shine so we can have our breakfast and get out on the beach. Surprise, surprise, the sun is shining. We can be out for several hours and still get back in time for the fish fry we are hosting tonight. All I have to prepare is the salad. Big Captain Larry just got in a couple days ago and he's not only bringing the shrimp, but he's going to cook it for us. You won't believe it, but they're so big that four of them will fill a dinner plate! He always brings us several pounds each time he comes back from a shrimp run."

Then during the day, Janice and Ric lathered up with suntan lotion, fell asleep on the beach while their parents and grandmother waded near shore and walked on the warm sand. By the time they got back to the river house, Janice's skin had begun to turn pink but fortunately it hadn't yet started to bother her as the party progressed. They soon discovered that Polly hadn't exaggerated about the shrimp, and they understood why the shrimp boat captain was called Big Larry. A gentle giant, he must have tipped the scales at four-hundred pounds or over.

As they consumed shrimp as fast as Captain Larry could cook it, June looked around at the group of characters Polly and Captain Bob had as friends. A few minutes after Ruby had arrived with her son and a couple teenage boys, a man named John, Captain Bob's former first mate, arrived with a twelve pack of beer. His slurred speech and teetering walk demonstrated that he'd had a few brews before he got there. Then when he launched into a monologue about what he'd said to the cat that hung out at the dock, Dick jokingly asked, "What did the cat say to you?"

Everyone laughed when John pulled himself to his full six-foot height, stood ramrod straight, and in a voice as dignified as that of a Supreme Court Justice announcing an important decision, he slowly proclaimed, "Cats don't talk."

Dick muttered to June, "He sure put me down with just three words, didn't he?" Then during the course of the party while an array of shrimp and fishing boat captains, mates, and dock-workers wandered in and out, June, Dick, Janice, and Ric were fascinated by the colorful people they met.

The next day Janice's sunburn prevented them from going to the beach, so they hung around the house and relaxed. While Polly, June, and Dick sat on the screened-in porch, they watched the antics of Ric and Janice as they wandered around in the shade while they picked up the coconuts that had fallen to the ground. Polly called out for them to be careful when one fell from a tree and narrowly missed hitting Ric on the head. They watched in amusement as Ric impersonating a monkey, with arms akimbo, jumped around the yard while he grunted, scratched himself, and made monkey faces. Polly laughingly remarked, "That boy should be a comedian!"

June replied, "He gets it from his father."

Later, after Janice and Ric joined them on the screened-porch, while they sipped lemonade, and ate the sandwiches Polly had prepared, she told them about shrimp-boat Captain Larry. "He was raised in Atlanta by his two unmarried aunts with all the advantages they could give him. Until about four years ago, when he was twenty-five, he had everything a young man could want; a pretty wife and two little girls, a nice job as a stockbroker, and a home in the suburbs. Then one night on a narrow curvy road a few miles from their home, his world came crushing down on him when a drunken driver barreled around one of the curves and crashed head-on into his car. When Big Larry came out of his coma a couple weeks later, his aunts broke the news to him that his wife and daughters had been killed outright. Big Larry wanted to die too, but after weeks in the hospital, he recovered physically, but the emotional scars are there to stay. Then when he got home, in spite of his aunts' objections, he quit his job, sold his home, bought the shrimp-boat and started a new life. He's never talked about it, but last summer when the aunts came for a visit, they told me. In my opinion, he tries to fill his life with food, his work, and the friends he's made here, but the pain never quite seems to leave his eyes." While they talked for awhile about this tragic young man, her listeners were reminded of how painful it had been for them when they lost Dick's brother Eddie in an automobile accident. The enormity of losing an entire family, though, was hard to comprehend.

⁓

They all were going to a party that night at the home of friends of Polly and Captain Bob. By evening, though, Janice's sunburn was making her too miserable to go, so Ric decided to stay home and keep her company. He and his sister had always been best friends, and he didn't want her to spend the last evening of their vacation alone. Another reason that he didn't want to go was that he didn't want to spend another evening trying to avoid Ruby's advances and his mother's displeasure.

While the adults enjoyed their party, Ric and Janice had a party of their own. They sat on the porch and watched the activities on the river, ate pizza, and listened to some records they'd brought along. While Ric looked through the stack of records, Janice had gone into the house for ice-cubes for their cokes. Seconds later, Ric heard a bloodcurdling scream from inside the house and took off running to his sister's rescue. Instead of being met by something life threatening, he found Janice staring down at a bug the size of a small mouse. "By the sound of that scream, I thought someone had broken into the house and was about to kill you," Ric said.

Some of the color under her sunburn had drained from her face as she pointed at the scurrying creature and announced, "That is the biggest cockroach I've ever seen!"

However when the partygoers returned and Janice told her grandmother about it, Polly grinned saucily and informed Janice that she hadn't seen a cockroach. "Since we're in the semi-tropics surrounded by palm trees, we don't have roaches, the bug you saw was a palmetto bug. They won't hurt you, but the next time you come, I'll be sure the landlord has just exterminated for them."

On the way home, the next day, as they were ready to cross the border from Florida into Georgia, Dick pulled into the Florida Welcoming Station when he saw a large sign that proclaimed "ALL THE ORANGE JUICE YOU CAN DRINK FOR A DIME." They all remembered Captain Bob's story about his first trip to Florida when he'd stopped at this station and, being thirsty, had quickly downed a cup of juice. Then since his thirst wasn't quenched, he took his cup to the counter and asked for another. When the counterman refused to give him a refill, he'd pointed to the sign and reminded the surly man that the sign said all the juice you can drink for a dime. To his surprise, the man informed them that since their policy was only one cup to a customer, "That IS all the juice you can drink for a dime!"

After they'd each downed their second drink and gone back and had their cups refilled, they realized the sign meant what it said and they could have all the juice they wanted for a dime. They felt foolish when it dawned on them that Captain Bob had taken a common Florida sign and turned it into a joke. "Since we won't be back for a year, I'll have plenty of time to come up with a gotcha for him the next time we see him," Dick jokingly remarked, as with cups in hand, they returned to the car and resumed their trip.

During the trip home, June took over at the wheel, while Dick rested. The eight cylinder engine purred as June drove through the tunnel of pine trees that lined the four-lane highway, while Dick dozed and Ric and Janice talked about what they planned to do when they got home. Then as June started to pass an eighteen-wheeler, Dick opened his eyes and glanced at the speedometer and asked if she knew how fast she was going. "The speed limit is seventy, and I don't think I'm going over it," she replied.

His response, "June you are going one-hundred miles an hour," startled and frightened her enough that she pulled into the next rest area and turned the driving back over to her husband.

She realized her close call the next day, while in the Smokey Mountains, when they saw several cars parked along the roadside and a cluster of people looking over the side of the mountain. Although there were no warning signs posted, they felt danger in the air, so Dick stopped behind the parked cars and they made their way to the front of the line. To their shock and amazement, they saw that a fifty-foot section of the highway was gone. As they looked down into the gaping hole, June moaned, "I'm thankful that we didn't arrive at this dangerous site while I was barreling down the road at one hundred miles an hour." While they were surrounded by the peaceful beauty of the mountains, they marveled that the collapse of the highway hadn't taken place at night and that no lives had been lost.

June wistfully noted, "A guardian angel certainly must have been watching over the travelers today. Just think, with as much traffic as there is on this road that there weren't any cars on it when it collapsed."

SIGNS OF PEACE

In the spring of nineteen seventy, shortly after they'd returned from the Florida trip, Janice and her friends were on their way to school, when her friend Shelley's Mustang blew a tire. As they opened the trunk to get out the spare tire, they discovered that it was flat also.

Janice announced, "We're going to have to start walking, or we'll be tardy."

Shelly voiced in with, "Let's not be tardy, let's skip school today! That's one notch we don't have on our gun-belt. Everyone should play hooky at least once in their life. Here we are seniors with only a few months to go."

Each wrestled with her own conscience. Janice felt the weight of Jiminy Cricket perched on her shoulder whispering, "Be a good girl and go to school."

Then she came out with, "What do you mean play hooky? We wouldn't do that, but we did have a flat tire, so we have to walk home, don't we?"

Janet chirped in with, "Right! We do have to walk home."

To which Diane, rolling her eyes heavenward, added, "That darn tire!" As they turned to walk the five miles home instead of the two blocks to school, their spirits were high. As they walked, they talked away the miles with the main topic being teenage boys.

Diane said, "Yesterday I saw Mike driving that blue convertible of his. He is such a cool guy!"

Janice heartily agreed, "When he drove his Falcon to my house the other day, he was so tanned and he smelled like the fresh air. He is so handy with cars. He took out the automatic transmission and put in a standard one he got at the junkyard. There's something about that gearshift on the floor that the guys really like."

Marsha asked, "Did his brother Tom help him with it? I think he's such a doll!"

Shelly added, "His brother Andy is so handsome too! We had such a blast when he visited from Germany. Does Mike have any other brothers?"

Diane joked, "Well, there's always his little brother Jon."

Janice teased, "Yeah, he's in the first grade. You'll have to wait awhile 'til he starts dating."

Janet announced to Janice, "Well I sure am glad that you and Mike fixed me up with my Tom. Those boys from McDonalds are pretty sharp! In a few months when you and Mike head off for college, I think Tom and I will be heading down the aisle." That brought an excited response from all the girls as they continued their trek toward home.

As they came to the country road near Horn's Hill, Janice pointed out the general area where, a few years earlier, Sis and Larry had car trouble and got stuck for five hours one night. Diane remarked, "I bet Larry was just faking car trouble to get Sis to park with him."

Janice informed her, "No, it was real. His dad had to get the transmission repaired."

Janet moaned, "I couldn't believe what happened to Larry. That was so awful!"

Janice sadly reminisced, "The night before his wedding, following his bachelor's party, Larry was celebrating with his buddies. Then, in front of Moundbuilder's Park, the driver lost control and slammed into a tree. The driver and all the passengers survived with only minor injuries, but Larry was killed instantly." She sighed deeply before she went on, "He never made it to his wedding day. I felt so bad for his bride."

They walked silently for a while, each thinking about this terrible tragedy. Then Marsha groaned, "My legs are tired of walking."

As Janice assured her that they only had a few miles to go, a car pulled up beside them with a tiny elderly woman behind the steering wheel. She smiled pleasantly and asked, "Do you girls need some help?"

After hearing their explanation about the flat tire, she coaxed them to get into the car. She said, "I'll be happy to give you a ride home."

Though none of them would normally accept a ride from a stranger, this friendly little old lady was not threatening at all, so the five girls piled into her car. First the sweet old lady introduced herself. Then Janice, who had been raised to be polite, returned the favor by introducing herself and each of her fellow truants. The white haired woman impressed them with what must have been a photographic memory when she repeated each of their names, first and last, and said she was glad to meet them. Next, she informed them that she was the principal of a neighborhood elementary school. The name of the school didn't even register, as all eyes glared accusingly at Janice, their betrayer, who had just provided this principal with all their names. They hadn't realized it, but they had just gone through an interrogation, instead of an introduction. That innocent looking lady had just gotten all the pertinent information, tried them, and found them guilty. Then she pronounced their sentence when she sweetly said, "I'm sure you will each find a way to return to school as soon as possible. I'll be checking up on you later to make sure you made it back safely."

When she got home, Janice explained their misfortune about having a flat tire, and June took them to school. They did keep their slate clean for never playing hooky, but had to chalk one up for being tardy.

This close group of friends would soon miss another day of school, but for a much more important reason than a flat tire.

∼

There was much fighting raging in the world at that time…the war in Vietnam, the Arab and Jewish conflict in the Middle East, and the bombings between Catholics and Protestants in Ireland.

Janice, Ric, and their teenaged friends didn't feel they had any power to control this, but they did what they could to improve the world around them. Janice volunteered to help with younger Girl Scouts when possible. She and Ric still tutored underprivileged children in the neighborhood on a weekly basis at their church, and they and their friends collected for UNICEF each year to help alleviate world hunger. That spring, Janice and Janet had gone by bus, with other Christian teens, to a conference in Washington, D.C. and to the United Nations in New York City to hear discussions about the Arab/Jewish conflict in the Middle East.

Many young people, who knew they were going to be asked to give their lives for the "Police Action" in Vietnam had protested the fighting. Then in April of 1970 when President Nixon announced the expansion of U.S. military involvement into Cambodia, the protests escalated.

On May 4th, the family was remembering that this would have been Rowie's sixty-fifth birthday. It had always been such a happy occasion, but this was the first birthday since her sudden death in October. Janice confided in her mother that she was trying to think of happier times but it just made her miss her grandmother more. One spark to cheer her was the thought that this was also her Uncle Bill's twenty-fourth birthday.

But the date, May 4th took on a new meaning forever when the unthinkable happened during a student demonstration against our country's involvement in Vietnam and Cambodia. At Kent State University in Ohio, students participating in the demonstration, plus innocent bystanders, and those walking to and from classes were involved in a confrontation with the skittish young National Guardsmen. Apparently without orders, the troops fired upon the crowd, killing four and wounding others. As Janice and her friends rode to school the next day, she informed the others that there was a peace rally planned that day at Denison University in nearby Granville. With much resolve, they unanimously agreed to go to Denison University instead of Newark High School. With a feeling of utter helplessness to stop this senseless killing, they wanted to band together with other peace seeking souls.

They certainly achieved their goal, as they walked around the campus with other high school and college students, listening to poetry about peace, singing peace songs, hearing memorials to the Kent State students, and to our boys in Vietnam. All day the tranquil sounds of the flutes could be heard playing in the background.

That evening as she sat in the kitchen at Mike's house, talking to his mother Heidi, who was eight months pregnant, Mike remarked, "Mom, I wonder if you'll have this baby before I graduate on May 31st."

Janice teasingly added, "Or maybe you'll get an award as the only mom there who is nine months pregnant, and has two sons graduating."

Mike's sister, fourteen year old Patty injected, "How embarrassing, Mom!"

Janice joked, "Heidi, did you know that my sister was born the same month and year that you had Andy? I was thinking the other day that you've had babies in the forties, fifties, sixties, and now in the seventies. Sounds like you should be in the Guinness Book of World Records." They all laughed, but all kidding aside, they were excitedly looking forward to the birth of this new baby.

Janice was eager to tell them about her incredible experience at the peace rally. After listening to her, Heidi told her, "It would be better if you didn't mention this to Al." Janice thought of how Mike's father, Al, had served in the military for twenty-one years, first in Europe, right after World War II, returning German Prisoners-Of-War to their country. Then in the Korean War, he had been in the Military Police. This was quite a contrast to her own father who had been such a pacifist that he'd been a medic in World War II administering to the wounded and dying, carrying stretchers rather than a gun.

The worried look on Heidi's face reminded the teenager of the intense discussion she and Al had a few weeks earlier about the draft of young men into the military. Al, like many other veterans, saw the draft as a duty these male citizens had toward their country. He whole-heartedly believed the slogan, "My country right or wrong."

Janice perceived the draft as an injustice where the government plucked these young men out of their everyday lives and plunked them down in a far-away country to possibly die for a war they didn't believe in. To Al, any boys who went to Canada to avoid the draft were draft-dodgers who were a shame to their country. To Janice, anyone who could avoid the fighting in Vietnam was exercising his right to lead a life free of being forced to kill or be killed needlessly. Both Al and Janice held strongly to their beliefs and no amount of discussion would sway either to the other's point of view.

Janice thought about the guys she knew who had been sent to Vietnam. Her friend, Gib, who'd been with them on their canoe trip last spring, had been there for months. She and Ric both wrote to him and she often sent newspaper cartoons to him to lift his spirits. Older boys she knew had returned and told her terrible stories about the atrocities taking place in that jungle war. Then there was her cousin Karen's young husband who'd been killed just days before he was to return to her and their two young sons.

With these thoughts in mind, Janice went into the living room to again talk to Al. As he sat watching the evening news, with pictures of the war filling the screen, she earnestly looked at him and said, "Al, I know what you think about the draft, but what do you really think about the war in Vietnam?"

Surprised by her question, he answered in his soft voice, "I have mixed feelings about that war. When I was in the service, as a military man, I couldn't counter-guess my superiors. But actually, as a soldier in the ranks, I felt that war in Vietnam was unnecessary. I don't think we have any right to be there. I feel that in Cambodia and Vietnam there are differences that they need to solve themselves. But if you are in the service, you must follow orders."

"I just wondered if you were for this war, since you are a military man," she responded.

His answer was, "Janice, I've never been for any war. But when you are in the service, you go where they send you. When the time came that the army was sending me to Vietnam soon, I was in the midst of deciding whether to re-enlist or not. I had my family in Germany with me, and I felt my place was with them. My decision was not to serve in that war, so I retired."

Then she told him, "There was a peace rally at Denison University today."

With eyebrows raised, he asked, "Were you there?"

She responded, "Yes, I was, and it was very impressive to be with so many young people whose lives could be changed forever by this war."

Then with a far-away look in his eyes, he added, "Some of my buddies and my superiors volunteered to go to Vietnam, and some of them didn't come back, but that was their decision."

As the young girl with her sights set high on hopes of world peace, and the retired career army veteran sat side-by-side in his living room, they had come to an agreement that our country was wrong to be in this war.

Later when Mike was driving her home, she said, "I was surprised at how your dad feels about the war in Vietnam."

Mike responded with, "Dad told me that since he spent so many years in the military, he thinks he's served enough time for all his sons. He hopes that none of us will have to go in."

The entire family at the house on Oakwood Avenue shared Janice's feeling about Vietnam. For the first time, the horror of war was brought into the living room as graphic scenes were shown and daily body counts were given. Two of the dead were friends of Sharlyn, and others were boys whose hair Dick had cut since they'd been babies. Very few families were untouched by what was happening in that distant land.

Alongside the scenes they saw on their television sets of men fighting and dying, were others of young men burning their draft cards or chanting, "Hell no! We won't go!" Like many mothers, June found this war to be beyond understanding. Almost like a game (a deadly one), young people were sent into the fighting zone for a year. If they survived, they came home, and someone else took their place. As in the Korean War, there was a line that could not be crossed. Unlike World War II, this wasn't an all out fight to the finish. There were too many rules.

She'd heard the phrase, "Cannon Fodder" used in reference to those who had been drafted. When she watched Ric, his friends, other boys in the neighborhood, and her nephews going about the business of growing up, she could only pray that before that term could apply to many more, the leaders of the United States and North Vietnam could bring this horrible war to a close. While Ric was only sixteen, time seemed to pass so fast that she was afraid he'd reach draft age before there was a sign of peace.

To show his opposition to the war, Ric painted peace signs on his and his friends' tee shirts, and they wore the symbol on a chain around their necks. While the young people sported these symbols, others taunted them by displaying bumper stickers of the peace sign with the motto, "A Sign of the American Chicken." Many veterans of World War II thought that when others protested this war, their own sacrifices were being negated. As a veteran, Dick didn't feel that way. "I felt our own country was in danger in World War II and we had no choice. Though I didn't want to take a life, I wanted to do what I could to save lives as a medic. If our country was in danger now I'd expect these young men to go, but I feel differently because of all the death and suffering I saw in the war." His family could see the pain of remembrance in his eyes when he added, "I've loaded young boys not much older than Ric into an ambulance with arms or legs blown off. I've held onto their hands as they called out for their mothers as they breathed their last breath. I don't want to see that happen to our son in a war our government doesn't even expect to win."

Dick concluded by saying, "I've heard people say that if you don't approve of the war that means that you don't support the ones who are fighting. I certainly don't feel that way! I know I just pray that they get home safely and that no others will have to die. I want to see this settled at the mediation table…the way sensible people solve their problems."

Some people thought that if you were for peace, you were unpatriotic. Though the family didn't agree with the war, they still supported the young men who were fighting over there.

One evening while watching a peace demonstration on television, June commented, "This generation is the first one to question having to fight. Do you think they might make our government more careful about getting involved in other country's problems?"

"I hope so," Dick responded, "but I wouldn't count on it. Maybe the leaders of these countries should put on boxing gloves and duke it out."

"That makes as much sense as what is going on," June said. "Maybe governments should learn from individuals who manage to co-exist. We have more sense than to get involved if our neighbors get into an argument. Remember when the woman up the street got mad when her husband came home drunk for the umpteenth time, and she chased him out of the house and hit him over the head with the coffee pot. We stayed out of it, and they worked it out."

"Yeah, as mad as she was, if I'd gone over, I'd probably have come home with a bump on my head to match his," Dick quipped.

Ric entered the conversation by saying, "I have been asked to speak at church next week for Youth Sunday. I'm going to talk about Vietnam. 'Thou Shall Not Kill' is going to be my title." When that Sunday rolled around, while his family and friends supported him in standing up and speaking from the heart about his convictions, not everyone in the congregation agreed with him. He learned the bitter lesson that the church, like the country, was divided in its opinion about the war. Although, in months to come, he got a few dirty looks from some of the men who had served in World War II, Ric's convictions didn't waver.

~

As his son grew tall and handsome, and more girls called, Dick sputtered that he was going to have the phone taken out so they could have a little peace. The girls all liked his wit, his good looks, and his dancing. Then when he met a boy named Cary at church camp, and they began to sing and play folk or religious music around town, he became even more popular. Janice had teased him when she'd heard one girl refer to him as "A real cool guy."

At first, Ric and Cary had only performed for their own youth group, but after awhile they decided to branch out. The first thing they did was to add a girl singer and name their trio "The God Squad." After weeks of practicing in the basement of the house on Oakwood Avenue, they set out to find some places to perform. With a list of churches in hand, they went to several to ask if they could sing during the services or for the youth group. They were generally well received by the minister or choir director and had secured several bookings the first day.

When he left the second day to join his singing partners, Ric was dressed in a pair of bell-bottom trousers, a long sleeved shirt, and a suede vest. As he did every day, he had showered, shampooed his hair until it was squeaky clean and brushed it until he could control the curls. Before he went out the door, June gave him a peck on the cheek and wished him luck.

The first place they stopped, they'd been asked to sing in a couple weeks, the second one had been pleasant, but hadn't hired them. The reaction from the third one was different from anything they'd ever encountered. When the church secretary had ushered them into the minister's study, they saw a short, stocky, middle aged man standing beside a massive desk. When he saw them, his eyebrows shot skyward, and his nostrils quivered as if a bad odor had invaded the room.

Ric tried to convince himself that he'd imagined the reaction, before he braced himself with a big gulp of air, and explained what they wanted. While

Ric talked, there was no warmth in the man's eyes. He didn't move, but glared at them through steel rimmed glasses. After Ric finished, the stern faced man tapped his fingers on the desk, pulled at a long hair that grew from a mole on his cheek, then pronounced, "I have to talk to God about it. I'm not sure this is something God would want this church to do." Thinking this was an odd statements, the trio followed his orders to wait outside until he got his answer from God.

Leading the way, Ric flung open the office door, and heard a squeal like that of a wounded animal from behind it. A young girl, who turned out to be the minister's daughter, had been listening outside the door, then when he'd thrown it open, it had hit her. "I don't think the guy liked us to start with, but clobbering his daughter certainly didn't win us any points," Cary muttered as they seated themselves in the straight-backed chairs that lined the wall.

When a few minutes later, the minister ushered them back into his study, it was to tell them that God's answer had been, "No!"

While Cary and the girl singer stood open mouthed, Ric blurted out, "Why? Why wouldn't God want us to sing here? We're Christians just like you."

The preacher was obviously displeased that Ric would dare to question him. Contempt dripped from each word when he explained that God didn't think they were the right kind of people to perform in their church. Ric had to hold his temper in check when he asked just what he meant by that. Although Cary gave Ric a warning look, curiosity got the better of him as he added his voice to his partner's and asked just what God had told him.

When the minister replied that God had informed him that he didn't want hippie looking boys with long hair to perform in His church, Ric protested, "How can you say such a thing? God's son, Jesus, had long hair!"

"That's where you're wrong!" The pompous little man exclaimed. As if to prove his point, he opened his desk drawer, pulled out a stack of Sunday school literature, and spread them on the desktop. To their surprise they saw that the familiar picture of a bearded Jesus with shoulder length hair was gone. He had been given a haircut, and his beard had been neatly trimmed.

June knew something was wrong when her son came home later that day. For the next few minutes, his mood swung from anger to amusement while he sat at the counter and chomped on a four-layer mayonnaise sandwich and told his mother what had happened. "He talked like he had a hot line in his office to God...like the red one President Nixon has to Khrushchev," he muttered. Then as he washed his last bite down with a swig of milk, he grinned and said, "Cary said that if we'd had a chance, I blew it when I hit the preacher's daughter."

After he explained that remark to his shocked mother, she told him that her mother had known that minister since he was a little boy. "From what she says, he sounds like a fanatic. You need to know, though, that since he doesn't approve of long hair, nothing you said or did would have made a difference. I think you'd better take Jesus' advice and shake the dust from your feet and go someplace else to sing."

That evening when his father returned from work, Ric met him at the car and spilled out the story to him. When he told his dad that the preacher had called them sinners, Dick said, "You need to remind him that churches are for sinners." He was astounded by his son's reply that the preacher had informed them that there were no sinners, only saints, in their congregation.

Dick exploded with, "Bull!" but he managed to restrain himself from expressing the rest of his opinion as he and his son walked up the porch steps and entered the house. Later that evening while he and June took a walk around the neighborhood, he said, "I have a good mind to have a talk with that man!"

"Won't do any good!" she replied. "There are a lot of people out there who are prejudiced against boys with long hair. Once they see that hair hit the shoulder, they close their mind to the fact that the boy is clean, or in Ric's case, active in church."

"If they don't think he's clean, all they have to do is look at the water bill. I think that boy washes his hair as often as the girls!" Dick quipped.

"Every day!" June replied. Seconds later, they dropped the subject as one of the neighbors called from the darkness of her porch and asked them to stop and visit for awhile. Although they didn't discuss it any more that night, for a long time to come, June continued to worry about the problems she knew her son would face because of other people's prejudices.

THEIR TOMORROWS

For now, though, she turned her attention to Janice's upcoming graduation from Newark High School. Then, in June while the family sat in the school auditorium with the background sound of the rain pelting the roof and watched Janice receive her diploma, June's mind wandered to former graduations; her own, her brothers, and her oldest daughter's. She turned and smiled warmly at Ric as she realized that in two short years he'd be part of that long processional.

When they returned to the house on Oakwood Avenue they were joined by Sharlyn, Charlie and toddler, Debbie. While Dick bounced baby Debbie on his knee, he jokingly said, "Mike, now that you've graduated I can get you a paint brush for each hand and make a fulltime painter out of you."

Mike's response was, "Thanks but I would rather be an engineer."

"B&O or Pennsylvania railroad?" Dick asked.

Janice grinned and said, "Electrical engineer, Dad!"

In a more serious vein, Charlie asked the graduates what they planned to do now that they were out of school. Janice replied that they both would be starting college in the fall. "Mike is going to be in school for his engineering studies, I am still deciding between nursing and dental hygiene."

Sharlyn turned to her brother and teased, "It looks like you will have Mom and Dad to yourself. Don't get too spoiled."

Ric responded, "Spoiled? Me? No way! Because I'll still have to share them with Mitzi." Ric grinned at his sister as he patted the sleek black dog at his side.

Sharlyn returned her brother's grin with a proud wide smile. Mitzi was Sharlyn's accomplishment, the second puppy she had successfully smuggled into her family's home. She fondly recalled the Christmas she had introduced Mitzi to the family. As she had revealed the small puppy hidden in her coat sleeve, she had seen excitement flash across her siblings' faces.

As the conversation swirled around her, June noticed Dick slip out of the room. "I wonder what he is up to," she mused.

She didn't give it another thought, though, when a few minutes later, Janice started to open her presents. The first one was from Mike. When she opened the large box, and with Mike's help lifted out a small wooden cabinet, her eyes widened in surprise and pleasure as she exclaimed, "It's a television set!"

Set within the beautiful cabinet was a small television screen. It was an exact miniature of the set in the family's living room.

June interjected with, "That screen is small like the first one your dad and I bought. That was before you were even born, Janice. The only difference was that the cabinets then were humongous! This one is perfectly beautiful. It's the right size to pick up and carry."

⁓

As Janice opened her last gift, they heard the persistent honking of a horn outside the house. "Go see who is making that racket," June instructed her son.

Ric went to the door to see what was happening. When he came back, he had a grin on his face when he said, "Mom, I think you had better come see this."

Curious, June went out on the porch where she was greeted by a sight she had never expected to see again. Her husband was sitting astraddle a beautiful Honda 350 motorcycle. Grinning, he called out, "Surprise! I missed my old blue Honda, so when I saw this, I couldn't resist buying it for us."

Janice acted like she was pouting when she said, "Aw, I thought it was for me."

Sharlyn elbowed Charlie, and lamented, "I used to own a Honda 50 but my husband gave it away to my sister on our wedding day."

Charlie snorted, "Oh, your Honda was no bigger than a scooter. That hardly counted as a motorcycle."

Mike countered his future brother-in-law saying, "The DMV disagrees. Janice and I both took our exam on that little Honda 50, and now we are licensed to drive *any* size cycle." Mike was rather emphatic in his pronunciation of the word "any".

Dick urged, "Jump on, June. I'll take you for a spin around the courthouse square."

June, feeling a little guilty about leaving the party, called out to her guests, "We'll be right back, and then we'll enjoy the cake."

Then she climbed on, wrapped her arms around her husband and said, "This sure beats our first motorcycle…the Popcorn Popper."

When they roared down Oakwood Avenue, their neighbors, Ginny and her husband, were sitting on the porch swing next door. Ginny turned to him and said, "That reminds me of when they first moved in. That little motorcycle they had really caused a lot of excitement in the neighborhood."

As they rode around the square past the Midland Theatre, June read the marquis announcing the new movie, Love Story. "I know another love story that began in that theatre," she said as she tightened her arms around his waist.

The motor noise almost drowned out his reply of, "And we owe it all to popcorn!"

When they returned to the house on Oakwood Avenue, June set out the graduation cake, and they all sat around the family's harvest table as they ate cake and ice cream. Among all the chatter, Dick added to the commotion by making bird sounds to entertain little Debbie. She laughingly said, "Mama June, Poppy Dick is so silly!"

June was tickled to hear her granddaughter calling her and Dick by their newest nicknames. How had they gone so quickly from being newlyweds, June and Dick, to Mama June and Poppy Dick?

Then with her family around her, her thoughts were filled with images of today and yesterday, of all their loved ones who had sat around this table, of herself and Dick as newlyweds coming to this house, and of their children growing up and becoming responsible young adults.

As she listened to their conversation and laughter, she couldn't help wonder what their tomorrows might bring. *Although she couldn't imagine it at the time, in the future when the family got together, the harvest table that seemed so large now wouldn't accommodate everyone.*

Thinking of the young usherette and the soldier who came along, she knew the future that had begun when she'd sold Dick those six boxes of popcorn would continue to live on in these young people and those still to come.

CPSIA information can be obtained
at www.ICGtesting.com
Printed in the USA
BVHW062258011221
622919BV00005B/20